LORNA
FIND

The Manual of Employment Appeals

First Edition

The Manual of Employment Appeals

First Edition

Patrick Green BA (Cantab), Barrister
Henderson Chambers
2 Harcourt Bulidings
Temple
London

Adam Heppinstall MA (Oxon), Barrister
Henderson Chambers
2 Harcourt Bulidings
Temple
London

JORDANS

Published by Jordan Publishing Limited
21 St Thomas Street
Bristol BS1 6JS

Whilst the publishers and the author have taken every care in preparing the material included in this work, any statements made as to the legal or other implications of particular transactions are made in good faith purely for general guidance and cannot be regarded as a substitute for professional advice. Consequently, no liability can be accepted for loss or expense incurred as a result of relying in particular circumstances on statements made in this work.

© Jordan Publishing Ltd 2008

All rights reserved. No part of this publication may be reproduced, stored in a retrieval system, or transmitted in any way or by any means, including photocopying or recording, without the written permission of the copyright holder, application for which should be addressed to the publisher.

British Library Cataloguing-in-Publication Data

A catalogue record for this book is available from the British Library.

ISBN 978 1 84661 090 5

Typeset by Letterpart Ltd, Reigate, Surrey
Printed and bound by CPI Antony Rowe, Chippenham, Wiltshire

FOREWORD

In a mature justice system busy appeal courts and tribunals are not necessarily a cause for congratulation. Their existence recognises the possibility that the system and those operating it are fallible and that the law itself, which was thought to be clear and certain, is neither, but is open to conflicting interpretations. Their busyness is a reflection of the growing complexity of the law, of increasing dissatisfaction with the performance of the system and of a greater inclination to question the authority of decision-makers.

The recognition of fallibility is realistic. All human beings and all human institutions, including the tribunal system, the appeal processes and even the law itself, are imperfect. However, the prospect of pursuing a case through two or more procedures in order to correct the errors that may occur in the handling of the case and to resolve uncertainties in the law is off-putting to tribunal users in terms of cost, time and effort. Sensible people want early closure for disputes that are potentially damaging to all concerned. They need to get on with their work and with life.

Nowhere is this need more evident than in disputes at and about work. It should not, therefore, be surprising to find that, although procedures for re-consideration of employment tribunal decisions by way of appeals, reviews and references exist, they are not there to encourage challenges. They are only intended for use by those that appear to have a sound legal basis for questioning the correctness of a reasoned decision.

The value of this new manual is in making that important fact clear both to the losers, who think that they should have won, and to the winners, who got what they thought they deserved in the tribunal, but face the prospect of having it taken from them by a different tribunal on appeal.

For the first time the losers and the winners can consult a handy comprehensive guide, which conveniently brings together in one place and clearly explains the procedures for all the different forms that further consideration of a case, or of an aspect of it, may take. This manual sets out, discusses and illustrates the procedures in more detail than has been possible in more comprehensive works on employment law generally.

As the authors emphasise in their key points, access to appeals is much more restricted than access to trial processes: for example, the sifting processes in the EAT and the requirement for permission to appeal to the Court of Appeal and beyond; the strict, short time limits, which are ignored or overlooked at peril;

grounds of appeal confined to errors of law; serious practical difficulties in mounting appeals on certain legal grounds, such as alleged bias of the tribunal and alleged perversity in their decisions; strict tests for the admission of new evidence after the tribunal decision; and the more severe costs regimes that exist in the appellate courts. Parties and their advisers are reminded that an appeal from an employment tribunal is not a re-trial, a re-run or a re-hearing of the original case. Nor is it an examination exercise in which the tribunal is assessed and marked and either passes or fails. It is tightly focused on specific legal aspects of the original decision, combined with a broad overview of the justice of the outcome. To adapt a saying of William James, appellate wisdom is 'the art of knowing what to overlook.'

The authors have collected together indispensable source materials, along with summaries of some Key Cases and a wealth of information and tips that originate in that source of useful knowledge for which there is no real substitute – solid and reliable personal experience of how the system of appeals, reviews and references works in practice.

For anyone proposing to contest the decision of an employment tribunal (or any decision on appeal or re-consideration) this excellent manual is highly recommended.

The Right Honourable Lord Justice Mummery
May 2008

PREFACE

Every appeal begins with the simple question: what can I do if I have lost in the Employment Tribunal? This book hopefully answers that question and all those likely to follow it.

The Employment Tribunals accepted 132,577 claims in 2006/7. About 32,000 were resolved after a final hearing. In the same year the EAT heard about 600 appeals (432 at a full hearing). So, around 2% of substantive Employment Tribunal judgments were appealed.

This book is devoted to those cases, to those who wish to appeal and to those who wish to resist an appeal. Perhaps, it will first appeal to those who are dissatisfied with the decision of an Employment Tribunal and are merely considering whether to appeal.

All the options are laid out: asking the Tribunal to look again at its decision by way of a review; an appeal to the EAT, on to the Court of Appeal or even House of Lords; even a trip to the European Court of Human Rights via the EAT and Court of Appeal, perhaps with a stop off at the European Court of Justice, if necessary. Whichever route the appeal may take, we hope this book will prove a faithful and helpful companion.

We have, perhaps ambitiously, tried to ride two horses, not always travelling in the same direction: accessibility to all and usefulness to the expert.

Without disrespect to the system of appeals and its architects, we have endeavoured to make fair criticisms and constructive suggestions in equal measure and identified where the system appears incomplete or obscure.

We are grateful, of course, to our publisher Jordans for their interest and enthusiasm for this book and our approach to it – and of course, their patience, especially when circumstances contrived to complicate things and the 2008 EAT Practice Direction emerged without warning. We thank the Right Honourable Lord Justice Mummery for his foreword.

We also owe thanks to Sarah Maddock and Kiran Goss (our commissioning editors); Kathleen Donnelly and Richard Roberts at Henderson Chambers (who ably assisted with Chapters 8 and 12 respectively); Niamh O'Reilly (who analysed the 2008 EAT PD); and Dr Diane Roberts (who nobly assisted with correcting the proofs).

We could not have written this book without the considerable forbearance of our families and it is devoted to our wives Leigh and Ruth and our daughters Sabina, Talulla and Hermione.

Any errors or omissions are our own and, generally, the law is stated as at 1 September 2008.

Patrick Green

Adam Heppinstall

Henderson Chambers
2 Harcourt Buildings
Temple, London EC4

CONTENTS

Foreword	v
Preface	vii
Table of Cases	xxi
Table of Statutes	xxix
Table of Statutory Instruments	xxxi

Chapter 1
Summary	**1**
Introduction	1
Key practice points	2
Source materials	2
Scope of this book	2
Typical appeal – an illustration	3
Summary of time limits	6
The Employment Appeal Tribunal	6
The Court of Appeal	6
House of Lords	7
Where to appeal	7
Nature of employment appeals	8
The Employment Appeal Tribunal	8
Limited powers	9
Effect on appeals	9
History	10
Grounds of appeal	11
Funding	12
Representation	12
Precedent and the hierarchy	12

Chapter 2
Review by the Employment Tribunal	**15**
Fresh evidence	16
The interests of justice	16
Review or appeal?	17
Procedure for review	18
An application for a review by a party	18
A review on the tribunal's own motion	18
Appealing and reviewing at the same time	19
The slip rule	19

Chapter 3
Employment Appeal Tribunal   21
Introduction   21
  Decision, order or judgment appealed   21
    Decisions   21
    Order or judgment?   21
    Reasons   23
  Errors of law   23
  Status   24
Overview of procedure   24
  Procedural rules   24
    Non-compliance with EAT Rules   25
    The registrar   26
      Interim applications   26
      Appeals from the registrar   28
      The register   28
  The overriding objective   29
  Other reference to the Civil Procedure Rules 1998   29
Lodging the appeal   29
  Time limits   30
    Forty-two days from when?   31
      Two regimes   31
    Illustrations   33
    Receipt   35
      Service   35
      Extensions of time   36
  Notice of appeal   45
  Drafting your grounds   46
    Perversity and bias   46
    Last minute appeals   47
  Documents required   47
    Appeal not validly lodged   47
    The documents   48
    Written reasons   49
    No reasons available   49
      What to do   50
Other time limits   52
Case tracks   53
The 'sift'   54
  Further reasons   55
  The rule 3(7) track   56
  Rule 3(10): oral hearing   56
    Purpose   56
    Submissions by the respondent   56
    Participation by the respondent   57
Preliminary hearing   57
  Purpose   57

Directions and cross-appeals	58
Importance of submissions	58
Cross-appeals	58
Further reasons	59
No further action on the appeal	59
Appealing a rule 3(10) decision	59
Proceeding to a full hearing	61
Respondent's answer and cross-appeals	61
Answer	61
When required	61
Documents received	62
Lodging and serving the answer	62
Content	63
Cross-appeals	64
Drafting the cross-appeal	64
Sift of the cross-appeal	64
Appellant's reply	65
Directions	65
Parallel appeals	65
How they arise	65
Guidance in *Plummer Parsons v Wight*	66
Separate parallel appeals	67
Amending grounds of appeal	68
New points on appeal	70
New evidence	71
The chairman's/judge's notes	72
Chairman now an employment judge	72
Requirement for notes	72
A practical approach	74
Provisions of the Practice Direction	76
Application with notice of appeal	76
Application after notice of appeal	76
Respondent's application	76
Content of the application	77
Further application	77
Directions	78
Provision of notes to the parties	78
Criticism: litigants in person	79
Challenging the notes	80
Other applications for interim orders	80
Applications	80
Appeals from the registrar	81
Stays	81
Witness orders and production of documents	82
Waiving the rules	82
Debarring orders	82
Sitting in private	83
Restricted reporting orders	83

Controlling vexatious parties or proceedings	84
Joining parties	85
Appeals involving national security	85
Full hearing	86
Preparation	86
Listing	86
Bundles	87
Skeleton arguments	89
Lodging the skeleton argument	90
Terminology	91
Authorities	92
The hearing	92
The members of the panel	92
Representation and assistance	93
Non-lawyers	93
Pro bono representation	93
What to expect	93
Presenting your case	93
Judgment	94
Giving judgment	94
Reserved judgment	94
Remission	96
Disposal of appeal by consent	98
Costs	99
Generally	99
Procedure	100
Assessment	100
Wasted costs orders	100
Costs of litigants in person	102
Costs of assisted person	102
Review	103
Appealing to Court of Appeal	103
Time limit	103
Not a second appeal	104
Permission to appeal	104
No leapfrog to the House of Lords	104
Enforcement of orders and awards	105
Funding	105
Legal expenses insurance	105
After the event insurance	105
Legal aid	105
Equality and Human Rights Commission	106
Chapter 4	
The Court of Appeal	**107**
Appealing to the Court of Appeal	107
Overview	108

The right of appeal	108
Not a 'second appeal'	109
Permission to appeal	110
Obtaining permission to appeal from the Employment Appeal Tribunal	110
Obtaining permission to appeal from the Court of Appeal	112
Must permission be sought from the EAT first?	112
Time limit for obtaining permission from the Court of Appeal	113
How to make the application for permission to the Court of Appeal	113
The appellant's skeleton argument	114
Serving the respondent	115
Grounds for granting permission to appeal	115
The decision	116
The decision 'on the papers'	117
Permission granted 'on the papers'	117
Permission refused	117
The oral permission hearing	117
Permission granted	118
Permission refused	119
Setting aside permission to appeal	119
Permission given by Employment Appeal Tribunal	119
Limited permission	120
If the Employment Appeal Tribunal grants limited permission to appeal	120
If the Court of Appeal grants limited permission	120
Conditional permission	121
Cross-appeals or 'seeking to uphold the EAT decision on different or additional grounds'	121
All respondent's must give notice	123
Appealing out of time – extending time for filing and serving appellant's or respondent's notice	123
Hearing permission applications and appeals together	125
Where the appeal is from a preliminary hearing or interim hearing of the Employment Appeal Tribunal	125
Preparation for the full hearing of the appeal	125
Step 1 – serve the appeal bundle	125
Step 2 – serve a supplemental bundle	126
Step 3 – a core bundle?	126
Step 4 – the appeal questionnaire	126
Step 5 – listing	127
Step 6 – date of hearing notified	127
Step 7 – file and serve appellant's supplementary skeleton argument	127
Step 8 – file and serve respondent's skeleton argument or supplementary skeleton argument	128
Step 9 – bundles of authorities	128
Step 10 – final filing of documents	128
Step 11 – final bundle of authorities	129

Step 12 – If the appeal is listed for one day or less – serve a costs schedule in accordance with para 14.1(5) and 14.2 of the PD to CPR Part 52 and see para 4.145 below – 24 hours before the hearing	129
Miscellaneous case management powers of the Court of Appeal	129
Varying time limits, stays, strike outs and civil restraint orders	129
Amendment of appellant's or respondent's notices	129
Security for costs	130
Master and Deputy Masters of the Court of Appeal	130
The hearing of the appeal	130
The test	130
The nature of the appeal	131
No oral evidence or re-hearing	131
Trying to introduce new evidence	131
New argument	132
Powers of the Court of Appeal	132
Remitting back to the employment tribunal	132
Remitting back to the EAT	132
What will the final hearing be like?	133
The reserved judgment	134
Appeals by consent	135
Dismissal by consent	135
Allowing the appeal by consent	135
Patients and children	135
Appeals totally without merit	136
Costs	136
Generally	136
Costs orders	136
The assessment of costs	136
Wasted costs orders	136
Costs of litigants in person	137
Costs of an assisted person	137
Re-opening an appeal	137
Statistics	137
Next stop – European Court of Justice, House of Lords or European Court of Human Rights	138
The Court of Appeal – miscellaneous	138

Chapter 5
The House of Lords	**139**
Overview	139
The right of appeal	139
Leave to appeal	140
Stay of Court of Appeal's order	140
Leave from the House of Lords	140
Time limit for presenting petition for leave to appeal	140
Presenting a petition for leave to appeal	140
Respondent's response	141

Deciding the petition for leave to appeal	141
Leave obtained	142
If you have the Court of Appeal's leave	143
Appealing out of time	143
Consolidation and conjoinder	143
Cross-appeals	143
The appeal hearing procedure	144
Step 1 – lodge the petition of appeal	144
Step 1A – notifiy the Judicial Office of any HRA point	144
Step 1B – intervention	144
Step 2 – lodge £25,000 security for costs or obtain a waiver	144
Step 3 – lodge any petition to cross-appeal	145
Step 3A – lodge statement of facts and issues and an appendix	145
Step 3B – setting the appeal down for hearing	146
Step 4 – submit time estimates	146
Step 5 – appellant submits case	147
Step 6 – respondent submits case	147
Step 7 – appellants lodge 15 bound volumes and 10 copies of every authority	148
Step 8 – receive notice of hearing	148
The hearing	149
The approach	149
Costs	149
New submissions	150
Judgment	150
The order of the House	151
Disposal by consent	151
The end of the road	151
References to the European Court of Justice	151
The Supreme Court of the United Kingdom	152

Chapter 6
References to the European Court of Justice	**153**
Introduction	153
Reference not an appeal	153
Employment tribunal, Employment Appeal Tribunal and Court of Appeal	154
Reference procedure	154
House of Lords	155
Procedure for reference made by House of Lords	155
Proceedings before the European Court of Justice	156
Post European Court of Justice judgment	156
New Article 234 EC	156

Chapter 7
The European Convention for the Protection of Human Rights and Fundamental Freedoms 1950 and taking a case to the European Court of Human Rights — 159
The European Convention for the Protection of Human Rights and Fundamental Freedoms 1950 — 159
Human Rights Act 1998 — 159
Rights relevant to employment law — 160
Human Rights Act 1998 didn't work? — 161
Admissibility — 162
Victim of a European Convention violation — 162
Exhaustion of domestic remedies — 162
The 6-month time limit — 162
Anonymity — 163
Matter already examined by the court — 163
The same matter has been submitted to another procedure of international investigation or settlement — 163
Incompatibility with the provisions of the European Convention — 163
Manifestly ill-founded — 164
Abuse of right of application — 164
Making a complaint — 164
The admissibility decision — 165
If the application is declared admissible — 166
Just satisfaction — 166
Friendly settlement — 166
Final hearing — 167
Judgments — 167
The outcome — 167

Chapter 8 — 169
Grounds of Appeal — 169
Scope of this chapter — 169
Overview — 169
  Law not fact — 169
    Approach — 170
      Live issue — 170
      Disposal — 171
  Key task — 171
Errors of law — 172
  Identifying errors of law — 172
    Difficult cases — 172
Grounds of appeal — 173
Misdirection, misunderstanding or misapplication — 173
  Illustrations — 173
Perversity — 175
  Categories of perversity challenge — 178
    On the evidence — 178
      No evidence — 178

Some evidence	179
Particulars must be given	179
Evidence must be agreed or chairman's notes produced	179
Reliance on the documents before the tribunal	180
A high hurdle	180
Inferences	180
Overall conclusion	181
Exercising a discretion	183
Inadequate reasons	183
Introduction	183
The duty to give reasons	184
Rule 30(1): the duty	184
Rule 30(6): written reasons for a judgment	184
Interim decisions	185
What is required	186
Meek-compliance	186
Courts and tribunals	186
Desirable reasons	188
Development of principles	189
Illustrations	190
Law or test applied	190
Unresolved issue	190
Unexplained decision not to draw inferences	191
Unexplained drawing of inferences	192
No reasoning	193
Where reasons are required	193
Rule 30(6)(a): issues relevant to the claim	194
Rule 30(6)(b): issues not determined and why	194
Rule 30(6)(c): relevant findings of fact	194
Rule 30(6)(d): concise statement of the applicable law	196
Rule 30(6)(e): how facts and law applied	196
Rule 30(6)(f): calculation of compensation	196
Additional Reasons	197
Obtaining additional reasons	198
Procedural irregularity	198
Bias	198
The test	199
Hearing evidence	200
Personal relationships	201
Personal interest	201
Conduct in previous cases	201
Closed mind and pre-judging	202
Prejudices	202
Excessive intervention	203
Unfairness of hearing	203
Representation	204
Evidence	204
Moving the goal posts	205

Tribunal's inattention	206
Public hearing	206
Delay	206
Errors of jurisdiction	207
Composition of employment tribunal	207
Employment judge sitting alone	207
Territorial jurisdiction	209
Jurisdiction on remission	210
Further reasons: Barke v SEETEC Business Technology Centre Ltd	211
The procedure	211
The power	211
Justification in *Burns* was wrong	211
The *Barke* justification	212
Critical analysis	213
Critique of the key points	213
A new theory	214
Aparau	214
Tran	214
Leverton	215
Reuben	215
Lambe	216
Employment tribunal	216
The statutory scheme	218
Confined jurisdiction	218
Conclusion	219

Chapter 9
The Employment Appeal Tribunal's Jurisdiction, Constitution and Powers — 221

Overview	221
Issues on jurisdiction	221
Territorial jurisdiction	223
UK rights – unfair dismissal	224
Peripatetic employees	225
Posted and expatriate employees	226
EU rights – sex discrimination	226
Period of employment	226
Holis and *Bleuse*	227
Sex discrimination claims now	228
Human rights	228
The Employment Appeal Tribunal's original and appellate jurisdictions	229
Original jurisdiction	232
Employment Appeal Tribunal – constitutional and administrative arrangements	232
Tribunals, Courts and Enforcement Act 2007	234
General powers	234
Appeals from employment tribunals to the High Court	235
National security	235

Appealing interim orders of the Employment Appeal Tribunal – EAT or Court of Appeal?	235

Chapter 10
Key Case Summaries — 237

Yeboah v Crofton [2002] IRLR 634	237
Meek v City of Birmingham District Council [1987] IRLR 250	239
Anya v University of Oxford and another [2001] IRLR 377	239
Burns v Consignia (No 2) [2004] IRLR 425	240
Barke v SEETEC [2005] IRLR 633	240
Sinclair Roche and Temperley (a firm) and others v Heard and another [2004] IRLR 763	241
Lambe v 186K Ltd [2004] EWCA Civ 1045	244

Appendix 1
Review in the Employment Tribunals — 249

Employment Tribunals (Constitution and Rules of Procedure) Regulations 2004	249

Appendix 2
The Employment Appeal Tribunal — 253

Employment Tribunals Act 1996	253
Employment Appeal Tribunal Rules 1993	269
Practice Direction (Employment Appeal Tribunal – Procedure) 2008	306
Practice Statement	330
Employment Appeal Tribunal Conciliation Protocol	332

Appendix 3
The Court of Appeal — 335

Employment Tribunals Act 1996	335
Supreme Court Act 1981	336
Access to Justice Act 1999	338
Civil Procedure Rules 1998	339

Appendix 4
The House of Lords and Supreme Court — 375

Appellate Jurisdiction Act 1876	375
Administration of Justice Act 1934	376
Constitutional Reform Act 2005	377
House of Lords Practice Directions Applicable to Civil Appeals	378

Appendix 5
References to the European Court of Justice — 407

Article 234 EC Treaty pre-Treaty of Lisbon	407
Article 234 EC Treaty post-Treaty of Lisbon	408
Civil Procedure Rules 1998	409

Appendix 6
The European Court of Human Rights 415
European Convention on Human Rights 415

Appendix 7
Precedents 419
Notice of Appeal from Decision of Employment Tribunal 419
Rule 3(10) Letter 423
EAT Form 3 424
EAT Respondent's Answer 425
CA Form N161 428
Court of Appeal Grounds 434
CA Form N162 436
Order Remitting Appeal to EAT 444
Reference to ECJ order 446
Petition for Leave to Appeal 448
Petition to Appeal 453
Application to ECtHR 455

Index 463

TABLE OF CASES

References are to paragraph numbers.

A v B ex parte News Group Newspapers Ltd [1998] ICR 55, (1997) *The Times*, July 4, EAT	3.315
Abbey National plc v Fairbrother [2007] IRLR 320	8.23
Adams v West Sussex County Council [1990] ICR 546	3.14, 8.47
Adivar and Others v Turkey (Application No 21893/93) (1996) 23 EHRR 143	7.20
Adjaho v Bariyendeza UKEAT/0137/04 [2005] All ER (D) 76 (Mar)	8.8
Advance Security UK v Musa UKEAT/0611/07, 21 May 2008	8.138
Alexander Machinery (Dudley) Ltd v Crabtree [1974] ICR 120	8.69, 8.77, 8.86
Alstom Transport v Tilson UKEAT/0532/07, 4 December 2007	8.136
Amy Services Limited v Cardigan [2008] IRLR 279	3.14
Ansar v Lloyds TSB Bank plc and Others [2006] EWCA Civ 1462, [2007] IRLR 211	8.128, 8.129, 8.131, 8.135
Anthony v Governors of Hillcrest School EAT/1193/00, 28 November 2001	8.137
Anya v University of Oxford and Another [2001] EWCA Civ 405, [2001] ICR 847, [2001] IRLR 377	8.51, 8.67, 8.103, 10.3
Aparau v Iceland Frozen Foods plc (No 2) [2000] 1 All ER 228, [2000] ICR 341, [2000] IRLR 196	8.166, 8.187, 8.199, 8.201, 9.6
Asda Stores Ltd v Thompson [2004] IRLR 598	3.239
Ashbourne v Department of Education and Skills and Another UKEAT/0123/07 [2007] All ER (D) 390 (Nov)	9.33
Assessor for Renfrewshire v Mitchell and Others 1965 SC 271, Lands Val AC	8.47
Associated Provincial Picture Houses Ltd v Wednesbury Corporation [1948] 1 KB 223, [1947] 2 All ER 680, CA	8.47
Atkins v Wiltshire Primary Care Trust UKEAT/0566/07, 14 February 2008	8.15
Attorney-General v Ayouvare UKEAT/0614/03 [2004] All ER (D) 80 (Apr)	3.322
Attorney-General v Barker [2000] 1 FLR 759	3.321, 3.322
Attorney-General v Bruce UKEAT/0586/05 [2006] All ER (D) 70 (Mar)	3.322
Attorney-General v Covey; Attorney-General v Matthews [2001] EWCA Civ 254, [2001] All ER (D) 222 (Feb)	3.322
Attorney-General v D'Souza UKEAT/0139/04 [2004] All ER (D) 322 (Jul)	3.322
Attorney-General v Deman UKEAT/0113/06 [2006] All ER (D) 337 (Oct)	3.318
Attorney-General v Jones [1990] 1 WLR 859, [1990] 2 All ER 636, CA	3.322
Attorney-General v Kuttappan UKEAT/0478/05 [2005] All ER (D) 301 (Dec)	3.322
Attorney-General v Perotti [2006] EWHC 1002 (Admin)	3.322
Attorney-General v Roberts UKEAT/0058/05 [2005] All ER (D) 138 (Jul)	3.322
Attorney-General v Tyrrell UKEAT/0236/03 [2004] All ER (D) 470 (Mar)	3.322
Attorney-General v Wheen [2000] IRLR 461, EAT, affirmed [2001] IRLR 91, CA	3.321, 3.322
Aziz v Bethnal Green City Challenge Co Ltd [2000] IRLR 111	3.91, 3.100, 3.103, 3.240
Babula v Waltham Forest College [2007] EWCA Civ 174, [2007] ICR 1026	8.23
Bache v Essex County Council [2000] ICR 313, [2000] IRLR 251	8.141
Bagga v Heavy Electricals (India) Ltd [1972] ICR 118	2.5
Bahl v Law Society [2004] EWCA Civ 1070, [2004] IRLR 799	8.149
Baker and Others v Superite Tools Ltd [1986] ICR 189	8.10

Balfour Beatty Power Networks v Wilcox [2006] EWCA Civ 1240, [2007]
  IRLR 63   4.121, 8.76
Balmoral Group v Borealis (UK) Ltd [2006] EWHC 2998, [2006] All ER
  (D) 135 (Aug)   4.18
Bansai v Alpha Flight Services [2007] ICR 308   8.120
Bansal v Cheema [2001] CP Rep 6, CA   4.88
Barke v SEETEC Business Technology Centre Ltd [2005] EWCA Civ 578,
  [2005] ICR 1373, [2005] IRLR 633   3.160, 3.171, 3.189, 3.382, 8.2, 8.80, 8.117, 8.174,
      8.188, 8.202, 8.203, 10.5
Barlow v Clifford & Co (Sidcup) Ltd UKEAT/0910/04, [2005] All ER (D)
  02 (Oct)   8.42, 8.62
Beasley v National Grid UKEAT/0626/06 [2007] All ER (D) 110 (Aug)   1.8, 3.65
Biwater Ltd v Bell EAT 218/89   8.10
Blackburn v Chief Constable of West Midlands Police [2007] All ER (D)
  250 (Dec)   8.23
Blackpole Furniture v Sullivan [1978] ICR 558   2.17
Bleuse v MBT Transport and Another UKEAT/0632/06 [2008] IRLR 264,
  [2008] ICR 488 [2007] All ER (D) 392 (Dec)   3.252, 8.164, 9.15, 9.31
Bolton School v Evans [2007] IRLR 140   8.23
Botham v Ministry of Defence UKEAT/0503/04 [2004] All ER (D) 210
  (Nov)   3.416, 4.22
Brenan and Ging v Edward (Lancs) Ltd [1976] IRLR 378   2.6
British Gas plc v Sharma [1991] IRLR 101, EAT   8.110
British Publishing Co Ltd v Fraser [1987] ICR 517   3.387
British Telecommunications plc v Sheridan [1990] IRLR 27, CA   8.36, 10.1
BUPA Care Homes (BNH) Ltd v Cann; Spillett v Tesco Stores Ltd [2006]
  IRLR 248   9.14
Burns v Consignia (No 2) [2004] IRLR 425   10.4, 10.5, 10.6
Burns v Royal Mail Group plc (formerly Consignia plc) and Another [2004]
  ICR 1103   3.189, 8.117, 8.174, 8.175, 8.176, 8.180, 8.183, 8.184, 8.186, 8.201, 8.202, 8.203
Burton v British Railways Board [1983] ICR 544   6.18
Butlins Skyline v Beynon EATUK/0042-0045/06 [2007] ICR 121   2.10, 8.23

Carmichael v National Power plc [1999] 1 WLR 2042, [1999] 4 All ER 897,
  [1999] ICR 1226, HL   8.24
Carter v Credit Change Ltd [1980] 1 All ER 252, [1979] ICR 908, [1979]
  IRLR 361, CA   8.32
Carver v Saudi Arabian Airlines [1999] 3 All ER 61, [1999] ICR 991, [1999]
  IRLR 370, CA   9.21, 9.29
Chapman v Simon [1994] IRLR 124   8.51, 8.107
Chiu v British Aerospace plc [1982] IRLR 56   3.125, 8.42
CILFIT Srl and Lanificio di Gavardo v Ministry of Health (Case C-283/81)
  [1982] ECR 3415   6.13
Clark v Midland Packaging Ltd [2005] 2 All ER 266   3.49, 3.66
Comfort v Lord Chancellor's Department [2004] EWCA Civ 349, CA   8.93
Conlin v United Distillers [1992] IRLR 503   8.57
Connex South Eastern Ltd v Bangs [2005] EWCA Civ 14, [2005] ICR 763   8.153
Cooke v Secretary of State for Social Security; *sub nom* Cooke v Social
  Security Commissioner [2001] EWCA Civ 734, [2002] 3 All ER 279,
  (2001) *The Daily Telegraph*, May 1, CA   4.41
Copsey v WWB Devon Clays Ltd [2005] EWCA Civ 932, [2005] ICR 1789,
  [2005] IRLR 811, CA   7.6
Costello-Roberts v United Kingdom (Application No 13134/87) (1995) 19
  EHRR 112, [1994] ELR 1, ECHR   7.18
Costellow v Somerset County Council [1993] 1 All ER 952   3.98, 3.99
Crofton v Yeboah [2002] EWCA Civ 794, [2002] IRLR 634, [2002] All ER
  (D) 512 (May), CA   1.31, 3.124, 3.265, 8.36, 8.43, 8.47
Crofts and Others v Cathay Pacific Airways Ltd [2005] EWCA Civ 599,
  [2005] ICR 1436   9.22

Case	Reference
D'Silva v Manchester Metropolitan University UKEAT/0024/07 [2007] All ER (D) 10 (Oct)	8.76, 8.150
Da'Bell v NSPCC UKEAT/0044/08, 13 February 2008	8.127
Darr v LRC Products Ltd [1993] IRLR 257, EAT	8.114
Davies v Presbyterian Church of Wales [1986] 1 WLR 323, [1986] 1 All ER 705, [1986] ICR 280, [1986] IRLR 194, HL	8.24
De Haney v Brent Mind and Another [2003] EWCA Civ 1637, [2004] ICR 348	9.44
Deman v Association of University Teachers [2003] EWCA Civ 329, [2003] 20 LS Gaz R 27	8.94
DeMarco Almeida v Opportunity Equity Partners Ltd [2006] UKPC 44	8.139
Dexine Rubber Co Ltd v Alker [1977] ICR 434	3.293
Dickie and Others v Cathay Pacific Airways Ltd [2004] ICR 1733	9.12
Diem v Crystal Services plc [2006] All ER (D) 84 (Feb)	8.138
Dignity Funerals v Bruce [2005] IRLR 189	8.116
Dore v Aon Training Ltd (formerly Totalamber Plc); *sub nom* Aon Training Ltd (formerly Totalamber Plc) v Dore [2005] EWCA Civ 411, [2005] IRLR 891, CA	8.115
Dunnachie v Kingston-upon-Hull City Council [2004] EWCA Civ 84, [2004] IRLR 287	8.114
Earl v Slater and Wheeler (Airlyne) Ltd [1973] 1 WLR 51, [1973] 1 All ER 145, [1972] ICR 508, [1972] IRLR 115, NIRC	3.215
Eckersley v Binnie (1988) 18 Con LR 1	8.82
Eclipse Blinds Ltd v Wright [1992] IRLR 133	8.42
Eden v Humphries and Glasgow Ltd [1981] ICR 183	3.391
Effa v Alexandra Health Trust and Another [1999] All ER (D) 1229	8.97
Ellis v M&P Steelcraft Ltd and Another UKEAT/0536/07, UKEAT/0537/07, [2008] All ER (D) 353 (Feb)	8.23
English Royal Mail Group Ltd UKEAT/0027/08, 3 July 2008	8.93
English v Emery Reimbold & Strick Ltd; DJ & C Withers (Farms Ltd) v Ambic Equipment Ltd; Verrechia v Commissioner of Police of the Metropolis (Practice Note) [2002] EWCA Civ 605, [2002] 1 WLR 2409, [2002] UKHRR 957, [2002] 3 All ER 385, CA	8.80, 8.83, 8.181, 8.185
Ezsias North Glamorgan NHS Trust [2007] EWCA Civ 330, [2007] 4 All ER 940	8.56, 8.137
Facey v Midas Retail Security Ltd and Another [2001] ICR 287	8.124
Gilham and Others v Kent County Council (No 2) [1985] ICR 233	8.29
Gizbert v ABC News International Inc [2006] All ER (D) 98 (Aug)	9.4
Gladwell v Secretary of State for Trade and Industry [2007] ICR 264	8.157
Glasgow City Council v Zafar [1997] 1 WLR 1659, [1998] ICR 120, [1998] IRLR 36, [1998] 2 All ER 953, HL	8.108
GMB v Holis Metal Industries Ltd UKEAT/0171/07 [2007] All ER (D) 304 (Dec)	8.164, 9.15, 9.31
Gover v Propertycare Ltd [2006] EWCA Civ 286, [2006] ICR 1073	4.121
Governors of Warwick Park School v Hazlehurst [2001] EWCA Civ 2056, [2001] All ER (D) 39 (Dec)	8.95
Grady v Prison Service [2003] EWCA Civ 527, [2003] 3 All ER 745, [2003] ICR 753, CA	3.198, 4.130, 10.7
Greenaway Harrison Ltd v Wiles [1994] IRLR 380, EAT	8.137
Guest v Alpine Soft Drinks Ltd [1982] ICR 110	8.69, 8.77
Gydnia American Shipping Lines (London) Ltd v Chelminski [2004] EWCA Civ 871, [2004] ICR 1523, [2004] IRLR 725	3.55, 3.132
Hafele v Nolan UKEATPA/0354/08, 23 July 2008	1.20, 3.43, 3.106, 3.134
Hamilton v GMB (Northern Region) [2007] IRLR 391	8.132
Hammond Suddards Solicitors v Agrichem International Holdings Ltd [2002] EWCA Civ 2065, [2001] All ER (D) 258 (Dec)	4.114
Haritaki v South East England Development Agency UKEATPA/0006/08	1.14

Hartel v Al-Ghazali Multi-Cultural Centre and Another UKEAT/0064/07, [2007] All ER (D) 244 (Dec)	8.98
Hawkins v Ball and Barclays Bank plc [1996] IRLR 258, EAT	3.263, 3.266
Haydock v GD Cocker and Sons Ltd EAT1143/99, EAT215/02 [2003] All ER (D) 438 (Mar)	3.7
Hertfordshire Investments Ltd v Bubb [2000] 1 WLR 2318	3.261
Hough and APEX v Leyland DAF Ltd [1991] IRLR 194	8.49
Houston v Lightwater Farms Ltd; Walker v Lakhadari [1990] ICR 502	3.262, 3.295
Hunt v Market Force (UK) Ltd; *sub nom* Market Force (UK) Ltd v Hunt [2002] IRLR 863, EAT	8.114
Interbulk Ltd v Aiden Shipping Co Ltd (The "Vimeira" (No.1)) [1985] 2 Lloyd's Rep 410	8.171
Iron and Steel Trades Confederation v ASW Ltd [2004] IRLR 926	3.394
J Sainsbury plc v Moger [1994] ICR 800	3.205, 3.387
Jackson v Ghost Ltd; Jackson v Ghost Inc [2003] IRLR 824, EAT	9.22
James v Baily Gibson & Co (a firm) [2002] EWCA Civ 1690, [2002] All ER (D) 454 (Oct)	4.68
James v Greenwich Borough Council [2007] ICR 577	8.24
Johnston and Others v Ireland (Application No 9697/82) (1987) 9 EHRR 203	7.12
Jones and Baird v TGWU UKEATS/0003/07 and UKEATS/0004/07, 6–7 February 2008	8.132
Jones v DAS Legal Expenses Insurance Co Ltd [2003] EWCA Civ 1071, [2004] IRLR 218	8.132
Jones v Governing Body of Burdett Coutts School [1999] ICR 38, [1998] IRLR 521, (1998) 142 SJLB 142, CA	3.251
Jones v MBNA International Bank (unreported) 30 June 2000	4.127
Judge v Crown Leisure Limited [2005] IRLR 823	8.140
Jurkowska v HLMAD Ltd [2008] EWCA Civ 231, [2008] ICR 841, [2008] IRLR 430	1.7, 3.43, 3.91, 3.94, 3.98, 3.104
Kanapathiar v Harrow London Borough Council [2003] IRLR 571	3.131
Khudados v Leggate and Others [2005] ICR 1013	3.245
King v Eaton (No 2) [1998] IRLR 686, [1999] SLT 656	10.7
Klusova v Hounslow London Borough Council [2007] EWCA Civ 1127, [2007] All ER (D) 105 (Nov)	8.45
Knight v Clifton [1971] 2 All ER 378	8.82
Knight v Harrow London Borough Council [2003] IRLR 140	8.113
Ladd v Marshall [1954] 1 WLR 1489, [1954] 3 All ER 745, (1954) 98 SJ 870, CA	3.254, 4.126
Ladup Ltd v Barnes [1982] ICR 107, [1982] IRLR 7, EAT	2.6
Lambe v 186K Ltd [2004] EWCA Civ 1045, [2005] ICR 307	3.198, 4.131, 8.92, 8.100, 8.192
Lawal v Northern Spirit Ltd [2003] UKHL 35, [2003] IRLR 538	9.43
Lawrence v HM Prison Service [2007] IRLR 468	8.157
Lawson v Serco Ltd, Botham v Ministry of Defence Crofts v Veta Ltd [2006] UKHL 3, [2006] IRLR 289	9.20, 9.21, 9.22, 9.23
Lear v Key Recruitment UK Ltd UKEAT/0597/07, [2008] All ER (D) 362 (Feb)	8.23
Leofelis SA v Lonsdale Sports Ltd (2008) *The Times*, July 23	4.94
Leverton v Clwyd County Council [1989] IRLR 28	8.189
Levy v Marrable & Co Ltd [1984] ICR 583	8.104
Lindsay v Ironsides Ray & Vials; Ironsides Ray & Vials v Lindsay [1994] ICR 384	2.6
Lloyd Jones v T Mobile (UK) Ltd [2003] EWCA Civ 1162, [2003] EGLR 55	4.71
Locabail (UK) Ltd v Bayfield Properties Ltd and Another; Locabail (UK) Ltd and Another v Waldorf Investment Corporation and Others; Timmins v Gormley; Williams v HM Inspector of Taxes and Others;	

Table of Cases xxv

Locabail (UK) Ltd v Bayfield Properties Ltd and Another; Locabail (UK) Ltd and Another v Waldorf Investment Corporation and Others; Timmins v Gormley; Williams v HM Inspector of Taxes and Others; —*continued*
R v Bristol Betting and Gaming Licensing Committee ex parte O'Callaghan [2000] QB 451, [2000] 2 WLR 870, [2000] UKHRR 300, [2000] 1 All ER 65, [2000] IRLR 96, CA 8.126
Lodwick v London Borough of Southwark [2004] EWCA Civ 306, [2004] ICR 884 .... 8.127
London Borough of Hackney v Sagnia [2005] All ER (D) 61 (Oct) 8.130, 8.131

Mackenzie v Billing Aquadrome UKEAT/0238/08, 21 August 2008 .... 8.93
Marks and Spencer plc v Martins [1998] IRLR 326 .... 8.108
Martin v British Railways Board [1989] ICR 24 .... 3.107, 3.129
Martin v Glynwed Distribution Ltd (t/a MBS Fastenings) [1983] ICR 511, [1983] IRLR 198, CA 3.266, 8.42, 8.44, 8.90
Masin v Bryn Howel Hotel Ltd UKEAT/0831/04 [2005] All ER (D) 350 (Feb) 3.304
McGowan v Scottish Water [2005] IRLR 167 .... 7.6
Meek v City of Birmingham District Council [1987] IRLR 250, CA   8.1, 8.54, 8.79, 8.92, 10.2
Melon and Others v Hector Powe Ltd [1981] ICR 43 .... 8.33
Melstar Ltd v Rix UKEAT/0701/04 [2005] All ER (D) 348 (Feb) 3.304
Mercy v Northgate HR Ltd [2007] EWCA Civ 1304, [2007] All ER (D) 196 (Dec) 3.386
Miller v Community Links Trust Ltd UKEAT/0486/07 [2007] All ER (D) 196 (Nov) 1.8, 3.65
Ministry of Defence v Wheeler [1996] ICR 554 .... 3.264
Miriki v Bar Council [2001] EWCA Civ 1973, [2002] ICR 505, (2002) *The Times*, January 22 .... 8.94
Morris v London Iron and Steel Co Ltd [1988] QB 493 .... 8.88
Mortimer v Reading Windings Ltd [1977] ICR 511 .... 8.136
Moult v East Sussex County Council UKEAT10329/07 .... 3.125

Neale v Hereford and Worcester County Council [1986] ICR 471, [1986] IRLR 168, CA 8.28, 8.30

Onwuka v Spherion Technology UK Ltd [2005] ICR 567 .... 2.2

Paragon Finance plc v Noueiri [2001] EWCA Civ 1402, [2001] 1 WLR 2357 ... 4.117
Parkers Bakeries Ltd v Palmer [1977] IRLR 215 .... 8.114
Patel v Gorai UKEAT/0052/07, [2007] All ER (D) 190 (Nov) 8.84
Pay v Lancashire Probation Service [2004] ICR 187, [2004] IRLR 129, (2003) *The Times*, November 27, EAT 7.4
Peter Simper & Co Ltd v Cooke [1986] IRLR 19 .... 8.136
Piggott Bros & Co Ltd v Jackson [1991] IRLR 309 .... 1.31, 3.266, 8.34
Pinnington v City and Council of Swansea UKEAT/0561/03 [2004] All ER (D) 564 (May) 3.289
Plummer Parsons v Wight UKEAT/0403/06 (unreported) 3.169, 3.196, 3.228
Portec (UK) Ltd v Mogensen [1976] 3 All ER 565, [1976] ICR 396, [1976] IRLR 209, EAT 1.57
Porter v Magill, Weeks v Magill [2001] UKHL 67, [2002] 2 WLR 37, [2002] 1 All ER 465, HL 8.125
Portsea Island Mutual Co-operative Society Ltd v Rees [1980] ICR 260 .... 8.101
Post Office v Howell [2000] ICR 913 .... 8.158, 8.159, 8.160
Prater v Cornwall County Council [2006] EWCA Civ 102, [2006] IRLR 362 ...... 9.4
Przybylska v Modus Telecom Ltd EAT/0566/06, [2007] All ER (D) 06 (May) 8.157

Qureshi v Victoria University of Manchester [2001] ICR 863, EAT 8.51, 8.107

R (Equal Opportunities Commission) v Secretary of State for Trade and Industry [2007] EWHC 483 (Admin), [2007] ICR 1234 .... 8.23

R (National Union of Journalists) v Central Arbitration Committee [2005] EWCA Civ 1309, [2006] IRLR 53	7.6
R v Bow Street Metropolitan Stipendiary Magistrate ex parte Pinochet Ugarte (No 2) [2000] AC 119	8.134
Rabahallah v British Telecom plc UKEAT/0382/04 [2005] ICR 440	9.4
Rance v Secretary of State for Health [2007] IRLR 665	1.3, 2.20, 3.135, 3.250
Raybright TV Services Ltd v Smith [1973] ICR 640	2.10
Regalbourne Ltd v East Lindsey District Council (1993) *The Times*, March 16	3.98
Reuben v Brent London Borough Council [2000] IRLR 176	8.190
Ridehalgh v Horsefield [1994] 3 WLR 462	3.398, 3.399
Roberts v Skelmersdale College [2003] EWCA Civ 954, [2003] ICR 1127	8.63, 8.78
Robinson v Fernsby [2003] EWCA Civ 1820, 148 Sol Jo LB 59	4.137
Saggar v Ministry of Defence [2005] EWCA Civ 413, [2005] IRLR 618	9.29
Saif Ali v Sydney Mitchell & Co [1978] 3 All ER 1033 at 1041, 1043, [1980] AC 198	3.399
Sandhu v Jan De Rijk Transport Ltd [2007] EWCA Civ 430, [2007] ICR 1137	8.23
Savoia v Chiltern Herb Farms Ltd [1981] IRLR 65	8.114
Scottish & Newcastle Beer Production Ltd v Cannon EAT 254/90	8.111
Secretary of State for Trade and Industry v Langridge [1991] Ch 402, [1991] 2 WLR 1343, [1991] 3 All ER 591, CA	8.157
Setiya v East Yorkshire Health Authority [1995] ICR 799	3.109
Sian v Abbey National plc [2004] ICR 55	3.55
Sinclair Roche and Temperley (a firm) and others v Heard and another [2004] IRLR 763	3.349, 3.382, 8.11, 10.6
Slee v Secretary of State for Justice [2007] EWHC 2717 (Admin), [2007] All ER (D) 303 (Nov)	3.384
Slingsby v Griffith Smith UKEAT/0619/07, UKEATPA/0735/07 (unreported)	3.53, 3.182, 3.206, 8.153
Smith v City of Glasgow District Council [1987] ICR 796, [1987] IRLR 326, HL	8.61
Sogbetun v Hackney London Borough Council [1998] ICR 1264	8.159, 9.4
Solani Tirado v St George's Healthcare NHS Trust UKEATPA/0669/05 [2005] All ER (D) 12 (Nov)	3.52, 3.103, 3.132
Southwark London Borough Council v Jiminez [2003] EWCA Civ 502, [2003] ICR 1176	8.136
Speciality Care plc v Pachela and Another [1996] ICR 633, [1996] IRLR 248, [1995] TLR 177, EAT	8.105
Stanley Cole (Wainfleet) Ltd v Sheridan; *sub nom* Sheridan v Stanley Cole (Wainfleet) Ltd [2003] EWCA Civ 1046, [2003] 4 All ER 1181, [2003] ICR 1449, CA; affirming [2003] ICR 297, [2003] IRLR 52, EAT	8.148
Stansbury v Dataplus plc [2003] EWCA Civ 1951, [2004] ICR 523, [2004] IRLR 466	7.6, 8.151
Sterling Developments (London) Ltd v Pagano [2007] IRLR 471	8.162
Stewart v Cleveland Guest (Engineering) Ltd [1994] IRLR 440	8.35
Storer v British Gas plc [2000] ICR 603	8.152
Sukul-Lennard v Croydon Primary Healthcare Trust [2003] All ER (D) 369 (Jul), (2003) *The Times*, July 22	4.130, 10.7
T (a child: contact: alienation: permission to appeal), Re [2002] EWCA Civ 1736, [2003] 1 FLR 531	4.23
Tanfern Ltd v Cameron-MacDonald and Another (Practice Note) [2000] 1 WLR 1311	4.42
Taylor v Lawrence [2002] EWCA Civ 90, [2003] QB 528, [2002] 3 WLR 640, [2002] 2 All ER 353, CA	4.149
Times Newspapers Ltd v Fitt [1981] ICR 637	2.21
Todd v British Midland Airways Ltd [1978] ICR 959	9.25
Training in Compliance Ltd v Drewse [2001] CP Rep 46	4.88

Table of Cases xxvii

Tran v Greenwich Vietnam Community Council [2002] EWCA Civ 553, [2002] ICR 1101	8.179, 8.188
Trimble v Supertravel Ltd [1982] ICR 440, [1982] IRLR 451, EAT	2.6, 2.7
Unilever v Chefaro Proprietaries Ltd and Others Practice Note [1995] 1 WLR 243	4.99
Union of Construction, Allied Trades and Technicians v Brain [1981] IRLR 225	8.85
Unison v Leicestershire County Council [2006] EWCA Civ 825, [2006] IRLR 810	8.5
United Arab Emirates v Abdelghafar [1995] ICR 65, [1995] IRLR 243, EAT	3.91, 3.93, 3.103, 3.105, 3.134, 3.240, 3.246, 3.316, 8.165
United Distillers v Conlin [1994] IRLR 169, Ct of Sess	8.111
Uyamnwa-Odu v Schools Offices Services Ltd EAT/0294/05 [2005] All ER (D) 377 (Nov)	3.10
Varma v North Cheshire Hospitals NHS Trust UKEAT/0264/05 [2006] All ER (D) 203 (Oct)	3.251
Varndell and Others v Kearney and Trecker Marwin Ltd [1983] ICR 683	8.86, 8.88
Vento v Chief Constable of the West Yorkshire Police [2002] ICR 318	10.7
Vernazza, Re [1959] 1 WLR 622, [1959] 2 All ER 200, QBD	3.322
Vincent v MJ Gallagher Contractors Ltd [2003] EWCA Civ 640, [2003] ICR 1244	4.130, 10.7
Voteforce Associates Ltd v Quinn [2002] ICR 1	8.91
Wadman v Carpenter Farrer Partnership [1993] IRLR 374, [1993] 3 CMLR 93, [1993] TLR 306, EAT	8.110
Welsh v Parnianzadeh [2004] EWCA Civ 1832, [2004] All ER (D) 170 (Dec)	4.88
Wheeler v Quality Deep Limited (trading as Thai Royale Restaurant) [2004] EWCA Civ 1085, [2005] ICR 265	3.291
Whittaker v P & D Watson (Trading as P & M Watson Haulage) and Another [2002] ICR 1244	7.3, 9.37
Wileman v Minilec Engineering Ltd [1988] ICR 318, [1988] IRLR 144, EAT	3.254
Williams v Cowell and Another [2000] ICR 85	9.47
Williams v Ferrosan [2004] IRLR 607	2.8
Williams v University of Nottingham [2007] IRLR 660	9.33
Wilson v Liverpool Corporation [1971] 1 WLR 302	4.127
Woodhouse School v Webster UKEAT/0459/07, 24 April 2008	8.140
Woodward v Abbey National plc; JP Garrett Electrical Ltd v Cotton [2005] IRLR 782	3.49, 3.66
X v Commissioner of the Police of the Metropolis [2003] ICR 1031	3.316
X v Y [2004] EWCA Civ 662, [2004] IRLR 625	7.4
Yeboah v Crofton [2002] IRLR 634	10.1
Yorkshire Engineering v Burnham [1973] IRLR 316	2.6
Young v Bristol Aeroplane Co Ltd [1944] KB 718, CA; affirmed [1946] AC 163, HL	1.56
Yusuf and Others v Aberplace Ltd [1984] ICR 850	8.190
Zargaran v Zargaran London EAT/1062/01 [2003] All ER (D) 140 (Mar)	8.8, 8.143

TABLE OF STATUTES

References are to paragraph numbers.

Access to Justice Act 1999	3.411
s 11	4.148
s 54(4)	4.59
s 55	3.411, 4.11, 4.12, 4.21, 4.41
s 55(1)	1.23
Administration of Justice Act 1934	
s 1	5.2
Administration of Justice Act 1960	
s 13	4.10
Administration of Justice Act 1969	
s 12	3.415
s 12(3)	3.415
Appellate Jurisdiction Act 1876	
s 3	5.2
s 4	5.2
Constitutional Reform Act 2005	
s 40(2)	5.76
Disability Discrimination Act 1995	9.39
s 68(2)	9.28
s 68(2A)	9.28
Employment Act 2002	9.14
Employment Protection (Consolidation) Act 1978	
s 57(3)	8.111
Employment Protection Act 1975	1.34, 9.42
Employment Relations Act 1999	9.39
Employment Rights Act 1996	8.163
s 13	8.23
s 14	8.23
s 94(1)	9.16, 9.17, 9.23
s 98	7.4
s 196	9.20, 9.21, 9.22
s 203	8.23
s 204	9.18
ss 221–224	8.91
s 228	8.91
Employment Tribunals Act 1996	3.22, 9.42
s 4(5)	8.158, 8.160
s 15	3.417
ss 20–37	1.35
s 20(3)	3.19
s 21	1.8, 9.39
s 21(1)	3.6, 3.7, 8.4, 8.16
s 24	9.43
s 28	9.44
s 29	9.50

Employment Tribunals Act 1996—*continued*	
s 29(2)	3.19, 3.300
s 30(3)	3.23, 8.181, 8.183, 8.185, 10.5
s 31	3.41, 3.307
s 32	3.41, 3.307
s 33	3.402, 3.404, 4.10
s 33(1)	3.41, 3.296, 3.406
s 33(1)(a)	3.319
s 33(1)(a)–(c)	3.406
s 33(2)	3.405
s 33(3)	3.403
s 33(4)	3.41, 3.296, 3.407
s 35	1.39, 8.188
s 35(1)	3.17, 8.176, 8.179, 10.4, 10.5
s 37	4.10, 4.13, 4.122
Equal Pay Act 1970	9.39
Equality Act 2006	9.39
European Communities Act 1972	
s 3(1)	6.1
Health and Safety at Work Act 1974	
s 24	9.51
Human Rights Act 1998	1.55, 3.184, 4.21, 5.9, 7.2, 7.4, 7.6
s 1	7.3
s 2	7.3, 7.8, 8.70
s 3	7.3
s 4	5.32, 7.3, 9.38
s 4(4)	9.37
s 4(5)	3.19, 9.37
s 6	7.3, 8.70
s 7	7.3
s 10	7.32
National Minimum Wage Act 1998	
s 19	9.39
Race Relations Act 1976	8.138, 9.39
s 8(1)	9.28
s 8(1A)	9.28
Sex Discrimination Act 1975	8.17, 9.39
s 10(1)	9.28
Sex Discrimination Act 1976	8.163
Supreme Court Act 1981	
s 2	4.10
s 3	4.10
s 9	9.43
s 54(6)	4.59

Supreme Court Act 1981—*continued*		Tribunals, Courts and Enforcement Act 2007—*continued*	
s 58(2)	4.117	s 5	9.48
Trade Union and Labour Relations (Consolidation) Act 1992	9.39	s 27	3.417
		s 30	9.48
Tribunals and Inquiries Act 1992		Sch 8, paras 36–39	3.262
s 1	9.51		
Tribunals, Courts and Enforcement Act 2007	9.49	Welsh Language Act 1993	9.47
s 2	9.48		

TABLE OF STATUTORY INSTRUMENTS

References are to paragraph numbers.

Civil Legal Aid (General) Regulations 1989, SI 1989/339	
reg 149	3.421
Civil Procedure Rules 1998, SI 1998/3132	3.46, 3.48
r 3.9	4.87, 4.88
r 3.11	4.142
r 19.4A	4.28
Pt 23	4.149
r 44.14	4.146
Pt 44	4.144, 4.145
r 47.17	3.401, 4.148
r 48.6	4.147
r 48.7	4.146
r 52.3(2)	4.23
r 52.3(4)	4.51
r 52.3(6)	4.40
r 52.3(7)	4.67
r 52.3(7)(b)	4.70
r 52.3(4A)	4.51
r 52.4	4.27
r 52.4(2)(a)	4.26, 4.62
r 52.4(2)(b)	4.62
r 52.4(3)	4.39
r 52.5	4.75
r 52.5(4)	4.76
r 52.5(5)	4.76
r 52.5(6)	4.79
r 52.6	4.86
r 52.8	4.115
r 52.9	4.60
r 52.9(1)(c)	4.74
r 52.9(3)	4.73
r 52.10	4.128
r 52.11	4.125
r 52.11(3)	4.119
r 52.16	4.117
r 52.17	4.149
Pt 68	6.9
Companies (Cross-Border Mergers) Regulations 2007, SI 2007/2974	9.39
Employment Appeal Tribunal (Amendment) Rules 1996, SI 1996/3216	1.9
Employment Appeal Tribunal (Amendment) Rules 2001, SI 2001/1128	1.9
Employment Appeal Tribunal (Amendment) Rules 2004, SI 2004/2526	1.9
Employment Appeal Tribunal (Amendment) Rules 2005, SI 2005/1871	1.9
Employment Appeal Tribunal Rules 1993, SI 1993/2854	1.9, 3.22, 3.23, 3.24, 3.25
r 2(1)	3.33
r 2A	3.29, 3.40, 3.46, 3.106
r 2A(2)	3.46
r 2A(3)	3.47
r 3	3.6
r 3(1)	3.50, 3.134
r 3(1)(b)	3.135
r 3(3)	3.56, 3.70
r 3(3)(a)(iii)	3.145
r 3(5)	3.393
r 3(6)	3.393
r 3(7)	1.16, 3.159, 3.165, 3.166, 3.173, 3.174, 3.175, 3.176, 3.231, 3.234, 3.355, 8.8, 8.130
r 3(7)–(10)	3.170
r 3(8)	1.16, 3.127, 3.167, 3.174, 3.175, 3.202, 3.231, 3.233, 3.234, 3.235
r 3(9)	3.175
r 3(10)	1.13, 1.16, 3.167, 3.178, 3.179, 3.180, 3.182, 3.183, 3.192, 3.194, 3.197, 3.198, 3.199, 3.200, 3.202, 3.231, 3.233, 3.234, 3.235, 8.130
r 4(1)	3.207
r 4(1)(c)–(e)	3.81
r 6(2)	3.212
r 6(3)	3.220
r 6(5)	3.204
r 6(7)	3.393
r 6(8)	3.393
r 18	3.315, 3.323
r 19	3.36, 3.296
r 20(1), (2)	3.40
r 20(3)	3.41
r 20(4)	3.41, 3.296
r 21	3.43, 3.297
r 21(2)	3.43, 3.297
r 23	3.41, 3.308
r 23(3)	3.312
r 23(4)	3.311
r 23(5)	3.310
r 23(5A)	3.312

Employment Appeal Tribunal Rules 1993,
SI 1993/2854—continued

r 23(5B)	3.312
r 23(5C)	3.312
r 23(7)	3.313
r 23(8)	3.314
r 23(9)	3.312
r 23A	3.41, 3.308
r 23A(4)	3.310
r 25	3.28
r 26	3.208, 3.304
r 27	9.50
r 27(1)	3.299
r 27(2)	3.300
r 28	9.50
r 29(2)	3.306
r 30(3)	3.143
r 30A	9.52
r 30A(2)	3.325
r 31A	9.52
r 34(4)	3.394, 3.395
r 34(5)	3.395
r 34A	3.392
r 34B(2)	3.395
r 34C	3.397
r 35(1)	3.44
r 35(5)	3.30, 3.302
r 37	3.43, 3.297
r 37(1)	3.84, 3.211
r 37(1A)	3.52, 3.76
r 37(3)	3.85
r 37(4)	3.85
r 39(1)	3.29, 3.302
r 39(2)	3.29, 3.301
r 39(3)	3.31, 3.32, 3.111, 3.112, 3.113, 3.114, 3.115, 3.149, 3.303

Employment Equality (Age)
Regulations 2006, SI 2006/1031   9.39
Employment Equality (Religion or
Belief) Regulations 2003,
SI 2003/1660   9.39
Employment Equality (Sexual
Orientation) Regulations 2003,
SI 2003/1661   9.39
Employment Tribunals (Constitution
and Rules of Procedure)
(Amendment) (No 2)
Regulations 2005, SI 2005/1865

reg 2(1)	3.143, 10.5
reg 4(h)	3.143

Employment Tribunals (Constitution
and Rules of Procedure)
Regulations 2004, SI 2004/1861   8.168

reg 17	8.194
reg 18	8.194
reg 19(1)	9.10, 9.13, 9.14
reg 19(1)(b)	9.12
Sch 1, r 10	1.5
Sch 1, r 10(2)(n)	2.2
Sch 1, r 11(1)	2.2
Sch 1, r 12	1.5
Sch 1, r 12(2)(b)	2.2
Sch 1, r 13(2)	3.10

Employment Tribunals (Constitution and
Rules of Procedure) Regulations 2004,
SI 2004/1861—continued

Sch 1, r 28	8.195
Sch 1, r 28(1)(a)	3.9, 3.10
Sch 1, r 29	8.195
Sch 1, r 30	8.71, 8.185, 8.195, 10.5
Sch 1, r 30(1)	8.72, 8.181, 8.185
Sch 1, r 30(1)(b)	8.68, 8.73
Sch 1, r 30(3)	10.5
Sch 1, r 30(3)(b)	8.181, 8.185, 10.5
Sch 1, r 30(6)	8.75, 8.76, 8.77, 8.93, 8.99, 8.137
Sch 1, r 30(6)(a)	8.100
Sch 1, r 30(6)(b)	8.101, 8.102
Sch 1, r 30(6)(c)	8.104, 8.105, 8.106, 8.107, 8.108, 8.109, 8.110
Sch 1, r 30(6)(d)	8.111
Sch 1, r 30(6)(e)	8.112, 8.113
Sch 1, r 30(6)(f)	8.114, 8.115, 8.116
Sch 1, r 32	8.195
Sch 1, r 33	2.2
Sch 1, r 34	1.5, 2.2, 8.196
Sch 1, r 34(3)	2.3
Sch 1, r 34(5)	2.11
Sch 1, r 35	1.5, 8.196
Sch 1, r 35(1)	2.12
Sch 1, r 35(2)	2.12
Sch 1, r 35(3)	2.13
Sch 1, r 36	1.5, 2.16, 8.196
Sch 1, r 37	2.21, 8.197
Sch 1, r 49	8.195

European Cooperative Society
(Involvement of Employees)
Regulations 2006, SI 2006/2059   9.39
European Public Limited-Liability
Company Regulations 2004,
SI 2004/2326

reg 33	1.12, 9.39, 9.40
reg 47(6)	3.50

Fishing Vessels (Working Time:
Sea-fishermen) Regulations
2004, SI 2004/1713   9.39
Fixed-term Employees (Prevention of
Less Favourable Treatment)
Regulations 2002, SI 2002/2034   9.39

Information and Consultation of
Employees Regulations 2004,
SI 2004/3426   1.9

reg 11	9.39
reg 22	1.12, 9.40
reg 35(6)	3.50

Justices of the Peace Act 1949
(Compensation) Regulations
1978, SI 1978/1682   3.384

Merchant Shipping (Working Time: Inland Waterways) Regulations 2003, SI 2003/3049	9.39
Occupational and Personal Pension Schemes (Consultation by Employers and Miscellaneous Amendment) Regulations 2006, SI 2006/349	9.39
Part-time Workers (Prevention of Less Favourable Treatment) Regulations 2000, SI 2000/1551	9.39
Transfer of Undertakings (Protection of Employment) Regulations 2006, SI 2006/246	
reg 3(4)	9.32

Transfer of Undertakings (Protection of Employment) Regulations 2006, SI 2006/246—*continued*	
reg 16(2)	9.39
Transnational Information and Consultation of Employees Regulations 1999, SI 1999/3323	
reg 20	1.12, 9.40
reg 20(1)	9.39
reg 21	1.12, 9.40
reg 21(1)	9.39
reg 38(8)	3.50
Working Time Regulations 1998, SI 1998/1833	9.16, 9.33, 9.39
reg 16	8.91

Chapter 1

SUMMARY

INTRODUCTION

1.1

'What can you do when you lose a case in the employment tribunal?'

This is a question that is often asked: employment disputes that go all the way to a full tribunal hearing tend to generate strong feelings, and in every case somebody has to lose.

1.2 If you lose there are two options, but they are only available in certain limited circumstances. First, you can ask the employment tribunal itself to review its decision (see Chapter 2).[1] Secondly, you can appeal to the Employment Appeal Tribunal (EAT) (see Chapter 3), which is the main subject of this book.

1.3 Those are the options when you wish to challenge a judgment, order or decision of the employment tribunal. Note that it is possible to do both in parallel.[2]

1.4 Since the basis upon which you can pursue each of these options is strictly limited, it is important to understand the grounds on which they might be available to you.

1.5 In short, a review is an opportunity for the same tribunal to re-consider its decision, where there are special reasons for doing so.[3] By contrast, an appeal is an opportunity for the EAT to consider whether or not the original employment tribunal made an error of law in arriving at its decision.

1.6 This book is intended to provide an accessible guide to employment appeals, while at the same time, providing sufficient detail to serve as a useful reference for experienced practitioners.

---

[1] Although a review is not strictly an appeal, it is a re-consideration of a judgment or order and is included within the scope of this work.
[2] 'However, where an application has also been made for a review, the reasons for granting or refusing a review will also be relevant' per McMullen J in *Rance v Secretary of State for Health* [2007] IRLR 665 at para 33.
[3] Employment Tribunals Rules of Procedure, in Sch 1 to the Employment Tribunals (Constitution and Rules of Procedure) Regulations 2004 (SI 2004/1861), rr 10, 12 and 34–36.

1.7 The law is stated as we understand it to be on 1 September 2008, including recent cases such as *Jurkowska v HLMAD Ltd*[4] and the new 2008 EAT Practice Direction which came into force on 22 May 2008.

Key practice points

1.8 We decided to pick out three key practice points to highlight at the very outset. It was a difficult choice, but we have settled on the following:

(1) The normal time limit for sending your notice of appeal and accompanying documents to the EAT is 42 days. When that period begins is complicated and is explained below (Chapter 3). Do not leave it to the last minute.[5]

(2) You can only appeal to the EAT on a point of law.[6] An appeal is therefore not an opportunity to re-argue the facts. Your notice of appeal should identify errors of law clearly and it is worthwhile drafting it with care.

(3) Alleging bias against the employment tribunal is even more difficult than alleging that the decision (or part of it) is perverse. In each case (bias or perversity), you have to give very full details of your complaint.

Source materials

1.9 The Employment Appeal Tribunal Rules 1993 (the EAT Rules)[7] and the Employment Appeal Tribunal Practice Direction 2008 (EAT PD) and other important source materials are included at the back of this book, in the Appendices, for reference.

SCOPE OF THIS BOOK

1.10 This book covers employment appeals in England and Wales, from the employment tribunal all the way through to the House of Lords, if necessary via the European Court of Justice (ECJ). It also looks at taking a case to the European Court of Human Rights (ECtHR). In this first edition, we have not covered procedure which is unique to Scottish cases, but we have dealt briefly with questions of territorial jurisdiction more generally.[8]

---

[4] [2008] ICR 841, [2008] IRLR 430.
[5] Eighty-eight seconds late was too late in *Beasley v National Grid* UKEAT/0626/06 [2007] All ER (D) 110 (Aug); followed in respect of a claim form in the employment tribunal which was just 9 seconds late in *Miller v Community Links Trust Ltd* UKEAT/0486/07 [2007] All ER (D) 196 (Nov).
[6] Employment Tribunals Act 1996 (ETA 1996), s 21.
[7] As amended by the following statutory instruments, which remain the authoritative sources of each provision: SI 1993/2854, SI 1996/3216, SI 2001/1128, SI 2004/2526, SI 2004/3426 and SI 2005/1871.
[8] See Chapter 9 – Jurisdiction at para **9.8**.

1.11 In principle it is limited to appeals, but we have included the procedure for a review in the employment tribunal, references to the ECJ and taking a case to the ECtHR which are not strictly appeals at all – though they may appear similar to non-lawyers for whom the employment tribunal jurisdiction was originally designed.

1.12 We have not covered the EAT's 'original' jurisdiction to hear cases at first instance about information and consultation[9] or failure to comply with an employee involvement agreement, which fall outside the scope of this work.

1.13 The book is structured to begin with an accessible introduction and, thereafter, to provide increasing levels of detail, including on some of the more awkward procedural points to which answers may not readily be found elsewhere (eg, on overlapping appeals or on appeals against an adverse r 3(10) decision[10] to the Court of Appeal). Where this results in the same point being made several times, we hope that this will be more help than hindrance.

TYPICAL APPEAL – AN ILLUSTRATION

1.14 Before diving into the detail, it is helpful to consider an overview of the procedural steps which a typical appeal from the employment tribunal to the EAT might follow.[11]

---

[9] Transnational Information and Consultation of Employees Regulations 1999 (SI 1999/3323), regs 20 and 21; Information and Consultation of Employees Regulations 2004 (SI 2004/3426), reg 22; and European Public Limited-Liability Company Regulations 2004 (SI 2004/2326), reg 33.
[10] EAT Rules.
[11] For a judicial overview of the EAT's procedures, see the recent judgment of HHJ McMullen QC in *Haritaki v South East England Development Agency* UKEATPA/0006/08.

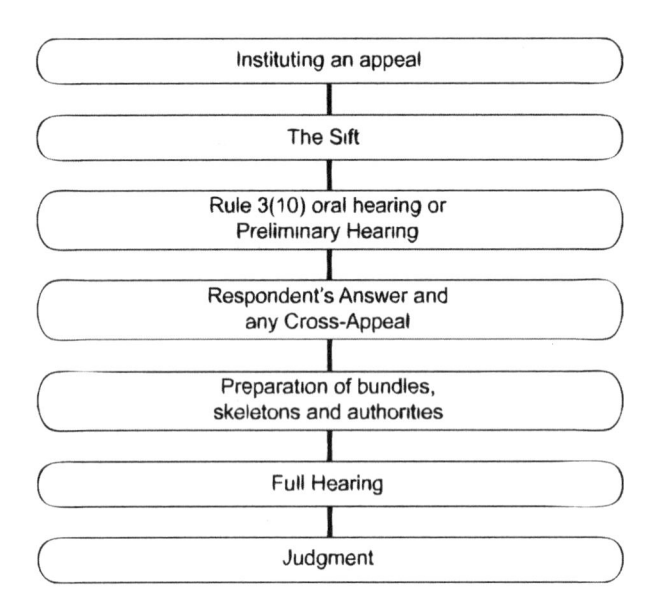

```
┌─────────────────────────────────┐
│      Instituting an appeal      │
└─────────────────────────────────┘
                 │
┌─────────────────────────────────┐
│            The Sift             │
└─────────────────────────────────┘
                 │
┌─────────────────────────────────┐
│   Rule 3(10) oral hearing or    │
│      Preliminary Hearing        │
└─────────────────────────────────┘
                 │
┌─────────────────────────────────┐
│    Respondent's Answer and      │
│        any Cross-Appeal         │
└─────────────────────────────────┘
                 │
┌─────────────────────────────────┐
│      Preparation of bundles,    │
│     skeletons and authorities   │
└─────────────────────────────────┘
                 │
┌─────────────────────────────────┐
│          Full Hearing           │
└─────────────────────────────────┘
                 │
┌─────────────────────────────────┐
│            Judgment             │
└─────────────────────────────────┘
```

1.15 However, it is important to stress that this illustration is not intended to be a substitute for referring to the detailed explanation of the provisions elsewhere in this book. The procedural course of appeals differs quite widely and it is important to consider each step with care.

1.16 What is set out below is therefore no more than an illustrative overview, which may help put what follows in context. With that warning in mind, a typical appeal will involve the following steps:

(1) **Instituting the appeal:** Serving a notice of appeal (together with accompanying documents) on the EAT within the 42-day time limit.

(2) **The 'sift':** A judge or the registrar looks at the papers to see if the notice of appeal discloses reasonable grounds for bringing the appeal and to make sure the appeal is not an abuse of process.
   (a) If the judge or registrar is satisfied that it does, the case will usually proceed straight to a full hearing of the appeal and the EAT will give directions about the necessary preparation for that hearing.
   (b) If not, the person appealing (the appellant) will receive a letter giving reasons for the view formed by the judge or registrar, and stating that no further action will be taken on the appeal.[12]
   (c) If the appellant takes no further action, that is the end of the appeal.
   (d) However, if the appellant wishes to pursue the appeal despite this, there are two options available at this juncture. First, a new notice of appeal can be served, usually within 28 days of the date of the letter being sent by the EAT.[13] Secondly, the appellant can 'express dissatisfaction' with the reasons provided in a letter, again with 28

---

[12] EAT Rules, r 3(7).
[13] EAT Rules, r 3(8).

days, and seek an oral hearing before a judge.[14] At that hearing, the respondent need not attend and will not make submissions.

(e) Where a new notice of appeal is served, the sift process is repeated and the appeal may go forward to a full hearing, if the judge or registrar takes a different view. Where there is an oral hearing, the appeal may come to life in oral argument in a way that was not apparent on the papers and result in the judge being persuaded that there are reasonable grounds for brining the appeal, in which case, the judge will usually order that the appeal go forward to a full hearing.

(3) **Preliminary hearing:** Occasionally, a preliminary hearing will be ordered,[15] which will enable the respondent to put in written submissions as to whether there are reasonable grounds for bringing the appeal.[16] Except when the respondent has served (or intends to serve) a cross-appeal, the respondent may or may not be permitted to take part in the preliminary hearing.

(4) **Respondent's answer and cross-appeal:** If an appeal is to proceed to a full hearing, the respondent must serve an answer (with any cross-appeal). If the respondent serves a cross-appeal, then that will go through the sift (above) as if it were a separate notice of appeal in its own right and it will either go on to a full hearing or not, as the case may be.

(5) **Preparation:** The parties will then prepare their bundle of documents (normally limited to 100 pages), their skeleton arguments and authorities in good time before the hearing.[17]

(6) **Full hearing:** There will be a full hearing. The EAT will give its judgment at or after the hearing and any party may wish to appeal to the Court of Appeal, for which the normal time limit is now 21 days (under the 2008 Practice Direction) from the date of the judgment – it was formerly 14 days, which was out of step with the 21 days allowed in other civil cases.

1.17 A common problem arises when one party wishes to rely on evidence that was given orally before the employment tribunal. The parties should try to agree what the evidence was, so as to avoid the employment tribunal chairman being asked to provide his notes of evidence (see paras **3.262** to **3.295**, especially **3.268** and **8.44**).[18]

1.18 Two areas which are procedural minefields in the EAT (see Chapter 3) are:

---

[14] EAT Rules, r 3(10).
[15] EAT PD, paras 9.6 and 9.7.
[16] EAT PD at para 9.8.
[17] EAT PD at para 6 (papers for use at the hearing).
[18] EAT PD, para 7.

(1) where there are overlapping appeals by both parties, ie both the claimant and the respondent are dissatisfied with different aspects of the same judgment (see para **3.223**); and

(2) in relation to notices of appeal lodged either out of time or without all the required documents (see para **3.130**).

SUMMARY OF TIME LIMITS

1.19 This section provides only a summary of relevant time limits and the more detailed sections for the EAT (Chapter 3), Court of Appeal (Chapter 4), and House of Lords (Chapter 5) are important.

The Employment Appeal Tribunal

1.20 Forty-two days (ie six weeks) is the normal time limit for appealing from the employment tribunal to the EAT. (Do not leave your Notice of Appeal to the last minute: for reasons which are hard to justify, extensions of time which would be granted without hesitation in the Court of Appeal are routinely refused in the EAT.[19]) However, the important question is when that period of 42 days begins.

1.21 The basic rule is that the 42 days runs from the day on which the tribunal sends the order, decision or written record of the judgment to the parties. However, there are special rules for judgments, depending on if, when and how written reasons are provided by the employment tribunal.[20] Those rules are fully explained below (see para **3.51**).

The Court of Appeal

1.22 Permission to appeal is required from either the EAT of the Court of Appeal. The 2008 EAT Practice Direction has introduced new provisions about the time for applying to the EAT for permission. An application to the EAT for permission to appeal must be made at the hearing, when a reserved judgment is handed down or in writing within seven days thereafter.[21]

1.23 The time limit for applying to the Court of Appeal for permission to appeal is now 21 days. (Prior to 22 May 2008, it was 14 days, unlike the 21 days allowed in other cases. This laid a trap for the unwary which the new PD has removed.) 21 days runs from the EAT's sealed order, even if the transcript of the judgment has not been sent out or received (see para **4.26**). The first draft of this book (just before the 2008 Practice Direction was published) argued for the harmonisation of the time limit to 21 days. Given that litigants are moving

---

[19] See judgment of Bean J in *Hafele v Nolan* UKEATPA/0354/08, 23 July 2008.
[20] EAT PD at para 3.3.
[21] EAT PD at para 21.1.

from a (mainly) costs free jurisdiction to the Court of Appeal where they may be at risk of substantial costs liability, there are sound policy and practical reasons why a longer period than 21 days might be justified. Against that background, the change to 21 days is to be welcomed.

It is important to note that an appeal to the Court of Appeal is not a 'second appeal' for the purposes of of s 55(1) of the Access to Justice Act 1999 and CPR r.52.13(1). The significance of this is that 'second appeals' must normally show a point of public importance: this is not necessary in an appeal from the EAT to the Court of Appeal and parties appealing are advised to state this in any skeleton argument in support of an application for permission to appeal.

House of Lords

1.24 If you have the Court of Appeal's leave to appeal to the House of Lords then a petition to appeal must be lodged within three months of date of the making of the order appealed. If you do not have the Court of Appeal's leave then a petition for leave must be lodged within one month of the Court of Appeal's making of the order appealed (see Chapter 5).

WHERE TO APPEAL

1.25 A party can challenge (or try to change) a decision of the employment tribunal:

(1) by applying to the employment tribunal for a review, which means asking the employment tribunal to change its mind (see Chapter 2); or

(2) by appealing to the EAT (see Chapter 3).

1.26 A party can challenge (or try to change) a decision of the EAT:

(1) by applying to the EAT for a review (see Chapter 3); or

(2) by appealing to the Court of Appeal[22] – for which permission is necessary from either the EAT or the Court of Appeal, as noted above at paras **1.22** and **1.23** (see also Chapter 4).

1.27 If the Court of Appeal refuses permission when a judge first looks at the papers, a party is entitled to request an oral hearing (see para **4.51**). However, if the Court of Appeal refuses permission to appeal at that oral hearing, there is no further appeal available.

---

[22] In Scotland, to the Inner House of the Court of Session, showing probabilis causa – not within the scope of this book.

1.28 If the Court of Appeal gives permission to appeal, the appeal will then go to a full hearing.

1.29 Once permission to appeal has been given, the Court of Appeal's decision can then be appealed to the House of Lords. Again, permission is required, this time either from the Court of Appeal or, failing that, from the House of Lords. The House of Lords will not normally hear any appeal that does not involve a point of public importance. Even if a point of public importance is involved, it is still entirely a matter for the House of Lords whether to hear (or consider hearing) the appeal (see Chapter 5).

NATURE OF EMPLOYMENT APPEALS

1.30 Employment appeals are not like normal civil appeals because they are only concerned with errors of law. It is not a proper ground of appeal in an employment appeal that the tribunal made a decision 'against the weight of the evidence', whereas it might be a proper ground of appeal in an ordinary civil case in the High Court or county court.

1.31 In an employment appeal, the hurdle is higher and some cases suggest, much higher. The equivalent ground of appeal in an employment appeal is that the tribunal's finding or decision was 'perverse', which probably means that it was so plainly wrong that no reasonable tribunal could have found as it did (although some cases suggest this is too harsh a test).[23]

1.32 If truth be told, the harshness of the test applied in a perversity appeal may well depend as much on the overall quality of the decision appealed and the sympathy of the court or tribunal hearing the appeal as it does on the different formulations of the test in the decided cases.

1.33 What is clear is that it is not enough that the court or tribunal hearing the appeal would have arrived at a different view. That does not establish that the decision is perverse and parties should be particularly conscious of this. This is explained more fully in Chapter 3.

THE EMPLOYMENT APPEAL TRIBUNAL

1.34 The EAT was established under the Employment Protection Act 1975, as an improvement on the appeal to a single judge (which had itself replaced the old National Industrial Relations Court), see Chapter 9.

---

[23] See generally *Crofton v Yeboah* [2002] EWCA Civ 794, [2002] IRLR 634; and as to the harshness of the test, *Piggott Bros & Co Ltd v Jackson* [1991] IRLR 309.

1.35 The EAT's jurisdiction is currently provided by Part II of the Employment Tribunals Act 1996 (ETA 1996),[24] which is found at Chapter 10.

1.36 The hierarchy of the main source materials affecting the EAT is as follows:

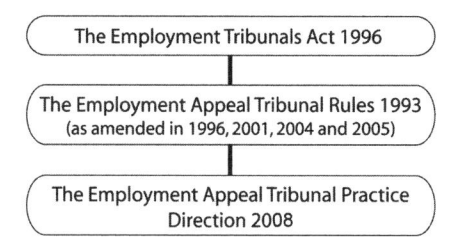

```
The Employment Tribunals Act 1996
            |
The Employment Appeal Tribunal Rules 1993
  (as amended in 1996, 2001, 2004 and 2005)
            |
The Employment Appeal Tribunal Practice
              Direction 2008
```

Limited powers

1.37 The EAT has limited powers, namely those specifically provided by Part II of ETA 1996 (as amended).

1.38 As already stated, the EAT only has jurisdiction to correct errors of law.

1.39 In correcting any error of law, under s 35 of ETA 1996, the EAT's powers are limited to:

(1) do anything which the employment tribunal which made the decision would have had power to do (ie the EAT may substitute its decision for that of the employment tribunal);

(2) remit the case to the employment tribunal which made the decision, or to a newly constituted employment tribunal (ie one comprising different members).

Effect on appeals

1.40 The combined effect of these limitations (above) plays out in appeals before the EAT as follows:

(1) the EAT is unwelcoming to appeals which involve any significant factual enquiry – even if only to identify properly an error of law;

(2) the EAT is particularly wary of allegations of 'perversity' as these often mask a wish to re-argue the facts;

(3) the EAT is wary of falling into the trap of substituting its own views for those of the employment tribunal when seeking to discern whether the employment tribunal has made an error of law; and therefore, is also wary

---

[24] ETA 1996, Pt II, ss 20–37, especially s 21.

of overturning an employment tribunal's decision on reasonableness, fairness or (especially in discrimination cases) the grounds on which something was done (or not done);

(4) new evidence which was not put before the employment tribunal will not normally be allowed by the EAT;

(5) the EAT will not normally allow new points of law to be raised, if they were not raised before the employment tribunal;

(6) the EAT will only very rarely overturn an exercise of discretion on a case management decision;

(7) the EAT is very wary of allegations of bias against employment tribunals.[25]

History

1.41 Historically, the EAT has had periods when it struggled to meet the increasing demand for its time, especially on budgets which were not increasing accordingly. This has led to an emphasis on efficient case management which, for the most part, is to be welcomed; and the EAT presently functions with admirable productivity. Cases which go straight to a full hearing are often heard within 3 months.

1.42 The present procedure of the EAT includes the system of the 'sift' of appeals as they come in. This resulted from trial and error and a wish to shorten the time between the service of a notice of appeal and the hearing and disposal of the appeal. Broadly speaking, it has worked, helped by the hard work of the EAT's staff.

1.43 The most recent published figures for appeals to the EAT for 2006/2007 showed the number of appeals heard by the EAT, down by over 20%. The figures for 2006/2007 are as follows:[26]

Table 9: Cases dealt with at preliminary hearings by the EAT

	Brought by employers	**Brought by employees**	**All**
Dismissed at hearing	18	40	58

---

[25] EAT PD at para 11, especially paras 11.2 NS 11.6.3.
[26] Employment tribunal and EAT Statistics (GB), 1 April 2006 to 31 March 2007.

Allowed to full hearing	60	54	114
All	78	94	172

Table 10: Appeals disposed of by the EAT at a full hearing

	Brought by employers	**Brought by employees**	**All**
Dismissed at hearing	92 (46.7% of 197)	113 (48.1% of 235)	205 (47.4% of 432)
Allowed	59 (29.9% of 197)	59 (25.1% of 235)	118 (27.3% of 432)
Allowed & remitted	46 (23.3% of 197)	63 (26.8% of 235)	109 (25.2% of 432)
All	197	235	432

1.44 So employers did only very marginally better than employees, in their appeals, overall, with employers winning 105/197 appeals (53.3%) and employees winning 113/235 (51.9%). The only real disparity between employers and employees was in *how* they succeeded with employees having 1.7% more appeals allowed and remitted for a re-hearing than simply allowed and employers having the opposite: 6.6% more appeals allowed outright than those allowed and remitted.

Grounds of appeal

1.45 The grounds of appeal available in an appeal to the EAT are those which disclose an error of law by the employment tribunal. Those grounds are briefly considered in Chapter 3 (at para **3.120**) and extensively in Chapter 8 (see para **8.21** and, on jurisdiction, para **9.4**).

1.46 The grounds of appeal are vital. The appeal often stands or falls on the drafting of the grounds. They should be carefully drafted. This in turn requires very detailed consideration of the employment tribunal's judgment and written reasons and, in particular, analysis of how the employment tribunal actually reached the decision appealed.

1.47 It is important to remember that it is not enough to identify an error of law: it must be a *material* error of law.

1.48 The grounds of appeal must clearly identify an error of law and if it is contended to be 'perversity' or bias, full particulars must be given at the outset.

Funding

1.49 Limited funding is available for appeals to the EAT. Since costs orders are not normally made against the losing party, appeals to the EAT do not obviously lend themselves to funding under a conditional fee agreement ('no win, no fee') since any fee paid in the event of a 'win' has to come out of the winning party's pocket, rather than from the other side.

1.50 Funding in the EAT is dealt with in more detail in Chapter 3 below.

Representation

1.51 A party may appear before the EAT in person, without a lawyer or be represented, for example, by a union representative or a friend. This was the original idea in both the employment tribunal and the EAT; however, it has become increasingly unrealistic in the many cases, especially in the EAT.

1.52 Alternatively, a party may instruct:

(1) a solicitor or barrister to appear for them;[27]

(2) a non-lawyer representative, who is not charging any fee (on any basis) for this service;

(3) a non-lawyer who is charging for the service but is registered under the Compensation Act 2006 with the Regulator of Regulated Claims Management Services (presently, the Right Honourable Jack Straw MP, Secretary of State for Justice) – it being a criminal offence to charge for such services when not registered.

1.53 Before the Court of Appeal and the House of Lords parties may appear in person or be represented by a lawyer. Non-lawyer representation is not usually allowed by the court may permit it on a case by case basis.

Precedent and the hierarchy

1.54 The House of Lords is at the top of the judicial ladder in the UK and the Court of Appeal, EAT and the tribunals are bound to follow its judgments. The House of Lords can depart from its earlier decisions.[28]

1.55 The ECJ is paramount in its field of EC law and the House of Lords, Court of Appeal, EAT and the tribunals must follow its judgments in those fields. The ECtHR's judgments must be taken into account but are not binding, although there is a statutory duty under the Human Rights Act 1998 imposed

---

[27] Since 23 April 2007, the provisions of the Compensation Act 2006 apply a 'new regime' regulating those providing claims services for reward in the employment tribunal and EAT.

[28] See *Practice Note (Judicial Precedent)* [1966] 3 All ER 77, sub nom *Practice Statement* [1966] 1 WLR 123.

on the courts (and other public bodies) to give effect to the Convention rights which it is the function of the European Court of Human Rights to interpret.

1.56 The Court of Appeal's judgments are binding on the EAT and the tribunals and the Court of Appeal does not usually depart from one of its own decisions. The Court of Appeal will depart from one of its own decisions where it has to decide between its own judgments which are conflicting[29] or where it is bound to refuse to follow a decision of its own which, although not expressly overruled, cannot, in its opinion, stand with a decision of the House of Lords; and further is not bound by one of its decisions if the House of Lords has decided the case on different grounds, ruling that the issue decided by the Court of Appeal did not arise for decision; and the Court of Appeal is not bound to follow a decision of its own if given per incuriam (without considering all of the relevant cases and materials).

1.57 The EAT is bound by judgments of the House of Lords, Court of Appeal, but not decisions of the High Court the former National Industrial Relations Court and most importantly of all it is not bound by its own previous decision, although they are to be treated as being persuasive.[30] The EAT often decides cases not in accordance with its previous decisions, leaving the Court of Appeal to sort out the resulting confusion.

---

[29] *Young v Bristol Aeroplane Co Ltd* [1944] KB 718, CA (where the exceptions are set out); affirmed [1946] AC 163, HL.
[30] *Portec (UK) Ltd v Mogensen* [1976] ICR 396, at 400.

Chapter 2

REVIEW BY THE EMPLOYMENT TRIBUNAL

2.1 The employment tribunals are one of a very few number of courts and tribunals which can review their own judgments once they have been issued. Accordingly, in some limited circumstances loosing parties can have a second bite of the cherry and can ask the tribunal to reconsider. The scope of this power of review is, however, very limited and in practice rarely exercised. Clearly, it would undermine the administration of justice if a tribunal issued a judgment and then performed a volte face on a regular basis. This chapter will seek to address those opportunities when a loosing party can ask a tribunal to review a judgment or order which it has made.

2.2 The tribunal can review its judgment after a contested hearing of a case. The tribunal can also review a decision not to accept a claim, response or counter-claim (eg, on technical grounds). It can also review a default judgment the Employment Tribunals (Constitution and Rules of Procedure) Regulations 2004 (the ET Rules),[1] r 33. It cannot, however, review any other order (ET Rules, r 34), although case management orders can be revisited.[2] It is therefore important to consider whether the 'order' that you wish to review can be fitted into one of the above categories. Furthermore, rr 10(2)(n), 11(1) and 12(2)(b) of the ET Rules should be noted as examples of situations in which the tribunal can vary and revoke orders without a review.

2.3 This section will concern itself with reviews of judgments made after full contested hearings of employment claims. Such reviews can only be done on specified grounds (ET Rules, r 34(3)). These are:

(a) the decision was wrongly made as a result of an administrative error;

(b) a party did not receive notice of the proceedings leading to the decision;

(c) the decision was made in the absence of a party;

(d) new evidence has become available since the conclusion of the hearing to which the decision relates, provided that its existence could not have been reasonably known of or foreseen at that time.

---

[1] SI 2004/1861.
[2] *Onwuka v Spherion Technology UK Ltd* [2005] ICR 567.

(e) the interests of justice require such a review.

2.4 This chapter will concentrate on grounds (d) and (e), above: new evidence and the interests of justice. The others are largely self-explanatory: (a) includes error by a party (sending a document to a wrong address) as well as error by the tribunal; (c) will only be invoked where the absent party can give a cogent and acceptable reason for absence, for example, merely forgetting to tell the tribunal your new address is insufficient. In one case in which one of the authors appeared, a Tribunal joined various new parties (including the respondent's worldwide Chairman personally) in the absence of the respondent, the Chairman or any representative. The respondent had not attended because the notice of hearing confined the hearing to an issue of disclosure to which the respondent had agreed by letter. The respondent was entirely unaware that any other application was to be made. The Order was something of a surprise; but it was set aside on a review under ground (c) above.

FRESH EVIDENCE

2.5 The evidence must be credible, might have had a decisive bearing on the tribunal's judgment and there must be a reasonable explanation for the failure to make it available for the hearing.[3] The fresh evidence must be adduced with the application for a review. Clearly, where a party has made an obvious choice not to adduce a certain piece of evidence it is very unlikely to be adduced under this procedure regardless of that choice being a product of professional negligence.

THE INTERESTS OF JUSTICE

2.6 This is a wide discretion. There is no need for the applicant to show exceptional circumstances. Errors of law as well as procedural errors can form the basis of a review under this head.[4] The width of the discretion can be shown by the following examples:

(1) An employer successfully argued that compensation awarded by an employment tribunal based upon the assumption that an employee would not be re-employed in the imminent future should be reduced on review after adducing evidence that the employee was re-employed swiftly after the hearing.[5]

---

[3] *Bagga v Heavy Electricals (India) Ltd* [1972] ICR 118.
[4] *Trimble v Supertravel Ltd* [1982] IRLR 451.
[5] *Yorkshire Engineering v Burnham* [1973] IRLR 316.

(2) A review has, however, been held to have been inappropriate where the tribunal had been asked to increase a loss of earnings award where it had underestimated the amount of time the claimant would be unemployed for.[6]

(3) In a case in which an employer alleged that claimant had committed a criminal offence and the employment tribunal found that he was unfairly dismissed. The EAT has stated that upon being convicted by a criminal court of the offence the tribunal should have held a review and ordered 100% contribution.[7]

(4) Where the need for a review arises because of professional negligence by a representative; rarely will a review be granted – the proper remedy is against the legal representative.[8]

REVIEW OR APPEAL?

2.7 The EAT said in *Trimble v Supertravel Ltd*[9] that a party should appeal to the EAT on a point of law and should not seek a review where the point had been fully argued and ventilated before the tribunal, whereas if oversight or procedural irregularity prevents a party arguing the point of law then a review would be appropriate.

2.8 Having said that, in *Williams v Ferrosan*[10] the EAT made clear that the rules contained no such distinction as was set out in *Trimble* and that the review power was to be used whenever the interests of justice required.

2.9 Quite simply there are no hard and fast rules. At the end of the day if the tribunal is implacably against the party who could seek an appeal then there is no point arguing the same point twice, and the ET should not be offered a second bite at the cherry – the right course it to appeal to the EAT. If, however, the tribunal has made an obvious mistake which it can rectify there should be no need to appeal and a review is appropriate. The parties and the tribunal will usually know instinctively whether a problem is to be cured by appeal or review. For example, as set out in *Trimble* if the tribunal has decided a point of law after exhaustive argument then there is little point in asking it to re-decide the issue.

2.10 Where a decision is both reviewable and appealable, the guidance from the EAT is that the review should take place first as it is viewed by the EAT as quicker and less expensive than an appeal to the EAT.[11] More than one review

---

[6] *Brenan and Ging v Edward (Lancs) Ltd* [1976] IRLR 378.
[7] *Ladup Ltd v Barnes* [1982] IRLR 7.
[8] *Lindsay v Ironsides Ray & Vials; Ironsides Ray & Vials v Lindsay* [1994] ICR 384.
[9] [1982] IRLR 451.
[10] [2004] IRLR 607.
[11] *Butlins Skyline v Beynon* EATUK/0042-0045/06 [2007] ICR 121.

can be applied for – but this should be reserved for exceptional circumstances – once a review has failed then an appeal should be next option.[12] All that said, if there is a real error of law, it is usually sensible to put in a Notice of Appeal in parallel with the application for a review. If you do this, a copy of the application for a review should accompany the Notice of Appeal and other required documents.[13]

PROCEDURE FOR REVIEW

2.11 A review comes before the tribunal in two ways – via an application made by a party and on the tribunal's own motion (ET Rules, r 34(5)).

An application for a review by a party

2.12 This must be made within 14 days of the decision being sent to the parties (ET Rules, r 35(1)). The application can be made both orally at the hearing at which the decision was made or subsequently in writing (r 35(2)) and the time limit is capable of extension (r 35(1)). The application must make clear which ground or grounds are relied upon.

2.13 If the application is made after the hearing at which the decision is made then it is referred to an employment judge on the papers who decides whether one of the grounds set out above is made out and whether there is a reasonable prospect of the decision being varied or revoked (r 35(3)). Written reasons are given for refusal at this stage.

2.14 If the employment judge does not refuse the review on the papers then it is listed before the employment judge and lay members who originally heard the case or if not practicable before a differently constituted tribunal appointed by the regional chairman or vice-president of the employment tribunals.

2.15 The tribunal can confirm, vary or revoke the original decision. If revoked the matter will be reheard.

A review on the tribunal's own motion

2.16 The tribunal must send, within 14 days of the decision that is to be reviewed, to each party, a notice explaining in summary form the grounds upon which the tribunal is proposing to review it decision. The parties should be invited to say whether they agree or not that a review should take place. The review must be heard by the tribunal which made the decision under review (ET Rules, r 36).

---

[12] *Raybright TV Services Ltd v Smith* [1973] ICR 640.
[13] EAT PD, para 2.2.

Appealing and reviewing at the same time

2.17 An employment judge who is worried that a party is both applying for a review and has appealed to the EAT should seek the guidance of the registrar to the EAT,[14] although a review can take place in such circumstances.

2.18 As noted above, an appellant before the EAT must disclose any application for a review to the EAT. Paragraph 2.2 of the EAT Practice Direction requires a copy of any relevant application for a review to accompany the Notice of Appeal. In the case of any doubt as to relevance, you are advised to err on the side of caution and send any possibly relevant application to the EAT with the Notice of Appeal. As the Practice Direction makes clear, it is important for case management at the EAT for it to be known whether or not an application has been made for a review, for notices of appeal are often stayed pending the outcome of any such application.

2.19 Where the case is stayed and the review takes place and the appellant is not satisfied with the decision on review then the tribunal's reasons given for or against reviewing a judgment ought to be considered by the EAT with the substantive judgment. A separate notice of appeal should perhaps be lodged in respect of the review decision but may not be necessary.

2.20 Since reviews are decided on different principles to appeals then an appeal could succeed against the substantive judgment of the tribunal before the EAT in circumstances where the EAT also dismisses the appeal against a negative review decision because the substantive decision was not properly amendable to review.[15]

THE SLIP RULE

2.21 Where a genuine slip or omission has occurred with a tribunal's order or decision then the correct course is not to apply for a review but to have it corrected by certificate under r 37 of the ET Rules. The other party must always be notified and be given an opportunity to comment on such an application.[16]

---

[14] *Blackpole Furniture v Sullivan* [1978] ICR 558.
[15] *Rance v Secretary of State for Health* [2007] IRLR 665, at para 33.
[16] *Times Newspapers Ltd v Fitt* [1981] ICR 637.

Chapter 3

EMPLOYMENT APPEAL TRIBUNAL

INTRODUCTION

3.1 The EAT hears appeals from the employment tribunal.[1]

3.2 You can only appeal to the EAT on a question of law. It is important to understand what that means.

3.3 As explained in Chapter 1, it means that you cannot simply reargue the facts to try to get a different decision.

3.4 Chapter 1 provides a useful summary of the practice and procedure of the EAT. This chapter considers the role and procedure of the EAT in more detail than in Chapter 1 and seeks to explain it all step-by-step, beginning with identifying the decision being appealed. Note that there is a new Practice Direction in the EAT which came into force on 22 May 2008.

3.5 Grounds of appeal are dealt with in detail in Chapter 8.

Decision, order or judgment appealed

3.6 An appeal lies to the EAT 'from any decision of, or arising in any proceedings before, an employment tribunal', ETA 1996, s 21(1). See also the EAT Rules, r 3.

Decisions

3.7 'Decision' in s 21(1) is construed widely. It includes not just orders and judgments, but any interim decision or refusal to make such a decision or order.[2]

Order or judgment?

3.8 Both orders and judgments are plainly appealable. However, because different rules apply to orders and judgments (eg, as to what documents to be

---

[1] For the EAT's very limited original jurisdiction, see Chapter 9.
[2] *Haydock v GD Cocker and Sons Ltd* EAT1143/99 and EAT215/02 [2003] All ER (D) 438 (Mar), which concerned the employment tribunal's refusal to grant a witness order.

lodged and the provision of the employment tribunal's written reasons), it is important to identify whether you are appealing a judgment or an order.

3.9 This will normally be fairly obvious. A judgment is defined by r 28(1)(a), which provides:

> 'A judgment which is a final determination of the proceedings, or of a particular issue in those proceedings. It may include an award of compensation, a declaration or recommendation and it may also include orders for costs, preparation time, or waste of costs.'

3.10 However, the case of *Uyamnwa-Odu v Schools Offices Services Ltd*[3] illustrates one situation when it is not obvious. The issue of construction raised in that appeal concerned the status of a r 13(2) 'unless order', which would have the effect of striking out the proceedings automatically if the claimant did not comply with the order. The short point was whether this was an order or a judgment. His Honour Judge Peter Clark gave the judgment of the EAT. He

---

[3] EAT/0294/05 [2005] All ER (D) 377 (Nov).

noted that costs orders were amongst the items in the non-exhaustive list of judgments in r 28(1)(a) and concluded that an order may be a judgment. The EAT held[4] that:

> 'a Rule 13(2) "unless order" amounts to a conditional judgment. It becomes a final determination of the proceedings if the party fails to comply with the underlying order.'

3.11 It is therefore worth giving some thought to whether you are appealing an order or a judgment.

Reasons

3.12 Because you can only appeal a 'decision' of the employment tribunal (which includes judgments and orders) the question arises as to whether you can appeal a finding of fact, about which you are unhappy. The answer is, no: you cannot appeal the findings or *reasons* of employment tribunal, in themselves, except where they are inadequate (see Chapter 8).

3.13 For example, if you win your case, but in the course of the employment tribunal's reasoning, it makes adverse findings against you, to which you strongly object, you cannot appeal against the adverse factual findings. You can only appeal a decision, order or judgment (or a refusal to make a decision etc).

3.14 It is therefore always important to identify precisely what you are appealing. For example, if an employment tribunal makes a decision in the course of a hearing that you are not entitled to cross-examine a witness on the other side, you may wish to appeal that decision[5] or the judgment which results, or both. Appealing case management decisions was also considered in *Amy Services Limited v Cardigan*.[6]

Errors of law

3.15 The jurisdiction of the EAT is only to correct errors of law (although this may include findings of fact which are 'perverse' – a high hurdle).

3.16 The EAT will only correct *material* errors of law. This means that the error must be operative in the employment tribunal's reasoning so as to affect the result.

---

[4] EAT/0294/05 [2005] All ER (D) 377 (Nov) at para 25.
[5] Appealing a discretionary procedural decision by an employment tribunal is just as difficult as appealing a judgment, and provided the employment tribunal (a) had power to do what it did, and (b) approach its exercise of discretion on correctly stated principles, an appellant has to show that the decision was such that no reasonable tribunal could have made it (ie it was not an option reasonably open to the tribunal): *Adams v West Sussex County Council* [1990] ICR 546, per Wood J at 551–552.
[6] [2008] IRLR 279.

3.17 Where a material error of law is identified by the employment tribunal, the powers of the EAT are to do anything which the employment tribunal could have done or to remit the case (or one or more issue) back to the employment tribunal for a decision: ETA 1996, s 35(1).

3.18 Errors of law as grounds of appeal are considered in detail in Chapter 8.

Status

3.19 The EAT is a superior court of record[7] and has the same powers as the High Court to compel the attendance of witnesses, the production of documents and other matters incidental to its jurisdiction.[8] However, the EAT has no jurisdiction to make a declaration that legislation is incompatible with the provisions of the European Convention for the Protection of Human Rights and Fundamental Freedoms 1950 (the European Convention), under the Human Rights Act 1998 (HRA 1998).[9]

3.20 At the time of writing, the EAT president is the Honourable Mr Justice Elias, but it has been announced that Mr Justice Underhill will take over as President from January 2009. It is not always the case that the President of the EAT practised in the field of employment law before becoming a judge, but this is the case with both the present President and Mr Justice Underhill. The registrar is Ms Pauline Donleavy.

3.21 Full hearings are normally conducted by a judge and two lay members who have practical experience of employment relations and are often very distinguished in their field. One of the lay members will have experience of the employer's perspective and the other will have experience from the employee's perspective. Some hearings will be conducted by a judge alone, who will normally be a High Court or circuit judge. However, on an appeal from a full employment tribunal, a judge sitting alone does not have jurisdiction.[10] The jurisdiction and composition of the EAT is dealt with more fully in Chapter 9.

OVERVIEW OF PROCEDURE

Procedural rules

3.22 As noted in Chapter 1, the EAT's procedure governed by the following provisions:

(1) the ETA 1996;

---

[7] ETA 1996, Pt II, s 20(3).
[8] ETA 1996, Pt II, s 29(2).
[9] HRA 1998, s 4(5) – since the EAT is not a 'court' for this purpose.
[10] See *D'Silva v Manchester Metropolitan University* UKEAT/0024/07 [2007] All ER (D) 10 (Oct) for a recent example of this.

(2) the EAT Rules 1993 (as amended in 1996, 2001, 2004 and 2005);

(3) the EAT Practice Direction 2008 (the EAT PD).[11]

3.23 The EAT has power to regulate its own procedure, subject to the EAT Rules[12] and, of course, within the limits of its powers under the ETA 1996.[13]

3.24 The EAT PD is a very helpful starting point for any appeal and it provides a commentary on how some of the EAT Rules apply. A copy of both the EAT Rules and the EAT PD is found in the Appendix of Statutory Materials.

3.25 Parties should always remember that:

(1) the EAT Rules always apply; and

(2) the EAT PD only applies in so far as the EAT has not given any specific directions in the case which conflict with the provisions of the Practice Direction.[14]

3.26 Where the EAT has given specific directions in a case, those will prevail over what is set out in the Practice Direction. But note, where no specific directions have been given by the EAT, the parties will be expected to follow the provisions of the Practice Direction.

3.27 Where specific directions have been given on some procedural steps only, the Practice Direction will govern any steps not specifically provided for by the EAT's directions.

3.28 The EAT has a wide discretion under r 25 to give any party directions as to any steps to be taken, whether on an application for such directions by one of the parties or on its own initiative.

Non-compliance with EAT Rules

3.29 By r 39(1), a failure to comply with the EAT Rules will not invalidate the proceedings unless the EAT directs otherwise. Under r 39(2), the EAT may dispense with any procedural step that might otherwise be taken or required under the EAT Rules, or direct that it be taken differently, if it considers that:

---

[11] Replacing the EAT PD 2004 from 22 May 2008.
[12] ETA 1996, Pt II, s 30(3).
[13] See, eg, the criticism of the Burns/Barke procedure for the EAT to obtain further written reasons from an employment tribunal in Chapter 8.
[14] However, in national security appeals, and appeals from the Certification Officer and the Central Arbitration Committee, the EAT Rules set out different procedures to be followed and the EAT will normally give specific directions.

(1) it would lead to the more expeditious or economical disposal of any proceedings;

(2) it would otherwise be desirable in the interests of justice.[15]

3.30 Rule 35(5) makes specific provision for dispensing with service or effecting it otherwise than as prescribed by the EAT Rules.

3.31 Rule 39(3) also specifically provides power for the EAT to allow the bringing of an appeal before the period for doing so has commenced. This obviously makes good sense, especially in the case of appeals against judgments, where the time period for appealing runs from the date the written reasons are sent to the parties. If a tribunal refused to provide reasons – despite being asked – then the aggrieved party would need the permission of the EAT to bring the appeal *before* the period for bringing it had commenced.

3.32 A party in this position should include with the notice of appeal and other documents, a request for the EAT to exercise its power under r 39(3) in these circumstances, as a matter of good practice (together with a copy of any relevant request for written reasons); although it is clear that the EAT can exercise these powers on its own initiative.

The registrar

3.33 It is important to note that 'the registrar' means the person appointed to be the registrar of the EAT, but this definition also includes any officer authorised by the president of the EAT to act on behalf of the registrar.[16] This is why you may find yourself corresponding with someone whose name is not (presently) Ms Donleavy, but who appears to you to be the registrar.

Interim applications

3.34 Interim applications are written requests for the EAT to do something (eg, make an order or give directions) after a notice of appeal has been lodged but before the appeal has been determined and disposed of. An example would be an application to the EAT to request the production of part of the employment judge's notes of evidence (from the employment tribunal hearing) if those are relevant and necessary to the appeal and the evidence cannot be agreed between the parties.[17] It is better to make all interim applications together, where possible, and the Practice Direction encourages parties 'to

---

[15] This criterion overlaps with the overriding objective in r 2A which the registrar must take into account in any decision on a request for such a waiver, but you should look at r 2A in full if making such an application.
[16] See the definition of 'the registrar' in the EAT Rules, r 2(1).
[17] Before making any application for the employment judge's notes, see para 7 of the EAT PD which makes detailed provision for the procedure to be followed.

make any such applications at a Preliminary Hearing ("PH") or an Appointment for Directions if one is ordered'.[18]

3.35 This is slightly confusing, since on the one hand these applications have to be made in writing and, on the other, they are to be made a preliminary hearing or an appointment for directions. What this really means is that it is sensible to make all interim applications in advance of a preliminary hearing or appointment for directions, so that they can all be determined together, with the benefit of any representations by the parties, thereby avoiding endless correspondence and allowing all the directions to be given in one order. This saves time for the EAT and the parties and helps the appeal to progress without unnecessary delay.

3.36 Any application should be copied to the other parties, so that they have a chance to consider the application at the earliest opportunity, if it has not been canvassed with them before. In fact, r 19 provides that the registrar will serve a copy of any application on every other party to the proceedings, but it is still courteous good practice to send a copy direct to other parties when making the application.

How to apply

3.37 In this respect, the EAT does not have the formality of a civil court and so any interim application can be made in a letter, setting out carefully what is sought and the reasons supporting the application. It may also be necessary to attach any relevant correspondence or documents, but these should be kept to a minimum.

3.38 There are no specified forms for making interim applications. No fees are payable for making an application (unlike in civil courts – the Court of Appeal, for example).

3.39 An interim application should always be made in writing and will be initially referred to the registrar.

3.40 The registrar considers all interim applications made to the EAT, including those for adjournments, and decides most of them, unless she thinks that it should be referred to the president or a judge[19] who may either deal with it or decide how it should be dealt with: by the registrar herself or by the president, a judge or a full tribunal. Under r 20(1) the registrar is obliged to have regard to the overriding objective in r 2A when considering an interim application.

3.41 Some interim applications have to be decided by the president or a judge:

---

[18] EAT PD at para 4.1, which has remained unchanged in the 2008 EAT PD.
[19] EAT Rules, r 20(1) and (2).

(1) restricted reporting orders;[20] and

(2) permission to a person subject to a restriction of proceedings order.[21]

3.42 The registrar also has power to reject notices of appeal on basis that the EAT has no jurisdiction to hear them.

Appeals from the registrar

3.43 Rule 21 of the EAT Rules provides for appeals against the decisions of the registrar:

(1) The time limit for appealing is 5 days,[22] not counting weekends etc.[23]

(2) Notice of appeal may be given orally or in writing,[24] ie you can telephone and ask to appeal any decision to the judge. Writing is preferable since there is less room for any misunderstanding and you can state your reasons for appealing with precision.

(3) The registrar informs the appellant and other parties concerned with the appeal of the arrangements for determining the appeal.

(4) The appeal is heard by the judge as a re-hearing.[25] It is therefore not necessary to show that the registrar exercised her discretion perversely – it is sufficient to persuade the judge to exercise his discretion differently.

The register

3.44 A register of cases is kept in the central office of the EAT and in Edinburgh or in the file which forms part of that register and all documents sent to the EAT are addressed to the registrar,[26] and their date of delivery recorded in the register. The public can inspect any notice of appeal or respondent's answer and any judgment or order of the EAT during office hours,[27] although any copies required will be charged for.[28]

---

[20] EAT Rules, r 20(3), where an order is sought under ETA 1996, s 31 or 32 (see rr 23 and 23A).
[21] EAT Rules, r 20(4), where the order has been made under ETA 1996, s 33(1) and application is made under s 33(4).
[22] EAT Rules, r 37 and EAT PD, para 4.3.
[23] Not counting weekends, Christmas Day, Good Friday and Bank Holidays: EAT PD, para 1.8.4.
[24] EAT Rules, r 21(2).
[25] See eg *Jurkowska v HLMAD Ltd* [2008] ICR 841, [2008] IRLR 430 and *Hafele v Nolan* UKEATPA/0354/08, 23 July 2008.
[26] EAT Rules, r 35(1).
[27] EAT PD, para 5.3.
[28] EAT PD, para 5.4.

3.45 If a member of the public wishes to inspect any other document, an application should be made to do so.[29] In practice, this means that the application should be in writing and it is sensible to specify clearly what documents.

The overriding objective

3.46 The EAT's regulation of its procedure is subject to r 2A of the EAT Rules, which introduced the 'overriding objective' into the procedure of the EAT. The overriding objective is to deal with cases 'justly'. In a way, it is perhaps surprising that this had to be expressly introduced into the EAT Rules. However, it is derived from the Civil Procedure Rules 1998[30] which apply in the civil proceedings in the County Courts and High Court and helpfully sets out criteria by which justice in dealing with cases will be assessed. Rule 2A(2) provides as follows:

> (2) Dealing with a case justly includes, so far as practicable—
>
> (a) ensuring that the parties are on an equal footing;
> (b) dealing with the case in ways which are proportionate to the importance and complexity of the issues;
> (c) ensuring that it is dealt with expeditiously and fairly; and
> (d) saving expense.

3.47 Rule 2A(3) and para 1.5 of the EAT PD both make clear that the parties are required to help the EAT to further the overriding objective.

Other reference to the Civil Procedure Rules 1998

3.48 Paragraph 1.8 of the EAT PD sets out examples of where the EAT is guided by the CPR (at paras 1.8.1–1.8.4 – provisions as to time), para 1.8 itself making the more general point that the EAT will be guided by the CPR where that is appropriate to the EAT's jurisdiction, procedure, unrestricted rights of representation and restricted costs regime.

LODGING THE APPEAL

3.49 If you are even considering appealing (or seeking a review by the employment tribunal – Chapter 2), make sure that you obtain the written reasons of the employment tribunal and check the relevant time limits. Appealing requires you to send a notice of appeal and some accompanying documents (including the written reasons, where available) to the EAT and they *all* have to arrive at the EAT within the time limit for your appeal.[31] If they arrive after the time limit has expired, your appeal is out of time and the EAT

---

[29] EAT PD, para 5.3.3.
[30] SI 1998/3132.
[31] *Woodward v Abbey National plc; JP Garrett Electrical Ltd v Cotton* [2005] IRLR 782, disapproving *Clark v Midland Packaging Ltd* [2005] 2 All ER 266.

will not normally accept it or extend the time limit. It is difficult to appeal with the written reasons of the employment tribunal.

3.50 Rule 3(1) of the EAT Rules provides as follows:

3. Institution of appeal

(1) Every appeal to the Appeal Tribunal shall, subject to paragraphs (2) and (4), be instituted by serving on the Tribunal[32] the following documents—

- (a) a notice of appeal in, or substantially in, accordance with Form 1, 1A or 2 in the Schedule to these rules;
- (b) in the case of an appeal from a judgment of an employment tribunal a copy of any claim and response in the proceedings before the employment tribunal or an explanation as to why either is not included; and;
- (c) in the case of an appeal from a judgment of an employment tribunal a copy of the written record of the judgment of the employment tribunal which is subject to appeal and the written reasons for the judgment, or an explanation as to why written reasons are not included;
- (d) in the case of an appeal made pursuant to regulation 38(8) of the 1999 Regulations or regulation 47(6) of the 2004 Regulations or regulation 35(6) of the Information and Consultation Regulations from a declaration or order of the CAC, a copy of that declaration or order; and
- (e) in the case of an appeal from an order of an employment tribunal a copy of the written record of the order of the employment tribunal which is subject to appeal and (if available) the written reasons for the order;
- (f) in the case of an appeal from a decision or order of the Certification Officer a copy of the decision or order of the Certification Officer which is subject to appeal and the written reasons for that decision or order.

Time limits

3.51 An appeal to the EAT from a decision, order or judgment of an employment tribunal must be *received* by the EAT within 42 days (ie 6 weeks).

3.52 Note also the following:

(1) Do **not** leave it to the last minute.[33] Remember that 'by 4 pm' means 'before 4 pm'.[34]

(2) The relevant time limit applies even if other aspects of the case have still not been determined (eg, remedy and assessment of compensation, or an application for a review): para 3.4 of the EAT PD.

---

[32] The 'Tribunal' here means the EAT.
[33] For example, *Solani Tirado v St George's Healthcare NHS Trust* UKEATPA/0669/05 [2005] All ER (D) 12 (Nov), per His Honour Judge Peter Clark.
[34] EAT Rules, r 37(1A) introduced the 4 pm deadline to the Rules in 2004. The 2008 EAT PD now refers to the 4 pm deadline expressly at para 1.8.1.

(3) If you are in any doubt or difficulty, lodge the notice of appeal and accompanying documents in time and apply to the registrar for directions, explaining your doubts or difficulties fully (para 3.9).

3.53 As explained below, the time limits are very strict for appeals and extensions of time are only very rarely granted. Oddly, the approach is stricter than the court of appeal and this approach applies to lodging cross-appeals in time, just as it does to lodging the original appeal in time.[35]

Forty-two days from when?

3.54 As noted above, the basic rule is that the 42 days runs from the day on which the tribunal sends the order, decision or written record of the judgment to the parties. However, there are special rules for judgments, which depend on if, when and how written reasons are provided by the employment tribunal.

3.55 Before you read anything more, find the date on which the order, decision or written record of the judgment was *sent to you by the employment tribunal*.[36] This is normally expressly recorded on the face of the order or record of the judgment sent to the parties. Do not rely on the date when you received it, or the date on the postmark. That is a schoolboy error. The date that you should rely on is the date when it was sent to you by the employment tribunal. This is an important point.

3.56 Rule 3(3) of the EAT Rules makes provision for the relevant time limits for lodging the notice of appeal. As stated, it is important to distinguish between an appeal against a judgment and other appeals, as explained below.

Two regimes

3.57 There are basically two regimes for working out the date on which your 42 days for appealing beings. One applies to decisions or orders and the other applies to judgments.

3.58 For orders and decisions (including refusing to make orders), para 3.2 of the EAT PD provides as follows:

> '3.2 If the appeal is against an order or decision, the appeal must be instituted within 42 days of the date of the order or decision. The EAT will treat a Tribunal's refusal to make an order or decision as itself constituting an order or decision. The date of an order or decision is the date when the order or decision was sent to the parties, which is normally recorded on or in the order or decision.'

---

[35] *Slingsby v Griffith Smith (No 1)* UKEAT/0619/07, per HHJ Burke QC.
[36] What was once a matter of some uncertainty on the authorities was resolved definitively by the Court of Appeal: *Gydnia American Shipping Lines (London) Ltd v Chelminski* [2004] EWCA Civ 871, [2004] ICR 1523, upholding, among other EAT decisions, *Sian v Abbey National plc* [2004] ICR 55 (Burton P presiding) – this observation is taken from the judgment of His Honour Judge Peter Clark in *Solani*, above.

3.59 The guidance on the EAT's website is, unsurprisingly, correct; but it may be slightly confusing, as it says the following:

> 'The usual rule is that your appeal must be received complete by the EAT no later than 16:00 on the 42nd day after the date on which the ET sent you the judgment, decision, direction or order.
>
> The judgment, decision, direction or order is not the same as the reasons. You may need to ask the ET for the reasons, but (unless one of the circumstances below applies) you should not wait until you receive them before sending your appeal, or it may be out of time.
>
> Under these circumstances you may count the 42 days from the date the reasons were sent to you – if:
>
> - you requested written reasons at the employment tribunal hearing; or
> - you wrote to request written reasons from the employment tribunal within 14 days of the date the judgment was sent to you; or
> - the employment tribunal reserved its reasons and gave them subsequently in writing.'

3.60 The date when written reasons are sent to the parties can only affect the time limit for appealing where a judgment is being appealed, and then only in certain circumstances. In the case of decisions, directions and orders (mentioned in the same breath in the guidance above), the date of the decision, direction or order itself is the date from which the 42 days runs. The guidance on the EAT's website is perhaps not quite as clear on this point as it could be.

3.61 Paragraph 3.3 of the EAT PD provides for the time limit for appealing judgments, and again the starting point is the date on which the written record of the judgment was sent to the parties. However, as para 3.3 explains, there are three situations in which the 42 days will run from the date on which written reasons are provided. Paragraph 3.3 provides as follows:

> '3.3 If the appeal is against a judgment, the appeal must be instituted within 42 days from the date on which the written record of the judgment was sent to the parties. However in three situations the time for appealing against a judgment will be 42 days from the date when written reasons were sent to the parties. This will be the case only if (1) written reasons were requested orally at the hearing before the Tribunal or (2) written reasons were requested in writing within 14 days of the date on which the written record of the judgment was sent to the parties or (3) the Tribunal itself reserved its reasons and gave them subsequently in writing: such exception will not apply if the request to the Tribunal for written reasons is made out of time (whether or not such request is granted). The date of the written record and of the written reasons is the date when they are sent to the parties, which is normally recorded on or in the written record and the written reasons.'

3.62 So, when the employment tribunal reaches the end of the case, there are basically three options for the employment tribunal to communicate its judgment to the parties. First, it can give its judgment and full reasons there and then, orally. Secondly, it can announce the result with no reasons and leave it to the parties to ask for reasons (asking either then and there, or within 14 days of the written record of the judgment being sent to the parties). Thirdly, the employment tribunal can reserve its judgment and send it to the parties in the post, so that they only find out whether they have won or lost at a later date. If this course is taken, the employment tribunal may or may not provide their written reasons at the same time and, if not, the parties have to request them.

3.63 The crucial point is whether (and when) written reasons, necessary for any appeal, were provided by the employment tribunal and, if they have not been provided, whether they had been properly requested by either party.

3.64 The important thing to note is that if you are aggrieved by a judgment in the employment tribunal, it is wise to seek the reasons either at the hearing or within 14 days of the judgment being sent to you, so that you at least have the opportunity to consider whether or not to appeal.

3.65 Finally, before giving two illustrations below, we reiterate: remember not to leave it too late; it is best to get your appeal in well within the 42 days. There have been a number of recent cases in which time limits have been missed by only days, hours, minutes or even seconds: 88 seconds late was too late in *Beasley v National Grid*.[37] This case was relied on by the EAT when considering an appeal concerning a claim form in the employment tribunal, which was just 9 seconds late. The EAT held that the employment tribunal was right to conclude that this was too late: *Miller v Community Links Trust Ltd*.[38] And note that a computer or fax machine problem at the last minute will be no excuse! Do not leave it to the last minute.

3.66 Note also that the notice of appeal and accompanying documents (specified below at para **3.130** et seq, especially para **3.135**) must all be received by the expiry of the time limit for appealing. It is not good enough that they are in the course of being received when the time limit expires: *Woodward v Abbey National plc; JP Garrett Electrical Ltd v Cotton*,[39] (effectively overturning *Clark v Midland Packaging Ltd*,[40] which had suggested that beginning sending a fax or email before the deadline would suffice).

Illustrations

3.67 Although these illustrations may seem obvious, time limits tend to generate considerable anxiety and we therefore give two worked illustrations of time limits in two different situations. To illustrate the operation of the time limits for a typical appeal to the EAT, we take the example of two separate unfair dismissal claims brought by Mrs Jones and Mr Singh against their employer, Fresco Ltd.

---

[37] UKEAT/0626/06 [2007] All ER (D) 110 (Aug).
[38] UKEAT/0486/07 [2007] All ER (D) 196 (Nov).
[39] [2005] IRLR 782.
[40] [2005] 2 All ER 266.

Judgment with full written reasons

3.68 Mrs Jones (the employee or 'claimant') loses her case against Fresco (the employer or 'respondent'). Mrs Jones receives a full written judgment from the employment tribunal. On the last page of the judgment, it states that the judgment was sent to the parties on **Tuesday, 1 April 2008**.

3.69 Mrs Jones reads the judgment. She is disappointed and says to herself, 'They must be joking'. Sadly for her, this is not the case. So, she decides to appeal.

3.70 Her notice of appeal and accompanying documents must be with the EAT within 42 days of that date,[41] not counting the date on which the judgment was sent, which means **before 4 pm**[42] **on Tuesday, 13 May 2008**.

Judgment without reasons

3.71 Mr Singh wins his case against Fresco. Fresco receives a judgment on **Thursday, 3 April 2008**. Neither Mr Singh nor Fresco has asked the tribunal for written reasons at the hearing.

3.72 Fresco must therefore request the written reasons with 14 days of the date when the judgment was **sent** to the parties. Fresco's solicitors look at the judgment and see that it was sent to the parties on **Tuesday, 1 April 2008**. Therefore, Fresco must ask for the tribunal's written reasons and ensure that the request is received by the employment tribunal before midnight[43] on **Tuesday, 15 April 2008**.

3.73 Fresco's solicitors are very efficient and ask for written reasons immediately, well within time and the employment tribunal send them to the parties on **Tuesday, 10 June 2008**.

3.74 The parties then receive the tribunal's written reasons on **Thursday, 12 June 2008**.

3.75 Fresco's notice of appeal (together with all the necessary documents) must be received by the EAT **by 4 pm on Tuesday, 22 July 2008**, which is 6 weeks (42 days) after the written reasons were **sent to the parties**. Not Thursday, 24 July 2008! Note that the time for appealing does not run from *receipt* of the reasons by the parties, but from when they are *sent to the parties* by the employment tribunal. That is a date which will be stated on the document containing the written reasons. One cannot emphasise this enough. This is an easy mistake to make. Do not make it.

---

[41] EAT Rules, r 3(3).
[42] EAT PD, para 1.8.1.
[43] Do not leave it this late; we recommend trying to ensure that it is clearly received by the employment tribunal during working hours before the due date.

Receipt

3.76 Anything that you send to the EAT must be received by the EAT **by 4 pm**,[44] which means **before 4 pm**; otherwise it will be regarded as arriving the following day.[45] This applies to your notice of appeal and all the necessary accompanying documents, just as it does to other documents that the parties will send the EAT as the appeal proceeds towards a hearing.

3.77 If you send your notice of appeal (rather than delivering it by hand) make sure that you check with the EAT that it has been successfully received.

3.78 Even if you hand deliver your notice of appeal and accompanying documents, make sure you look at the receipt when you are given it and check the date and time stamp. One of the authors encountered a particular problem, unlikely to arise very often, but to which parties should be alert. We therefore include this cautionary tale.

3.79 A notice of appeal was due by 4 pm on the Wednesday. It was delivered by hand to the EAT at 4.05 pm on the preceding day, the Tuesday and was therefore 23 hours and 55 minutes early, and could have been lodged in time the following day, before 4 pm. However, because this was after 4 pm, it was stamped with Wednesday's date, but the time stamp still showed 4.05 pm. So, it looked as if it had been lodged at 4.05 pm on the Wednesday. The EAT therefore treated it as having been lodged out of time! Fortunately, the mistake was corrected and the appeal proceeded.

3.80 However, parties beware; check the time and date stamp on your receipt from the EAT, immediately you receive it. Make sure there has been no error. It is much easier to correct any error or misunderstanding immediately, than it is later on.

Service

3.81 Following the 'sift' procedure, the EAT Rules make provision for the registrar of the EAT to seal the notice of appeal and serve a sealed copy on the respondent(s) to the appeal and the secretary of the employment tribunals (or, in special cases, the person specified in r 4(1)(c)–(e)).

3.82 So, if the appellant serves a copy of the notice of appeal on you (as respondent) out of courtesy and the EAT does not serve a copy, you know that the appeal is still going through the sift procedure.

3.83 Following service of the notice of appeal on the respondent by the EAT; EAT PD, para 10.1 requires the respondent then to lodge a respondent's notice at the EAT and serve it on all other parties, within 14 days of the seal date of the order setting the appeal (see below).

---

[44] EAT Rules, r 37(1A).
[45] EAT PD, paras 1.8.1 and 1.8.2.

Extensions of time

Power to extend time

3.84 Although this is not controversial, the EAT has power to extend any time limit, whether or not it has already expired. Rule 37(1) provides as follows:

> '37(1) The time prescribed by these Rules or by order of the Appeal Tribunal for doing any act may be extended (whether it has already expired or not) or abridged, and the date appointed for any purpose may be altered, by order of the Tribunal.'

Not before lodging notice of appeal

3.85 Paragraph 3.5 of the EAT PD makes it clear that an application for an extension of time 'cannot be considered until a Notice of Appeal ... has been lodged with the EAT'. This reflects the fact that r 37(4) provides that an application for an extension of time under r 37(3) 'shall not be heard until the notice of appeal has been served on the Appeal Tribunal'.

3.86 So, there is no opportunity to apply for an extension to put in your notice of appeal before the time limit has expired. Applying for an extension will therefore always mean that the time limit has expired already. This is not a situation which is desirable. Nor is it an advantageous standpoint from which to seek the indulgence of the EAT.

3.87 This underlines the point made in para 3.9 that:

> 'In any case of doubt or difficulty, a notice of appeal should be lodged in time and an application made to the registrar for directions'.

Application

3.88 An application for extension of time for appealing is made to the registrar, in writing as an interim application.[46]

3.89 The registrar will normally invite and consider representations from each side about any application for an extension of time, before determining it.[47]

3.90 As noted above, there is a right of appeal to a judge but it must be notified 'orally or in writing' within 5 days of the registrar's decision being sent to the parties.[48]

Criteria

3.91 Paragraph 3.7 of the 2008 EAT PD makes clear that:

---

[46] EAT Rules, rr 37(3) and 20; and EAT PD, paras 3.6 and 4.2.
[47] EAT PD, para 3.6.
[48] EAT PD, para 4.3.

'particular attention will be paid to whether any good excuse[49] for the delay has been shown and to the guidance contained in the decisions of the EAT and the Court of Appeal, as summarised in *United Arab Emirates v Abdelghafar* [1995] ICR 65, *Aziz v Bethnal Green City Challenge Co Ltd* [2000] IRLR 111 and *Jurkowska v HLMAD Ltd* [2008] EWCA Civ 231[50].'

3.92 It is convenient first to identify the key criteria upon which the discretion to extend time will (rarely) be exercised.

3.93 The key questions[51] are as follows:

(1) What is the explanation for the default?

(2) Does it provide a good excuse for the default?

(3) Are there circumstances which justify the EAT taking the exceptional step of granting an extension of time?

(4) In the absence of the above, is there an overriding duty[52] binding on (at least) the employment tribunal and the EAT to give effect to the rights of the appellant, in circumstances where allowing the appeal is the only way in which that could be achieved?

3.94 It is arguable that this last question might fall within the third question as being circumstances which justify the taking of the exceptional step of extending time. However, it does seem that this last question raises issues which are not merely different by degree but in nature. 'Circumstances' seems a wide word to allow justice to be done as a matter of discretion. The last question (overriding duty) suggests a hard-edged duty, which has wrongly not been discharged by the UK (through the employment tribunal) as it should have been. This is a category of case which may grow in years to come. In any event, following *Jurkowska*, it seems likely that there may need to be some further clarification or rationalisation of the EAT's practice on this point, since the present state of affairs seems odd and unclear for reasons explained below.

Explanation

3.95 The appellant must provide a 'full and honest' explanation of the reason for failing to lodge the notice of appeal and accompanying documents in time.

---

[49] The fact than an application for litigation support from public funds has been made, but not yet determined; or that other support is being sought is unlikely to be regarded as a good excuse: EAT PD, para 3.8.

[50] Since reported at [2008] ICR 841, [2008] IRLR 430.

[51] The first three key questions are derived directly from para 30 of the judgment in *United Arab Emirates v Abdelghafar* [1995] ICR 65.

[52] In *Abdelghafar*, there was such an overriding duty, to accord the United Arab Emirates rights of state immunity.

Good excuse

3.96 The following points should be noted about how the EAT approaches the issue of 'a good excuse':

(1) Since parties are informed of the 42-day time limit for appealing when judgments and orders are sent out to the parties, ignorance of the time limit is no excuse, even for an unrepresented party.

(2) Nor are the following likely to be regarded as 'a good excuse':
  (a) oversight of the passing of the time limit, for example, by a solicitor under pressure of work;
  (b) prior notification sent of the intention to appeal, sent to the EAT or the employment tribunal or the successful party;
  (c) a pending application for review of the decision;
  (d) a forthcoming remedies hearing (when liability is being appealed);
  (e) delay in an application for public (or other funding) for litigation support or other assistance.

Discretion

3.97 Even where a full and honest explanation for the delay is put forward, the EAT may have regard to a wide range of other factors in the exercise of its discretion, such as:

(1) conduct of the appellant, meaning any evidence of:
  (a) procedural abuse,
  (b) questionable tactics,
  (c) or intentional delay,

(2) the length of the delay;

(3) the merits of the appeal;[53] and

(4) any prejudice or injustice to the successful party.

General principles

3.98 The general principle are to be found in the EAT's decision in *Abdleghafar*, which should now be read in the light of *Jurkowska v HLMAD Ltd*.[54] The EAT in *Abdelghafar* considered two (then recent) decisions of the Court of Appeal outside the area of employment law, which it

---

[53] Although the EAT will not normally hold 'a mini-hearing of the substantive appeal'.
[54] [2008] EWCA Civ 231, [2008] ICR 841, [2008] IRLR 430.

regarded as relevant to the approach to the question of extensions of time: *Costellow v Somerset County Council*[55] and *Regalbourne Ltd v East Lindsey District Council.*[56]

3.99 At paras 22–29, the EAT outlined the principles which govern the exercise of the EAT's discretion to extend time and those factors which are relevant to it from which the criteria above are derived (at para 30 in the judgment). Any explanation seeking to show a good excuse should have in mind these principles and factors as the proper background to any consideration of an application to extend time for lodging a notice of appeal:

> '(1) The grant or refusal of an extension of time is a matter of judicial discretion to be exercised, not subjectively or at whim or by rigid rule of thumb, but in a principled manner in accordance with reason and justice. The exercise of the discretion is a matter of weighing and balancing all the relevant factors which appear from the material before the Appeal Tribunal. The result of an exercise of a discretion is not dictated by any set factor. Discretions are not packaged, programmed responses.
>
> (2) As Sir Thomas Bingham MR pointed out in *Costellow v Somerset CC*, supra, at 959C, time problems arise at the intersection of two principles, both salutary, neither absolute:
>
>> '... The first principle is that the rules of court and the associated rules of practice, devised in the public interest to promote the expeditious dispatch of litigation, must be observed. The prescribed time limits are not targets to be aimed at or expressions of pious hope but requirements to be met ...'
>
> The second principle is that:
>
>> '... a plaintiff should not in the ordinary way be denied an adjudication of his claim on its merits because of procedural default, unless the default causes prejudice to his opponent for which an award of costs cannot compensate ...'

24

> (3) The approach indicated by these two principles is modified according to the stage which the relevant proceedings have reached. If, for example, the procedural default is in relation to an interlocutory step in proceedings, such as a failure to serve a pleading or give discovery within the prescribed time limits, the court will, in the ordinary way and in the absence of special circumstances, grant an extension of time. Unless the delay has caused irreparable prejudice to the other party, justice will usually favour the action proceeding to a full trial on the merits. The approach is different, however, if the procedural default as to time relates to an appeal against a decision on the merits by the court or tribunal of first instance. The party aggrieved by that decision has had a trial to hear and determine his case. If he is dissatisfied with the result he should act promptly. The grounds for

---

[55] [1993] 1 All ER 952.
[56] (1993) *The Times*, March 16.

extending his time are not as strong as where he has not yet had a trial. The interests of the parties and the public in certainty and finality of legal proceedings make the court more strict about time limits on appeals. An extension may be refused, even though the default in observing the time limit has not caused prejudice to the party successful in the original proceedings.

25

(4) An extension of time is an indulgence requested from the court by a party in default. He is not entitled to an extension. He has no reasonable or legitimate expectation of receiving one. His only reasonable or legitimate expectation is that the discretion relevant to his application to extend time will be exercised judicially in accordance with established principles of what is fair and reasonable. In those circumstances, it is incumbent on the applicant for an extension of time to provide the court with a full, honest and acceptable explanation of the reasons for the delay. He cannot reasonably expect the discretion to be exercised in his favour, as a defaulter, unless he provides an explanation for the default.

26

Application of principles by the EAT

In accordance with the general principles stated above, the Appeal Tribunal follows the guidelines for the exercise of its discretion to extend time. They are only guidelines. They do not fetter the exercise of the discretion. They are intended to ensure, as far as possible, consistency of treatment, predictability of result and the attainment of justice.

27

(1) The timetable set by the EAT Rules should be observed by the parties and their lay and professional advisers. Although more sympathy may be shown to a party who is unrepresented, as many are, there is no excuse, even in the case of an unrepresented party, for ignorance of the time limit or of the importance of compliance. When parties are notified of the reasons for the industrial tribunal's decision they are informed of the 42-day time limit for appealing. The limits will, therefore, only be relaxed in rare and exceptional cases where the tribunal is satisfied that there is a reason which justifies departure from the time limits laid down in the Rules.

28

(2) The tribunal's discretion will not be exercised, unless the appellant provides the tribunal with a full and honest explanation of the reason for non-compliance. If the explanation satisfies the tribunal that there is a good excuse for the default, an extension of time may be granted. Experience has shown that most of the explanations offered do not in fact excuse the delay which has occurred. For example, the following explanations have been rejected by the Appeal Tribunal as excuses for delay: ignorance of the time limit; oversight of the passing of the limit, for example, by a solicitor under pressure of work; prior notification to the Employment Appeal Tribunal or the Industrial Tribunal or to the successful party of the intention to appeal; the existence of pending applications for review of the

decision or for remedies; delay in the processing of an application for legal aid or of an application for advice or support from elsewhere, such as the Equal Opportunities Commission or the Commission for Racial Equality. It is always possible, in cases where there may be unavoidable delay, for an extension to be agreed between the parties or granted by order of the Appeal Tribunal *before* the period has expired. Alternatively, a notice of appeal may be served in order to comply with the Rules, with a covering letter saying that it may be necessary to apply to amend it later.

29

(3) If an explanation for the delay is offered, other factors may come into play in the exercise of the discretion. It is, of course, impossible to make an exhaustive list of factors. The Appeal Tribunal will be astute to detect any evidence of procedural abuse, questionable tactics or intentional default. The Tribunal will look at the length of the delay which has occurred, though it may refuse to grant an extension even where the delay is very short. Extensions have been refused, even where the notice of appeal was served only one day out of time. Parties who have decided to appeal are also strongly advised not to leave service of the notice of appeal until the last few days of the 42-day period. If they do, they run the risk of delay in the delivery of post or of the misdirection of mail. That risk can be avoided by service of the notice of appeal well within the period. The merits of the appeal may be relevant, but are usually of little weight. It is not appropriate on an application for leave to extend time for the Tribunal to be asked to investigate in detail the strength of the appeal. Otherwise there is a danger that an application for leave will be turned into a mini-hearing of the substantive appeal. Lack of prejudice or of injustice to the successful party in the original proceedings is also a factor of little or no significance. If there is irreparable concrete prejudice, that will strengthen the opposition to the application for extension; but even if there is no prejudice, the application may still be refused.

30

Thus, the questions which must be addressed by the Appeal Tribunal, the parties and their representatives on an application for an extension are: (a) What is the explanation for the default? (b) Does it provide a good excuse for the default? (c) Are there circumstances which justify the Tribunal taking the exceptional step of granting an extension of time?'

Other cases

3.100 In *Aziz v Bethnal Green City Challenge Co Ltd*,[57] the Court of Appeal affirmed the approach in The guidance in *Abdelghafar* as providing a perfectly acceptable formula for the EAT's exercise of its discretion whether to allow an extension of time for appealing.

3.101 However, the Court of Appeal noted that the approach in *Abdelghafar* may be stricter than the one adopted by the Court of Appeal in hearing

---

[57] [2000] IRLR 111 – the other case mentioned in the EAT PD, para 3.7.

applications out of time, but accepted that it was not necessary for the EAT to follow exactly the way in which the Court of Appeal deals with prospective appeals.

3.102 The Court of Appeal accepted that there were significant distinctions between the EAT and the Court of Appeal, not least that the EAT only has power to hear appeals on points of law, not fact. Furthermore, unlike the Court of Appeal, the EAT is a statutory body set up under a statutory framework and has the power to regulate its own procedure. It has its own good reasons for requiring the parties to deal with proposed appeals expeditiously and these factors taken together justify a stricter approach as permissible.

3.103 In subsequent case of *Solani Tirado v St George's Healthcare NHS Trust*,[58] the EAT was considering a situation in which His Honour Judge Peter Clark gave the judgment of the EAT and held[59] that:

> 'The EAT time limits must be strictly observed. See *United Arab Emirates v Abdelghafar* [1995] ICR 65, [1995] IRLR 243 approved in *Aziz v Bethnal Green City Challenge Co Ltd* [2000] IRLR 111 (Court of Appeal). Potential Appellants should not leave it until the last minute; else they run the risk of finding themselves time-barred. I am satisfied that applying the EAT Rules and Practice Direction, this appeal was out of time, albeit by only one day. The question then ... is whether the Appellant has provided an honest explanation amounting to a good excuse for the delay. In the present case, in my judgment, no good explanation is proffered. There is no excuse. In these circumstances I see no reason to differ from the view taken by the registrar. This appeal fails and is dismissed.'

Jurkowska

3.104 As noted above,[60] the 2008 EAT PD specifically refers to the Court of Appeal's decision in *Jurkowska v HLMAD Ltd*[61] in which the Court of Appeal considered whether or not the decision of Underhill J (upholding the registrar) to allow an extension of time was permissible, ie within the judge's discretion. The case is interesting for three reasons. First, it shows up the oddity of a stricter regime in the EAT than in the Court of Appeal again. Second, to the extent that the members of the court agreed with each other, the agreement was pretty threadbare. Third, the background facts were odd, even if the real issue involved was more commonplace, namely the omission of a document by mistake. The short facts were that solicitors DLA failed to lodge a copy of the judgment with the Notice of Appeal and other documents. So the appeal was not validly lodged and an extension was necessary. Even though the judgment and the written reasons are clearly distinguished in the EAT Rules, and in the Practice Direction, both the registrar and Underhill J were prepared to extend time. What had happened was that the ET had handed a copy of the judgment to DLA's barrister, who (understandably) did not appreciate that this was

---

[58] UKEATPA/0669/05 [2005] All ER (D) 12 (Nov).
[59] UKEATPA/0669/05 [2005] All ER (D) 12 (Nov) at para [13].
[60] See para **3.98**.
[61] [2008] EWCA Civ 231, [2008] ICR 841, [2008] IRLR 430.

intended by the ET to be a substitute for sending a copy to the parties (or their solicitors). The barrister was unaware that his solicitors and client would not receive a copy and DLA failed to spot the absence of the judgment, when putting together the bundle of documents to be lodged with the Notice of Appeal.

3.105 The Court of Appeal upheld the decision of Underhill J but each of the three members of the court took a different approach. Although the Court of Appeal endorsed the strict approach in *Abdelghafar*, they nonetheless felt that Underhill J had been entitled to depart from the policy behind *Abdelghafar*, on the particular facts of the case – although Sedley LJ was very reluctant to do so.

At para [19], Rimer LJ said:

> 'The *Abdelghafar* principles reflect that rules as to time limits are expected to be respected, and there is precisely nothing unjust or unfair about that. Litigants are not entitled to expect rules of practice to be re-written so as to accommodate their own negligence, idleness or incompetence. But the principles also recognise that nobody is perfect, that errors will happen, that time limits will be missed and that in appropriate circumstances it may therefore be just to extend time for compliance. That, however, is in the nature of an indulgence and the guidelines are directed at outlining the approach to the question of whether it will or may be fair so to indulge the appellant. In the ordinary case a good explanation and excuse will have to be shown. But even if the explanation does not amount to a good excuse, there may be exceptional circumstances which anyway justify an extension. The guidelines are not rigid but they do prescribe a principled approach to an application for an extension of time. Nothing less should be expected from a developed system of civil law.'

Hooper LJ clearly felt that lack of prejudice (said to be of 'little or no significance' in *Abdelghafar*) was plainly material. At para [61], he said:

> 'I do not follow why a lack of prejudice is an irrelevant factor if an application is to be dealt with justly. I would be concerned if any desire on the part of the EAT to reduce the work involved in handling applications for extensions of time was given undue weight.'

3.106 The authors respectfully sympathise with the view that the present state of the law on this issue makes little practical sense and is not clearly underpinned by principle. Hooper LJ must be right that there is no justification for holding that lack or prejudice is a factor of little or no significance, certainly since the introduction of the overriding objective in r 2A in 2004, long after *Abdelghafar* was decided. As noted below at **3.134**, it is surprising that the EAT should be stricter than the Court of Appeal in relation to extensions of time arising from errors or oversights (see Bean J in *Hafele v Nolan*).[62]

---

[62] UKEATPA/0354/08, 23 July 2008.

Consent

3.107 A party in difficulties may seek the agreement to an extension of time for appealing from the other party to the proposed appeal. It should be noted that the parties do not themselves have power to extend the time for appealing, since this is a matter for the exercise of the powers and discretion of the EAT. However:

(1) the agreement of the parties will be a relevant consideration in the exercise of the EAT's discretion; and

(2) a party agreeing to an extension of time will be estopped from objecting to it on any application for it made by the proposed appellant: *Martin v British Railways Board*.[63]

Change in the law

3.108 A change in the law is one of life's risks: it will seldom justify an extension of time for appealing to the EAT.

3.109 Even where the law changes on a matter of Community law, public policy considerations of certainty and the finality of litigation weigh heavily against granting an extension of time for appealing. The position may be different where the consequences of the decision appealed are continuing, as between the parties. In *Setiya v East Yorkshire Health Authority*,[64] Mummery J (as he then was) held that:

> 'It cannot be right, in my view, to extend the time for appealing on the basis that two years after the decision the law appeared to the House of Lords to be different from what it appeared to the tribunal to be in 1992. Life, including the law, is subject to the chance of change. Dr Setiya's claim, against the authority was subject to the 'hazards of time' inherent in change. It is true that, if Dr Setiya had been dismissed in October 1994, instead of October 1991, he would have had a right to have his claim for unfair dismissal heard by the industrial tribunal. That does not, however, justify an extension of time for appealing, so as to question the validity of an unappealed decision, which was final and binding between these parties when it was decided. I am as reluctant to disturb that decision as I would be to question a compromise reached between the two parties at that time, which it was sought to set aside subsequently on the basis that the legal position was now different from it was thought to be when the parties settled their differences. Life, including the law, is subject to the chance of change. Dr Setiya's claim against the authority was subject to the "hazards of time" inherent in change.'

3.110 Mummery J went on to question whether it could still be said that the role of the courts is declaratory, that is to state the law as it has always been, and whether there 'may no longer be a sound theoretical or practical basis for treating the effect of all judicial decisions as retrospective, particularly in an

---

[63] [1989] ICR 24, at 32.
[64] [1995] ICR 799.

area such as Community law, which emerges and changes direction and shape, sometimes unpredictably'. But that question is for another book. For present purposes, a change in the law will not usually operate as a powerful reason to extend time for lodging a valid notice of appeal.

Before the period for appealing

3.111 Strictly this is not an extension of time and certainly, this is not applicable to appeals which are late. Rather, r 39(3) applies to the situation in which the notice of appeal is lodged early! That is to say, the period for lodging the appeal has not yet begun.

3.112 Rule 39(3) deals with this problem expressly, by providing the EAT with power to allow the bringing of an appeal before the period for doing so has commenced.

3.113 As noted above, this obviously makes good sense, especially in the case of appeals against judgments where the employment tribunal has refused or failed to provide its written reasons to the parties. The period for appealing runs from the date on which the written reasons are sent to the parties, and would therefore never begin if the tribunal was never to send the written reasons out to the parties, as requested. If there were no power under r 39(3) to deal with this situation, an aggrieved party would be left waiting indefinitely for the employment tribunal to provide its written reasons and for the period for appealing to begin. That would be plainly both unsatisfactory and unfair.

3.114 Anyone seeking to institute an appeal to the EAT before the period for appealing has begun would be well advised, as a matter of good practice, to include with the notice of appeal and other documents, a request for the EAT to exercise its power under r 39(3), along with an explanation of what has happened.

3.115 Although the EAT can exercise its powers under r 39(3) on its own initiative, para 2.3 of the EAT PD provides that where written reasons of the employment tribunal are not attached to the notice of appeal, an appellant must set out the full grounds of any application under r 39(3) when lodging the notice of appeal.

Notice of appeal

3.116 There are basically three forms on which parties can set out their notice of appeal, but the notice of appeal does not have to follow the forms absolutely precisely. Paragraph 2.1 of the EAT PD provides that the notice of appeal 'must be, or be substantially, in accordance with Form 1 (in the amended form annexed to this Practice Direction) or Forms 1A or 2 of the Schedule to the EAT Rules and must identify the date of the judgment, decision or order being appealed'.

3.117 An acceptable form for the notice of appeal can be found on the EAT's website, www.employmentappeals.gov.uk. However, you will need Adobe Acrobat Reader (which is free) or similar software to be able to open it. Once on the EAT's website, you can find the form by clicking on the 'How to appeal' link and then clicking on the 'EAT Form 1' link. Alternatively, you can go straight to it at the following address: www.employmentappeals.gov.uk/how_to_appeal/how_to_appeal.html.

3.118 A clean copy of this form is found in the Schedule to the EAT Rules, Form 1. An example of a completed notice of appeal is included in Appendix 7 below.

3.119 The notice of appeal must state the date of the judgment, decision or order being appealed and, as explained below at para **3.135**, a copy of the judgment, decision or order appealed must be provided with the notice of appeal and other required documents. If written reasons are not provided, there must be an explanation for this and a request either for the EAT to deal with the appeal without the reasons or to request the employment tribunal to provide its reasons.

Drafting your grounds

3.120 As noted already, the EAT only has jurisdiction to hear appeals on questions of law, as opposed to questions of fact, although where a finding of fact is 'perverse' this can also amount to an error of law and so be appealable. Available grounds of appeal, generally, are dealt with in detail in Chapter 8 and specific issues of jurisdiction in Chapter 9.

3.121 The notice of appeal must set out the grounds of appeal, which are very important, since whether or not the EAT allows the appeal to proceed to a full hearing will depend upon how the grounds of appeal are formulated.

3.122 Non-lawyers and lawyers alike are advised to consider their grounds very carefully, especially as para 2.4 of the EAT PD requires that the appellant's notice of appeal:

> 'must clearly identify the points of law which form(s) the ground(s) of appeal. It should also state the order which the appellant will ask the EAT to make at the hearing'.

Perversity and bias

3.123 Both these allegations require special care before they are pleaded.[65]

---

[65] A specific warning about unfounded allegations of bias or misconduct was added in the 2008 EAT PD, paras 11.2 and 11.6. A party making such allegations may have costs ordered against it.

3.124 Any allegation that any of the employment tribunal's findings or conclusions were perverse must be properly explained in detail,[66] as must any allegation that the employment tribunal (or any of its members) was biased.

3.125 The contention that the employment tribunal's conclusion was 'contrary to the weight of the evidence' is not sufficient to constitute perversity[67] and is not a proper ground of appeal before the EAT.

3.126 Grounds of appeal are addressed in detail in Chapter 8.

Last minute appeals

3.127 If for reasons beyond your control, you are in desperate circumstances and need to send your notice of appeal to the EAT very quickly, so that you do not have time to do a masterful job on drafting your grounds of appeal, ensure that you send all the necessary documents which must accompany the grounds and set out your grounds very briefly but clearly. If the EAT decides that your grounds are very poor, you may have a further chance to draft them under r 3(8) of the EAT Rules, or you may apply to amend your notice of appeal. Neither of these courses is ideal or recommended in any way, but an appeal which is out of time has much less chance than a poorly drafted appeal which is in time.

3.128 Alternatively, if you really cannot get your notice of appeal (and accompanying documents) to the EAT on time, then you can always try to seek the consent of the other side to an extension of the period for appealing. Good luck! The other side will, more often than not, be delighted that you are in difficulties and may well be unwilling to help.

3.129 However, it is possible that the other side might agree to an extension,[68] in which case refer to the issues on consent, above.

Documents required

Appeal not validly lodged

3.130 The documents accompanying a notice of appeal are crucial since a notice of appeal without the required documentation will not be validly lodged. If the appellant is unaware of this or if there is insufficient time to put it right, the appeal will be out of time and will normally not proceed.

---

[66] EAT PD, para 2.6; *Crofton v Yeboah* [2002] EWCA Civ 794, [2002] IRLR 634, at para [92], per Mummery LJ.
[67] *Chiu v British Aerospace plc* [1982] IRLR 56; *Moult v East Sussex County Council* UKEAT10329/07.
[68] The EAT has to grant any extension but a party agreeing to an extension of time will be estopped from later objecting to it: *Martin v British Railways Board* [1989] ICR 24, at 32.

3.131 In the case of *Kanapathiar v Harrow London Borough Council*,[69] the EAT made clear that a failure to lodge the written reasons required with the notice of appeal in time would mean that the notice of appeal had not been validly lodged in time. On 3 February 2005, the president handed down a Practice Note to emphasise the point, ending with the following statement:

> 'From the date of this Practice Statement, ignorance or misunderstanding of the requirements as to service of the documents required to make a notice of appeal within the 42 days valid will not be accepted by the registrar as an excuse.'

3.132 In *Solani Tirado v St George's Healthcare NHS Trust*,[70] His Honour Judge Peter Clark observed that any controversy over the need to lodge documents with the notice of appeal had been resolved definitively by the Court of Appeal in *Gydnia American Shipping Lines (London) Ltd v Chelminski*.[71]

3.133 The short point is: make sure you lodge the documents required, as set out below.

The documents

3.134 The documents which are required are set out in r 3(1) of the EAT Rules and paras 2.1–2.3 of the EAT PD. You need only provide copies, not the originals, but the copies must all be received by the EAT *within* the applicable time limit. If, for any reason, a copy of one of the required documents cannot be provided, a written explanation must always be given for this. Check that all the documents you are lodging are complete. The EAT is, perhaps surprisingly, stricter than the Court of Appeal in relation to any errors or oversights. For example, in *Hafele v Nolan*,[72] Bean J considered an application for an extension of time which was necessary because three pages of the ET3 had not been sent with all the other documents and the Notice of Appeal. This was put right immediately, the following day. Bean J held that he would have granted the necessary extension 'without hesitation' if unconstrained by authority, but felt unable to do so in the light of the guidelines in *Abdelghafar* and other cases (above).

3.135 Here is a convenient list of the necessary documents, copies of which must accompany the notice of appeal:

(1) the judgment, decision or order appealed against;

(2) the employment tribunal's written reasons (if available);[73]

---

[69] [2003] IRLR 571.
[70] UKEATPA/0669/05 [2005] All ER (D) 12 (Nov).
[71] [2004] EWCA Civ 871, [2004] ICR 1523.
[72] UKEATPA/0354/08, 23 July 2008.
[73] If the written reasons are not available, see the procedure explained in para **3.136** et seq below.

(3) the claim (ET1) – when appealing a judgment;[74]

(4) the response (ET3) – when appealing a judgment;

(5) any relevant orders, including case management orders, made by the employment tribunal;

(6) any application to the employment tribunal for a review of its judgment, decision or order appealed;[75]

(7) any judgment and written reasons of the employment tribunal on any such review application, or a statement that a judgment and/or written reasons are awaited.

3.136 You should always include any explanation for anything you do not have together with an application to the EAT for it to extend time for you to provide it.

3.137 You should also include a request for any particular directions that you would wish the judge or registrar to consider on the sift.[76]

Written reasons

3.138 If you are considering appealing, remember to keep a clean copy of the employment tribunal's written reasons, since you will need this to accompany your notice of appeal.

3.139 It is not desirable or helpful for the EAT to be furnished with your angry annotations all over the employment tribunal's written reasons; however justified you may feel them to be. (It is equally worth keeping a clean copy of the ET1 Claim and ET3 Response for the same purpose.)

No reasons available

3.140 If the employment tribunal's written reasons are not available, there are special procedures which may apply, as explained below.

3.141 There are five situations in which the employment tribunal's reasons may not be available to send to the EAT:

(1) the appellant has wrongly failed to ask the employment tribunal to provide written reasons;

---

[74] A copy of the claim and response are required by the EAT Rules, r 3(1)(b).
[75] EAT PD, para 2.2. See also *Rance v Secretary of State for Health* [2007] IRLR 665, at para 33.
[76] EAT PD, para 9.2.

(2) the appellant has correctly asked the employment tribunal to provide its written reasons but the employment tribunal has not yet done so;

(3) the appellant has correctly asked the employment tribunal to provide its written reasons but the employment tribunal has refused to provide them;

(4) the employment tribunal has provided its written reasons and sent them to the parties, but the appellant has not received them;

(5) last, the 'my dog ate my homework' situation: the appellant has received the employment tribunal's written reasons but no longer has them.

3.142 The first and the last of these situations are the least desirable, since the EAT will normally ensure that the other three situations are not fatal to the appeal, provided that he appellant follows the correct procedures when the notice of appeal is submitted and explains exactly what has happened, why and what the appellant is asking the EAT to do about it. This overview is explained further below.

What to do

Powers of the Employment Appeal Tribunal

3.143 Paragraph 2.3 of the EAT PD provides as follows:

> '2.3 Where written reasons of the employment tribunal are not attached to the notice of appeal, either (as set out in the written explanation) because a request for written reasons has been refused by the employment tribunal or for some other reason, an appellant must, when lodging the notice of appeal, apply in writing to the EAT to exercise its discretion to hear the appeal without written reasons or to exercise its power to request written reasons from the employment tribunal, setting out the full grounds of that application.'

The EAT's power to seek written reasons where only oral reasons have been provided is confirmed by the amendment made to r 30(3)[77] which now provides:

> '(3) [[Where oral reasons have been provided], written reasons shall only be provided]—
>
> (a) in relation to judgments if requested by one of the parties within the time limit set out in paragraph (5); or
> (b) in relation to any judgment or order if requested by the Employment Appeal Tribunal at any time.'

Reasons not sought

3.144 There must be an excellent explanation of why reasons were not sought or very special circumstances to have even a faint hope of successfully

---

[77] By SI 2005/1865, reg 2(1) and (4)(h).

persuading the EAT either to hear the appeal without the tribunal's full written reasons or to request them from the tribunal. Subject to the circumstances, we would recommend applying for both options.

3.145 Note that where the written reasons for the judgment have not been sought in accordance with the EAT Rules or provided by the employment tribunal, the time limit for appealing is 42 days from the written record of the judgment being sent to the parties.[78]

3.146 If the tribunal's judgment is obviously wrong on its face, regardless of the reasoning (eg, dismissing a claim under the wrong Act) then there is a prospect that the EAT might be persuaded to hear the appeal without written reasons. However, where the reasons would or might have any bearing on the EAT's understanding of the lawfulness of what the employment tribunal has done (which will almost always be the case) the EAT will be extremely reluctant to hear the appeal without the written reasons.

Waiting for reasons

3.147 If reasons have been requested but not provided, on a practical note, the EAT will usually expect the appellant to have tried to find out from the employment tribunal when the reasons might be forthcoming, before seeking to appeal without the reasons.

3.148 Where repeated indications of when to expect the reasons are given but not honoured by the employment tribunal or there has been unconscionable delay, the EAT may be prepared to request the reasons from the employment tribunal and, if they are not forthcoming within a reasonable period, hear the appeal without the written reasons.

3.149 In the case of a judgment, this effectively means allowing the institution of an appeal before the period for appealing has begun. The EAT has express power to do this under r 39(3). Paragraph 2.3 of the EAT PD provides that where written reasons of the employment tribunal are not attached to the notice of appeal, an appellant must set out the full grounds of any application under r 39(3) when lodging the notice of appeal.

Reasons refused

3.150 As the employment tribunal is required to provide written reasons, a refusal to do so is itself appealable. However, for practical purposes, the EAT will request the employment tribunal to provide its written reasons, so that the appeal can be heard and determined.

---

[78] EAT Rules, r 3(3)(a)(iii).

Lost in the post

3.151 Where the written reasons have been sent by the employment tribunal but not received by the parties, a copy of the written reasons must be requested as soon as this situation has been discovered. This is why it is worth enquiring as to when the written reasons are expected to be sent to the parties, so that in the case of a judgment being appealed, the time limit for appealing is not missed because the parties are awaiting the written reasons.

3.152 The important thing to note is that an appellant will be expected to act quickly and efficiently, where it is discovered that the written reasons appear to have been lost or delayed in the post.

'My dog ate my homework'

3.153 This is not good. A further copy of the written reasons should be requested from the employment tribunal in good time, so that the reasons can accompany the notice of appeal. If they have not been received and therefore cannot be lodged with the notice of appeal, then a full and candid explanation for what has happened should accompany the notice of appeal, explaining when the copy of the written reasons will be available, where this is known.

OTHER TIME LIMITS

3.154 The EAT PD explains how the time for serving documents, required by an order made by the EAT, will be calculated. Unfortunately, one particular paragraph (1.8.4) is badly drafted and may be confusing. Given that this paragraph was revised in the 2008 Practice Direction, it is a shame that this was not addressed at the same time.

3.155 The relevant paragraphs of the EAT PD are as follows:

> '1.8.2 When a date is given for serving of a document or for doing some other act, the complete document must be received by the EAT or the relevant party by 4.00 pm on that date. Any document received after 4.00 pm will be deemed to be lodged on the next working day.
>
> 1.8.3 Except as provided in 1.8.4 below, all days count, but if a time limit expires on a day when the central office of the EAT, or the EAT office in Edinburgh (as appropriate), is closed, it is extended to the next working day.
>
> 1.8.4 Where the time limit is 5 days (eg an appeal against a registrar's order or direction), Saturdays, Sundays, Christmas Day, Good Friday and Bank Holidays do not count. [For example an appeal against an order made on a Wednesday must arrive at the EAT on or before the following Wednesday.[79]]

---

[79] These words were added in the 2008 EAT PD.

1.9 In this PD any reference to the date of an order shall mean the date stamped upon the relevant order by the EAT ("the seal date").'

3.156 So, as with the notice of appeal, any document must be served before 4 pm on the relevant day.

3.157 However, when the time limit is 5 days or less, weekends and Bank Holidays (plus Christmas day and Easter) are not counted in calculating when the 5 days expires. Unhelpfully, para 1.8.4 states that this is only the case 'Where the time limit is 5 days'. This is obviously wrong (or incomplete) and parties should take comfort that the normal practice of the EAT is to apply this paragraph as if it said 'Where the time limit is 5 days *or less*'. Given that this jurisdiction was designed for non-lawyers, it is unsatisfactory that this has not been corrected.

CASE TRACKS

3.158 Paragraph 9.5 of the EAT PD provides that there are effectively four case tracks and one set of traffic lights, as it were. A judge or registrar will decide into which track the appeal will go on the 'sift', which is explained further below.

3.159 The four case tracks are:

(1) Rule 3(7) cases (EAT PD, paras 9.5.1 and 9.6) – as will be seen below, this is usually more of a dead end than a track;

(2) Preliminary hearing cases (paras 9.5.2, and 9.7–9.18);

(3) Full hearing cases (paras 9.5.3 and 9.19); and

(4) Fast track full hearing cases (paras 9.5.4 and 9.20–9.21).

3.160 The set of traffic lights is the possibility that the judge or registrar may stay an appeal pending the making or outcome of a review application before the employment tribunal, or pending a response by the employment tribunal to an invitation to provide additional or clarifying reasons for its decision,[80] under the procedure in *Barke v SEETEC Business Technology Centre Ltd*.[81] A stay for these purposes is often for 21 days for a review. It is sometimes longer for the provision of further reasons.

3.161 After the stay is lifted, then the case will then be directed to proceed on one of the four tracks above, as a result of the 'sift'.

---

[80] Under the 2004 EAT PD, the provisions of further or clearer (or any) reasons and a stay of 21 days was expressly provided for at para 9.5. However, this reference has now disappeared in the 2008 EAT PD.

[81] [2005] EWCA Civ 578, [2005] ICR 1373.

THE 'SIFT'

3.162 The 'sift' is the gateway to getting your appeal heard.

3.163 The procedure is that a judge or the registrar looks at the papers you have sent to the EAT:

(1) to see if the notice of appeal discloses reasonable grounds for bringing the appeal; and

(2) to make sure the appeal is not an abuse of process.

3.164 If the judge or registrar is satisfied that the notice of appeal does disclose reasonable grounds for bringing the appeal and is not an abuse of process, the case will usually be directed to proceed straight to a full hearing of the appeal and the EAT will give directions about the necessary preparation for that hearing.

3.165 If not, the person appealing (the appellant) will receive a letter giving reasons for the view formed by the judge or registrar, and stating that no further action will be taken on the appeal.[82]

3.166 If the appellant takes no further action, that is the end of the appeal. (Hence, as noted above, the r 3(7) procedure is often more of a dead end than a track.)

3.167 However, if the appellant wishes to pursue the appeal despite this, there are two options available at this juncture. First, a new notice of appeal can be served, usually within 28 days of the date of the letter being sent by the EAT.[83] Secondly, the appellant can 'express dissatisfaction' with the reasons provided in a letter, again with 28 days, and seek an oral hearing before a judge.[84] At that hearing, the respondent need not attend and will not make submissions.

3.168 Where a new notice of appeal is served, the sift process is repeated and the appeal may go forward to a full hearing, if the judge or registrar takes a different view.

3.169 Where there is an oral hearing, the appeal may come to life in oral argument in a way that was not apparent on the papers and result in the judge being persuaded that there are reasonable grounds for bringing the appeal, in which case, the judge will usually order that the appeal go forward to a full hearing. Indeed, oral advocacy may equally persuade a judge that the appeal is not an abuse of process.[85]

---

[82] EAT Rules, r 3(7).
[83] EAT Rules, r 3(8).
[84] EAT Rules, r 3(10).
[85] *Plummer Parsons v Wight* UKEAT/0403/06.

3.170 For convenience, r 3(7)–(10) provides as follows:

'(7) Where it appears to a judge or the registrar that a notice of appeal or a document provided under paragraph (5) or (6)—

(a) discloses no reasonable grounds for bringing the appeal; or
(b) is an abuse of the Appeal Tribunal's process or is otherwise likely to obstruct the just disposal of proceedings,

he shall notify the Appellant or special advocate accordingly informing him of the reasons for his opinion and, subject to paragraphs (8) and (10), no further action shall be taken on the notice of appeal or document provided under paragraph (5) or (6).

(7A) In paragraphs (7) and (10) reference to a notice of appeal or a document provided under paragraph (5) or (6) includes reference to part of a notice of appeal or document provided under paragraph (5) or (6).

(8) Where notification has been given under paragraph (7), the appellant or the special advocate, as the case may be, may serve a fresh notice of appeal, or a fresh document under paragraph (5) or (6), within the time remaining under paragraph (3) or (6) or within 28 days from the date on which the notification given under paragraph (7) was sent to him, whichever is the longer period.

(9) Where the appellant or the special advocate serves a fresh notice of appeal or a fresh document under paragraph (8), a judge or the registrar shall consider such fresh notice of appeal or document with regard to jurisdiction as though it were an original notice of appeal lodged pursuant to paragraphs (1) and (3), or as though it were an original document provided pursuant to paragraph (5) or (6), as the case may be.

(10) Where notification has been given under paragraph (7) and within 28 days of the date the notification was sent, an appellant or special advocate expresses dissatisfaction in writing with the reasons given by the judge or registrar for his opinion, he is entitled to have the matter heard before a judge who shall make a direction as to whether any further action should be taken on the notice of appeal or document under paragraph (5) or (6).'

Further reasons

3.171 Even during the sift, the EAT may request further reasons from the employment tribunal, to supplement those provided in the decision, order or judgment and written reasons which are the subject of the appeal: *Barke v SEETEC Business Technology Centre Ltd*.[86]

3.172 This is explained slightly more fully below, and discussed in much greater detail, with a critical analysis, in Chapter 8.

---

[86] [2005] EWCA Civ 578, [2005] ICR 1373.

The rule 3(7) track

3.173 Before deciding to send a r 3(7) letter to the appellant and allocate the potential appeal to the r 3(7) track, the judge or registrar may require the appellant to provide further amplification or clarification of the notice of appeal.[87]

3.174 As set out above, the r 3(7) letter states that no further action will be taken on the appeal and gives reasons. The options available to a recipient of a r 3(7) letter are:

(1) to put in a new notice of appeal (under r 3(8));

(2) to request an oral hearing to decide whether your appeal discloses reasonable grounds for bringing the appeal (or, as the case may be, is not an abuse of process).

3.175 There is nothing in the EAT Rules to suggest that these options are alternatives and there may well be cases in which it is appropriate to do both, although r 3(9) provides that the new notice of appeal served under r 3(8) will then go back into the sift procedure again for assessment under r 3(7).

3.176 Paragraph 9.6 of the EAT PD makes clear that a case may be allocated to the r 3(7) track at any stage in the proceedings, not just at the stage of the sift, 'if appropriate'.

Rule 3(10): oral hearing

Purpose

3.177 The purpose of the hearing is to revisit the assessment made by the judge or the registrar on the 'sift' in order to ascertain whether the notice of appeal discloses reasonable grounds for bringing the appeal and whether or not the appeal is an abuse of process. The difference is that the decision is made with the benefit of representation, usually by a barrister or solicitor, and in the light of written submissions from the respondent.

3.178 It is important to distinguish between an oral hearing under r 3(10) and a preliminary hearing at which both parties are represented and heard.

Submissions by the respondent

3.179 The EAT will not normally accept any written submissions by the respondent, prior to a r 3(10) hearing. Respondents have occasionally sought to put written submissions before the EAT at this stage, usually without any acknowledged success.

---

[87] EAT PD, para 2.5.

Participation by the respondent

3.180 The respondent is not permitted to take part in a r 3(10) hearing. However, it is often advisable for the respondent's representative to attend the hearing for two reasons:

(1) It is sometimes useful to know how the appellant put the case at the r 3(10) hearing in order to persuade the judge to allow the appeal to go forward to a full hearing.

(2) Occasionally, if the appellant has persuaded the EAT that the appeal should go forward to a hearing, the EAT will ask the appellant's representative if he would object to the respondent's representative making submissions as to the directions which would be appropriate in order to progress.

3.181 At that hearing the judge may confirm the earlier decision or order that the appeal proceeds to a preliminary hearing or full hearing.

3.182 Normally, success at a r 3(10) hearing results in the appeal going forward to a full hearing; however, a preliminary hearing may be appropriate where:

(1) the EAT finds that the balance is only just tipped in favour of the appeal proceeding at all;

(2) the appeal is one which might look very different with the benefit of submissions of both parties; and

(3) the preliminary hearing will neither take all the time not incur all the costs which a Full Hearing would.[88]

PRELIMINARY HEARING

3.183 Occasionally, a preliminary hearing will be ordered,[89] either on the 'sift' or as a result of a r 3(10) hearing, as above.

Purpose

3.184 As para 9.7 of the EAT PD makes clear, the purpose of a preliminary hearing is to revisit whether the appeal should go forward to a full hearing and, more specifically, to determine whether:

---

[88] For example, *Slingsby v Griffith Smith* UKEATPA/0735/07 (unreported), per His Honour Judge Reid QC.
[89] EAT PD, paras 9.6 and 9.7.

(1) the grounds in the notice of appeal raise a point of law which gives the appeal a reasonable prospect of success at a full hearing (para 9.7.1); or

(2) the appeal should be heard for some other compelling reason (such as the appellant seeking a declaration of incompatibility under HRA 1998; or arguing that a decision binding on the EAT should be considered by the Court of Appeal or House of Lords – para 9.7.2).

Directions and cross-appeals

3.185 Prior to the preliminary hearing, the EAT will give automatic directions, and will send a copy of the notice of appeal to the respondent to the appeal. When these directions are given, there are normally then three things that a respondent must or may then do:

(1) As para 9.8 makes clear, the respondent may be permitted (or sometimes required) to lodge and serve on the appellant 'concise written submissions ... dedicated to showing that there is no reasonable prospect of success for all or any [of the appellant's] grounds'.

(2) The respondent may also wish to cross-appeal (see below for more detail). Or the respondent may wish to cross-appeal, only if the appellant's appeal is to proceed to a full hearing. Either way, any cross-appeal must be accompanied by written submissions and must be lodged and served within 14 days of service of the notice of appeal. The respondent must then make clear his intentions on the cross-appeal:

(3) if he will cross-appeal in any event (an unconditional cross-appeal – para 9.9.1); or

(4) if he will only cross-appeal if the appellant's appeal is to go forward to a full hearing (a conditional cross-appeal – para 9.9.2).

Importance of submissions

3.186 Note that the submissions accompanying the cross-appeal are important since the 'sift' process is applied to cross-appeals in the same way as to appeals, although in practice a more generous approach to a cross-appeal is sometimes discernable, where the appeal itself is going to a full hearing.

3.187 Well argued and cogent written submissions accompanying the cross-appeal pay dividends.

Cross-appeals

3.188 When the respondent has served (or intends to serve) a cross-appeal, the respondent will usually attend and make submissions at the hearing. Where the respondent has not served a cross-appeal, the respondent may or may not be permitted to take part in the preliminary hearing. The respondent may make representations to the registrar or the judge, in advance of the preliminary hearing, as to whether or not the respondent should be allowed to appear and be heard at the preliminary hearing. However, the respondent's written submissions will be taken into account.

Further reasons

3.189 Before finally determining the appeal the EAT may refer specific questions back to the employment tribunal and, if necessary, seek further reasons from the employment tribunal. What was formerly known as the *Burns* procedure, following *Burns v Royal Mail Group plc (formerly Consignia plc) and Another*[90] is now often referred to as the Burns/Barke procedure, following the Court of Appeal's decision in *Barke v SEETEC Business Technology Centre Ltd*,[91] confirming yet qualifying the approach in *Burns*.

3.190 This is explained in slightly more detail below, but more extensively, with a critical analysis, in Chapter 8. A brief case summary of *Burns* and a more extensive case summary of *Barke* appear in Chapter 10 below.

3.191 The Court of Appeal in *Barke* reframed the supposed justification for the provision of additional reasons. However, with all due respect to the Court of Appeal, the authors have reservations about this procedure, which are set out in the critical analysis of this procedure in Chapter 8.

NO FURTHER ACTION ON THE APPEAL

3.192 Where the EAT orders no further action on the appeal as the outcome of a r 3(10) hearing or a preliminary hearing, that is an end of the appeal, unless the disappointed appellant appeals to the Court of Appeal (or, even less likely, seeks a review).

Appealing a rule 3(10) decision

3.193 As with any other appeal from the EAT, it is necessary to obtain permission to appeal either from the EAT or from the Court of Appeal. This is explained later in this chapter and more fully in Chapter 4.

3.194 The oddity which arises in these appeals is that the test on the granting of permission to appeal to the Court of Appeal is, for practical purposes, barely distinguishable from the test being applied by the EAT at a r 3(10) hearing or a preliminary hearing.

---

[90] [2004] ICR 1103.
[91] [2005] EWCA Civ 578, [2005] ICR 1373.

3.195 Thus, if the Court of Appeal gives permission to appeal, the logical course may be for the Court of Appeal to remit the appeal back to the EAT for it to go forward to a full hearing.

3.196 This odd situation is well illustrated by the case of *Plummer Parsons v Wight*,[92] in which Plummer Parsons appealed a finding of unfair dismissal and Mr Wight cross-appealed the dismissal of his whistleblowing claim.[93]

3.197 At a r 3(10) hearing on Mr Wight's cross-appeal, His Honour Judge Reid QC held that there was 'no arguable basis on which the cross-appeal should be allowed to go forward'.

3.198 Mr Wight sought permission to appeal to the Court of Appeal, which was granted by Laws LJ on paper, commenting that that the cross-appeal should be heard together with the appeal before the EAT. This obviously made very good sense. However, two points arise from it:

(1) The single judge in the Court of Appeal has no power to allow the appeal alone. A consent order is required, so that the full court can allow the appeal against the r 3(10) decision of the EAT and remit the case for full hearing before the EAT. (A precedent of the unusual order to effect this is included in Appendix 7 below.)

(2) This is not the course which is always (or even often) followed, as also explained in Chapter 4. In *Lambe v 186k Limited*,[94] the Court of Appeal directed that the appeal go forward to a full hearing before the Court of Appeal, rather than sending it back for a full hearing before the EAT, this having been a matter of some controversy between the parties. In a postscript to the judgment dealing specifically with this point, the Court of Appeal explained this position as follows:

> '[83] The circumstances in which this court will remit an appeal to the EAT are, we think, limited. Examples are, of course, provided by the two cases to which we have referred. Another example is where the EAT dismisses an appeal from the Tribunal on the grounds that the EAT does not have jurisdiction to hear it. In such circumstances, if this court on appeal from the EAT takes the view that the EAT does have jurisdiction to entertain the appeal, it will remit the appeal to the EAT for hearing – see, for example, *Grady v Prison Service* [2003] EWCA Civ 527, [2003] 3 All ER 745, where the EAT held that it did not have jurisdiction to entertain an appeal by a bankrupt appellant whose claim for unfair dismissal had been dismissed by the Tribunal.
>
> [84] Where, however, under the PH procedure the EAT, as here, dismisses an appeal on the basis that none of the grounds of appeal raises a point of law

---

[92] UKEAT/0403/06.
[93] The procedural history of his cross-appeal is discussed in more detail under 'Parallel appeals' at para **3.228** below.
[94] [2004] EWCA Civ 1045, [2005] ICR 307.

which gives the appeal a reasonable prospect of success at a Full Hearing, and the disappointed appellant obtains the permission of this court to appeal to the Court of Appeal, this court will hear the appeal in the normal way and will either dismiss it or allow it. If it does the latter, and upsets the Tribunal's decision, it will either impose its own order; alternatively, as here, it will remit the decision, or a relevant part of it, to the ET for reconsideration.'

3.199 So, it is worth considering very carefully what directions you are seeking if you are appealing a Rule 3(10) or preliminary hearing decision to the Court of Appeal.

PROCEEDING TO A FULL HEARING

3.200 Where the EAT is satisfied (at a r 3(10) hearing or preliminary hearing – or on the papers during the 'sift') that the notice of appeal does disclose reasonable grounds for brining the appeal and that it is not an abuse of process.[95]

3.201 As noted above, following service of the notice of appeal on the respondent, the respondent must serve an answer and any cross-appeal.

RESPONDENT'S ANSWER AND CROSS-APPEALS

Answer

When required

3.202 A respondent will only be required to lodge and serve an answer if:

(1) the appeal has been directed to proceed straight to a full hearing on the sift; or

(2) the appeal has been directed to proceed to a full hearing after:
   (a) a new notice of appeal has replaced the original notice of appeal (under r 3(8)) and that the appeal proceeds on that new notice of appeal,
   (b) following a r 3(10) hearing, requested by the appellant, the EAT so directs, or
   (c) following a preliminary hearing, the EAT so directs.

3.203 A respondent should not lodge and serve an answer if he has merely received a copy of the notice of appeal from the appellant.

---

[95] See one of the issues arising in the 'Parallel appeals' commentary at para **3.223** below, by way of example of an issue on abuse of process.

3.204 If a respondent does not wish to contest the appeal, r 6(5) and para 15 of the EAT PD makes provision disposal of appeals by consent. Rule 6(5) and para 15.3 provide for an agreed draft order allowing the appeal to be delivered to the EAT by the parties, for the EAT to make, 'if it considers it right to do so' on the terms agreed. There will usually be a hearing to determine this.

3.205 Paragraph 15 of the EAT PD makes more detailed provision for abandonment, withdrawal and settlement of the appeal. In *J Sainsbury plc v Moger*,[96] the EAT held that it will not normally make an order by consent, where there is no overall settlement and the parties are asking that the case be remitted for a rehearing.

3.206 If the Respondent does wish to contest the appeal, it is important to lodge the Respondent's Answer (including any cross-appeal) in time. It is particularly important to lodge this document in time if it does include a cross-appeal, since the approach to strict time limits adopted in relation to lodging the original appeal is also applicable to lodging any cross-appeal. A different and more liberal approach will be adopted in relation to the lodging of the Answer itself (excluding the cross-appeal).[97]

Documents received

3.207 The respondent will usually receive the following documents from the registrar, triggering the obligation to lodge and serve an answer, if the respondent wishes to resist the appeal:

(1) a sealed copy of the notice of appeal,[98] with any amendments;

(2) any written submissions or skeleton arguments lodged by the appellant;

(3) an order giving any directions made on the sift; and

(4) a letter enclosing the above.

Lodging and serving the answer

3.208 If the respondent wishes to resist the appeal, he must send an answer to both the EAT and any other parties, so that it is received by the EAT within 14 days of the seal date of the order.[99]

3.209 The answer should be substantially in accordance with Form 3, in the Schedule to the EAT Rules.

---

[96] [1994] ICR 800.
[97] *Slingsby v Griffith Smith (No 1)* UKEAT/0619/07, per HHJ Burke QC.
[98] EAT Rules, r 4(1).
[99] Failing to lodge the answer in time may lead to an order debarring the respondent from taking any further part in the appeal, or such other order as is thought just: EAT Rules, r 26 and EAT PD, para 2.8.

3.210 The answer is the respondent's opportunity to state why the appeal should not succeed, and its content is considered further below.

3.211 Again, as with any other document, it must reach the EAT by 4 pm on the due date. If the respondent needs an extension of time for serving the answer, under r 37(1), the application should be made before the time limit has expired,[100] in writing, to the registrar, with a full explanation for the delay.

Content

3.212 Rule 6(2) requires the respondent to set out the grounds on which the respondent resists the appeal. The first choice that the respondent has to make, from a strategic point of view, is whether:

(1) to rely entirely on the reasons given for the decision appealed (eg, the employment tribunal's written reasons);

(2) to put forward additional grounds why the result was correct, even if not fully demonstrated or justified on the face of the reasons given;

(3) to do both, in combination for all or different parts of the decision appealed.

3.213 The second choice is more a matter of emphasis, but requires careful thought. Should the answer emphasise:

(1) why the decision is right;

(2) why the complaints in the grounds of appeal are without merit;

(3) or both.

3.214 The inclusion of a cross-appeal is dealt with below. This is obviously an important consideration.

3.215 However, further points to consider when drafting grounds of resistance in the respondent's answer are as follows:

(1) Is the appeal merely an attempt to reargue the facts? This is commonly asserted by respondents, sometimes with greater and sometimes with lesser justification.

(2) Is the aspect of the decision appealed one of the classic areas which are not usually susceptible to appeal, such as whether or not a dismissal is fair

---

[100] To avoid the risk of an order under EAT PD, para 2.8.

on the facts,[101] whether an employee has resigned or has been dismissed or whether a claimant is an employee or self-employed?

(3) Is the appellant taking new points (or old points in new ways) not argued below? If so and the respondent wishes to object, the respondent should normally indicate this in the answer or, if a preliminary hearing has been ordered, in writing to the EAT.[102]

(4) Is the appellant alleging perversity? If so, have the full particulars required by para 2.6 of the EAT PD been provided. Is any further information about this allegation reasonably required by the respondent so that he can consider and answer it? If so, it should be requested.

(5) Is there an allegation of bias or misconduct by the tribunal? If so, have the requirements of para 11 of the EAT PD been complied with? Has an affidavit been provided, in support of the allegations? And, is the bias or misconduct properly particularised in the grounds? Have comments been sought from the tribunal?[103]

(6) Can the complaints in the appellant's grounds of appeal be defeated by a fair, or even generous, reading of the reasons for the decision appealed? If so, identify how.

Cross-appeals

3.216 If the respondent decides to cross-appeal, the cross-appeal must be included in the Form 3 together with the answer and sent to the EAT within the 14 days, as for the answer.

Drafting the cross-appeal

3.217 The same rules apply to drafting the grounds of a cross-appeal as to drafting grounds of appeal. Chapter 8 provides a detailed consideration of grounds of appeal.

Sift of the cross-appeal

3.218 A cross-appeal is treated as if it were an appeal in its own right for the purposes of the 'sift' procedure, as para 9.12 of the EAT PD makes clear by requiring a respondent who has put in a cross-appeal to apply for directions as to whether there should be a preliminary hearing, in cases where there is not

---

[101] For example, 'In determining any question "in accordance with equity", a court or tribunal should adopt a broad approach of common sense and common fairness, eschewing all legal or other technicality' in *Earl v Slater and Wheeler (Airlyne) Ltd* [1973] 1 WLR 51, per Sir John Donaldson.
[102] EAT PD, para 8.5.
[103] NB a respondent alleging bias must also comply with para 11.

going to be a preliminary hearing on the main appeal (ie if the main appeal has been assigned to the full hearing track and directed to proceed to a full hearing without a preliminary hearing).

3.219 Paragraph 9.12 also requires that the respondent's application for directions should be made:

(1) in writing;

(2) on notice to the other parties; and

(3) 'immediately'.

Appellant's reply

3.220 Where the respondent's answer contains a cross-appeal, r 6(3) of the EAT Rules and para 10.1 of the EAT PD require the appellant to lodge and serve[104] a reply, within 14 days of service of the answer including the cross-appeal.[105]

Directions

3.221 After the respondent's answer and any reply have been lodged with the EAT and served on all parties, the registrar will normally invite the parties to agree or apply for directions to be made.

3.222 Usually, directions will be given without the need for the attendance of the parties, although an appointment for directions[106] or preliminary hearing to deal with directions and other matters will be much more common where there is a cross-appeal than where there is not.

Parallel appeals

3.223 Parallel appeals present special procedural considerations. When they do, this commentary may be extremely useful, since there is little to be found elsewhere on this area.

How they arise

3.224 There are two ways in which parallel appeals can arise:

---

[104] The phrase 'lodge and serve' means send or deliver to the EAT and to the other parties, but imports the requirement that the EAT should actually receive what is lodged, rather than it just being sent.
[105] Unless the EAT otherwise directs, which the EAT PD appears to anticipate by making this specific provision in para 10.1.
[106] EAT PD, para 10.2.

(1) **Unitary parallel appeals**: Two parties (eg, the claimant and the respondent before the employment tribunal) are both aggrieved by different aspects of the *same* decision. They both appeal within the time limit for appealing that decision, each putting in a notice of appeal.

(2) **Separate parallel appeals**: Two parties are both aggrieved about different decisions of the employment tribunal. They each appeal *different* orders, made by the same tribunal between the same parties.

3.225 The significance of the distinction becomes important in other contexts too, since a respondent *can* cross-appeal against the same order but cannot cross-appeal against a different order.

3.226 So, unitary parallel appeals could in principle be consolidated or directed to be heard together. Alternatively, there is a powerful case that it is more procedurally convenient for them to be dealt with as an appeal and a cross-appeal in the same proceedings, rather than as separate appeals.

3.227 But how should the parties proceed?

Guidance in Plummer Parsons v Wight

3.228 This issue reared its head in the case of *Plummer Parsons v Wight*.[107]

3.229 In that case, Mr Wight (W) had won on unfair dismissal before the employment tribunal, but had lost his whistleblowing claim. Plummer Parsons (PP) appealed the finding of unfair dismissal and W appealed the dismissal of his whistleblowing claim, by a notice of appeal which W drafted himself.

3.230 Both appeals were in time. Both appeals were considered on the sift, but only PP's appeal was directed to proceed to a full hearing.

3.231 On 21 July 2006, W received a r 3(7) letter, in which it was stated that no further action would be taken on W's appeal and His Honour Judge Serota QC's reasons for this were stated. This letter also pointed out the possibility of submitting a fresh notice of appeal in accordance with r 3(8) or requesting an oral hearing in accordance with r 3(10).

3.232 On the same day, W also received notice that PP's appeal was to proceed to a full hearing and that he was required to lodge his answer, including any cross-appeal within 14 days.

3.233 On 2 August 2006, less than 14 days later, W lodged his answer and cross-appeal in PP's appeal, this time drafted by counsel. He took no action on his own appeal, under r 3(8) or (10).

---

[107] UKEAT/0403/06 (unreported).

3.234 His cross-appeal was then considered on the sift by His Honour Judge McMullen QC who held it to be an abuse of process, stating in a r 3(7) letter as follows:

> 'It is an abuse of process of the Employment Appeal Tribunal under Rule 3 for an Appellant, whose notice of appeal was taken no further by direction of an Employment Appeal Tribunal Judge under Rule 3, and who did not pursue the matter under Rule 3(8) or (10), to raise a complaint against the same aspect (the whistleblowing finding) of the Judgment by cross appeal against a notice of appeal.'

3.235 W then applied for a r 3(10) hearing on his cross-appeal. That hearing took place before His Honour Judge Reid on 21 December 2006. Having heard submissions on behalf of W, His Honour Judge Reid held that the course which W had followed was (in W's case) not an abuse of process at all, but in fact both proper and procedurally convenient:

> '8. In my judgment, the question of whether or not an attempt to do by cross-appeal that which it has been proved impossible to dot on appeal is an abuse of process is something which is case-specific. There is no general rule that it is always an abuse of process or that it is never an abuse or process. It would, in my view, be an abuse of process simply to regurgitate by way of cross-appeal those same grounds which have been rejected when presented as the grounds of the appeal. In those circumstances, what the litigant ought to do is to go by way of either rule 3(8) or rule 3(10) in respect of his own proposed appeal. On the other hand, it does not seem to me automatically an abuse of process to seek to go by way of cross-appeal on grounds other than the grounds which have already been rejected. That same course could have been taken under rule 3(8).
>
> 9. [...] There may well be procedural conveniences in going by way of cross-appeal in the other side's appeal, by having the whole appeal and cross-appeal, so to speak, in one file (as opposed to going by way of a rule 3(10) application in the prosective Appellant's own appeal, thereby creating two appeals which then have to be brought together). The essential test, it seems to me, is whether when one looks at the grounds of the proposed cross-appeal they are grounds different from those which were originally propounded and which themselves should be allowed to go to either a preliminary hearing or a full hearing. If that be the case, it seems to me that it is not an abuse of process to go by means of cross-appeal. The procedural effect is substantially the same.'

Separate parallel appeals

3.236 The key point in separate parallel appeals is that the time for appealing runs, in each case, from the date applicable to the decision appealed in each case. That date cannot be effectively extended by cross-appealing.

3.237 This is tactically important since, if two different orders are made at different times and sent to the parties say 7 days apart, the time for appealing those two orders will expire on different dates, 42 days later, 7 days apart.

3.238 Assuming that both parties are each aggrieved by one order, but would live with it if the other party did not appeal, the party aggrieved by the earlier order would normally have to lodge a protective notice of appeal, since the other party would otherwise be able to take the benefit of the first order but appeal the second.

3.239 This issue arose in *Asda Stores Ltd v Thompson*.[108] In that case, three managers had been dismissed without having had sight of statements made against them confidentially by other employees. The EAT had directed the employment tribunal to re-consider the statements and their confidentiality on established principles, but the parties were at odds as to how the employment tribunal should approach this task. The employer appealed a decision by the employment tribunal rejecting a suggested course proposed by the employer. The employees sought to cross-appeal (back to the EAT) the EAT's previous decision on the basis that it was ambiguous and wrong. The reality of this was that it was far out of time.

3.240 Burton P gave the judgment of the EAT and held as follows at paras 26 and 27, indicating the possibility of a more lenient approach to extending time in such cases:

> 'The course in our judgment would and should have been that consideration should have been given, or would be given, in an ordinary case, to whether a 'cross-appeal' in respect of a different order was in time, addressing its own time limit, namely the time running from the order complained of in the 'cross-appeal'. If such a 'cross-appeal' is out of time, it may be that the existence of an appeal against a different Order on the same topic may well be a good justification for allowing an *extension* of time, and it may well be, in an appropriate case, that the extremely strict consequences of being out of time on such an appeal, such as are laid down in *United Arab Emirates v Abdelghafar* [1995] IRLR 243 and *Aziz v Bethnal Green City Challenge Co Ltd* [2000] IRLR 111, where of course without the appropriate time limit being complied with by an *appellant* there would be no appeal at all, would not be applied to a time limit on such a cross-appeal.
>
> It may thus in appropriate cases be a justification for an extension if there already is an appeal and no prejudice is caused to the appellant by an extension of time in respect of the cross-appeal. Good reasons will always have to be given, but it may be the existence of an appeal might of itself amount to an exceptional reason in an appropriate case. However it is apparent that this is another reason for proper compliance with paragraph 4 of the ordinary order, to which we have already referred, made either on a sift or indeed on a preliminary hearing, so that that question too can be addressed by the Employment Appeal Tribunal with the benefit of any submissions from the original appellant, who would of course have been served with notice, as the order requires.'

3.241 It would seem that this approach would only apply where the separate parallel appeals relate to the same point, albeit in different orders.

---

[108] [2004] IRLR 598.

3.242 It is far less clear that any leniency would be shown where the separate parallel appeals related to different (even if loosely related) points, in different orders.

AMENDING GROUNDS OF APPEAL

3.243 Paragraph 2.7 of the EAT PD provides as follows:

> '2.7 A party cannot reserve a right to amend, alter or add, to a notice of appeal or a respondent's Answer. Any application for leave to amend must be made as soon as practicable and must be accompanied by a draft of the amended notice of appeal or amended Answer which makes clear the precise amendments for which permission is sought.'

3.244 Although it is clear that a party cannot reserve the right to amend, it is equally clear that a party in difficulties in lodging a valid notice of appeal in time should lodge as best it can and apply to the registrar for directions including any request for permission to amend the notice of appeal, giving an explanation for the situation.

3.245 In *Khudados v Leggate and Others*,[109] the EAT held that the principle that amendments should generally be allowed, provided the public interest in the efficient administration of justice is not harmed and any prejudice to the other party caused by the amendment can be compensated for in costs, could not be applied in the EAT without some modification.

3.246 The EAT set out the principles to be applied on an application to amend (while refusing Mrs Khudados's application). Those principles echoed, at least to some extent, those applied in extending time for lodging a notice of appeal, as set forth in *United Arab Emirates v Abdelghafar*,[110] but the requirements in that case should not be applied in their entirety or full rigour.

3.247 His Honour Judge Serota gave the judgment of the EAT. He said that the relevant considerations would include the following:

(1) Whether the applicant was in breach of the EAT Rules or the EAT PD. Compliance with the requirement to make an application for permission to amend a notice of appeal as soon as a need for amendment is known, is of considerable importance.

(2) Any extension of time is an indulgence and the EAT is entitled to a full, honest and acceptable explanation for any delay or failure to comply with the EAT Rules or the EAT PD.

---

[109] [2005] ICR 1013.
[110] [1995] ICR 65.

(3) The extent to which the amendment, if allowed, would cause any delay. Proposed amendments that raise a crisp point of law closely related to existing grounds of appeal, or offering limited particulars which flesh out existing grounds, are more likely to be allowed than wholly new grounds of perversity raising issues of complex fact and requiring consideration of a volume of documents, including witness statements and notes of evidence.

(4) Whether allowing the amendment will cause prejudice to the opposite party, and whether refusing the amendment will cause prejudice to the applicant by depriving him of fairly arguable grounds of appeal.

(5) In some cases, it may be necessary to consider the merits of the proposed amendments, although these would not be determining factors.

(6) Regard must be had to the public interest in ensuring that business in the EAT is conducted expeditiously and that its resources are used efficiently. This was in accordance with the overriding objective.

NEW POINTS ON APPEAL

3.248 A party is not normally allowed to argue a new point that was not argued or determined below in the employment tribunal. New points will only be entertained on appeal in exceptional circumstances.

3.249 If the appellant is taking a new point and the respondent wishes to object on that basis, para 8.5 of the EAT PD provides that the respondent should give notice of that as follows:

> '8.5 If a respondent intends to contend at the FH that the appellant has raised a point which was not argued below, the respondent shall so state:
>
> 8.5.1 if a PH has been ordered, in writing to the EAT and all parties, within 14 days of receiving the notice of appeal;
> 8.5.2 if the case is listed for a FH without a PH, in a respondent's Answer.
>
> In the event of dispute the Chairman should be asked for his/her comments as to whether a particular legal argument was deployed.'

3.250 The practice of the EAT was set out in *Rance v Secretary of State for Health*.[111]

---

[111] [2007] IRLR 665.

3.251 Where additional findings of fact would need to be made to resolve a new point, it is unlikely that the EAT will give permission for it to be raised for the first time on appeal. That would require exceptional circumstances.[112]

3.252 In *Bleuse v MBT Transport and Another*,[113] the president of the EAT (Elias J) allowed a new point to be raised that had not been raised below, namely that different rules about territorial jurisdiction ought to apply to employment rights derived from directly effective EU provisions than would apply to domestic rights. At para 58 of his judgment, Elias J noted that there had been 'no reliance on any submission based on directly effective rights in the employment tribunal'. He continued:

> 'However, I think that this is a case where I should allow the point to be argued now. Both parties below acted on the assumption that English law was the appropriate law relating to the relationship, as I think it is. The fresh argument is then simply a matter of law, determining whether the Working Time Regulations can be construed compatibly with the right to holiday pay derived from the Directive. No further finding of fact is necessary and in my judgment it would be unjust to deny the claimant the opportunity to advance that claim.'

3.253 This case is illustrative of the factors to which the EAT will have regard in deciding whether or not to allow a new point to be taken, which was not argued or determined in the employment tribunal.

NEW EVIDENCE

3.254 The principles upon which the EAT will exercise its discretion in granting or refusing an application to adduce new evidence on appeal are set out in *Wileman v Minilec Engineering Ltd*,[114] following the well known statement of practice in *Ladd v Marshall*.[115]

3.255 Fresh evidence will only be admitted on appeal in exceptional circumstances. The test is threefold:

(1) the evidence could not have been obtained with reasonable diligence for use at the employment tribunal;

(2) the evidence must be relevant and would have had an important, although not necessarily decisive influence on the outcome of the hearing below; and

---

[112] See: *Jones v Governing Body of Burdett Coutts School* [1999] ICR 38; *Varma v North Cheshire Hospitals NHS Trust* UKEAT/0264/05 [2006] All ER (D) 203 (Oct).
[113] UKEAT/0632/06 [2007] All ER (D) 392 (Dec).
[114] [1988] IRLR 144.
[115] [1954] 1 WLR 1489.

(3) the evidence must be apparently credible, although it need not be incontrovertible.

3.256 This is confirmed by para 8.2 of the EAT PD.

3.257 Paragraph 8.1 requires a party wishing to put in new documentary or witness evidence to make an application (enclosing any relevant new documents) which must be lodged at the EAT with notice of appeal together with a statement of:

(1) the nature and substance of the evidence;

(2) the date when the party first became aware of its existence;

(3) any reason why it was not put before the employment tribunal (other than arising from (2) above).

3.258 The statement may be included in a witness statement, but must be similarly lodged and served, however it is provided.

3.259 Paragraph 8.3 provides that a party wishing to resist an application to admit new evidence must lodge and serve any representations within 14 days of the application being sent.

3.260 The discretion must be exercised in accordance with the overriding objective of doing justice between the parties, balancing public policy considerations of certainty and finality in litigation with the particular circumstances of the case.

3.261 It is, however, important that parties bear the responsibility to bring forward their own case to the tribunal and must put their full case at trial. They should not be allowed a second bite of the cherry without very good reason: *Hertfordshire Investments Ltd v Bubb*.[116]

THE CHAIRMAN'S/JUDGE'S NOTES

Chairman now an employment judge

3.262 Since 1 December 2007, chairmen of employment tribunals have the new title of 'employment judge'. In many of the cases cited in this book, they will be referred to as chairmen.[117] They take a note of evidence during the hearing before the employment tribunal, which the EAT may request them to produce if there is an issue about what evidence was given which cannot be resolved by agreement.[118]

---

[116] [2000] 1 WLR 2318, per Hale LJ at 2324B–C, 2325–F.
[117] Schedule 8 to the Tribunals, Courts and Enforcement Act 2007, at paras 36–39.
[118] *Houston v Lightwater Farms Ltd; Walker v Lakhadari* [1990] ICR 502: an employment judge

Requirement for notes

3.263 A party alleging perversity will often[119] have to seek to rely on evidence that was given before the tribunal, in order to establish perversity of the tribunal's decision. If the alleged perversity is not obvious on the face of the reasons for the decision, it is frequently impossible to demonstrate it without reference to the evidence given before the tribunal.[120] Some of that evidence will be in witness statements and documents which were before the tribunal. However, an overwhelming case must be shown for an allegation of perversity to succeed and this will almost always mean contending that either:

(1) there was no evidence from which the employment tribunal could have concluded as it did; or

(2) there was some evidence, but no reasonable tribunal could have concluded as this employment tribunal did.

3.264 This ground of appeal is explored further in Chapter 8 (see paras **8.25** to **8.64**); however, it is important to set the issue of the production of the judge's notes in context:

(1) on the one hand, identifying what evidence was given (or not given) may be crucial to the appeal: for example, *Ministry of Defence v Hunt*; *Ministry of Defence v Wheeler*; *Ministry of Defence v George*; *Ministry of Defence v Donald Anderson*; *Ministry of Defence v Stuart*;[121]

(2) on the other hand, seeking the production of judge's notes smacks of an appeal on the facts and would often impose a huge burden on the judge.

3.265 Against that background, the EAT requires an allegation of perversity to be fully particularised 'so that the respondent can be fully prepared to meet it and in order to deter attempts to pursue hopeless and impermissible appeals on factual points': para 2.6 of the EAT PD and *Crofton v Yeboah*.[122]

3.266 In *Hawkins v Ball and Barclays Bank plc*,[123] the EAT refused to order the production of the (then) chairman's notes of evidence. Keene J gave the following helpful illustrative guidance at paras 15–18:

'15. The EAT Practice Direction of 17 February 1981 makes it clear that notes of evidence would only be ordered where they are necessary for the purpose of the

---

has a judicial duty to make an appropriate note of evidence for the assistance of an appellate court in the event of an appeal; the EAT is entitled to require the chairman's notes of evidence; they are not supplied on appeal merely as a matter of courtesy.

[119] But not always: *Hawkins v Ball and Barclays Bank plc* [1996] IRLR 258. See also para **8.44** for rationale.
[120] EAT PD, para 7.1.
[121] [1996] ICR 554.
[122] [2002] EWCA Civ 794, [2002] IRLR 634, at para [92], per Mummery LJ.
[123] [1996] IRLR 258.

appeal. We do not accept that such notes become necessary automatically upon an allegation of perversity being raised. Nor do we read the decision in *Piggott Brothers & Co Ltd* [1991] IRLR 309 as suggesting anything to the contrary. In that case, the tribunal below had found that the dismissals were unfair in all the circumstances. The appeal against that decision alleged that that finding was perverse. The Court of Appeal, perhaps not surprisingly, took the view that that ground of appeal could only be considered if all the chairman's notes were available. The Court of Appeal did so because that argument required a consideration of all the evidence so as to assess the fairness or otherwise of the dismissal. That is not this case. It is important to recognise, in our view, that allegations of perversity on appeal may take different forms and we do not read Lord Donaldson's comments as intending to apply to all cases where such an allegation is made, whatever may be the basis for it. In the present case, the allegation of perversity rests upon a specific and much more limited platform as we have already indicated. Nor is the appellant assisted by *Martin v MBS Fastenings (Glynwed) Distribution Ltd* [1983] IRLR 198. The passage from that decision which is relied upon by the appellant also say this:

> "If it is intended to appeal upon the ground that there was not evidence to support the tribunal's findings, the appellant must take the necessary steps to obtain a note of the evidence."

16. That is essentially dealing with a particular kind of perversity argument, namely, one where it is said, in effect, that there was no evidence for a particular finding or findings reached by the tribunal below. In those circumstances, it may often be the case that it will be necessary to produce the chairman's notes. An allegation that there was no evidence for a particular finding will often necessitate looking at all the evidence and that can only be done by obtaining the chairman's notes but, again, that is not this case.

17. It is important to bear in mind what was said in *Webb v Anglian Water Authority* [1981] IRLR 494 and, in particular, at p 496, 8:

> "Before any such order is made, the party seeking the notes should specify the exact finding which is attacked or the finding which he says ought to have been made. After all, the parties have been present at the industrial tribunal, they know the evidence which was given to the industrial tribunal and, before raising any allegations as to the findings of fact, they ought to know which findings they are challenging. If a party cannot, or does not, narrow down in this way the allegations of fact which are to be challenged, in general we think the notes ought to be refused."

18. We are firmly of the view that general allegations of perversity are not enough. Such allegations will frequently merely be a pretext for a fishing expedition.'

3.267 The reality is that the wider the application for the employment judge's notes is, the less likely it is to be granted. Parties seeking the employment judge's notes should therefore have every incentive to try to agree as much as possible before making any application for their production – not least because the parties are under a duty to co-operate in reaching such agreement.

A practical approach

3.268 The standard directions[124] given where an allegation of perversity is made require the parties to co-operate in seeking to agree a note of the relevant parts of the evidence before the tribunal.

3.269 As explained below, this is not always an easy exercise. The authors favour this exercise being carried out on a table of evidence (example below) with three main columns: the first column is the relevant evidence that the parties agree on, the second column contains the comments or additional evidence contended for by the party alleging perversity; and the third column contains the comments or additional evidence contended for by the party responding to the allegation of perversity. An additional column on the left numbering each row is helpful.

3.270 Below is an example, part way through the process of agreement of the evidence.

	Agreed evidence	**C comments**	**R comments**
1.	Mrs Smith ('C') gave oral evidence (i/c and XX) that Mr Smug had said her dismissal was a foregone conclusion.	–	C was not able to explain (in XX) why she had not mentioned this at the disciplinary hearing or the appeal hearing.
2.	Mr Smug denied saying this (i/c and XX). He was not at work on the day it was supposedly said. P.43 of the bundle shows his diary, confirming this.	C gave oral evidence that it may have been a conversation by telephone.	C could not explain (in XX) why her ET1 and her witness statement explained in detail how this conversation had happened beside the water cooler in the office.

3.271 It may be that, with some work, the table of evidence will record all items that can be recorded in an agreed form of words in the column headed 'Agreed Evidence'. More likely, there will be some matters which cannot be agreed. At least, the areas of disagreement can be defined and the relevant parts of the evidence readily identified. It is useful to distinguish between evidence given in chief ('i/c'), in cross-examination ('XX') and in re-examination ('rx'), in respect of each witness. This concentrates the minds of

---

[124] See EAT PD, para 7.3.

the parties, helps to avoid misunderstandings between them, and naturally helps to identify the relevant parts of the notes evidence which might need to be produced.

3.272 Doubtless, it would be possible to construct a more refined or complicated structure, but the table above has been found to work well in practice, with anything not dealt with on the table being a matter for oral submissions and, if necessary, an application for the employment judge's notes.

3.273 The advantage of this approach is that it is often possible to arrive at a workable, if incomplete, agreement as to the effect of the evidence before the tribunal on specific relevant points particularised in the grounds of appeal, such that it would be disproportionate to seek the judge's notes of evidence on the remaining, perhaps minor points, especially if this would delay the hearing of the appeal. If the notes are required, they need only be produced on the remaining narrow issues.

3.274 If an application is made for their production, it is infinitely easier to show the EAT a table of evidence, prepared as above, than to trawl through lengthy correspondence,[125] canvassing the items agreed or not agreed.

Provisions of the Practice Direction

3.275 Paragraph 7 of the EAT PD provides a fairly complicated procedure, at which the practical approach above is aimed. However, it is worth considering the issues that arise in stages.

Application with notice of appeal

3.276 Paragraph 7.1 states that an appellant should submit an application with the notice of appeal where:

(1) the appellant considers that a point of law raised in the notice of appeal cannot be argued without reference to evidence given (or not given) at the employment tribunal;

(2) because the nature or substance of which does not, or does not sufficiently, appear from the written reasons, must ordinarily submit an application with the notice of appeal; and

(3) the appellant wishes either to:
    (a) admit evidence given (or not given) before the tribunal and/or,
    (b) seek the production of the relevant parts of the chairman's notes of evidence (which should be clearly identified).

---

[125] Required to accompany any application: EAT PD, para 7.4.

Application after notice of appeal

3.277 Paragraph 7.1 goes on to make provision for the application to be made after the lodging of the notice of appeal. This is sensible, since the scope of the issues on appeal is not always clear in advance. Two alternative courses are provided for:

> '7.1.1 if a PH is ordered, in the skeleton or written submissions lodged prior to such PH; or
> 7.1.2 if the case is listed for FH without a PH, then within 14 days of the seal date of the order so providing.'

Respondent's application

3.278 The respondent should apply as early as possible, but in any event, in the respondent's answer. This provision makes more sense of the provisions above, allowing a later application by the appellant, making provision for dealing with the issue at a preliminary hearing where one has been ordered.

Content of the application

3.279 Paragraph 7.2 states that the application 'must explain why such a matter is considered necessary in order to argue the point of law raised in the notice of appeal or respondent's Answer'.

3.280 It is vital to tie in any application with the grounds of appeal and/or the grounds of resistance, identifying precisely which points in issue cannot be dealt with without notes of evidence.[126] Where a respondent's answer has been served, a party should not restrict their analysis of the issues on which the evidence is necessary merely to the issues in their *own* grounds (of appeal or resistance, as the case may be). While it is vital to identify properly how the issues arise on their own grounds, parties should look at the issues as they arise on reading *both* the notice of appeal and the respondent's answer, since this is the lens through which the EAT will look at the application and may also narrow the issues.

3.281 Paragraph 7.2 goes on to require that the application identifies:

> '7.2.1 the issue(s) in the notice of appeal or respondent's Answer to which the matter is relevant;
> 7.2.2 the names of the witnesses whose evidence is considered relevant, alternatively the nature of the evidence the absence of which is considered relevant;
> 7.2.3 (if applicable) the part of the hearing when the evidence was given;
> 7.2.4 the gist of the evidence (or absence of evidence) alleged to be relevant; and

---

[126] EAT PD, para 7.2.1.

7.2.5 (if the party has a record), saying so and by whom and when it was made, or producing an extract from a witness statement given in writing at the hearing.'

3.282 Paragraph 7.3 provides the requirement for the parties to co-operate and use their best endeavours to agree the note of evidence.

Further application

3.283 Paragraph 7.4 contemplates the need for a further application, for directions, to be made to the EAT, where agreement cannot be reached within 21 days, or any shorter period ordered.

3.284 Any party may make that application within 7 days of the expiry of that period (ie the 21 days or less).

3.285 The party applying for directions must enclose all relevant correspondence and give notice to the other parties. A party wishing to provide a table of evidence, as suggested above, in lieu of the correspondence required by para 7.4 should request permission to do so from the registrar, copying all other parties with that request. Ideally, such a request should be made with the support and prior agreement of the other parties.

Purpose of notes of evidence

3.286 Paragraph 7.7 recites that the purpose of providing the employment judge's notes is not 'to enable the parties to embark on a "fishing expedition" to establish grounds or additional grounds of appeal or because they have not kept their own notes of the evidence'.

Costs risk

3.287 Paragraph 7.7 also provides that a party behaving unreasonably is at a specific risk of an order for costs for either:

(1) making unreasonable applications for the employment judge's notes; or

(2) unreasonably causing applications to be made by the other side by an unreasonable lack of co-operation in agreeing the note of the evidence.

Directions

3.288 The directions which the EAT may give include the following:[127]

(1) the resolution of the disagreement on the papers or at a hearing;

---

[127] EAT PD, para 7.4.

(2) the administration by one party to the others of, or a request to the employment judge to respond to, a questionnaire; or

(3) if the EAT is satisfied that such notes are necessary, a request that the employment judge produce his notes of evidence either in whole or in part.

Provision of notes to the parties

3.289 Paragraph 7.5 provides that if the EAT requests any documents from the employment judge, it will supply copies to the parties upon receipt. If you are expecting to receive the employment judge's notes of evidence, do make sure that they have been sent to you. In *Pinnington v City and Council of Swansea*,[128] the EAT provided the respondent's counsel with the notes by fax but sent the appellant's lay representative a copy by second class post the following day (a Saturday). This was shortly before the full hearing of the appeal. At the hearing, it was accepted that it is plainly desirable that both parties to have access to the notes at the same time, especially if time is short in which to consider them.

Criticism: litigants in person

3.290 The procedure set out above is fairly complicated, especially for parties representing themselves ('litigants in person'). On one view, it is unnecessary complicated.

3.291 This was acknowledged by the Court of Appeal in *Wheeler v Quality Deep Limited (trading as Thai Royale Restaurant)*,[129] in which Hooper LJ said commented on para 7.1 of the EAT PD as follows:

> 66. Whilst I, as a judge who has sat in the EAT, understand this [paragraph], I am not sure that the average lay litigant would understand it. Many litigants might not even understand that there is no record of the proceedings in the Tribunal other than the Chairman's notes. An explanatory note might help. I would also invite the President to consider whether the judge who conducts the "sift" and orders a full hearing might not also be asked to consider whether the Chairman's notes could be required in the light of the grounds of appeal (assuming that this is not already done).
>
> 67. Peter Gibson LJ said that it seemed open to argument whether paragraph 2 of the Grounds of the notice of appeal prepared not by lawyers but by a lay person should have been construed as coming within the paragraph 7 of the Practice Direction. He also said that it was open to argument whether the EAT should have considered ordering the Chairman's notes of evidence.
>
> 68. Whilst fully accepting the difficulties faced by the EAT in dealing with a large volume of appeals and whilst fully accepting the important role which the Practice

---
[128] UKEAT/0561/03 [2004] All ER (D) 564 (May).
[129] [2004] EWCA Civ 1085, [2005] ICR 265.

Direction plays, it seems to me that the EAT should not have peremptorily dismissed this ground. Nor am I able to say that the result would necessarily have been the same even if the Chairman's notes of evidence had been made available.

3.292 It seems to the authors that there is an opportunity to streamline this vexed part of the EAT's procedures, along the following lines:

(1) Amend the standard forms for the notice of appeal and respondent's answer, to require each party to state which grounds of appeal can (in that party's opinion) be determined without the need to agree a note of evidence or seek production of the employment judge's notes and which cannot (with permission to amend that statement available from the registrar).

(2) Impose a duty to co-operate in agreeing any note of evidence where either party has indicated it is necessary, without the need to apply to the EAT.

(3) Allow the parties to set out the evidence agreed or not agreed in some form of table or schedule (such as that set out above), so that lengthy correspondence need not always be produced to the EAT, as presently happens.

(4) Require any party who is not content to rely on the table of evidence (which need not necessarily reflect complete agreement) to apply for directions within a sensible timescale applicable to all appeals.

Challenging the notes

3.293 If a party disputes the note of evidence provided by the chairmen then there is a procedure set down in the case of *Dexine Rubber Co Ltd v Alker*.[130] The overriding point to note is that the chairman is going to win any dispute. The disputing party can try and persuade him to change his note, but if they will not, the EAT will accept the chairman's version.

3.294 The procedure operates as follows:

(1) The criticism of the note should be sent to the other party to the appeal to try and secure agreement between the parties on whether the note is accurate.

(2) The criticising party should then send the criticism (either its own or if agreed, of both parties) to the Employment Judge.

(3) The Employment Judge should then respond either accepting the criticism or confirming the accuracy of the note.

---

[130] [1977] ICR 434.

(4) The Employment Judge's response is final and the notes cannot thereafter be challenged.

3.295 An Employment Judge cannot refuse to disclose his notes – see *Houston v Lightwater Farms Ltd; Walker v Lakhdari*.[131]

OTHER APPLICATIONS FOR INTERIM ORDERS

Applications

3.296 Applications to the registrar have been dealt with above but in brief any application for an interim order should:

(1) be in writing;

(2) be addressed to the registrar (save in special cases);[132]

(3) state what order is sought and the reasons for the application;

(4) be made at a convenient moment in the proceedings, where possible, so that interim applications can be dealt with together;

(5) be accompanied by any necessary documents or correspondence but this should be kept to a minimum;

(6) be copied to the other parties, out of courtesy, so that they have a chance to consider the application at the earliest opportunity (although r 19 of the EAT Rules provides that the registrar will serve copies of the application on the other parties).

Appeals from the registrar

3.297 As noted above, r 21 of the EAT Rules provides for appeals against the decisions of the registrar:

(1) The time limit for appealing is 5 days,[133] not counting weekends etc.[134]

(2) Notice of appeal may be given orally or in writing,[135] ie you can telephone and ask to appeal any decision to the judge. Writing is preferable since

---

[131] [1990] ICR 502.
[132] EAT Rules, r 20(4): restricted reporting orders and permission to a person subject to a restriction of proceedings order where the order has been made under ETA 1996, s 33(1) and application is made under s 33(4).
[133] EAT Rules, r 37.
[134] Not counting weekends, Christmas Day, Good Friday and Bank Holidays: EAT PD, para 1.8.4.
[135] EAT Rules, r 21(2).

there is less room for any misunderstanding and you can state your reasons for appealing with precision.

(3) The registrar informs the appellant and other parties concerned with the appeal of the arrangements for determining the appeal.

Stays

3.298 As noted above, the judge or registrar may stay an appeal for a period (normally 21 days) pending a review or the provision of further reasons by the employment tribunal. Provision for this was formerly expressly made in the 2004 EAT Practice Direction at para 9.5, but this has disappeared from the 2008 EAT Practice Direction, perhaps because the powers necessary are inherent in the rules.

Witness orders and production of documents

3.299 Under r 27(1), the EAT may order any person to attend before it as a witness or to produce any document.

3.300 Enforcing these orders is dependent upon the witness having been offered sufficient 'conduct money' to cover the costs of his attending at the hearing when the order was served on him. Unless this has been offered, he will not be held to have failed to comply with the order: r 27(2). If he has been offered sufficient 'conduct money', failure to comply with the order will be a contempt of court, under s 29(2) of ETA 1996.

Waiving the rules

3.301 As noted above, under r 39(2), the EAT may dispense with any procedural step that might otherwise be taken or required under the EAT Rules, or direct that it be taken differently, if it considers that:

(1) it would lead to the more expeditious or economical disposal of any proceedings;

(2) it would otherwise be desirable in the interests of justice.

3.302 By r 39(1), a failure to comply with the EAT Rules will not invalidate the proceedings unless the EAT directs otherwise. Rule 35(5) makes specific provision for dispensing with service or effecting it otherwise than as prescribed by the EAT Rules.

3.303 Rule 39(3) also specifically provides power for the EAT to allow the bringing of an appeal before the period for doing so has commenced, which is discussed more fully above.

Debarring orders

3.304 Under r 26, the EAT has power to make an order debarring the respondent from taking any further part in the appeal,[136] or such other order as is thinks just (such as an order striking out allegations of bias or misconduct in a notice of appeal after the appellant failed to provide the required affidavit to support those allegations, but where there were nonetheless other grounds: *Masin v Bryn Howel Hotel Ltd*.[137]

3.305 The EAT also has power to make a costs order against a party that does not comply with an order or Practice Direction under r 40(4). It would seem that the costs awarded need not be incurred as a result of the non-compliance, on the face of the rule.

Sitting in private

3.306 Sitting in private is not the same as the restriction of reporting. However, it seems appropriate to mention these points together. Rule 29(2) provides that the EAT may sit in private in certain circumstances, including for the purpose of hearing evidence from someone who would be breaking the law or breaking a confidence by disclosing it.

Restricted reporting orders

3.307 Sections 31 and 32 of ETA 1996 give the EAT the power to make rules allowing the making of restricted reporting orders in two types of case:

(1) cases involving sexual misconduct; and

(2) disability.

3.308 Rules 23 and 23A make that provision.

3.309 These rules apply where either:

(1) a decision of an employment tribunal to make or not to make a restricted reporting order is appealed; or

(2) an interlocutory (or interim) decision of a tribunal in a case where the tribunal has made such an order which has not been revoked is being appealed.

3.310 The EAT may make such an order at any time prior to making the order disposing of the appeal, whether on the application of a party or on its

---

[136] For example, *Melstar Ltd v Rix* UKEAT/0701/04 [2005] All ER (D) 348 (Feb).
[137] UKEAT/0831/04 [2005] All ER (D) 350 (Feb).

own initiative, provided that it first gives the parties the opportunity to advance oral argument at a hearing if they so wish, before making a full order: rr 23(5) and 23A(4).

3.311 A restricted reporting order must state the persons who may not be identified: r 23(4).

3.312 The order may be temporary or full:

(1) A temporary restricted reporting order:
   (a) may be made by the EAT without a hearing: r 23(5A);
   (b) lasts 14 days unless a party applies to have converted into a full order: r 23(5B);
   (c) continues to have effect after 14 days, if an application to convert it to a full order has been made, until the application is determined: r 23(5C);
   (d) must be notified to the parties in writing as soon as possible, together with the right of the parties to apply to have it revoked or converted into a full order within 14 days of it having been made;

(2) a full order takes effect until the final order disposing of the appeal is sent to the parties: r 23(3) and (9).

3.313 The EAT may revoke a restricted reporting order at any time where it thinks fit: r 23(7). This is plainly a very wide discretion.

3.314 The fact that it has been made must be displayed at the EAT, on the notice board and on the door of the room where the hearing is taking place: r 23(8).

3.315 Any party wishing to make representations about a restricted reporting order should apply to be joined as a party pursuant to r 18, showing a good case for joinder: *A v B ex parte News Group Newspapers Ltd*.[138]

3.316 *X v Commissioner of the Police of the Metropolis*[139] was an overriding public duty case, rather like *Adbelghafar*, in that the EAT observed that whether or not the EAT had obligation to protect the identity of claimants who would otherwise be deterred from bring sex discrimination claims, in order to render effective the rights conferred by the Equal Treatment Directive,[140] even though this went beyond the provisions in the EAT Rules.

---

[138] [1998] ICR 55.
[139] [2003] ICR 1031.
[140] Council Directive 76/207/EEC of 9 February 1976 on the implementation of the principle of equal treatment for men and women as regards access to employment, vocational training and promotion, and working conditions (1976) OJ L 39/40.

Controlling vexatious parties or proceedings

3.317 Litigants who bring rafts of claims, in large numbers and without regard to their merits or their impact on the respondents risk eventually becoming the subject of an order preventing them from starting any new proceedings without the permission of the EAT.

3.318 *Attorney-General v Deman*[141] is a good illustration. In that case, Mr Deman had brought 40 claims in the employment tribunal, mainly for race discrimination against higher education institutions, trade unions and others.

3.319 With equal vigour, he had made over 40 appeals to the EAT and had been repeatedly criticised for his conduct of those proceedings and appeals. The EAT found him to have habitually and persistently:

(1) instituted vexatious 'proceedings', which included both the institution of the initial proceedings and the institution of the appeals; and

(2) made vexatious applications in the course of those proceedings

within the meaning of s 33(1)(a) and (b) of the ETA 1996.

3.320 The timing and facts of this case show how far an enthusiasm for the tribunals will be tolerated before the Attorney-General will seek such an order.

3.321 The considerations as to the exercise of this power were examined by both the EAT and the Court of Appeal in *Attorney-General v Wheen*,[142] Lindsay J adopted Lord Bingham LCJ's formulation of the meaning of 'vexatious proceedings', from *Attorney-General v Barker*,[143] characterising them as:

(1) having little or no basis in law (or at least no discernible basis);

(2) subjecting the defendant to inconvenience, harassment and expense out of all proportion to any gain likely to accrue to the claimant; and

(3) involving an abuse of the process of the court, meaning by that a use of the court process for a purpose or in a way which is significantly different from the ordinary and proper use of the court process ...'

3.322 Such applications and orders are relatively rare but apparently becoming less so. While broadly similar considerations apply across all jurisdictions, proper notice should be taken of the peculiarities of the employment jurisdiction.[144]

---

[141] UKEAT/0113/06 [2006] All ER (D) 337 (Oct).
[142] [2000] IRLR 461, EAT, affirmed [2001] IRLR 91, CA.
[143] [2000] 1 FLR 759.
[144] Relevant cases include: *Re Vernazza* [1959] 1 WLR 622; *Attorney-General v Jones* [1990]

Joining parties

3.323 Rule 18 gives the EAT power to join a party to proceedings and give consequential directions, either on the application of a party or on its own initiative.

APPEALS INVOLVING NATIONAL SECURITY

3.324 Rules 30A and 31A provide special rules for dealing with appeals involving questions of national security, designed to allow the cases to be brought without inappropriate disclosure of sensitive information, allowing a Minister of the Crown to direct the EAT to sit in private for all or part of a hearing, where he considers is to be expedient in the interests of national security to do so.

3.325 Equally, the EAT may make such orders itself: r 30A(2).

3.326 If an order is made excluding a party or his representative from a hearing, the EAT must inform the Attorney-General who may appoint a special advocate to represent his interests, albeit without communicating directly or indirectly with anyone including the excluded party about the grounds of appeal or resistance, nor any matter raised during the private sitting. This makes taking instructions from your client (if you are the special advocate) impossible, by definition. But it is better than nothing.

FULL HEARING

Preparation

Listing

3.327 If an appeal is permitted to go forward to a full hearing, it will be assigned a listing category which will affect the composition of the Tribunal before which it will be heard. The 2008 EAT PD has reduced the number of categories to which a case may be assigned to three (although the President has expressly reserved the discretion to alter any relevant category as circumstances require). Paragraph 9.18 of the EAT PD identifies these as follows:

P   (recommended to be heard in the President's list);

---

1 WLR 859; *Attorney-General v Barker* [2000] 1 FLR 759; *Attorney-General v Covey; Attorney-General v Matthews* [2001] EWCA (Civ) 254, [2001] All ER (D) 222 (Feb); *Attorney-General v Wheen* (above); *Attorney-General v Tyrrell* UKEAT/0236/03 [2004] All ER (D) 470 (Mar); *Attorney-General v Ayovuare* UKEAT/0614/03 [2004] All ER (D) 80 (Apr); *Attorney-General v D'Souza* UKEAT/0139/04 [2004] All ER (D) 322 (Jul); *Attorney-General v Roberts* UKEAT/0058/05 [2005] All ER (D) 138 (Jul); *Attorney-General v Kuttappan* UKEAT/0478/05 [2005] All ER (D) 301 (Dec); *Attorney-General v Bruce* UKEAT/0586/05 [2006] All ER (D) 70 (Mar); and *Attorney-General v Perotti* [2006] EWHC 1002 (Admin).

A (complex, and raising point(s) of law of public importance);

B (any other cases).

3.328 Full hearings normally run in the order in which the Notice of Appeal is received, unless one of the factors in paras 9.20.1–9.20.5 or 9.21 applies. The use of lay members to hear appeals in the EAT means that the hearing estimate set for a hearing must be absolutely accurate. If hearing overruns it will be adjourned part heard to the next time that the judge and the wing members can sit together again, which may be some time in the future. Paragraph 12.1 of the EAT PD states: 'Any change in such estimate, or disagreement with an estimate made by the EAT on a sift or at a PH, is to be notified immediately to the Listing Officer'.

3.329 The EAT has power to restrict the time given to parties to make submissions during the case to avoid an adjournment – see para 12.2 of the EAT PD. The EAT, cannot of course use this power to procure an unfair hearing contrary to Art 6 of the European Convention and at some point the EAT will have to face the consequences of an adjournment rather than allow an injustice to occur. The EAT may visit in costs however, any adjournment caused by a failure of a representative or party.

3.330 A case will be listed for a date which is 'as soon as practicable' after the preliminary hearing or if there was no preliminary hearing after the sift. There are basically three lists into which a case will go. There is a fixed date list, which speaks for itself, and a warned list. The warned list consists of cases which are 'short' or are those in which expedition has been ordered. Basically these cases could come on for hearing at any time. As much notice as possible will be given of the hearing. The parties may inform the listing officer that a case is going to be very short because the appeal is to be withdrawn or has settled and he may list the case at very short notice. The parties may object to being in the warned list or for being told of a hearing at short notice and may apply for another fixed date. This should be done by way of a written application on notice to the listing officer. There is a right of appeal to the registrar or a judge.

3.331 The listing officer will usually co-operate with the parties to fix a convenient date in most cases but is not bound to do so. Once the date is fixed in the list then the parties can only have it changed by making an application to the listing officer on notice to all other parties setting out their reasons. If a party receives such an application then they must immediately and in any event within not less than 7 days notify their views to the listing officer.

3.332 The list can be found on the EAT website and is updated each week. See Part 12 of the EAT PD for full details on listing.

BUNDLES

3.333 The EAT PD requires the production of a bundle for the full hearing. The ultimate responsibility is for the appellant to prepare this, but it is a joint bundle which must be produced with the co-operation and consent of the respondent. The documents included must be certified by the parties as strictly only those which are relevant to the points of law raised in the appeal and which are likely to be referred to at the hearing. The parties cannot merely reproduce the bundle which was used before the employment tribunals. They must produce new bundles and fillet out any extraneous documents outside of the criteria of relevance to the point of law in issue and which are likely to be referred to. All documents must be legible and unmarked.[145]

3.334 The documents must be numbered by item and paginated continuously. They should appear in the following order:

(1) Judgment, decision or order appealed from and written reasons.

(2) Sealed notice of appeal.

(3) Respondent's answer if a full hearing, respondent's submissions if a preliminary hearing.

(4) ET1 claim (and any additional information or written answers).

(5) ET3 response (and any additional information or written answers).

(6) Questionnaire and replies (discrimination and equal pay cases).

(7) Relevant orders, judgments and written reasons of the employment tribunal.

(8) Relevant orders and judgments of the EAT.

(9) Affidavits and employment tribunal comments (where ordered).

(10) Any documents relating to evidence before the ET, which may have been agreed (ie a note of oral evidence given by one or more of the witnesses, voluntarily agreed between the parties) or ordered by the EAT.

3.335 Any other relevant documents should then follow on in the bundle. These could include the contract of employment and any policies etc, but only so far as these are relevant. There is a maximum of 100 pages. To lodge a bundle of more than 100 pages the permission of the registrar or a judge's order will be required.[146] If permission is given then the additional pages

---

[145] EAT PD, para 6.4.
[146] EAT PD, para 6.3.

should follow in a separate bundle. In the event of such additional bundles then an essential reading list must be produced. All documents must be legible and unmarked.

3.336 Four copies (two if a judge is hearing the case alone) of the bundle should be lodged with the EAT. The timing for lodging the bundles has changed in the 2008 EAT Practice Direction. For a full hearing (FH), the bundle must be lodged by no later than 28 days after the seal date of the order, which sets down the case for final hearing (or within such other period as is otherwise ordered).[147] If the case is in the warned list then the bundles should be lodged as soon as possible and in any event within 7 days after the parties have been told that their case is in such a list.[148] If the hearing is going to take place within 7 days then the bundle must be lodged as soon as possible.

3.337 For all other hearings, bundles should be prepared and lodged 'as soon as possible after service of the Notice of Appeal and no later than 21 days from the seal date of the relevant order unless otherwise directed.'

3.338 If the parties cannot agree the bundle or otherwise fall into difficulties they should seek the direction of the registrar by written application on notice to the other parties. The registrar may give such direction of her own initiative.

3.339 Estimate of length of hearing: the lay members of the EAT are part-time members. They attend when available on pre-arranged dates. They do not sit for continuous periods. Consequently, appeals which run beyond their estimated length have to be adjourned part-heard (often with substantial delay) until a day on which the judge and members are all available. To avoid inconvenience to the parties and to the EAT, and to avoid additional delay and costs suffered as a result of adjournment of part-heard appeals, all parties are required to ensure that the estimates of length of hearing (allowing for the fact that the parties can expect the EAT to have pre-read the papers and for the giving of a judgment) are accurate when first given. Any change in such estimate, or disagreement with an estimate made by the EAT on a sift or at a preliminary hearing, is to be notified immediately to the listing officer.

3.340 If the EAT concludes that the hearing is likely to exceed the estimate, or if for other reasons the hearing may not be concluded within the time available, it may seek to avoid such adjournment by placing the parties under appropriate time limits in order to complete the presentation of the submissions within the estimated or available time.

3.341 Subject to para 12.6 of the EAT PD, below, a date will be fixed for a preliminary hearing as soon as practicable after the sift (referred to in para 9.5, above) and for a full hearing as soon as practicable after the sift if no preliminary hearing is ordered, or otherwise after the preliminary hearing.

---

[147] EAT PD, para 6.6.
[148] EAT PD, para 6.7.

3.342 The listing officer will normally consult the parties on dates, and will accommodate reasonable requests if practicable, but is not bound to do so. Once the date is fixed, the appeal will be set down in the list. A party finding that the date which has been fixed causes serious difficulties may apply to the listing officer for it to be changed, having first notified all other parties entitled to appear on the date of their application and the reasons for it.

Skeleton arguments

3.343 A well structured and concise skeleton argument, gives you a chance to help the EAT understand exactly how you put your case, before you arrive at the tribunal. It should be cross-referenced to the page numbers in the hearing and should identify any relevant parts of any table or note of evidence which has been agreed or produced.

3.344 A poor skeleton argument is an opportunity missed.

3.345 A chronology should always be provided with the skeleton argument: para 13.4 of the EAT PD.

3.346 Paragraph 13 of the EAT PD sets out what is required in relation to skeleton arguments, which must be provided by all parties in all hearings, unless:

(1) the EAT is notified by a party or representative in writing that the notice of appeal or respondent's answer or relevant application contains the full argument; or

(2) the EAT directs otherwise.

3.347 Paragraph 13.2 identifies the following features which should characterise a good skeleton:

(1) should be concise;

(2) should identify and summarise:
 (a) the relevant points of law,
 (b) the steps in the legal argument, and
 (c) the statutory provisions and authorities to be relied upon, identifying them by name, page and paragraph and stating the legal proposition sought to be derived from them.

3.348 An important point is that the skeleton argument should state the form of order which the party will ask the EAT to make at the hearing.

3.349 As an aside, the normal order in the majority of cases is to remit back to the same tribunal. If the appellant is seeking a different order, such as remission to a fresh tribunal or substitution of the EAT's decision for the employment tribunal's decision, that should be stated but the appellant should go on to set out, at least briefly, why a different order is sought and justified. This should make reference to the principles set out in *Sinclair Roche & Temperley v Heard* (see para **3.382** below).[149]

Lodging the skeleton argument

3.350 Paragraphs 13.6–13.12 of the EAT PD deal with lodging the skeleton argument and, in short, para 13.9 provides that it must be lodged and served on any party attending the hearing in good time, which means:

(1) not less than 10 days (unless otherwise ordered) before the date fixed for a preliminary hearing, appeal against registrar's order, r 3(10) hearing or appointment for directions;[150]

(2) not less than 14 days before the full hearing;[151]

(3) as soon as possible and (unless the hearing date is less than 7 days later) in any event within 7 days after the parties have been notified that the case is expedited as a fast track full hearing case or in the warned list.[152]

3.351 Paragraph 13.10 of the EAT PD makes clear that failure to follow the above procedure may lead to an adjournment of an appeal or to dismissal for non-compliance with the Practice Direction, and to an award of costs. The party in default may also be required to attend before the EAT to explain their failure. It will always mean that the defaulting party must immediately despatch any delayed skeleton argument to the EAT by hand or by fax or by email to londoneat@ets.gsi.gov.uk or, as appropriate, edinburgheat@ets.gsi.gov.uk and (unless notified by the EAT to the contrary) bring to the hearing sufficient copies (a minimum of six) of the skeleton argument and any authorities referred to. The EAT staff will not be responsible for supplying or copying these on the morning of the hearing.

Terminology

Parties

3.352 One party will be the appellant and the other will be the respondent to the appeal. The good sense of referring to parties as appellant and respondent in the skeleton argument is clear where the employee is appealing and the employer remains the respondent. However, where the employer appeals, there is room for confusion since the employer was the respondent before the employment tribunal and is now the appellant.

---

[149] [2004] IRLR 763 at paras 46 and 47.
[150] Or, if the hearing is fixed at less than 7 days' notice, as soon as possible after the hearing date has been notified: EAT PD, para 13.9.1.
[151] EAT PD, para 13.9.2.
[152] EAT PD, para 13.9.3.

3.353 The 2004 EAT PD met this problem, at the end of para 13.2, by providing that: 'The parties can be referred to by name or as they appeared at the employment tribunal'.

3.354 This provision was permissive rather than mandatory. However, the 2008 EAT PD has made this mandatory and now states at para 13.5 that:

> 'The parties should be referred to by name or as they appeared at the Employment Tribunal ie Claimant (C) and Respondent (R).'

Rules and Practice Direction

3.355 Rule 3(7) of the EAT Rules should never be referred to as 'r 3.7' – it is simply confusing because it looks like one of the paragraphs of the EAT PD, which are numbered that way.

3.356 Similarly, para 3.7 of the EAT PD should never be referred to as 'para 3(7)'.

3.357 This confusion has grown up as a result of some commentators failing to make this distinction. This is not helpful to the parties or the members of the EAT.

Authorities

3.358 Paragraph 14 of the EAT PD provides for the citation of authorities. Note that the time limits for lodging bundles of authorities have changed in the 2008 EAT PD. The key provisions of para 14 can be summarised as follows:

(1) bundles of authorities should be properly prepared, paginated and agreed, so as not to cite the same case twice or more than one case for one proposition;

(2) sufficient copies should always be provided for the tribunal members and for any parties attending the hearing;

(3) key passages relied on should be sidelined;

(4) identify and highlight to the EAT the principle(s) you seek to derive from the authority;

(5) for decisions of the ECJ, the official report should be used where possible.

(6) oddly, bundles of authorities have to be lodged not less than seven days before a full hearing, but not less than 10 days before all other hearings – the reason for this is perhaps that skeleton arguments for these other

hearings are normally due 10 days before the hearing too, although this does not allow for including authorities that deal with a point raised by the other side in their skeleton.[153]

The hearing

The members of the panel

3.359 The members of the panel will be a judge and two lay members.

3.360 The judge will be either a High Court judge or a circuit judge. One lay member is drawn from those with experience of the employer's perspective and one is drawn from those with experience of the employee's perspective. More detail is set out in Chapter 9. The judge is addressed as 'sir' or 'madam'.

Representation and assistance

Non-lawyers

3.361 Non-lawyers should be particularly careful since under the Compensation Act 2006, it is now a criminal offence for anyone to provide advocacy services in an employment case for reward (eg, money) if the person providing those services is not registered to do so.

Pro bono representation

3.362 There are various schemes which provide free advice and representation to parties in the EAT. They are: the Bar Pro Bono Unit, the Free Representation Unit and ELAAS. They are manned by lawyers who voluntarily give their time and services to those who need them, without charge. Further details are available from the EAT.

What to expect

3.363 The day before the hearing, check which court you are listed in and before which members. There may be more than one case listed before the same tribunal, so you may not be first on.

3.364 When you arrive on the day of the hearing, you will sign in, giving your name. If you are presenting the case, you will need to fill in three forms with your name and that of your opponent for the members of the tribunal.

3.365 You then need to ask which court you are in (if you do not know already) and ask where the waiting room is. The EAT staff are very helpful and will normally make sure you know where you are going. Be aware that you may

---

[153] EAT PD, paras 14.7 (FH cases) and 14.6 (headed 'PH cases' but applicable to all other cases) – these standard time limits are new in the 2008 EAT PD.

be waiting in the same room as your opponent, so do not discuss your case unguardedly, without checking who is in earshot.

3.366 If you have not appeared in the EAT before, it is a good idea either to go to watch someone who has to do a case there before it is your turn or, at the very least, go in and sit at the back of the court to watch any cases coming on before you, just to get your eye in.

Presenting your case

3.367 Do not expect to command the EAT like Laurence Olivier playing Hamlet or Cicero addressing his fellow Athenians. The EAT will not expect you to read long tracts of your skeleton argument or judgments out.

3.368 You are there to *argue* your case, courteously, carefully but firmly. You will be interrupted, in all probability, fairly early on in your submissions. Usually, the interruptions will come from the judge, but be prepared to answer questions from the lay members.

3.369 Look on frequent interruptions as helpful, even if you hear the oft repeated refrain, 'This is just an appeal on the facts isn't it, Mr Bloggs?' when you think it is not. At least this way you know what the EAT's concerns are and how you can usefully deploy your best advocacy to best advantage.

3.370 Make sure that you make your important points early and clearly. Be sure to make any point that you may wish to make again on appeal the Court of Appeal.

3.371 Listen to your opponent and try to narrow the issues, even during the course of argument to those things that really matter, without wanton surrender.

3.372 When you cite authorities, just tell the EAT what the principle is in case it is uncontroversial, rather than reading out the relevant passages. That said, if the precise formulation of what is said is important to your case, do not be afraid to say so and to read out the relevant passage, even if the tribunal appears to be familiar with it.[154]

3.373 Last but not least; be brief.

---

[154] EAT PD, para 14.4 provides: 'It is unnecessary for a party citing a case in oral argument to read it in full to the EAT. Whenever a case is cited in a skeleton argument or in an oral argument it is helpful if the legal proposition for which it is cited is stated. References need only be made to the relevant passages in the report. If the formulation of the legal proposition based on the authority cited is not in dispute, further examination of the authority will often be unnecessary'.

Judgment

Giving judgment

3.374 The EAT typically gives judgment in one of two ways. First, it may given an ex tempore judgment, that is one in which it explains, there and then, what its reasons are. These may later be transcribed. Otherwise, it may be given as a reserved judgment.

Reserved judgment

3.375 In plain English, a reserved judgment is one that comes out later. After the hearing, there will be a gap of perhaps a few weeks, following which the judgment will be handed down.

Handing down

3.376 The procedure for handing down judgments is not without its difficulties for lawyers. It is helpfully summarised in para 18 of the EAT PD. In summary, it is as follows:

(1) the parties are notified of the date when the judgment will be handed down;

(2) the parties only need attend if they intend to make an application, either for costs or to appeal to the Court of Appeal – although a party will not know whether they intend to make such an application because they will not yet know the result of the hearing;

(3) if it is intended to make an application, notice of that fact should be given to the EAT and the other parties, together with any necessary particulars specified in para 19.3 (for any costs application), 48 hours before that date;

(4) copies of the judgment will be available to the parties or their representatives on the morning on which it is handed down or, if so directed by a judge, earlier to the parties' representatives in draft subject to terms as to confidentiality. Where a draft judgment has been provided in advance, any intended application for permission to appeal referred to in para 18.1 of the EAT PD, above, must be accompanied by a draft notice of appeal. This means that the lawyer drafting the notice of appeal has no way of knowing whether the client would like to appeal or not and has no way of finding out, certainly not in the light of the way the case has, in fact, been decided;

(5) the judgment will be pronounced without being read aloud, by the judge who presided or by another judge, on behalf of the EAT. The judge may

deal with any application or may refer it to the judge and/or the tribunal who heard the appeal, whether to deal with on the papers or at a further oral hearing on notice;

(6) paras 18.4–18.8 make detailed provision for whether or not there will be a transcript of the judgment.

Problems arising

3.377 As may be apparent from the above, lawyers who are sent a draft copy of the judgment in confidence are put in an awkward position, in that they have to prepare a notice of appeal to the Court of Appeal or an application for costs, without the client having had the chance to consider whether any such application should proceed in the light the judgment – as the client cannot, of course, see the judgment or be told about it.

3.378 One answer is that it is always part of a barrister's or solicitor's implied retainer to make such application as are necessary on the handing down of the judgment.

3.379 However, comforting that analysis may be on an academic level, it is extremely unsatisfactory for a client to have no informed input into authorising a decision which may result in the otherwise unnecessary attendance of the other side's lawyers.

3.380 The authors respectfully regard the present practice of the EAT on this point alone as uncharacteristically unsatisfactory.

REMISSION

3.381 The aim of saving costs and the principle of proportionality both tend to favour remission of cases back to the same, rather than a different, tribunal.

3.382 The seminal guidance on remission is that of Burton P in *Sinclair Roche & Temperley v Heard*[155] (subsequently approved and endorsed by the Court of Appeal in *Barke v SEETEC Business Technology Centre Ltd*).[156]

3.383 A case summary of *Sinclair Roche & Temperley* is included in Chapter 10. However, in outline, the relevant factors are as follows:

(1) proportionality: although where sufficient money is at stake, this would not necessarily be a decisive, or even an important, factor;

---

[155] [2004] IRLR 763, at paras 46 and 47.
[156] [2005] EWCA Civ 578, [2005] ICR 1373.

(2) distress and inconvenience of the parties: this must carefully considered, as to the extent by which this is actually caused by full or partial remission and by remission to a fresh rather than the original tribunal;

(3) passage of time: a case should not be sent back to the same tribunal if there is a real risk that it will have forgotten about it;

(4) bias or partiality: it would not be appropriate to send the matter back to the same tribunal where there was a real question of bias or the risk of pre-judgment or partiality;

(5) totally flawed decision: it is not normally appropriate to send a case back to a tribunal where the first hearing was wholly flawed or completely mishandled;

(6) second bite: the EAT should only send the matter back if it has confidence that, with guidance, the tribunal would be prepared to look fully at further matters and thus be willing to come to a different conclusion;

(7) presumption of tribunal professionalism: in the absence of clear indicators to the contrary, it should be assumed that the original tribunal would be capable of approach to matter professionally on remission.

3.384 In the more recent case of *Slee v Secretary of State for Justice*,[157] Silber J heard an appeal in the Administrative Court from a decision of an employment tribunal under the Justices of the Peace Act 1949 (Compensation) Regulations 1978.[158] Allowing the appeal, the judge had to consider whether it should be remitted to the original or a fresh tribunal.

3.385 Silber J identified the following considerations weighing against remission back to the original tribunal:

> 57. There are important countervailing submissions of which the first is that the Tribunal service has informed the respondent's solicitors that, if the rehearing were listed immediately, the earliest date on which the same Tribunal could rehear the claim would be in January or February 2008, which would be about two years after the original hearing. In the light of the length of this period, the Tribunal which heard the original claim would have little advantage over a freshly constituted tribunal especially as there are agreed notes of the evidence at the first hearing.
>
> 58. The second countervailing factor is that the question to be remitted (viz. what tasks the appellant performed on 2 February 1995 and at the material date, and whether they were wholly or predominately devoted to assisting the Justices Clerk) is both narrow and discrete from the majority of the evidence which was heard by

---

[157] [2007] EWHC 2717 (Admin), [2007] All ER (D) 303 (Nov).
[158] SI 1978/1682 (the Crombie regulations).

the original tribunal. The evidence which the employment tribunal heard concerning the claim for constructive unfair dismissal and the other issue before it would not assist in determining the question to be remitted. Any tribunal would need to hear evidence on the remitted question. So there would be little advantage in remitting this case to the same employment tribunal.

59. The third and crucial countervailing factor is that this is an old claim which should be resolved as soon as possible and it would obviously be possible to obtain an earlier hearing date in front of any employment tribunal rather than the three members of the original employment tribunal In those circumstances, I have concluded that the need for this matter to be resolved speedily together with the factors set out in paragraphs 57 and 58 above satisfy me that this matter should be remitted to a differently constituted employment tribunal but I stress that this decision is not any form of criticism of the Tribunal which originally dealt with this matter ...'

3.386 The decision as to where to remit a case following an appeal is a classic discretionary decision with which an appellate court (usually the Court of Appeal) will be reluctant to interfere. In *Mercy v Northgate HR Ltd*,[159] the Court of Appeal refused to overturn the EAT's decision to remit the case back to a new tribunal, despite the fact that 'it could not be said that it would have been inappropriate to remit the matter to the same tribunal'. The approach of the Court of Appeal acknowledged the wide discretion of the EAT on a decision to remit, applying the principles in *Sinclair Roche & Temperley*.

DISPOSAL OF APPEAL BY CONSENT

3.387 In *J Sainsbury plc v Moger*,[160] the EAT held that it will not normally make an order by consent where there is no overall settlement and the parties are asking that the case be remitted for a rehearing. In those circumstances, the EAT will need to hear the appeal.[161]

3.388 This is now reflected in para 15 of the EAT PD, which provides as follows:

'15.1 An appellant who wishes to abandon or withdraw an appeal should notify the other parties and the EAT immediately. If a settlement is reached, the parties should inform the EAT as soon as possible. The appellant should submit to the EAT a letter signed by or on behalf of the appellant and signed also by or on behalf of the respondent, asking the EAT for permission to withdraw the appeal and to make a consent order in the form of an attached draft signed by or for both parties dismissing the appeal, together with any other agreed order.

15.2 If the other parties do not agree to the proposed order the EAT should be informed. Written submissions should be lodged at the EAT and served on the

---

[159] [2007] EWCA Civ 1304, [2007] All ER (D) 196 (Dec), per Maurice Kay LJ, at paras [24]–[26].
[160] [1994] ICR 800.
[161] See also: *British Publishing Co Ltd v Fraser* [1987] ICR 517.

parties. Any outstanding issue may be determined on the papers by the EAT, particularly if it relates to costs, but the EAT may fix an oral hearing to determine the outstanding matters in dispute between the parties.

15.3 If the parties reach an agreement that the appeal should be allowed by consent, and that an order made by the employment tribunal should be reversed or varied or the matter remitted to the employment tribunal on the ground that the decision contains an error of law, it is usually necessary for the matter to be heard by the EAT to determine whether there is a good reason for making the proposed order. On notification by the parties, the EAT will decide whether the appeal can be dealt with on the papers or by a hearing at which one or more parties or their representatives should attend to argue the case for allowing the appeal and making the order that the parties wish the EAT to make.

15.4 If the application for permission to withdraw an appeal is made close to the hearing date the EAT may require the attendance of the Appellant and/or a representative to explain the reasons for delay in making a decision not to pursue the appeal.'

3.389 By way of overview, the disposal of an appeal by consent can arise in three broad categories of case:

(1) the parties agree that the appeal should be allowed in whole or in part (reversing, setting aside or otherwise overturning the employment tribunal's decision);

(2) the appellant wishes to abandon or withdraw the appeal (leaving the employment tribunal decision undisturbed); or

(3) the parties wish to compromise the entire dispute on agreed terms (effectively avoiding the need to disturb the employment tribunal decision).

3.390 On the face of para 15 of the EAT PD, a hearing will only be necessary in the first category of case: where the EAT is reversing, setting aside or otherwise overturning the employment tribunal's decision at the invitation of the parties.

3.391 *Eden v Humphries and Glasgow Ltd.*[162]

---

[162] [1981] ICR 183.

COSTS

Generally

3.392 The EAT can make costs orders but only in limited circumstances. These are set out at r 34A of the EAT Rules. The following are the grounds for a costs order:

(1) the proceedings brought by the paying party were:
  (a) unnecessary,
  (b) improper,
  (c) vexatious, or
  (d) misconceived, or

(2) a party:
  (e) has caused unreasonable delay, or
  (f) is guilty of unreasonable conduct.

3.393 In particular, costs orders may be made where there has been a failure to comply with the EAT PD or where a party has caused any adjournment of the case or where a party has amended one of the following documents:

(a) Notice of appeal.

(b) Respondent's answer.

(c) Respondent's statement of cross-appeal.

(d) Rule 3(5) document.

(e) Rule 3(6) document.

(f) Rule 6(7) document.

(g) Rule 6(8) document.

3.394 Costs orders can be made at any stage in the proceedings (EAT Rules, r 34(4)). They remain unusual. Key points to note are:

(1) They can be made at a preliminary hearing where the appeal is misconceived which can be defined as not having a reasonable prospect of success. This is especially the case where a respondent has made a written submission stating that there is no reasonable prospect of success.

(2) They can be made at full hearing even though the case got through a preliminary hearing. See *Iron and Steel Trades Confederation v ASW Ltd*.[163]

Procedure

3.395 Costs orders are usually sought at the end of a hearing or can be sought by way of an application in writing to the registrar within 14 days of the order finally disposing of the proceedings being sent to the parties (EAT Rules, r 34(4)). Notice will be given to the other parties of any written application so that they can be given an opportunity to make representations (r 34(5)). The application will be dealt with on the papers if made in writing or may be referred to an oral hearing. The party seeking an order must state the legal ground upon which the application is made and the facts upon which it is based. They should also provide a costs schedule. The paying party should serve a witness statement with relevant exhibits if they wish the EAT to take into account their means and inability to pay (see r 34B(2)). See generally, para 19.3 of the EAT PD.

Assessment

3.396 Costs will either be assessed by the EAT itself or sent off for detailed assessment under the CPR at the Supreme Court Costs Office.

Wasted costs orders

3.397 The EAT has the same power as the Court of Appeal to award wasted costs where a legal representative acting for profit (including on a CFA) causes wasted costs by way of improper, unreasonable or negligence acts or omissions which the EAT thinks its reasonable for that representative to pay. The representative must be allowed to make representations and will be sent a 'show cause notice'. Ability to pay may be taken into account (r 34C). Where an application is made for a wasted costs order then this will be served on the legal representatives and must set out the basis of the application (EAT PD, para 19.5).

3.398 A three-stage test is usually used in these circumstances. It is taken from the case of *Ridehalgh v Horsefield*:[164]

(1) Has the legal representative of whom complaint is made acted improperly, unreasonably or negligently?

(2) If so, did such conduct cause the applicant to incur uncessary costs?

---

[163] [2004] IRLR 926.
[164] [1994] 3 WLR 462.

(3) If so, is it in all the circumstances just to order the legal representative to compensate the applicant for the whole or any part of the relevant costs?

3.399 There must in all cases be a breach of duty to the court. Moreover, the following guidance was given in *Ridehalgh:*

> "'Improper' means what it has been understood to mean in this context for at least half a century. The adjective covers, but is not confined to, conduct which would ordinarily be held to justify disbarment, striking off, suspension from practice or other serious professional penalty. It covers any significant breach of a substantial duty imposed by a relevant code of professional conduct. But it is not in our judgment limited to that. Conduct which would be regarded as improper according to the consensus of professional (including judicial) opinion can be fairly stigmatised as such whether or not it violates the letter of a professional code.
>
> "Unreasonable" also means what it has been understood to mean in this context for at least half a century. The expression aptly describes conduct which is vexatious, designed to harass the other side rather than advance the resolution of the case, and it makes no difference that the conduct is the product of excessive zeal and not improper motive. But conduct cannot be described as unreasonable simply because it leads in the event to an unsuccessful result or because other more cautious legal representatives would have acted differently. The acid test is whether the conduct permits of a reasonable explanation. If so, the course adopted may be regarded as optimistic and as reflecting on a practitioner's judgment, but it is not unreasonable.
>
> The term "negligent" was the most controversial of the three. It was argued that the 1990 Act, in this context as in others, used "negligent" as a term of art involving the well-known ingredients of duty, breach, causation and damage. Therefore, it was said, conduct cannot be regarded as negligent unless it involves an actionable breach of the legal representative's duty to his own client, to whom alone a duty is owed. We reject this approach. (1) As already noted, the predecessor of the present Ord 62, r 11 made reference to "reasonable competence". That expression does not invoke technical concepts of the law of negligence. It seems to us inconceivable that by changing the language Parliament intended to make it harder, rather than easier, for courts to make orders. (2) Since the applicant's right to a wasted costs order against a legal representative depends on showing that the latter is in breach of his duty to the court it makes no sense to superimpose a requirement under this head (but not in the case of impropriety or unreasonableness) that he is also in breach of his duty to his client.
>
> We cannot regard this as, in practical terms, a very live issue, since it requires some ingenuity to postulate a situation in which a legal representative causes the other side to incur unnecessary costs without at the same time running up unnecessary costs for his own side and so breaching the ordinary duty owed by a legal representative to his client. But for whatever importance it may have, we are clear that "negligent" should be understood in an untechnical way to denote failure to act with the competence reasonably to be expected of ordinary members of the profession.

In adopting an untechnical approach to the meaning of negligence in this context, we would however wish firmly to discountenance any suggestion that an applicant for a wasted costs order under this head need prove anything less than he would have to prove in an action for negligence—

"advice, acts or omissions in the course of their professional work which no member of the profession who was reasonably well-informed and competent would have given or done or omitted to do ... [an error of judgment] such as no reasonably well informed and competent member of that profession could have made." (See *Saif Ali v Sydney Mitchell & Co* [1978] 3 All ER 1033 at 1041, 1043, [1980] AC 198 at 218, 220 per Lord Diplock.)

We were invited to give the three adjectives (improper, unreasonable and negligent) specific, self-contained meanings, so as to avoid overlap between the three. We do not read these very familiar expressions in that way. Conduct which is unreasonable may also be improper, and conduct which is negligent will very frequently be (if it is not by definition) unreasonable. We do not think any sharp differentiation between these expressions is useful or necessary or intended.'

Costs of litigants in person

3.400 Costs of litigants in person can be awarded. This includes any disbursements and any financial loss which the party has incurred preparing for the case or an hourly rate of £28 (it increases by £1 per annum on 6 April each year). Litigants in person include company or corporation representatives.

Costs of assisted person

3.401 The costs of an assisted person are assessed by way of detailed assessment by the Supreme Court Costs Office pursuant to CPR r 47.17.

REVIEW

3.402 Section 33 of ETA 1996 makes provision for the EAT to review its decisions and correct any errors.

3.403 Section 33(3) expressly confirms the 'slip rule', in this case, the EAT's statutory power at any time to correct a clerical mistake in any order arising from an accidental slip or omission may be corrected on the authority of a judge or member.

3.404 The rest of s 33 concerns the procedure for seeking a review of any order made by the EAT, upon which the EAT may revoke or vary the order.

3.405 Any application must be made within 14 days of the date of the order: s 33(2). This is now reflected in the 2008 EAT PD, which provides as follows:[165]

---

[165] EAT PD, para 20.

'A request to review a judgment or order of the EAT must be made within 14 days of the seal date of the order, or must include an application, with reasons for an extension of time copied to all parties.'

3.406 However, note also that the EAT is not limited to reviewing an order on the application of a party, but may do so on its own initiative: s 33(1). The grounds upon which such an application can be made are set out in s 33(1)(a)–(c) as follows:

'(a) the order was wrongly made as the result of an error on the part of the Tribunal or its staff;
(b) a party did not receive proper notice of the proceedings leading to the order; or
(c) the interests of justice require such review.'

3.407 Section 33(4) provides that the decision to grant or refuse an application for review may be made by a judge.

APPEALING TO COURT OF APPEAL

3.408 This is fully dealt with in Chapter 4, but a few short points to note are set out below.

Time limit

3.409 21 days. The 2008 EAT PD[166] has now harmonised the time for appealing to the Court of Appeal from the EAT with the 21-day time limit which applies to appeals from the High Court or County Court. Under the 2004 EAT PD, the time limit was 14 days, which effectively varied the standard 21-day period which would otherwise have prevailed. For more detail on this, see Chapter 4.

Not a second appeal

3.410 An appeal to the Court of Appeal from the EAT need not involve a point of public importance, which is a requirement for second appeals in many other civil cases.

3.411 This is because an appeal to the Court of Appeal is not classified as a 'second appeal' under s 55 of the Access to Justice Act 1999.

Permission to appeal

3.412 Permission to appeal is required either from the EAT or from the Court of Appeal. It is now dealt with under EAT PD, paras 18.3 and 21.1 and 21.2. The amendments to para 21.1 introduced in the 2008 EAT PD, particularly the

---

[166] EAT PD, para 21.1.

provision which allows an application in writing within seven days after a reserved decision is handed down,[167] at least partially deals with a problem which advocates have encountered in the EAT for years: where the judgment is disclosed confidentially to counsel (or other advocate) in advance of the hearing, unlike the Court of Appeal, the EAT prohibits disclosure of the judgment to the parties until one hour before the hearing. This means that the client used to have just one hour to decided whether to appeal a judgment which may run to many pages. Frankly, this was always unsatisfactory. It has now been partially addressed.

3.413 It may be difficult to persuade the EAT to grant permission but it is more inclined to do so where the point raised is one of wider importance.[168]

3.414 However, it is not necessary to ask for permission to appeal from the EAT. It may be sought direct from the Court of Appeal, as explained in Chapter 4.

No leapfrog to the House of Lords

3.415 Unlike in the civil courts,[169] it is not possible to 'leapfrog' directly to the House of Lords from the EAT, no matter how important the case. The power to grant the necessary certificate for a 'leapfrog' appeal applies only in proceedings before a single judge of the High Court or a Divisional Court, but not in the EAT.

3.416 In *Botham v Ministry of Defence*,[170] the EAT 'venture[d] to suggest that consideration be given to whether the EAT, which did not exist in 1969, might be brought within the scope of the section'. That suggestion has not yet been taken up.

ENFORCEMENT OF ORDERS AND AWARDS

3.417 Judgments of the EAT are enforceable in the same way as judgments of the employment tribunals. This is because the EAT is exercising the power of the tribunal below when it gives judgment (see para **1.39**). Section 15 of the Employment Tribunals Act 1996 sets out the current enforcement procedure for tribunal judgments, which involves registering the judgment with the county courts. This cumbersome system for enforcement is about to be replaced by a

---

[167] As provide for, somewhat circularly, by para 18.3 which refers back to para 21 itself.
[168] For example, *Jackson v Computershare Investor Services plc* UKEAT/0503/06 [2007] All ER (D) 67 (Feb).
[169] With a certificate under s 12 of the Administration of Justice Act 1969 permitting a petition to be presented to their Lordships for leave to bring a 'leapfrog' appeal direct to the House of Lords, the court being satisfied that the conditions in s 12(3) are met.
[170] UKEAT/0503/04 [2004] All ER (D) 210 (Nov).

more direct method which will deem tribunal judgments to be county court judgments without the need for any registration.[171]

FUNDING

Legal expenses insurance

3.418 Many individuals and some companies nowadays litigate with the benefit of legal expenses insurance. For individuals, this is often part of the cover provided with their household insurance policy. It is important to check this at an early stage (preferably before bringing a claim in the employment tribunal) if you want the insurers to accept your claim on the policy and provide the cover.

After the event insurance

3.419 It is possible to obtain insurance against any costs order which might be made against you, after the dispute has arisen. This is called 'after the event' or ATE insurance. ATE insurance in civil cases in the courts is typically obtained where the lawyers have agreed to act on a conditional fee or 'no win, no fee' basis.

3.420 However, as costs orders are fairly rare in the EAT, for the reasons explained above, such policies are not commonly used in cases in the EAT.

Legal aid

3.421 Subject to means, litigation support from public funds is available, in principle, for representation in proceedings in the EAT.[172]

3.422 Note that, as spelt out in para 3.8 of the EAT PD, the fact that an application for such support has been made but not determined is' not usually a good reason for late lodgment of a notice of appeal'.

3.423 Any party applying for such support from public funds, should state this in their application, in support of a request for their entitlement to be determined as a matter of urgency.

Equality and Human Rights Commission

3.424 Funding support for cases is sometimes available from the Equality and Human Rights Commission, depending on the type of case. The Equality and Human Rights Commission came into being on 1 October 2007, established by the Equality Act 2006 as a non-departmental public body. According to its website, it 'champions equality and human rights for all, working to eliminate

---

[171] See s 27 of the Tribunals, Courts and Enforcement Act 2007.
[172] Civil Legal Aid (General) Regulations 1989 (SI 1989/339), reg 149.

discrimination, reduce inequality, protect human rights and to build good relations, ensuring that everyone has a fair chance to participate in society'.

3.425 The Equality and Human Rights Commission brings together three previous Commissions: the Commission for Racial Equality (CRE), the Disability Rights Commission (DRC) and the Equal Opportunities Commission (EOC), as well as having a remit to take up human rights cases. The Equality and Human Rights Commission may be contacted via its website www.equalityhumanrights.com or by telephone, on 0845 604 6610 for England or 0845 604 8810 for Wales.

Chapter 4

THE COURT OF APPEAL

APPEALING TO THE COURT OF APPEAL

4.1 If all did not go accordingly to plan in the EAT then the next rung on the appeal ladder is the Court of Appeal. The way to the Court of Appeal is blocked by the need to have permission to go there. Either the EAT can give that permission or the Court of Appeal. The permission stage is all important in the Court of Appeal. Obtaining it is far from easy, but once obtained your case's passage through to the final hearing of the appeal is at least eased by at least one Lord or Lady Justice of Appeal believing that your case has or had at least a realistic prospect of success or otherwise ought to be heard. The permission stage also keeps the respondents' costs to a minimum as they do not usually become involved at that stage.

4.2 Obtaining permission to appeal from the EAT has become very difficult as there are some practical problems in the way. Even if these can be overcome persuading a tribunal which has just dismissed your appeal that there is realistic prospect of the Court of Appeal disagreeing is not an easy task and one which is only usually successful where an important point of principle is at issue or where the EAT has just delivered a judgment patently at odds with other EAT judgments and the Court of Appeal needs to referee. Accordingly, for these reasons it can often be a lot easier and more productive to seek permission from the Court of Appeal rather than the EAT.

4.3 The Court of Appeal can only intervene if the EAT has made an error of law, which usually means that the Court of Appeal should focus upon whether the employment tribunal made an error of law at first instance, and it is in that way that the Court of Appeal usually looks at an appeal from the EAT.

4.4 Appealing to the Court of Appeal also marks the departure of an employment case from a 'no costs' (save in defined circumstances) jurisdiction to a largely 'looser pays' arena. Accordingly, unsuccessfully appealing or resisting an appeal can be very expensive and is not to be done lightly.

4.5 The Court of Appeal's procedure is somewhat complex and onerous. The following is as simplified a guide as can be managed to a Byzantine procedure.

OVERVIEW

4.6 As set out above the first stage is the permission stage. If the EAT refuse permission or if you did not seek it from the EAT then it must be sought from the Court of Appeal. There is no requirement to ask the EAT before asking the Court of Appeal and if the EAT gives permission then there is no need for the Court of Appeal to be troubled by a further permission application.

4.7 There was a big red herring when appealing from the EAT to the Court of Appeal which was that the 21-day time limit that usually applies for bringing an appeal before the Court of Appeal in most civil cases, did not apply when seeking permission to appeal from the Court of Appeal in an EAT case as the EAT had directed that such applications must be made to the Court of Appeal in 14 and not 21 days from the date of the EAT's sealed order. This red herring has now been caught and poached by the new 2008 EAT Practice Direction (coming into force on 22 May 2008) which replaces the 14-day time limit with the orthodox 21-day limit.

Therefore the position now is that if the EAT's sealed order is dated on or after 22 May 2008 then you have 21 days from the date of the sealed order to apply to the Court of Appeal, for permission to appeal to the Court of Appeal. If the date of the EAT's sealed order is before 22 May 2008 then the anomalous time limit of 14 days remains.

4.8 The other slightly smaller but just as misleading red herring is that notwithstanding that the decision being appealed to the Court of Appeal was decided on appeal to the EAT, and thus is 'a second appeal', the rules relating to 'second appeals' before the Court of Appeal **do not apply to appeals from the EAT.**

4.9 The application for permission to appeal is usually considered on the papers by a single Court of Appeal judge and if refused the appellant can seek an oral hearing. Once the permission stage is past then most of the subsequent work goes into the appeal bundles and listing. For the advocate the greatest attention must be paid to the skeleton arguments, which can be put before the court both at the permission and final appeal hearing stages. Busy appeal judges rely heavily on advocates highlighting the merits or problems with an appeal in the first few paragraphs of a skeleton and for all the oral dexterity and flair which can be deployed at oral hearing, cases are usually won or lost on the skeletons.

THE RIGHT OF APPEAL

4.10 The Court of Appeal is a creature of statute, created by s 2 of the Supreme Court Act 1981. It has a civil and a criminal division and appeals from the EAT are allocated to the civil division (s 3). The right of appeal from the EAT to the Court of Appeal is to be found in s 37 of THE ETA 1996 which is set out below. It is to be noted that the appeal does not have to be from a final judgment or order of the EAT but can be from '*any decision or order of the Appeal Tribunal*'.

37. Appeals from Appeal Tribunal

(1) Subject to subsection (3), an appeal on any question of law lies from any decision or order of the Appeal Tribunal to the relevant appeal court with the leave of the Appeal Tribunal or of the relevant appeal court.

(2) In subsection (1) the "relevant appeal court" means—

> (a) in the case of proceedings in England and Wales, the Court of Appeal, and
> (b) in the case of proceedings in Scotland, the Court of Session.

(3) No appeal lies from a decision of the Appeal Tribunal refusing leave for the institution or continuance of, or for the making of an application in, proceedings by a person who is the subject of a restriction of proceedings order made under section 33.

(4) This section is without prejudice to section 13 of the Administration of Justice Act 1960 (appeal in case of contempt of court).

Not a 'second appeal'

4.11 Section 55 of the Access to Justice Act 1999 introduced a higher hurdle for those who wished to appeal to the Court of Appeal in most civil cases where the appeal was a second appeal:

55. Second appeals

(1) Where an appeal is made to a county court or the High Court in relation to any matter, and on hearing the appeal the court makes a decision in relation to that matter, no appeal may be made to the Court of Appeal from that decision unless the Court of Appeal considers that—

> (a) the appeal would raise an important point of principle or practice, or
> (b) there is some other compelling reason for the Court of Appeal to hear it.

(2) This section does not apply in relation to an appeal in a criminal cause or matter.

4.12 As can be seen from the wording of s 55, however, this higher hurdle only applies where the appeal before the Court of Appeal relates to a decision which itself was heard on appeal in the High Court or county court but not where it was heard in the EAT and, accordingly, the 'higher hurdle' does not apply to an appeal from the EAT to the Court of Appeal. Equally s 55 requires permission to appeal from the Court of Appeal and not the court below; clearly this does not apply to employment appeals where the EAT can give permission to appeal.

Permission to appeal

4.13 Section 37 of ETA 1996 requires either the permission (referred to as leave in the Act but now referred to as permission to appeal) of the EAT or the Court of Appeal to be given before the Court of Appeal can hear an appeal from the EAT.

Obtaining permission to appeal from the Employment Appeal Tribunal

4.14 Once the EAT has given judgment or made its order then the parties can make an application for permission to appeal to the Court of Appeal. The basic rule is that permission to appeal should be sought orally immediately after judgment is given, whether or not judgment is reserved. There are two exceptions to this. First, you can ask the EAT if it would adjourn the hearing at which judgment has been given to allow the application to be made later, either at a further oral hearing or by way of a paper application. Second, if the judge or tribunal handing down the judgment is different than that which heard the case then the judge or tribunal handing down judgment can either determine the application for permission to appeal or can direct that it be considered by the judge or tribunal who heard the case either at a further oral hearing at a later date or on the papers; in that event the application should be made in writing, seven days after the reserved judgment hearing (EAT PD, para 21). If it is not a judgment which is being appealed but another decision or order then the application should be made at the hearing at which the order or decision is made.

4.15 It used to be the case, prior to the coming into force of the 2008 EAT Practice Direction, that if judgment was reserved then any party seeking permission to appeal had to give notice of their application for permission, pursuant to para 18.1 of the old EAT PD, to the EAT and to all other parties, 48 hours before the hearing. Where a draft judgment had been made available in advance then notice of the application for permission had to be accompanied with a draft appellant's notice. These rules are no longer in force as from 22 May 2008. Parties should, however, try and give notice to each other of such applications as a matter of courtesy but it seems that such notice is no longer required.

4.16 The EAT can, by order, vary this procedure. For example, the EAT could give a party extra time to make an application for permission to appeal or could allow a paper application as opposed to an oral application to be made.

4.17 Under the old Practice Direction parties struggled to give 48 hours notice of an application for permission to appeal because para 18.2 of the old Practice Direction stated that copies of the judgment to be handed down would not be available to the parties or their representatives until the morning of the handing down hearing. Clearly this prevented giving notice of an application of permission to appeal 48 hours before that hearing. This problem sometimes was solved by the parties asking the EAT to avail itself of its power (old para 18.2) to permit the judgment to be seen in draft earlier by the legal representatives. This, however, did not quite solve the problem as the terms upon which the draft was disclosed very often prevented representatives from showing it to their clients (compare this with the standard direction in the Court of Appeal which does usually permit clients to see the draft judgment – see para 15.15 PD to CPR Part 52). Accordingly, seeking instructions as to whether permission to appeal was to be sought in time to serve the 48 hours notice was often practically impossible.

4.18 The New Practice Direction, as has been mentioned above, has gone some way to dealing with this problem. There is no longer any need to give notice of an application for permission to appeal. There does remain however, the problem of only receiving the judgment on the morning of the hearing or if the EAT direct that it is to be seen earlier, it usually does not order that the representative's clients can be shown the judgment (the parties could make an application for their clients to see the draft in advance of the handing down hearing). In these situations where consideration of the transcript of the judgment or the taking of instructions from clients means that it is impracticable to make an application for permission to appeal at the handing down hearing, an application should be made at the handing down hearing to effectively adjourn that hearing to permit the application for permission to be made at a later date or by way of a paper application. This is permitted by para 21.1 of the new Practice Direction. A note of caution is to be sounded in relation to this latter course. The case of *Balmoral Group v Borealis (UK) Ltd*[1] is authority for the proposition that once judgment has been handed down and the handing down hearing is over, the opportunity to obtain the EAT's permission to appeal is lost and any application must then be made to the Court of Appeal, hence the importance of adjourning the handing down hearing to a later date, to keep that hearing alive, rather than asking the EAT to list a fresh hearing at some later date.

4.19 Another way around the above problem is to effectively ignore the EAT and make no application for permission, making an application to the Court of Appeal as set out below at para **4.23**.

4.20 As mentioned above, if at the handing down of a reserved judgment the tribunal is differently constituted from that which heard the appeal then the judge may either determine any application to permission to appeal or refer it to the tribunal which heard the appeal whether for a further hearing or for consideration of the matter on receipt of written submissions (para 18.3).

4.21 The EAT has provided no guidance on when it will grant permission to appeal. While s 55 of the Access to Justice Act 1999 does not apply as set out at para **4.11** above, the EAT is likely to grant permission to appeal where an important point of principle or practice is raised or where there is some other

---

[1] [2006] EWHC 2998, [2006] All ER (D) 135 (Aug).

compelling reason for permission to be given. As noted above, the EAT is most likely to grant permission where its decision is at odds with other judgments of the EAT on the same or similar issues and, accordingly, the Court of Appeal needs to adjudicate (see para **4.2** above). Or where the EAT had to decide a case in a particular way because of a Court of Appeal authority which the EAT thinks that the Court of Appeal or the House of Lords should look at again. Furthermore, the EAT should usually give permission to appeal to the Court of Appeal if they are being asked to make a declaration of incompatibility under HRA 1998 as the EAT has no power but the Court of Appeal has, to make such a declaration notwithstanding the presence of a High Court judge in the tribunal which heard the appeal (see para **7.3** below). Parties are required to explicitly set out the point of law in issue and the grounds of appeal when making their application to the EAT (EAT PD, para 21.2) and careful thought must given as to why a second appeal should be permitted. Regard should also be had to the Court of Appeal's own approach to its jurisdiction – see paras **4.40** and **4.45** below – which the EAT is likely to bear in mind.

4.22 The EAT has no power to give permission to appeal to the House of Lords.[2]

Obtaining permission to appeal from the Court of Appeal

Must permission be sought from the EAT first?

4.23 If permission is not obtained from the EAT then it must be obtained from the Court of Appeal. There is no rule that an application must be made to the EAT before one can be made to the Court of Appeal. CPR r 52.3(2) states that the application may be made either to the EAT or the Court of Appeal. In *Re T (a child: contact: alienation: permission to appeal)*[3] the Court of Appeal stated that permission to appeal **should** be sought from the lower court first, in this case, the EAT, because it saves costs and will be dealt with by the judge who decided the case.

4.24 On the other hand, in the EAT, the judge handing down judgment is very often not he who heard the case and where a reserved judgment is handed down and the parties have no reason to attend the handing down save for the application for permission to appeal, then it may well be the case that costs will be wasted in an oral application for permission to appeal which could be made in writing to the Court of Appeal. Furthermore, the party may not wish the Court of Appeal to have the 'benefit' of the EAT's reasons for refusing permission to appeal. Further as noted above (para **4.18**) it may be impossible to make the application to the EAT due to the parties not having seen the EAT's judgment in advance of the time when the application must be made.

4.25 Accordingly it may be more cost effective and tactically more advantageous to proceed directly to the Court of Appeal; on the other hand the

---

[2] *Botham v Ministry of Defence* UKEAT/0503/04 [2004] All ER (D) 210 (Nov).
[3] [2002] EWCA Civ 1736, [2003] 1 FLR 531.

litigant could miss an opportunity to persuade the EAT to give permission which the Court of Appeal may not have given; it is all a question of judgment.

Time limit for obtaining permission from the Court of Appeal

4.26 Using the power set out at CPR r 52.4(2)(a) the EAT has directed in para 21.1 of EAT PD that an application for permission must be made to the Court of Appeal **within 21 days of date of the EAT's sealed order**. As noted above, the 21-day period came into force on 22 May 2008, replacing a 14-day period. The EAT (a judge or the Registrar) may extend this period of time on application by the parties. Paragraph 21.1 of the new Practice Direction states that this discretion is likely to be exercised where a case is made out that there is a need to extend time until the transcript of the judgment is obtained. Otherwise the EAT is likely to direct that such an application be made to the Court of Appeal (see para **4.86** below).

How to make the application for permission to the Court of Appeal

4.27 Permission is sought in an appellant's notice (CPR r 52.4). The prescribed form is N161. This is the pleading, statement of case or originating document which commences the appeal to the Court of Appeal. It contains the grounds of appeal which must comprehensively set out the reasons why the EAT is said to have fallen into error of law.

4.28 Where the appellant is seeking to rely on any issue under HRA 1998 or is seeking a remedy under that Act then the appellant's notice must comply with paras 15.1 and 15.2 of the PD to CPR Part 16. Note that CPR r 19.4A will also apply.

4.29 When commencing an appeal in the Court of Appeal the following documents must be filed:

- the original appellant's notice and two copies and one copy for each respondent;

- plus one copy of the appellant's skeleton argument for every notice filed;

- a sealed copy of the EAT's order being appealed;

- an appeal bundle containing the following:
  – a sealed copy of the appellant's notice
  – a sealed copy of the EAT's order being appealed
  – a copy of the skeleton argument
  – the judgment of the EAT
  – the notice of appeal before the EAT
  – the judgment of the employment tribunal
  – the ET1 and the ET3

- if thought necessary – the skeleton arguments of both parties before the EAT and the tribunal, if any
- if any, other documents relevant to the appeal.

4.30 Obtaining the judgment of the EAT is not straightforward if judgment was not handed down in writing. See paras 18.3–18.6 of the EAT PD on the procedure for obtaining a written copy of the EAT's judgment.

4.31 The appeal bundle must be filed with a certificate from a solicitor, counsel or other representative, where the appellant is represented, which confirms that para 5.6A(2) of the PD to CPR Part 52 has been complied with. This paragraph states that all extraneous documents must be excluded from the appeal bundle and the certificate states that this has occurred.

4.32 Where some of the above items are unavailable, then the court should be informed as to when they will be filed (there is space for this in the appellant's notice).

4.33 All documents for filing at the Court of Appeal should be filed at the Civil Appeals Office Registry, Room E307, Royal Courts of Justice, Strand, London, EC2A 2LL. The appellant's notice can be filed by email – see para 15.1A of the PD to CPR Part 52.

4.34 All bundles in the Court of Appeal must strictly comply with para 15.4 of the PD to CPR Part 52. This guidance must be taken very seriously as non-compliance will incur judicial and civil service wrath. Paragraph 15.4(1) states that non-compliance may result in a 'special' (probably adverse) costs order and the bundles may also be rejected.

The appellant's skeleton argument

4.35 This, without doubt, is the most important document which the appellant will file with the court. It is to this document that the court will turn first when considering whether to grant permission to appeal. It must comply with para 5.10 of the PD to CPR Part 52 and failure to do so will incur the wrath of the court if not also an adverse costs order. Note particularly the injunction against citing more than one authority in support of a proposition without stating the justification for doing so.[4]

4.36 Prolixity is to be avoided, the judge reading the skeleton in the first instance is likely to have many cases before him and will not be impressed with irrelevant material. The document should use abbreviations like 'C' for claimant and 'R' for respondent. The appellant's best points should be put first and boldly to catch attention. The document is the argument upon which the

---

[4] See also *Practice Note* [2001] 2 All ER 510, sub nom *Practice Direction (citation of authorities)* [2001] 1 WLR 1001.

application will be based, whether or not an oral hearing takes place. The court will not be impressed with and may disallow oral argument that was not raised in the skeleton argument.

4.37 The skeleton should not only address the reasons why permission to appeal should be granted, although this should be its focus, it should also address the question of the appeal itself. It should, however, be borne in mind that if the case proceeds to a full appeal hearing the appellant can file a supplementary skeleton argument once the respondent has filed its skeleton;[5] and therefore, it will not necessarily be limited to the points raised in the initial skeleton.

4.38 The skeleton argument, as set out above, should be filed with the appellant's notice (provision is made for it to be contained within that form, although it can be and normally is provided separately) but can be filed up to 14 days afterwards.[6] An unrepresented party is not compelled to file a skeleton argument but is encouraged to do so.

Serving the respondent

4.39 The Court of Appeal does not serve documents; this must be arranged by the parties. The appellant, at this stage need only serve the respondent with the appellant's notice. This must be done as soon as practicable after filing and within 7 days at the latest, see CPR r 52.4(3). The rules of service set out at CPR Part 6 must be followed.

Grounds for granting permission to appeal

4.40 The court will grant permission where it considers that an appeal real prospects of success or where there is some other compelling reason why the appeal should be heard (CPR r 52.3(6)).

4.41 In *Cooke v Secretary of State for Social Security*[7] Hale LJ suggested that while s 55 of the Access to Justice Act 1999 did not apply (see para **4.11** above) to second appeals from specialist tribunals the standard grounds for granting permission to appeal should be applied with a '*robust attitude*' (at para 17). Hale LJ was hearing an appeal from the Social Security Appeal Tribunal. Hale LJ's justification for her gloss on the test was that social security law was not encountered by many lawyers in practice. It is respectfully submitted that the EAT is not to be considered to be a rarefied specialist tribunal and accordingly no such gloss should be applied to the standard test.

---

[5] See para 15.11A of the PD to CPR Part 52.
[6] See para 5.9 of the PD to CPR Part 52.
[7] [2001] EWCA Civ 734, [2002] All ER 279.

4.42 There is little guidance as to how the grounds should be applied save that in the case of *Tanfern Ltd v Cameron-MacDonald and Another (Practice Note)*[8] the court confirmed that 'real prospect of success' meant realistic as opposed to fanciful.

4.43 It is submitted that whereas Hale LJ's suggested gloss should not be applied the parties must consider that they have already had their case heard by at least a leading QC, circuit or High Court judge in the EAT and that some weight is going to be given to such a judgment by the court, which will not lightly grant permission to appeal.

4.44 The most important consideration is clearly the court's assessment of whether or not there is a real prospect that the court will find that the EAT has failed to spot an error of law made by the tribunal at first instance or has spotted an error of law which was not made by the tribunal at first instance. Or the court must be satisfied that there is some other reason that the appeal be heard, one such reason may be that the EAT's decision is at odds with other EAT decision and accordingly the Court of Appeal must intervene to provide consistency. Reference has to be had to the way in which the court deals with appeals from the EAT. In that regard see paras **4.119** to **4.127** below.

4.45 Where a case management decision of either the employment tribunal or the EAT is under appeal then the court, when deciding the issue of permission to appeal, will take into account whether the issue is of insufficient significance to justify the costs or the appeal, whether the procedural consequences of an appeal outweigh the significance of the decision under appeal or whether it would be more convenient to consider the issue after the final hearing of the tribunal or EAT has taken place (see paras 4.4–4.5 of the PD to CPR Part 52).

4.46 Particular considerations will also apply where the court is considering an application for permission to appeal a decision of the EAT made at a preliminary hearing or other interim hearing – see para **4.90** below.

The decision

4.47 The court has a wide discretion as to how it deals with applications for permission to appeal. It can first consider the application on the papers without an oral hearing (para 4.11 of the PD to CPR Part 52). This is the most usual route. It can, however, decide to hold an oral hearing to decide the issue. Furthermore, it can direct that the oral hearing for permission be listed immediately before the hearing of the full appeal (which of course, would not proceed, if the application for permission failed). All of these options are considered below.

---

[8] [2000] 1 WLR 1311.

The decision 'on the papers'

4.48 The papers will usually come before a single Lord or Lady Justice of Appeal, who will decide whether to grant permission to appeal based upon the appellant's notice, the skeleton argument and the appeal bundle.

4.49 The respondent will not usually have any role to play at this stage (para 4.22 of the PD to CPR Part 52). Exceptionally, the judge may request written submissions from the respondent. If this occurs the judge will probably direct them to be served on the appellant and may allow a right of reply. At this point, however, it will be open for the court to direct an oral hearing as this may be more appropriate. It should be noted that if the court requests the respondent's involvement at this stage, it can make an order in respect of the parties' costs (para 4.24(1)). If the respondent has no involvement then there is no order for costs and if permission is granted the costs of seeking it become costs in the appeal (para 4.23). As noted above, it is likely that it most cases and where the respondent has no involvement, the greatest attention will be paid to the appellant's skeleton argument.

Permission granted 'on the papers'

4.50 If permission is granted then the Lord or Lady Justice will record the fact in an order which will also state their reasons (para 4.12 of the PD to CPR Part 52). The matter will now proceed to a full appeal and the procedure set out in para **4.92** et seq applies.

Permission refused

4.51 If the single Lord or Lady Justice refuses permission to appeal on the papers then they can either decide that the application was totally without merit and that the decision is final (CPR r 52.3(4A)) or can permit the appellant to have the right to request an oral hearing to renew their application (r 52.3(4)). The order refusing permission will state whether the appellant has the right to request an oral hearing and will record the reasons for the order made (para 4.13 of the PD to CPR Part 52).

4.52 If the appellant is given this right, and wishes to request an oral hearing, then they must do so within seven days after service upon them of the notice stating that permission to appeal has been refused (see para 4.14). A copy of the request for an oral hearing must be served on the respondent.

The oral permission hearing

4.53 The oral permission hearing may be the first time the application has been considered or may be a renewal of the application which has been previously rejected 'on the papers'. In the later case it may be before the same single Lord or Lady Justice who made the decision to refuse permission on the papers or it may be before a different judge (para 4.13 of the PD to

CPR Part 52). It can be before more than one judge. Where the judge who made the decision on the papers expressed himself or herself forcefully against the appeal then the court may direct an oral hearing before a differently constituted court.

4.54 The usual position is that a respondent does not attend such a hearing (para 4.15). The court can require the respondent to attend (para 4.22) and the respondent can attend voluntarily. If the court does so require the respondent to attend then it will direct the appellant to serve a copy of the appeal bundle on the respondent, either within 7 days of the order or within such other period at the court will direct (para 4.16).

4.55 If the respondent does attend the hearing then it will not be allowed the costs of doing so unless the court requested the attendance and permission is refused (if permission is granted then the respondent can be ordered to pay the costs of the hearing if the application has been actively resisted) (paras 4.24 of the PD to CPR Part 52). As noted there is nothing to stop the respondent voluntarily attending the oral hearing to listen and take notes or to volunteer submission or assistance; however, the costs of doing so will be irrecoverable (para 4.23).

4.56 If the appellant is to be represented before the oral permission hearing then his or its advocate must 4 days before the hearing file at court and serve on the respondent a brief written statement setting out which points he intends to raise at the hearing, setting out why permission should be granted, notwithstanding the reasons for refusal on paper and confirming, where public funding is being used, that para 4.17 of the PD to CPR Part 52 has been complied with (this is unlikely to apply in employment cases) (see para 4.14).

4.57 The appellant can expect a short and punchy hearing. The judges will not wish to explore all areas of the case and will focus upon the reasons why permission should be granted in the brief written notice set out above. The judges will not hold back in testing the arguments attached, and the advocate must be ready to robustly defend any submissions made. These hearings can be very quick and unforgiving.

Permission granted

4.58 If permission is granted then the matter will proceed as set out at para **4.92** below.

Permission refused

4.59 If permission is refused after an oral hearing then the end of the line is reached.[9] Accordingly, upon refusal the appeal is brought to an end and no recourse can be had to the House of Lords. Recourse can be had to the ECtHR (see Chapter 7).

SETTING ASIDE PERMISSION TO APPEAL

4.60 CPR r 52.9 gives the Court of Appeal a power to set aside permission to appeal. This cannot and must not be used by a respondent to set aside permission to appeal with which it is unhappy. It has no right of appeal against the order granting permission. An application to set aside must only be made where there the permission has been obtained via an abuse of the process (eg, the court has been misled) or where a clear and unambiguous point of law has been overlooked, which would obviously mean that permission should not have been given, for example, where a statute or precedent has been overlooked. The power can also be used where a mistake has been made or where the court did not have power to grant permission. If the respondent was present at a permission hearing then it cannot make a subsequent application to set aside (CPR r 52.9(3)). The court will only set aside permission on compelling grounds (r 52.9(2)).

PERMISSION GIVEN BY EMPLOYMENT APPEAL TRIBUNAL

4.61 If the EAT gave permission to appeal, then there is no reason to additionally seek it from the Court of Appeal. An appellant who has obtained the EAT's permission should commence the appeal by filing and serving an appellant's notice and bundle as set out above at para **4.27** et seq above, but should include in addition the sealed order of the EAT granting permission and the notice, order or transcript giving its reasons for doing so. This should be filed as an accompaniment to the appellant's notice and appear in the appeal bundle. The procedure set out at para **4.92** below should then be followed.

4.62 The time limit for filing the appellant's notice after obtaining permission to appeal from the EAT is regrettably unclear. The default position is 21 days after the date of the decision (date of it being made not sealed) of the EAT being appealed (CPR r 52.4(2)(b)). However, the EAT is free to make its own direction as to when the notice is to be filed (CPR r 52.4(2)(a)). **Accordingly, it is submitted that a direction pursuant to CPR r 52.4(2)(a) should be sought from the EAT in every case in which it grants permission to appeal and the notice should be filed in accordance with that direction.**

---

[9] See s 54(6) of the Supreme Court Act 1981 and s 54(4) of the Access to Justice Act 1999.

LIMITED PERMISSION

4.63 Both the EAT and the Court of Appeal do not have to grant permission to appeal in respect of the all the grounds of the appeal raised by the appellant. They can choose to limit the permission to certain grounds alone.

If the Employment Appeal Tribunal grants limited permission to appeal

4.64 If the EAT does this and the appellant wishes to renew his application in respect of the rejected grounds before the Court of Appeal then he is open to do so, and in respect of those grounds he should follow the procedure set out above for obtaining permission to appeal from the Court of Appeal, while also filing and serving his appellant's notice and appeal bundle making clear that he already has limited permission to appeal from the EAT and supplying the relevant order as set out above at para **4.61** (note that the 21-day time limit will apply for filing this appellant's notice as it relates to permission which has been refused by the EAT).

4.65 If the Court of Appeal grants permission on some or all of the additional grounds rejected by the EAT then the EAT and Court of Appeal 'grounds' will be considered together before the Court of Appeal.

4.66 If the Court of Appeal rejects the additional grounds sought, after an oral permission hearing, then they cannot be raised before the court at the full appeal.

If the Court of Appeal grants limited permission

4.67 If the Court of Appeal exercises its power under CPR r 52.3(7)(a) to limit the grounds of appeal when considering the application on the papers then the appellant may renew the application in respect of the additional grounds at an oral hearing (if not certified totally without merit) as set out at para **4.53** above. If that application at the oral hearing fails then the grounds cannot be raised subsequently.

4.68 If there was no oral hearing of the permission application and the court granted limited permission to appeal 'on the papers' then at the final hearing of the appeal the court can permit the appellant to argue the additional grounds (see *James v Baily Gibson & Co (a firm)*).[10]

4.69 The above is a little curious as you appear to be in a better position at the final hearing if you don't request an oral hearing where limited permission is given on the papers, than if you do.

---

[10] [2002] EWCA Civ 1690, [2002] All ER (D) 454 (Oct).

CONDITIONAL PERMISSION

4.70 The Court of Appeal can by, CPR r 52.3(7)(b) order that permission to appeal be subject to conditions. It is doubtful whether the EAT has this power and a respondent seeking conditions should urge the EAT to reject any application for permission to enable it to be made to the Court of Appeal. The conditions to be attached are not limited in any way. They will usually, however, relate to costs. In EAT appeals there will rarely have been any costs orders below and the infrequency of costs orders before the tribunals will probably make the court wary about requiring security for costs from impecunious appellants, as access to justice could be stifled.

4.71 On the other hand, the court has made orders against large commercial organisations seeking to bring an appeal against impecunious respondents. In *Lloyd Jones v T Mobile (UK) Ltd*,[11] the Court of Appeal made a conditional permission to appeal order in circumstances in which a big corporation was seeking to appeal a decision obtained by two individual claimants acting in person which would have a far wider effect across all their business. It was reported that T Mobile's solicitors has already spent £50,000 preparing the appeal. The court granted permission to T Mobile on condition that it would not be entitled to its costs if successful, to prevent the appeal effectively putting the respondents under unbearable pressure to concede the appeal.

4.72 In the employment law context rich employers regularly appeal EAT decisions obtained by impecunious employees because the decision will have a wider effect across its organisation. In these circumstances employee-respondents may wish to consider applying for conditions to be attached to any permission to appeal which is granted by the Court of Appeal.

4.73 The respondent needs to be careful about when he seeks conditions. If the respondent attends an oral permission hearing and does not seeks conditions he will be unable to do so at a later date (CPR r 52.9(3)).

4.74 Conditions may be varied under r 52.9(1)(c) where there are compelling reasons for doing so.

CROSS-APPEALS OR 'SEEKING TO UPHOLD THE EAT DECISION ON DIFFERENT OR ADDITIONAL GROUNDS'

4.75 If a respondent, on receipt of the appellant's notice wishes to cross-appeal, that is, make its own appeal against the EAT's decision. Or, if the respondent wishes to submit that while he is happy with the result of the EAT's decision, the EAT should have decided the matter on different or additional grounds. Then that respondent must file and serve a respondent's notice

---

[11] [2003] EWCA Civ 1162, [2003] EGLR 55.

(CPR r 52.5). A respondent who is happy with both the result of the EAT's decision and its reasoning need not file and serve a respondent's notice.

4.76 The respondent's notice should be filed within 14 days of one of the following dates, whichever is applicable (or by such date as the EAT directs):

- Where the appellant has the EAT's permission to appeal, the date of service of the appellant's notice.

- Where the appellant has the Court of Appeal's permission to appeal, the date of service of notification that the permission has been granted.

- Where the court has decided to hear the permission application and the full appeal together then it is the date of service of the notification that this is to take place.

See CPR r 52.5(4) and (5).

4.77 This effectively means that if the EAT grants permission to appeal, the respondent will then have 14 days from service of the appellant's notice to decide whether to file and serve a respondent's notice. Whereas if the Court of Appeal is being asked to give permission to appeal to the appellant, the respondent can wait until 14 days after being informed that that permission has been granted.

4.78 The respondent's notice must be accompanied with the following:

- two additional copies of the notice;

- one copy for each appellant and any other respondent;

- a supplemental bundle of documents if the respondent believes that the appeal bundle does not contain all the relevant documents and he cannot agree an amendment of it with the appellant;

- a skeleton argument.

See para 7.10 of the PD to CPR Part 52.

4.79 The notice and accompaniments must be served on the appellant and any other respondent as soon as practicable or in any event not less than 7 days of filing. It is to be recalled that the court does not serve documents and that CPR Part 6 applies (r 52.5(6)).

4.80 The respondent's skeleton argument must conform with the same rules as the appellant's (see paras **4.35** to **4.38** above) and must be filed and served with the respondent's notice as set out above or separately within 14 days of the filing of the notice. The skeleton must answer the arguments set out in the appellant's skeleton (para 7.8 of the PD to CPR Part 52).

4.81 In respect of a cross-appeal, where permission from the court is sought, the respondent will be treated like an appellant seeking permission to appeal and the same procedure as is set out above for appellants will be followed. Accordingly, if the EAT granted the appellant permission, and the respondent did not obtain permission for a cross-appeal from the EAT, then the respondent will make an application to the Court of Appeal which will be considered as set out above. If the appellant obtains permission from the Court of Appeal, then before the cross-appeal can be heard with the appellant's appeal the permission to appeal procedure will have to be gone through by the respondent.

ALL RESPONDENT'S MUST GIVE NOTICE

4.82 In every appeal the respondent must inform the Civil Appeals Office whether he intends to file a respondent's notice or whether he seeks merely to rely on the reasons given by the lower court, within 21 days of notification being given that the appellant has obtained permission to appeal (whether from the EAT or the Court of Appeal) or within 21 days of being notified that the appeal and permission to appeal application are going to be heard together. This requirement is in addition to the requirement to file and serve a respondent's notice.

APPEALING OUT OF TIME – EXTENDING TIME FOR FILING AND SERVING APPELLANT'S OR RESPONDENT'S NOTICE

4.83 As set out at paras **4.26** and **4.62** above the appellant has 21 days or such other period as the EAT directs to file his appellant's notice. This period can be extended by the EAT (see paras **4.26** and **4.62** above) but only while the EAT is still seized of the case. Once the EAT is no longer seized of the case then an application to extend time must be made to the Court of Appeal. If the application is being made after the expiry of the time period then it should be included in the appellant's notice. The notice should state the reason for the delay and the steps taken prior to the application being made (see para 5.2 of the PD to CPR Part 52). If the application is being made before the expiry of the time period then it should be made in accordance with para **4.86** below.

4.84 If the EAT gave permission to appeal but the appellant's notice was not filed in time at the Court of Appeal then the respondent has the right to be heard upon the application to extend time for filing. He must be served with a copy of the appeal bundle. If the respondent resists the application then costs are in issue although a respondent whose resistance is judged unreasonable may end up paying the appellant's costs (para 5.3).

4.85 If the respondent needs such an extension of time he too should seek it in his respondent's notice – see paras 7.4 and 7.5 of the PD to CPR Part 52. Curiously, if the respondent has the EAT's permission the rules do not make any express provision for the appellant to fight any application for an extension in the same as set out in the last preceding paragraph. If an appellant wishes to resist such an application they should make written representations to the court for an oral hearing which they can attend.

4.86 An application can be made to the Court of Appeal to extend time before it has expired. This should be done pursuant to CPR r 52.6 and be by way of an application complying with Part 23. The applicant will need to show good grounds for such an application and will also, if no previous application to extent time has been made to the EAT, have to address the issue of why an application to extend time was not made to the EAT.

4.87 Where the application is being made after time has expired then it is treated as an application for relief from sanctions and CPR r 3.9 applies. If the application is made prior to the time expiring then r 3.9 does not apply. Time limits cannot be extended by consent.

4.88 All of the circumstances listed at r 3.9 must be considered in turn and none should be omitted from consideration – see *Bansal v Cheema*.[12] The court should also all other circumstances of each case. As to (f), below, see *Training in Compliance Ltd v Drewse*[13] and *Welsh v Parnianzadeh*:[14]

3.9

(1) On an application for relief from any sanction imposed for a failure to comply with any rule, practice direction or court order the court will consider all the circumstances including–

- (a) the interests of the administration of justice;
- (b) whether the application for relief has been made promptly;
- (c) whether the failure to comply was intentional;
- (d) whether there is a good explanation for the failure;
- (e) the extent to which the party in default has complied with other rules, practice directions, court orders and any relevant preaction protocol (GL);
- (f) whether the failure to comply was caused by the party or his legal representative;
- (g) whether the trial date or the likely trial date can still be met if relief is granted;
- (h) the effect which the failure to comply had on each party; and
- (i) the effect which the granting of relief would have on each party.

---

[12] [2001] CP Rep 6.
[13] [2001] CP Rep 46, at para 66.
[14] [2004] EWCA Civ 1832, [2004] All ER (D) 170 (Dec).

(2) An application for relief must be supported by evidence.

Hearing permission applications and appeals together

4.89 There is nothing to stop and the court does commonly list oral applications for permission to appeal together with the full appeal hearing which is to go ahead in the event that permission is granted. This is usually done where after considering the application for permission on the paper, the court comes to the conclusion that permission is likely to be given and, accordingly, it is expedient for the appeal to be held immediately after the permission hearing. If this is done then the hearing is to be treated as if it were a listing for a full appeal hearing and the procedure set out below at para **4.92** et seq is to be followed.

WHERE THE APPEAL IS FROM A PRELIMINARY HEARING OR INTERIM HEARING OF THE EMPLOYMENT APPEAL TRIBUNAL

4.90 When an appeal is effectively complaining that the EAT rejected certain or all of the grounds of appeal which the appellant tried to argue before the EAT without the EAT hearing full argument upon them and effectively the Court of Appeal in granting permission to appeal has expressed the view that the EAT was wrong to reject such grounds of appeal, then respondents should consider whether or not to concede the appeal to allow the matter to be remitted back to the EAT for the rejected grounds of appeal to be considered. The Court of Appeal when giving permission to appeal may invite the respondent to so present a consent order. This effectively would avoid the wasting of costs in holding a full appeal hearing merely for the purposes of remitting the case back to the EAT. Once the consent order has been made by the court the parties should contact the EAT to have the matter re-listed or seek directions from the president.

4.91 The limits to when the Court of Appeal will remit back to the EAT are set out below at para **4.130** and the procedure for dealing with an appeal by consent is set out at para **4.139** et seq below.

PREPARATION FOR THE FULL HEARING OF THE APPEAL

Step 1 – serve the appeal bundle

4.92 If the respondent has not yet had the appeal bundle (ie did not participate at the permission stage), then it must be served upon him within 7 days of the order giving permission to appeal (para 6.2 of the PD to CPR Part 52). Regardless of whether or not the bundle has to be served at this stage the following items must be added to the bundle at this point (para 6.3A):

- The respondent's notice and skeleton argument if any.

- Transcripts of evidence relevant to the appeal.

- The order granting permission to appeal, and if given at an oral hearing the judgment of the court.

- Any document which the appellant and respondent have agreed to add.

4.93 If the appeal bundle has already been served then it should be updated within the same 7-day period with the above items. Paragraph 15.4(10) of the PD to CPR Part 52 should be complied with.

Step 2 – serve a supplemental bundle

4.94 If the respondent has not yet agreed an amendment of the appeal bundle with the appellant (see para **4.78** above) and has not served a supplemental bundle then he must either agree such an amendment of the appeal bundle, if necessary, or file and serve a Supplemental Bundle within 21 days of service of the appeal bundle (see para 7.12 of the PD to CPR Part 52). The parties must co-operate in putting together the bundles and if it is the most practical thing to do, they should, in a complex case put together bundles which do not comply with the Practice Direction. If this course is going to be taken they should apply to the Court for directions by consent.[15]

Step 3 – a core bundle?

4.95 If the appeal bundle goes over 500 pages (exclusive of transcripts of evidence) then the appellant's solicitors should consult with those of the respondent and prepare and file at court (in addition to the appeal bundles) copies of a core bundle. The core bundle should contain those documents considered to be central to the appeal and must not exceed 150 pages. Paragraph 15.4 of the PD to CPR Part 52 will apply to the core bundle. The core bundle must be filed within 28 days of the order giving permission to appeal or where the EAT gave permission, within 28 days of the service of the appellant's notice upon the respondent (see paras 15.2 to 15.3).

Step 4 – the appeal questionnaire

4.96 The Court of Appeal will notify the parties of the date by which the appeal will be heard and at the same time will send a questionnaire which will include questions about time estimates, which parts of any transcript of evidence the court should read and the availability of the appeal bundles for use of the court (paras 6.4 and 6.5 of the PD to CPR Part 52).

---

[15] See *Leofelis SA v Lonsdale Sports Ltd* (2008) *The Times*, July 23.

4.97 The time estimate is all important as the court will strictly adhere to it. It must be given by the advocate who will attend the appeal. It should exclude time for giving judgment.

4.98 The appeal questionnaire must be filed and served on the respondents who have seven days of receipt to object to the time estimate.

Step 5 – listing

4.99 The Civil Appeals Office will use the information in the appeals questionnaire to place the case into one of the lists. There is a general appeals list in which cases are placed after permission to appeal has been granted and are called on for hearing in turn. There is an expedited list, which as the name suggests contains cases where the court has ordered expedition. The case of *Unilever v Chefaro Proprietaries Ltd and Others Practice Note*[16] sets out the test which the court will apply when considering whether to order expedition. Those seeking expedition should seek it in their notice or subsequently in an application to the court complying with CPR Part 23. The stand out list contains those appeals which a judge has ordered are not ready to proceed. The special fixtures list contains those cases which need special arrangements, such as where a group of appeals is being heard together. The second fixtures list contains cases which are double booked with others, and will be listed at short notice if a gap occurs. And finally the short-warned list contains cases which the court has determined can be prepared for by the advocate (this does not assume that the advocate is the one who was originally instructed) with half a day's notice and the cases are called on with that notice (see paras 15.7–15.9A of the PD to CPR Part 52).

4.100 The legal representatives or litigant should keep in close contact with the listing officer who will allocate a date of hearing as soon as possible.

Step 6 – date of hearing notified

Step 7 – file and serve appellant's supplementary skeleton argument

4.101 It is to be recalled that the appellant will have filed and served his skeleton argument either with his appellant's notice or within 14 days of that filing and, accordingly, much water may have passed under the bridge since that date including possibly the institution of a cross-appeal. Accordingly, the appellant is entitled to file and serve a supplementary skeleton within 14 days of the hearing date (para 15.11A(1) of the PD to CPR Part 52).

---

[16] [1995] 1 WLR 243.

Step 8 – file and serve respondent's skeleton argument or supplementary skeleton argument

4.102 This is the only substantive step which a respondent need take if they wish to address the court at the final appeal hearing. Before now a respondent has been able to stay away from the permission hearing, refrain from filing any documents and has merely been required to inform the Civil Appeals Office as to whether or not he intends to file a respondent's notice (see para **4.82** above). If the respondent wishes to oppose the appeal on the basis of supporting the EAT's reasoning then he must file and serve a skeleton argument at this point, within seven days of the hearing (para 7.7 of the PD to CPR Part 52). Failure to serve a skeleton will probably render the respondent silent if he attends the hearing! The skeleton argument must comply with the rules set out at para **4.35** et seq above and must answer the appellant's arguments.

4.103 If the respondent has already filed and served a skeleton with a respondent's notice then the respondent can file and serve an supplementary skeleton argument 7 days before the hearing (para 15.11A(2) of the PD to CPR Part 52).

4.104 Both the appellant and respondent may be prevented from arguing a point before the court which is not raised in a skeleton argument (para 15.11A(4)).

Step 9 – bundles of authorities

4.105 The appellant's advocate must in consultation with his opponent(s) file a bundle of authorities upon which they wish to rely at the hearing, which should not include authorities for propositions not in dispute and not contain more than 10 authorities unless the scale of the appeal warrants more extensive citation. The relevant passages should be marked if attention has not be drawn to specific passages in the skeleton arguments.

4.106 The bundle must be filed at least seven days prior to the hearing or where notice of the hearing is less than seven days, it must be filed 'immediately'.

4.107 The bundle must carry a certificate from the advocates responsible for arguing the case stating that the above requirements have been complied with.

4.108 See para 15.11 of the PD to CPR Part 52.

Step 10 – final filing of documents

4.109 The parties must ensure that all documents necessary for the appeal are filed within 7 days of the hearing.

4.110 Failure to comply with this rule can result in a hearing before the presiding Lord Justice to show cause as to why the appeal should proceed.

4.111 It is worth considering putting together agreed chronologies, dramatis personae, reading lists etc to assist the court. These documents of assistance can be filed and served at any time. The court may direct that these are filed and served, especially in the case of a reading list in a complex appeal.

4.112 See para 15.11B of the PD to CPR Part 52.

Step 11 – final bundle of authorities

4.113 To take account of any last minute thoughts of the advocates the court will accept a second bundle of agreed bundle of authorities which the appellant's advocate must file within 48 hours of the commencement of the appeal (see para 15.11(5) of the PD to CPR Part 52).

Step 12 – If the appeal is listed for one day or less – serve a costs schedule in accordance with para 14.1(5) and 14.2 of the PD to CPR Part 52 and see para 4.145 below – 24 hours before the hearing

Miscellaneous case management powers of the Court of Appeal

Varying time limits, stays, strike outs and civil restraint orders

4.114 The court has all the many case management powers set out at CPR Part 3. The court can hold hearings to give directions in complex appeals. It can vary the time limits applicable, including the time limit for filing the appellant's notice (see para **4.83** et seq above), the parties may not agree any such variation. If a party is in breach of a time limit or other requirement the court can give relief from sanctions under CPR r 3.9 (see para **4.88** above). As appeals do no stay the effect of the order below, a party must apply for a stay to either the EAT or the Court of Appeal. Stays will be granted where a successful appellant may be unable to reclaim monies paid under a judgment to the respondent. Equally, a stay will not be granted if the respondent, if successful will loose the ability to enforce a good judgment.[17] The court can also strike out a notice usually as a sanction for non-compliance with orders or for abuse of the process. If the court thinks that an appeal is totally without merit then it should certify so and should consider whether to make a civil restrain order (CPR r 3.11).

---

[17] See *Hammond Suddards Solicitors v Agrichem International Holdings Ltd* [2002] EWCA Civ 2065, [2001] All ER (D) 258 (Dec).

Amendment of appellant's or respondent's notices

4.115 If a party wishes to amend their appellant's or respondent's notice to add or delete a ground of appeal or make another change then they should make an application to the court for permission (CPR r 52.8). The application should be made in accordance with CPR Parts 17 and 23 and the application notice should include a copy of the notice with the proposed amendments. The application will normally be heard at the hearing of the full appeal unless this would cause unnecessary expense or delay and in these circumstances the parties separately or together may request that the application be heard earlier (see para 5.25 of the PD to CPR Part 52).

Security for costs

4.116 An application for security for costs can be made either in the appellant's or respondent's notices or separately in compliance with CPR Parts 23 and 25.

Master and Deputy Masters of the Court of Appeal

4.117 These officers can make case management orders including the dismissal of any appeal where a breach of the procedural rules or practice direction has occurred, including the breach of an order of the court (CPR r 52.16). Any decision made by such an officer may be reconsidered by a single appeal judge or by a full court if a party requests within seven days of service of notice of the officer's decision. If a single judge considers the matter on the papers then an oral hearing may be held to re-consider the matter. Where a hearing takes place or none is requested then no further re-hearing or appeal will take place and the end of the road is reached as if an appeal ends as a result of an order of such an officer or a single judge, and that order does not involve the determination of an appeal or an application for permission to appeal and which can be or has been reviewed by the court as set out above, then no appeal from such an order can be made to the House of Lords – see s 58(2) of the Supreme Court Act 1981.[18]

4.118 Take careful note of the above as if you do not abide by the procedural rules or directions or orders of the Court of Appeal then your case could be struck out or dismissed and the next stop has to be the ECtHR!

THE HEARING OF THE APPEAL

The test

4.119 The Court of Appeal can only set aside a decision of the EAT if it is satisfied that the decision was wrong or unjust because of a serious procedural or other irregularity (CPR r 52.11(3)).

---

[18] See *Paragon Finance plc v Noueiri* [2001] EWCA Civ 1402, [2001] 1 WLR 2357.

4.120 The scope of this test is more or less limitless and no gloss is placed on the test of 'wrong' or 'unjust'.

The nature of the appeal

4.121 Before Buxton LJ threw doubt on the matter in the cases of *Gover v Propertycare Ltd*[19] and *Balfour Beatty Power Networks v Wilcox*,[20] it was always thought that the Court of Appeal was not conducting a review of the EAT's decision to see if there was an error of law, but was conducting a review of the employment tribunal's decision to see if there was an error of law. The received wisdom was that if the employment tribunal got the decision correct then the Court of Appeal should uphold the decision regardless of the EAT's response in between. Accordingly, appeals to the Court of Appeal usually focus upon the tribunal's and not the EAT's decision.

4.122 Buxton LJ's rationale is that the Court of Appeal's power to hear an appeal from the EAT is set out in s 37 of ETA 1996 (set out in para **4.10** above) and that power only permits an appeal from an error of law made by the EAT and not the employment tribunal.

4.123 It seems to the authors of this work that the answer lies between these two positions. An appeal to the EAT is based upon an error of law by the employment tribunal. Accordingly, if the EAT fail to recognise an error of law made by the tribunal or wrongly characterise a decision of the employment tribunal as an error of law, then the EAT has failed to exercise its jurisdiction properly and itself has made an error of law. Accordingly it is a useful shorthand in coming to a decision as to whether the EAT has made an error of law to look at the employment tribunal's decision and decide whether it made an error of law.

4.124 This methodology should not be taken to the extreme that the EAT's judgment should just be ignored. The EAT could easily make an error of judgment, of approach or of procedure which could amount to an error of law which had nothing to do with the employment tribunal's decision. Accordingly both the employment tribunal's and EAT's errors of law are relevant.

No oral evidence or re-hearing

4.125 It is hard to conceive of an occasion when the Court of Appeal would hold a re-hearing and/or hear oral evidence on an appeal from the EAT as in such circumstances, such as the admission of new evidence, the court is likely to remit the case back to the employment tribunal to hear the evidence (CPR r 52.11).

---

[19] [2006] EWCA Civ 286, [2006] ICR 1073.
[20] [2006] EWCA Civ 1240, [2007] IRLR 63.

Trying to introduce new evidence

4.126 As to an attempt to introduce new evidence before the Court of Appeal, the *Ladd v Marshall*[21] test will apply being the need to demonstrate:

(1) that the evidence could not have been obtained with reasonable diligence for use before the employment tribunal;

(2) the new evidence must be such that, if given, it would probably have had an important influence on the result of the case (though it need not be decisive); and

(3) the evidence must be credible although it need not be incontrovertible.

New argument

4.127 The Court of Appeal will not usually entertain any argument which has not been argued in the EAT. It has a discretion to allow such argument as set out in the case of *Wilson v Liverpool Corporation*,[22] in which it was said that the court will not permit new arguments unless the court is in possession of all the material necessary to enable it to dispose of the matter finally without injustice to the other party and without recourse to a further hearing. May LJ sounded a more discouraging note in *Jones v MBNA International Bank*,[23] but these are obiter remarks. If a new argument is going to be put forward it must be denoted as such in the skeleton arguments.

POWERS OF THE COURT OF APPEAL

4.128 By CPR r 52.10 the Court of Appeal has all the powers of the EAT which itself has all the powers of the employment tribunal (see para **3.17** above), and hence the Court of Appeal is vested with all the powers of an employment tribunal. The court will usually either uphold the EAT or restore the order of the employment tribunal. It may substitute the tribunal's order with one of its own or may remit the case back the tribunal.

Remitting back to the employment tribunal

4.129 Where the Court of Appeal has identified an error of law with the way in which the employment tribunal dealt with the case and which requires the tribunal to apply the law in a different way to the findings of fact or indeed for new findings of fact to be made the court usually remits the case back to the tribunal for a re-hearing.

---

[21] [1954] 3 All ER 745.
[22] [1971] 1 WLR 302.
[23] (unreported) 30 June 2000.

Remitting back to the EAT

4.130 The court will very rarely remit the case back the EAT. It has only ever done so in the following circumstances:

(1) Where the EAT wrongly found that it had no jurisdiction.[24]

(2) Where the EAT at preliminary hearing ordered that the appeal before it could only proceed on three of five grounds of appeal and that decision was appealed the Court of Appeal remitted the case back to be argued before the EAT on all five grounds of appeal.[25]

(3) Where at a preliminary hearing the EAT had found that the appeal was totally unarguable the Court of Appeal remitted the case back to the EAT for it to hear the appeal based on grounds of appeal which had not been before it.[26]

4.131 Where however, the EAT has decided that all the grounds of appeal before it could not go beyond a preliminary hearing, but the Court of Appeal decides to give permission to appeal on all those same grounds, it should not remit the matter back to the EAT but proceed to hear the appeal in the usual way.[27]

What will the final hearing be like?

4.132 The final hearing will usually be heard by two or three Lord or Lady Justices of Appeal or High Court judges sitting as judges of the Court of Appeal. There is no guarantee of any of the judges having any employment experience and background (equally former presidents of the EAT or High Court judges who have sat in the EAT may be members of the court, Mummery LJ (formerly Mummery P of the EAT) regularly presides over employment appeals). Neither will they have a copy of anything other than the White Book to hand. Extracts from things like *Butterworths Employment Law Handbook*[28] will have to be provided. Enquiries should be made with the presiding judge's clerk in cases of doubt. The court will be presided over or chaired by one of the members of the court (usually the most senior), who will take the lead on how the court deal with the case. That said, the members of the court are all equal, having the same voting power in the result and will exercise the powers to question advocates equally robustly (a majority vote decides the appeal – if a two-judge court divides then the matter can be re-heard by a court with an odd number). The judges will usually have done some pre-reading and there is often no need for the case to be opened. Advocates should caution against reading out drafted texts; the judges will set

---

[24] *Grady v Prison Service* [2003] EWCA Civ 527, [2003] All ER 745.
[25] *Vincent v MJ Gallagher Contractors Ltd* [2003] EWCA Civ 640, [2003] ICR 1244.
[26] *Sukul-Lennard v Croydon Primary Healthcare Trust* [2003] All ER (D) 369 (Jul).
[27] *Lambe v 186K Ltd* [2004] EWCA Civ 1045, [2005] ICR 307.
[28] LexisNexis, 16th edn (2008).

the agenda of the hearing and will invite submissions on matters they think are important and in the order that they see fit. They will usually allow the advocate an opportunity at the end to cover any points not raised which he wishes to address. One way of dealing with this often disconcerting experience is to write down all of the points one wishes to address and to tick them off as they are dealt with so that the advocate can ensure that all have been covered. Some advocates use cards which they take from one pile to another to record the point having being covered.

4.133 The appellant will go first, followed by the respondent, followed by the appellant, with a right of reply limited to the matters raised by the respondent. This order may be changed at the direction of the court and it often invites advocates to address them on particular topics one by one rather than hearing the whole of the appeal together. If the court is against the appellant it may not call upon the respondent to make any submissions at all.

4.134 Once the submissions have been heard the court will indicate whether it will give judgment extemporaneously or whether it will be reserved and handed down on another day. Reserved judgments are now very common and in many employment cases, the norm.

4.135 Once judgment has been given, whether reserved or otherwise, the court will ask for the parties' assistance and submissions on the proper form of the order, which can be agreed by the parties and will decide the issue of costs and whether leave should be granted to appeal to the House of Lords.

The reserved judgment

4.136 Where the presiding Lord or Lady Justice is satisfied that no special degree of confidentiality or sensitivity will attach to the result of the appeal the court will make available the draft judgment to the parties' legal advisers by 4 pm on the second working day before the judgment is due to be pronounced (or by some other interval as may be directed by the court). The judgment can be shown to the parties for the purposes of obtaining instructions only and not for any other purpose and is not to be disclosed to any other person (paras 15.12 and 15.13 of the PD to CPR Part 52).

4.137 Any formal or typographical amendments should be notified by the advocates to the clerk to the judge who prepared the judgment (now usually sent by email to the advocate or their clerk with instructions on how to reply) usually by 12 noon on the working day before the judgment is due to be handed down. This is not the time for making new submissions. There, remains, however, power for the court to change its judgment right up to the time of sealing of the order of the court. Accordingly, if an advocate thinks that there is a glaring problem with the judgment he should notify the court and his opponent and the court can invite further submissions and argument if necessary. This, however, will be rare and advocates should refrain from raising substantive points at this stage unless absolutely necessary.[29]

4.138 The case is then listed and the judgment is pronounced and handed down on the appointed day (para 15.14 of the PD to CPR Part 52). It is rarely read out. If it may attract public attention a press statement may be released by the court to explain the judgment if the only matter between the parties consequent upon the judgment is whether the court should grant leave to appeal to the House of Lords then the parties need not attend. Instead by 12 noon on the working day before judgment is to be handed down the parties must fax to the clerk to the presiding Lord Justice and file at the Civil Appeal Office, four copies of the draft agreed order and written submissions on the application for leave to appeal. If the parties cannot agree the order or costs then they should inform the court and attend the oral hearing (paras 15.15 and 15.16 and 19–21 of the PD to CPR Part 52).

Appeals by consent

Dismissal by consent

4.139 Where the appellant seeks for the appeal to be dismissed because it is abandoned or otherwise and it is prepared to pay the respondent's costs then he should file and serve a request for such an order with the court, which will be usually granted. Where the appellant does not wish to pay the respondent's costs then the request must be consented to by the respondent (paras 12.2 and 12.3 of the PD to CPR Part 52). Where a settlement has been reached between the parties which does not require the varying or setting aside of the EAT's order then a joint request to the court should be made that the appeal be dismissed by consent (paras 12.4 and 13.1).

Allowing the appeal by consent

4.140 The court will not normally allow an appeal by consent unless satisfied that the EAT's decision was wrong. Where the parties can show 'good and significant reasons for doing so' the court may accede to a request which carries the consent of all parties, to set aside or vary the order, the EAT without determining the merits of the appeal. The request will usually be dealt with on the papers. The application must set out the relevant history of the proceedings and the matters relied on in justification for the request together with a draft order. See para **4.90** above for a good example of when this procedure may be used.

---

[29] *Robinson v Fernsby* [2003] EWCA Civ 1820, 148 Sol Jo LB 59. See para 15.18 of the PD to CPR Part 52.

Patients and children

4.141 In the unlikely event of a patient or child appealing from the EAT the procedure for appeals by consent is at paras 13.2–13.5 of the PD to CPR Part 52.

Appeals totally without merit

4.142 Where the appeal is certified by the Court of Appeal to be totally without merit then the court must record its certificate on the face of the order and should consider whether it is appropriate to make a civil restraint order to prohibit further appeals or applications (CPR r 3.11).

Costs

Generally

4.143 The Court of Appeal has a free hand when it comes to costs. Unlike employment tribunals and the EAT it does not have a fettered discretion. Costs following the event are the norm and hence the loosing party can expect to be ordered to pay its own and the other side's costs. The court can also make orders in respect of any orders for the payment of costs made by the EAT or the employment tribunal.

Costs orders

4.144 The court can exercise its very wide discretion to reduce the amount of costs awarded to a successful party based upon the extent of its success. So if an appellant only succeeds on some of its grounds it may only be awarded a concomitant proportion of its costs. Further, if the successful party has misconducted himself then he cannot expect to receive a full costs order. The court will have to decide whether to order costs on the standard or indemnity basis (CPR Part 44).

The assessment of costs

4.145 Costs will be subject to detailed assessment by the Supreme Court Costs Office unless the hearing (whether a contested permission hearing or full appeal hearing or other hearing) lasted for one day or less. If one day or less, summary assessment may take place (para 14.1 of the PD to CPR Part 52). The summary assessment procedure as set out at para 14 of the PD to CPR Part 44 applies. Particular regard should be had to para 13.5 of the PD to CPR Part 44, which requires the service of a costs schedule 24 hours before the hearing.

Wasted costs orders

4.146 By CPR rr 44.14 and 48.7 the court can impose a wasted costs order upon a legal representative. Legal representatives have the right to be given a reasonable opportunity to attend a hearing to give reasons why the court should not make an order against them. The normal course is for an order to be issued requiring the legal representative to attend a further hearing to show cause why they should not pay the costs of the other parties. The jurisdiction should be exercised in the same way as that of the EAT's and accordingly the material at para **3.397** above should be carefully considered.

Costs of litigants in person

4.147 CPR r 48.6 applies and litigants in person are entitled to claim for their disbursement and any financial loss they can prove they have incurred by working on their claim or £9.25 per hour. Their costs cannot exceed two-thirds of what a legal representative would have claimed for conducting the case on the litigant's behalf. Litigants in person should take notice of the difference in hourly rate which can be claimed in the Court of Appeal and the EAT, see para **3.400** above.

Costs of an assisted person

4.148 The costs of an assisted person (assistance by the Legal Services Commission) are assessed by way of detailed assessment by the Supreme Court Costs Office pursuant to CPR r 47.17. To obtain the protection of s 11 of the Access to Justice Act 1999, the funding certificate needs to be in court.

Re-opening an appeal

4.149 The Court of Appeal has an extremely limited power to re-open an appeal after judgment. Under CPR r 52.17 the court will re-open an appeal where it is necessary to do so to avoid real injustice, where the circumstances are exceptional and make it appropriate to re-open the appeal and where there is no effective alternative remedy. An application for permission to re-open an appeal should be made pursuant to CPR Part 23 and be supported by written evidence. The application should not be served on anybody else unless the court so directs. If it is served on another party they have 14 days to make written representations. The application will be considered by a single judge who may deal with it on the papers or direct an oral hearing. The decision is final and there is no right of appeal to the House of Lords against a refusal of permission to re-open. If the appeal is re-opened then the matter will proceed to a full hearing of the court pursuant to directions issued by the court. Reference should be had to *Taylor v Lawrence*[30] and para 25 of the PD to CPR Part 52.

Statistics

4.150 The most recent published statistics for appeals from the EAT to the Court of Appeal (for 2006) are as follows:[31]

---

[30] [2002] EWCA Civ 90, [2003] QB 528.

Appeals Filed[32]	Allowed	Dismissed	Dismissed by consent	Struck out	Total
40	16	33	12	—	61

NEXT STOP – EUROPEAN COURT OF JUSTICE, HOUSE OF LORDS OR EUROPEAN COURT OF HUMAN RIGHTS

4.151 If you lost before the Court of Appeal after a final hearing of an appeal then the next stop is the House of Lords – see Chapter 5. If you did not get so far as a final hearing of the appeal then the next stop is the ECtHR – see Chapter 7. If you successfully managed to get the Court of Appeal to refer questions to the ECJ then the next stop that court, although you'll be coming back to the Court of Appeal thereafter – see Chapter 6.

THE COURT OF APPEAL – MISCELLANEOUS

4.152 The Master of Rolls (Right Honourable Sir Anthony Clarke) presides over the civil division of the Court of Appeal assisted by a deputy (Waller LJ). It usually sits in the Royal Courts of Justice but can also sat in Birmingham, Newcastle and Cardiff or indeed at any other major civil court centre. The present fees for appeals are £200 for an application for permission to appeal and £400 for a full appeal hearing. Practitioners should seek up-to-date fees information. Mummery LJ is the only former president of the EAT currently sitting in the Court of Appeal.

---

[31] Source: Judicial and Court Statistics 2006, Chapter 1, Tables 1.8 and 1.91, at pp 23 and 24.
[32] Including two interlocutory appeals, both of which were dismissed, Table 1.9, at p 24.

Chapter 5

THE HOUSE OF LORDS

OVERVIEW

5.1 Appealing to the House of Lords is not a step to be taken lightly. The fees and costs, even without legal representation are enormous and the amount of preparation is colossal. For these reasons only the most important cases will be permitted to be heard by the House. Either the Court of Appeal or the House of Lords can give that permission or leave. Once leave is obtained then a large amount of paper has to be marshalled and assembled and the procedure is not for the feint hearted. Neither are the hearings themselves, held before the leading judges of the land; for even the most able QC these hearing are usually the greatest test of any advocate's skills. Having said that the House of Lords is just as open to litigants in person. What follows is our best attempt to explain the House's procedures in the context of an employment appeal.

THE RIGHT OF APPEAL

5.2 By s 3 of the Appellate Jurisdiction Act 1876 and s 1 of the Administration of Justice Act 1934 there is a right of appeal from the Civil Division of the Court of Appeal to 'Her Majesty the Queen in her Court of Parliament'. It is the chamber of the House of Lords which deals with such appeals. Section 4 of the Appellate Jurisdiction Act 1876 states:

> 'Every appeal shall be brought by way of petition to the House of Lords, praying that the matter of the order or judgment appealed against may be reviewed before Her Majesty the Queen in her Court of Parliament, in order that the said Court may determine what of right, and according to the law and custom of this realm, ought to be done in the subject-matter of such appeal.'

5.3 The procedure of the House of Lords is to be found in the 'Blue Book' (BB) on the Parliament.uk website or it can be obtained from the Judicial Office of the House of Lords. Extracts also appear in the collection of statutory materials to be found in the Appendices to this book.

5.4 While the House of Lords in its judicial capacity is part of the legislature the relevant committees which hear judicial appeals can act while Parliament is prorogued or adjourned. Since 1948 the appeals have been heard by committees in committee rooms outside of the chamber of the House of Lords. Judgments are still given in the chamber. Twelve Lords of Appeal in Ordinary, led by a Senior Law Lord now hear appeals. Lord Chancellors have not heard appeals since 25 October 2001.

LEAVE TO APPEAL

5.5 The right of appeal can only be exercised with the leave of the Court of Appeal or the House of Lords. Unlike appeals from the EAT to the Court of Appeal it is necessary to ask the Court of Appeal for leave before asking the House of Lords (BB, para 1.6). The procedure for asking the Court of Appeal for leave is set out at paras **4.135** and **4.138** above.

STAY OF COURT OF APPEAL'S ORDER

5.6 Only the Court of Appeal can grant such a stay and not the House of Lords (BB, para 43.1).

LEAVE FROM THE HOUSE OF LORDS

5.7 If the Court of Appeal has refused leave to appeal, then there is no right of appeal from that decision. Instead leave is sought from the House of Lords by presenting a petition for leave to appeal.

TIME LIMIT FOR PRESENTING PETITION FOR LEAVE TO APPEAL

5.8 Within one month of the date of the Court of Appeal's order (the date it was made not the date it was sealed) (BB, para 2.1) the appellant must lodge a petition for leave to appeal at the Judicial Office of the House of Lords.

PRESENTING A PETITION FOR LEAVE TO APPEAL

5.9 This is known as 'lodgment'. The petition must be in a prescribed format. The rules are to be found at section 3 of the BB and a pro forma is annexed to the BB. The petition should briefly set out the facts and points of law and conclude with a summary of reasons why leave should be granted. If the appellant asks the House to depart from one of its own decisions, or raises issued under HRA 1998 or seeks a reference to the ECJ the petition must clearly state this.

5.10 Before lodging the petition, it must be served on the other parties and a certificate of service endorsed on the back of the petition (BB, para 3.12).

5.11 Lodgment is effected by taking:

(1) Two original copies of the petition.

(2) A copy of the Court of Appeal's order.

(3) And if separate, a copy of the Court of Appeal's order refusing leave to appeal.

(where such orders are not available then they should be lodged as soon as possible thereafter) to the Judicial Office of the House of Lords. This is usually done in person and the person attending the office should be familiar with the subject matter of the petition. A non-refundable fee is payable if a waiver cannot be obtained. Waivers are granted where parties would suffer financial hardship if they had to pay. The fee in 2008 is £570 (BB, paras 3.13–13.17). It may also be convenient to lodge the documents set out at para **5.13** below, at the same time.

RESPONDENT'S RESPONSE

5.12 The respondent need not react to the petition for leave to appeal. If they wish to take part in the proceedings and be kept informed of progress and if they may ever wish to seek a costs order then they should enter an appearance. This takes the form of informing the Judicial Office by post of name and address (or representatives' details) and paying the prescribed fee (£115 in 2008) (BB, paras 3.18–3.20).

DECIDING THE PETITION FOR LEAVE TO APPEAL

5.13 The petition comes before the appeal committee composed of three Lords of Appeal in Ordinary. They consider the case on the papers, in the first instance. To enable this the following must be lodged at the Judicial Office within 7 days of presentation of the petition: four copies of:

(1) the petition;

(2) the Court of Appeal's order;

(3) if separate, a copy of its order refusing leave to appeal;

(4) the Court of Appeal's judgment (official copy);

(5) the orders and judgments of the employment tribunal and the EAT;

(6) any unreported judgments cited in any of the above.

These must be lodged in the form set out at para 4.3 of the BB. Other documents must not be lodged unless requested by the appeal committee (BB, para 4.2).

5.14 The respondent may submit written objections as to why leave to appeal should not be granted either within 14 days of service of the petition or within 14 days of being invited to by the committee or within 14 days of referral to an oral hearing.

5.15 The committee will only grant leave to appeal to those petitions which raise an important point of law of general public importance which ought to be considered by the House at that time.

5.16 If the committee is unanimous and judge that no further argument is necessary then it will either grant or refuse leave to appeal.

5.17 If the committee is not unanimous or if it judges that further argument is necessary then the petition will be referred to an oral hearing. The parties attend a short hearing before the committee. Only one person may speak per side and authorities are not usually cited (BB, paras 4.1–4.21). The committee will then decide the petition, a majority of 2:1 is required.

5.18 If it refused leave to appeal, that is the end of the road and no further right of appeal in the UK is available. It may well be that an application may be made to the ECtHR (see Chapter 7).

5.19 Leave may be given on only some grounds of appeal or may be given on terms. If it is to be given on terms then the parties can make submissions on the proposed terms within 14 days of the decision to give leave. If an appellant is not prepared to accept the terms they can withdraw the appeal.

5.20 If leave is granted then the costs of the petition become costs in the appeal. If leave is refused on the papers then costs may only awarded for preparing the papers for the appeal committee, attending the client, the other side, perusing the petition and preparing respondent's objections as applicable. An application should be made by letter or by bill of costs to the Judicial Office (BB, para 5.1). For costs following an oral hearing, the application must be made at the hearing (BB, paras 5.4–5.5 for the assessment of costs procedure).

LEAVE OBTAINED

5.21 A petition of appeal must be lodged within 14 days of the appeal committee's decision and within 3 months of the Court of Appeal's order that is under appeal (BB, paras 4.22–7.1).

IF YOU HAVE THE COURT OF APPEAL'S LEAVE

5.22 A petition to appeal must be lodged at the Judicial Office within 3 months of the date of the Court of Appeal's order that is being appealed against. The Court of Appeal has power to reduce this time but not to extend it (BB, paras 7.1–7.2).

APPEALING OUT OF TIME

5.23 If you do not have the Court of Appeal's leave and are presenting a petition for leave outside of the one month period then you should lodge a petition for leave to appeal out of time. This will be the same as a petition for leave to appeal as described above but with an extra paragraph seeking leave to appeal out of time. The appeal committee will consider the petition and either refuse leave to appeal out of time or grant leave to appeal in the manner set out above. If leave is obtained then the procedure set out at para **5.28** below will apply (BB, paras 2.2–3).

5.24 If you do have the Court of Appeal's leave and do not lodge a petition of appeal within the 3-month time limit set out above then you must lodge a petition to present an appeal out of time, which will be dealt with by an appeal committee in a similar manner to a petition for leave to appeal (BB, para 7.3).

CONSOLIDATION AND CONJOINDER

5.25 Where the issues in one or more appeals are similar they may be heard together. This is achieved by consolidation or conjoinder. The former is where the appeals are presented by one team of counsel only each side and a single set of appendicies are used (see para **5.37** et seq below). The latter is where there is a looser connection between linked cases. Many variations are possible with conjoinder, each party may remain with their own counsel or they may share leading counsel or juniors etc. The Judicial Office will strive to eliminate unnecessary duplication where possible.

5.26 Consolidation or conjoinder are achieved by petition which if the parties do not consent, is referred to the appeal committee (BB, section 29).

CROSS-APPEALS

5.27 These are treated in the same way as an appeal. They can only be brought with the leave of the Court of Appeal or the House. Where leave is sought from the House, the petition should be lodged in the same manner as an appeal but after the granting of leave to the appellant. One master plus five copies of the petition for leave must be lodged. Cross-appeals may be presented out of time and paras **5.23** and **5.24** above applies.

THE APPEAL HEARING PROCEDURE

Step 1 – lodge the petition of appeal

5.28 Petitions of appeal must be in a prescribed format (BB, paras 9.1–9.11).

5.29 Lodgment is by way of taking the original and seven copies to the Judicial Office with the prescribed fee (£1,140 if appealing with the Court of Appeal's leave and £570 without). If appealing with the Court of Appeal's leave then a copy of the order appealed against and if separate a copy of the order granting leave should also be lodged. If the orders are not available then they should be lodged as soon as possible after lodging the petition.

5.30 The petition should be served prior to lodging, by personal or first class post service on the respondents (BB, para 9.12).

5.31 The respondents should enter an appearance (as set out above at para **5.12**) to remain a part of the proceedings. A fee of £230 is paid (BB, para 9.15).

Step 1A – notifiy the Judicial Office of any HRA point

5.32 Appellants must notify the Judicial Office in writing where the House is being asked to make, uphold or reverse any declaration of incompatibility made under s 4 of HRA 1998 or seeks to challenge the act of a public authority under HRA 1998 or relies in any way upon the Act. The notification should briefly set out the arguments involved and whether the point was taken in the courts below.

5.33 In the case of notification that the House is being asked to make, uphold or reverse any declaration of incompatibility then the Crown has the right to be joined into the appeal (BB, section 33).

Step 1B – intervention

5.34 Once the petition to appeal has been lodged any person may petition to intervene in the appeal. This must be done within 6 weeks of the hearing of any appeal (BB, section 37).

Step 2 – lodge £25,000 security for costs or obtain a waiver

5.35 Within 7 days of the presentation of the petition to appeal the appellant must lodge £25,000 with the House of Lords security fund account. Payment must be by banker's draft or cheque or by instalments of less than £10,000 in cash. This requirement can be waived by the appeal committee or by consent of all the respondents. Those with public funding are exempt as are government departments (BB, paras 10.1–10.6).

Step 3 – lodge any petition to cross-appeal

5.36 If leave to cross-appeal is obtained whether from the Court of Appeal or the House then the petition of cross-appeal must be lodged within 6 weeks of the lodging of the petition to appeal. One master plus seven copies is required. No security for costs is required.

Step 3A – lodge statement of facts and issues and an appendix

5.37 The appellant must lodge a statement of facts and issues within 6 weeks of lodging the petition to appeal. The appellant draws up a statement of the facts in the case and a record of the judicial proceedings so far. This is served on the respondent. The parties must agree the statement and all disputed items must be removed (see BB, paras 11.1 and 11.2 for the format). Where a cross-appeal is also lodged and there is insufficient time to include its detail in the statement, then the statement may be delayed with the consent of all parties. The Judicial Office should be consulted in this event.

5.38 The appendix to the statement is put together by the appellant in consultation with the respondents. It should deal with both the appeal and any cross-appeal. The appendix, in a typical employment claim would probably look something like this:

Part 1 must contain:

- ET1 and ET3 and any other pleadings at first instance – such as response to request of further and better particulars etc.

- Judgments and orders of tribunal, EAT and Court of Appeal. Judgments must, if they have been published be taken from the unbound parts of the law reports (ie including ICR), WLR or from All ER. Curiously no provision is made for using the IRLR. If unpublished an official copy of the judgment must be used. Fifteen copies of the judgments are required.

- All relevant legislative provisions (either the official printed Act or Regulations or if too large, copies of extracts from Halsbury's Statutes or Statutory Instruments).

- Any central relevant document upon which the appeal is based – a contract of employment, harassment policy etc.

The further parts of the appendix could be composed of the following:

- The bundles used in the tribunal hearing.

- The witness statements used in the tribunal hearing.

- Any new evidence admitted before the EAT and the Court of Appeal.

- Any other documentary evidence (that has already been used below) which is necessary for the determination of the appeal.

5.39 See para 12.7 of the BB for the form of the appendix and para 12.8 for how the parties should agree its contents.

5.40 The appellant must do all of this work with the co-operation of the respondents. If the parties cannot agree then the respondents should lodge their own bundle.

5.41 If the parties cannot meet the deadline for submitting the statement and appendix then it may be extended three times by consent and the respondents are not expected to unreasonably withhold consent. If consent is withheld or on the fourth request for an extension the matter will be referred to an appeal committee (see BB, paras 13.3–13.6 for the procedure).

5.42 A master and seven copies of the statement plus eight copies of part 1 of the appendix and 15 copies of all other Parts and 15 copies of the respondent's bundle if any must be lodged at the Judicial Office together with a fee of £3,420.

Step 3B – setting the appeal down for hearing

5.43 While the appellant is at the Judicial Office lodging the statement and the appendix he should also set down the appeal and cross-appeal for hearing.

5.44 This is done by a form of application which is found at Appendix A, Form 13, of the BB.

5.45 Once the appeal is set down it can be called on for hearing at short notice. Provisional dates for the hearing set at the parties' convenience will be given as soon as possible. See para **5.59** below.

Step 4 – submit time estimates

5.46 Within 7 days of setting down the parties submit their time estimates for presenting their appeals. The maximum time estimate is 2 days. If more time is needed an explanation should be given to head of the Judicial Office (BB, paras 14.3–14.4).

Step 5 – appellant submits case

5.47 The case is the most important document in the appeal. It is essentially a super-skeleton argument that addresses the heads of argument which counsel proposes to submit at the hearing. It omits anything already in the statement. It must contain the following.

- Give notice that a party is abandoning a point taken below.

- Give notice that the party is taking a point not taken below. The Judicial Office should also be informed.

- Make any application to adduce new evidence.

- Give notice that a party intends to persuade the House to depart from one of its earlier decisions. Special attention must be drawn to this part of the case.

- Transcripts of unreported cases may only be cited where necessary.

- It should end with a numbered summary of the reasons upon which the argument is founded.

5.48 The case should address any cross-appeal.

5.49 No later than 5 weeks before the hearing the appellant must lodge one master plus seven copies at the Judicial Office and serve a sufficient number of copies for use by the respondent's counsel (maximum eight) on the respondent.

5.50 All appellants must join in one case.

5.51 See section 15 of the BB.

Step 6 – respondent submits case

5.52 Three weeks before the hearing the respondents must serve on the appellant 16 copies of their case and lodge at the Judicial Office a master and seven copies. Any intervenor or amicus curiae should do the same.

5.53 The respondent's case should take the same format of the appellant's case as set out above, save that it should also state whether or not the respondent is seeking to uphold the Court of Appeal's judgment or whether it is seeking to support it with new or other grounds.

5.54 The case should deal with any cross-appeal and in that event should comply with para **4.57** et seq above.

5.55 Once the respondent has submitted its case, there can be no further arguments submitted without leave.

5.56 The respondents should all join in one case. A procedure applies if they cannot (BB, para 15.9).

Step 7 – appellants lodge 15 bound volumes and 10 copies of every authority

5.57 No later than 14 days before the hearing the appellants must lodge 15 bound volumes containing:

- Petitions of appeal/cross-appeal.

- The statement.

- The cases with cross references on the outside margins to the appendix and authorities. If there is a cross-appeal, the appellants may answer any points made by the respondent on the cross-appeal in the case which the appellants place in the bound volume at this stage (BB, para 30.5).

- Case of intervenor or amicus.

- Part 1 of the appendix.

- Index to authorities.

It must be in the form set out at para 16.2 of the BB.

5.58 At the same time as lodging the bound volumes the appellants must lodge 10 copies of all authorities needed bound together in one or more volumes. The respondents must give the appellants 10 copies of authorities they wish to rely on and the appellants do not. The first volume should contain authorities from those sources set out at para 17.3 of the BB. The form and content of the volumes is otherwise dictated by paras 17.1–17.8.

Step 8 – receive notice of hearing

5.59 Appeals are listed at the convenience of the parties and provisional dates will be notified to the parties in advance. The parties are asked to keep themselves free in the week before and after the provisional dates and, essentially, the case can be called on at short notice with a notice of hearing at any time within this 3-week period (BB, paras 18.1–18.3).

THE HEARING

5.60 The appeal will be heard by five Lords of Appeal in Ordinary or Lords of Appeal (retired but otherwise qualified peers). In exceptional cases it may be heard by more – seven or nine. The hearings take place 10.30 am to 1 pm and 2 pm to 4 pm (save for Mondays when they start at 11 am) Monday to Thursday in Committee Rooms 1 and 2 on the Committee Corridor of the Palace of Westminster.

5.61 Hearings before the Lords are strangely informal. Robes are only worn by counsel. The Lords will focus in upon the fundamentals of each party's case and will test those fundamentals mercilessly.

THE APPROACH

5.62 The House is supreme within the jurisdiction of the UK in the area of employment law. It is unbound by precedent and can depart from an earlier decisions *Practice Note (Judicial Precedent)*.[1] It is bound by decisions of the ECJ (see para **6.2** below). Its powers and jurisdiction as noted above is to 'determine what of right, and according to the law and custom of this realm, ought to be done in the subject matter of such appeal'. This essentially means that it has the same power as the Court of Appeal to set aside such decisions as are necessary to procure the right result where an error of law has been identified. Subject to the Court of Appeal making its own error of procedure or law, the House of Lords is as much concerned with the judgment of the employment tribunal as the Court of Appeal, and will substitute its own judgment or remit back to the employment tribunal in a similar manner to the Court of Appeal. It will rarely if ever remit back to the Court of Appeal or the EAT.

COSTS

5.63 Contrary to normal practice before the civil court, costs should be dealt with before judgment in the House of Lords. Essentially in the absence of any submissions the Lords will assume that costs should follow the event and that the winning party should be paid his costs by the others. If a different order is sought then the parties should make written submissions within 14 days of the conclusion of the hearing and before judgment is given. If the content of the judgment is such that the parties think that a particular costs order is called for which has not been previously canvassed then the Lords may postpone making a costs order to allow the parties to make written submissions within 14 days of judgment. Special procedures are involved where a conditional fee agreement is involved (BB, section 19).

---

[1] [1966] 3 All ER 77, sub nom *Practice Statement* [1966] 1 WLR 123.

5.64 If costs are granted then bills of costs for taxation should be lodged within 3 months from the date of judgment. Regard should be had to the Practice Directions relating to judicial taxation and forms of bills of costs which are available from the Judicial Office or www.parliament.uk. Instruction of a costs draftsman with experience of the House of Lords would seem to be a wise course at this stage where possible.

NEW SUBMISSIONS

5.65 If after conclusion of oral argument a party wishes to bring to the attention of the House new circumstances which have arisen and which might affect the decision or order of the House then an application should be made by letter to the head of the Judicial Office without delay with copies to the other parties (BB, para 38.1).

JUDGMENT

5.66 It is when judgment is given that the parties are reminded that they have just litigated not before a court but before a part of the legislature, for judgment is given in and as part of the proceedings of the legislative chambers of the House of Lords. Strictly speaking there is no judgment. The Lords deliver their opinions to the House and put questions to it, the answers to which dispose of the case if they are carried by a vote of the House (although those voting are the 'judges' who heard the appeal). One week's notice is given of a hearing in the chamber of the House of Lords usually on Wednesdays at 9.45 am. Counsel attend at the Bar of the House. The opinions of the Lords in draft and the questions that it is proposed to put to the House are made available from 10.30 am the previous morning. They are disclosed to counsel and representatives but may not usually be shown to clients. They may only be shown to in-house legal advisers where they are in a government department. Accredited members of the media also receive the judgment under strict embargo. Usually only junior counsel attend the hearing in the chamber. If leading counsel attends, then a full bottomed wig is worn. In contrast to all other judicial proceedings in the UK the hearing is broadcast as part of the proceedings of Parliament.

5.67 Counsel should inform the Lords of any apparent errors or ambiguity in the opinions or questions to be put and should email them to lawlords@parliament.uk by 4 pm on the Monday before judgment is given.

5.68 The Lords will usually hand down or read their opinions. A majority of the panel decides the matter and minority judgments are quite normal.

5.69 See section 20 of the BB.

THE ORDER OF THE HOUSE

5.70 Once the House has given judgment then drafts of the order are sent to all parties. They must be returned to the Judicial Office within 7 days with amendments or approval. Where amendments are made agreement should be reached with the other parties. Where the amendments amount to a change to the questions put and agreed to by the House then a petition must be lodged (BB, para 21.1).

DISPOSAL BY CONSENT

5.71 A petition for leave to appeal or a petition to appeal not yet set down for hearing may be withdrawn by writing to the Head of the Judicial Office stating that the parties have agreed costs (including what should happen to any security for costs) upon withdrawal. The respondents should notify the Judicial Office of their agreement.

5.72 A petition to appeal which has been set down for hearing can only be withdrawn by order of the House after a petition to withdraw has been made. The petition should include submissions on costs and state any consent from the other parties.

5.73 Where there has been a settlement between the parties which involves more than mere withdrawal and provisions about costs on withdrawal the parties should bring the settlement to the notice of the Judicial Office and seek directions. The House is very unlikely to allow an appeal by consent without determining the merits of the decision below.

THE END OF THE ROAD

5.74 The conclusion of an appeal to the House of Lords marks the end of the road for an employment appeal within the legal system of the UK. At a minimum the case will have been dealt with by 10 judges and four lay people by the time it reaches this stage. Aggrieved parties by this stage are left with seeking relief from international tribunals, such as the ECtHR. See Chapter 7 below.

REFERENCES TO THE EUROPEAN COURT OF JUSTICE

5.75 The House of Lords can refer questions to the ECJ (see Chapter 6 below).

THE SUPREME COURT OF THE UNITED KINGDOM

5.76 From October 2009 the judicial jurisdiction of the House of Lords will be transferred to a new Supreme Court of the United Kingdom. This reform is to be found in the Constitutional Reform Act 2005. Section 40(2) states that an appeal will lie to the Supreme Court from any order of judgment of the Court of Appeal in civil proceedings. As now an appeal will only lie with the permission of the Court of Appeal or the Supreme Court. Initially the justices of the Supreme Court will be the same as the Lords of Appeal in Ordinary.

5.77 Draft rules for the court were issued in January 2007, but their final form has yet to be set. The procedure looks like it will be very similar to the procedure of the House of Lords set out above. Principal matters in the draft rules include:

- Applications for permission to appeal to be brought before the Supreme Court within one month of the decision appealed from. The Supreme Court will be able to extend this time limit.

- Three justices will consider any application for permission to appeal on the papers or by way of oral hearing. The oral hearing will be limited to 30 minutes and only one counsel will be heard.

- If permission to appeal is granted then the application will stand as the notice of appeal.

- The statement and appendix, cases and bound volume requirements in the BB will largely continue to apply.

- Appeals shall be heard in open court. Only two counsel will appear per party.

- Security of costs will only be ordered on the application of the respondents.

Chapter 6

REFERENCES TO THE EUROPEAN COURT OF JUSTICE

INTRODUCTION

6.1 Section 3(1) of European Communities Act 1972 states:

> 'For the purposes of all legal proceedings any question as to the meaning or effect of any of the Treaties, or as to the validity, meaning or effect of any Community instrument, shall be treated as a question of law (and, if not referred to the European Court, be for determination as such in accordance with the principles laid down by and any relevant [decision of the European Court or any court attached thereto)].'

6.2 This essentially means that any ruling of the ECJ is binding upon all the courts and tribunals of England and Wales. Accordingly, if a question of EC Law comes before an employment tribunal, the EAT, Court of Appeal or House of Lords, they must decide the question in accordance with the judgments of the ECJ.

6.3 Where there is no such binding ruling on the question before the court or tribunal then the ECJ can be called by any such court or tribunal to make such a ruling. This is known as making a reference to the ECJ and is provided for in Art 234 of the Treaty Establishing the European Communities 1957 (the EC Treaty).

REFERENCE NOT AN APPEAL

6.4 It important to understand that a reference to the ECJ is not an appeal. There is a three-stage process. The referring court makes all the necessary findings of fact, it then refers the question of EC law to the ECJ, the ECJ then decide the question and the referring court applies the law as found by the ECJ to the facts it has found and decides the case accordingly. An employment tribunal can so make a reference. If it did then the ruling from the ECJ would bind the EAT, Court of Appeal and House of Lords if they went on to hear the case. Equally, if the EAT refers a matter to the ECJ then once the ECJ has decided the reference and the case is back before the EAT then it is for the EAT to decide the appeal before it, not the ECJ. The ECJ's role is limited to deciding the question sent to it by the referring court, it has no role in deciding the issue before the referring court.

EMPLOYMENT TRIBUNAL, EMPLOYMENT APPEAL TRIBUNAL AND COURT OF APPEAL

6.5 Article 234 EC gives these three 'tribunals' the discretion to refer any question they think is necessary to enable it to give judgment on the matter before it. The question may not be necessary to dispose of the whole matter or appeal, it need only be necessary to dispose of at least one issue before the referring tribunal.

6.6 The tribunals will usually refer any question of EC Law which is not free from doubt. The referring tribunal may well have its own view of the answer to the question, but may nonetheless refer the matter to the ECJ.

6.7 The other key issue is – when a question should be referred to the ECJ. Many times employment tribunals and the EAT will be nervous about referring a question and will leave it to the Court of Appeal or House of Lords. However, given that it can take two years for a reference to be determined by the ECJ, it is submitted that the reference should take place as soon as it becomes apparent that a reference is necessary, no matter at what stage and before which tribunal this becomes apparent.

6.8 The parties before the relevant tribunal or court should ask for a reference should they think one necessary. It is for the tribunal or court to then deicide whether one is necessary.

REFERENCE PROCEDURE

6.9 CPR Part 68 should be used as a procedure, notwithstanding that it only formally applies to the Court of Appeal. It is a useful procedure guide for use in the employment tribunals and the EAT. Reference should also be had to the Information Note of References from National Courts for a Preliminary Ruling (2005) OJ C 143/01 (IN) (replicated in the Appendices to this book).

6.10 The Practice Direction to CPR Part 68 states that the parties should assist the tribunal with the setting of the terms of the reference to the ECJ, but that the terms remain ultimately a matter for the referring tribunal. The reference should identify as clearly and as succinctly as possible the question upon which the tribunal seeks the ruling of the ECJ. It must be recalled that it will be translated into many languages.

6.11 The reference will be made by order of the tribunal together with a schedule which sets out the following:

(1) the full name of the referring tribunal;

(2) the full name of the parties;

(3) summary of the nature and history of the proceedings, including the salient facts, indicating whether these are proved or admitted or assumed;

(4) setting out the relevant rules of national law;

(5) summarising the relevant contentions of the parties;

(6) explaining why a ruling of the ECJ is sought; and

(7) identifying the provisions of EC law, which the ECJ is being requested to interpret.

6.12 If an employment tribunal wishes to make a reference then the secretary of the employment tribunals will send a copy of the tribunal's order and schedule to the registrar of the ECJ (ET Rules, r 58). A proper officer of the EAT should do likewise (no rules of the EAT make any provision). If the Court of Appeal is making the reference then the Senior Master of the Queen's Bench Division transmits it to the ECJ (see para 21–22 of the PD to CPR Part 68). The new 2008 EAT Practice Direction states that cases where a reference to the ECJ is sought will probably be placed in the EAT's fast-track for listing purposes – see para 9.20.4 of the PD.

HOUSE OF LORDS

6.13 Unlike inferior courts and tribunals the House of Lords has no discretion to refuse to make a reference to the ECJ where one is required. There are only really two exceptions to the obligation (see *CILFIT Srl and Lanificio di Gavardo v Ministry of Health*):[1]

(1) Where there is no reasonable doubt as to the manner in which the question of EC Law should be resolved (also known as *Acte clair*).

(2) Where the answer can be found in a previous ruling of the ECJ.

PROCEDURE FOR REFERENCE MADE BY HOUSE OF LORDS

6.14 The Lords can refer a question to the ECJ at any stage of its proceedings – even before granting leave to appeal. The hearing of an appeal is adjourned and the parties are invited to submit a draft of the questions to be referred. A further statement of facts and issues for the use of the ECJ may be ordered. The House will then make the reference to the ECJ (BB, s 34).

---

[1] (Case C-283/81) [1982] ECR 3415.

PROCEEDINGS BEFORE THE EUROPEAN COURT OF JUSTICE

6.15 The reference will be allocated to a chamber of the ECJ and to an Advocate-General. The parties, all Member States and the European Commission (the Commission) will be invited to make written submissions. There is then a short oral hearing in the language of the referring court at which advocates of the parties, any Member State and/or the Commission are heard. The Advocate-General then publishes an opinion for the benefit of the judges assigned to hear the reference. The parties cannot comment upon this. The judges then issue a judgment of the court.

POST EUROPEAN COURT OF JUSTICE JUDGMENT

6.16 Once the judgment of the ECJ has been received the referring court or tribunal must then resume the proceedings and decide the case, whether with further submissions or hearings or otherwise, in accordance with the ECJ's judgment.

6.17 In the House of Lords it will be decided by the Lords whether a further hearing is necessary. If the reference took place during proceedings before the appellate committee and a further hearing is necessary then further supplemental cases will be lodged together with new bound volumes (BB, paras 34.6–34.9).

6.18 The costs of the reference and the proceedings before the ECJ are treated as costs in the domestic proceedings and awarded and assessed accordingly. The ECJ has no power to make orders about costs. This has led to some injustice in the EAT where the costs jurisdiction is limited. The proper course may be for the parties to give cross-undertakings as to costs of a reference from the EAT to the ECJ (see *Burton v British Railways Board*).[2]

NEW ARTICLE 234 EC

6.19 This chapter is based upon Art 234 of the EC Treaty. This Treaty has been renamed the Treaty on the functioning of the European Union by the Treaty of Lisbon signed on 13 December 2007. Article 234 EC has been amended by the Treaty of Lisbon. That Treaty is the reform treaty which replaced the failed constitution. At the time of writing it is subject to the ratification procedures of the Member States and as there is no guarantee of ratification the text of this section will be based upon the current version of

---

[2] [1983] ICR 544.

Art 234 EC which is enforce at this time. In any event the new text of the Article is unlikely to make any substantive change to the procedure set out above.

Chapter 7

THE EUROPEAN CONVENTION FOR THE PROTECTION OF HUMAN RIGHTS AND FUNDAMENTAL FREEDOMS 1950 AND TAKING A CASE TO THE EUROPEAN COURT OF HUMAN RIGHTS

THE EUROPEAN CONVENTION FOR THE PROTECTION OF HUMAN RIGHTS AND FUNDAMENTAL FREEDOMS 1950

7.1 The Convention for the Protection of Human Rights and Fundamental Freedoms 1950 (the European Convention) signed at Rome on 4 November 1950 and brought into force on 3 September 1953 is a creation of the Council of Europe which was established after the Second World War in 1949 to among other things protect human rights in Europe. The Council has a Committee of Ministers, a Parliamentary Assembly and a Court of Human Rights (ECtHR) which sits in Strasbourg and is made up of judges elected by the Parliamentary Assembly and one judge represents each of the 47 Member States (but need not be from that Member State – the judge representing Lichtenstein is from Switzerland). Pursuant to Art 34 of the European Convention individuals may bring claims against Member States that their Convention rights have been violated. This chapter will be largely devoted to such claims.

HUMAN RIGHTS ACT 1998

7.2 HRA 1998 came into force on 2 October 2000 and in effect permits parties in employment litigation to rely on certain Articles of the European Convention in employment cases before domestic courts and tribunals rather than having to bring cases before the ECtHR.

7.3 HRA 1998 only incorporates the following parts of the European Convention into UK law – Arts 2–12 and 14 and Arts 13 of Protocol 1 and Art 1 of Protocol 13 (s 1). All courts and tribunals are required to take into account any judgment of the ECtHR (s 2). All legislation must be read and given effect in a way which is compatible with Convention rights (s 3) and all public authorities including courts and tribunals must not act in a way which is incompatible with a Convention right (s 6). Actions for damages resulting from a violation of a right by a public authority (but not a court or tribunal) may be brought (but not in an employment tribunal or the EAT) (s 7), and the High Court, Court of Appeal and House of Lords can declare primary legislation incompatible with Convention rights but may not strike such legislation down (s 4). Where a party seeks to have employment legislation declared incompatible and appeals to the EAT, the proper course is probably for the EAT to dismiss the appeal but grant permission to appeal to the Court of Appeal. This would appear to be an anomaly as a High Court judge sitting alone in the High Court could make a declaration but cannot when sitting with specialist lay members in the EAT – see Lindsay P in *Whittaker v P & D Watson (Trading as P & M Watson Haulage) and Another*.[1]

7.4 Accordingly, employment tribunals, the EAT, the Court of Appeal and the House of Lords are, since the coming into force of HRA 1998 all bound to apply employment law in a way which is compatible with the European Convention. For guidance as to how this is to be done see *X v Y*.[2] In effect in cases involving private and public employers' tribunals and courts must blend Convention rights with the substantive law. Accordingly, a dismissal in breach of a Convention right must be unfair pursuant to s 98 of the Employment Rights Act 1996 (ERA 1996) – see *Pay v Lancashire Probation Service*[3] for a public employer and *X v Y* above for a private employer.

RIGHTS RELEVANT TO EMPLOYMENT LAW

7.5 The following Convention rights are probably more applicable to employment law cases that the others:

- Article 4 – prohibiting forced labour;
- Article 6 – right to a fair trial;
- Article 8 – right to respect for private and family life;
- Article 9 – freedom of thought, conscience and religion;
- Article 10 – freedom of expression;
- Article 11 – freedom of assembly and association;
- Article 14 – prohibition of discrimination.

7.6 The following are good examples of how the European Convention can be used in employment proceedings:

---

[1] [2002] ICR 1244, at 1249.
[2] [2004] EWCA Civ 662, [2004] IRLR 625.
[3] [2004] IRLR 129.

(1) *McGowan v Scottish Water*.[4] Unfair dismissal case. Employee accused of falsifying his time sheets. Employer monitored him and his family in their home to prove their case. EAT held that violation of Art 8 of the European Convention – right to respect of private and family life was justified as in effect the employer had been investigating a criminal offence.

(2) *Stansbury v Dataplus plc*.[5] Employment tribunal member not appearing to be alert – breach of Art 6 – right to a fair trial.

(3) *Copsey v WWB Devon Clays Ltd*.[6] Breach of Art 9 – freedom of thought and religion – said to have been breached because of forced working on a Sunday.

(4) *R (National Union of Journalists) v Central Arbitration Committee*.[7] Breach of Art 11 – freedom of association, argued where employer recognised union of minority of workers.

HUMAN RIGHTS ACT 1998 DIDN'T WORK?

7.7 Where, however, a party has argued a human rights point before all of the tribunals and courts of the UK and still feels that he has not secured his rights under the European Convention he can complain to the ECtHR.

7.8 The important point to realise is that taking a case before the ECtHR is not an appeal from the House of Lords or indeed from any other court or tribunal in the UK. The ECtHR is an international court which sits outside of the judicial system in this country although is judgments are now persuasive but not binding (HRA 1998, s 2). Accordingly, the ECtHR cannot directly overturn an employment law judgment or decision made in the UK. It can merely point out that they were wrong or right and award limited compensation and costs. Nevertheless, by way of international treaty obligations in the European Convention ECtHR judgments are binding on the UK and the government of the day will usually enact relevant legislative changes to ensure that a further breach of the European Convention does not recur. Accordingly, the ECtHR really is not a court from which a meaningful remedy can be obtained but is a forum for proving a point or to secure the reform of domestic law.

7.9 Article 34 of the European Convention states that the ECtHR may 'receive applications from any person, non-governmental organisation or group of individuals claiming to be the victim of a violation by one of the High Contracting Parties of the rights set forth in the Convention or the Protocols

---

[4] [2005] IRLR 167.
[5] [2003] EWCA Civ 1951, [2004] IRLR 466.
[6] [2005] EWCA Civ 932, [2005] IRLR 811.
[7] [2005] EWCA Civ 1309, [2006] IRLR 53.

thereto'. Thus a party may bring an application before the court that the UK as a High Contracting Party has not secured his Convention rights; in the employment context this is likely to amount to a claim that the employment law of the UK has failed to secure the complainant's Convention rights. It is proceedings under Art 34 which are the focus of this chapter.

7.10 Legal aid can be obtained for these proceedings from the court directly – see Chapter X of the Rules of the European Court of Human Rights (the Rules).

ADMISSIBILITY

7.11 Article 35 of the European Convention sets out which claims the ECtHR will hear and which it will not – which are admissible before it and those which are not. The criteria of admissibility are as follows.

VICTIM OF A EUROPEAN CONVENTION VIOLATION

7.12 The complainant must be a victim of a European Convention violation. The complainant must be personally or directly affected by the violation. Potential victims may complain so long as they can show that there is a real risk of them being directly affected by a violation (*Johnston and Others v Ireland*).[8]

EXHAUSTION OF DOMESTIC REMEDIES

7.13 The burden is on the respondent (usually the UK) to demonstrate that the complainant has not exhausted all of the available domestic remedies before coming to the ECtHR. In the employment context this will usually mean that the complainant must have had permission to appeal refused or dismissed or struck out on procedural grounds by the Court of Appeal or the House of Lords or their appeal refused by the House of Lords.

THE 6-MONTH TIME LIMIT

7.14 The application to the ECtHR must be brought within 6 months of the final decision which constituted the exhaustion of domestic remedies. In reality and in the context of this book this amounts to a time limit that the complaint be brought within 6 months of the judgment of the House of Lords or refusal of permission to appeal/dismissal/strike out order made by the Court of Appeal or of leave to appeal by the House of Lords.

---

[8] (Application No 9697/82) (1987) 9 EHRR 203.

ANONYMITY

7.15 The application must disclose the identity of the applicant. Confidentiality can later be granted by the court.

MATTER ALREADY EXAMINED BY THE COURT

7.16 An applicant cannot keep bringing the same matter before the ECtHR. The same matter will only be admissible if new facts have emerged since the last time the case was before the court.

THE SAME MATTER HAS BEEN SUBMITTED TO ANOTHER PROCEDURE OF INTERNATIONAL INVESTIGATION OR SETTLEMENT

7.17 For example, petitions to the Human Rights Committee under the United Nations International Covenant on Civil and Political Rights 1966. In the employment context individuals may bring a complaint relating to a matter which the Trade Union Congress has already brought before the International Labour Organisation.[9]

INCOMPATIBILITY WITH THE PROVISIONS OF THE EUROPEAN CONVENTION

7.18 This has four aspects, which have been given a latin shorthand:

(1) *ratione loci* – incompatibility because of the limit of the state's jurisdiction. In other words the violation occurred outside of the territorial jurisdiction of the Member State. In the employment context UK employment law can apply outside of the territorial limits of the UK, see Chapter X of the Court's Rules;

(2) *ratione materiae* – incompatibility because the complaint is outside the limits of what is covered by the European Convention and its Protocols;

(3) *ratione temporis* – incompatibility because the allegedly violating state has not ratified the European Convention or the right to present complaints to the court. This would not apply to the UK;

(4) *ratione personae* – incompatibility because the complaint is not directed against an emanation of the Contracting State. This would not apply where the violation was caused by a private body which a public body was

---

[9] See (1987) 50 DR 228.

using to discharge its functions – *Costello-Roberts v United Kingdom*[10] (eg, a private training company discharging the UK Government's training of the young function). This does not apply merely because an employee has suffered a violation at the hands of a private company – the UK state is then under an obligation to provide a means of redress against such a violation – for example, a claim to the employment tribunal – if that claim is insufficient to protect the Convention right concerned then there will have been a violation which can, if otherwise admissible, be brought before the ECtHR.

MANIFESTLY ILL-FOUNDED

7.19 Article 35(3) states that an application may be declared inadmissible as being manifestly unfounded or in other words for not raising a prima facie case that there has been a breach of Convention rights. Many cases are declared inadmissible on this ground. This is the main filter which the court applies and is a merits test. This test is often applied by the court itself and can often attract a split vote, the complaint being declared inadmissible on a majority vote of the court.

ABUSE OF RIGHT OF APPLICATION

7.20 Article 35(3) permits applications to be declared inadmissible where they are an abuse of the process. This will occur where they are vexatious, written in abusive language, concealing facts or where a breach of the court's confidentiality occurs by reason of the party revealing details of the case to the press. It is not used where the contracting party is merely embarrassed about the criticism of it in the application – *Adivar and Others v Turkey*.[11]

MAKING A COMPLAINT

7.21 Rule 47 of the 2006 Rules state that any application under Art 34 shall be made on the application form provided by the registry of the court. The applicant is required to set out:

(1) the name, date of birth, nationality, sex, occupation and address of the applicant;

(2) the name, occupation and address of the representative, if any;

(3) the name of the contracting party or parties against which the application is made;

---

[10] (Application No 13134/87) (1995) 19 EHRR 112.
[11] (Application No 21893/93) (1996) 23 EHRR 143.

(4) a succinct statement of the facts;

(5) a succinct statement of the alleged violation(s) of the European Convention and the relevant arguments;

(6) a succinct statement on the applicant's compliance with the admissibility criteria (exhaustion of domestic remedies and the 6-month rule) laid down in Art 35(1) of the European Convention; and the object of the application;

(7) and be accompanied by copies of any relevant documents and in particular the decisions, whether judicial or not, relating to the object of the application;

(8) applicants are also required to provide information, enabling it to be shown that the admissibility criteria (exhaustion of domestic remedies and the 6-month rule) have been satisfied; and applicants should indicate whether they have submitted their complaints to any other procedure of international investigation or settlement.

7.22 Applicants who do not wish their identity to be disclosed to the public should say so on the form and should submit a statement of the reasons justifying such a departure from the normal rule of public access to information in proceedings before the court.

7.23 On receipt of an application the ECtHR opens a file and considers whether the application is inadmissible.

THE ADMISSIBILITY DECISION

7.24 Admissibility is decided either by a committee of three judges of the court who can order it inadmissible if they are unanimous. This will occur whether either the information submitted by the applicant is sufficient for such a decision to be taken or where a judge rapporteur appointed by the court has after, asking for further information and documents from the party, decided that the matter should be decided by committee. Otherwise the admissibility decision is taken by a chamber of the court (see r 49 of the Rules).

7.25 Under r 54 admissibility decisions taken by the court will be made by seven judges either on written representations or after an oral hearing attended by the parties. The court can decide matters on a majority basis.

7.26 If the application is declared inadmissible then it ends and goes no further. This really can be seen as the litigious end of the road for employment claims.

IF THE APPLICATION IS DECLARED ADMISSIBLE

7.27 Then the application proceeds to a final hearing. The court under r 59 will give directions for the submission of further evidence and representations and give directions for an oral hearing.

JUST SATISFACTION

7.28 At this stage if an applicant wishes to seek an award of compensation pursuant to Art 41 of the European Convention he must give full particulars of the nature of his claim. Compensation will be awarded where the applicant has not obtained any or a full remedy in the domestic legal system. This can take the form of pecuniary or non-pecuniary compensation (ie it includes injury to feelings) and has in the past been awarded under the following heads:

(1) loss of earnings;

(2) refund of fines and taxes paid;

(3) domestic costs incurred;

(4) medical expenses;

(5) pain and suffering;

(6) anguish and distress;

(7) trauma;

(8) embarrassment, frustration and inconvenience;

(9) loss of opportunity, relationships and reputation;

(10) costs and expenses of the ECtHR proceedings.

FRIENDLY SETTLEMENT

7.29 A little like the ACAS procedure before the employment tribunal the registrar of the ECtHR will try to settle the proceedings in advance of the final hearing by way of a friendly settlement. The negotiations are confidential and without prejudice. Should a settlement be reached then the proceedings are struck out. See r 62 of the Rules and Art 38(1) of the European Convention.

FINAL HEARING

7.30 The final hearing will usually be before a chamber of seven judges of the court. If the point to be decided requires an important ruling on the European Convention then a grand chamber of 17 judges may hear it. This can happen even if a chamber has already heard the case; the grand chamber can re-hear it (Chapter VII of the Rules). The hearings are in public but can be in camera where required. The president of the chamber has power to organise and direct the hearings and usually rules on who will be called on to address the court and when. The court can decide a case in the absence of the parties. A verbatim record of the hearing is made.

JUDGMENTS

7.31 The judgment will usually deal with all matters before the court but the question of just satisfaction can be adjourned to another hearing. Where this happens the parties will usually agree the level of compensation in line with the judgment and the court will usually ratify this agreement so long as it is 'equitable'. Judgments are delivered in English and French and are either read out at an oral hearing or more usually sent to the parties in writing. The parties can seeks clarification of the judgment if they do not understand a part of it or can ask for a revision of it, in the event of the discovery of a fact which might by its nature have had a decisive influence and which, when a judgment was delivered, was unknown to the court and could not reasonably have been known to that party. The request for a revision must be made within a period of 6 months after that party acquired knowledge of the fact (Chapter VIII of the Rules).

THE OUTCOME

7.32 The court makes a declaration as to whether there has been a violation of Convention rights or not and can make an award of compensation. It cannot strike down any law or decision or judgment made in the domestic arena. However, the UK comes under an international obligation to take such action as is necessary to remedy the violations identified (see Art 46) and the Committee of Ministers of the Council of Europe can apply pressure where this does not happen. Section 10 of HRA 1998 permits the UK Government to use delegated legislation to amend primary legislation to implement a judgment of the ECtHR (or indeed to implement a declaration of incompatibility made in by a domestic court).

7.33 The applicant can write to the committee if they are not happy with the UK's response to the judgment or if they have not been paid compensation which has been ordered. The committee will apply diplomatic pressure by passing strongly worded resolutions against the offending party. In the end, apart from ejection from the Council of Europe and widespread condemnation there is no actual enforcement mechanism of judgments. Ultimately a failure to implement a judgment is a breach of the European Convention and can be submitted to the court in a fresh application. The committee can also bring a Member State before the court for non-compliance with a judgment.

7.34 Litigants cannot enforce any judgment in the UK. UK courts cannot enforce monetary orders made by the ECtHR nor force implementation of any necessary legislation as that is solely a question for the Government and Parliament. If the Government ignored an ECtHR judgment then the litigants should contact MPs and pressure groups as well as the Committee of Ministers to obtain compliance.

7.35 It is very important that litigants before the ECtHR realise the limited nature of its powers and its position outwith the domestic legal system.

7.36 For example, say an unfair dismissal claimant is refused permission to be heard on a particular question by an employment tribunal and say that this results in a finding that he was not unfairly dismissed. The EAT, Court of Appeal and House of Lords do not hold this a breach of Art 6 and do not interfere with the tribunal's decision. An application to the ECtHR may result in a declaration that Art 6 has been breached and an award some compensation and costs but the ECtHR has no power to set aside the decision of the tribunal or to required the UK Government or other domestic court, tribunal or other organ to secure the setting aside of the decision. The UK Government will be required to pay the compensation and costs awarded and to consider examining what measures can be take to ensure the violation does not happen again. This will, however, be the limit of the remedy obtained.

CHAPTER 8

GROUNDS OF APPEAL

SCOPE OF THIS CHAPTER

8.1 The only proper grounds of appeal are errors of law and this chapter deals with those grounds: amongst others, misdirection, misapplication of the law, perversity and the complaint that an employment tribunal has failed to provide adequate reasons.[1] It also deals with the less favoured ground of misconduct or bias by an employment tribunal.

8.2 At the end of this chapter there is also a commentary and an analysis of the procedure for seeking additional reasons from the employment tribunal under the procedure in *Barke v SEETEC Business Technology Centre Ltd*[2] (also briefly covered in Chapter 3 and even more briefly referred to in Chapter 1). We have also included a detailed critical analysis of the *Barke* procedure.

8.3 The reasons for including the Barke procedure here are twofold. First, there is an overlap with considerations relevant to the 'inadequate reasoning' ground of appeal. Secondly, the provision of additional reasons can sometimes generate new grounds of appeal which either did not exist or were not apparent before.

OVERVIEW

Law not fact

8.4 As noted above, you can only appeal from the decision of an employment tribunal on a point of law.[3]

8.5 In *Unison v Leicestershire County Council*,[4] considering the test for perversity (below) Laws LJ stated:

> '... with respect authority is hardly needed. The EAT's limited role, dealing with law only, is plain and obvious.'

8.6 That said, there is sometimes considerable difficulty in defining or identifying what is and is not a point of law.

---

[1] See, for example, the classic formulation of this ground in *Meek v City of Birmingham District Council* [1987] IRLR 250.
[2] [2005] EWCA Civ 578, [2005] ICR 1373.
[3] An aggrieved party may appeal to the EAT on 'any question of law arising from any decision of, or arising in any proceedings before, an employment tribunal': ETA 1996, s 21(1).
[4] [2006] EWCA Civ 825, [2006] IRLR 810.

8.7 What is or may be an error of law is explored in detail in this chapter. However, it is worth first setting out the context in which the EAT will be considering the grounds of appeal.

Approach

8.8 In summary, the questions which the EAT will ask itself on hearing any appeal and, barring perhaps the fifth question, on looking at the notice of appeal under the 'sift' procedure (see Chapter 3) are as follows:

(1) Questions of law: Do the grounds of appeal in the notice of appeal raise questions of law at all?[5]

(2) Error: If so, do the grounds of appeal disclose apparent or potential errors on those questions?

(3) Materiality: If so, were any such errors of law *material* to the decision appealed?[6]

(4) Live issue: Do the grounds of appeal refer to a matter which is still a live issue between the parties?

(5) Disposal: If so, should the EAT substitute a decision or remit the case back to the original or a new employment tribunal?

8.9 The first three of those issues hinge on the content and drafting of the grounds of appeal. The central question of what amounts to an identifiable error of law is canvassed extensively below.

Live issue

8.10 The fourth issue is mentioned particularly to caution against attractive grounds concealing appeals which are flawed because they do not relate to a live issue between the parties, such as where the proceedings (or the issues in the appeal) have been settled by a valid compromise agreement;[7] where your only

---

[5] A failure to raise questions of law on the face of the grounds of appeal will normally mean that the appeal will be weeded out during the 'sift' (see Chapter 3) and a r 3(7) letter sent saying that no further action will be taken on the appeal.
[6] See *Zargaran v Zargaran London* EAT/1062/01 [2003] All ER (D) 140 (Mar), in which Burton P found that the tribunal had erred in refusing to allow some cross-examination but held the error not material; and *Adjaho v Bariyendeza* UKEAT/0137/04 [2005] All ER (D) 76 (Mar), in which His Honour Judge Serota QC held that, although the employment tribunal misdirected itself as to certain evidence, the misdirection was not a sufficient error of law to render its decision flawed.
[7] *Biwater Ltd v Bell* EAT 218/89, where the employer had settled the dispute with the employee but wished to appeal an issue of territorial jurisdiction to get a definitive (and binding) answer on the contract which affected other employees ordinarily working outside Great Britain.

complaint is as to *how* the employment tribunal found in your favour; or where you won but would like the EAT to give greater authority to your victory.[8]

Disposal

8.11 An extra point to note is that although disposal is essentially a procedural issue (covered in detail in Chapter 3), it will sometimes depend, at least in part, upon what grounds were advanced or established, in particular whether:

(1) bias or misconduct of the case has been alleged as a ground; or

(2) the employment tribunal's decision can be said to be entirely flawed.[9]

8.12 If either of the above two conditions applies, the case will not normally be remitted to the same employment tribunal if the appeal is allowed. Rather, if it has to be remitted to the employment tribunal, the employment tribunal will be freshly constituted, ie will be composed of different members.

8.13 However, it is quite improper to make an unfounded allegation of bias merely to try to avoid going back in front of the same tribunal.

Key task

8.14 Against that background, the key task of anyone wishing to appeal a decision of any employment tribunal is to identify:

(1) a question of law;

(2) that was material to the decision;

(3) on which the employment tribunal's fell into error.

8.15 It is also important to stress that grounds of appeal should echo the case that was argued before the employment tribunal, rather than advancing a wholly new case, not argued before.[10] The EAT will only rarely allow new points to be taken on appeal that were not argued below.

---

[8] *Baker and Others v Superite Tools Ltd* [1986] ICR 189.
[9] *Sinclair Roche & Temperley v Heard* [2004] IRLR 763.
[10] See *Atkins v Wiltshire Primary Care Trust* UKEAT/0566/07 (unreported) 14 February 2008.

ERRORS OF LAW

8.16 The most important point in this book is that it is only possible to appeal from the decision, order or judgment of an employment tribunal on a point of law[11] – although there is sometimes considerable difficulty in defining or identifying a point of law.

Identifying errors of law

8.17 Some issues are easy to recognise a point of law, for example, whether the employment tribunal applied the correct section of the Sex Discrimination Act 1975. That is, perhaps obviously, a question of law.

8.18 Common grounds of appeal are discussed below. However, at the other end of the spectrum, there are cases which are much more difficult confidently to identify as points of law, for example, where perversity is alleged.

Difficult cases

8.19 There are three categories of case which are particularly difficult to characterise as raising a point of law and particularly awkward for appellants:

(1) where the employment tribunal simply ignores one party's case but claims in its reasons to have 'heard and considered the evidence and submissions for both the claimant and the respondent';

(2) where there is no actual reasoning, despite perhaps quite long written reasons, reciting, for example, lots of documentary evidence;

(3) where there is clear and sometimes lengthy reasoning but it results in findings of fact or conclusions which are 'perverse' (ie not permissible on the evidence – a high hurdle).

8.20 The difficulty in these cases arises because:

(1) any error must be characterised as one or more recognisable errors of law; and

(2) it is difficult to establish that the employment tribunal has made an error of law without a close and careful reading of the employment tribunal's written reasons and an analysis of the issues and evidence before the employment tribunal, which can quickly begin to look like an appeal on the facts.

---

[11] An aggrieved party may appeal to the EAT on 'any question of law arising from any decision of, or arising in any proceedings before, an employment tribunal': ETA 1996, s 21(1).

GROUNDS OF APPEAL

8.21 The following are commonly recognised as potential grounds of appeal which disclose (or may disclose) errors of law:

(1) Misdirection, misunderstanding or misapplication of the law;

(2) Perversity:
    (a) On the facts;
    (b) In exercising a discretion;
    (c) In reaching a conclusion.

(3) Failures of reasoning:
    (a) failure to make necessary findings;
    (b) failure to resolve issues;
    (c) failure to give reasons.

(4) Procedural irregularity:
    (a) bias;
    (b) unfairness of hearing;
    (c) delay;
    (d) tribunal's composition;
    (e) tribunal's inattention.

MISDIRECTION, MISUNDERSTANDING OR MISAPPLICATION

8.22 Where the employment tribunal has misdirected itself on the law or has misapplied the law, this will be a proper ground of appeal and will be easy to recognise. Where an employment tribunal has approached its application of the law incorrectly or misunderstood the nature of the scope or content of the law, this will sometimes be less clear.

Illustrations

8.23 The following variety of recent examples illustrates where the appellate courts have held the tribunal to have misdirected itself or misunderstood or misapplied the law:

(1) *Lear v Key Recruitment UK Ltd*,[12] ss 13 or 14 of the ERA 1996 were capable of justifying the deduction of a commission payment, on termination of the employee's contract, on the grounds that he was not entitled to it because the client had failed to pay the fee due to them.

---

[12] UKEAT/0597/07, [2008] All ER (D) 362 (Feb).

(2) *Ellis v M&P Steelcraft Ltd and Another*,[13] s 203 of the ERA 1996 would render void a clause designed to defeat the contractual effect and statutory protection afforded by an agreement whose purpose was the provision of personal service typical of an employment relationship.

(3) *Blackburn v Chief Constable of West Midlands Police*,[14] the tribunal had misunderstood the nature of the justification defence in an equal pay claim.

(4) *R (Equal Opportunities Commission) v Secretary of State for Trade and Industry*,[15] the Tribunal had wrongly applied a 'but for' test to the question of whether or not sex discrimination had occurred.

(5) *Butlins Skyline Ltd and Another v Beynon*,[16] the tribunal was wrong to hold that the Secretary's administrative decision not to accept the response was not a 'decision' that could be the subject of a review under the ET Rules.

(6) *Abbey National plc v Fairbrother*,[17] the tribunal failed to apply the 'range of reasonable responses' test to the employer's operation of the grievance procedure.

(7) *Sandhu v Jan De Rijk Transport Ltd*,[18] the tribunal had misdirected itself as to the law in as to whether or not the employee had resigned, the only conclusion which it could properly have reached was that the employee had been dismissed.

(8) *Bolton School v Evans*,[19] the tribunal was wrong in a whistleblowing case to adopt a purposive interpretation of 'disclosure' which paid no respect to the wording of the statute.

(9) *Babula v Waltham Forest College*,[20] the tribunal erred in striking out the claimant's claim where he reasonably believed that a criminal offence had been committed, even though it turned out to be wrong, the tribunal having applied the wrong test by requiring there to have been a breach of a legal obligation.

8.24 Where the issue concerns solely the interpretation of a written legal contract, an appeal falls within the definition of a question of law: *Carmichael*

---

[13] UKEAT/0536/07 and UKEAT/0537/07, [2008] All ER (D) 353 (Feb).
[14] [2007] All ER (D) 250 (Dec).
[15] [2007] EWHC 483 (Admin), [2007] ICR 1234.
[16] [2007] ICR 121.
[17] [2007] IRLR 320.
[18] [2007] EWCA Civ 430, [2007] ICR 1137.
[19] [2007] IRLR 140.
[20] [2007] EWCA Civ 174, [2007] ICR 1026.

v *National Power*[21] and *Davies v Presbyterian Church of Wales*[22] – but see also *James v Greenwich Borough Council*,[23] where the question whether it is necessary to imply a contractual relationship between an agency worker and an end-user is a question of fact – although the requirement of necessity was a question of law.

PERVERSITY

8.25 Perversity means that the decision or finding was not 'a permissible option': it is difficult to establish perversity in an employment appeal.

8.26 Perversity is the principal basis upon which the appellate courts can entertain a challenge to an employment tribunal's findings of primary fact, inferences and exercises of discretion.

8.27 However, the appellate courts should not find perversity lightly.

8.28 In *Neale v Hereford and Worcester County Council*,[24] May LJ warned of the dangers of strong views on the facts at para 45:

> 'The danger in that approach is that an appellate court can very easily persuade itself that, as it certainly would not have reached the same conclusion, the Tribunal that did so was "certainly wrong". The more dogmatic the temperament of the judges, the more likely they are to take that view. That is a classic non sequitur ... What matters is whether the decision under appeal is a permissible option. To answer that question in the negative in the context of employment law, the EAT will almost always have to be able to identify a finding of fact which was unsupported by any evidence or a clear self-misdirection in law by the tribunal. If it cannot do this, it should re-examine with the greatest care its preliminary conclusion that the decision under appeal was not a permissible option and has to be characterised as "perverse".'

8.29 As Griffiths LJ (as he then was) said in *Gilham and Others v Kent County Council (No 2)* at p 22:[25]

> 'It is therefore important that this Court should resist the temptation to seek to overturn a factual decision with which it may not agree by searching for some shadowy point of law on which to hang its hat for the purpose of bringing uniformity to the differing decisions. If we were to take this course, it would have the very undesirable effect of encouraging innumerable appeals which raised no point of law, but depended upon comparative findings of fact.'

---

[21] [1999] 1 WLR 2042.
[22] [1986] ICR 280.
[23] [2007] ICR 577.
[24] [1986] ICR 471.
[25] [1985] ICR 233.

8.30 One well-known common sense test was expressed by May LJ in *Neale v Hereford and Worcester County Council*[26] at 483:

> 'Deciding these cases is the job of industrial tribunals and when they have not erred in law neither the appeal tribunal nor this court should disturb their decision unless one can say in effect: "My goodness, that was certainly wrong".'

8.31 Findings of fact for which there is no supporting evidence are sometimes treated as a species of perversity and sometimes as a separate category of error.

8.32 Given that the EAT's jurisdiction is limited to questions of law, the fact that establishing perversity is a high hurdle is a common theme in the cases. In *Carter v Credit Change Ltd*,[27] the Court of Appeal adopted and affirmed Arnold J's explanation of when a tribunal's decision could be reversed:

> 'Either we must find, in order so to do, that the tribunal, or its chairman, has taken into account some matter which it was improper to take into account or has failed to take into account some matter which it was necessary to take into account in order that the discretion might be properly exercised; or, alternatively if we do not find that, that the decision which was made by the tribunal, or its chairman, in the exercise of its discretion was so far beyond what any reasonable tribunal or chairman could have decided that we are entitled to reject it as perverse.'

8.33 An allegation of perversity will only succeed where it is shown that no reasonable tribunal, properly directed in law, could have reached the decision which the particular tribunal has reached: *Melon and Others v Hector Powe Ltd* at p 48.[28]

8.34 In *Piggott Bros & Co Ltd v Jackson*,[29] the Court of Appeal formulated this test as whether the decision was a permissible option:

> 'What matters is whether the decision under appeal was a permissible option. To answer that question in the negative in the context of employment law, the EAT will almost always have to be able to identify a finding of fact which was unsupported by any evidence or a clear self-misdirection in law by the Industrial Tribunal.'

8.35 Mummery J held in *Stewart v Cleveland Guest (Engineering) Ltd* at p 443:[30]

> 'This Tribunal should only interfere with the decision of the [employment] tribunal where the conclusion of that tribunal on the evidence before it is "irrational", "offends reason", "is certainly wrong" or "is very clearly wrong" or "must be

---

[26] [1986] ICR 471.
[27] [1980] 1 All ER 252.
[28] [1981] ICR 43.
[29] [1991] IRLR 309.
[30] [1994] IRLR 440.

wrong" or "is plainly wrong" or "is not a permissible option" or "is fundamentally wrong" or "is outrageous" or "makes absolutely no sense" or "flies in the face of properly informed logic".'

8.36 The seminal authority now is the decision of the Court of Appeal in *Crofton v Yeboah*,[31] in which Mummery LJ emphasised that an appeal should not turn into a rehearing of the evidence, and that a perversity appeal ought only to succeed where 'an overwhelming case is made out that the employment tribunal reached a decision which no reasonable tribunal, on a proper application of the law, would have reached'. It is worth perhaps quoting from Mummery LJ's judgment, from paras [93]–[96], more extensively, to give the flavour of the approach of the appellate courts:

'93. Such an appeal ought only to succeed where an overwhelming case is made out that the employment tribunal reached a decision which no reasonable tribunal, on a proper appreciation of the evidence and the law, would have reached. Even in cases where the Appeal Tribunal has "grave doubts" about the decision of the Employment Tribunal, it must proceed with "great care": *British Telecommunications plc v Sheridan* [1990] IRLR 27 at paragraph 34.

94. Over the years there have been frequent attempts, consistently resisted by the Employment Appeal Tribunal, to present appeals on fact as questions of law. The technique sometimes employed is to trawl through the extended reasons of an employment tribunal, selecting adverse findings of fact on specific issues on which there was a conflict of oral evidence, and alleging, without adequate particulars, supporting material or even proper grounds, that these particular findings of fact are perverse and that therefore the overall decision is perverse. An application is often made to obtain the notes of evidence made by the chairman in the hope of demonstrating that the notes are silent or incomplete on factual points, that the findings of fact were not therefore supported by the evidence and that a question of law accordingly arises for the determination of the Employment Appeal Tribunal.

95. Inevitably, there will from time to time be cases in which an employment tribunal has unfortunately erred by misunderstanding the evidence, leading it to make a crucial finding of fact unsupported by evidence or contrary to uncontradicted evidence. In such cases the appeal will usually succeed. But no appeal on a question of law should be allowed to be turned into a rehearing of parts of the evidence by the Employment Appeal Tribunal. I am, of course, well aware that this is easier said than done, especially when, as here, neither side was legally represented on the first level of appeal. As the Employment Appeal Tribunal was well aware, unrepresented litigants have understandable problems in separating questions of law from proof of facts and in distinguishing the making of legal submissions from submissions of fact, even giving evidence in the course of submissions.

96. In my judgment, the mass of detail in which the unrepresented parties advanced their written and oral arguments on the appeals over a 12-day hearing led the Employment Appeal Tribunal to reach the unjustified conclusion that

---

[31] [2002] EWCA Civ 794, [2002] IRLR 634.

specific decisions on fact, and therefore ultimate decisions on liability, were perverse, following a consideration of only part of the vast expanse of evidence available to the employment tribunal.'

Categories of perversity challenge

8.37 There are essentially three broad categories of perversity challenge and those drafting (or responding to) perversity grounds would be well advised to consider carefully into which category their case may properly fall:

(1) **No evidence:** there was no evidence at all to support the employment tribunal's finding or conclusion.

(2) **Some evidence:** no reasonable tribunal could have made the finding that it did on the totality of the evidence, despite the existence of some evidence to support it.

(3) **Employment practice:** whether or not there was evidence to support the conclusion, the decision flies in the face of the basic principles of acknowledged employment practice.

8.38 There is also sometimes an overlap between perversity appeals and 'inadequate reasons' appeals, which are dealt with below.

On the evidence

8.39 The first two categories allege perversity on the evidence and will almost always require the EAT to consider what evidence was or was not before the employment tribunal, unless the perversity is plain on the face of the employment tribunal's written reasons, which is unusual.[32]

No evidence

8.40 Where there is no evidence at all to support a finding made by the tribunal, this is a clear case of perversity.

8.41 However, it is sometimes difficult to prove a negative and it is often the case that the absence of evidence is best proved by identifying the evidence that was given on the issue and showing, in each case, how it contradicted the relevant finding or conclusion of the employment tribunal, ie that not only was there *no* evidence to support the finding, but the evidence which there was contradicts it.

---

[32] The procedure for agreeing a note of evidence and, where agreement is not possible, applying for the production of the chairman's notes of evidence is dealt with in Chapter 3.

Some evidence

8.42 'Some evidence' cases are difficult for the following reasons:

(1) It is not a proper or admissible ground of appeal that the employment tribunal 'failed to give sufficient weight' to particular evidence: *Eclipse Blinds Ltd v Wright* at p 135;[33] and *Chiu v British Aerospace plc*.[34] The hurdle is much higher.

(2) The instinctive reflex of the EAT will be that they are being invited to consider an (inadmissible) appeal seeking to reargue the facts.[35]

(3) The Court of Appeal has warned that appellate courts and tribunals should not be tempted to find that, merely because they are certain that they would have arrived at a different conclusion, the employment tribunal's conclusion is perverse.

(4) It is usually extremely difficult to agree a note, table or summary of the evidence given before the tribunal with sufficient precision to avoid the need for the EAT to trawl through a considerable volume of evidence. This presents problems of presentation and an impression of an appeal on the facts (as indicated above).

Particulars must be given

8.43 As noted in Chapter 3, para 2.6 of the EAT PD requires any perversity allegation in a notice of appeal to be accompanied by full particulars of the allegation. These should be set out in sufficient detail for the respondent to be able to consider and respond to the allegation of perversity: *Crofton v Yeboah*.[36]

Evidence must be agreed or chairman's notes produced

8.44 Certainly in 'some evidence' appeals and often in 'no evidence' appeals, it will be necessary to agree or obtain a note of the evidence that was before the tribunal. The procedure for doing so is dealt with in detail in Chapter 3 (at paras **3.262** to **3.295**), but the rationale for it is set out by Lord Dondaldson in *Martin v Glynwed Distribution Ltd*,[37] at para 18:

---

[33] [1992] IRLR 133.
[34] [1982] IRLR 56.
[35] See *Martin v Glynwed Distribution Ltd* [1983] IRLR 198, at para 17 and, for a striking example, *Barlow v Clifford & Co (Sidcup) Ltd* UKEAT/0910/04, [2005] All ER (D) 02 (Oct), also at para 17: 'We will deal with the grounds separately but we wish to make it clear that our overall impression of this appeal, having considered both the written and oral submissions from the Appellant is that this appeal, in general, has been no more than a thinly veiled attempt to re-litigate the facts of the case and at the outset, we remind ourselves that we should only interfere with the Tribunal's decision if there has been a clear error of law or an erroneous conclusion on the facts which would satisfy the high standard of a perversity appeal.'
[36] [2002] EWCA Civ 794, [2002] IRLR 634.
[37] [1983] IRLR 198.

'It was also submitted that the Tribunal's findings of fact were perverse. This involves the proposition that on the evidence no reasonable Tribunal could have reached the same conclusion. But neither we nor the Employment Appeal Tribunal had any note of the evidence which the Tribunal heard. It is no part of the duty of a Tribunal in setting out its reasons to record all the evidence. In practice, in telling the story, the Tribunal will often advert to parts of the evidence, but no court having an appellate jurisdiction limited to question of law is entitled to assume that this is the totality of the evidence. If it is intended to appeal upon the ground that there was no evidence to support the Tribunal's findings, the appellant must take the necessary steps to obtain a note of the evidence.'

Reliance on the documents before the tribunal

8.45 As Mummery LJ made clear in *Klusova v Hounslow London Borough Council*,[38] where perversity is alleged 'it is normally necessary to have available for the Court of Appeal all the relevant documents that were before the ET'. Note that this does not mean all the documents. The emphasis is on the *relevant* documents.

8.46 When drafting grounds of appeal alleging perversity, regard should therefore be had to all the documents from which the tribunal could have concluded as it did. If there is documentary support for the finding to be appealed, the appeal will not normally succeed.

A high hurdle

8.47 Although the *Wednesbury* test used in judicial review,[39] has been referred to in some of the cases[40] there is a sense from some cases that the bar for perversity appeals in *Crofton v Yeboah* is set, if anything, higher in employment appeals.

8.48 On any view, it is a high hurdle.

Inferences

8.49 A finding or conclusion will not be held to be perverse merely because there was no direct oral evidence to support it. An inference may properly be drawn from documentary evidence before the tribunal, despite there having been no oral evidence to support it: *Hough and APEX v Leyland DAF Ltd* at p 196.[41]

---

[38] [2007] EWCA Civ 1127, [2007] All ER (D) 105 (Nov).
[39] To treat a relevant factor as irrelevant is wrong under *Wednesbury* principles (*Associated Provincial Picture Houses Ltd v Wednesbury Corporation* [1948] 1 KB 223), as is reaching a decision which no reasonable decision maker, properly directing himself, could make.
[40] See *Adams v West Sussex County Council* [1990] ICR 546, considering appeals against interim orders
[41] [1991] IRLR 194.

8.50 The drawing of inferences is particularly important in discrimination cases and some other cases, such as whistleblowing, where the real reason for an act or omission by the employer is in issue. However, the drawing of inferences is quintessentially a matter for the tribunal hearing the case and is difficult to appeal.

8.51 Although the decision in *Chapman v Simon*[42] makes clear that an employment tribunal can only hold a person liable for acts of discrimination set out in the claimant's ET1, it is equally clear that it is permissible for the employment tribunal to have regard to discrimination allegations raised in evidence and going beyond those pleaded in the ET1. These evidential allegations often go back much earlier in time than the events pleaded in the ET1, but can play a highly material part in a tribunal's decision by setting the scene for the pleaded events and providing primary facts from which adverse inferences may be drawn: *Qureshi v Victoria University of Manchester*,[43] approved in *Anya v University of Oxford and Another*.[44]

8.52 Against this background, although inferences may be very important in a tribunal's decision, they will usually be very difficult to appeal.

8.53 However, as is made clear below, an inference may be challenged on appeal where the reason for drawing (or not drawing) the inferences is unexplained.

8.54 This reflects both the pivotal role that inferences may play in certain cases, as well as the important principle that parties should know why they won or lost.[45] If a key inference is wholly unexplained, it is difficult to say that the parties know why they won or, as the case may be, lost.

Overall conclusion

8.55 If the tribunal's overall conclusion defies logic or flies in the face of acknowledged employment practice, it will be appealable either on grounds of misdirection or perversity.

8.56 In *Ezsias North Glamorgan NHS Trust*,[46] the Court of Appeal held that the tribunal's decision to strike out a whistleblowing claim as having no reasonable prospects of success was 'legally perverse', on the basis that there were diametrically opposed cases on the reason for the dismissal and serious disputes on a crucial core of material facts. The court went on to say that it would only be in an exceptional case that an application to an employment tribunal will be struck out as having no reasonable prospect of success when the central facts are in dispute.

---

[42] [1994] IRLR 124.
[43] [2001] ICR 863.
[44] [2001] EWCA Civ 405, [2001] ICR 847.
[45] *Meek v City of Birmingham District Council* [1987] IRLR 250, per Bingham LJ.
[46] [2007] EWCA Civ 330, [2007] 4 All ER 940.

8.57 In *Conlin v United Distillers*,[47] the tribunal made three important findings, namely that:

(1) the employee had received a formal written warning that the likely consequence of further misconduct was dismissal;

(2) the employee had subsequently committed a deliberate fraud; and

(3) the employer had carried out a fair investigation.

8.58 Despite these findings (and the correct test for unfair dismissal being that the dismissal was outside the range of reasonable responses), the employment tribunal held the dismissal to be unfair, on the basis of various other factors, including that the fraud involved the sum of only £3. On appeal, the EAT overturned the decision. The Court of Session upheld the EAT's decision.[48]

8.59 However, it is important to note that both the EAT and the Court of Session upheld the appeal on the basis that the employment tribunal had misdirected itself as to the proper test to be applied, although it is clear that there is a strong sense in both judgments that the result reached was not a permissible option if the tribunal had directed itself correctly.[49]

8.60 So, this is perhaps a case which shows the perversity of the result underpinning parallel complaints that the employment tribunal did not set out the correct test for unfair dismissal and did not apply it. Had the result not seemed perverse, the appeal would not have succeeded as it did.

8.61 In *Smith v City of Glasgow District Council*,[50] Mr Smith was dismissed and the Council set out their reasons for dismissing him in a letter. The tribunal found that one of the alleged reasons which the employer relied was neither established as a matter of fact nor something which the employer had reasonable grounds to believe to be true. Nonetheless, the tribunal held the dismissal to have been fair. The House of Lords held that the dismissal was unfair, overturning the original tribunal's decision, since the flawed reason had been one of the most serious allegations against the employee and must have formed an important part of the Council's reason for dismissing him.

8.62 This is illustrates when the appellate courts will interfere with the conclusion reached by the tribunal (although a similar argument in relation to an allegation of dishonesty failed in *Barlow v Clifford & Co (Sidcup) Ltd*).[51]

---

[47] [1992] IRLR 503.
[48] [1994] IRLR 169.
[49] [1994] IRLR 169, see Lord Coulsfield's judgment in the Court of Session, at para 4.
[50] [1987] ICR 796, [1987] IRLR 326, HL.
[51] UKEAT/0910/04, [2005] All ER (D) 02 (Oct).

Exercising a discretion

8.63 The exercise of a discretion will rarely be appealed successfully. The proper approach to appealing an exercise of discretion is clearly and succinctly stated by Mummery LJ in *Roberts v Skelmersdale College* at para [29]:[52]

> '... I turn to the principles on which this court acts when there is an appeal against an exercise of discretion. I have already mentioned that rule 9(3) confers a wide discretion on an employment tribunal. In reviewing an exercise of discretion, the Court of Appeal acts in accordance with the general principle that it has to be shown by the appellant that the tribunal has either erred in principle in its approach to the case in the exercise of its discretion, or has left out of account or taken into account some feature which it should or should not have considered, or that its decision is plainly wrong because the court is forced to the conclusion that the various factors relevant to the exercise of discretion have not been fairly balanced in the scale.'

8.64 The difficulty is showing that material matters were not taken into account when they have been expressly mentioned by the employment tribunal. Showing that the exercise of a discretion is plainly wrong is equally difficult – it is the same high hurdle as an appeal on the ground of perversity. Therefore, appellants should be cautious about basing their appeal on a challenge to the exercise of a discretion. Respondents should alight upon any ground of appeal attacking the exercise of a discretion and look carefully at what the appellant's underlying complaint really is.

INADEQUATE REASONS

Introduction

8.65 A failure to provide adequate reasons for a decision may be a good ground of appeal.

8.66 However, like perversity, it should not be used as an opportunity to re-argue the facts. Nor is a perfectionist approach to the tribunal's reasons appropriate.

8.67 As Sedley LJ observed at para [26] of his judgment in *Anya v University of Oxford and Another*:[53]

> 'The courts have repeatedly told appellants that it is not acceptable to comb through a set of reasons for hints of error and fragments of mistake, and to try to assemble these into a case for oversetting the decision. No more is it acceptable to comb through a patently deficient decision for signs of the missing elements, and to try to amplify these by argument into an adequate set of reasons. Just as the courts will not interfere with a decision, whatever its incidental flaws, which has

---

[52] [2003] EWCA Civ 954, [2003] ICR 1127.
[53] [2001] EWCA Civ 405, [2001] ICR 847.

covered the correct ground and answered the right questions, so they should not uphold a decision which has failed in this basic task, whatever its other virtues.'

The duty to give reasons

8.68 The employment tribunal, like any statutory tribunal, must give reasons for its decisions.[54]

8.69 A failure to give any reasons will render a judgment a nullity: *Guest v Alpine Soft Drinks Ltd*,[55] and *Alexander Machinery (Dudley) Ltd v Crabtree*.[56]

8.70 As a public body determining the civil rights and obligations of the parties, an employment tribunal must also observe its obligations and accord the parties their fair trial rights under Art 6(1) of the European Convention, which is given effect in domestic law by HRA 1998.[57] These provisions give rise to a parallel duty to give reasons.

8.71 The duty to give reasons is also now found in r 30 of the ET Rules.

Rule 30(1): the duty

8.72 Rule 30(1) of the ET Rules provides:

'(1) A tribunal or chairman must give reasons (either oral or written) for any—

    (a)   judgment; or

    (b)   order, if a request for reasons is made before or at the hearing at which the order is made.'

8.73 Rule 30(1)(b) therefore represents an important qualification to the principle that an employment tribunal must give its reasons for any decision.

8.74 It is therefore important to seek the tribunal's reasons if you are not content with an order made by an employment tribunal. Failure to do so will make appealing considerably more difficult, as explained in Chapter 3.

Rule 30(6): written reasons for a judgment

8.75 Rule 30(6) of the ET Rules, provides as follows:

'(6) Written reasons for a judgment shall include the following information—

    (a)   the issues which the tribunal or chairman has identified as being relevant to the claim;

    (b)   if some identified issues were not determined, what those issues were and why they were not determined;

---

[54] This obligation is now qualified for interim decisions, such as orders, by r 30(1)(b) so that tribunals need only give reasons where they are sought at or before the hearing.
[55] [1982] ICR 110.
[56] [1974] ICR 120.
[57] Especially, ss 2 and 6.

(c) findings of fact relevant to the issues which have been determined;
(d) a concise statement of the applicable law;
(e) how the relevant findings of fact and applicable law have been applied in order to determine the issue;
(f) where the judgment includes an award of compensation or a determination that one party make a payment to the other, a table showing how the amount or sum has been calculated or a description of the manner in which it has been calculated.'

8.76 However, the rule is apparently 'a guide not a straightjacket'. A failure by an employment tribunal expressly to tick every box in r 30(6) will not necessarily amount to an error of law. As Buxton LJ commented in *Balfour Beatty Power Networks v Wilcox*:[58]

'I do not doubt that in future employment tribunals would be well advised to recite the terms of rule 30(6) and to indicate serially how their determination fulfils its requirements, if only to avoid unmeritorious appeals. But the rule is surely intended to be a guide and not a straitjacket. Provided it can be reasonably spelled out from the determination of the employment tribunal that what rule 30(6) requires has been provided by that tribunal, then no error of law will have been committed.'[59]

8.77 While the advice to tribunals to identify serially how their reasons fulfil the requirements of r 30(6) is plainly right and very sensible, the suggestion that the rule is intended to be a 'guide not a straitjacket' should not be taken out of context and regarded as undermining the requirements of r 30(6), for three reasons:

(1) first, because it is immediately followed by a requirement to identify how the tribunal has provided what *is* required by the rule;

(2) secondly, because the origins of the 'failure to give adequate reasons' ground of appeal lie in cases such as *Guest v Alpine Soft Drinks Ltd*,[60] and *Alexander Machinery (Dudley) Ltd v Crabtree*,[61] in which the requirement to give reasons was held to be mandatory, so that a failure to give any reasons will render the judgment a nullity; and

(3) it is practically difficult to see how a tribunal can explain to the parties why they have won or lost without satisfying the requirements of r 30(6).

Interim decisions

8.78 As noted above, reasons need only be given for orders and decisions other than judgments if they are requested at or before the hearing. However,

---

[58] [2006] EWCA Civ 1240, [2007] IRLR 63, at para [25].
[59] More recently applied in *D'Silva v Manchester Metropolitan University* UKEAT/0024/07 [2007] All ER (D) 10 (Oct), per His Honour Judge Peter Clark.
[60] [1982] ICR 110.
[61] [1974] ICR 120.

once reasons are so requested, the authors submit that the tribunal's duty to explain its reasoning is then the same as it was previously (eg, in cases such as *Roberts v Skelmersdale College*,[62] at para [13]), and the duty is to provide the parties with an explanation of why they won or lost, sufficiently clearly to show an appellate court that no error of law has been made.

What is required

Meek-compliance

8.79 Tribunals' reasons are sometimes referred to as being 'Meek-compliant' which is shorthand for satisfying the well known requirements in the case of *Meek v City of Birmingham District Council*.[63] In that case, Bingham LJ explained the requirement to give reasons as follows, at para 8:

> 'It has on a number of occasions been made plain that the decision of an Industrial Tribunal is not required to be an elaborate formalistic product of refined legal draftsmanship, but it must contain an outline of the story which has given rise to the complaint and a summary of the Tribunal's basic factual conclusions and a statement of the reasons which have led them to reach the conclusion which they do on those basic facts. The parties are entitled to be told why they have won or lost. There should be sufficient account of the facts and of the reasoning to enable the EAT or, on further appeal, this court to see whether any question of law arises; and it is highly desirable that the decision of an Industrial Tribunal should give guidance both to employers and trade unions as to practices which should or should not be adopted.'

Courts and tribunals

8.80 In *English v Emery Reimbold & Strict Ltd*,[64] the Court of Appeal considered the requirement of the courts to give reasons in a personal injury case. Although the statutory remit of employment tribunals may be different for some purposes,[65] it is clear that this case is regarded as the leading authority on the duty to give reasons generally.

8.81 Lord Phillips MR gave the judgment of the Court of Appeal and adopted Lord Bingham's formulation in *Meek* that 'The parties are entitled to be told why they have won or lost' when he held at para [16] that 'We would put the matter at its simplest by saying justice will not be done if is not apparent to the parties why one has won and the other has lost'.

8.82 He went on to consider what that meant in practice, albeit in an appeal concerning a judge's decision to prefer the evidence of one expert over another:

---

[62] [2003] EWCA Civ 954, [2003] ICR 1127.
[63] [1987] IRLR 250.
[64] [2002] EWCA Civ 605, [2003] IRLR 710.
[65] See the critical analysis of the *Barke v SEETEC Business Technology Centre Ltd* [2005] EWCA Civ 578, [2005] ICR 1373, procedure for the provision of further reasons by an employment tribunal, below.

'17. As to the adequacy of reasons, as has been said many times, this depends on the nature of the case: see for example Flannery at p 382. In the Eagil Trust case, Griffiths LJ stated that there was no duty on a judge, in giving his reasons, to deal with every argument presented by counsel in support of his case:

> "When dealing with an application in chambers to strike out for want of prosecution, a judge should give his reasons in sufficient detail to show the Court of Appeal the principles on which he has acted, and the reasons which led him to his decision. They need not be elaborate. I cannot stress too strongly that there is no duty on a judge in giving his reasons to deal with every argument presented by counsel in support of his case. It is sufficient if what he says shows the parties, and if need be the Court of Appeal, the basis on which he acted ... (see Sachs LJ in Knight v Clifton [1971] 2 All ER 378 at 392–393, [1971] Ch 700 at 721)" (p 122).

18. In our judgment, these observations of Griffiths LJ apply to judgments of all descriptions. But when considering the extent to which reasons should be given it is necessary to have regard to the practical requirements of our appellate system. A judge cannot be said to have done his duty if it is only after permission to appeal has been given and the appeal has run its course that the court is able to conclude that the reasons for the decision are sufficiently apparent to enable the appeal court to uphold the judgment. An appeal is an expensive step in the judicial process and one that makes an exacting claim on judicial resources. For these reasons permission to appeal is now a nearly universal prerequisite to bringing an appeal. Permission to appeal will not normally be given unless the applicant can make out an arguable case that the judge was wrong. If the judgment does not make it clear why the judge has reached his decision, it may well be impossible within the summary procedure of an application for permission to appeal to form any view as to whether the judge was right or wrong. In that event permission to appeal may be given simply because justice requires that the decision be subjected to the full scrutiny of an appeal.

19. It follows that, if the appellate process is to work satisfactorily, the judgment must enable the appellate court to understand why the judge reached his decision. This does not mean that every factor which weighed with the judge in his appraisal of the evidence has to be identified and explained. But the issues the resolution of which were vital to the judge's conclusion should be identified and the manner in which he resolved them explained. It is not possible to provide a template for this process. It need not involve a lengthy judgment. It does require the judge to identify and record those matters which were critical to his decision. If the critical issue was one of fact, it may be enough to say that one witness was preferred to another because the one manifestly had a clearer recollection of the material facts or the other gave answers which demonstrated that his recollection could not be relied upon.

20. The first two appeals with which we are concerned involved conflicts of expert evidence. In Flannery, Henry LJ quoted from the judgment of Bingham LJ in *Eckersley v Binnie* (1988) 18 Con LR 1 at 77–78 in which he said that "a coherent reasoned opinion expressed by a suitably qualified expert should be the subject of a coherent reasoned rebuttal". This does not mean that the judgment should contain a passage which suggests that the judge has applied the same, or even a superior, degree of expertise to that displayed by the witness. He should simply

provide an explanation as to why he has accepted the evidence of one expert and rejected that of another. It may be that the evidence of one or the other accorded more satisfactorily with facts found by the judge. It may be that the explanation of one was more inherently credible than that of the other. It may simply be that one was better qualified, or manifestly more objective, than the other. Whatever the explanation may be, it should be apparent from the judgment.

21. When giving reasons a judge will often need to refer to a piece of evidence or to a submission which he has accepted or rejected. Provided that the reference is clear, it may be unnecessary to detail, or even summarise, the evidence or submission in question. The essential requirement is that the terms of the judgment should enable the parties and any appellate tribunal readily to analyse the reasoning that was essential to the judge's decision.'

Desirable reasons

8.83 It is clear that the mere fact the further reasoning would have been desirable or would have assisted an appellate court in understanding the basis of the decision will not, without more, amount to an error of law. This is clear from the result in *English v Emery Reimbold & Strict Ltd*,[66] at paras 89 and 90:

'Summary

89. There were shortcomings in the judgment in this case. On a number of occasions we have had to consider the underlying material to which the judge referred in order to understand his reasoning. On one occasion, the significance of the fact that the milking cups were perpetually full of milk, we failed to follow his reasoning even with the benefit of the underlying material. At the end of the exercise, however, we have been able to identify reasons for the judge's conclusions which cogently justify his decision. While he did not express all of these with clarity in his judgment, he made sufficient reference to the evidence that had weighed with him to enable us, after considering that evidence, to follow that reasoning with confidence.

90. It follows that the appeal based on inadequacy of the reasons fails and must be dismissed.'

8.84 *Patel v Gorai*[67] is a good example of this proposition in action in the employment arena. It is a case in which further reasoning would have been useful but it was not an error of law for the tribunal not to have provided it. The EAT held:

'We accept that further detailed reasoning could usefully have been provided by the Tribunal. However, we bear in mind the approach of the Court of Appeal in English, see particularly the judgment of the Master of the Rolls paragraph 89.'

---

[66] [2002] EWCA Civ 605, [2003] IRLR 710.
[67] UKEAT/0052/07, [2007] All ER (D) 190 (Nov).

Development of principles

8.85 In *Union of Construction, Allied Trades and Technicians v Brain*,[68] Donaldson LJ said at p 227:

> 'Industrial Tribunals' reasons are not intended to include a comprehensive and detailed analysis of the case, either in terms of fact or in law ... The reasons are then recorded and no doubt tidied up for differences between spoken English and written English. But their purpose remains what it has always been, which is to tell the parties in broad terms why they lose or, as the case may be, win. I think it would be a thousand pities if these reasons began to be subjected to a detailed analysis and appeals were to be brought based upon any such analysis. This, to my mind, is to misuse the purpose for which the reasons are given.'

8.86 In *Varndell and Others v Kearney and Trecker Marwin Ltd*,[69] Eveleigh LJ adopted reasoning in Alexander Machinery (Dudley) Ltd v Crabtree,[70] stating as follows:

> 'It is impossible for us to lay down any precise guidelines. The overriding test must always be: is the Tribunal providing both parties with the materials which will enable them to know that the Tribunal has made no error of law in reaching its findings of fact? We do not think that the brief reasons set out here suffice for that purpose.'

8.87 Eveleigh LJ adds, at p 694G:

> 'He is not, as I read that judgment, saying that in every case all these points to which I refer must be adhered to, otherwise there will be an error of law in the decision of the Tribunal.'

8.88 In *Morris v London Iron and Steel Co Ltd*,[71] May LJ cited Eveleigh LJ in *Varndell*, at p 693:

> 'It seems to me that the arguments put forward on behalf of the employees in effect require, not a statement of reasons, but an analysis of the facts and arguments on both sides, with reasons for rejecting the arguments of the employees and reasons for accepting the facts relied upon in support of the tribunal's conclusion ... There is no right of appeal on a question of fact, so of what use, generally speaking, is it to have a detailed recitation of the evidence? A conclusion of fact with which this court or the appeal tribunal might disagree, provided it is justifiable on the evidence, gives rise to no ground of appeal.'

8.89 In the light of more recent cases, the emphasis is now on providing sufficient reasons for an appellate court to see that the finding or conclusion is 'justifiable on the evidence'.

---

[68] [1981] IRLR 225.
[69] [1983] ICR 683.
[70] [1974] ICR 120.
[71] [1988] QB 493.

8.90 In *Martin v Glynwed Distribution Ltd*[72] at p 202, Lord Donaldson identified the tribunal's duty as follows:

> 'The duty of an Industrial Tribunal is to give reasons for its decision. This involves making findings of fact and answering a question or questions of law. So far as the findings of fact are concerned, it is helpful to the parties to give some explanation of them, but it is not obligatory. So far as the questions of law are concerned, the reasons should show expressly or by implication what were the questions to which the Industrial Tribunal addressed its mind and why it reached the conclusions which it did, but the way in which it does so is entirely a matter for the Industrial Tribunal.'

Illustrations

Law or test applied

8.91 Just one example is *Voteforce Associates Ltd v Quinn*[73] in which His Honour Judge Peter Clark gave the judgment of the EAT:

> '[16] As to that, we begin with the tribunal's reasoning. First, we are quite unable to see the relevance of the provisions relating to the calculation of a week's pay, to be found in reg 16, to the question of continuity. Regulation 16 provides that ss 221–224 of the Employment Rights Act 1996 (ERA) shall apply for the purpose of determining the amount of a week's pay for paid leave, with certain modifications. In particular, the reference in those provisions to s 228 does not apply.'

Unresolved issue

8.92 In *Lambe v 186k Limited*,[74] the Court of Appeal considered a failure to resolve an issue between the parties, as follows:

> '[63] This leaves the pension issue. In our judgment, this is a question in which the Appellant succeeds on a *Meek v City of Birmingham District Council* basis. We have set out how the issue arises in paras 17 to 21 of this judgment. The Tribunal deals with the matter in the following way:
>
> > "[9] There was an issue as to whether Mr Lambe was misled as to his pension entitlement by opting to take a sum in lieu of notice rather then remaining employed until the end of his notice period [...] However, we have heard no evidence today to make us believe that he would have done anything different then to what he did in February. At that time he made his own enquiries of the Pension Administrator and made the decision that he would take the cash option and we think that the same thing would have happened had he been making that decision at the end of March. On that basis, there is no further compensation payable in relation to the pension."

---

[72] [1983] IRLR 198.
[73] [2002] ICR 1.
[74] [2004] EWCA Civ 1045, [2005] ICR 307.

[64] We agree with Mr Green that this paragraph of the Tribunal's reasons neither identifies the issue nor addresses it. The reasoning appears to be that if the Appellant had had (as he should have done) an additional seven weeks with the Respondent before his employment terminated he would still have taken the cash option. This thinking not only piles hypothesis upon hypothesis, but does not address the case, which was being advanced by the Appellant.

[65] Furthermore, the matter is not cured by the EAT, which itself appears to misunderstand the issue since it records the Tribunal as "not persuaded on the evidence that (the Appellant) would have taken that option (ie the deferred pension) in February 2002 when dismissal took place". The EAT also deals inadequately with the issue, stating shortly: "No doubt the Tribunal balanced in their minds the options available to the Appellant" and going on to say that the question seemed to them a matter of judgment for the Tribunal, and one moreover which did not give rise to an issue of law. We do not agree. It is axiomatic that a failure properly both to identify and address an important issue, with the consequence that neither side can understand clearly why it won or lost, is clearly an error of law.'

8.93 This was a fairly clear case of a failure to resolve an issue, although it was not appreciated by the EAT. Equally clear but different is the situation where one party's case is effectively ignored and the employment tribunal simply adopts the other party's case wholesale, without any scrutiny, analysis or explanation. Such a situation arose in *English Royal Mail Group Ltd*,[75] where the employment tribunal simply repeated one side's closing written submissions and ignored the other side's, compounding this by failing to distinguish in the reasons between submissions and findings of fact. This decision, perhaps unsurprisingly failed to comply with the requirements of r 30(6) to give adequate reasons. Where, for example, the constructive dismissal is in issue, it is plainly important for the tribunal to make proper findings of fact before reaching a conclusion of law as to effect of those findings of fact – you cannot do the second without the first exercise. In *Comfort v Lord Chancellor's Department*,[76] Peter Gibson LJ held as follows, at para 32:

'With all respect to the EAT in arriving at a different conclusion, in the circumstances it seems to me plain that the ET erred in coming to its decision on constructive dismissal without making findings on the evidential dispute about the meetings and without explaining why it left that factual dispute out of account. That failure on so important a matter in controversy constitutes, in my judgment, an error of law ...'

Unexplained decision not to draw inferences

8.94 It seems that the level of detail required in the employment tribunal's reasons may be less than in straightforward unfair dismissal cases. In *Deman v Association of University Teachers*,[77] the Court of Appeal considered a failure

---

[75] UKEATPA/0098/08/MAA; UKEAT/0027/08//MAA 3 July 2008, per Bean J.
[76] [2004] EWCA Civ 349, CA, LTL 16/3/2004, recently applied in *Mackenzie v Billing Aquadrome* UKEAT/0238/08, heard on 21 August 2008.
[77] [2003] EWCA Civ 329, [2003] 20 LS Gaz R 27.

by the employment tribunal to explain why it had not drawn inferences that could permissibly have been drawn from the evidence, in a race discrimination case:

> '46. In our judgment, the first and most obvious criticism of the ET's decision is the assertion in paragraph 21 of the reasons that "the Tribunal is unable to find any evidence from which an inference of race discrimination or victimisation could be drawn against the Respondents". That is manifestly incorrect. The findings made in paragraphs 17 and 18 of the reasons (recorded at paragraph 16 onwards of this judgment) provide abundant material, in our view, from which inferences of discrimination could properly be drawn. "Could", of course, is the operative word. It is for the Tribunal, who heard and saw the witnesses to assess their credibility and their motivation. It is for this reason that an analysis of the evidence, and the provision of reasons explaining why inferences have or have not been drawn, is so important.
>
> 47. The EAT regarded the appellant's attack on paragraph 21 of the ET's reasons as little more than a quibble". It said:
>
> "The Tribunal was surely saying that looking at the evidence as a whole, including that which it accepted as to incompetence and corner cutting, there was nothing left which was unaccounted for on those grounds from which the inference can be drawn. That is not a conclusion which, as to the first two key events, we can say was in error of law."
>
> 48. That analysis was, of course, enthusiastically adopted by counsel for the Respondent in this appeal. With great respect, however, we are unable to accept it. Bearing in mind, as we do, the caution given by Peter Gibson LJ in *Miriki v Bar Council* cited at paragraph 32 of this judgment, that the Chairman, whilst a lawyer is not a full time judge, there is, we suggest, a very substantial difference between, on the one hand, there being no evidence from which inferences of race discrimination or victimisation can properly be drawn; and, on the other a situation in which there was evidence from which such inferences could properly be drawn, but where the Tribunal had come to the conclusion that it was not appropriate to draw them. To give paragraph 21 of the ET's reasons the interpretation which the EAT gave it is, in our judgment, impermissibly to re-write them.
>
> 49. Even if paragraph 21 is given the meaning the EAT ascribed to it, the mischief, in our judgment, is not cured. If what the Tribunal was saying was that there was evidence from which inferences could properly be drawn, it was under a clear obligation to explain fully why it had decided not to draw them. In other words, it had to give reasons for its decision.'

Unexplained drawing of inferences

8.95 In *Governors of Warwick Park School v Hazlehurst*,[78] Pill LJ said at para [28]:

---

[78] [2001] EWCA Civ 2056, [2001] All ER (D) 39 (Dec).

'In my judgment, it is quite impossible, looking at the detailed findings as a whole, to find a decisive pointer towards a racially discriminatory attitude. It is impossible to find in the judgment of the employment tribunal any reason why they drew the inference they did from the facts they found. Bingham LJ stated in *Meek* that a party before an employment tribunal is entitled to know why it lost. The respondents in this case have no sufficient indication of that from the judgment of the employment tribunal. In the absence of reasoning, there is a real danger that the inference has been wrongly drawn.'

8.96 This is also a good example of the need for an appellate court to be able to see from the employment tribunal's reasoning whether or not the employment tribunal has erred in law.

8.97 There are numerous cautions in other cases, warning against an employment tribunal drawing an inference of discrimination without explaining the factual basis from which that inference can properly be drawn: for example, *Effa v Alexandra Health Trust and Another*.[79]

No reasoning

8.98 In *Hartel v Al-Ghazali Multi-Cultural Centre and Another*,[80] His Honour Judge Pugsley gave the judgment of the EAT and specifically contrasted two different types of inadequacy of reasoning:

'8. We accept the point made by Mr Thacker that this Tribunal decision does not fall into the error which is unhappily commonly the case where a Tribunal decision faithfully and methodically records the evidence it hears on one side and then the evidence of the other, but at no stage makes findings of fact as to what it accepts with sufficient clarity so that one can see why they have reached the conclusion they did.

9. However, we are concerned that the decision falls into another error namely of allowing its conclusions to become its reasons. We are all of the view that having read this decision the way in which it emerges does not enable us to follow a chain of reasoning that leads either to the majority decision or the minority decision. Whilst it is abundantly clear that the majority view accepted the evidence of the Claimant on crucial issues and the minority Chairman did not, it is not possible to identify the route by which this destination was arrived at by either majority or the minority members of the Tribunal. We are united in saying that at times the judgment comes across as though its conclusions have become its reasons.'

Where reasons are required

8.99 The following headings are taken from r 30 and are illustrated by examples which might fall under those headings, although most of the cases have been decided on general principles and before r 30 was introduced. Laying these examples out in this way is therefore intended to be illustrative only.

---

[79] [1999] All ER (D) 1229.
[80] UKEAT/0064/07, [2007] All ER (D) 244 (Dec).

Rule 30(6)(a): issues relevant to the claim

8.100 *Lambe v 186k Limited*,[81] provides a good example of a failure to identify (or determine) an issue at para [64] of the judgment.

Rule 30(6)(b): issues not determined and why

8.101 If an issue has been raised and identified by the tribunal, it is an error of law simply to fail to decide it: *Lambe* (above) and *Portsea Island Mutual Co-operative Society Ltd v Rees*.[82]

8.102 There may be cases where an issue ceases to be relevant, perhaps because it is overtaken by the evidence, for example, where a claimant in an unfair dismissal case agrees that a fair procedure would have made no difference. However, where any matter which was clearly in issue is no longer material it is incumbent on the tribunal to say why, either expressly or at the very least, implicitly in its reasons.

8.103 It is important for tribunals to show their reasoning, particularly in discrimination cases, and to follow their findings through to a reasoned conclusion. As Sedley LJ explained in *Anya v University of Oxford and Another*:[83]

> 'It is simply that it is the job of the tribunal of first instance not simply to set out the relevant evidential issues, as this industrial tribunal conscientiously and lucidly did, but to follow them through to a reasoned conclusion except to the extent that they become otiose; and if they do become otiose, the tribunal needs to say why. But the single finding of the industrial tribunal in this case on Dr Roberts's honesty as a witness, while important, does not make the other issues otiose: on the contrary, it begs all the questions they pose. Mr Underhill's reliance on it as effectively dispositive overlooks what Lord Goff said in *The Ocean Frost* [1985] I Lloyds LR 1, 57:
>
>> "It is frequently very difficult to tell whether a witness is telling the truth or not; and where there is a conflict of evidence ... reference to the objective facts and documents, to the witnesses' motives and to the overall probabilities can be of very great assistance to a judge in ascertaining the truth".'

Rule 30(6)(c): relevant findings of fact

8.104 Where there are conflicts of evidence on 'significant issues of fact', the tribunal must make clear its finding on that issue so that its conclusion can be readily ascertained from a reading of the decision as a whole: *Levy v Marrable & Co Ltd*,[84] at p 587E.

---

[81] [2004] EWCA Civ 1045, [2005] ICR 307.
[82] [1980] ICR 260.
[83] [2001] EWCA Civ 405, [2001] ICR 847.
[84] [1984] ICR 583.

8.105 For example, while it is well known that a tribunal should expressly state the principal reason for the dismissal in an unfair dismissal case, where there is more than one operative reason, the tribunal's duty is to explain how it arrived at its conclusion on which was the principal reason: *Speciality Care plc v Pachela and Another*.[85]

8.106 The relevant findings of fact will not just be the facts which are directly in dispute between the parties, but will also include those facts which provide the basis for any inferences drawn by the tribunal.

8.107 In *Qureshi v Victoria University of Manchester*,[86] Mummery J explained this as follows:

> 'The process of making inferences or deductions from primary facts is itself a demanding task, often more difficult than deciding a conflict of direct oral evidence. In *Chapman v Simon* [1994] IRLR 124 (supra) at paragraph 43, Peter Gibson LJ gave a timely reminder of the importance of having a factual basis for making inferences. He said–
>
>> "... Racial discrimination may be established as a matter of direct primary fact. For example, if the allegation made by Ms Simon of racially abusive language by the headteacher had been accepted, there would have been such a fact. But that allegation was unanimously rejected by the tribunal. More often racial discrimination will have to be established, if at all, as a matter of inference. It is of the greatest importance that the primary facts from which such inference is drawn are set out with clarity by the tribunal in its fact-finding role, so that the validity of the inference can be examined. Either the facts justifying such inference exist or they do not, but only the tribunal can say what those facts are. A mere intuitive hunch, for example, that there has been unlawful discrimination is insufficient without facts being found to support that conclusion" (see also Balcombe LJ at paragraph 33(3)).'

8.108 As Sedley LJ held in Anya v University of Oxford and Another,[87] at para [10]:

> 'Running through this guidance, and the guidance cited in it, is the ubiquitous need to make the findings of primary fact without which it is impossible to consider the drawing of relevant inferences. It can be found again in this court's judgment in *Marks and Spencer plc v Martins* [1998] IRLR 326, which cites Lord Browne-Wilkinson's reminder in *Glasgow City Council v Zafar* [1998] IRLR 36, 38–39 that:
>
>> "Claims [of race and sex discrimination] present special problems of proof for complainants since those who discriminate on grounds of race or gender do not in general advertise their prejudices".'

---

[85] [1996] ICR 633.
[86] [2001] ICR 863.
[87] [2001] EWCA Civ 405, [2001] ICR 847.

8.109 In discrimination cases, preferring one witness to another baldly will be insufficient.

8.110 Hence, it is vital that a tribunal should clearly identify the factual findings from which it draws any inferences.[88]

Rule 30(6)(d): concise statement of the applicable law

8.111 In *United Distillers v Conlin*,[89] Lord Coulsfield endorsed the suggestion that the employment tribunal should refer to or summarise the relevant provisions:

> 'In *Scottish & Newscastle Beer Production Ltd v Cannon*, the Employment Appeal Tribunal emphasised that unless the Industrial Tribunal does refer to s 57(3) or at least summarise the wording, the Employment Appeal Tribunal may have difficulty in concluding that the Industrial Tribunal has applied its mind to the statutory requirements. That is no doubt so, and we agree with what the Employment Appeal Tribunal has said regarding this matter in this case.'

Rule 30(6)(e): how facts and law applied

8.112 It is helpful and will sometimes be vital for the tribunal to set out how it has applied the facts and the relevant law to arrive at its conclusions.

8.113 A good example is whistleblowing cases, in which a tribunal should set out the necessary elements in turn, considering each one separately and thereby explaining how the law and facts have been applied to reach the decision: *Knight v Harrow London Borough Council*.[90]

Rule 30(6)(f): calculation of compensation

8.114 The principle that the parties should know why they have won or lost applies equally to each element and the overall calculation of any compensation. An employment tribunal must properly explain how it has arrived at any sum it awards by way of compensation and should identify, for example, the following:

(1) how it has calculated any components of the award, including pension loss, any credit for sums paid by the employer;

---

[88] See also *British Gas plc v Sharma* [1991] IRLR 101 at 105; *Wadman v Carpenter Farrer Partnership* [1993] IRLR 374.
[89] [1994] IRLR 169.
[90] [2003] IRLR 140.

(2) 'a recital of or a reference to the facts which justify the award, accompanied by any necessary indication of the scale of quantification which is being used' where applying guidelines to assessing compensation at large;[91]

(3) the basis of any Polkey reduction;[92]

(4) the basis of any reduction for contributory conduct;[93]

(5) whether and how any relevant statutory maximum has been applied (eg, on a week's pay or the total amount of the compensatory award for unfair dismissal).[94]

8.115 In *Dore v Aon Training Ltd*[95] the employment tribunal effectively made two errors in its decision on the claimant's loss of earnings: first, it ignored the actual loss of earnings and secondly, it had failed to give its reasons for doing so.

8.116 In *Dignity Funerals v Bruce*[96] (Court of Session), the tribunal's decision gave no adequate reasons for not awarding compensation for the period from the dismissal to the hearing.

Additional Reasons

8.117 The present state of the law is that where the EAT finds a possible inadequacy in the reasons provided by the employment tribunal, it may seek further reasons from the employment tribunal. For some time, this was known as the *Burns* procedure, following *Burns v Royal Mail Group plc (formerly Consignia plc) and Another*[97] but is now often referred to as the *Burns/Barke procedure*, following the Court of Appeal's decision in *Barke v SEETEC Business Technology Centre Ltd*[98] confirming yet qualifying the approach in *Burns*.

8.118 The authors respectfully doubt the correctness of the decision in *Barke* and their critical analysis of it is set out below. However, the *Burns/Barke* procedure remains the law.

---

[91] *Dunnachie v Kingston-upon-Hull City Council* [2004] EWCA Civ 84, [2004] IRLR 287 at para [55], per Sedley LJ.
[92] *Market Force (UK) Ltd v Hunt* [2002] IRLR 863.
[93] *Parkers Bakeries Ltd v Palmer* [1977] IRLR 215; *Savoia v Chiltern Herb Farms Ltd* [1981] IRLR 65.
[94] *Darr v LRC Products Ltd* [1993] IRLR 257.
[95] [2005] EWCA Civ 411, [2005] IRLR 891.
[96] [2005] IRLR 189.
[97] [2004] ICR 1103.
[98] [2005] EWCA Civ 578, [2005] ICR 1373.

Obtaining additional reasons

8.119 Where you are considering bringing an appeal on the basis of inadequate reasons, you should consider carefully whether further reasons should be sought from the employment tribunal while the case is fresh in its mind.

8.120 In *Bansai v Alpha Flight Services*,[99] the EAT said at para 22 that it was good practice to do so:

> 'In our opinion it is certainly good practice, where parties are legally represented in employment tribunals, for advocates to ask the tribunal to amplify its reasoning where it is considered that there has been a material omission in its findings of fact or in its consideration of the issues of fact and law before it. Where reasons are given ex tempore the application should be made at the time. If reasons are given in writing the request should be made as soon as possible after the reasons are received. We would encourage advocates to seek clarification from the employment tribunal promptly in any case where there might otherwise be an appeal based on alleged insufficiency of reasons. It is much easier for tribunals to deal with requests for clarification when they are fresh in their minds and the amplification of insufficient reasons and findings will save the parties time and expense and may in some cases obviate the need for an appeal and subsequent remission of the case.'

PROCEDURAL IRREGULARITY

8.121 Paragraph 11.1 of the EAT PD requires an appellant who intends to complain about the conduct of the employment tribunal (eg, bias, apparent bias or improper conduct by the chairman or lay members or any procedural irregularity at the hearing) to include in the notice of appeal full particulars of each complaint made.

8.122 By paragraph 11.1, at the sift stage or before, the judge or registrar may postpone a decision as to track, and direct that the appellant or a representative provide an affidavit setting out full particulars of all allegations of bias or misconduct relied upon. Paragraph 11.2 of the 2008 EAT PD introduces a specific provision[100] permitting the registrar to enquire of the party making any complaint of bias whether it is intended to proceed with it and to draw the party's attention to the costs warning in para 11.6. This reflects the (possibly increasing) unpopularity of allegations of bias or misconduct. They are serious allegations and should not be made without cause.

---

[99] [2007] ICR 308.
[100] EAT PD, para 11.2.

Bias

8.123 Bringing an appeal on the ground of bias (usually apparent bias rather than actual bias) is another case where you face a high hurdle.

8.124 There are detailed procedural requirements for such appeals, as to which see Chapter 3, para 11 of the EAT PD and *Facey v Midas Retail Security Ltd and Another*.[101]

The test

8.125 The well known test of bias was expressed by Lord Hope of Craighead in *Porter v Magill, Weeks v Magill*[102] at para [103], in these terms:

> 'The question is whether the fair-minded and informed observer having considered the facts, would conclude that there was a real possibility that the tribunal was biased.'

8.126 While recognising that each case must be carefully considered on its own facts, it has been said that a real danger of bias might well be thought to arise if:[103]

(1) there were personal friendship or animosity between the judge and any member of the public involved in the case; or

(2) the judge were closely acquainted with any member of the public involved in the case, particularly if the credibility of that individual could be significant in the decision of the case; or

(3) in a case where the credibility of any individual were an issue to be decided by the judge, the judge had in a previous case rejected the evidence of that person in such outspoken terms as to throw doubt on his ability to approach such person's evidence with an open mind on any later occasion; or

(4) on any question at issue in the proceedings before him the judge had expressed views, particularly in the course of the hearing, in such extreme and unbalanced terms as to throw doubt on their ability to try the issue with an objective judicial mind; or

(5) for any other reason, there were real grounds for doubting the ability of the judge to ignore extraneous considerations, prejudices and predilections and bring an objective judgment to bear on the issues.

---

[101] [2001] ICR 287.
[102] [2001] UKHL 67, [2002] 2 AC 357.
[103] *Locabail (UK) Ltd v Bayfield Properties Ltd* [2000] IRLR 96, at para 25.

8.127 In *Lodwick v London Borough of Southwark*,[104] the Court of Appeal again applied the same test to determine whether an employment tribunal chairman (now judge) should stand down, ie whether a fair-minded and informed observer, having considered the facts, would conclude that there was a real possibility that the tribunal was biased. Previous adverse findings or comments by a judge or lay member do not establish, bias, without more. However, if there is apparent bias of a chairman, that is not negated by the fact that he sits with two lay members who could outvote him.[105]

8.128 Note, however, that the mere making of a complaint about the conduct of the tribunal is not sufficient to require the tribunal to decide to recuse itself and the substance of the complaint must be analysed with care: *Ansar v Lloyds TSB Bank plc and Others*.[106]

Hearing evidence

8.129 In *Ansar v Lloyds TSB Bank plc and Others*,[107] His Honour Judge Burke QC delivered the EAT's judgment after a hearing over 4 days spent analysing a whole series of alleged incidents over a 36-day hearing in the employment tribunal. These incidents were alleged to establish apparent bias on the part of the tribunal, including alleged inconsistent conduct between the parties, and alleged unfairness in how the appellant's case was treated.

8.130 It is clear from para 57 of the judgment that the EAT did not feel that it had received much benefit from oral evidence from the witnesses (including cross-examination):

> 'We would not wish to end without taking the opportunity to express our concern, after an appeal which has lasted three and a half days of judicial time at the Employment Appeal Tribunal, time which is valuable, not for itself, but because of the other cases that need to be dealt with, mostly dedicated to the consideration of the allegations of bias and misconduct. There is no need for us once again to repeat the scriptures of Rimer J in *London Borough of Hackney v Sagnia*, paragraphs 63 to 66, or the warning contained in paragraph 11 of the EAT practice direction. We do not seek to discourage properly arguable appeals, and loyally follow the guidance of the Court of Appeal that the Employment Appeal Tribunal must resolve material disputes of fact where there is a complaint about the behaviour of a member of the Employment Tribunal ... and must, unless the allegation is totally without merits on its face, exercise its powers in the manner contemplated in the practice direction before reaching its decision, thus giving the Claimant, the Respondent and members of the Tribunal the opportunity to say what happened. But there is no reason why this cannot be done – and, in our judgment, this should have been such a case – by way of a consideration under

---

[104] [2004] EWCA Civ 306, [2004] ICR 884.
[105] Any decision on recusal of one member should generally be made by the whole tribunal: *Da'Bell v NSPCC* UKEAT/0044/08, 13 February 2008.
[106] [2006] EWCA Civ 1462, [2007] IRLR 211.
[107] [2006] ICR 1565.

Rule 3(7) and (10) of the Employment Appeal Tribunal Rules, and the same goes for a preliminary hearing, without a full hearing and without cross-examination.'

8.131 This case points towards a practice of weeding out weak or unmeritorious bias appeals[108] before they are allowed to go to a full hearing, and certainly without the EAT hearing oral evidence unless this is absolutely necessary.

Personal relationships

8.132 In *Jones v DAS Legal Expenses Insurance Co Ltd*,[109] the Court of Appeal held that there was no bias established in a case where a tribunal chairman's husband was a barrister who was occasionally instructed by the respondent company. In any event, the applicant had waived his right to object by not raising any objection when given the opportunity to do so. Equally in *Jones and Baird v TGWU*,[110] Lady Smith gave the EAT's judgment in which it roundly rejected an allegation of an appearance of bias arising from the Chairman having been formerly employed by another union (Unison) as its legal officer.

Personal interest

8.133 A direct financial interest in the outcome of a case will be enough to engage the duty to disclose the interest and usually enough to constitute apparent bias.

8.134 However, a personal interest may be relevant even if much more remote. In the well known case of *R v Bow Street Metropolitan Stipendiary Magistrate ex parte Pinochet Ugarte (No 2)*,[111] Lord Hoffman should have recused himself because of his wife's link with commercial arm of an intervening party, the charity Amnesty International.

Conduct in previous cases

8.135 In *Ansar v Lloyds TSB Bank plc and Others*,[112] the Court of Appeal held that a chairman had been entitled to refuse a request to recuse himself from sitting at a pre-hearing review. Even though there were outstanding complaints of bias against him relating to his dismissal of the claimant's earlier case against the same respondents, those allegations were not of a kind that

---

[108] Allegations of bias require proof and generalised assertions of an alleged lack of even-handedness from a group of dissatisfied witnesses will not suffice: *London Borough of Hackney v Sagnia* [2005] All ER (D) 61 (Oct), applied in *Ansar v Lloyds TSB Bank plc and Others* [2006] ICR 1565.
[109] [2003] EWCA Civ 1071, [2004] IRLR 218. A similar point also arose in *Hamilton v GMB (Northern Region)* [2007] IRLR 391.
[110] UKEATS/0003/07 and UKEATS/0004/07, 6–7 February 2008.
[111] [2000] AC 119.
[112] [2006] EWCA Civ 1462, [2007] IRLR 211.

would lead a fair-minded observer to conclude that there was any real possibility that the chairman was biased against the claimant in the second set of proceedings.

Closed mind and pre-judging

8.136 The premature expression of a concluded view or the manifesting of a closed mind by the tribunal may amount to the appearance of bias.[113]

8.137 That was held to be the case in *Ezsias North Glamorgan NHS Trust*[114] in which the tribunal's decision to strike out a whistleblowing claim was vitiated by apparent bias. Previous statements by the judge to the effect that the claimant had no reasonable prospect of success were such that a fair-minded and informed observer would conclude that there was very little prospect that the claimant would be able to shift her from her view. The employment judge's view in the case was plainly intended to be a conclusive view of the claimant's prospects of success. Any comments alleged to constitute bias must be judged in the context of the hearing as a whole.[115] What might indicate bias before a hearing will be judged differently if said after the conclusion of a hearing.[116] As noted above in relation to inadequate reasons, an employment tribunal simply repeating verbatim the closing written submissions of one party and ignoring those of the other party without distinguishing between submissions and findings of fact, will not comply with the requirements of due process and of r 30(6) of the ET Rules of Procedure. This may evidence apparent bias in the sense of not approaching the resolution of the issues even-handedly.[117]

Prejudices

8.138 In *Diem v Crystal Services plc*,[118] the chairman sought to establish if the claimant was seeking to expand her claim of race discrimination to include less favourable treatment on the grounds of her colour as well as her Vietnamese national origin. He asked whether she was claiming to be non-white and said that her skin colour was as white as the English, pointing to the skin of his other hand to stress the point and adding that 'your skin looks whiter than mine'. The EAT held the fair-minded observer would have concluded that the remarks made were likely to cause the claimant to feel unsettled, humiliated and embarrassed, and the case was remitted to a fresh tribunal. Contrast this

---

[113] Peter Gibson LJ in *Southwark London Borough Council v Jiminez* [2003] EWCA Civ 502, [2003] ICR 1176 at para [25]. See also *Mortimer v Reading Windings Ltd* [1977] ICR 511 (prejudging issue of resignation); *Peter Simper & Co Ltd v Cooke* [1986] IRLR 19 (uninformed unqualified remarks hostile to employer's case); and *Alstom Transport v Tilson* UKEAT/0532/07, 4 December 2007 (reference to evidence not relied upon by parties on joinder issue effectively (or apparently) prejudged issue on pre-hearing review).
[114] [2007] EWCA Civ 330, [2007] 4 All ER 940.
[115] *Anthony v Governors of Hillcrest School* EAT/1193/00, 28 November 2001.
[116] *Greenaway Harrison Ltd v Wiles* [1994] IRLR 380.
[117] *English Royal Mail Group Ltd* UKEATPA/0098/08; UKEAT/0027/08, 3 July 2008, per Bean J.
[118] [2006] All ER (D) 84 (Feb).

with the EAT's decision in *Advance Security UK v Musa*,[119] which held that an employment tribunal did not give the appearance of bias when the Employment Judge clarified for the Claimant-in-person the racial group he belonged to for the purposes of the Race Relations Act 1976.

Excessive intervention

8.139 Excessive intervention by a tribunal may, but will not always, be capable of establishing a claim of bias. It is always necessary to apply the 'fair-minded and informed observer' standard, and also to consider whether the interventions are in fact an indication of bias, rather than, for example, over-zealous case management or an enthusiasm for understanding the evidence: *DeMarco Almeida v Opportunity Equity Partners Ltd*.[120]

Unfairness of hearing

8.140 This category of grounds covers a variety of issues and has some overlap with situations in which bias might be alleged (see, for example: 'Excessive intervention' above). It is important to note that where unfairness would be a sufficient ground it may be neither necessary or desirable to allege bias (see, eg the requirements of the EAT PD for allegations of bias, and especially EAT PD, paras 11.2 and 11.6 noted above). Parties should however expect the EAT and Court of Appeal to take a realistic (if not robust) approach on some questions of unfairness, particularly having regard to whether any error amounting to unfairness was material[121] . One example was *Judge v Crown Leisure Limited*,[122] in which the Court of Appeal adopted a robust approach to what was, on the face of it, an unfair failure by the employment tribunal to invite submissions from the parties on a finding of fact which neither side had contended for (recently applied in *Woodhouse School v Webster*[123]). Smith LJ held as follows:

> '[20] Mr Mulholland now accepts that it was open to the ET to make the findings of the fact that it made about what had been said at the Christmas party. He complains, and plainly with justification, that neither the Appellant nor the Respondent had contended for that finding and had not anticipated it. They had not had the opportunity to address the Tribunal upon the legal impact of that finding. Mr Mulholland submits that it is a cardinal principle of fairness that the parties should have the opportunity to be heard on any issue that is likely to be relevant to the decision. As a general proposition, that is obviously right. It is highly desirable that if a Tribunal foresees that it might make a finding of fact which has not been contended for, that possible finding should be raised with the parties during closing submissions. If the Tribunal does not realise what its findings of fact are likely to be until after the hearing has finished, it will usually

---

[119] UKEAT/0611/07, 21 May 2008.
[120] [2006] UKPC 44.
[121] UKEAT/0225/07, 29 February 2008.
[122] [2005] IRLR 823.
[123] UKEAT/0459/07, 24 April 2008.

be necessary to give the parties the opportunity to make further submissions, at least in writing, although not, in my view, necessarily by oral argument.

[21] However, the giving of such an opportunity is not, in my judgment, an invariable requirement. That is so for two reasons. First, paragraph 11 of the Employment Tribunal Regulations gives the ET a wide discretion on procedural matters. It seems to me that that discretion is wide enough to encompass a decision as to the appropriate course to take where this kind of situation arises. In any event, if the legal effect of the findings of fact that are to be made is obviously and unarguably clear, no injustice will be done if the decision is promulgated without giving that opportunity. Even if an opportunity should have been given and was not, the consequence will not necessarily be that an appellate court will set aside the decision of the lower court. It will only do so if it concludes that the lower court's application of the law was wrong.'

Sir Martin Nourse said (at para [26]):

'I read again what the Employment Tribunal said at the end of paragraph 9 of their extended reasons: "The Tribunal was not, however, satisfied that Mr Fannon, particularly in an environment such as that described above, either would have or indeed did enter into any legally binding contractual commitment to the applicant whatsoever". That view, a perfectly tenable one to be taken by a Tribunal whose composition includes two industrial members, was formed after they had heard both Mr Judge and Mr Fannon give evidence. The ultimate question is whether there is any real possibility that if Mr Mulholland had been given the opportunity to make the submissions he now seeks to make at a rehearing, the Employment Tribunal would have come to a different view. Mr Mulholland has failed to satisfy me that there is such a possibility. The Employment Tribunal's view must have been based on their impression of the evidence of Mr Judge and Mr Fannon and it is unrealistic to suppose that any submissions by counsel, however persuasive, would have been able to change it.'

Representation

8.141 In *Bache v Essex County Council*,[124] the Court of Appeal held that an employment tribunal had acted outside its powers in ruling that the employee's representative could no longer represent her on her complaint of unfair dismissal and directing that she should represent herself.

Evidence

8.142 If an employment tribunal wrongly excludes evidence or prevents a party from adducing evidence which is both relevant and admissible, this may be an error of law. It is possible to characterise it as an erroneous exercise of discretion, but where it results in unfairness, it may be equally appropriate to characterize it as unfairness at the hearing.

---

[124] [2000] ICR 313, [2000] IRLR 251.

8.143 *Zargaran v Zargaran London*[125] is a good example of unfairness in the way the hearing was conducted. In that case, the employment tribunal wrongly held that the claimant's representative could not ask any questions about differences between the witness statement originally exchanged by the respondent and the materially different statements which the tribunal had permitted the respondent's witnesses to rely on at the hearing.

8.144 It was not a question of bias. The employment tribunal was simply wrong on this point. In the event, on appeal, Burton P took a very robust view indeed and found that the tribunal had made an error of law in refusing to allow that cross-examination but held the error not material, which was an interesting decision.

Moving the goal posts

8.145 In most cases nowadays, a list of issues will be prepared before the full hearing in the employment tribunal. This helps the parties and the employment tribunal to concentrate on those issues and serves as a useful reference point for the closing submissions of the parties and the judgment and written reasons of the employment tribunal.

8.146 Against that background, it is obvious that the parties will each conduct their case on the basis of the issues before the employment tribunal, as they understand them to be – indeed, this is the case even when there is no list of issues.

8.147 It is a basic principle of natural justice that the employment tribunal should not decide the case (or any issue) on a basis which the parties have not had an opportunity to address.

8.148 In *Sheridan v Stanley Cole (Wainfleet) Ltd*[126] the Court of Appeal considered the test to be applied in determining whether failure by a tribunal to alert parties to a relevant authority[127] renders the decision appealable. The test, was ultimately one of unfairness was includes the following elements:

(1) the authority must be central to the employment tribunal's decision and play an influential part in shaping the judgment;

(2) in the mind of a fair-minded observer, it must significantly alter the way in which parties might have wished to address the case, in a way that the appellant could not reasonably have anticipated.

---

[125] EAT/1062/01, [2003] All ER (D) 140 (Mar).
[126] [2003] EWCA Civ 1046, [2003] IRLR 885.
[127] Ie decided case, setting a relevant principle of law.

8.149 The need for a tribunal to raise an issue with the parties, so that they may address it is well established. In *Bahl v Law Society*[128] the Court of Appeal approved the judgment of Elias J in the EAT.

8.150 A similar issue arose in the unusual case of *D'Silva v Manchester Metropolitan University*,[129] in which the claimant succeeded in a race discrimination case without actually attending the hearing. The natural justice point was explained by His Honour Judge Peter Clark in the following terms at para 31:

> '... we recognise the possibility in the unique circumstances of the present case that, in the absence of the Claimant, it was open to the Employment Tribunal to raise with the Respondent an actual or hypothetical comparator not identified by the Claimant on his case on paper and if necessary to consider that comparison. What, in our view, is impermissible as a matter of natural justice is to construct some different comparator without giving the Respondent an opportunity to deal with the point.'

Tribunal's inattention

8.151 In *Stansbury v Datapulse*,[130] Mr Stansbury lost his unfair dismissal case before the employment tribunal and essentially complained that one of the members of the employment tribunal had been drunk and had fallen asleep. He first applied to the employment tribunal for a review of its decision on various grounds including the member being drunk and asleep but the tribunal rejected this, the tribunal chairman stating that the member's conduct should have been drawn to the attention of the tribunal at the hearing. He appealed to the EAT, which dismissed his appeal, declining to make any findings about the member being 'apparently in a drunken state' despite having called for comments for many of those who were there. The Court of Appeal allowed his appeal, holding that it was the duty of the employment tribunal to be (and to appear to be) alert during the whole of the hearing. A member of a tribunal who does not appear to be alert may cause that hearing to be held to be unfair, both under English law and under Art 6(1) of the Human Rights Convention, on balance accepting that the allegations of drunkenness and falling asleep had been made out. Peter Gibson LJ concluded as follows (at para [33]):

> 'In my judgment, a hearing by a tribunal which includes a member who has been drinking alcohol to the extent that he appeared to fall asleep and not to be concentrating on the case does not give the appearance of the fair hearing to which every party is entitled. Public confidence, as Mr Kibling pointed out, in the administration of justice would be damaged were we to take the view that such behaviour by a member of the tribunal did not matter. In my judgment, we should say firmly that the conduct of [the lay member] at the hearing was wholly inappropriate for any member of a tribunal.'

---

[128] [2004] EWCA Civ 1070, [2004] IRLR 799, at para 156.
[129] UKEAT/0024/07 [2007] All ER (D) 10 (Oct).
[130] [2003] EWCA Civ 1951, [2004] ICR 523.

Public hearing

8.152 A failure to hold a hearing in public as required may breach the requirements of fairness (see *Storer v British Gas plc*).[131] Employment tribunals are now careful to ensure that the doors to the tribunal remain unlocked!

Delay

8.153 An appeal on the ground of delay by a tribunal will normally succeed only where there is a real risk that a party has been denied or substantially deprived of his rights, under Art 6 of the European Convention, to a fair trial, so that it would be unfair and unjust to allow the delayed decision to stand.[132] In *Connex*, the delay did not create such a risk and it was therefore fair to allow the decision to stand. The reality is normally that in order to establish the necessary evidence of unfairness, an appellant will have to demonstrate facts which would probably establish other appealable errors. In most cases, therefore, delay as a ground of appeal will usually add very little to an appeal.[133] That said, there will be rare cases where the delay is so extreme that the delay itself may establish the necessary unfairness.

ERRORS OF JURISDICTION

8.154 Errors of jurisdiction are classic errors of law, rather than errors of fact.

8.155 Since the employment tribunal and the EAT are created by statute, they have no powers or jurisdiction beyond what is conferred by various Acts of Parliament and subsidiary legislation (such as Regulations etc).

8.156 This means that if an employment tribunal exercises jurisdiction which it does not have, its decision is a nullity and of no effect.[134] Whether or not an employment tribunal has made an error of jurisdiction is a question of law (although it may depend on findings of fact by the employment tribunal which are much more difficult to overturn on appeal, since they have to be perverse before they can amount to an error of law).

Composition of employment tribunal

8.157 Improper constitution of the employment tribunal is a matter which may go to the jurisdiction of the employment tribunal. Even if it does not go to jurisdiction, it is an appealable irregularity which will often result in a rehearing of the case.[135]

---

[131] [2000] ICR 603.
[132] *Connex South Eastern Ltd v Bangs* [2005] EWCA Civ 14, [2005] ICR 763.
[133] See eg *Slingsby v Griffith Smith* UKEAT/0619/07 per HHJ McMullen QC.
[134] See the criticism of the *Burns/Barke* procedure, for obtaining additional reasons from the employment tribunal, in Chapter 8.
[135] See *Secretary of State for Trade and Industry v Langridge* [1991] Ch 402 in particular at pp

Employment judge sitting alone

8.158 In a case where the views and experience of the lay members are likely to be of assistance to the decision-making process, a chairman should generally decide, pursuant to s 4(5) of ETA 1996, that the case be heard by a full tribunal.[136]

8.159 In *Sogbetun v Hackney London Borough Council*[137] the EAT adopted a very strict approach and held that a failure by a chairman (now employment judge) expressly to exercise his discretion to sit alone rendered went directly to his jurisdiction and rendered his decision a nullity, on the following basis:[138]

'Paragraphs 9, 13 and 14 of the judgment in the *Sogbetun* [1998] IRLR 676 case are to the effect that:

(a) before he sits alone in the qualifying proceedings identified by s.4(3) Industrial Tribunals Act 1996 a chairman must have exercised his discretion conferred by s.4(5) negatively (our emphasis),

(b) a case cannot be heard by a chairman sitting alone without the matters referred to in s.4(5) having been evaluated by a chairman,

(c) the consent of the parties is not determinative as to how the discretion of the chairman concerning whether or not he, or she, should sit alone should be exercised,

(d) unless the chairman exercises his, or her, discretion under s.4(5) an employment tribunal comprising a chairman sitting alone that adjudicates on a qualifying case is not properly constituted in accordance with the statute,

(e) if the employment tribunal is not for that reason properly constituted its decision is a nullity, and

(f) the points as to the proper constitution of the employment tribunal, and its effect, are ones of jurisdiction and the parties cannot confer jurisdiction by consent, waiver, acquiescence or estoppel.'

8.160 In *Post Office v Howell*,[139] the EAT again held that the employment tribunal chairman had erred in sitting alone to hear a complaint of unlawful deduction from wages, without having first considered whether to exercise his discretion under s 4(5) of ETA 1996 to sit with lay members, and again allowed the appeal, remitting the case for hearing by a full employment tribunal.

8.161 While following *Sogbetun* that it was an error of law not to exercise the discretion, the EAT adopted a much more liberal approach:

410F–411G and also the recent cases of *Gladwell v Secretary of State for Trade and Industry* [2007] ICR 264; *Przybylska v Modus Telecom Ltd* EAT/0566/06, [2007] All ER (D) 06 (May), and *Lawrence v HM Prison Service* [2007] IRLR 468.

[136] *Post Office v Howell* [2000] ICR 913.
[137] [1998] ICR 1264.
[138] This is the summary of the reasoning made by the EAT in *Post Office v Howell* [2000] ICR 913, below.
[139] See fn 138 above.

(1) this error did not go to his jurisdiction and the decision was therefore not a nullity; and

(2) as to the test of whether the discretion had, in fact, been exercised or not, the EAT held:

'Greater flexibility as to the stance of the parties would be introduced. For example, if they formally agreed and consented to the chairman sitting alone, this might be treated as an exercise of discretion by an overt, or tacit, acceptance of the agreement, or in some circumstances the irregularity might be held to have been waived.'

8.162 In *Sterling Developments (London) Ltd v Pagano*,[140] the EAT held that if a party wishes to challenge the composition of the tribunal, it must do so before the full hearing on liability takes place. Any reasoned judicial decision taken after representations on the point will be susceptible to appeal, but a judgment on the substantive issues in a case presided over by a lone chairman whose jurisdiction has not been questioned will not to be open to challenge on the basis that it was made by an incompetent tribunal.

Territorial jurisdiction

8.163 The statutory provisions providing employment protection (such as ERA 1996, the Sex Discrimination Act 1976, etc) are all limited in the geographical or territorial scope of their application, although not all in the same way. If an employee's employment falls outside the territorial scope of the relevant statutory provisions, it will be a clear error of law for a tribunal to purport to exercise jurisdiction by hearing the substantive case and making any award in favour of the employee (or for that matter, any other substantive order). The tribunal may however hold a hearing to determine whether it has jurisdiction or not.

8.164 That question will depend on:

(1) the scope of the substantive rights conferred by the statute itself; and,

(2) since the recent cases of in *Bleuse v MBT Transport and Another*[141] and *GMB v Holis Metal Industries*,[142] upon whether the rights conferred are primarily domestic rights or EU-derived rights (eg, rights now found in UK legislation, but originating in the Treaty, an EC Regulation or Directive, which the domestic legislation purports to implement).

8.165 Another jurisdiction issue (not technically territorial jurisdiction) arose in the well known case of *United Arab Emirates v Abdelghafar*,[143] in which the

---

[140] [2007] IRLR 471.
[141] UKEAT/0632/06, [2007] All ER (D) 392 (Dec).
[142] UKEAT/0171/07, [2007] All ER (D) 304 (Dec).
[143] [1995] ICR 65.

United Arab Emirates asserted State immunity, at a very late stage. The notice of appeal was very late, but as the issue went to jurisdiction of the original tribunal and the UK had international obligations to respect State immunity, an extension of time was granted to allow this point to be determined on appeal. The issue of territorial jurisdiction is dealt with fairly fully in Chapter 9, but the short point for the purposes of this chapter is simply to identify that an error of jurisdiction is a classic error of law.

Jurisdiction on remission

8.166 A classic example is the well known case of In *Aparau v Iceland Frozen Foods plc*[144] in which the Court of Appeal considered a situation in which a case had been remitted to the employment tribunal by the EAT and on remission, the employment tribunal had, with the agreement of both parties, re-considered an issue which the EAT had not remitted to it.

8.167 The Court of Appeal held that, like any other tribunal, an employment tribunal (then called an industrial tribunal) had exhausted its jurisdiction once it had delivered a final decision disposing of all the issues before it.[145]

8.168 After that, it only retained the limited power of review given by the relevant procedural rules (then the 1993 Regulations, now the 2004 Regulations – see Chapter 2) and therefore the tribunal had no power to reopen the hearing or reconsider its decision unless the matter had been remitted to it by the EAT.

8.169 The Court of Appeal was clear that a decision outside the employment tribunal's jurisdiction was a nullity.

8.170 The Court of Appeal held in particular that:

(1) that the jurisdiction of the tribunal was derived wholly from statute and that the lack of objection on the part of the employee to the course taken by the tribunal (considering an issue not remitted to it by the EAT) could not confer jurisdiction on the employment tribunal which did not otherwise exist;

(2) that on a remission the tribunal had no power to reconsider any matter other than that or those specifically remitted to it; and

(3) that in all other respects the tribunal had exhausted their jurisdiction.

8.171 Moore-Bick J, with whom Mance LJ and Peter Gibson LJ expressly agreed, held at para [25]:

'The effect of an order remitting a case to a tribunal which had otherwise exhausted its jurisdiction was considered by this court in the context of arbitral

---

[144] [2000] 1 All ER 228 at 235J–236A.
[145] The Latin term for this exhaustion of jurisdiction being *'functus officio'*.

proceedings in *Interbulk Ltd v Aiden Shipping Co Ltd (The "Vimeira" (No.1))* [1985] 2 Lloyd's Rep. 410. Ackner L.J. pointed out that the extent to which the tribunal's jurisdiction is revived in consequence of an order remitting the matter to it depends entirely on the scope of the remission.

If, as occurred in the present case, the matter is remitted for the Tribunal to consider certain specific issues, it will have no jurisdiction to hear or determine matters outside the scope of those issues and it must follow that it has no power to allow one party to amend its case to raise issues which were not previously before it.

In the present case it is clear from the passages in the judgment of the Employment Appeal Tribunal to which I have already referred that remission was ordered in very limited terms simply to enable the Employment Tribunal to reconsider whether Iceland's new terms of employment had been accepted by Mrs Aparau.

That being so, the Tribunal did not by virtue of the remission have jurisdiction to reopen the case generally, nor did it have jurisdiction to hear or determine any argument on the part of Iceland relating to the fairness of any dismissal. Although Mr Glennie sought to persuade us to the contrary, I for my part am quite satisfied that that was not an issue which had previously been raised in the proceedings and it was certainly not within the scope of the remission.'

8.172 Errors of jurisdiction may be raised at any time[146] and the EAT and appellate courts have been much more sympathetic to entertaining points on jurisdiction as new points, not raised in the employment tribunal, than to any other alleged error of law. This is for good public policy reasons and reflects the fact that if the argument that there is no jurisdiction is correct, then the decision being appealed is a nullity.

8.173 The circumstances in which the appellate courts can disturb an employment tribunal's findings of primary fact, inferences and exercises of discretion are far more difficult to define.

FURTHER REASONS: BARKE V SEETEC BUSINESS TECHNOLOGY CENTRE LTD

The procedure

8.174 The EAT has the power to invite an employment tribunal to amplify its reasons, in accordance with the procedure explained in *Burns v Royal Mail Group plc (formerly Consignia plc) and Another*.[147]

---

[146] When there remains a live issue between the parties, but not after settlement.
[147] [2004] ICR 1103.

The power

Justification in Burns was wrong

8.175 The power justifying the procedure was not that adopted by that EAT in *Burns*.

8.176 In *Burns*, the EAT had held that the power to use this procedure was derived from the provision in s 35(1) of ETA 1996, that:

> '(1) For the purposes of disposing of an appeal, the Appeal Tribunal may—
>
> (a) exercise any of the powers of the body or officer from whom the appeal was brought, or
> (b) remit the case to that body or officer.'

8.177 The Court of Appeal held this was a straightforward matter of statutory construction and that the words 'for the purpose of disposing of an appeal' referred to the final disposal of the appeal and no other stage.

8.178 If those words had a wider meaning, they were 'surplusage' on the basis that:[148]

> 'It goes without saying that everything that the Employment Appeal Tribunal does when it is seised of an appeal is done with a view to the eventual disposing of the appeal. If it had been intended that these powers could be exercised at any stage of the process, then the words "for the purpose of disposing of an appeal" would serve no useful purpose.'

8.179 Therefore, the majority view of the Court of Appeal in *Tran v Greenwich Vietnam Community Council*,[149] that the EAT does not have power under s 35(1) to remit a case to the employment tribunal for fuller reasons prior to a further hearing of the appeal, was correct.

The Barke justification

8.180 The Court of Appeal identified an alternative power justifying the use of the *Burns* procedure, which requires careful scrutiny.

8.181 The Court of Appeal relied in its decision on four key points:

(1) Rule 30(3)(b) of the ET Rules, which provides that written reasons will be provided 'in relation to any judgment or order if requested by the EAT at any time'.

(2) Rule 30(1) provides that the employment tribunal 'must give reasons (either oral or written) for any judgment ...'. If the employment tribunal

---

[148] Barke, at para 20.
[149] [2002] EWCA Civ 553, [2002] ICR 1101.

has provided no or no adequate reasons, it has not complied with this duty, 'it cannot be said to be *functus officio*'.

(3) Section 30(3) of ETA 1996 provides that 'subject to Appeal Tribunal procedure rules, the Appeal Tribunal has the power to regulate its own procedure'. The *Burns* procedure, 'codified in the 2004 Practice Direction', therefore, amounted to the exercise of a discretionary case management power.

(4) The employment tribunal is able to correct slips in its judgment or reasons and review any decision. Both of these powers are exercisable after its decision has been entered on the register and sent to the parties. This shows that it retains jurisdiction in the case.

(5) In *English v Emery Reimbold & Strick Ltd*[150] the Court of Appeal indicated that this procedure was applicable in the courts and it should apply equally in the employment tribunal jurisdiction.

8.182 The Court of Appeal also noted that the overriding objective required the EAT to deal with cases justly which included saving expense.

Critical analysis

8.183 In reaching its decision, the Court of Appeal repeatedly observed that there was nothing in the statutory scheme to prohibit the *Burns* procedure. An alternative view is that this is a distraction from the crucial questions:

(1) Is such a procedure specifically authorised by ETA 1996 or the relevant tribunal Rules?

(2) If not, is it inconsistent with any provisions of the statutory scheme viewed as a whole?

8.184 If the *Burns* procedure is inconsistent with the statutory scheme as a whole, individual provisions should not be stretched unnaturally to accommodate it.

Critique of the key points

8.185 Following the three key points of the Court of Appeal's reasoning, the author's alternative view is as follows:

(1) Rule 30(3)(b) of the ET Rules clearly contrasts the EAT's ability to request the tribunal's reasons *at any time*, on the one hand, with the time limits imposed upon the parties r 30 for requesting the tribunal's reasons, on the other. This is clear from the fact that r 30 begins 'Subject to

---

[150] [2002] EWCA Civ 605, [2003] IRLR 710 at 714, per Lord Phillips MR, paras [24] and [25].

paragraph (1), written reasons shall only be provided'. Rule 30(3)(b) does not provide a power for the tribunal to provide a second, third or fourth raft of reasoning for the EAT or the parties.

(2) The obligation in r 30(1) to give reasons is clear. However, to say that if the employment tribunal has provided no or no adequate reasons, it has not complied with this duty and therefore 'it cannot be said to be *functus officio*' is to confuse the doing of an act with the adequacy of correctness of it. It cannot be said that a tribunal can reserve jurisdiction to itself to provide further reasons (beyond that specifically provided by the rules for a slip or a review) simply by giving inadequate reasons, in breach of its duty to give adequate reasons.

(3) While s 30(3) of ETA 1996 gives the EAT the power to regulate its own procedure, subject to the EAT Rules, it does not give the EAT power to extend its own jurisdiction or that of the employment tribunal.

(4) The employment tribunal is able to correct slips in its judgment or reasons and review any decision. However, the ET Rules make specific and detailed provision for these powers and the procedure by which they are exercised. No such provision is made for the *Burns* procedure. The need to make such provision for the correction of slips (by way of example) shows why the absence of such provision for the *Burns* procedure is significant.

(5) Dicta in *English v Emery Reimbold & Strick Ltd*[151] were wrongly regarded as applying equally to the statutory framework of the employment tribunals and EAT, without reference to the statutory limitations which apply to these particular tribunals.

A new theory

8.186 It is fair to say that the Court of Appeal's justification of the *Burns* procedure relied on an entirely new theory (not that expressed in *Burns*), as the following earlier cases illustrate.

Aparau

8.187 Once the employment tribunal has given its decision, it is *functus officio*, subject to the limited and clearly defined provisions for review and correction of slips: *Aparau v Iceland Frozen Foods plc*.[152]

Tran

8.188 In *Tran v Greenwich Vietnam Community Council*,[153] the majority of the Court of Appeal disagreed with what is now the practice in the EAT but,

---

[151] [2003] IRLR 710 at p 714, per Lord Phillips MR at paras [24] and [25].
[152] [2000] 1 All ER 228, at 235J–236A.
[153] [2002] EWCA Civ 553, [2002] ICR 1101.

significantly, was only considering it on the basis of the power suggested to exist in s 35 which in *Barke* was rejected. At para [36], Arden LJ stated:

> 'I am satisfied that the power of remission in s.35 of the Employment Tribunals Act 1996 can only be utilised where the employment tribunal is making a final order on an appeal, generally an order allowing the appeal. I do not consider that a court or tribunal can be said to be "disposing" of an appeal if it simply makes an interim order such as would be involved in remitting a case to the employment tribunal to clarify its reasons prior to a further hearing of the appeal. As Brooke LJ observes, retaining an appeal is not the same thing as disposing of it.'

Leverton

8.189 That majority view echoed the judgment of May LJ in *Leverton v Clwyd County Council*:[154]

> '... in my respectful opinion, an appeal to the Employment Appeal Tribunal should be decided upon the Industrial Tribunal's reasons as originally drafted, and I deprecate any procedure whereby these may be supported or enlarged by any direct communication between the Industrial Tribunal on the one hand and the Employment Appeal Tribunal on the other.'

Reuben

8.190 Morrison J, as president of the EAT, carefully analysed the issue and agreed in *Reuben v Brent London Borough Council*.[155] He regarded *Yusuf and Others v Aberplace Ltd*[156] as wrongly decided and held:

> '15. It is the Employment Tribunal's function to give a decision in accordance with their Rules of Procedure. The decision, once given, is promulgated to the parties and entered in the Register. The Register contains all promulgated decisions and is open to public scrutiny. Apart from correcting any error under the slip rule [which correction would be added to the Register] once a decision has been entered in the Register, the Employment Tribunal is "functus officio". If it became aware that an appeal had been made, it would be quite improper for the ET to seek to comment on the grounds of appeal or try and improve the decision or to fill in gaps. The only circumstance in which a Tribunal may make comment is when there is an allegation of bias [...]
>
> 16. If the EAT, as in this case, asks the Chairman to amplify his decision then there is immediately a problem. What status do the Chairman's additional words have? They are not entered in the Register. Under what principle of law may a decision maker in the judicial field be given a second chance to get his decision right, in the light of the notice of appeal? Of course, if the EAT considered on the hearing of the appeal that the ET had not, but should have, dealt with a particular point then it could allow the appeal and remit the matter back to determine particular issues. By that process, the Employment Tribunal has been re-invested

---

[154] [1989] IRLR 28.
[155] [2000] IRLR 176.
[156] [1984] ICR 850.

with the power to consider the case further, and is no longer functus officio. Any further decision would be required to be entered in the Register and there could be a further appeal against the new decision. The short-cut route adopted in this case ignores the status of a Tribunal which has concluded its task, and gives it a chance to make another, informal decision which has no legal status and deprives the appellant of a separate right of appeal against the "second attempt".'

8.191 One view is that Morrison J's jurisdictional analysis is soundly based on the express provisions of the statutory framework and merits consideration.

Lambe

8.192 In *Lambe v 186k Limited*[157] the Court of Appeal held that that the EAT had exhausted its jurisdiction in dismissing the appeal at a preliminary hearing, and that the proper course was for the appeal to proceed on its merits in the Court of Appeal. (This is not the same point, but reinforces the continued application of the doctrine of exhaustion of jurisdiction by the Court of Appeal.)

8.193 The doctrine of exhaustion of jurisdiction applies in this situation. It circumscribes the employment tribunal's powers and jurisdiction. The employment tribunal's jurisdiction, function and powers are only those provided for by Parliament, which do not admit the later provision of 'supplemental material' in a letter or other communication from the chairman.

Employment tribunal

8.194 The relevant Regulations in the employment tribunal are as follows:

'**17. Register**

(1) The Secretary shall maintain a Register which shall be open to the inspection of any person without charge at all reasonable hours.

(2) The Register shall contain a copy of all judgments and any written reasons issued by any tribunal or chairman which are required to be entered in the Register in accordance with the rules in Schedules 1 to 5.

(3) The Register, or any part of it, may be kept by means of a computer.

18. Proof of decisions of tribunals

The production in any proceedings in any court of a document purporting to be certified by the Secretary to be a true copy of an entry of a judgment in the Register shall, unless the contrary is proved, be sufficient evidence of the document and of the facts stated therein.'

8.195 The relevant rules (in addition to r 30) are as follows:

---

[157] [2004] EWCA Civ 1045, [2005] ICR 307.

'28. Orders and judgments

(1) Chairmen or tribunals may issue the following—

  (a) a "judgment", which is a final determination of the proceedings or of a particular issue in those proceedings; it may include an award of compensation, a declaration or recommendation and it may also include orders for costs, preparation time or wasted costs;
  (b) an "order", which may be issued in relation to interim matters and it will require a person to do or not to do something ...

(3) At the end of a hearing the chairman (or, as the case may be, the tribunal) shall either issue any order or judgment orally or shall reserve the judgment or order to be given in writing at a later date ...

29. Form and content of judgments

(1) When judgment is reserved a written judgment shall be sent to the parties as soon as practicable. All judgments (whether issued orally or in writing) shall be recorded in writing and signed by the chairman.

(2) The Secretary shall provide a copy of the judgment to each of the parties and, where the proceedings were referred to the tribunal by a court, to that court. The Secretary shall include guidance to the parties on how the judgment may be reviewed or appealed.

(3) Where the judgment includes an award of compensation or a determination that one party is required to pay a sum to another (excluding an order for costs, expenses, allowances, preparation time or wasted costs), the document shall also contain a statement of the amount of compensation awarded, or of the sum required to be paid.

32. The Register

(1) Subject to rule 49, the Secretary shall enter a copy of the following documents in the Register—

  (a) any judgment (including any costs, expenses, preparation time or wasted costs order); and
  (b) any written reasons provided in accordance with rule 30 in relation to any judgment.

(2) Written reasons for judgments shall be omitted from the Register in any case in which evidence has been heard in private and the tribunal or chairman so orders. In such a case the Secretary shall send the reasons to each of the parties and where there are proceedings before a superior court relating to the judgment in question, he shall send the reasons to that court, together with a copy of the entry in the Register of the judgment to which the reasons relate.'

8.196 Rules 34–36 make express and detailed provision for review by the employment tribunal.

8.197 However, correction of slips or errors is specifically provided for:

'**37. Correction of judgments, decisions or reasons**

(1) Clerical mistakes in any order, judgment, decision or reasons, or errors arising in those documents from an accidental slip or omission, may at any time be corrected by certificate by the chairman, Regional Chairman, Vice President or President.

(2) If a document is corrected by certificate under paragraph (1), or if a decision is revoked or varied under rules 33 or 36 or altered in any way by order of a superior court, the Secretary shall alter any entry in the Register which is so affected to conform with the certificate or order and send a copy of any entry so altered to each of the parties and, if the proceedings have been referred to the tribunal by a court, to that court.

(3) Where a document omitted from the Register under rules 32 or 49 is corrected by certificate under this rule, the Secretary shall send a copy of the corrected document to the parties; and where there are proceedings before any superior court relating to the decision or reasons in question, he shall send a copy to that court together with a copy of the entry in the Register of the decision, if it has been altered under this rule ...'

The statutory scheme

8.198 The effect of the Regulations and Rules above is that express provision is made for the judgment and reasons of an employment tribunal to be entered on the register and to have status as such and express provision is made for both review and the correction of any slips or errors. No such provision is made for providing additional reasons after the tribunal has purported to dispose of the case finally (see the definition of 'judgment').

Confined jurisdiction

8.199 As discussed above in relation to jurisdiction on remission,[158] it is clear that the employment tribunal and EAT have no powers or jurisdiction outside those provided in the statutory framework. Neither the EAT nor the employment tribunal may assume them. As noted above, in *Aparau v Iceland Frozen Foods plc*[159] the Court of Appeal held that, like any other tribunal, an industrial tribunal *exhausted its jurisdiction once it had delivered a final decision* disposing of all the issues before it. Thereafter, apart from the limited power of review given by the relevant procedural rules (then the 1993 Regulations), the employment tribunal has no power to reopen the hearing or reconsider its decision unless the matter had been remitted to it by the EAT. The Court of Appeal was clear that a decision outside the employment tribunal's jurisdiction was a nullity (see para **8.169** above, per Moore-Bick J).

8.200 The Court of Appeal held in particular:

(1) that the jurisdiction of the tribunal was derived wholly from statute and that the lack of objection on the part of the employee to the course taken

---

[158] See paras **8.18.1** to **8.170**.
[159] [2000] 1 All ER 228, at 235J–236A.

by the tribunal (considering an issue not remitted to it by the EAT) could not confer jurisdiction on the tribunal which did not otherwise exist;

(2) that on a remission the tribunal had no power to reconsider any matter other than that or those specifically remitted to it; and

(3) that in all other respects the tribunal had exhausted their jurisdiction.

8.201 The authors' view is that neither the reasoning in *Aparau* nor the statutory scheme of the employment tribunals is readily reconcilable with the practice approved in *Burns*.

CONCLUSION

8.202 There is much more to say about the *Burns/Barke* procedure, especially as to the analysis of the power of different statutory tribunals and the practical consequences of such a procedure. However, that will have to wait for any further edition of this book or a brave advocate before the Court of Appeal or House of Lords.

8.203 In conclusion, it is the authors' view that although the *Burns/Barke* procedure is both expedient and convenient, there is no clear lawful jurisdiction for the EAT to seek or rely on 'supplementary material' containing necessary additional reasons which the employment tribunal failed to give on an issue which the employment tribunal purports to have determined and on which it has given a judgment (with reasons) which has been sent to the parties and entered in the register. Equally, there is no jurisdiction in the employment tribunal to provide it.

Chapter 9

THE EMPLOYMENT APPEAL TRIBUNAL'S JURISDICTION, CONSTITUTION AND POWERS

OVERVIEW

9.1 This chapter will deal with the jurisdiction of the EAT and will also consider the constitution and administrative arrangements of the EAT in more detail than set out in Chapter 3 above. It also briefly considers what impact, if any, the Government's proposed administrative tribunals reforms will have on the EAT.

9.2 Apart from the EAT's 'original' jurisdiction which does not fall within the scope of this book, employment appeals arising from cases in the employment tribunal are:

- necessarily limited (in their scope and subject matter) to the jurisdiction of the employment tribunal;

- further limited, by the nature of the appellate jurisdiction of the EAT (ie questions of law only), which defines the limits of any appeals to the Court of Appeal or House of Lords thereafter.

9.3 There are two ways that the question of jurisdiction can therefore arise in an employment appeal:

- as a ground of appeal that the employment tribunal did not have jurisdiction to make the order it did; or

- as to whether the EAT (or a higher court) has jurisdiction to entertain the appeal.

ISSUES ON JURISDICTION

9.4 The employment tribunal's jurisdiction mainly concerns unfair dismissal claims, a wide range of discrimination claims, whistleblowing, wages claims and breach of contract claims. These matters are well covered by commentators on procedure in the employment tribunal and it would not be possible to cover every aspect of employment tribunal's jurisdiction in this book and so we only briefly mention the most common ways that the question of jurisdiction arises in the employment tribunal. These are as follows:

- the claimant was not an employee nor 'worker';

- the claimant does not have sufficient period of continuous employment with the respondent;[1]

- the claim was not presented in time (including any extensions allowed);

- the statutory grievance or disciplinary procedures have not been correctly followed;

- the constitution (ie membership) of the employment tribunal was unlawful;[2]

- the claim did not fall within the employment tribunal's territorial jurisdiction.

9.5 As is made clear in Chapter 8, jurisdiction is a 'hard edged' question of law; in that the tribunal either does have jurisdiction, or it does not. If the tribunal does not have jurisdiction, then any decision, order or judgment by the tribunal is a nullity.

9.6 Since a jurisdictional question may be raised much more readily at any stage of the appeal process, even if it was not raised in the employment tribunal below, the jurisdiction generally should always be carefully considered. It is clear that a party may raise the issue of jurisdiction even where that party has consented to the tribunal exercising the jurisdiction which the party is now challenging.[3]

9.7 While other aspects of jurisdiction are too broad to cover in detail here, the *territorial* limits on the jurisdiction of the employment tribunal (and therefore, also on any appeal) are briefly explained below, since they are becoming increasingly relevant and the law is developing in this area.

---

[1] For example, *Prater v Cornwall County Council* [2006] EWCA Civ 102, [2006] IRLR 362; *Gizbert v ABC News International Inc* [2006] All ER (D) 98 (Aug).

[2] *Sogbetun v Hackney London Borough Council* [1998] ICR 1264 – concerning when an employment tribunal chairman may determine a case sitting on his own; *Rabahallah v British Telecom plc* UKEAT/0382/04 [2005] ICR 440, holding that a party consenting to a two-member tribunal is entitled to know from what panel (employers or employees) the remaining lay member is drawn in the employment tribunal as well as in the EAT.

[3] *Aparau v Iceland Frozen Foods plc* [2000] IRLR 196.

Territorial jurisdiction

9.8 Whether or not a claimant has any substantive rights before a tribunal may be a question of the territorial scope of protection afforded by the Act in question. This important question is explained and illustrated below.

9.9 However, it is sensible to consider that question against the background of the relevant procedural provisions as to jurisdiction.

9.10 Regulation 19(1) of the ET Rules effectively makes provision for the allocation of jurisdiction as between England and Wales on the one hand and Scotland on the other in the following terms:

> **19. Jurisdiction of tribunals in Scotland and in England & Wales**
>
> (1) An employment tribunal in England or Wales shall only have jurisdiction to deal with proceedings (referred to as 'English and Welsh proceedings') where—
>
> (a) the respondent or one of the respondents resides or carries on business in England and Wales;
> (b) had the remedy been by way of action in the county court, the cause of action would have arisen wholly or partly in England and Wales;
> (c) the proceedings are to determine a question which has been referred to the tribunal by a court in England and Wales; or
> (d) in the case of proceedings to which Schedule 3, 4 or 5 applies, the proceedings relate to matters arising in England and Wales.

9.11 Although these provisions appear to be allocating jurisdiction between parts of Great Britain, they are not expressly confined to that purpose and would appear, on their face, to define more generally the limits of territorial jurisdiction.

9.12 However, it is clear that reg 19(1)(b) throws the procedural question of jurisdiction back onto the question of whether or not there would have been jurisdiction in the county court (which brings into play the *forum* rules of private international law[4] that are, subject to the discussion below, generally beyond the scope of this book).

9.13 So, the primary underlying question is whether the claimant has any substantive rights before the employment tribunal at all. If not, reg 19(1) cannot confer on the tribunal jurisdiction, which it would not otherwise have.

9.14 In any event, the authors submit that reg 19(1) should not be construed so as to restrict substantive rights which a claimant may have. Rather, its provisions should be construed as primarily allocating jurisdiction within England and Wales. This approach to construing procedural provisions (being hesitant to diminish substantive rights[5] by procedural restrictions) is illustrated, albeit in a different context, by the EAT's approach in *BUPA Care Homes*

---

[4] *Dickie and Others v Cathay Pacific Airways Ltd* [2004] ICR 1733.
[5] Particularly where conferred by or originating in EC law.

(BNH) Ltd v Cann; Spillett v Tesco Stores Ltd[6] which concerned the Employment Act 2002 and pre-action requirements of the statutory grievance procedures.

9.15 Whether an employee has any rights in the employment tribunal at all will depend upon:

- the scope of the substantive rights conferred by the statute itself; and,

- since the recent cases of in *Bleuse v MBT Transport and Another*[7] and *GMB v Holis Metal Industries Ltd*,[8] upon whether the rights conferred are primarily domestic rights or EU-derived rights (eg, rights now found in UK legislation, but originating in the Treaty, an EC Regulation or Directive, which the domestic legislation purports to implement).

9.16 This distinction can be briefly but, we hope, helpfully illustrated by contrasting two examples: UK rights exemplified by the right not to be unfairly dismissed and EU rights exemplified by the right not to be dismissed on the grounds of gender (ie sex discrimination).[9]

UK rights – unfair dismissal

9.17 Section 94(1) of ERA 1996 provides that 'an employee has the right not to be unfairly dismissed'.

9.18 Section 204 of ERA 1996 is as follows:

'(1) For the purposes of this Act it is immaterial whether the law which (apart from this Act) governs any person's employment is the law of the United Kingdom, or of a part of the United Kingdom, or not.'

9.19 But what about *where the person is* employed?

9.20 The reason that uncertainty in this area arose at all (and had to be decided in the end by the House of Lords)[10] is that the relevant provisions in s 196 of ERA 1996 were repealed in October 1999 and were not replaced.

---

[6] [2006] IRLR 248.
[7] UKEAT/0632/06 [2007] All ER (D) 392 (Dec).
[8] UKEAT/0171/07 [2007] All ER (D) 304 (Dec).
[9] In *Bleuse* above, the president (Elias J) distinguished the EU-derived rights under the Working Time Regulations 1998 (SI 1998/1833) from the domestic right not to be unfairly dismissed under ERA 1996, s 94(1).
[10] In *Lawson v Serco Ltd, Botham v Ministry of Defence Crofts v Veta Ltd* [2006] UKHL 3, [2006] IRLR 289, at para 9.17.

9.21 The reason that s 196 was repealed may have been to meet the requirements of the Posted Workers Directive, Council Directive 96/71/EC[11] and, possibly, to mitigate the effect of the decision in *Carver v Saudi Arabian Airlines*[12] which was widely thought to be unsatisfactory.[13]

9.22 In *Lawson v Serco Ltd, Botham v Ministry of Defence, Crofts v Veta Ltd*,[14] the House of Lords held that jurisdiction depends on the substantive provisions of the statute under which the claim is brought and not on the procedural rules.[15] Since there was no express limitation to the right not to be unfairly dismissed, due to the repeal of s 196, the House of Lords considered that there must be an implied limitation.[16]

9.23 Lord Hoffmann gave the leading speech and held that the scope of the right under s 94(1) depended on 'what Parliament may reasonably be supposed to have intended and attributing to Parliament a rational scheme',[17] and that rather than focusing on the employee's place of work in the contract of employment, the basic test should be 'whether the employee was working in Great Britain at the time of his dismissal',[18] although this might have to qualified for two special categories of employee, namely employees with no fixed place of work ('peripatetic' employees) and expatriate employees, working overseas.

Peripatetic employees

9.24 Examples of peripatetic employees might include airline pilots, international management consultants or salesmen, and they should be treated as if the place that they were based was their place of employment. If that place was England and Wales, then the employment tribunals of England and Wales would have jurisdiction.

9.25 As to where an employee was based, in *Serco* Lord Hoffmann adopted Lord Denning's test in *Todd v British Midland Airways Ltd*,[19] which concerned an airline pilot who typically worked 53% of his time outside Great Britain. Lord Denning held that in such a case, the provisions of the contract did not determine the issue as 'simply' as in other cases. Lord Denning himself adopted

---

[11] Directive 96/71/EC of the European Parliament and of the Council of 16 December 1996 concerning the posting of workers in the framework of the provision of services (1997) OJ L 18/1.
[12] [1999] ICR 991.
[13] *Lawson v Serco Ltd* [2004] EWCA Civ 12, [2004] ICR 204, CA, per Pill LJ, at para [10].
[14] [2006] UKHL 3, [2006] IRLR 289.
[15] See also *Jackson v Ghost Ltd* [2003] IRLR 824, at para 79.
[16] In *Crofts and Others v Cathay Pacific Airways Ltd* [2005] EWCA Civ 599, [2005] ICR 1436, the Court of Appeal had held that was a need for a degree of flexibility in applying the *Serco* test laid down in the Court of Appeal.
[17] *Lawson v Serco Ltd, Botham v Ministry of Defence Crofts v Veta Ltd* [2006] UKHL 3, [2006] IRLR 289 at para [24].
[18] [2006] UKHL 3 at para [27].
[19] [1978] ICR 959, and *Serco*, at para [40].

what he called 'the "base" test' from a judgment of Megaw LJ in an earlier case and said 'You have to go by the conduct of the parties and the way they have been operating the contract. You have to find at the material time where the man is based'.[20]

> 'A man's base is the place where he should be regarded as ordinarily working, even though he may spend days, weeks or months working overseas. I would only make this suggestion. I do not think that the terms of the contract help much in these cases. As a rule, there is no term in the contract about exactly where he is to work. You have to go by the conduct of the parties and the way they have been operating the contract. You have to find at the material time where the man is based.'

Posted and expatriate employees

9.26 Lord Hoffman identified two further special cases, when an employee based overseas might nonetheless bring proceedings in an employment tribunal: first, an employee posted abroad for the purpose of a business carried on in Great Britain; and secondly, an expatriate employee of a British employer in a British enclave in a foreign country. Lord Hoffman held that any other special cases would have to have 'equally strong connections with Great Britain and British employment law'.[21]

9.27 The bottom line is that, subject to some exceptions, the *Serco* test is fairly restrictive.

EU rights – sex discrimination

9.28 The Sex Discrimination Act 1975 provides that a tribunal may only hear a claim of sex discrimination if it relates to employment at an establishment in Great Britain and 'employment is to be regarded as at an establishment in Great Britain unless the employee does his work *wholly outside* Great Britain'.[22]

Period of employment

9.29 In *Saggar v Ministry of Defence*,[23] the Court of Appeal held that it was right to consider the whole period of the employment relationship, not merely the period during which the alleged race discrimination had taken place. *Carver*

---

[20] [1978] ICR 959 at 964F–G.
[21] *Serco*, above, at para [40].
[22] Sex Discrimination Act 1975, s 10(1) – note that, eg, the Race Relations Act 1976 (RRA 1976), is not unusual in making more generous provision on territorial jurisdiction, to expressly include employees sent to foreign offices of businesses in Great Britain, where the employee does his work wholly outside Great Britain and (i) the employer has a place of business at an establishment in Great Britain, (ii) the work is for the purposes of the business carried there, and (iii) the employee is ordinarily resident in Great Britain either when he applies for or is offered the employment, or at any time during the course of his employment (RRA 1976, s 8(1), (1A), Disability Discrimination Act 1995, s 68(2), (2A): s 8(1) and (1A)).
[23] [2005] EWCA Civ 413, [2005] IRLR 618.

v *Saudi Arabian Airlines*,[24] had been understood as authority for the proposition that, for the purposes of establishing jurisdiction, it was necessary to consider where the employee was wholly or mainly working, *at the time of the alleged discrimination*. The Court of Appeal held that this was the wrong approach.

9.30 This suggests that an employee who has been working in Great Britain and is then posted overseas may still retain the protection of the discrimination legislation, as if still working in Great Britain, when the period of employment is viewed as a whole.

Holis and Bleuse

9.31 There have been some recent cases on territorial jurisdiction. Including *GMB v Holis Metal Industries Ltd*,[25] and *Bleuse v MBT Transport and Another*.[26] In each case, a purposive interpretation of the EU-derived rights was adopted, so enlarging the protection (or confirming a wider scope of protection) afforded by the domestic legislation.

9.32 *Holis* was a judgment of His Honour Judge Ansell, also sitting alone, in which he held that the provisions of the Transfer of Undertakings (Protection of Employment) Regulations 2006 (TUPE)[27] may apply to transfers of businesses to locations outside the UK and outside the EU, (in this case Israel) on the basis of a purposive interpretation of TUPE in the light of its EU origins. His Honour Judge Ansell held that:

> '[41] I am persuaded that the wording of both the [Acquired Rights Directive] and Regulation 3 [of TUPE] is precise in setting the application of the regulation to transfers of undertakings situated immediate before the transfer in the UK. Set against the purpose of protecting the rights of workers in the event of change of employer it seems to me that a purposeful approach requires that those employees should be protected even if the transfer is to be across borders outside the EU. It is not a case of either the UK or the EU seeking to legislate outside their jurisdictions without good reason. I am satisfied that the pre-transfer requirement of location in the UK acts as a significant limitation which should that not offend against the comity of notions. Mr Siddall in his written submissions compared Holis's position to a foreign person committing a tort while present in the UK and then asserting that it is an exorbitant exercise of discretion that they should be held to account for the same.
>
> [42] Further I regard it also significant that regulation 3(4) makes it clear that an international element can be governed by TUPE and I am also satisfied that the service provision changes brought into the 2006 regulations, where again the only limitation is that there should have been an organised group of employees situated

---

[24] [1999] ICR 991.
[25] UKEAT/0171/07 [2007] All ER (D) 304 (Dec).
[26] UKEAT/0632/06 [2007] All ER (D) 392 (Dec).
[27] SI 2006/246.

in Great Britain immediately before the service provision change, is clearly aimed at the modern outsourcing of service provision, particularly call centres, whether inside or outside the EU.'

9.33 *Bleuse* was a judgment of the president, Elias J, sitting alone. He held that the employment tribunal had been right to apply the old *Serco* test to the claims for unfair dismissal and unlawful deduction from wages and therefore to reject them. But he went on to hold that the employment tribunal had been wrong to reject the claim for holiday pay because there was a directly effective right derived from the Directive, to which proper effect could be given by construing the Working Time Regulations 1998[28] in a manner which was compatible with the terms of the Directive. Therefore, even if the protection of the Working Time Regulations 1998 would otherwise have been confined to those who had a base in the UK, the wider construction (informed by the Directive) had the effect of extending the protection more widely. In doing so, the president departed from the approach in two previous decisions of the EAT[29] in which *Serco* had been applied in EU-derived rights cases.

Sex discrimination claims now

9.34 In the light of the above cases, it is likely that a sex discrimination claim brought by an employee whose employment has a substantial connection to (say) England would be much more likely to be able to bring a claim in an employment tribunal in England than prior to these cases.

9.35 More specifically, the provision that 'employment is to be regarded as at an establishment in Great Britain unless the employee does his work *wholly outside* Great Britain' is likely to be interpreted to give effect to the protective purpose behind the Equal Treatment Directive.[30]

9.36 This is likely to be a fertile area for development in the law, especially given the increased mobility of the workforce.

Human rights

9.37 For the purposes of s 4(5) of HRA 1998, the EAT is not a 'court', so it is unable to entertain a question concerning the incompatibility of legislation with the European Convention, or to make a finding that an Act of Parliament, for example, is incompatible under s 4(4) of HRA 1998.[31] Lindsay P held this to be the case although, 'It does give rise to some puzzlement as to whether that effect was truly intended'.

---

[28] SI 1998/1833.
[29] *Ashbourne v Department of Education and Skills and Another* UKEAT/0123/07 [2007] All ER (D) 390 (Nov) and *Williams v University of Nottingham* [2007] IRLR 660.
[30] Council Directive 76/207/EEC of 9 February 1976 on the implementation of the principle of equal treatment for men and women as regards access to employment, vocational training and promotion, and working conditions.
[31] *Whittaker v P & D Watson (Trading as P & M Watson Haulage) and Another* [2002] ICR 1244.

9.38 The proper course in such cases is for the EAT to dismiss the appeal and grant permission to appeal to the Court of Appeal which then consider the claim for a declaration of incompatibility under s 4 of HRA 1998 (see Chapter 4 above).

THE EMPLOYMENT APPEAL TRIBUNAL'S ORIGINAL AND APPELLATE JURISDICTIONS

9.39 The EAT's jurisdiction is as follows:

STATUTE	COMMENTS
APPELLATE JURISDICTIONS	
Section 21 of ETA 1996:	This is the main head of jurisdiction under which the EAT hears appeals on any question of law from the decisions of the employment tribunals in the United Kingdom. Not only is jurisdiction founded on the list of statutes but also in respect of any secondary legislation made thereunder such a breach of contract claims under the Extension of Jurisdiction Orders 1994.
(1) An appeal lies to the Appeal tribunal on any question of law arising from any decision of, or arising in any proceedings before, an [employment tribunal] under or by virtue of—	
(a) the Equal Pay Act 1970,	
(b) the Sex Discrimination Act 1975,	
(c) the Race Relations Act 1976,	
(d) the Trade Union and Labour Relations (Consolidation) Act 1992,	
(e) the Disability Discrimination Act 1995, …	
(f) the Employment Rights Act 1996 […	
[(ff …]	
[(fg …]	
[(g) this Act,]	
[([ga) the National Minimum Wage Act 1998,	NB – where an employer appeals an Enforcement Notice pursuant to s 19 of the 1998 Act to the Employment Tribunal, there is right of appeal to the EAT by virtue of s 21 of the 1996 Act.

(gb)	the Employment Relations Act 1999][,
[(gc)	the Equality Act 2006,]]
(h)	the Working Time Regulations 1998, …
(i)	the Transnational Information and Consultation of Employees Regulations 1999]] […
(j)	the Part-time Workers (Prevention of Less Favourable Treatment) Regulations 2000] […
(k)	the Fixed-term Employees (Prevention of Less Favourable Treatment) Regulations 2002] […
(l)	the Employment Equality (Sexual Orientation) Regulations 2003] […
(m)	the Employment Equality (Religion or Belief) Regulations 2003],
[(n)	the Merchant Shipping (Working Time: Inland Waterways) Regulations 2003], […
(o)	the European Public Limited-Liability Company Regulations 2004]
[[(p)]	the Fishing Vessels (Working Time: Sea-fishermen) Regulations 2004], […
(q)	the Information and Consultation of Employees Regulations 2004][, …

	(r)	the Schedule to the Occupational and Personal Pension Schemes (Consultation by Employers and Miscellaneous Amendment) Regulations 2006],[...
	(s)	the Employment Equality (Age) Regulations 2006][, ...
	(t)	the European Cooperative Society (Involvement of Employees) Regulations 2006], [or
	(u)	the Companies (Cross-Border Mergers) Regulations 2007].
(2)		No appeal shall lie except to the Appeal tribunal from any decision of an [employment tribunal] under or by virtue of the Acts listed [or the Regulations referred to] in subsection (1).
(3)		Subsection (1) does not affect any provision contained in, or made under, any Act which provides for an appeal to lie to the Appeal tribunal (whether from an [employment tribunal], the Certification Officer or any other person or body) otherwise than on a question to which that subsection applies.
[(4)		The Appeal tribunal also has any jurisdiction in respect of matters other than appeals which is conferred on it by or under—
	(a)	the Trade Union and Labour Relations (Consolidation) Act 1992,
	(b)	this Act, or
	(c)	any other Act.]

Reg 16(2), TUPE Regulations	This creates a right of appeal in a TUPE case.
Sections 9, 45D, 56A, 95, 104, 108C, 126	These are all rights of appeal from the Certification Office to the EAT in respect of trade unions.

Transnational Information and Consultation of Employees Regulations 1999	A limited right of appeal from the Central Arbitration Committee (CAC) in respect of European Works Councils. Other challenges to the CAC decisions is by way of judicial review in the Administrative Court of the Queen's Bench Division of the High Court of Justice.

ORIGINAL JURISDICTION

Regulations 20(1) and 21(1) Transnational Information and Consultation of Employees Regulations 1999	Relates to failures to establish a European Works Council or information or consultation procedures. The EAT has powers to fine and make orders requiring compliance.
Regulation 33, European Public Limited-Liability Company Regulations 2004	The EAT can issue a penalty notice if the CAC has declared that there has been a failure to comply with an employee involvement agreement of the standard rules on employee involvement.
Regulation 11, Information and Consultation of Employees Regulations 2004	Penalty notice can be issued following a CAC declaration that there has been a failure to comply with a negotiated agreement ore the standard information and consultation provisions.

Original jurisdiction

9.40 The original jurisdiction of the EAT covers issues on the provision of information and worker consultation and involvement under the Transnational Information and Consultation of Employees Regulations 1999, regs 20 and 21; the Information and Consultation of Employees Regulations 2004, reg 22, and the European Public Limited-Liability Company Regulations 2004, reg 33.

9.41 In this context, 'original jurisdiction' means that the EAT is the first tribunal to hear any issue arising under those provisions and is therefore not hearing an appeal. For that reason, the original jurisdiction of the EAT falls outside the scope of this work.

EMPLOYMENT APPEAL TRIBUNAL – CONSTITUTIONAL AND ADMINISTRATIVE ARRANGEMENTS

9.42 As explained in Chapter 3, the EAT is the successor to the National Industrial Relations Court which heard appeals from industrial tribunals from 1971–1974. From 1964–1971 appeals were heard by the Divisional Court of the High Court and in 1974 a single judge of the High Court heard appeals until the establishment of the EAT by the Employment Protection Act 1975. It is now established by ETA 1996.

9.43 The tribunal consists of:

(a) Judges of the High Court and Court of Appeal (including judges appointed under s 9 of the Supreme Court Act 1981, ie Deputy High Court judges) nominated by the Lord Chief Justice.

(b) At least one judge of the Court of Session nominated by the Lord President of the Court of Session.

(c) Temporary judicial members appointed under s 24 of ETA 1996 (in reality QCs) (such QCs now rarely sit as by doing so they cannot appear before the EAT with the lay members they have sat with – *Lawal v Northern Spirit Ltd*).[32]

(e) Persons appointed by the Queen on the joint recommendation of the Lord Chancellor and the Secretary of State for Business, Enterprise and Regulatory Reform who represent employers and employees.

9.44 The EAT is properly constituted where a judicial member in the chair and is sitting with two or four lay members, where equal numbers represent employees and employers. The parties can consent to a judge and one lay member or by a judge and three lay members (although they need to know whether the lay members are employee or employer representatives before consenting – see *de Haney v Brent Mind and Another*).[33] Where an employment judge heard a case alone in the employment tribunal then a judicial member can hear the appeal from the decision alone (see s 28). The lay members can out vote the judicial member. The judicial member will give a single judgment but express the minority view where there is one.

9.45 The EAT is presided over by a president. The following have been office holders, Phillips J, Slynn J, Browne-Wilkinson J, Waite J, Popplewell J, Wood J, Mummery J, Morrison J, Lindsay J and Burton J. The present President is Elias J. In Scotland the following Court of Session judges have presided Lord MacDonald, Lord Mayfield, Lord Coulsfield, Lord Johnson and at present Lady Smith.

9.46 The registrar of the EAT has specific powers under the EAT Rules. Presently she is Ms P Dunleavy.

9.47 The EAT sits usually in four or five courts at Audit House, 58 Victoria Embankment, London, EC4Y 0DS and in one court at 11 Melville Crescent, Edinburgh, EH3 7LU. The EAT can also sit in Wales with a Welsh speaking judge presiding although the Welsh Language Act 1993 does not apply and there is no right to have a hearing in welsh (see *Williams v Cowell and*

---

[32] [2003] UKHL 35, [2003] IRLR 538.
[33] [2003] EWCA Civ 1637, [2004] ICR 348.

Another).[34] Appeals from Northern Irish employment tribunals are heard by the Court of Appeal in Northern Ireland and not the EAT.

TRIBUNALS, COURTS AND ENFORCEMENT ACT 2007

9.48 The Tribunals, Courts and Enforcement Act 2007 creates a new administrative justice tribunal service. Section 2 creates the new office of senior president (Lord Justice Carnwath has been appointed). He will be senior to the president of the employment tribunals and the president of the EAT. By s 5 it would appear that judges and members of the EAT are to be also members of the new upper-tier tribunal that will hear appeals from a first-tier tribunal, which will be composed of amongst others, employment tribunal judges and members. Section 30 does provide for the augmentation of the EAT's jurisdiction by secondary legislation but the Act does not provide for the transfer of the employment tribunals' and the EAT's jurisdictions to other bodies, such as first-tier and the upper-tier tribunals. Thus it seems that the 'employment tribunals' are not going to be subsumed into the new tribunal structure. Accordingly, it remains to be seen as to why EAT judges and members may sit in the upper-tier tribunal. The Act does provide for the administration and rule making power in respect of the EAT to be vested entirely in the Lord Chancellor rather to be shared with the Secretary of State for Business, Enterprise and Regulatory Reform, as at present.

9.49 We will have to wait to see how the Government implements the new Act which has yet to come into force. In a consultation paper issued in November 2007 the Government stated this:[35]

> 'The 2007 Act makes a number of changes to the employment tribunals Act 1996. These changes put employment tribunals and the EAT on a par with the First-tier tribunal and the Upper tribunal in terms of the powers and duties of the Senior President, removal from office, taking the judicial oath and mediation. The implementation of the 2007 Act will create a shared pool of tribunal members and "cross ticketing", so that suitably qualified members may consider cases from more than one jurisdiction. However, the existing statutory requirements for sitting on the employment tribunals and the EAT will be retained. These will be operated in a way which will ensure that employment expertise will not be diluted.'

GENERAL POWERS

9.50 The EAT has the 'powers, rights, privileges and authority' as the High Court of Justice when it sits in England and Wales and as the Court of Session when it sits in Scotland in relation to the attendance and examination of witnesses, the production and inspection of documents and all other matter

---

[34] [2000] ICR 85.
[35] Para 105, Transforming Tribunals: Implementing Part 1 of the Tribunals, Courts and Enforcement Act 2007, Consultation Paper Co Number: CP 30/07.

incidental to its jurisdiction. See s 29 of ETA 1996. Rule 27 of the EAT Rules provides the mechanism by which summonses may be issued. These power are very rarely used as evidence is not usually called in the EAT. The EAT can require evidence to be heard on oath (EAT Rules, r 28).

APPEALS FROM EMPLOYMENT TRIBUNALS TO THE HIGH COURT

9.51 Employment tribunals hear appeals against prohibition and improvement notices imposed by the Health and Safety Executive pursuant to s 24 of the Health and Safety at Work Act 1974. An appeal against a decision of a tribunal under this provision does not lie in general to the EAT, but to the High Court pursuant to s 1 of the Tribunals and Inquiries Act 1992.

NATIONAL SECURITY

9.52 Rules 30A and 31A of the EAT Rules permit a Minister of the Crown and the EAT to direct the EAT to sit private, exclude the claimant and his representatives and conceal the identity of witness in appeals concerning Crown employment. The EAT can also prevent the disclosure of any documents or decision to any person and can keep secret its decision. Where a person is excluded from a hearing the Attorney-General can appoint a special advocate to represent the interests of the excluded person.

APPEALING INTERIM ORDERS OF THE EMPLOYMENT APPEAL TRIBUNAL – EAT OR COURT OF APPEAL?

9.53 The EAT has power to review its own interim orders (see Chapter 3 above) and equally the Court of Appeal will consider appeals against such orders and is able to remit the case back to the EAT for further consideration or go on to decide the case itself (see Chapter 3 above). Accordingly, it would seem that both the EAT and the Court of Appeal have jurisdiction to deal with errors made by the EAT when making interim orders (see Chapters 3 and 4 respectively).

Chapter 10

KEY CASE SUMMARIES

YEBOAH V CROFTON [2002] IRLR 634

10.1 Claimant made six applications to the ET alleging race discrimination. The Respondent was found liable by the Tribunal. The EAT found that the Tribunal's findings of fact were perverse and set aside its decision. The Court of Appeal held that the EAT had been wrong to make a finding of perversity and gave the following guidance (Mummery LJ):

Paragraph 12:

> 'When the principal ground of appeal is, as here, perversity of the decision of the fact-finding tribunal, there is an increased risk that the appellate body's close examination of the evidence and of the findings of fact by the employment tribunal may lead it to substitute its own assessment of the evidence and to overturn findings of fact made by the employment tribunal. Only the employment tribunal hears all the evidence first hand. The evidence available to the Employment Appeal Tribunal and to the Court of Appeal on an appeal on a question of law is always seriously and incurably incomplete. Much as one, or sometimes both, of the parties would like it to be so, an appeal from an employment tribunal is not a re-trial of the case. The scope of the appeal is limited to consideration of questions of law, which it is claimed arise on the conduct of the proceedings and the decision of the employment tribunal. The legal points must, of course, be considered in the context of the entirety of the proceedings and the whole of the decision, but with an awareness of the limitations on the court's competence to question the evidential basis for findings of fact by the employment tribunal. It is a rare event for the appellate body to have all the documents put in evidence in the employment tribunal. No official transcript of the oral evidence exists. If an order is made for production of the chairman's notes, it is usually on a selective basis, related to the particular grounds of appeal, which should always be particularised on a perversity challenge. Most important of all, none of the witnesses give oral evidence on an appeal.'

Paragraph 92:

> 'A ground of appeal based on perversity should always be fully particularised, so that the respondent can be fully prepared to meet it and in order to deter attempts to pursue hopeless and impermissible appeals on factual points. Paragraph 2(5) of the *Employment Appeal Tribunal Practice Direction – Procedure* (29 March 1996) provides:

"It is not acceptable for an appellant to state as a ground of appeal simply that 'the decision was contrary to the evidence' or that 'there was no evidence to support the decision' or that 'the decision was one that no reasonable tribunal could have reached and was perverse' or similar general grounds, unless the notice of appeal also sets out full and insufficient particulars of the matters relied on in support of those general grounds.'"

Paragraph 93:

'Such an appeal ought only to succeed where an overwhelming case is made out that the employment tribunal reached a decision which no reasonable tribunal, on a proper appreciation of the evidence and the law, would have reached. Even in cases where the Appeal Tribunal has "grave doubts" about the decision of the Employment Tribunal, it must proceed with "great care": *British Telecommunications plc v Sheridan* [1990] IRLR 27 at paragraph 34.'

Paragraph 94:

'Over the years there have been frequent attempts, consistently resisted by the Employment Appeal Tribunal, to present appeals on fact as questions of law. The technique sometimes employed is to trawl through the extended reasons of an employment tribunal, selecting adverse findings of fact on specific issues on which there was a conflict of oral evidence, and alleging, without adequate particulars, supporting material or even proper grounds, that these particular findings of fact are perverse and that therefore the overall decision is perverse. An application is often made to obtain the notes of evidence made by the chairman in the hope of demonstrating that the notes are silent or incomplete on factual points, that the findings of fact were not therefore supported by the evidence and that a question of law accordingly arises for the determination of the Employment Appeal Tribunal.'

Paragraph 95:

'Inevitably, there will from time to time be cases in which an employment tribunal has unfortunately erred by misunderstanding the evidence, leading it to make a crucial finding of fact unsupported by evidence or contrary to uncontradicted evidence. In such cases the appeal will usually succeed. But no appeal on a question of law should be allowed to be turned into a rehearing of parts of the evidence by the Employment Appeal Tribunal. I am, of course, well aware that this is easier said than done, especially when, as here, neither side was legally represented on the first level of appeal. As the Employment Appeal Tribunal was well aware, unrepresented litigants have understandable problems in separating questions of law from proof of facts and in distinguishing the making of legal submissions from submissions of fact, even giving evidence in the course of submissions.'

MEEK V CITY OF BIRMINGHAM DISTRICT COUNCIL [1987] IRLR 250

10.2 The Industrial Tribunal found that the claimant has been unfairly dismissed. The EAT set aside its decision on the basis that its decision was flawed 'by the absence of factual determination which would have enabled the parties to know what it was that they could or should have done'. The EAT remitted the case back to the Tribunal. The claimant appealed that decision to the Court of Appeal. The Court of Appeal upheld the EAT. The now President of the EAT appeared for the City Council. The Court of Appeal agreed with the EAT that the Tribunal's decision was flawed for lack of reasons and gave the following guidance (Bingham LJ):

Paragraph 8:

> 'It has on a number of occasions been made plain that the decision of an Industrial Tribunal is not required to be an elaborate formalistic product of refined legal draftsmanship, but it must contain an outline of the story which has given rise to the complaint and a summary of the Tribunal's basic factual conclusions and a statement of the reasons which have led them to reach the conclusion which they do on those basic facts. The parties are entitled to be told why they have won or lost. There should be sufficient account of the facts and of the reasoning to enable the EAT or, on further appeal, this court to see whether any question of law arises; and it is highly desirable that the decision of an Industrial Tribunal should give guidance both to employers and trade unions as to practices which should or should not be adopted.'

ANYA V UNIVERSITY OF OXFORD AND ANOTHER [2001] IRLR 377

10.3 The claimant commenced proceedings against the University for race discrimination arising out of his failure to secure a research assistants position. He lost in the Employment Tribunal and unsuccessfully appealed to the EAT. He was then subsequently successful in the Court of Appeal which found that the Tribunal on the grounds that the Tribunal had considered the relevant evidence but failed to resolve material disputes of fact and come to reasoned conclusions based on those findings. The case was remitted to a new Tribunal and the following guidance was given (Sedley LJ):

Paragraph 25:

> 'It is simply that it is the job of the tribunal of first instance not simply to set out the relevant evidential issues, as this industrial tribunal conscientiously and lucidly did, but to follow them through to a reasoned conclusion except to the extent that they become otiose; and if they do become otiose, the tribunal needs to say why.'

BURNS V CONSIGNIA (NO 2) [2004] IRLR 425

10.4 In *Burns v Consignia (No 2)*, the EAT held that where an employment tribunal was alleged to have failed to give adequate reasons for a decision, the EAT could invite the tribunal to clarify, supplement or give its written reasons before proceeding to a final determination of the appeal.

The EAT held that such practice was permissible under s 35(1) of the Employment Tribunals Act, which provides that:

> 'For the purposes of disposing of an appeal, the Appeal Tribunal may – (a) exercise any of the powers of the body or officer from whom the appeal was brought, or (b) remit the case to that body or officer.'

The so-called '*Burns* procedure' was subsequently included in the *EAT Practice Direction 2004*.

BARKE V SEETEC [2005] IRLR 633

10.5 In this case, the Court of Appeal considered the practice established in *Burns v Consignia (No 2)* of seeking further reasons from the employment tribunal. The *Burns* decision had been followed by the EAT in *Barke* and the Court of Appeal approved the procedure but on different grounds by the Court of Appeal.

The Court of Appeal held that the power to remit for further reasons did not derive from the provision in s 35(1) of the Employment Tribunals Act, as had been held in *Burns*. Dyson LJ found that the EAT did however have such a power under r 30 of Sch 1 to the Employment Tribunals (Constitution and Rules of Procedure) Regulations 2004:

Paragraph 22:

> 'In our judgment, there is nothing in the language of these rules which prohibits the Employment Appeal Tribunal from making a request for further written reasons under rule 30(3)(b) where the employment tribunal has already provided some written reasons.'

Rule 30 provides as follows:

> **'30. Reasons**
>
> (1) A tribunal chairman must give reasons (either oral or written) for any—
>
>   (a)   judgment; or
>   (b)   order, if a request for reasons is made before or at the hearing at which the order is made.'

Dylon LJ went on to state at para 29:

'Jurisdiction outside the rules

Even if there were no power to request further reasons pursuant to rule 30, the Employment Appeal Tribunal would in our view be acting lawfully in inviting the employment tribunal to clarify, supplement or give its written reasons. As we have said, there is no prohibition in the statute or rules against such a request. Indeed, s 30(3) of the 1996 Act provides that "Subject to Appeal Tribunal procedure rules, the Appeal Tribunal has power to regulate its own procedure."'

However, since the Court of Appeal's decision in *Barke* r 30(3) has been amended by SI 2005/1865, reg 2(1), (4)(h). It now provides:

(3) [[Where oral reasons have been provided], written reasons shall only be provided]—

- (a) in relation to judgments if requested by one of the parties within the time limit set out in paragraph (5); or
- (b) in relation to any judgment or order if requested by the Employment Appeal Tribunal at any time.

It is interesting that this amendment to the rules still provides no express authority for this somewhat problematic procedure and merely deals (so far as material) with the EAT's power to require reasons from the employment tribunal. This leaves open the decision in *Barke* open to argument by a brave advocate at a future date.

This leaves open the question of whether the EAT still has jurisdiction outside the rules to remit a decision in cases when written reasons were given.

SINCLAIR ROCHE AND TEMPERLEY (A FIRM) AND OTHERS V HEARD AND ANOTHER [2004] IRLR 763

10.6 The former partners of the respondent solicitors firm sued the firm and current partners alleging sex discrimination. They were successful before the Employment Tribunal but lost the respondent's appeal. The EAT found that the Tribunal had not made sufficient findings and had not completed 'their job'. The respondents wanted the case remitted back to a new Tribunal whereas using the reasoning in *Burns v Consignia (No 2)* the claimant wanted a carefully controlled remission of the case remitted back to the same Tribunal. The EAT found that the case was to be distinguished from *Burns* because this was not a case of inadequacy of reasoning or an absence of a finding in which the Tribunal could be called upon to answer specific questions based on its existing notes of evidence. Nevertheless the EAT decided to send it back to the same Tribunal and not to a new Tribunal. The following guidance, which will be useful at the end of most successful appeals, was given (Burton P):

Paragraph 45:

'We are satisfied that the tribunal's conclusions that there was direct discrimination against SF and SH (the referrals issue) and indirect discrimination of SF (the part-time working issue) cannot stand. Mr Gatt QC submits that the case should be remitted for hearing before a different tribunal. Mr Bean QC submits that this would be catastrophic for his clients, and in any event unnecessary. He refers to the somewhat different procedure which we have been adopting at the preliminary hearing, and indeed sift, stages, by reference to English, as explained in *Burns v Consignia (No 2)* [2004] IRLR 425, by way of what he referred to as a carefully controlled remission. That however is a practice which is adopted at the interlocutory stage where, inter alia, there is a case alleged of inadequacy of reasoning, or absence of a finding, and the case is sent back to the same tribunal simply to answer specific questions, based on its existing notes of evidence. That is not the case here, where we have concluded that the tribunal has in fact not done, or at any rate finished, its job. This is not a question of what has been described in Burns as a referral back, but of a straightforward remission. The issue nevertheless remains as to whether it should be remitted back to the same tribunal, which, subject to our guidance, will be able to make use of its existing knowledge of the case and notes of evidence, or a fresh tribunal to start again.'

Paragraph 46:

'There is no authority which has been cited to us, or of which we ourselves know, which would assist us in such a situation, and we set out what appear to us to be relevant factors:

46.1 Proportionality must always be a relevant consideration. Here the award was for £900,000, and although we are conscious that ordering a fresh hearing in front of a different tribunal would add considerably to the cost to parties on both sides who have already invested in solicitors and counsel, both at the tribunal and on appeal (in the case of the applicants, two counsel for the appeal), sufficient money is at stake that the question of costs would from the one point of view not offend on the grounds of proportionality and from the other not be a decisive, or even an important, factor. Similarly the distress and inconvenience of the parties in reliving a hearing must be weighed up, but (a) are rendered necessary in any event by the decision to set aside the original decision and (b) will not be greatly less by virtue of the extra time taken by a fully, rather than partially remitted, hearing, the main distress and inconvenience being caused by the matter being reopened at all.

46.2 Passage of time. The appellate tribunal must be careful not to send a matter back to the same tribunal if there is a real risk that it will have forgotten about the case. Of course, tribunals deal with so many different cases per month that it is impossible for them to carry the facts in their minds, nor would they be expected to do so. But they can normally refresh those minds from the notes of evidence and submissions if the case occurred relatively recently. This case was a relatively long one, and will not on that basis alone have completely evanesced from the minds of the tribunal. It was only just over a year ago. That in itself is quite a long time, though the lengthy reserved decision sent to the parties on 30 July 2003 would have kept the case in the minds of the tribunal at least until then: but in addition they have held a remedies hearing which began in October 2003, the hearing lasting until 18 December, and then required consideration in chambers' meetings in January and March, and did not result in a promulgated decision until as recently as 19 March 2004. We are satisfied therefore that the question of delay and loss of recollection is not a material factor in this case one way or the other.

46.3 Bias or partiality. It would not be appropriate to send the matter back to the same tribunal where there was a question of bias or the risk of pre-judgment or partiality. This would obviously be so where the basis of the appeal had depended upon bias or misconduct, but is not limited to such a case.

46.4 Totally flawed decision. It would not ordinarily be appropriate to send the matter back to a tribunal where, in the conclusion of the appellate tribunal, the first hearing was wholly flawed or there has been a complete mishandling of it. This of course may come about without any personal blame on the part of the tribunal. There could be complexities which had not been appreciated, authorities which had been overlooked or the adoption erroneously of an incorrect approach. The appellate tribunal must have confidence that, with guidance, the tribunal can get it right second time.

46.5 Second bite. There must be a very careful consideration of what Lord Phillips in English (at paragraph 24) called "A second bite at the cherry". If the tribunal has already made up its mind, on the face of it, in relation to all the matters before it, it may well be a difficult if not impossible task to change it: and in any event there must be the very real risk of an appearance of pre-judgment or bias if that is what a tribunal is asked to do. There must be a very real and very human desire to attempt to reach the same result, if only on the basis of the natural wish to say "I told you so". Once again the appellate tribunal would only send the matter back if it had confidence that, with guidance, the tribunal, because there were matters which it had not, or had not yet, considered at the time it apparently reached a conclusion, would be prepared to look fully at such further matters, and thus be willing or enabled to come to a different conclusion, if so advised.

46.6 Tribunal professionalism. In the balance with all the above factors, the appellate tribunal will, in our view, ordinarily consider that, in the absence of clear indications to the contrary, it should be assumed that the tribunal below is capable of a professional approach to dealing with the matter on remission. By professionalism, we mean not only the general competence and integrity of the members as they go about their business, but also their experience and ability in doing that business in accordance with the statutory framework and the guidance of the higher courts. Employment law changes; indeed it has been a rapidly developing area of the law. Employment tribunals are therefore all too familiar with the need to apply a different legal approach to a case today from that which they applied last year, or even last week, where the law has changed, although the cases may be on all fours as regards their facts. Some areas of employment law have not been easy, and the approach to be adopted in considering whether there has been race or sex discrimination in a case such as this is just such a matter which has understandably caused problems for tribunals. It follows that where a tribunal is corrected on an honest misunderstanding or misapplication of the legally required approach (not amounting to a 'totally flawed' decision described at 46.4), then, unless it appears that the tribunal has so thoroughly committed itself that a rethink appears impracticable, there can be the presumption that it will go about the tasks set them on remission in a professional way, paying careful attention to the guidance given to it by the appellate tribunal.'

Paragraph 47:

'We are satisfied that this is a case where we can and should remit the matter to the same tribunal:

47.1 Although this will not be in any way analogous to a Burns situation of simply sending back the matter with a question or list of questions, but will be a genuine rehearing with fresh evidence, and certainly fresh submissions, a great deal of time will be saved by leaving the evidence which has already been taken where it is, namely in the tribunal's notes of evidence and, after sufficient refreshing of recollection, in the minds of the tribunal and the parties. None of the evidence so far given will be wasted, although in the light of the issues which have now become clear, and the guidance from this Appeal Tribunal, by no means all of it will be relevant. Much of it can simply be taken for granted as the tribunal and the parties move on.

47.2 As can be seen from this judgment, we are satisfied that the reality of this case is that there is unfinished business to be done. So far as the indirect discrimination case is concerned, now clarified, the tribunal has not in our judgment even reached the halfway point. As for the referrals issue, the tribunal is more or less at halfway, although it needs to set out clearly its conclusions, after hearing further evidence, as to the nature and extent of the unfavourable treatment in so far as it so finds it, but it will in any event need then to move on to consider in detail the respondents' explanations. In our judgment this will not involve the tribunal in an exercise either of straining to change its mind or straining not to change its mind (as was canvassed before us), but rather to realise that it was previously making a decision without all the necessary information or ammunition.

47.3 We are satisfied that this is not a case either where bias or partiality is or was involved, or indeed prejudgment, nor where there was a complete mishandling of the case. We are confident that, like any judge or judicial body, this tribunal will approach its renewed task, free of preconceptions and with an open mind. In any event the reopening of their conclusions may not go only one way. While the respondents will be persuading the tribunal that there was no unfavourable treatment and/or there was a non-discriminatory explanation in respect of events after January 2000, the applicants will also be seeking to persuade the tribunal to come to a different conclusion, namely in relation to events prior to January 2000 – with the consequent need, in that event, to look at the respondents' case in that regard. As we are about to say in respect of ground 2, all bets will be off and the book will be open.'

LAMBE V 186K LTD [2004] EWCA CIV 1045

10.7 The following excerpt from the judgment of Wall J provides an excellent summary of the circumstances when the Court of Appeal will remit back to the EAT (Wall LJ):

'**Footnote: the preliminary procedural point arising in this appeal**

70. In granting permission to appeal in this case on paper, Peter Gibson LJ stated:

"The points which Mr. Lambe wishes to raise cannot be said to have no prospect of success, and the point on the Polkey practice in the light of *King v Eaton (No 2)* is one of some general importance to practice in the ET."

71. This formulation of permission led to a dispute between the parties as to the future of the appeal, which we determined administratively prior to the appeal being heard. Mr. Lambe wanted his appeal heard and decided by this court in the normal way. The Respondent, however, suggested that since Peter Gibson LJ's had said that the points raised by the Appellant could not be said to have no real prospects of success, the proper course was for the matter to be remitted to the EAT (which had said none of the points was arguable) for that Tribunal to conduct a full hearing of the appeal.

72. It was suggested that this course would be appropriate in the light of two decisions of this court, namely *Vincent v MJ Gallagher Contractors Ltd* [2003] ICR 1244 and *Sukul-Lennard v Croydon Primary Care Trust* (*The Times* 22 July 2003). Having raised the point however, the Respondent made it clear that if we did not think it appropriate for the matter to be remitted to the EAT for a full hearing, it would be content to argue the appeal before this court on its merits.

73. We took the view, on the facts of this case, that the EAT had exhausted its jurisdiction, and that the proper course was for the appeal to proceed on its merits in this court. We took that view for the several reasons, which we need briefly to explain.

74. Firstly, because there is no requirement for permission to appeal from the ET to the EAT, the EAT has introduced various procedures which endeavour to sift out those appeals which, on paper, it does not think contain an arguable point of law. One of the ways this is done is by way of PH. The term is, perhaps, slightly misleading. The hearing is only preliminary in the sense that, if the appeal is found to contain an arguable point of law, it goes forward to a full hearing with both parties present. If, in the judgment of the EAT and after the appellant has been heard the appeal is held not to raise an arguable point of law, it is dismissed then and there and that subject to any question of permission to appeal to this court, is the end of the matter.

75. Neither of the cases cited is, in our judgment, applicable to the facts of this case. In *Vincent v MJ Gallagher Contractors Ltd* the EAT, at a preliminary hearing, allowed the appeal to go forward to a full hearing on two of the five grounds advanced. There was an appeal to this court against that ruling. This court took the view that, since the compass of the appeal was a narrow one, the EAT should have allowed the appeal to be argued before it on all five grounds. It therefore allowed the appeal and remitted the matter to the EAT for the full appeal to be conducted on that basis.

76. In our judgment, that is a quite different situation to that which appertains here. In Vincent's case there had been no adjudication by the EAT on the appellant's appeal. This court was astute to point out that the outcome of the appeal was at large. This court was being asked to decide how the EAT should go about hearing the appeal. That is manifestly not this case, where the EAT dismissed Mr. Lambe's appeal on the basis that in its view it contained no arguable point of law.

77. Equally, it does not seem to us that Sukul-Lennard is in point In that case the ET had struck out Mrs. Sukul-Lennard's application. She appealed to the EAT which dismissed her appeal at a PH. She applied to this court for permission to appeal. This court (Peter Gibson LJ and Hooper J) identified three grounds of appeal, which either had not been argued at all; alternatively, one had (possibly) been argued in rather a different form. Permission to appeal having been given, the appeal subsequently came on for hearing before a constitution of this court comprising Peter Gibson, Mance and Longmore LJJ.

78. Counsel for the Respondent in Sukul-Lennard conceded that the points identified by this court were arguable. This court accordingly allowed the appeal against the EAT's preliminary ruling. The Respondent had not, of course, been either present or represented at the preliminary hearing. The question for the court was whether to remit the matter to the EAT or the ET. The court remitted the matter to the EAT. It did so (1) because the EAT had not adjudicated on the points identified by this court as arguable, and (2) because this court said it would find it of assistance to have the decision of the EAT on them in the event that the matter were to return to the Court of Appeal. The appellant wanted the matter remitted to the ET. Peter Gibson LJ said at paragraph 5 of his judgment:

> "To my mind, given the nature of this case and the procedural issues involved, it is plain that it would be better that the EAT should consider the arguments now sought to be advanced for the respondent. The preliminary hearing procedure for appeals to the EAT does have the consequence that this court may have an appeal from the decision reached at a preliminary hearing without the benefit of the views of the specialist tribunal, the EAT on the respondent's case. It may well be that the respondent could have advanced points in writing to the EAT for the preliminary hearing, but if it had done so it would have been responding to what were the points taken by the appellant, not trying to anticipate what this court might consider to offer a real prospect of success on an appeal. in my view, there must be power for this court to achieve the result that the EAT will, at a full hearing, consider points such as now arise in this case. It seems to me that the appropriate order is to set aside the decision of the EAT and to direct that Mrs. Sukul-Lennard's appeal from the Tribunal should go to a full hearing of the EAT so that both sides can advance the arguments which they wish to advance but which have not yet been heard in contested litigation."

79. The critical point in Sukul-Lennard seems to us to be that the EAT had not had the opportunity to consider the points identified by this court as arguable. Here, of course, the EAT has dealt fully with Mr. Lambe's appeal, and dismissed it. In our judgment it would be inappropriate for this court to remit the appeal to the EAT simply the basis that this court had taken the view on paper that the points the Appellant wished to raise could not be said to have no real prospect of success. In our judgment, in these circumstances, both good practice and good sense dictated that this court should proceed to hear and determine Mr. Lambe's appeal on its merits.

80. We are fortified in that view by the fact that it is, of course, the original decision of the ET with which we are concerned: see *Vento v Chief Constable of the*

West Yorkshire Police [2002] ICR 318 at 326 paragraph 25 per Mummery LJ. Thus if this court finds an error of law in a Tribunal's decision, it is to the Tribunal which it remits the matter.

81. Mr. Moretto submitted, in his skeleton argument on this point, that for this court to hear the full appeal on its merits rather than remitting it to the EAT would prejudice the Respondent by preventing it from; (1) having an opportunity fully to argue the merits of the Tribunal's decision in front of the EAT; and (2) doing so in what is a costs free jurisdiction. The purpose of the PH system, he argued, was to save the Respondent to an appeal having to incur unnecessary costs.

82. We do not accept these arguments. The Respondent has in fact so benefited. It has not had to pay the costs of being represented before the EAT, where, of course, it succeeded. Had the Appellant not obtained this court's permission to appeal that would have been the end of the matter. To have remitted this appeal to the EAT without a hearing – assuming such a course was open to us – would, in our view, have been to duplicate proceedings and to incur unnecessary costs.

83. The circumstances in which this court will remit an appeal to the EAT are, we think, limited. Examples are, of course, provided by the two cases to which we have referred. Another example is where the EAT dismisses an appeal from the Tribunal on the grounds that the EAT does not have jurisdiction to hear it. In such circumstances, if this court on appeal from the EAT takes the view that the EAT does have jurisdiction to entertain the appeal, it will remit the appeal to the EAT for hearing – see, for example, *Grady v Prison Service* [2003] 3 All ER 745, where the EAT held that it did not have jurisdiction to entertain an appeal by a bankrupt appellant whose claim for unfair dismissal had been dismissed by the Tribunal.

84. Where, however, under the PH procedure the EAT, as here, dismisses an appeal on the basis that none of the grounds of appeal raises a point of law which gives the appeal a reasonable prospect of success at a Full Hearing, and the disappointed appellant obtains the permission of this court to appeal to the Court of Appeal, this court will hear the appeal in the normal way and will either dismiss it or allow it. If it does the latter, and upsets the Tribunal's decision, it will either impose its own order; alternatively, as here, it will remit the decision, or a relevant part of it, to the ET for reconsideration.'

For *Abelghafar* and *Jurkowska*, see Chapter 3.

Appendix 1

REVIEW IN THE EMPLOYMENT TRIBUNALS

CONTENTS

Employment Tribunals (Constitution and Rules of Procedure) Regulations 2004 (SI 2004/1861), Sch 1

EMPLOYMENT TRIBUNALS (CONSTITUTION AND RULES OF PROCEDURE) REGULATIONS 2004

SI 2004/1861

Schedule 1
The Employment Tribunals Rules of Procedure

How to bring a claim

****

33 Review of default judgments

(1) A party may apply to have a default judgment against or in favour of him reviewed. An application must be made in writing and presented to the Employment Tribunal Office within 14 days of the date on which the default judgment was sent to the parties. The 14 day time limit may be extended by a chairman if he considers that it is just and equitable to do so.

(2) The application must state the reasons why the default judgment should be varied or revoked. When it is the respondent applying to have the default judgment reviewed, the application must include with it the respondent's proposed response to the claim, an application for an extension of the time limit for presenting the response and an explanation of why rules 4(1) and (4) were not complied with.

(3) A review of a default judgment shall be conducted by a chairman in public. Notice of the hearing and a copy of the application shall be sent by the Secretary to all other parties.

(4) The chairman may

    (a)   refuse the application for a review;
    (b)   vary the default judgment;

(c) revoke all or part of the default judgment;
(d) confirm the default judgment;

and all parties to the proceedings shall be informed by the Secretary in writing of the chairman's judgment on the application.

(5) A default judgment must be revoked if the whole of the claim was satisfied before the judgment was issued or if rule 8(6) applies. A chairman may revoke or vary all or part of a default judgment if the respondent has a reasonable prospect of successfully responding to the claim or part of it.

(6) In considering the application for a review of a default judgment the chairman must have regard to whether there was good reason for the response not having been presented within the applicable time limit.

(7) If the chairman decides that the default judgment should be varied or revoked and that the respondent should be allowed to respond to the claim the Secretary shall accept the response and proceed in accordance with rule 5(2).

34 Review of other judgments and decisions

(1) Parties may apply to have certain judgments and decisions made by a tribunal or a chairman reviewed under rules 34 to 36. Those judgments and decisions are –

(a) a decision not to accept a claim, response or counterclaim;
(b) a judgment (other than a default judgment but including an order for costs, expenses, preparation time or wasted costs); and
(c) a decision made under rule 6(3) of Schedule 4;

and references to "decision" in rules 34 to 37 are references to the above judgments and decisions only. Other decisions or orders may not be reviewed under these rules.

(2) In relation to a decision not to accept a claim or response, only the party against whom the decision is made may apply to have the decision reviewed.

(3) Subject to paragraph (4), decisions may be reviewed on the following grounds only –

(a) the decision was wrongly made as a result of an administrative error;
(b) a party did not receive notice of the proceedings leading to the decision;
(c) the decision was made in the absence of a party;
(d) new evidence has become available since the conclusion of the hearing to which the decision relates, provided that its existence could not have been reasonably known of or foreseen at that time; or
(e) the interests of justice require such a review.

(4) A decision not to accept a claim or response may only be reviewed on the grounds listed in paragraphs (3)(a) and (e).

(5) A tribunal or chairman may on its or his own initiative review a decision made by it or him on the grounds listed in paragraphs (3) or (4).

35 Preliminary consideration of application for review

(1) An application under rule 34 to have a decision reviewed must be made to the Employment Tribunal Office within 14 days of the date on which the decision was sent to the parties. The 14 day time limit may be extended by a chairman if he considers that it is just and equitable to do so.

(2) The application must be in writing and must identify the grounds of the application in accordance with rule 34(3), but if the decision to be reviewed was made at a hearing, an application may be made orally at that hearing.

(3) The application to have a decision reviewed shall be considered (without the need to hold a hearing) by the chairman of the tribunal which made the decision or, if that is not practicable, by –

(a) a Regional Chairman or the Vice President;
(b) any chairman nominated by a Regional Chairman or the Vice President; or
(c) the President;

and that person shall refuse the application if he considers that there are no grounds for the decision to be reviewed under rule 34(3) or there is no reasonable prospect of the decision being varied or revoked.

(4) If an application for a review is refused after such preliminary consideration the Secretary shall inform the party making the application in writing of the chairman's decision and his reasons for it. If the application for a review is not refused the decision shall be reviewed under rule 36.

36 The review

(1) When a party has applied for a review and the application has not been refused after the preliminary consideration above, the decision shall be reviewed by the chairman or tribunal who made the original decision. If that is not practicable a different chairman or tribunal (as the case may be) shall be appointed by a Regional Chairman, the Vice President or the President.

(2) Where no application has been made by a party and the decision is being reviewed on the initiative of the tribunal or chairman, the review must be carried out by the same tribunal or chairman who made the original decision and –

(a) a notice must be sent to each of the parties explaining in summary the grounds upon which it is proposed to review the decision and giving them an opportunity to give reasons why there should be no review; and
(b) such notice must be sent before the expiry of 14 days from the date on which the original decision was sent to the parties.

(3) A tribunal or chairman who reviews a decision under paragraph (1) or (2) may confirm, vary or revoke the decision. If the decision is revoked, the tribunal or chairman must order the decision to be taken again. When an order is made that the original decision be taken again, if the original decision was

taken by a chairman without a hearing, the new decision may be taken without hearing the parties and if the original decision was taken at a hearing, a new hearing must be held.

37 Correction of judgments, decisions or reasons

(1) Clerical mistakes in any order, judgment, decision or reasons, or errors arising in those documents from an accidental slip or omission, may at any time be corrected by certificate by the chairman, Regional Chairman, Vice President or President.

(2) If a document is corrected by certificate under paragraph (1), or if a decision is revoked or varied under rules 33 or 36 or altered in any way by order of a superior court, the Secretary shall alter any entry in the Register which is so affected to conform with the certificate or order and send a copy of any entry so altered to each of the parties and, if the proceedings have been referred to the tribunal by a court, to that court.

(3) Where a document omitted from the Register under rules 32 or 49 is corrected by certificate under this rule, the Secretary shall send a copy of the corrected document to the parties; and where there are proceedings before any superior court relating to the decision or reasons in question, he shall send a copy to that court together with a copy of the entry in the Register of the decision, if it has been altered under this rule.

(4) In Scotland, the references in paragraphs (2) and (3) to superior courts shall be read as referring to appellate courts.

****

Appendix 2

THE EMPLOYMENT APPEAL TRIBUNAL

CONTENTS

Employment Tribunals Act 1996
Employment Appeal Tribunal Rules 1993 (SI 1993/2854)
Practice Direction (Employment Appeal Tribunal – Procedure) 2008
President's Practice Statement (EAT) (3 February 2005)
Employment Appeal Tribunal Conciliation Protocol

EMPLOYMENT TRIBUNALS ACT 1996

****

PART II
THE EMPLOYMENT APPEAL TRIBUNAL

Introductory

20 The Appeal Tribunal

(1) The Employment Appeal Tribunal ('the Appeal Tribunal') shall continue in existence.

(2) The Appeal Tribunal shall have a central office in London but may sit at any time and in any place in Great Britain.

(3) The Appeal Tribunal shall be a superior court of record and shall have an official seal which shall be judicially noticed.

(4) Subsection (2) is subject to regulation 34 of the Transnational Information and Consultation of Employees Regulations 1999, regulation 46(1) of the European Public Limited-Liability Company Regulations 2004, regulation 36(1) of the Information and Consultation of Employees Regulations 2004, regulation 37(1) of the European Cooperative Society (Involvement of Employees) Regulations 2006 and regulation 58(1) of the Companies (Cross-Border Mergers) Regulations 2007.

Amendments—SI 1999/3323, reg 35(1), (2); SI 2004/3426, reg 36(2)(a), (b); SI 2004/2326, reg 48(2); SI 2006/2059, reg 37(2)(a), (b); SI 2007/2974, reg 58(2)(a), (b).

Jurisdiction

21 Jurisdiction of Appeal Tribunal

(1) An appeal lies to the Appeal Tribunal on any question of law arising from any decision of, or arising in any proceedings before, an employment tribunal under or by virtue of –

(a) the Equal Pay Act 1970,
(b) the Sex Discrimination Act 1975,
(c) the Race Relations Act 1976,
(d) the Trade Union and Labour Relations (Consolidation) Act 1992,
(e) the Disability Discrimination Act 1995,
(f) the Employment Rights Act 1996
(ff) ...
(fg) ...
(g) this Act,
(ga) the National Minimum Wage Act 1998,
(gb) the Employment Relations Act 1999,
(gc) the Equality Act 2006,
(h) the Working Time Regulations 1998,
(i) the Transnational Information and Consultation of Employees Regulations 1999,
(j) the Part-time Workers (Prevention of Less Favourable Treatment) Regulations 2000,
(k) the Fixed-term Employees (Prevention of Less Favourable Treatment) Regulations 2002,
(l) the Employment Equality (Sexual Orientation) Regulations 2003,
(m) the Employment Equality (Religion or Belief) Regulations 2003,
(n) the Merchant Shipping (Working Time: Inland Waterways) Regulations 2003,
(o) the European Public Limited-Liability Company Regulations 2004,
(p) the Fishing Vessels (Working Time: Sea-fishermen) Regulations 2004,
(q) the Information and Consultation of Employees Regulations 2004,
(r) the Schedule to the Occupational and Personal Pension Schemes (Consultation by Employers and Miscellaneous Amendment) Regulations 2006,
(s) the Employment Equality (Age) Regulations 2006,
(t) the European Cooperative Society (Involvement of Employees) Regulations 2006, or
(u) the Companies (Cross-Border Mergers) Regulations 2007.

(2) No appeal shall lie except to the Appeal Tribunal from any decision of an employment tribunal under or by virtue of the Acts listed or the Regulations referred to in subsection (1).

(3) Subsection (1) does not affect any provision contained in, or made under, any Act which provides for an appeal to lie to the Appeal Tribunal (whether from an employment tribunal, the Certification Officer or any other person or body) otherwise than on a question to which that subsection applies.

(4) The Appeal Tribunal also has any jurisdiction in respect of matters other than appeals which is conferred on it by or under –

(a) the Trade Union and Labour Relations (Consolidation) Act 1992,
(b) this Act, or
(c) any other Act.

Amendments—Employment Rights (Dispute Resolution) Act 1998, ss 1(2)(a), 15, Sch 1, para 17(2), (3), Sch 2; National Minimum Wage Act 1998, ss 29, 53, Sch 3; Tax Credits Act 1999, ss 60, 7, Sch 3, para 5, Sch 6; Employment Relations Act 2004, s 38; Equality Act 2006, s 40, Sch 3, para 57; SI 1998/1833, reg 34(a), (b); SI 1999/3323, reg 35(1), (3)(b); SI 2000/1551, reg 10, Schedule, para 1(b)(i), (ii); SI 2002/2034, reg 11, Sch 2, Pt 1, para 2(b)(i), (ii); SI 2003/1661, reg 39, Sch 5, para 1(b)(i), (ii); SI 2003/1660, reg 39(2), Sch 5, para 1(b)(i), (ii); SI 2003/3049, reg 20, Sch 2, para 2(1), (3); SI 2004/2326, reg 49; SI 2004/3426, reg 37(a), (b), (c); SI 2004/1713, reg 21, Sch 2, para 1(1), (3); SI 2006/349, reg 17, Schedule, para 10(a), (b); SI 2006/1031, reg 49(1), Sch 8, Pt 1, paras 18, 20(1), (2), (3); SI 2006/2059, reg 38(a), (b); SI 2007/2974, reg 59(a), (b).

Membership etc

22 Membership of Appeal Tribunal

(1) The Appeal Tribunal shall consist of –

(a) such number of judges as may be nominated from time to time by the Lord Chief Justice, after consulting the Lord Chancellor, from the judges of the High Court and the Court of Appeal,

(b) at least one judge of the Court of Session nominated from time to time by the Lord President of the Court of Session, and

(c) such number of other members as may be appointed from time to time by Her Majesty on the joint recommendation of the Lord Chancellor and the Secretary of State ('appointed members').

(2) The appointed members shall be persons who appear to the Lord Chancellor and the Secretary of State to have special knowledge or experience of industrial relations either –

(a) as representatives of employers, or

(b) as representatives of workers (within the meaning of the Trade Union and Labour Relations (Consolidation) Act 1992).

(3) The Lord Chief Justice shall appoint one of the judges nominated under subsection (1) to be the President of the Appeal Tribunal.

(3A) The Lord Chief Justice must not make an appointment under subsection (3) unless –

(a) he has consulted the Lord Chancellor, and

(b) the Lord President of the Court of Session agrees.

(4) No judge shall be nominated a member of the Appeal Tribunal except with his consent.

(5) The Lord Chief Justice may nominate a judicial office holder (as defined in section 109(4) of the Constitutional Reform Act 2005) to exercise his functions under this section.

(6) The Lord President of the Court of Session may nominate a judge of the Court of Session who is a member of the First or Second Division of the Inner House of that Court to exercise his functions under subsection (3A)(b).

Amendments—Constitutional Reform Act 2005, s 15(1), Sch 4, Pt 1, paras 245, 246(1), (2)(a), (b), (3), (4), (5), Sch 18, Pt 2.

23 Temporary membership

(1) At any time when –
- (a) the office of President of the Appeal Tribunal is vacant, or
- (b) the person holding that office is temporarily absent or otherwise unable to act as the President of the Appeal Tribunal,

the Lord Chief Justice may nominate another judge nominated under section 22(1)(a) to act temporarily in his place.

(2) At any time when a judge of the Appeal Tribunal nominated under paragraph (a) or (b) of subsection (1) of section 22 is temporarily absent or otherwise unable to act as a member of the Appeal Tribunal –
- (a) in the case of a judge nominated under paragraph (a) of that subsection, the Lord Chief Justice may nominate another judge who is qualified to be nominated under that paragraph to act temporarily in his place, and
- (b) in the case of a judge nominated under paragraph (b) of that subsection, the Lord President of the Court of Session may nominate another judge who is qualified to be nominated under that paragraph to act temporarily in his place.

(3) At any time when an appointed member of the Appeal Tribunal is temporarily absent or otherwise unable to act as a member of the Appeal Tribunal, the Lord Chancellor and the Secretary of State may jointly appoint a person appearing to them to have the qualifications for appointment as an appointed member to act temporarily in his place.

(4) A person nominated or appointed to act temporarily in place of the President or any other member of the Appeal Tribunal, when so acting, has all the functions of the person in whose place he acts.

(5) No judge shall be nominated to act temporarily as a member of the Appeal Tribunal except with his consent.

(6) The functions conferred on the Lord Chief Justice by the preceding provisions of this section may be exercised only after consulting the Lord Chancellor.

(7) The functions conferred on the Lord Chancellor by subsection (3) may be exercised only after consultation with the Lord Chief Justice.

(8) The Lord Chief Justice may nominate a judicial office holder (as defined in section 109(4) of the Constitutional Reform Act 2005) to exercise his functions under this section.

Amendments—Constitutional Reform Act 2005, s 15(1), Sch 4, Pt 1, paras 245, 247(1), (2), (3), (4).

24 Temporary additional judicial membership

(1) This section applies if both of the following conditions are met –

(a) the Lord Chancellor thinks that it is expedient, after consulting the Lord Chief Justice, for a qualified person to be appointed to be a temporary additional judge of the Appeal Tribunal in order to facilitate in England and Wales the disposal of business in the Appeal Tribunal;
(b) the Lord Chancellor requests the Lord Chief Justice to make such an appointment.

(1A) The Lord Chief Justice may, after consulting the Lord Chancellor, appoint a qualified person as mentioned in subsection (1)(a).

(1B) An appointment under this section is –

(a) for such period, or
(b) on such occasions,

as the Lord Chief Justice determines, after consulting the Lord Chancellor.

(2) In this section 'qualified person' means a person who –

(a) is qualified for appointment as a judge of the High Court under section 10 of the Supreme Court Act 1981 Senior Courts Act 1981, or
(b) has held office as a judge of the High Court or the Court of Appeal.

(3) A person appointed to be a temporary additional judge of the Appeal Tribunal has all the functions of a judge nominated under section 22(1)(a).

(4) The Lord Chief Justice may nominate a judicial office holder (as defined in section 109(4) of the Constitutional Reform Act 2005) to exercise his functions under this section.

Amendments—Constitutional Reform Act 2005, ss 15(1), 59(5), Sch 4, Pt 1, paras 245, 248(1), (2), (3), (4), Sch 11, Pt 1, para 1(2).

[24A Training etc of members of Appeal Tribunal]

[The Senior President of Tribunals is responsible, within the resources made available by the Lord Chancellor, for the maintenance of appropriate arrangements for the training, guidance and welfare of judges, and other members, of the Appeal Tribunal (in their capacities as members of the Appeal Tribunal).]

Prospective amendments—Prospectively inserted by Tribunals, Courts and Enforcement Act 2007, s 48(1), Sch 8, paras 35, 44.

[24B Oaths]

[(1) Subsection (2) applies to a person ('the appointee') –

(a) who is appointed under section 22(1)(c) or 23(3), or
(b) who is appointed under section 24(1A) and –
(i) falls when appointed within paragraph (a), but not paragraph (b), of section 24(2), and
(ii) has not previously taken the required oaths after accepting another office.

(2) The appointee must take the required oaths before –

- (a) the Senior President of Tribunals, or
- (b) an eligible person who is nominated by the Senior President of Tribunals for the purpose of taking the oaths from the appointee.

(3) If the appointee is a member of the Appeal Tribunal appointed before the coming into force of this section, the requirement in subsection (2) applies in relation to the appointee from the coming into force of this section.

(4) A person is eligible for the purposes of subsection (2)(b) if one or more of the following paragraphs applies to him –

- (a) he holds high judicial office (as defined in section 60(2) of the Constitutional Reform Act 2005);
- (b) he holds judicial office (as defined in section 109(4) of that Act);
- (c) he holds (in Scotland) the office of sheriff.

(5) In this section 'the required oaths' means –

- (a) the oath of allegiance, and
- (b) the judicial oath,

as set out in the Promissory Oaths Act 1868.]

Prospective amendments—Prospectively inserted by the Tribunals, Courts and Enforcement Act 2007, s 48(1), Sch 8, paras 35, 44.

25 Tenure of appointed members

(1) Subject to subsections (2) to (4), an appointed member shall hold and vacate office in accordance with the terms of his appointment.

(2) An appointed member –

- (a) may at any time resign his membership by notice in writing addressed to the Lord Chancellor and the Secretary of State, and
- (b) shall vacate his office on the day on which he attains the age of seventy.

(3) Subsection (2)(b) is subject to section 26(4) to (6) of the Judicial Pensions and Retirement Act 1993 (Lord Chancellor's power to authorise continuance of office up to the age of seventy-five).

(4) If the Lord Chancellor, after consultation with the Secretary of State, is satisfied that an appointed member –

- (a) has been absent from sittings of the Appeal Tribunal for a period longer than six consecutive months without the permission of the President of the Appeal Tribunal,
- (b) has become bankrupt or made an arrangement with his creditors, or has had his estate sequestrated or made a trust deed for behalf of his creditors or a composition contract,
- (c) is incapacitated by physical or mental illness, or
- (d) is otherwise unable or unfit to discharge the functions of a member,

the Lord Chancellor may declare his office as a member to be vacant and shall notify the declaration in such manner as the Lord Chancellor thinks fit; and when the Lord Chancellor does so, the office becomes vacant.

(5) The Lord Chancellor may declare an appointed member's office vacant under subsection (4) only with the concurrence of the appropriate senior judge.

(6) The appropriate senior judge is the Lord Chief Justice of England and Wales, unless the member whose office is to be declared vacant exercises functions wholly or mainly in Scotland, in which case it is the Lord President of the Court of Session.

Amendments—Constitutional Reform Act 2005, s 15(1), Sch 4, Pt 1, paras 245, 249.

26 Staff

The Secretary of State may appoint such officers and servants of the Appeal Tribunal as he may determine, subject to the approval of the Minister for the Civil Service as to numbers and terms and conditions of service.

Prospective amendments—Prospectively repealed from a date to be appointed by the Tribunals, Courts and Enforcement Act 2007, s 146, Sch 23, Pt 1.

27 Remuneration, pensions and allowances

(1) The Secretary of State shall pay –

    (a)   the appointed members, [and]
    (b)   any person appointed to act temporarily in the place of an appointed member, and
    (c)   *the officers and servants of the Appeal Tribunal,*

such remuneration and such travelling and other allowances as he may, with the relevant approval, determine; and for this purpose the relevant approval is that of the Treasury in the case of persons within paragraph (a) or (b) *and the Minister for the Civil Service in the case of persons within paragraph (c)*.

(2) A person appointed to be a temporary additional judge of the Appeal Tribunal shall be paid such remuneration and allowances as the Lord Chancellor may, with the approval of the Treasury, determine.

(3) If the Secretary of State determines, with the approval of the Treasury, that this subsection applies in the case of an appointed member, the Secretary of State shall –

    (a)   pay such pension, allowance or gratuity to or in respect of that person on his retirement or death, or
    (b)   make to the member such payments towards the provision of a pension, allowance or gratuity for his retirement or death,

as the Secretary of State may, with the approval of the Treasury, determine.

(4) Where –

(a) a person ceases to be an appointed member otherwise than on his retirement or death, and

(b) it appears to the Secretary of State that there are special circumstances which make it right for him to receive compensation,

the Secretary of State may make to him a payment of such amount as the Secretary of State may, with the approval of the Treasury, determine.

Prospective amendments—Sub-s (1) prospectively amended from a date to be appointed by Tribunals, Courts and Enforcement Act 2007, s 48(1), Sch 8, paras 35, 45; Tribunals, Courts and Enforcement Act 2007, s 146, Sch 23, Pt 1; Tribunals, Courts and Enforcement Act 2007, s 146, Sch 23, Pt 1; Tribunals, Courts and Enforcement Act 2007, s 146, Sch 23, Pt 1.

28 Composition of Appeal Tribunal

(1) The Appeal Tribunal may sit, in accordance with directions given by the President of the Appeal Tribunal, either as a single tribunal or in two or more divisions concurrently.

(2) Subject to subsections (3) to (5), proceedings before the Appeal Tribunal shall be heard by a judge and either two or four appointed members, so that in either case there is an equal number –

(a) of persons whose knowledge or experience of industrial relations is as representatives of employers, and

(b) of persons whose knowledge or experience of industrial relations is as representatives of workers.

(3) With the consent of the parties, proceedings before the Appeal Tribunal may be heard by a judge and one appointed member or by a judge and three appointed members.

(4) Proceedings on an appeal on a *question arising from any decision of, or arising in any proceedings before, an employment tribunal consisting of the person mentioned in section 4(1)(a) alone* [chairman-alone question] shall be heard by a judge alone unless a judge directs that the proceedings shall be heard in accordance with subsections (2) and (3).

[(4A) In subsection (4) 'chairman-alone question' means –

(a) a question arising from any decision of an employment tribunal that is a decision of –
   (i) the person mentioned in section 4(1)(a) acting alone, or
   (ii) any Employment Judge acting alone, or
(b) a question arising in any proceedings before an employment tribunal that are proceedings before –
   (i) the person mentioned in section 4(1)(a) alone, or
   (ii) any Employment Judge alone.]

(5) ...

Amendments—Employment Rights (Dispute Resolution) Act 1998, s 1(2)(a); Employment Relations Act 1999, ss 41, 44, Sch 8, para 4, Sch 9, Table 12; sub-s (4) Procedure.

Prospective amendments—prospectively amended and sub-s (4A) prospectively inserted by Tribunals, Courts and Enforcement Act 2007, s 48(1), Sch 8, paras 35, 46(1), (2), (3).

29 Conduct of hearings

(1) A person may appear before the Appeal Tribunal in person or be represented by –

- (a) counsel or a solicitor,
- (b) a representative of a trade union or an employers' association, or
- (c) any other person whom he desires to represent him.

(2) The Appeal Tribunal has in relation to –

- (a) the attendance and examination of witnesses,
- (b) the production and inspection of documents, and
- (c) all other matters incidental to its jurisdiction,

the same powers, rights, privileges and authority (in England and Wales) as the High Court and (in Scotland) as the Court of Session.

[29A Practice directions]

[(1) Directions about the procedure of the Appeal Tribunal may be given –

- (a) by the Senior President of Tribunals, or
- (b) by the President of the Appeal Tribunal.

(2) A power under subsection (1) includes –

- (a) power to vary or revoke directions given in exercise of the power, and
- (b) power to make different provision for different purposes.

(3) Directions under subsection (1)(a) may not be given without the approval of the Lord Chancellor.

(4) Directions under subsection (1)(b) may not be given without the approval of –

- (a) the Senior President of Tribunals, and
- (b) the Lord Chancellor.

(5) Subsection (1) does not prejudice any power apart from that subsection to give directions about the procedure of the Appeal Tribunal.

(6) Directions may not be given in exercise of any such power as is mentioned in subsection (5) without the approval of –

- (a) the Senior President of Tribunals, and
- (b) the Lord Chancellor.

(7) Subsections (3), (4)(b) and (6)(b) do not apply to directions to the extent that they consist of guidance about any of the following –

- (a) the application or interpretation of the law;
- (b) the making of decisions by members of the Appeal Tribunal.

(8) Subsections (3), (4)(b) and (6)(b) do not apply to directions to the extent that they consist of criteria for determining which members of the Appeal Tribunal may be chosen to decide particular categories of matter; but the directions may, to that extent, be given only after consulting the Lord Chancellor.

(9) Subsections (4) and (6) do not apply to directions given in a particular case for the purposes of that case only.

(10) Subsection (6) does not apply to directions under section 28(1).]

Prospective Amendments—Prospectively inserted by the Tribunals, Courts and Enforcement Act 2007, s 48(1), Sch 8, paras 35, 47.

30 Appeal Tribunal procedure rules

(1) The Lord Chancellor, after consultation with the Lord President of the Court of Session, shall make rules ('Appeal Tribunal procedure rules') with respect to proceedings before the Appeal Tribunal.

(2) Appeal Tribunal procedure rules may, in particular, include provision –

- (a) with respect to the manner in which, and the time within which, an appeal may be brought,
- (b) with respect to the manner in which any application or complaint to the Appeal Tribunal may be made,
- (c) for requiring persons to attend to give evidence and produce documents and for authorising the administration of oaths to witnesses,
- (d) for requiring or enabling the Appeal Tribunal to sit in private in circumstances in which an employment tribunal is required or empowered to sit in private by virtue of section 10A of this Act,
- (e) and
- (f) for interlocutory matters arising on any appeal or application to the Appeal Tribunal to be dealt with otherwise than in accordance with section 28(2) to (5) of this Act.

(2A) Appeal Tribunal procedure rules may make provision of a kind which may be made by employment tribunal procedure regulations under section 10(2), (5), (6) or (7).

(2B) For the purposes of subsection (2A) –

- (a) the reference in section 10(2) to section 4 shall be treated as a reference to section 28, and
- (b) the reference in section 10(4) to the President or a Regional Chairman shall be treated as a reference to a judge of the Appeal Tribunal.

(2C) Section 10B shall have effect in relation to a direction to or determination of the Appeal Tribunal as it has effect in relation to a direction to or determination of an employment tribunal.

(3) Subject to Appeal Tribunal procedure rules and directions under section 28(1) or 29A(1), the Appeal Tribunal has power to regulate its own procedure.

NOTES

Amendments—Employment Rights (Dispute Resolution) Act 1998, s 1(2)(a); Employment Relations Act 1999, s 41, Sch 8, paras 5(1), (2), (3); Employment Relations Act 2004, s 57, Sch 1, para 26, Sch 2; SI 1999/3323, reg 35(1), (4);

Prospective Amendments—sub-s (3) prospectively inserted by the Tribunals, Courts and Enforcement Act 2007, s 48(1), Sch 8, paras 35, 48.

31 Restriction of publicity in cases involving sexual misconduct

(1) Appeal Tribunal procedure rules may, as respects proceedings to which this section applies, include provision –

(a) for cases involving allegations of the commission of sexual offences, for securing that the registration or other making available of documents or divisions shall be so effected as to prevent the identification of any person affected by or making the allegation, and

(b) for cases involving allegations of sexual misconduct, enabling the Appeal Tribunal, on the application of any party to the proceedings before it or of its own motion, to make a restricted reporting order having effect (if not revoked earlier) until the promulgation of the decision of the Appeal Tribunal.

(2) This section applies to –

(a) proceedings on an appeal against a decision of an employment tribunal to make, or not to make, a restricted reporting order, and

(b) proceedings on an appeal against any interlocutory decision of an employment tribunal in proceedings in which the employment tribunal has made a restricted reporting order which it has not revoked.

(3) If any identifying matter is published or included in a relevant programme in contravention of a restricted reporting order –

(a) in the case of publication in a newspaper or periodical, any proprietor, any editor and any publisher of the newspaper or periodical,

(b) in the case of publication in any other form, the person publishing the matter, and

(c) in the case of matter included in a relevant programme –
   (i) any body corporate engaged in providing the service in which the programme is included, and
   (ii) any person having functions in relation to the programme corresponding to those of an editor of a newspaper,

shall be guilty of an offence and liable on summary conviction to a fine not exceeding level 5 on the standard scale.

(4) Where a person is charged with an offence under subsection (3) it is a defence to prove that at the time of the alleged offence he was not aware, and

neither suspected nor had reason to suspect, that the publication or programme in question was of, or included, the matter in question.

(5) Where an offence under subsection (3) committed by a body corporate is proved to have been committed with the consent or connivance of, or to be attributable to any neglect on the part of –

(a) a director, manager, secretary or other similar officer of the body corporate, or
(b) a person purporting to act in any such capacity,

he as well as the body corporate is guilty of the offence and liable to be proceeded against and punished accordingly.

(6) In relation to a body corporate whose affairs are managed by its members 'director', in subsection (5), means a member of the body corporate.

(7) 'Restricted reporting order' means –

(a) in subsections (1) and (3), an order –
  (i) made in exercise of a power conferred by rules made by virtue of this section, and
  (ii) prohibiting the publication in Great Britain of identifying matter in a written publication available to the public or its inclusion in a relevant programme for reception in Great Britain, and
(b) in subsection (2), an order which is a restricted reporting order for the purposes of section 11.

(8) In this section –

'identifying matter', in relation to a person, means any matter likely to lead members of the public to identify him as a person affected by, or as the person making, the allegation,
'relevant programme' has the same meaning as in the Sexual Offences (Amendment) Act 1992,
'sexual misconduct' means the commission of a sexual offence, sexual harassment or other adverse conduct (of whatever nature) related to sex, and conduct is related to sex whether the relationship with sex lies in the character of the conduct or in its having reference to the sex or sexual orientation of the person at whom the conduct is directed,
'sexual offence' means any offence to which section 4 of the Sexual Offences (Amendment) Act 1976, the Sexual Offences (Amendment) Act 1992 or section 274(2) of the Criminal Procedure (Scotland) Act 1995 applies (offences under the Sexual Offences Act 1956, Part I of the Criminal Law (Consolidation) (Scotland) Act 1995 and certain other enactments), and
'written publication' has the same meaning as in the Sexual Offences (Amendment) Act 1992.

Amendments—Employment Rights (Dispute Resolution) Act 1998, s 1(2)(a).

32 Restriction of publicity in disability cases

(1) This section applies to proceedings –

(a) on an appeal against a decision of an employment tribunal to make, or not to make, a restricted reporting order, or

(b) on an appeal against any interlocutory decision of an employment tribunal in proceedings in which the employment tribunal has made a restricted reporting order which it has not revoked.

(2) Appeal Tribunal procedure rules may, as respects proceedings to which this section applies, include provision for –

(a) enabling the Appeal Tribunal, on the application of the complainant or of its own motion, to make a restricted reporting order having effect (if not revoked earlier) until the promulgation of the decision of the Appeal Tribunal, and

(b) where a restricted reporting order is made in relation to an appeal which is being dealt with by the Appeal Tribunal together with any other proceedings, enabling the Appeal Tribunal to direct that the order is to apply also in relation to those other proceedings or such part of them as the Appeal Tribunal may direct.

(3) If any identifying matter is published or included in a relevant programme in contravention of a restricted reporting order –

(a) in the case of publication in a newspaper or periodical, any proprietor, any editor and any publisher of the newspaper or periodical,

(b) in the case of publication in any other form, the person publishing the matter, and

(c) in the case of matter included in a relevant programme –
   (i) any body corporate engaged in providing the service in which the programme is included, and
   (ii) any person having functions in relation to the programme corresponding to those of an editor of a newspaper,

shall be guilty of an offence and liable on summary conviction to a fine not exceeding level 5 on the standard scale.

(4) Where a person is charged with an offence under subsection (3), it is a defence to prove that at the time of the alleged offence he was not aware, and neither suspected nor had reason to suspect, that the publication or programme in question was of, or included, the matter in question.

(5) Where an offence under subsection (3) committed by a body corporate is proved to have been committed with the consent or connivance of, or to be attributable to any neglect on the part of –

(a) a director, manager, secretary or other similar officer of the body corporate, or

(b) a person purporting to act in any such capacity,

he as well as the body corporate is guilty of the offence and liable to be proceeded against and punished accordingly.

(6) In relation to a body corporate whose affairs are managed by its members 'director', in subsection (5), means a member of the body corporate.

(7) 'Restricted reporting order' means –

- (a) in subsection (1), an order which is a restricted reporting order for the purposes of section 12, and
- (b) in subsections (2) and (3), an order –
  - (i) made in exercise of a power conferred by rules made by virtue of this section, and
  - (ii) prohibiting the publication in Great Britain of identifying matter in a written publication available to the public or its inclusion in a relevant programme for reception in Great Britain.

(8) In this section –

'complainant' means the person who made the complaint to which the proceedings before the Appeal Tribunal relate,

'identifying matter' means any matter likely to lead members of the public to identify the complainant or such other persons (if any) as may be named in the order,

'promulgation' has such meaning as may be prescribed by rules made by virtue of this section,

'relevant programme' means a programme included in a programme service, within the meaning of the Broadcasting Act 1990, and

'written publication' includes a film, a sound track and any other record in permanent form but does not include an indictment or other document prepared for use in particular legal proceedings.

Amendments—Employment Rights (Dispute Resolution) Act 1998, s 1(2)(a).

33 Restriction of vexatious proceedings

(1) If, on an application made by the Attorney General or the Lord Advocate under this section, the Appeal Tribunal is satisfied that a person has habitually and persistently and without any reasonable ground –

- (a) instituted vexatious proceedings, whether before the Certification Officer, in an employment tribunal or before the Appeal Tribunal, and whether against the same person or against different persons, or
- (b) made vexatious applications in any proceedings, whether before the Certification Officer, in an employment tribunal or before the Appeal Tribunal,

the Appeal Tribunal may, after hearing the person or giving him an opportunity of being heard, make a restriction of proceedings order.

(2) A 'restriction of proceedings order' is an order that –

- (a) no proceedings shall without the leave of the Appeal Tribunal be instituted before the Certification Officer, in any employment tribunal or before the Appeal Tribunal by the person against whom the order is made,

(b) any proceedings instituted by him before the Certification Officer, in any employment tribunal or before the Appeal Tribunal before the making of the order shall not be continued by him without the leave of the Appeal Tribunal, and
(c) no application (other than one for leave under this section) is to be made by him in any proceedings before the Certification Officer, in any employment tribunal or before the Appeal Tribunal without the leave of the Appeal Tribunal.

(3) A restriction of proceedings order may provide that it is to cease to have effect at the end of a specified period, but otherwise it remains in force indefinitely.

(4) Leave for the institution or continuance of, or for the making of an application in, any proceedings before the Certification Officer, in an employment tribunal or before the Appeal Tribunal by a person who is the subject of a restriction of proceedings order shall not be given unless the Appeal Tribunal is satisfied –

(a) that the proceedings or application are not an abuse of process, and
(b) that there are reasonable grounds for the proceedings or application.

(5) A copy of a restriction of proceedings order shall be published in the London Gazette and the Edinburgh Gazette.

Amendments—Employment Rights (Dispute Resolution) Act 1998, s 1(2)(a); Employment Relations Act 2004, s 49(1), (2), (3), (4)–(6), (7)(a), (b).

34 Costs and expenses

(1) Appeal Tribunal procedure rules may include provision for the award of costs or expenses.

(2) Rules under subsection (1) may include provision authorising the Appeal Tribunal to have regard to a person's ability to pay when considering the making of an award against him under such rules.

(3) Appeal Tribunal procedure rules may include provision for authorising the Appeal Tribunal –

(a) to disallow all or part of the costs or expenses of a representative of a party to proceedings before it by reason of that representative's conduct of the proceedings;
(b) to order a representative of a party to proceedings before it to meet all or part of the costs or expenses incurred by a party by reason of the representative's conduct of the proceedings.

(4) Appeal Tribunal procedure rules may also include provision for taxing or otherwise settling the costs or expenses referred to in subsection (1) or (3)(b) (and, in particular in England and Wales, for enabling the amount of such costs to be assessed by way of detailed assessment in the High Court).

Amendments—Substituted by Employment Act 2002, s 23.

Decisions and further appeals

35 Powers of Appeal Tribunal

(1) For the purpose of disposing of an appeal, the Appeal Tribunal may –

    (a) exercise any of the powers of the body or officer from whom the appeal was brought, or

    (b) remit the case to that body or officer.

(2) Any decision or award of the Appeal Tribunal on an appeal has the same effect, and may be enforced in the same manner, as a decision or award of the body or officer from whom the appeal was brought.

36 Enforcement of decisions etc

(1) ...

(2) ...

(3) ...

(4) No person shall be punished for contempt of the Appeal Tribunal except by, or with the consent of, a judge.

(5) A magistrates' court shall not remit the whole or part of a fine imposed by the Appeal Tribunal unless it has the consent of a judge who is a member of the Appeal Tribunal.

Amendments—Employment Relations Act 2004, s 57, Sch 1, para 27, Sch 2.

EMPLOYMENT APPEAL TRIBUNAL RULES 1993

SI 1993/2854

1 Citation and commencement

(1) These Rules may be cited as the Employment Appeal Tribunal Rules 1993 and shall come into force on 16 December 1993.

(2) (not reproduced)

2 Interpretation

(1) In these rules –

'the 1992 Act' means the Trade Union and Labour Relations (Consolidation) Act 1992;
'the 1996 Act' means the Employment Tribunals Act 1996;
'the 1999 Regulations' means the Transnational Information and Consultation of Employees Regulations 1999;
'the 2004 Regulations' means the European and Public Limited-Liability Company Regulations 2004;
'the Information and Consultation Regulations' means the Information and Consultation of Employees Regulations 2004;
'the 2007 Regulations' means the Companies (Cross-Border Mergers) Regulations 2007;
'the Appeal Tribunal' means the Employment Appeal Tribunal established under section 87 of the Employment Protection Act 1975 and continued in existence under section 20(1) of the 1996 Act and includes the President, a judge, a member or the Registrar acting on behalf of the Tribunal;
'the CAC' means the Central Arbitration Committee;
'the Certification Officer' means the person appointed to be the Certification Officer under section 254(2) of the 1992 Act;
'costs officer' means any officer of the Appeal Tribunal authorised by the President to assess costs or expenses;
'Crown employment proceedings' has the meaning given by section 10(8) of the 1996 Act;
'document' includes a document delivered by way of electronic communication;
'electronic communication' shall have the meaning given to it by section 15(1) of the Electronic Communications Act 2000;
'excluded person' means, in relation to any proceedings, a person who has been excluded from all or part of the proceedings by virtue of –
   (a) a direction of a Minister of the Crown under rule 30A(1)(b) or (c); or
   (b) an order of the Appeal Tribunal under rule 30A(2)(a) read with rule 30A(1)(b) or (c);

'judge' means a judge of the Appeal Tribunal nominated under section 22(1)(a) or (b) of the 1996 Act and includes a judge nominated under section 23(2) of, or a judge appointed under section 24(1) of, the 1996 Act to be a temporary additional judge of the Appeal Tribunal;

'legal representative' shall mean a person, including a person who is a party's employee, who –
- (a) has a general qualification within the meaning of the Courts and Legal Services Act 1990;
- (b) is an advocate or solicitor in Scotland; or
- (c) is a member of the Bar of Northern Ireland or a Solicitor of the Supreme Court of Northern Ireland Solicitor of the Court of Judicature of Northern Ireland;

'member' means a member of the Appeal Tribunal appointed under section 22(1)(c) of the 1996 Act and includes a member appointed under section 23(3) of the 1996 Act to act temporarily in the place of a member appointed under that section;

'national security proceedings' shall have the meaning given to it in regulation 2 of the Employment Tribunals (Constitution and Rules of Procedure) Regulations 2004;

'the President' means the judge appointed under section 22(3) of the 1996 Act to be President of the Appeal Tribunal and includes a judge nominated under section 23(1) of the 1996 Act to act temporarily in his place;

'the Registrar' means the person appointed to be Registrar of the Appeal Tribunal and includes any officer of the Tribunal authorised by the President to act on behalf of the Registrar;

'the Secretary of Employment Tribunals' means the person acting for the time being as the Secretary of the Central Office of the Employment Tribunals (England and Wales) or, as may be appropriate, of the Central Office of the Employment Tribunals (Scotland);

'special advocate' means a person appointed pursuant to rule 30A(4);

'writing' includes writing delivered by means of electronic communication.

(2) …

(3) Any reference in these Rules to a person who was the claimant or, as the case may be, the respondent in the proceedings before an employment tribunal includes, where those proceedings are still continuing, a reference to a person who is the claimant or, as the case may be, is the respondent in those proceedings.

Amendments—Substituted by SI 2001/1128, r 2; amended by Constitutional Reform Act 2005, s 59(5), Sch 11, Pt 3, para 5; SI 2004/2526, r 2(1)(a), (b), (c), (d), (e), (2), (3); SI 2004/3426, reg 41(a); SI 2007/2974, reg 64(1).

2A Overriding Objective

(1) The overriding objective of these Rules is to enable the Appeal Tribunal to deal with cases justly.

(2) Dealing with a case justly includes, so far as practicable –

(a) ensuring that the parties are on an equal footing;
(b) dealing with the case in ways which are proportionate to the importance and complexity of the issues;
(c) ensuring that it is dealt with expeditiously and fairly; and
(d) saving expense.

(3) The parties shall assist the Appeal Tribunal to further the overriding objective.

Amendments—Inserted by SI 2004/2526, r 3.

3 Institution of Appeal

(1) Every appeal to the Appeal Tribunal shall, subject to paragraphs (2) and (4), be instituted by serving on the Tribunal the following documents –

(a) a notice of appeal in, or substantially in, accordance with Form 1, 1A or 2 in the Schedule to these rules;
(b) in the case of an appeal from a judgment of an employment tribunal a copy of any claim and response in the proceedings before the employment tribunal or an explanation as to why either is not included; and
(c) in the case of an appeal from a judgment of an employment tribunal a copy of the written record of the judgment of the employment tribunal which is subject to appeal and the written reasons for the judgment, or an explanation as to why written reasons are not included; and
(d) in the case of an appeal made pursuant to regulation 38(8) of the 1999 Regulations or regulation 47(6) of the 2004 Regulations or regulation 35(6) of the Information and Consultation Regulations or regulation 57(6) of the 2007 Regulations from a declaration or order of the CAC, a copy of that declaration or order; and
(e) in the case of an appeal from an order of an employment tribunal a copy of the written record of the order of the employment tribunal which is subject to appeal and (if available) the written reasons for the order;
(f) in the case of an appeal from a decision or order of the Certification Officer a copy of the decision or order of the Certification Officer which is subject to appeal and the written reasons for that decision or order.

(2) In an appeal from a judgment or order of the employment tribunal in relation to national security proceedings where the appellant was the claimant –

(i) the appellant shall not be required by virtue of paragraph (1)(b) to serve on the Appeal Tribunal a copy of the response if the response was not disclosed to the appellant; and
(ii) the appellant shall not be required by virtue of paragraph (1)(c) or (e) to serve on the Appeal Tribunal a copy of the written reasons for the judgment or order if the written reasons were not

sent to the appellant but if a document containing edited reasons was sent to the appellant, he shall serve a copy of that document on the Appeal Tribunal.

(3) The period within which an appeal to the Appeal Tribunal may be instituted is –

(a) in the case of an appeal from a judgment of the employment tribunal –
   (i) where the written reasons for the judgment subject to appeal –
      (aa) were requested orally at the hearing before the employment tribunal or in writing within 14 days of the date on which the written record of the judgment was sent to the parties; or
      (bb) were reserved and given in writing by the employment tribunal

   42 days from the date on which the written reasons were sent to the parties;
   (ii) in an appeal from a judgment given in relation to national security proceedings, where there is a document containing edited reasons for the judgment subject to appeal, 42 days from the date on which that document was sent to the parties; or
   (iii) where the written reasons for the judgment subject to appeal –
      (aa) were not requested orally at the hearing before the employment tribunal or in writing within 14 days of the date on which the written record of the judgment was sent to the parties; and
      (bb) were not reserved and given in writing by the employment tribunal

   42 days from the date on which the written record of the judgment was sent to the parties;
(b) in the case of an appeal from an order of an employment tribunal, 42 days from the date of the order;
(c) in the case of an appeal from a decision of the Certification Officer, 42 days from the date on which the written record of that decision was sent to the appellant;
(d) in the case of an appeal from a declaration or order of the CAC under regulation 38(8) of the 1999 Regulations or regulation 47(6) of the 2004 Regulations or regulation 35(6) of the Information and Consultation Regulations or regulation 57(6) of the 2007 Regulations, 42 days from the date on which the written notification of that declaration or order was sent to the appellant.

(4) In the case of an appeal from a judgment or order of the employment tribunal in relation to national security proceedings, the appellant shall not set out the grounds of appeal in his notice of appeal and shall not append to his notice of appeal the written reasons for the judgment of the tribunal.

(5) In an appeal from the employment tribunal in relation to national security proceedings in relation to which the appellant was the respondent in the proceedings before the employment tribunal, the appellant shall, within the

period described in paragraph (3)(a), provide to the Appeal Tribunal a document setting out the grounds on which the appeal is brought.

(6) In an appeal from the employment tribunal in relation to national security proceedings in relation to which the appellant was the claimant in the proceedings before the employment tribunal –

- (a) the appellant may, within the period described in paragraph 3(a)(ii) or (iii) or paragraph 3(b), whichever is applicable, provide to the Appeal Tribunal a document setting out the grounds on which the appeal is brought; and
- (b) a special advocate appointed in respect of the appellant may, within the period described in paragraph 3(a)(ii) or (iii) or paragraph 3(b), whichever is applicable, or within 21 days of his appointment, whichever is later, provide to the Appeal Tribunal a document setting out the grounds on which the appeal is brought or providing supplementary grounds of appeal.

(7) Where it appears to a judge or the Registrar that a notice of appeal or a document provided under paragraph (5) or (6) –

- (a) discloses no reasonable grounds for bringing the appeal; or
- (b) is an abuse of the Appeal Tribunal's process or is otherwise likely to obstruct the just disposal of proceedings,

he shall notify the Appellant or special advocate accordingly informing him of the reasons for his opinion and, subject to paragraphs (8) and (10), no further action shall be taken on the notice of appeal or document provided under paragraph (5) or (6).

(7A) In paragraphs (7) and (10) reference to a notice of appeal or a document provided under paragraph (5) or (6) includes reference to part of a notice of appeal or document provided under paragraph (5) or (6).

(8) Where notification has been given under paragraph (7), the appellant or the special advocate, as the case may be, may serve a fresh notice of appeal, or a fresh document under paragraph (5) or (6), within the time remaining under paragraph (3) or (6) or within 28 days from the date on which the notification given under paragraph (7) was sent to him, whichever is the longer period.

(9) Where the appellant or the special advocate serves a fresh notice of appeal or a fresh document under paragraph (8), a judge or the Registrar shall consider such fresh notice of appeal or document with regard to jurisdiction as though it were an original notice of appeal lodged pursuant to paragraphs (1) and (3), or as though it were an original document provided pursuant to paragraph (5) or (6), as the case may be.

(10) Where notification has been given under paragraph (7) and within 28 days of the date the notification was sent, an appellant or special advocate expresses dissatisfaction in writing with the reasons given by the judge or Registrar for his opinion, he is entitled to have the matter heard before a judge who shall make a direction as to whether any further action should be taken on the notice of appeal or document under paragraph (5) or (6).

Amendments—Substituted by SI 2001/1128, r 3; amended by SI 2004/2526, r 4(1)(a), (b), (c)(i), (ii), (d), (2), (3)(a), (b), (c), (4)(a), (b), (5), (6)(a), (b), (c), (7), (8), (9), (10), (11); SI 2004/3426, reg 41(b); SI 2007/2974, reg 64(2).

4 Service of notice of appeal

(1) On receipt of notice under rule 3, the Registrar shall seal the notice with the Appeal Tribunal's seal and shall serve a sealed copy on the appellant and on –

- (a) every person who, in accordance with rule 5, is a respondent to the appeal; and
- (b) the Secretary of Employment Tribunals in the case of an appeal from an employment tribunal; or
- (c) the Certification Officer in the case of an appeal from any of his decisions; or
- (d) the Secretary of State in the case of an appeal under ... Chapter II of Part IV of the 1992 Act or Part XI of the Employment Rights Act 1996 to which he is not a respondent; or
- (e) the Chairman of the CAC in the case of an appeal from the CAC under regulation 38(8) of the 1999 Regulations or regulation 47(6) of the 2004 Regulations or regulation 35(6) of the Information and Consultation Regulations or regulation 57(6) of the 2007 Regulations.

(2) On receipt of a document provided under rule 3(5) –

- (a) the Registrar shall not send the document to a person in respect of whom a Minister of the Crown has informed the Registrar that he wishes to address the Appeal Tribunal in accordance with rule 30A(3) with a view to the Appeal Tribunal making an order applicable to this stage of the proceedings under rule 30A(2)(a) read with 30A(1)(b) or (c) (exclusion of a party or his representative), at any time before the Appeal Tribunal decides whether or not to make such an order; but if it decides not to make such an order, the Registrar shall, subject to sub-paragraph (b), send the document to such a person 14 days after the Appeal Tribunal's decision not to make the order; and
- (b) the Registrar shall not send a copy of the document to an excluded person, but if a special advocate is appointed in respect of such a person, the Registrar shall send a copy of the document to the special advocate.

(3) On receipt of a document provided under rule 3(6)(a) or (b), the Registrar shall not send a copy of the document to an excluded person, but shall send a copy of the document to the respondent.

Amendments—Employment Rights (Dispute Resolution) Act 1998, s 1(2)(a), (b); SI 2001/1128, r 4(a), (b), (c), (d); SI 2004/2526, r 5; SI 2004/3426, reg 41(b); SI 2007/2974, reg 64(2).

5 Respondents to appeals

The respondents to an appeal shall be –

- (a) in the case of an appeal from an employment tribunal or of an appeal made pursuant to section 45D, 56A, 95, 104 or 108C of the 1992 Act

from a decision of the Certification Officer, the parties (other than the appellant) to the proceedings before the employment tribunal or the Certification Officer;
(b) in the case of an appeal made pursuant to section 9 or 126 of the 1992 Act from a decision of the Certification Officer, that Officer
(c) in the case of an appeal made pursuant to regulation 38(8) of the 1999 Regulations or regulation 47(6) of the 2004 Regulations or regulation 35(6) of the Information and Consultation Regulations or regulation 57(6) of the 2007 Regulations from a declaration or order of the CAC, the parties (other than the appellant) to the proceedings before the CAC.

Amendments—Employment Rights (Dispute Resolution) Act 1998, s 1(2)(a); SI 2001/1128, r 5(a), (b), (c); SI 2004/2526, r 6; SI 2004/3426, reg 41(b); SI 2007/2974, reg 64(2).

6 Respondent's answer and notice of cross-appeal

(1) The Registrar shall, as soon as practicable, notify every respondent of the date appointed by the Appeal Tribunal by which any answer under this rule must be delivered.

(2) A respondent who wishes to resist an appeal shall subject to paragraph (6), and, within the time appointed under paragraph (1) of this rule, deliver to the Appeal Tribunal an answer in writing in, or substantially in, accordance with Form 3 in the Schedule to these Rules, setting out the grounds on which he relies, so, however, that it shall be sufficient for a respondent to an appeal referred to in rule 5(a) or 5(c) who wishes to rely on any ground which is the same as a ground relied on by the employment tribunal, the Certification Officer or the CAC for making the judgment, decision, declaration or order appealed from to state that fact in his answer.

(3) A respondent who wishes to cross-appeal may subject to paragraph (6), do so by including in his answer a statement of the grounds of his cross-appeal, and in that event an appellant who wishes to resist the cross-appeal shall, within a time to be appointed by the Appeal Tribunal, deliver to the Tribunal a reply in writing setting out the grounds on which he relies.

(4) The Registrar shall serve a copy of every answer and reply to a cross-appeal on every party other than the party by whom it was delivered.

(5) Where the respondent does not wish to resist an appeal, the parties may deliver to the Appeal Tribunal an agreed draft of an order allowing the appeal and the Tribunal may, if it thinks it right to do so, make an order allowing the appeal in the terms agreed.

(6) In an appeal from the employment tribunal in relation to national security proceedings, the respondent shall not set out the grounds on which he relies in his answer to an appeal, nor include in his answer a statement of the grounds of any cross-appeal.

(7) In an appeal from the employment tribunal in relation to national security proceedings in relation to which the respondent was not the claimant in the

proceedings before the employment tribunal, the respondent shall, within the time appointed under paragraph (1), provide to the Registrar a document, setting out the grounds on which he intends to resist the appeal, and may include in that document a statement of the grounds of any cross-appeal.

(8) In an appeal from the employment tribunal in relation to national security proceedings in relation to which the respondent was the claimant in the proceedings before the employment tribunal –

- (a) the respondent may, within the time appointed under paragraph (1) provide to the Registrar a document, setting out the grounds on which he intends to resist the appeal, and may include in that document a statement of the grounds of any cross-appeal; and
- (b) a special advocate appointed in respect of the respondent may, within the time appointed under paragraph (1), or within 21 days of his appointment, whichever is the later, provide to the Registrar a document, setting out the grounds, or the supplementary grounds, on which the respondent intends to resist the appeal, and may include in that document a statement of the grounds, or the supplementary grounds, of any cross-appeal.

(9) In an appeal from the employment tribunal in relation to national security proceedings, if the respondent, or any special advocate appointed in respect of a respondent, provides in the document containing grounds for resisting an appeal a statement of grounds of cross-appeal and the appellant wishes to resist the cross-appeal –

- (a) where the appellant was not the claimant in the proceedings before the employment tribunal, the appellant shall within a time to be appointed by the Appeal Tribunal deliver to the Tribunal a reply in writing setting out the grounds on which he relies; and
- (b) where the appellant was the claimant in the proceedings before the employment tribunal, the appellant, or any special advocate appointed in respect of him, may within a time to be appointed by the Appeal Tribunal deliver to the Tribunal a reply in writing setting out the grounds on which the appellant relies.

(10) Any document provided under paragraph (7) or (9)(a) shall be treated by the Registrar in accordance with rule 4(2), as though it were a document received under rule 3(5).

(11) Any document provided under paragraph (8) or (9)(b) shall be treated by the Registrar in accordance with rule 4(3), as though it were a document received under rule 3(6)(a) or (b).

(12) Where it appears to a judge or the Registrar that a statement of grounds of cross-appeal contained in respondent's answer or document provided under paragraph (7) or (8) –

- (a) discloses no reasonable grounds for bringing the cross-appeal; or
- (b) is an abuse of the Appeal Tribunal's process or is otherwise likely to obstruct the just disposal of proceedings,

he shall notify the appellant or special advocate accordingly informing him of the reasons for his opinion and, subject to paragraphs (14) and (16), no further action shall be taken on the statement of grounds of cross-appeal.

(13) In paragraphs (12) and (16) reference to a statement of grounds of cross-appeal includes reference to part of a statement of grounds of cross-appeal.

(14) Where notification has been given under paragraph (12), the respondent or special advocate, as the case may be, may serve a fresh statement of grounds of cross-appeal before the time appointed under paragraph (1) or within 28 days from the date on which the notification given under paragraph (12) was sent to him, whichever is the longer.

(15) Where the respondent or special advocate serves a fresh statement of grounds of cross-appeal, a judge or the Registrar shall consider such statement with regard to jurisdiction as though it was contained in the original Respondent's answer or document provided under (7) or (8).

(16) Where notification has been given under paragraph (12) and within 28 days of the date the notification was sent, a respondent or special advocate expresses dissatisfaction in writing with the reasons given by the judge or Registrar for his opinion, he is entitled to have the matter heard before a judge who shall make a direction as to whether any further action should be taken on the statement of grounds of cross-appeal.

Amendments—Employment Rights (Dispute Resolution) Act 1998, s 1(2)(a); SI 2001/1128, r 6(a)(i), (ii), (iii), (iv), (b), (c); SI 2004/2526, r 7(1)(a), (b), (c), (2).

7 Disposal of appeal

(1) The Registrar shall, as soon as practicable, give notice of the arrangements made by the Appeal Tribunal for hearing the appeal to –

- (a) every party to the proceedings; and
- (b) the Secretary of Employment Tribunals in the case of an appeal from an employment tribunal; or
- (c) the Certification Officer in the case of an appeal from one of his decisions; or
- (d) the Secretary of State in the case of an appeal under Part XI of the Employment Rights Act 1996 or Chapter II of Part IV of the 1992 Act to which he is not a respondent; or
- (e) the Chairman of the CAC in the case of an appeal from a declaration or order of, or arising in any proceedings before, the CAC under regulation 38(8) of the 1999 Regulations or regulation 47(6) of the 2004 Regulations or regulation 35(6) of the Information and Consultation Regulations or regulation 57(6) of the 2007 Regulations.

(2) Any such notice shall state the date appointed by the Appeal Tribunal by which any interim application must be made.

Amendments—Employment Rights (Dispute Resolution) Act 1998, s 1(2)(a), (b); SI 2001/1128, r 7(a), (b); SI 2004/2526, r 8(1), (2); SI 2004/3426, reg 41(b); SI 2007/2974, reg 64(2).

8 Application in respect of exclusion or expulsion from, or unjustifiable discipline by, a trade union

Every application under section 67 or 176 of the 1992 Act to the Appeal Tribunal for:

(a) an award of compensation for exclusion or expulsion from a trade union; or

(b) one or both of the following, that is to say –
  (i) an award of compensation for unjustifiable discipline;
  (ii) an order that the union pay to the applicant an amount equal to any sum which he has paid in pursuance of any such determination as is mentioned in section 64(2)(b) of the 1992 Act;

shall be made in writing in, or substantially in, accordance with Form 4 in the Schedule to these Rules and shall be served on the Appeal Tribunal together with a copy of the decision or order declaring that the applicant's complaint against the trade union was well-founded.

9

If on receipt of an application under rule 8(a) it becomes clear that at the time the application was made the applicant had been admitted or re-admitted to membership of the union against which the complaint was made, the Registrar shall forward the application to the Central Office of Employment Tribunals.

Amendments—Employment Rights (Dispute Resolution) Act 1998, s 1(2)(b).

10 Service of application under rule 8

On receipt of an application under rule 8, the Registrar shall seal it with the Appeal Tribunal's seal and shall serve a sealed copy on the applicant and on the respondent trade union and the Secretary of Employment Tribunals.

Amendments—Employment Rights (Dispute Resolution) Act 1998, s 1(2)(b).

11 Appearance by respondent trade union

(1) Subject to paragraph (2) of this rule, a respondent trade union wishing to resist an application under rule 8 shall within 14 days of receiving the sealed copy of the application enter an appearance in, or substantially in, accordance with Form 5 in the Schedule to these Rules and setting out the grounds on which the union relies.

(2) Paragraph (1) above shall not require a respondent trade union to enter an appearance where the application is before the Appeal Tribunal by virtue of having been transferred there by an employment tribunal and, prior to that transfer, the respondent had entered an appearance to the proceedings before the employment tribunal.

Amendments—Employment Rights (Dispute Resolution) Act 1998, s 1(2)(a).

12

On receipt of the notice of appearance under rule 11 the Registrar shall serve a copy of it on the applicant.

13 Application for restriction of proceedings order

Every application to the Appeal Tribunal by the Attorney General or the Lord Advocate under section 33 of the 1996 Act for a restriction of proceedings order shall be made in writing in, or substantially in, accordance with Form 6 in the Schedule to these Rules, accompanied by an affidavit in support, and shall be served on the Tribunal.

Amendments—SI 2001/1128, r 8.

14 Service of application under rule 13

On receipt of an application under rule 13, the Registrar shall seal it with the Appeal Tribunal's seal and shall serve a sealed copy on the Attorney General or the Lord Advocate, as the case may be, on the Secretary of Employment Tribunals and on the person named in the application.

Amendments—Employment Rights (Dispute Resolution) Act 1998, s 1(2)(b).

15 Appearance by person named in application under rule 13

A person named in an application under rule 13 who wishes to resist the application shall within 14 days of receiving the sealed copy of the application enter an appearance in, or substantially in, accordance with Form 7 in the Schedule to these Rules, accompanied by an affidavit in support.

16

On receipt of the notice of appearance under rule 15 the Registrar shall serve a copy of it on the Attorney General or the Lord Advocate, as the case may be.

16A Complaints under regulations 20 and 21 of the 1999 Regulations

Every complaint under regulation 20 or 21 of the 1999 Regulations shall be made by way of application in writing in, or substantially in, accordance with Form 4A in the Schedule to these Rules and shall be served on the Appeal Tribunal.

Amendments—Inserted by SI 2001/1128, r 9.

16AA Applications under regulation 33(6) of the 2004 Regulations

Every application under regulation 33(6) of the 2004 Regulations or regulation 22(6) of the Information and Consultation Regulations or regulation 53(6) of the 2007 Regulations shall be made by way of application in writing in, or substantially in, accordance with Form 4B in the Schedule to these Rules and shall be served on the Appeal Tribunal together with a copy of the declaration referred to in regulation 33(4) of the 2004 Regulations or regulation 22(4) of the Information and Consultation Regulations or regulation 53(4) of the 2007 Regulations, or an explanation as to why none is included.

Amendments—Inserted by SI 2004/2526, r 9; amended by SI 2004/3426, reg 41(c)(i)(ii); SI 2007/2974, reg 64(3).

16B Service of application under rule 16A

On receipt of an application under rule 16A or 16AA, the Registrar shall seal it with the Appeal Tribunal's seal and shall serve a sealed copy on the applicant and on the respondent.

Amendments—Inserted by SI 2001/1128, r 9; amended by SI 2004/2526, r 10.

16C Appearance by respondent

A respondent wishing to resist an application under rule 16A or 16AA shall within 14 days of receiving the sealed copy of the application enter an appearance in, or substantially in, accordance with Form 5A in the Schedule to these Rules and setting out the grounds on which the respondent relies.

Amendments—Inserted by SI 2001/1128, r 9; SI 2004/2526, r 10.

16D

On receipt of the notice of appearance under rule 16C the Registrar shall serve a copy of it on the applicant.

Amendments—Inserted by SI 2001/1128, r 9.

17 Disposal of application

(1) The Registrar shall, as soon as practicable, give notice to the parties to an application under rule 8, 13, 16A or 16AA of the arrangements made by the Appeal Tribunal for hearing the application.

(2) Any such notice shall state the date appointed by the Appeal Tribunal by which any interim application must be made.

Amendments—SI 2001/1128, r 10; SI 2004/2526, rr 11, 12.

18 Joinder of parties

The Appeal Tribunal may, on the application of any person or of its own motion, direct that any person not already a party to the proceedings be added as a party, or that any party to proceedings shall cease to be a party, and in either case may give such consequential directions as it considers necessary.

19 Interlocutory applications

(1) An interim application may be made to the Appeal Tribunal by giving notice in writing specifying the direction or order sought.

(2) On receipt of a notice under paragraph (1) of this rule, the Registrar shall serve a copy on every other party to the proceedings who appears to him to be concerned in the matter to which the notice relates and shall notify the applicant and every such party of the arrangements made by the Appeal Tribunal for disposing of the application.

Amendments—SI 2004/2526, r 12.

20 Disposal of interim applications

(1) Every interim application made to the Appeal Tribunal shall be considered in the first place by the Registrar who shall have regard to rule 2A (the overriding objective) and, where applicable, to rule 23(5).

(2) Subject to sub-paragraphs (3) and (4), every interim application shall be disposed of by the Registrar except that any matter which he thinks should properly be decided by the President or a judge shall be referred by him to the President or judge who may dispose of it himself or refer it in whole or part to the Appeal Tribunal as required to be constituted by section 28 of the 1996 Act or refer it back to the Registrar with such directions as he thinks fit.

(3) Every interim application for a restricted reporting order shall be disposed of by the President or a judge or, if he so directs, the application shall be referred to the Appeal Tribunal as required to be constituted by section 28 of the 1996 Act who shall dispose of it.

(4) Every interim application for permission to institute or continue or to make a claim or application in any proceedings before an employment tribunal or the Appeal Tribunal, pursuant to section 33(4) of the 1996 Act, shall be disposed of by the President or a judge, or, if he so directs, the application shall be referred to the Appeal Tribunal as required to be constituted by section 28 of the 1996 Act who shall dispose of it.

Amendments—Substituted by SI 2004/2526, r 13.

21 Appeals from Registrar

(1) Where an application is disposed of by the Registrar in pursuance of rule 20(2) any party aggrieved by his decision may appeal to a judge and in that case the judge may determine the appeal himself or refer it in whole or in part to the Appeal Tribunal as required to be constituted by section 28 of the 1996 Act.

(2) Notice of appeal under paragraph (1) of this rule may be given to the Appeal Tribunal, either orally or in writing, within five days of the decision appealed from and the Registrar shall notify every other party who appears to him to be concerned in the appeal and shall inform every such party and the appellant of the arrangements made by the Tribunal for disposing of the appeal.

Amendments—SI 2001/1128, r 12(a), (b).

22 Hearing of interlocutory applications

(1) The Appeal Tribunal may, subject to any direction of a Minister of the Crown under rule 30A(1) or order of the Appeal Tribunal under rule 30A(2)(a) read with rule 30A(1), and, where applicable, to rule 23(6), sit either in private or in public for the hearing of any interim application.

(2) …

Amendments—SI 2001/1128, r 13(a), (b); SI 2004/2526, r 14.

23 Cases involving allegations of sexual misconduct or the commission of sexual offences

(1) This rule applies to any proceedings to which section 31 of the 1996 Act applies.

(2) In any such proceedings where the appeal appears to involve allegations of the commission of a sexual offence, the Registrar shall omit from any register kept by the Appeal Tribunal, which is available to the public, or delete from any order, judgment or other document, which is available to the public, any identifying matter which is likely to lead members of the public to identify any person affected by or making such an allegation.

(3) In any proceedings to which this rule applies where the appeal involves allegations of sexual misconduct the Appeal Tribunal may at any time before promulgation of its decision either on the application of a party or of its own motion make a restricted reporting order having effect, if not revoked earlier by the Appeal Tribunal, until the promulgation of its decision.

(4) A restricted reporting order shall specify the persons who may not be identified.

(5) Subject to paragraph (5A) the Appeal Tribunal shall not make a full restricted reporting order unless it has given each party to the proceedings an opportunity to advance oral argument at a hearing, if they so wish.

(5A) The Appeal Tribunal may make a temporary restricted reporting order without a hearing.

(5B) Where a temporary restricted reporting order has been made the Registrar shall inform the parties to the proceedings in writing as soon as possible of:

    (a)   the fact that the order has been made; and
    (b)   their right to apply to have the temporary restricted reporting order revoked or converted into a full restricted reporting order within 14 days of the temporary order being made.

(5C) If no such application is made under subparagraph (5B)(b) within the 14 days, the temporary restricted reporting order shall lapse and cease to have any effect on the fifteenth day after it was made. When such an application is made the temporary restricted reporting order shall continue to have effect until the Hearing at which the application is considered.

(6) Any hearing shall, subject to any direction of a Minister of the Crown under rule 30A(1) or order of the Appeal Tribunal under rule 30A(2)(a) read with rule 30A(1), or unless the Appeal Tribunal decides for any of the reasons mentioned in rule 29(2) to sit in private to hear evidence, be held in public.

(7) The Appeal Tribunal may revoke a restricted reporting order at any time where it thinks fit.

(8) Where the Appeal Tribunal makes a restricted reporting order, the Registrar shall ensure that a notice of that fact is displayed on the notice board of the Appeal Tribunal at the office in which the proceedings in question are being dealt with, on the door of the room in which those proceedings are taking place and with any list of the proceedings taking place before the Appeal Tribunal.

(9) In this rule, 'promulgation of its decision' means the date recorded as being the date on which the Appeal Tribunal's order finally disposing of the appeal is sent to the parties.

Amendments—SI 2001/1128, r 14(a), (b); SI 2004/2526, r 15(1), (2), (3).

23A Restricted reporting orders in disability cases

(1) This rule applies to proceedings to which section 32(1) of the 1996 Act applies.

(2) In proceedings to which this rule applies the Appeal Tribunal may, on the application of the complainant or of its own motion, make a restricted reporting order having effect, if not revoked earlier by the Appeal Tribunal, until the promulgation of its decision.

(3) Where the Appeal Tribunal makes a restricted reporting order under paragraph (2) of this rule in relation to an appeal which is being dealt with by the Appeal Tribunal together with any other proceedings, the Appeal Tribunal may direct that the order is to apply also in relation to those other proceedings or such part of them as it may direct.

(4) Paragraphs (5) to (9) of rule 23 apply in relation to the making of a restricted reporting order under this rule as they apply in relation to the making of a restricted reporting order under that rule.

Amendments—Inserted by SI 1996/3216, r 2; amended by Employment Rights (Dispute Resolution) Act 1998, s 1(2)(c); SI 2001/1128, r 15.

24 Appointment for direction

(1) Where it appears to the Appeal Tribunal that the future conduct of any proceedings would thereby be facilitated, the Tribunal may (either of its own motion or on application) at any stage in the proceedings appoint a date for a meeting for directions as to their future conduct and thereupon the following provisions of this rule shall apply.

(2) The Registrar shall give to every party in the proceedings notice of the date appointed under paragraph (1) of this rule and any party applying for

directions shall, if practicable, before that date give to the Appeal Tribunal particulars of any direction for which he asks.

(3) The Registrar shall take such steps as may be practicable to inform every party of any directions applied for by any other party.

(4) On the date appointed under paragraph (1) of this rule, the Appeal Tribunal shall consider every application for directions made by any party and any written representations relating to the application submitted to the Tribunal and shall give such directions as it thinks fit for the purpose of securing the just, expeditious and economical disposal of the proceedings, including, where appropriate, directions in pursuance of rule 36, for the purpose of ensuring that the parties are enabled to avail themselves of opportunities for conciliation.

(5) Without prejudice to the generality of paragraph (4) of this rule, the Appeal Tribunal may give such directions as it thinks fit as to –

- (a) the amendment of any notice, answer or other document;
- (b) the admission of any facts or documents;
- (c) the admission in evidence of any documents;
- (d) the mode in which evidence is to be given at the hearing;
- (e) the consolidation of the proceedings with any other proceedings pending before the Tribunal;
- (f) the place and date of the hearing.

(6) An application for further directions or for the variation of any directions already given may be made in accordance with rule 19.

25 Appeal Tribunal's power to give directions

The Appeal Tribunal may either of its own motion or on application, at any stage of the proceedings, give any party directions as to any steps to be taken by him in relation to the proceedings.

26 Default by parties

If a respondent to any proceedings fails to deliver an answer or, in the case of an application made under section 67 or 176 of the 1992 Act, section 33 of the 1996 Act, regulation 20 or 21 of the 1999 Regulations, regulation 33 of the 2004 Regulations regulation 22 of the Information and Consultation Regulations or regulation 53 the 2007 Regulations, a notice of appearance within the time appointed under these Rules, or if any party fails to comply with an order or direction of the Appeal Tribunal, the Tribunal may order that he be debarred from taking any further part in the proceedings, or may make such other order as it thinks just.

Amendments—SI 2001/1128, r 16; SI 2004/2526, r 17(1), (2); SI 2004/3426, reg 41(d)(i), (ii); SI 2007/2974, reg 64(4).

27 Attendance of witnesses and production of documents

(1) The Appeal Tribunal may, on the application of any party, order any person to attend before the Tribunal as a witness or to produce any document.

(1A) Where –
- (a) a Minister has at any stage issued a direction under rule 30A(1)(b) or (c) (exclusion of a party or his representative), or the Appeal Tribunal has at any stage made an order under rule 30A(2)(a) read with rule 30A(1)(b) or (c); and
- (b) the Appeal Tribunal is considering whether to impose, or has imposed, a requirement under paragraph (1) on any person,

the Minister (whether or not he is a party to the proceedings) may make an application to the Appeal Tribunal objecting to the imposition of a requirement under paragraph (1) or, where a requirement has been imposed, an application to vary or set aside the requirement, as the case may be. The Appeal Tribunal shall hear and determine the Minister's application in private and the Minister shall be entitled to address the Appeal Tribunal thereon. The application shall be made by notice to the Registrar and the Registrar shall give notice of the application to each party.

(2) No person to whom an order is directed under paragraph (1) of this rule shall be treated as having failed to obey that order unless at the time at which the order was served on him there was tendered to him a sufficient sum of money to cover his costs of attending before the Appeal Tribunal.

Amendments—SI 2001/1128, r 17.

28 Oaths

The Appeal Tribunal may, either of its own motion or on application, require any evidence to be given on oath.

29 Oral hearings

(1) Subject to paragraph (2) of this rule and to any direction of a Minister of the Crown under rule 30A(1)(a) or order of the Appeal Tribunal under rule 30A(2)(a) read with rule 30A(1)(a), an oral hearing at which any proceedings before the Appeal Tribunal are finally disposed of shall take place in public before, where applicable, such members of the Tribunal as (section 28 of the 1996 Act) the President may nominate for the purpose.

(2) Notwithstanding paragraph (1), the Appeal Tribunal may sit in private for the purpose of hearing evidence from any person which in the opinion of the Tribunal is likely to consist of –
- (a) information which he could not disclose without contravening a prohibition imposed by or by virtue of any enactment;
- (b) information which has been communicated to him in confidence or which he has otherwise obtained in consequence of the confidence reposed in him by another person; or
- (c) information the disclosure of which would, for reasons other than its effect on negotiations with respect to any of the matters mentioned in section 178(2) of the 1992 Act, cause substantial injury to any undertaking of his or in which he works.

Amendments—SI 2001/1128, r 18(a)(i), (ii), (b).

30 Duty of Appeal Tribunal concerning disclosure of information

When exercising its functions, the Appeal Tribunal shall ensure that information is not disclosed contrary to the interests of national security.

Amendments—Substituted by SI 2001/1128, r 19.

30A Proceedings in cases concerning national security

(1) A Minister of the Crown (whether or not he is a party to the proceedings) may, if he considers it expedient in the interests of national security, direct the Appeal Tribunal by notice to the Registrar to –

- (a) sit in private for all or part of particular Crown employment proceedings;
- (b) exclude any party who was the claimant in the proceedings before the employment tribunal from all or part of particular Crown employment proceedings;
- (c) exclude the representatives of any party who was the claimant in the proceedings before the employment tribunal from all or part of particular Crown employment proceedings;
- (d) take steps to conceal the identity of a particular witness in particular Crown employment proceedings.

(2) The Appeal Tribunal may, if it considers it expedient in the interests of national security, by order –

- (a) do in relation to particular proceedings before it anything of a kind which the Appeal Tribunal can be required to do in relation to particular Crown employment proceedings by direction under paragraph (1) of this rule;
- (b) direct any person to whom any document (including any decision or record of the proceedings) has been provided for the purposes of the proceedings not to disclose any such document or the content thereof –
    - (i) to any excluded person;
    - (ii) in any case in which a direction has been given under paragraph (1)(a) or an order has been made under paragraph (2)(a) read with paragraph (1)(a), to any person excluded from all or part of the proceedings by virtue of such direction or order; or
    - (iii) in any case in which a Minister of the Crown has informed the Registrar in accordance with paragraph (3) that he wishes to address the Appeal Tribunal with a view to the Tribunal making an order under paragraph (2)(a) read with paragraph (1)(b) or (c), to any person who may be excluded from all or part of the proceedings by virtue of such an order, if an order is made, at any time before the Appeal Tribunal decides whether or not to make such an order;
- (c) take steps to keep secret all or part of the reasons for any order it makes.

The Appeal Tribunal shall keep under review any order it makes under this paragraph.

(3) In any proceedings in which a Minister of the Crown considers that it would be appropriate for the Appeal Tribunal to make an order as referred to in paragraph (2), he shall (whether or not he is a party to the proceedings) be entitled to appear before and to address the Appeal Tribunal thereon. The Minister shall inform the Registrar by notice that he wishes to address the Appeal Tribunal and the Registrar shall copy the notice to the parties.

(4) In any proceedings in which there is an excluded person, the Appeal Tribunal shall inform the Attorney General or, in the case of an appeal from an employment tribunal in Scotland, the Advocate General for Scotland, of the proceedings before it with a view to the Attorney General (or, as the case may be, the Advocate General), if he thinks it fit to do so, appointing a special advocate to represent the interests of the person who was the claimant in the proceedings before the employment tribunal in respect of those parts of the proceedings from which –

(a) any representative of his is excluded;
(b) both he and his representative are excluded; or
(c) he is excluded, where he does not have a representative.

(5) A special advocate shall have a general qualification within the meaning of section 71 of the Courts and Legal Services Act 1990, or, in the case of an appeal from an employment tribunal in Scotland, shall be –

(a) an advocate; or
(b) a solicitor who has by virtue of section 25A of the Solicitors (Scotland) Act 1980 rights of audience in the Court of Session or the High Court of Justiciary.

(6) Where the excluded person is a party to the proceedings, he shall be permitted to make a statement to the Appeal Tribunal before the commencement of the proceedings, or the part of the proceedings, from which he is excluded.

(7) Except in accordance with paragraphs (8) to (10), the special advocate may not communicate directly or indirectly with any person (including an excluded person) –

(a) (except in the case of the Appeal Tribunal or the party who was the respondent in the proceedings before the employment tribunal) on any matter contained in the documents referred to in rule 3(5), 3(6), 6(7) or 6(8)(b); or
(b) (except in the case of a person who was present) on any matter discussed or referred to during any part of the proceedings in which the Appeal Tribunal sat in private pursuant to a direction of the Minister under paragraph (1)(a) or an order of the Appeal Tribunal under paragraph (2)(a) read with paragraph (1)(a).

(8) The special advocate may apply for directions from the Appeal Tribunal authorising him to seek instructions from, or otherwise to communicate with, an excluded person –

    (a) on any matter contained in the documents referred to in rule 3(5), 3(6), 6(7) or 6(8)(b); or

    (b) on any matter discussed or referred to during any part of the proceedings in which the Appeal Tribunal sat in private as referred to in paragraph (7)(b).

(9) An application under paragraph (8) shall be made by presenting to the Registrar a notice of application, which shall state the title of the proceedings and set out the grounds of the application.

(10) The Registrar shall notify the Minister of an application for directions under paragraph (8) and the Minister shall be entitled to address the Appeal Tribunal on the application.

(11) In these rules, in any case in which a special advocate has been appointed in respect of a party, any reference to a party shall (save in those references specified in paragraph (12)) include the special advocate.

(12) The references mentioned in paragraph (11) are those in rules 5 and 18, the first and second references in rule 27(1A), paragraphs (1) and (6) of this rule, the first reference in paragraph (3) of this rule, rule 34(1), the reference in item 4 of Form 1, and in item 4 of Form 1A, in the Schedule to these Rules.

Amendments—Substituted by SI 2001/1128, r 19; amended by SI 2004/2526, r 16; SI 2005/1871, r 2(a), (b).

31 Drawing up, reasons for, and enforcement of orders

(1) Every order of the Appeal Tribunal shall be drawn up by the Registrar and a copy, sealed with the seal of the Tribunal, shall be served by the Registrar on every party to the proceedings to which it relates and –

    (a) in the case of an order disposing of an appeal from an employment tribunal or of an order under section 33 of the 1996 Act, on the Secretary of the Employment Tribunals;

    (b) in the case of an order disposing of an appeal from the Certification Officer, on that Officer

    (c) in the case of an order imposing a penalty notice under regulation 20 or 21 of the 1999 Regulations, regulation 33 of the 2004 Regulations regulation 22 of the Information and Consultation Regulations or regulation 53 the 2007 Regulations, on the Secretary of State; or

    (d) in the case of an order disposing of an appeal from the CAC made under regulation 38(8) of the 1999 Regulations, on the Chairman of the CAC.

(2) Subject to rule 31A, the Appeal Tribunal shall, on the application of any party made within 14 days after the making of an order finally disposing of any proceedings, give its reasons in writing for the order unless it was made after the delivery of a reasoned judgment.

(3) Subject to any order made by the Court of Appeal or Court of Session and to any directions given by the Appeal Tribunal, an appeal from the Tribunal shall not suspend the enforcement of any order made by it.

Amendments—Employment Rights (Dispute Resolution) Act 1998, s 1(2)(a), (b); SI 2001/1128, r 20(a), (b), (c), (d); SI 2004/2526, r 18; SI 2004/3426, reg 41(d)(ii); SI 2007/2974, reg 64(4).

31A Reasons for orders in cases concerning national security

(1) Paragraphs (1) to (5) of this rule apply to the document setting out the reasons for the Appeal Tribunal's order prepared under rule 31(2) or any reasoned judgment of the Appeal Tribunal as referred to in rule 31(2), in any particular Crown employment proceedings in which a direction of a Minister of the Crown has been given under rule 30A(1)(a), (b) or (c) or an order of the Appeal Tribunal has been made under rule 30A(2)(a) read with rule 30A(1)(a), (b) or (c).

(2) Before the Appeal Tribunal gives its reasons in writing for any order or delivers any reasoned judgment, the Registrar shall send a copy of the reasons or judgment to the Minister.

(3) If the Minister considers it expedient in the interests of national security, he may –

- (a) direct the Appeal Tribunal that the document containing its reasons for any order or its reasoned judgment shall not be disclosed to any person who was excluded from all or part of the proceedings and to prepare a further document setting out the reasons for its order, or a further reasoned judgment, but with the omission of such reasons as are specified in the direction; or
- (b) direct the Appeal Tribunal that the document containing its reasons for any order or its reasoned judgment shall not be disclosed to any person who was excluded from all or part of the proceedings, but that no further document setting out the Appeal Tribunal's reasons for its order or further reasoned judgment should be prepared.

(4) Where the Minister has directed the Appeal Tribunal in accordance with paragraph (3)(a), the document prepared pursuant to that direction shall be marked in each place where an omission has been made. The document may then be given by the Registrar to the parties.

(5) The Registrar shall send the document prepared pursuant to a direction of the Minister in accordance with paragraph (3)(a) and the full document without the omissions made pursuant to that direction –

- (a) to whichever of the appellant and the respondent was not the claimant in the proceedings before the employment tribunal;
- (b) if he was not an excluded person, to the person who was the claimant in the proceedings before the employment tribunal and, if he was not an excluded person, to his representative;
- (c) if applicable, to the special advocate; and

(d) where there are proceedings before a superior court relating to the order in question, to that court.

(6) Where the Appeal Tribunal intends to take steps under rule 30A(2)(c) to keep secret all or part of the reasons for any order it makes, it shall send the full reasons for its order to the persons listed in sub-paragraphs (a) to (d) of paragraph (5), as appropriate.

Amendments—Inserted by SI 2001/1128, r 21; amended by SI 2004/2526, r 16.

32 Registration and proof of awards in respect of exclusion or expulsion from, or unjustifiable discipline by, a trade union

(1) This rule applies where an application has been made to the Appeal Tribunal under section 67 or 176 of the 1992 Act.

(2) Without prejudice to rule 31, where the Appeal Tribunal makes an order in respect of an application to which this rule applies, and that order –

(a) makes an award of compensation, or
(b) is or includes an order of the kind referred to in rule 8(b)(ii),

or both, the Registrar shall as soon as may be enter a copy of the order, sealed with the seal of the Tribunal, into a register kept by the Tribunal (in this rule referred to as 'the Register').

(3) The production in any proceedings in any court of a document, purporting to be certified by the Registrar to be a true copy of an entry in the Register of an order to which this rule applies shall, unless the contrary is proved, be sufficient evidence of the document and of the facts stated therein.

33 Review of decisions and correction of errors

(1) The Appeal Tribunal may, either of its own motion or on application, review any order made by it and may, on such review, revoke or vary that order on the grounds that –

(a) the order was wrongly made as the result of an error on the part of the Tribunal or its staff;
(b) a party did not receive proper notice of the proceedings leading to the order; or
(c) the interests of justice require such review.

(2) An application under paragraph (1) above shall be made within 14 days of the date of the order.

(3) A clerical mistake in any order arising from an accidental slip or omission may at any time be corrected by, or on the authority of, a judge or member.

(4) The decision to grant or refuse an application for review may be made by a judge.

Amendments—SI 2004/2526, r 19.

34 General power to make costs or expenses orders

(1) In the circumstances listed in rule 34A the Appeal Tribunal may make an order ('a costs order') that a party or a special advocate, ('the paying party') make a payment in respect of the costs incurred by another party or a special advocate ('the receiving party').

(2) For the purposes of these Rules 'costs' includes fees, charges, disbursements and expenses incurred by or on behalf of a party or special advocate in relation to the proceedings, including the reimbursement allowed to a litigant in person under rule 34D. In Scotland, all references to costs or costs orders (except in the expression 'wasted costs') shall be read as references to expenses or orders for expenses.

(3) A costs order may be made against or in favour of a respondent who has not had an answer accepted in the proceedings in relation to the conduct of any part which he has taken in the proceedings.

(4) A party or special advocate may apply to the Appeal Tribunal for a costs order to be made at any time during the proceedings. An application may also be made at the end of a hearing, or in writing to the Registrar within 14 days of the date on which the order of the Appeal Tribunal finally disposing of the proceedings was sent to the parties.

(5) No costs order shall be made unless the Registrar has sent notice to the party or special advocate against whom the order may be made giving him the opportunity to give reasons why the order should not be made. This paragraph shall not be taken to require the Registrar to send notice to the party or special advocate if the party or special advocate has been given an opportunity to give reasons orally to the Appeal Tribunal as to why the order should not be made.

(6) Where the Appeal Tribunal makes a costs order it shall provide written reasons for doing so if a request for written reasons is made within 21 days of the date of the costs order. The Registrar shall send a copy of the written reasons to all the parties to the proceedings.

Amendments—Substituted by SI 2004/2526, r 20.

34A When a costs or expenses order may be made

(1) Where it appears to the Appeal Tribunal that any proceedings brought by the paying party were unnecessary, improper, vexatious or misconceived or that there has been unreasonable delay or other unreasonable conduct in the bringing or conducting of proceedings by the paying party, the Appeal Tribunal may make a costs order against the paying party.

(2) The Appeal Tribunal may in particular make a costs order against the paying party when –

    (a)   he has not complied with a direction of the Appeal Tribunal;

(b) he has amended its notice of appeal, document provided under rule 3 sub-paragraphs (5) or (6), Respondent's answer or statement of grounds of cross-appeal, or document provided under rule 6 sub-paragraphs (7) or (8); or

(c) he has caused an adjournment of proceedings.

(3) Nothing in paragraph (2) shall restrict the Appeal Tribunal's discretion to award costs under paragraph (1).

Amendments—Inserted by SI 2004/2526, r 21.

34B The amount of a costs or expenses order

(1) Subject to sub-paragraphs (2) and (3) the amount of a costs order against the paying party can be determined in the following ways:

(a) the Appeal Tribunal may specify the sum which the paying party must pay to the receiving party;

(b) the parties may agree on a sum to be paid by the paying party to the receiving party and if they do so the costs order shall be for the sum agreed; or

(c) the Appeal Tribunal may order the paying party to pay the receiving party the whole or a specified part of the costs of the receiving party with the amount to be paid being determined by way of detailed assessment in the High Court in accordance with the Civil Procedure Rules 1998 or in Scotland the Appeal Tribunal may direct that it be taxed by the Auditor of the Court of Session, from whose decision an appeal shall lie to a judge.

(2) The Appeal Tribunal may have regard to the paying party's ability to pay when considering the amount of a costs order.

(3) The costs of an assisted person in England and Wales shall be determined by detailed assessment in accordance with the Civil Procedure Rules.

Amendments—Inserted by SI 2004/2526, r 21.

34C Personal liability of representatives for costs

(1) The Appeal Tribunal may make a wasted costs order against a party's representative.

(2) In a wasted costs order the Appeal Tribunal may disallow or order the representative of a party to meet the whole or part of any wasted costs of any party, including an order that the representative repay to his client any costs which have already been paid.

(3) 'Wasted costs' means any costs incurred by a party (including the representative's own client and any party who does not have a legal representative):

(a) as a result of any improper, unreasonable or negligent act or omission on the part of any representative; or

(b) which, in the light of any such act or omission occurring after they were incurred, the Appeal Tribunal considers it reasonable to expect that party to pay.

(4) In this rule 'representative' means a party's legal or other representative or any employee of such representative, but it does not include a representative who is not acting in pursuit of profit with regard to the proceedings. A person is considered to be acting in pursuit of profit if he is acting on a conditional fee arrangement.

(5) Before making a wasted costs order, the Appeal Tribunal shall give the representative a reasonable opportunity to make oral or written representations as to reasons why such an order should not be made. The Appeal Tribunal may also have regard to the representative's ability to pay when considering whether it shall make a wasted costs order or how much that order should be.

(6) When the Appeal Tribunal makes a wasted costs order, it must specify in the order the amount to be disallowed or paid.

(7) The Registrar shall inform the representative's client in writing –
- (a) of any proceedings under this rule; or
- (b) of any order made under this rule against the party's representative.

(8) Where the Appeal Tribunal makes a wasted costs order it shall provide written reasons for doing so if a request is made for written reasons within 21 days of the date of the wasted costs order. The Registrar shall send a copy of the written reasons to all parties to the proceedings.

Amendments—Inserted by SI 2004/2526, r 21.

34D Litigants in person and party litigants

(1) This rule applies where the Appeal Tribunal makes a costs order in favour of a party who is a litigant in person.

(2) The costs allowed under this rule must not exceed, except in the case of a disbursement, two-thirds of the amount which would have been allowed if the litigant in person had been represented by a legal representative.

(3) The litigant in person shall be allowed –
- (a) costs for the same categories of –
  - (i) work; and
  - (ii) disbursements,

which would have been allowed if the work had been done or the disbursements had been made by a legal representative on the litigant in person's behalf;
- (b) the payments reasonably made by him for legal services relating to the conduct of the proceedings;
- (c) the costs of obtaining expert assistance in assessing the costs claim; and
- (d) other expenses incurred by him in relation to the proceedings.

(4) The amount of costs to be allowed to the litigant in person for any item of work claimed shall be –

(a) where the litigant in person can prove financial loss, the amount that he can prove he had lost for the time reasonably spent on doing the work; or

(b) where the litigant in person cannot prove financial loss, an amount for the time which the Tribunal considers reasonably spent on doing the work at the rate of £25.00 per hour;

(5) For the year commencing 6th April 2006 the hourly rate of £25.00 shall be increased by the sum of £1.00 and for each subsequent year commencing on 6 April, the hourly rate for the previous year shall also be increased by the sum of £1.00.

(6) A litigant in person who is allowed costs for attending at court to conduct his case is not entitled to a witness allowance in respect of such attendance in addition to those costs.

(7) For the purpose of this rule, a litigant in person includes –

(a) a company or other corporation which is acting without a legal representative; and

(b) in England and Wales a barrister, solicitor, solicitor's employee or other authorised litigator (as defined in the Courts and Legal Services Act), who is acting for himself; and

(c) in Scotland, an advocate or solicitor (within the meaning of the Solicitors (Scotland) Act 1980) who is acting for himself.

(8) In the application of this rule to Scotland, references to a litigant in person shall be read as references to a party litigant.

Amendments—Inserted by SI 2004/2526, r 21.

35 Service of documents

(1) Any notice or other document required or authorised by these Rules to be served on, or delivered to, any person may be sent to him by post to his address for service or, where no address for service has been given, to his registered office, principal place of business, head or main office or last known address, as the case may be, and any notice or other document required or authorised to be served on, or delivered to, the Appeal Tribunal may be sent by post or delivered to the Registrar –

(a) in the case of a notice instituting proceedings, at the central office or any other office of the Tribunal; or

(b) in any other case, at the office of the Tribunal in which the proceedings in question are being dealt with in accordance with rule 38(2).

(2) Any notice or other document required or authorised to be served on, or delivered to, an unincorporated body may be sent to its secretary, manager or other similar officer.

(3) Every document served by post shall be assumed, in the absence of evidence to the contrary, to have been delivered in the normal course of post.

(4) The Appeal Tribunal may inform itself in such manner as it thinks fit of the posting of any document by an officer of the Tribunal.

(5) The Appeal Tribunal may direct that service of any document be dispensed with or be effected otherwise than in the manner prescribed by these Rules.

36 Conciliation

Where at any stage of any proceedings it appears to the Appeal Tribunal that there is a reasonable prospect of agreement being reached between the parties or of disposal of the appeal or a part of it by consensual means, the Tribunal may take such steps as it thinks fit to enable the parties to avail themselves of any opportunities for conciliation, whether by adjourning any proceedings or otherwise.

Amendments—SI 2004/2526, r 22.

37 Time

(1) The time prescribed by these Rules or by order of the Appeal Tribunal for doing any act may be extended (whether it has already expired or not) or abridged, and the date appointed for any purpose may be altered, by order of the Tribunal.

(1A) Where an act is required to be done on or before a particular day it shall be done by 4 pm on that day.

(2) Where the last day for the doing of any act falls on a day on which the appropriate office of the Tribunal is closed and by reason thereof the act cannot be done on that day, it may be done on the next day on which that office is open.

(3) An application for an extension of the time prescribed for the doing of an act, including the institution of an appeal under rule 3, shall be heard and determined as an interim application under rule 20.

(4) An application for an extension of the time prescribed for the institution of an appeal under rule 3 shall not be heard until the notice of appeal has been served on the Appeal Tribunal.

Amendments—SI 2001/1128, r 23; SI 2004/2526, r 23(1), (2).

38 Tribunal offices and allocation of business

(1) The central office and any other office of the Appeal Tribunal shall be open at such times as the President may direct.

(2) Any proceedings before the Tribunal may be dealt with at the central office or at such other office as the President may direct.

39 Non-compliance with, and waiver of, rules

(1) Failure to comply with any requirements of these Rules shall not invalidate any proceedings unless the Appeal Tribunal otherwise directs.

(2) The Tribunal may, if it considers that to do so would lead to the more expeditious or economical disposal of any proceedings or would otherwise be desirable in the interests of justice, dispense with the taking of any step required or authorised by these Rules, or may direct that any such steps be taken in some manner other than that prescribed by these Rules.

(3) The powers of the Tribunal under paragraph (2) extend to authorising the institution of an appeal notwithstanding that the period prescribed in rule 3(2) may not have commenced.

40 Transitional provisions

(1) Where, prior to 16th December 1993, an employment tribunal has given full written reasons for its decision or order, those reasons shall be treated as extended written reasons for the purposes of rule 3(1)(c) and rule 3(2) and for the purposes of Form 1 in the Schedule to these Rules.

(2) Anything validly done under or pursuant to the Employment Appeal Tribunal Rules 1980 shall be treated as having been done validly for the purposes of these Rules, whether or not what was done could have been done under or pursuant to these Rules.

Amendments—Employment Rights (Dispute Resolution) Act 1998, s 1(2)(a).

Schedule

Rule 3

FORM 1
Notice of Appeal from Decision of Employment Tribunal

1

The appellant is (name and address of appellant).

2

Any communication relating to this appeal may be sent to the appellant at (appellant's address for service, including telephone number if any).

3

The appellant appeals from (here give particulars of the judgment, decision or order of the employment tribunal from which the appeal is brought including the location of the employment tribunal and the date).

4

The parties to the proceedings before the employment tribunal, other than the appellant, were (name and addresses of other parties to the proceedings resulting in judgment, decision or order appealed from).

5

Copies of –

(a) the written record of the employment tribunal's judgment, decision or order and the written reasons of the employment tribunal;
(b) the claim (ET1);
(c) the response (ET3); and/or (where relevant)
(d) an explanation as to why any of these documents are not included;

are attached to this notice.

6

If the appellant has made an application to the employment tribunal for a review of its judgment or decision, copies of –

(a) the review application;
(b) the judgment;
(c) the written reasons of the employment tribunal in respect of that review application; and /or;
(d) a statement by or on behalf of the appellant, if such be the case, that a judgment is awaited

are attached to this Notice. If any of these documents exist but cannot be included, then a written explanation must be given.

7

The grounds upon which this appeal is brought are that the employment tribunal erred in law in that (here set out in paragraphs the various grounds of appeal).

Signed

Date

NB The details entered on your Notice of Appeal must be legible and suitable for photocopying or electronic scanning. The use of black ink or typescript is recommended.

Amendments—Substituted by SI 2005/1871, r 3(a).

FORM 1A
Notice of Appeal from the CAC Made Pursuant to Regulation 38(8) of the Transnational Information and Consultation of Employees Regulations 1999, ... regulation 47(6) of the European Public Limited-Liability Company Regulations 2004 regulation 35(6) of the Information and Consultation of Employees Regulations 2004 or regulation 57(6) of the Companies (Cross-Border Mergers) Regulations 2007

Rule 3

1

The appellant is (name and address of appellant).

2

Any communication relating to this appeal may be sent to the appellant at (appellant's address for service, including telephone number if any).

3

The appellant appeals from (here give particulars of the decision, declaration or order of the CAC from which the appeal is brought including the date).

4

The parties to the proceedings before the CAC, other than the appellant, were (names and addresses of other parties to the proceedings resulting in decision appealed from).

5

A copy of the CAC's decision, declaration or order appealed from is attached to this notice.

6

The grounds upon which this appeal is brought are that the CAC erred in law in that (here set out in paragraphs the various grounds of appeal).

Date

Signed

Amendments—Inserted by SI 2001/1128, r 24; amended by SI 2004/2526, r 25(1); SI 2004/3426, reg 41(e)(i), (ii); SI 2007/2974, reg 64(5).

FORM 2
Notice of Appeal from Decision of Certification Officer

Rule 3

1

The appellant is (name and address of appellant).

2

Any communication relating to this appeal may be sent to the appellant at (appellant's address for service, including telephone number if any).

3

The appellant appeals from

(here give particulars of the order or decision of the Certification Officer from which the appeal is brought).

4

The appellant's grounds of appeal are:

(here state the grounds of appeal).

5

A copy of the Certification Officer's decision is attached to this notice.

Date

Signed

FORM 3
Appeal from decision of employment tribunal / certification officer

Rule 6

Respondent's Answer

1

The respondent is (name and address of respondent).

2

Any communication relating to this appeal may be sent to the respondent at (respondent's address for service, including telephone number if any).

3

The respondent intends to resist the appeal of (here give the name of appellant). The grounds on which the respondent will rely are (the grounds relied upon by the employment tribunal/Certification Officer for making the judgment, decision or order appealed from) (and) (the following grounds):

(here set out any grounds which differ from those relied upon by the employment tribunal or Certification Officer, as the case may be).

4

The respondent cross-appeals from

(here give particulars of the decision appealed from).

5

The respondent's grounds of appeal are:

(here state the grounds of appeal).

Date

Signed

Amendments—Employment Rights (Dispute Resolution) Act 1998, s 1(2)(a); SI 2005/1871, r 3(b)(i), (ii).

FORM 4
Application to the Employment Appeal Tribunal for Compensation for Exclusion or Expulsion from a Trade Union or for Compensation or an Order in respect of Unjustifiable Discipline

Rule 8

1

My name is

My address is

2

Any communication relating to this application may be sent to me at

(state address for service, including telephone number, if any).

3

My complaint against (state the name and address of the trade union)

was declared to be well-founded by (state tribunal) on (give date of decision or order).

4

(Where the application relates to exclusion or expulsion from a trade union) I have not been admitted/re-admitted* to membership of the above-named trade union and hereby apply for compensation on the following grounds.

(Where the application relates to unjustifiable discipline) The determination infringing my right not to be unjustifiably disciplined has not been revoked./ The trade union has failed to take all the steps necessary for securing the reversal of things done for the purpose of giving effect to the determination.*

(*Delete as appropriate)

Date

Signed

NB. –A copy of the decision or order declaring the complaint against the trade union to be well-founded must be enclosed with this application.

FORM 4A
Application under Regulation 20 or 21 of the Transnational Information and Consultation of Employees Regulations 1999

Rule 16A

1

The applicant is (name and address of applicant).

2

Any communication relating to this application may be sent to the applicant at (state address for service, including telephone number, if any).

3

The application is made against (state identity or, where applicable, identities of respondents) who is/are, or is/are representative of, the central or local management/the European Works Council/one or more information and consultation representatives (delete what does not apply).

4

The address(es) of the respondent(s) is/are

5

My complaint against the respondent(s) is that it/they failed to comply with its/their obligations under regulation 20 or 21 of the Transnational Information and Consultation of Employees Regulations 1999 as follows (give particulars, set out in paragraphs and making reference to the specific provisions in the 1999 Regulations alleged to have been breached).

Date

Signed

Amendments—Inserted by SI 2001/1128, r 25.

FORM 4B
Applications under Regulation 33 of the European Public Limited–Liability Company Regulations 2004 or regulation 22 of the Information and Consultation of Employees Regulations 2004 or regulation 53 of the Companies (Cross-Border Mergers) Regulations 2007

Rule 16AA

1

The applicant's name is (name and address of applicant)

2

Any communication relating to this application may be sent to the applicant at (applicant's address for service, including telephone number if any).

3

The application is made against (state identity of respondent)

4

The address of the respondent is

5

The Central Arbitration Committee made a declaration in my favour on (insert date) and I request the Employment Tribunal to issue a penalty notice in accordance with regulation 33 of the European Public Limited–Liability Company Regulations 2004 or regulation 22 of the Information and Consultation of Employees Regulations 2004 or regulation 53 of the Companies (Cross-Border Mergers) Regulations 2007(delete which does not apply).

Date

Signed

Amendments—Inserted by SI 2004/2526, r 25(2); amended by SI 2004/3426, reg 41(f)(ii); SI 2007/2974, reg 64(6)(a), (b).

FORM 5
Notice of appearance to Application to Employment Appeal Tribunal for Compensation for Exclusion or Expulsion from a Trade Union or for Compensation or an Order in respect of Unjustifiable Discipline

Rule 11

1

The respondent trade union is (name and address of union).

2

Any communication relating to this application may be sent to the respondent at (respondent's address for service, including telephone number, if any).

3

The respondent intends to resist the application of (here give name of the applicant).

The grounds on which the respondent will rely are as follows:

4

(Where the application relates to exclusion or expulsion from the trade union, state whether or not the applicant had been admitted or re-admitted to membership on or before the date of application.)

(Where the application relates to unjustifiable discipline, state whether –

- (a) the determination infringing the applicant's right not to be unjustifiably disciplined has been revoked; and
- (b) the trade union has taken all the steps necessary for securing the reversal of anything done for the purpose of giving effect to the determination.)

Date

Signed

Position in union

FORM 5A
Notice of Appearance to the Employment Appeal Tribunal under Regulation 20 or 21 of the Transnational Information and Consultation of Employees Regulations 1999

Rule 16C

1

The respondent is (name and address of respondent).

2

Any communication relating to this application may be sent to the respondent at (respondent's address for service, including telephone number, if any).

3

The respondent intends to resist the application of (here give the name or description of the applicant).

The grounds on which the respondent will rely are as follows: (give particulars, set out in paragraphs and making reference to the specific provisions in the Transnational Information and Consultation of Employees Regulations 1999 alleged to have been breached).

Date

Signed

Position in respondent company or undertaking:

(Where appropriate give position in respondent central or local management or position held in relation to respondent Works Council)

Amendments—Inserted by SI 2001/1128, r 26.

FORM 6
Application to the Employment Appeal Tribunal Under Section 33 of the 1996 Act for a Restriction of Proceedings Order

Rule 13

1

The applicant is (the Attorney General/Lord Advocate).

2

Any communication relating to this application may be sent to the applicant at (state address for service, including telephone number).

3

The application is for a restriction of proceedings order to be made against (state the name and address of the person against whom the order is sought).

4

An affidavit in support of the application is attached.

Date

Signed

Amendments—SI 2001/1128, r 27.

FORM 7
Notice of appearance to Application to the Employment Appeal Tribunal under section 33 of the 1996 Act for a Restriction of Proceedings Order

Rule 15

1

The respondent is (state name and address of respondent).

2

Any communication relating to this application may be sent to the respondent at (respondent's address for service, including telephone number, if any).

3

The respondent intends to resist the application. An affidavit in support is attached to this notice.

Date

Signed

Amendments—SI 2001/1128, r 27.

PRACTICE DIRECTION (EMPLOYMENT APPEAL TRIBUNAL – PROCEDURE) 2008

1 Introduction and Objective

1.1 This Practice Direction ('PD') supersedes all previous Practice Directions. It comes into force on 22 May 2008.

1.2 The Employment Appeal Tribunal Rules 1993 (SI 1993/2854) as amended by the Employment Appeal Tribunal (Amendment) Rules 2001 (SI 2001/1128 and 2001/1476) and the Employment Appeal Tribunal (Amendment) Rules 2004 (SI 2004/2526) ('the Rules') apply to all proceedings irrespective of when those proceedings were commenced.

1.3 By s 30(3) of the Employment Tribunals Act 1996 ('ETA 1996') the Employment Appeal Tribunal ('the EAT') has power, subject to the Rules, to regulate its own procedure. In so doing, the EAT regards itself as subject in all its actions to the duties imposed by Rule 2A. It will seek to apply the overriding objective when it exercises any power given to it by the Rules or interprets any Rule.

1.4 The overriding objective of this PD is to enable the EAT to deal with cases justly. Dealing with a case justly includes, so far as is practicable:

1.4.1 ensuring that the parties are on an equal footing;
1.4.2 dealing with the case in ways which are proportionate to the importance and complexity of the issues;
1.4.3 ensuring that it is dealt with expeditiously and fairly;
1.4.4 saving expense.

1.5 The parties are required to help the EAT to further the overriding objective.

1.6 Where the Rules do not otherwise provide, the following procedure will apply to all appeals to the EAT.

1.7 The provisions of this PD are subject to any specific directions which the EAT may make in any particular case. Otherwise, the directions set out below must be complied with in all appeals from Employment Tribunals. In national security appeals, and appeals from the Certification Officer and the Central Arbitration Committee, the Rules set out the separate procedures to be followed and the EAT will normally give specific directions.

1.8 Where it is appropriate to the EAT's jurisdiction, procedure, unrestricted rights of representation and restricted costs regime, the EAT is guided by the Civil Procedure Rules. So, for example:

1.8.1 For the purpose of serving a valid Notice of Appeal under Rule 3 and para 3 below, when an Employment Tribunal decision is sent to parties on a Wednesday, that day does not count and the Notice of Appeal must arrive at the EAT by 4.00pm on or before the Wednesday 6 weeks (ie 42 days) later.

1.8.2 When a date is given for serving of a document or for doing some other act, the complete document must be received by the EAT or the relevant party by 4.00pm on that date. Any document received after 4.00pm will be deemed to be lodged on the next working day.

1.8.3 Except as provided in 1.8.4 below, all days count, but if a time limit expires on a day when the central office of the EAT, or the EAT office in Edinburgh (as appropriate), is closed, it is extended to the next working day.

1.8.4 Where the time limit is five days (eg an appeal against a Registrar's order or direction), Saturdays, Sundays, Christmas Day, Good Friday and Bank Holidays do not count. For example an appeal against an order made on a Wednesday must arrive at the EAT on or before the following Wednesday.

1.9 In this PD any reference to the date of an order shall mean the date stamped upon the relevant order by the EAT ('the seal date').

1.10 The parties can expect the EAT normally to have read the documents (or the documents indicated in any essential reading list if permission is granted under para 6.3 below for an enlarged appeal bundle) in advance of any hearing.

2 Institution of Appeal

2.1 The Notice of Appeal must be, or be substantially, in accordance with Form 1 (in the amended form annexed to this Practice Direction) or Forms 1A or 2 of the Schedule to the Rules and must identify the date of the judgment, decision or order being appealed. Copies of the judgment, decision or order appealed against and of the Employment Tribunal's written reasons, together with a copy of the claim (ET1) and the response (ET3) must be attached, or if not, a written explanation must be given. A Notice of Appeal without such documentation will not be validly lodged.

2.2 If the appellant has made an application to the Employment Tribunal for a review of its judgment or decision, a copy of such application should accompany the Notice of Appeal together with the judgment and written reasons of the Employment Tribunal in respect of that review application, or a statement, if such be the case, that a judgment is awaited. If any of these documents cannot be included, a written explanation must be given. The appellant should also attach (where they are relevant to the appeal) copies of any orders including case management orders made by the Employment Tribunal.

2.3 Where written reasons of the Employment Tribunal are not attached to the Notice of Appeal, either (as set out in the written explanation) because a request for written reasons has been refused by the Employment Tribunal or for some other reason, an appellant must, when lodging the Notice of Appeal, apply in writing to the EAT to exercise its discretion to hear the appeal without written reasons or to exercise its power to request written reasons from the Employment Tribunal, setting out the full grounds of that application.

2.4 The Notice of Appeal must clearly identify the point(s) of law which form(s) the ground(s) of appeal from the judgment, decision or order of the Employment Tribunal to the EAT. It should also state the order which the appellant will ask the EAT to make at the hearing.

2.5 Rules 3(7)-(10) give a judge or the Registrar power to decide that no further action shall be taken in certain cases where it appears that the Notice of Appeal or any part of it (a) discloses no reasonable grounds for bringing the appeal, or (b) is an abuse of the Employment Appeal Tribunal's process or is otherwise likely to obstruct the just disposal of proceedings. The Rules specify the rights of the appellant and the procedure to be followed. The appellant can request an oral hearing before a judge to challenge the decision. If it appears to the judge or Registrar that a Notice of Appeal or an application gives insufficient grounds of, or lacks clarity in identifying, a point of law, the judge or Registrar may postpone any decision under Rule 3(7) pending the appellant's amplification or clarification of the Notice of Appeal or further information from the Employment Tribunal.

2.6 **Perversity Appeals:** an appellant may not state as a ground of appeal simply words to the effect that "the judgment or order was contrary to the evidence", or that "there was no evidence to support the judgment or order", or that "the judgment or order was one which no reasonable Tribunal could have reached and was perverse" unless the Notice of Appeal also sets out full particulars of the matters relied on in support of those general grounds.

2.7 A party cannot reserve a right to amend, alter or add, to a Notice of Appeal or a respondent's Answer. Any application for permission to amend must be made as soon as practicable and must be accompanied by a draft of the amended Notice of Appeal or amended Answer which makes clear the precise amendments for which permission is sought.

2.8 A respondent to the appeal who wishes to resist the appeal and/or to cross-appeal, but who has not delivered a respondent's Answer as directed by the Registrar, or otherwise ordered, may be precluded from taking part in the appeal unless permission is granted to serve an Answer out of time.

2.9 Where an application is made for permission to institute or continue relevant proceedings by a person who has been made the subject of a Restriction of Proceedings Order pursuant to s 33 of ETA 1996, that application will be considered on paper by a judge, who may make an order granting, refusing or otherwise dealing with such application on paper.

3 Time for Instituting Appeals

3.1 The time within which an appeal must be instituted depends on whether the appeal is against a judgment or against an order or decision of the Employment Tribunal.

3.2 If the appeal is against an order or decision, the appeal must be instituted within 42 days of the date of the order or decision. The EAT will treat a Tribunal's refusal to make an order or decision as itself constituting an order or decision. The date of an order or decision is the date when the order or decision was sent to the parties, which is normally recorded on or in the order or decision.

3.3 If the appeal is against a judgment, the appeal must be instituted within 42 days from the date on which the written record of the judgment was sent to the parties. However in three situations the time for appealing against a judgment will be 42 days from the date when written reasons were sent to the parties. This will be the case only if (1) written reasons were requested orally at the hearing before the Tribunal or (2) written reasons were requested in writing within 14 days of the date on which the written record of the judgment was sent to the parties or (3) the Tribunal itself reserved its reasons and gave them subsequently in writing: such exception will not apply if the request to the Tribunal for written reasons is made out of time (whether or not such request is granted). The date of the written record and of the written reasons is the date when they are sent to the parties, which is normally recorded on or in the written record and the written reasons.

3.4 The time limit referred to in paras 3.1 to 3.3 above apply even though the question of remedy and assessment of compensation by the Employment Tribunal has been adjourned or has not been dealt with and even though an application has been made to the Employment Tribunal for a review.

3.5 An application for an extension of time for appealing cannot be considered until a Notice of Appeal in accordance with para 2(1) above has been lodged with the EAT.

3.6 Any application for an extension of time for appealing must be made as an interim application to the Registrar, who will normally determine the application after inviting and considering written representations from each side. An interim appeal lies from the Registrar's decision to a judge. Such an appeal must be notified to the EAT within 5 days of the date when the Registrar's decision was sent to the parties. [See para 4.3 below.]

3.7 In determining whether to extend the time for appealing, particular attention will be paid to whether any good excuse for the delay has been shown and to the guidance contained in the decisions of the EAT and the Court of Appeal, as summarised in *United Arab Emirates v Abdelghafar* [1995] ICR 65, *Aziz v Bethnal Green City Challenge Co Ltd* [2000] IRLR 111 and *Jurkowska v HLMAD Ltd* [2008] EWCA Civ 231.

3.8 It is not usually a good reason for late lodgment of a Notice of Appeal that an application for litigation support from public funds has been made, but not yet determined; or that support is being sought from, but has not yet been provided by, some other body, such as a trade union, employers' association or the Equality and Human Rights Commission.

3.9 In any case of doubt or difficulty, a Notice of Appeal should be lodged in time and an application made to the Registrar for directions.

4 Interim Applications

4.1 Interim applications should be made in writing (no particular form is required) and will be initially referred to the Registrar who after considering the papers may deal with the case or refer it to a judge. The judge may dispose of it himself or refer it to a full EAT hearing. Parties are encouraged to make any such applications at a Preliminary Hearing ('PH') or an Appointment for Directions if one is ordered (see paras 9.7–9.18 and 11.2 below).

4.2 Unless otherwise ordered, any application for extension of time will be considered and determined as though it were an interim application to the Registrar, who will normally determine the application after inviting and considering written representations from each side.

4.3 An interim appeal lies from the Registrar's decision to a judge. Such an appeal must be notified to the EAT within five days of the date when the Registrar's decision was sent to the parties.

5 The Right to Inspect the Register and Certain Documents and to Take Copies

5.1 Any document lodged in the Central Office of the EAT in London or in the EAT office in Edinburgh in any proceedings before the EAT shall be sealed with the seal of the EAT showing the date (and time, if received after 4.00 pm) on which the document was lodged.

5.2 Particulars of the date of delivery at the Central Office of the EAT or in the EAT office in Edinburgh of any document for filing or lodgment together with the time, if received after 4.00pm, the date of the document and the title of the appeal of which the document forms part of the record shall be entered in the Register of Cases kept in the Central Office and in Edinburgh or in the file which forms part of the Register of Cases.

5.3 Any person shall be entitled during office hours by appointment to inspect and request a copy of any of the following documents filed or lodged in the Central Office or the EAT office in Edinburgh, namely:

5.3.1 any Notice of Appeal or respondent's Answer or any copy thereof;
5.3.2 any judgment or order given or made in court or any copy of such judgment or order; and
5.3.3 with the permission of the EAT, which may be granted on an application, any other document.

5.4 A copying charge per page will be payable for those documents mentioned in para 5.3 above.

5.5 Nothing in this Direction shall be taken as preventing any party to an appeal from inspecting and requesting a copy of any document filed or lodged in the Central Office or the EAT office in Edinburgh before the commencement of the appeal, but made with a view to its commencement.

6 Papers for use at the Hearing

6.1 It is the responsibility of the parties or their advisers (see paras 6.5 and 6.6 below) to prepare a core bundle of papers for use at any hearing. Ultimate responsibility lies with the appellant, following consultation with other parties. The bundle must include only those exhibits (productions in Scotland) and documents used before the Employment Tribunal which are considered to be necessary for the appeal. It is the duty of the parties or their advisers to ensure that only those documents are included which are (a) relevant to the point(s) of law raised in the appeal and (b) likely to be referred to at the hearing. It is also the responsibility of parties to retain copies of all documents and correspondence, including hearing bundles, sent to EAT. Bundles (see para 6.2 below) used at one EAT hearing will not be retained by the EAT for a subsequent hearing.

6.2 The documents in the core bundle should be numbered by item, then paginated continuously and indexed, in the following order:

6.2.1 Judgment, decision or order appealed from and written reasons
6.2.2 Sealed Notice of Appeal
6.2.3 Respondent's Answer if a Full Hearing ('FH'), respondent's Submissions if a PH
6.2.4 ET1 claim (and any Additional Information or Written Answers)
6.2.5 ET3 response (and any Additional Information or Written Answers)
6.2.6 Questionnaire and Replies (discrimination and equal pay cases)
6.2.7 Relevant orders, judgments and written reasons of the Employment Tribunal
6.2.8 Relevant orders and judgments of the EAT
6.2.9 Affidavits and Employment Tribunal comments (where ordered)
6.2.10 Any documents agreed or ordered pursuant to para 7 below.

6.3 Other documents relevant to the particular hearing (for example the particulars or contract of employment and any procedures) referred to at the Employment Tribunal may follow in the core bundle, if the total pages do not exceed 100. No bundle containing more than 100 pages should be agreed or lodged without the permission of the Registrar or order of a judge which will not be granted without the provision of an essential reading list as soon as practicable thereafter. If permitted or ordered, further pages should follow, with consecutive pagination, in an additional bundle or bundles if appropriate.

6.4 All documents must be legible and unmarked.

6.5 **PH cases** (see para 9.5.2 below), **Appeals from Registrar's Order, Rule 3(10) hearings, Appointments for Directions:** the appellant must prepare and lodge four copies (two copies if judge sitting alone) of the bundle as soon as possible after service of the Notice of Appeal and no later than 28 days from the seal date of the relevant order unless otherwise directed.

6.6 **FH cases** (see para 9.5.3 below): the parties must co-operate in agreeing a bundle of papers for the hearing. By no later than 28 days from the seal date of the relevant order, unless otherwise directed, the appellant is responsible for ensuring that four copies (two copies if judge sitting alone) of a bundle agreed by the parties is lodged at the EAT.

6.7 **Warned List and Fast Track FH cases:** the bundles should be lodged as soon as possible and (unless the hearing date is within seven days) in any event within seven days after the parties have been notified that the case is expedited or in the Warned List.

6.8 In the event of disagreement between the parties or difficulty in preparing the bundles, the Registrar may give appropriate directions, whether on application in writing (on notice) by one or more of the parties or of his/her own initiative.

7 Evidence Before the Employment Tribunal

7.1 An appellant who considers that a point of law raised in the Notice of Appeal cannot be argued without reference to evidence given (or not given) at the Employment Tribunal, the nature or substance of which does not, or does not sufficiently, appear from the written reasons, must ordinarily submit an application with the Notice of Appeal. The application is for the nature of such evidence (or lack of it) to be admitted, or if necessary for the relevant parts of the employment judge's notes of evidence to be produced. If such application is not so made, then it should be made:

7.1.1 if a PH is ordered, in the skeleton or written submissions lodged prior to such PH; or

7.1.2 if the case is listed for FH without a PH, then within 14 days of the seal date of the order so providing.

Any such application by a respondent to an appeal, must, if not made earlier, accompany the respondent's Answer.

7.2 The application must explain why such a matter is considered necessary in order to argue the point of law raised in the Notice of Appeal or respondent's Answer. The application must identify:

7.2.1 the issue(s) in the Notice of Appeal or respondent's Answer to which the matter is relevant;

7.2.2 the names of the witnesses whose evidence is considered relevant, alternatively the nature of the evidence the absence of which is considered relevant;

7.2.3 (if applicable) the part of the hearing when the evidence was given;

7.2.4 the gist of the evidence (or absence of evidence) alleged to be relevant; and

7.2.5 (if the party has a record), saying so and by whom and when it was made, or producing an extract from a witness statement given in writing at the hearing.

7.3 The application will be considered on the papers, or if appropriate at a PH, by the Registrar or a judge. The Registrar or a judge may give directions for written representations (if they have not already been lodged), or may determine the application, but will ordinarily make an order requiring the party who seeks to raise such a matter to give notice to the other party(ies) to the appeal/cross-appeal. The notice will require the other party(ies) to co-operate in agreeing, within 21 days (unless a shorter period is ordered), a statement or note of the relevant evidence, alternatively a statement that there was no such evidence. All parties are required to use their best endeavours to agree such a statement or note.

7.4 In the absence of such agreement within 21 days (or such shorter period as may be ordered) of the requirement, any party may make an application within seven days thereafter to the EAT, for directions. The party must enclose all relevant correspondence and give notice to the other parties. The directions may include: the resolution of the disagreement on the papers or at a hearing; the administration by one party to the others of, or a request to the employment judge to respond to, a questionnaire; or, if the EAT is satisfied that such notes are necessary, a request that the employment judge produce his/her notes of evidence either in whole or in part.

7.5 If the EAT requests any documents from the employment judge, it will supply copies to the parties upon receipt.

7.6 In an appeal from an Employment Tribunal which ordered its proceedings to be tape recorded, the EAT will apply the principles above to any application for a transcript.

7.7 A note of evidence is not to be produced and supplied to the parties to enable the parties to embark on a 'fishing expedition' to establish grounds or additional grounds of appeal or because they have not kept their own notes of the evidence. If an application for such a note is found by the EAT to have been unreasonably made or if there is unreasonable lack of co-operation in agreeing a relevant note or statement, the party behaving unreasonably is at risk of being ordered to pay costs.

8 Fresh Evidence and New Points of Law

8.1 Where an application is made by a party to an appeal to put in, at the hearing of the appeal, any document which was not before the Employment Tribunal, and which has not been agreed in writing by the other parties, the application and a copy of the documents sought to be admitted should be lodged at the EAT with the Notice of Appeal or the respondent's Answer, as appropriate. The application and copy should be served on the other parties. The same principle applies to any oral evidence not given at the Employment Tribunal which is sought to be adduced on the appeal. The nature and substance of such evidence together with the date when the party first became aware of its existence must be disclosed in a document, where appropriate a witness statement from the relevant witness with signed statement of truth, which must be similarly lodged and served.

8.2 In exercising its discretion to admit any fresh evidence or new document, the EAT will apply the principles set out in *Ladd v Marshall* [1954] 1 WLR 1489, having regard to the overriding objective, ie:

8.2.1   the evidence could not have been obtained with reasonable diligence for use at the Employment Tribunal hearing;
8.2.2   it is relevant and would probably have had an important influence on the hearing;
8.2.3   it is apparently credible.

Accordingly the evidence and representations in support of the application must address these principles.

8.3 A party wishing to resist the application must, within 14 days of its being sent, submit any representations in response to the EAT and other parties.

8.4 The application will be considered by the Registrar or a judge on the papers (or, if appropriate, at a PH) who may determine the issue or give directions for a hearing or may seek comments from the employment judge. A copy of any comments received from the employment judge will be sent to all parties.

8.5 If a respondent intends to contend at the FH that the appellant has raised a point which was not argued below, the respondent shall so state:

8.5.1   if a PH has been ordered, in writing to the EAT and all parties, within 14 days of receiving the Notice of Appeal;
8.5.2   if the case is listed for a FH without a PH, in a respondent's Answer.

In the event of dispute the employment judge should be asked for his/her comments as to whether a particular legal argument was deployed.

9 Case Tracks and Directions: the Sift of Appeals

9.1 Consistent with the overriding objective, the EAT will seek to give directions for case management so that the case can be dealt with quickly, or better considered, and in the most effective and just way.

9.2 Applications and directions for case management will usually be dealt with on the papers ('the sift') by a judge, or by the Registrar with an appeal to a judge. Any party seeking directions must serve a copy on all parties. Directions may be given at any stage, before or after the registration of a Notice of Appeal. An order made will contain a time for compliance, which must be observed or be the subject of an application by any party to vary or discharge it, or to seek an extension of time. Otherwise, failure to comply with an order in time or at all may result in the EAT exercising its power under Rule 26 to strike out the appeal, cross-appeal or respondent's Answer or debar the party from taking any further part in the proceedings or to make any other order it thinks fit, including an award of costs.

9.3 Any application to vary or discharge an order, or to seek an extension of time, must be lodged at the EAT and served on the other parties within the time fixed for compliance. Such other parties must, if opposing the application and within 14 days (or such shorter period as may be ordered) of receiving it, submit their representations to the EAT and the other parties.

9.4 An application to amend a Notice of Appeal or respondent's Answer must include the text of the original document with any changes clearly marked and identifiable, for example with deletions struck through in red and the text of the amendment either written or underlined in red. Any subsequent amendments will have to be in a different identifiable colour.

9.5 Notices of Appeal are sifted by a judge or the Registrar so as to determine the most effective case management of the appeal. The sift will result in a decision as to which track the appeal will occupy, and directions will be given. There are four tracks:

9.5.1 Rule 3(7) cases [see para 9.6 below].
9.5.2 Preliminary Hearing (PH) cases [see paras 9.7–9.18 below]
9.5.3 Full Hearing (FH) cases [see para 9.19 below].
9.5.4 Fast Track Full Hearing ('FTFH') cases [see paras 9.20–9.21 below].

The judge or Registrar may also stay (or sist in Scotland) the appeal for a period, normally 21 days, pending the making or the conclusion of an application by the appellant to the Employment Tribunal (if necessary out of time) for a review or pending the response by the Employment Tribunal to an invitation from the judge or Registrar to clarify, supplement or give its written reasons.

Rule 3(7) Cases (9.5.1)

9.6 The judge or Registrar, having considered the Notice of Appeal and, if appropriate, having obtained any additional information, may decide that it or any of the grounds contained in it discloses no reasonable grounds for bringing the appeal or is an abuse of the process or otherwise likely to obstruct the just disposal of the proceedings. Reasons will be sent and within 28 days the appellant may submit a fresh Notice of Appeal for further consideration or request an oral hearing before a judge. At that hearing the judge may confirm the earlier decision or order that the appeal proceeds to a Preliminary or Full Hearing. A hearing under Rule 3(10), including judgment and any directions, will normally last not more than one and a half hours. A judge or Registrar may also follow the Rule 3(7) procedure, of his or her own initiative, or on application, at any later stage of the proceedings, if appropriate.

Preliminary Hearing Cases (9.5.2)

9.7 The purpose of a PH is to determine whether:

9.7.1 the grounds in the Notice of Appeal raise a point of law which gives the appeal a reasonable prospect of success at a FH; or
9.7.2 for some other compelling reason the appeal should be heard e g that the appellant seeks a declaration of incompatibility under the Human Rights Act 1998; or to argue that a decision binding on the EAT should be considered by a higher court.

9.8 Prior to the PH there will be automatic directions. These include sending the Notice of Appeal to the respondent(s) to the appeal. The direction may order or in any event will enable the respondent(s) to lodge and serve, within 14 days of the seal date of the order (unless otherwise directed), concise written submissions in response to the Notice of Appeal, dedicated to showing that there is no reasonable prospect of success for all or any grounds of any appeal. Such submissions will be considered at the PH.

9.9 If the respondent to the appeal intends to serve a cross-appeal this must be accompanied by written submissions and must be lodged and served within 14 days of service of the Notice of Appeal. The respondent to the appeal must make clear whether it is intended to advance the cross-appeal:

9.9.1   in any event (an unconditional cross-appeal); or
9.9.2   only if the Appellant succeeds (a conditional cross-appeal).

In either case the respondent is entitled to attend the PH, which will also amount to a PH of the cross-appeal, and make submissions.

9.10 All parties will be notified of the date fixed for the PH. In the normal case, unless ordered otherwise, only the appellant and/or a representative should attend to make submissions to the EAT on the issue whether the Notice of Appeal raises a point of law with a reasonable prospect of success:

9.10.1   Except where the respondent to the appeal makes a cross-appeal, or the EAT orders a hearing with all parties present, the respondent to the appeal is not required to attend the hearing and is not usually permitted to take part in it. But any written submissions as referred to in (8) above will be considered at the PH.

9.10.2   If the appellant does not attend, the appeal may nevertheless be dealt with as above on written submissions, and be wholly or in part dismissed or allowed to proceed.

9.11 The PH, including judgment and directions, will normally last no more than one hour.

9.12 The sift procedure will be applied to cross-appeals as well as appeals. If an appeal has been assigned to the FH track, without a PH, and the respondent includes a cross-appeal in the respondent's Answer, the respondent must immediately apply to the EAT in writing on notice to the appellant for directions on the papers as to whether the EAT considers that there should be a PH of the cross-appeal.

9.13 If satisfied that the appeal (and/or the cross-appeal) should be heard at a FH on all or some of the grounds of appeal, the EAT will give directions relating to, for example, a time estimate, any application for fresh evidence, a procedure in respect of matters of evidence before the Employment Tribunal not sufficiently appearing from the written reasons, the exchange and lodging of skeleton arguments and an appellant's Chronology, and bundles of documents and authorities.

9.14 Permission to amend a Notice of Appeal (or cross-appeal) may be granted:

9.14.1   **If the proposed amendment is produced at the hearing**, then, if such amendment has not previously been notified to the other parties, and the appeal (or cross-appeal) might not have been permitted to proceed but for the amendment, the opposing party(ies) will have the opportunity to apply on notice to vary or discharge the permission to proceed, and for consequential directions as to the hearing or disposal of the appeal or cross-appeal.

9.14.2 **If a draft amendment is not available at the PH**, an application for permission to amend, in writing on notice to the other party(ies) in accordance with para 9.4 above, will be permitted to be made within 14 days. Where, but for such proposed amendment, the appeal (or cross-appeal) may not have been permitted to proceed to a FH, provision may be made in the order on the PH for the appeal (or cross-appeal) to be dismissed if the application for permission to amend is not made. Where such an application is made and refused, provision will be made for any party to have liberty to apply, in writing on notice to the other party(ies), as to the hearing or disposal of the appeal.

9.15 If not satisfied that the appeal, or any particular ground of it, should go forward to a FH, the EAT at the PH will dismiss the appeal, wholly or in part, and give a judgment setting out the reasons for doing so.

9.16 If an appeal is permitted to go forward to an FH on all grounds, a reasoned judgment will not normally be given.

9.17 Parties who become aware that a similar point is raised in other proceedings at an Employment Tribunal or the EAT are encouraged to co-operate in bringing this to the attention of the Registrar so that consideration can be given to the most expedient way of dealing with the cases, in particular to the possibility of having two or more appeals heard together.

9.18 If an appeal is permitted to go forward to an FH, a listing category will be assigned ie:

P   (recommended to be heard in the President's list);
A   (complex, and raising point(s) of law of public importance);
B   (any other cases).The President reserves the discretion to alter any relevant category as circumstances require.

Full Hearing Cases (9.5.3)

9.19 If a judge or the Registrar decides to list the case for an FH without a PH s/he will consider appropriate directions, relating for example to amendment, further information, any application for fresh evidence, a procedure in respect of matters of evidence at the Employment Tribunal not sufficiently appearing from the written reasons, allegations of bias, apparent bias or improper conduct, provisions for skeleton arguments, appellant's Chronology and bundles of documents and of authorities, time estimates and listing category (as set out in para 9.18 above).

Fast Track Full Hearing Cases (9.5.4)

9.20 FH cases are normally heard in the order in which they are received. However, there are times when it is expedient to hear an appeal as soon as it can be fitted into the list. Appeals placed in this Fast Track, at the discretion of a judge or the Registrar, will normally fall into the following cases:

9.20.1 appeals where the parties have made a reasoned case on the merits for an expedited hearing;

9.20.2 appeals against interim orders or decisions of an Employment Tribunal, particularly those which involve the taking of a step in the proceedings within a specified period, for example adjournments, further information, amendments, disclosure, witness orders;

9.20.3 appeals on the outcome of which other applications to the Employment Tribunal or the EAT or the civil courts depend;

9.20.4 appeals in which a reference to the European Court of Justice (ECJ), or a declaration of incompatibility under the Human Rights Act 1998, is sought;

9.20.5 appeals involving reinstatement, re-engagement, interim relief or a recommendation for action (discrimination cases).

9.21 Category B cases estimated to take two hours or less may also be allocated to the Fast Track.

10 Respondent's Answer and Directions

10.1 After the sift stage or a PH, at which a decision is made to permit the appeal to go forward to an FH, the EAT will send the Notice of Appeal, with any amendments which have been permitted, and any submissions or skeleton argument lodged by the appellant, to all parties who are respondents to the appeal. Within 14 days of the seal date of the order (unless otherwise directed), respondents must lodge at the EAT and serve on the other parties a respondent's Answer. If it contains a cross-appeal, the appellant must within 14 days of service (unless otherwise directed), lodge and serve a Reply.

10.2 After lodgment and service of the respondent's Answer and of any Reply to a cross-appeal, the Registrar may, where necessary, invite applications from the parties in writing, on notice to all other parties, for directions, and may give any appropriate directions on the papers or may fix a day when the parties should attend on an Appointment for Directions.

10.3 A judge may at any time, upon consideration of the papers or at a hearing, make an order requiring or recommending consideration by the parties or any of them of compromise, conciliation, mediation or, in particular, reference to ACAS.

11 Complaints about the Conduct of the Employment Tribunal Hearing

11.1 An appellant who intends to complain about the conduct of the Employment Tribunal (for example bias, apparent bias or improper conduct by the employment judge or lay members or any procedural irregularity at the hearing) must include in the Notice of Appeal full particulars of each complaint made.

11.2 An appeal which is wholly or in part based on such a complaint will be sifted by a judge or the Registrar as set out in para 9.5 above and this may result in a decision as to the appropriate track which the appeal will occupy. At the sift stage or before, the judge or Registrar may postpone a decision as to track, and direct that the appellant or a representative provide an affidavit setting out full particulars of all allegations of bias or misconduct relied upon. At the sift stage the Registrar may enquire of the party making the complaint whether it is intended to proceed with it and may draw attention to para 11.6 below.

11.3 If the appeal is allocated to the PH or FH track, the EAT may take the following steps prior to such hearing within a time-limit set out in the relevant order:

11.3.1 require the appellant or a representative to provide, if not already provided, an affidavit as set out in para 11.2 above;

11.3.2 require any party to give an affidavit or to obtain a witness statement from any person who has represented any of the parties at the Tribunal hearing, and any other person present at the Tribunal hearing or a relevant part of it, giving their account of the events set out in the affidavit of the appellant or the appellant's representative. For the above purpose, the EAT will provide copies of any affidavits received from or on behalf of the appellant to any other person from whom an account is sought;

11.3.3 seek comments, upon all affidavits or witness statements received, from the employment judge of the Employment Tribunal from which the appeal is brought and may seek such comments from the lay members of the Tribunal. For the above purpose, copies of all relevant documents will be provided by the EAT to the employment judge and, if appropriate, the lay members; such documents will include any affidavits and witness statements received, the Notice of Appeal and other relevant documents.

11.3.4 the EAT will on receipt supply to the parties copies of all affidavits, statements and comments received.

11.4 A respondent who intends to make such a complaint must include such particulars as set out in paras 11.1 and 11.2 above:

11.4.1 (in the event of a PH being ordered in respect of the appellant's appeal, in accordance with para 9.5.2 above) in the cross-appeal referred to in para 9.9 above, or, in the absence of a cross-appeal, in written submissions, as referred to in para 9.8 above;

11.4.2 (in the event of no PH being ordered, in accordance with para 9.5.3 above) in his respondent's Answer.

A similar procedure will then be followed as in para 11.3 above.

11.5 In every case which is permitted to go forward to an FH the EAT will give appropriate directions, ordinarily on the papers after notice to the appellant and respondent, as to the procedure to be adopted at, and material to be provided to, the FH; but such directions may be given at the sift stage or at a PH.

11.6 Parties should note the following:

11.6.1 The EAT will not permit complaints of the kind mentioned above to be raised or developed at the hearing of the appeal unless this procedure has been followed.

11.6.2 The EAT recognises that employment judges and Employment Tribunals are themselves obliged to observe the overriding objective and are given wide powers and duties of case management (see Employment Tribunal (Constitution and Rules of Procedure) Regulations 2004 (SI No 1861)), so appeals in respect of the conduct of Employment Tribunals, which is in exercise of those powers and duties, are the less likely to succeed.

11.6.3 Unsuccessful pursuit of an allegation of bias or improper conduct, particularly in respect of case management decisions, may put the party raising it at risk of an order for costs.

12 Listing of Appeals

12.1 **Estimate of Length of Hearing:** the lay members of the EAT are part-time members. They attend when available on pre-arranged dates. They do not sit for continuous periods. Consequently appeals which run beyond their estimated length have to be adjourned part-heard (often with substantial delay) until a day on which the judge and members are all available. To avoid inconvenience to the parties and to the EAT, and to avoid additional delay and costs suffered as a result of adjournment of part-heard appeals, all parties are required to ensure that the estimates of length of hearing (allowing for the fact that the parties can expect the EAT to have pre-read the papers and for deliberation and the giving of a judgment) are accurate when first given. Any change in such estimate, or disagreement with an estimate made by the EAT on a sift or at a PH, is to be notified immediately to the Listing Officer.

12.2 If the EAT concludes that the hearing is likely to exceed the estimate, or if for other reasons the hearing may not be concluded within the time available, it may seek to avoid such adjournment by placing the parties under appropriate time limits in order to complete the presentation of the submissions within the estimated or available time.

12.3 Subject to para 12.6 below a date will be fixed for a PH as soon as practicable after the sift (referred to in para 9.5 above) and for an FH as soon as practicable after the sift if no PH is ordered, or otherwise after the PH.

12.4 The Listing Officer will normally consult the parties on dates, and will accommodate reasonable requests if practicable, but is not bound to do so. Once the date is fixed, the appeal will be set down in the list. A party finding that the date which has been fixed causes serious difficulties may apply to the Listing Officer for it to be changed, having first notified all other parties entitled to appear on the date, of their application and the reasons for it.

12.5 Parties receiving such an application must, as soon as possible and within seven days, notify the Listing Officer of their views.

12.6 In addition to this fixed date procedure, a list ('the warned list') may be drawn up. Cases will be placed in such warned list at the discretion of the

Listing Officer or may be so placed by the direction of a judge or the Registrar. These will ordinarily be short cases, or cases where expedition has been ordered. Parties or their representatives will be notified that their case has been included in this list, and as much notice as possible will be given of the intention to list a case for hearing, when representations by way of objection from the parties will be considered by the Listing Officer and if necessary on appeal to the Registrar or a judge. The parties may apply on notice to all other parties for a fixed date for hearing.

12.7 Other cases may be put in the list by the Listing Officer with the consent of the parties at shorter notice: for example, where other cases have been settled or withdrawn or where it appears that they will take less time than originally estimated. Parties who wish their cases to be taken as soon as possible and at short notice should notify the Listing Officer. Representations by way of objection may be made by the parties to the Listing Officer and if necessary by appeal to a judge or the Registrar.

12.8 Each week an up-to-date list for the following week will be prepared, including any changes which have been made, in particular specifying cases which by then have been given fixed dates. The list appears on the EAT website.

13 Skeleton Arguments

(This part of the Practice Direction does not apply to an appeal heard in Scotland, unless otherwise directed in relation to that appeal by the EAT)

13.1 Skeleton arguments must be provided by all parties in all hearings, unless the EAT is notified by a party or representative in writing that the Notice of Appeal or respondent's Answer or relevant application contains the full argument, or the EAT otherwise directs in a particular case. It is the practice of the EAT for all the members to read the papers in advance. A well-structured skeleton argument helps the members and the parties to focus on the point(s) of law required to be decided and so makes the oral hearing more effective.

13.2 The skeleton argument should be concise and should identify and summarise the point(s) of law, the steps in the legal argument and the statutory provisions and authorities to be relied upon, identifying them by name, page and paragraph and stating the legal proposition sought to be derived from them. It is not, however, the purpose of the skeleton argument to argue the case on paper in detail. The parties should be referred to by name or as they appeared at the Employment Tribunal ie Claimant (C) and Respondent (R).

13.3 The skeleton argument should state the form of order which the party will ask the EAT to make at the hearing: for example, in the case of an appellant, whether the EAT will be asked to remit the whole or part of the case to the same or to a different Employment Tribunal, or whether the EAT will be asked to substitute a different decision for that of the Employment Tribunal.

13.4 The appellant's skeleton argument must be accompanied by a Chronology of events relevant to the appeal which, if possible, should be agreed by the parties. That will normally be taken as an uncontroversial document, unless corrected by another party or the EAT.

13.5 Unless impracticable, the skeleton argument should be prepared using the pagination in the index to the appeal bundle. In a case where a note of the evidence at the Employment Tribunal has been produced, the skeleton argument should identify the parts of the record to which that party wishes to refer.

13.6 Represented parties should give the instructions necessary for their representative to comply with this procedure within the time limits.

13.7 The fact that conciliation or settlement negotiations are in progress in relation to the appeal does not excuse delay in lodging and exchanging skeleton arguments.

13.8 A skeleton argument may be lodged by the appellant with the Notice of Appeal or by the respondent with the respondent's Answer.

13.9 Skeleton arguments must (if not already so lodged):

13.9.1 be lodged at the EAT not less than 10 days (unless otherwise ordered) before the date fixed for the PH, appeal against Registrar's Order, Rule 3 (10) hearing or Appointment for Directions; or, if the hearing is fixed at less than seven days notice, as soon as possible after the hearing date has been notified. In the event that the hearing has been ordered to be heard with all parties present, the skeleton arguments must also then be exchanged between the parties;

13.9.2 be lodged at the EAT, and exchanged between the parties, not less than 14 days before the FH;

13.9.3 in the case of warned list and fast track FH cases be lodged at the EAT and exchanged between the parties as soon as possible and (unless the hearing date is less than seven days later) in any event within seven days after the parties have been notified that the case is expedited or in the warned list.

13.10 Failure to follow this procedure may lead to an adjournment of an appeal or to dismissal for non-compliance with the PD pursuant to Rule 26, and to an award of costs. The party in default may also be required to attend before the EAT to explain their failure. It will always mean that the defaulting party must immediately despatch any delayed skeleton argument to the EAT by hand or by fax or by email to londoneat@tribunals.gsi.gov.uk or, as appropriate, edinburgheat@tribunals.gsi.gov.uk and (unless notified by the EAT to the contrary) bring to the hearing sufficient copies (a minimum of 6) of the skeleton argument and any authorities referred to. The EAT staff will not be responsible for supplying or copying these on the morning of the hearing.

14 Citation of Authorities

General

14.1 It is undesirable for parties to cite the same case from different sets of reports. The parties should, if practicable, agree which report will be used at the hearing. Where the Employment Tribunal has cited from a report it may be convenient to cite from the same report.

14.2 It is the responsibility of a party wishing to cite any authority to provide photocopies for the use of each member of the Tribunal and photocopies or at least a list for the other parties. All authorities should be indexed and incorporated in an agreed bundle.

14.3 Parties are advised not to cite an unnecessary number of authorities either in skeleton arguments or in oral argument at the hearing. It is of assistance to the EAT if parties could highlight or sideline passages relied on within the bundle of authorities.

14.4 It is unnecessary for a party citing a case in oral argument to read it in full to the EAT. Whenever a case is cited in a skeleton argument or in an oral argument it is helpful if the legal proposition for which it is cited is stated. References need only be made to the relevant passages in the report. If the formulation of the legal proposition based on the authority cited is not in dispute, further examination of the authority will often be unnecessary.

14.5 For decisions of the ECJ, the official report should be used where possible.

PH Cases

14.6 If it is thought necessary to cite any authority at a PH, appeal against Registrar's Order, Rule 3(10) hearing or Appointment for Directions, three copies should be provided for the EAT (one copy if a judge is sitting alone) no less than 10 days before the hearing, unless otherwise ordered: and additional copies for any other parties notified. All authorities should be bundled, indexed and incorporated in one agreed bundle.

FH Cases

14.7 The parties must co-operate in agreeing a list of authorities and must jointly or severally lodge a list and three bundles of copies (one copy if judge sitting alone) of such authorities at the EAT not less than seven days before the FH, unless otherwise ordered.

15 Disposal of Appeals by Consent

15.1 An appellant who wishes to abandon or withdraw an appeal should notify the other parties and the EAT immediately. If a settlement is reached, the parties should inform the EAT as soon as possible. The appellant should submit to the EAT a letter signed by or on behalf of the appellant and signed also by or on behalf of the respondent, asking the EAT for permission to withdraw the appeal and to make a consent order in the form of an attached draft signed by or for both parties dismissing the appeal, together with any other agreed order.

15.2 If the other parties do not agree to the proposed order the EAT should be informed. Written submissions should be lodged at the EAT and served on the parties. Any outstanding issue may be determined on the papers by the EAT, particularly if it relates to costs, but the EAT may fix an oral hearing to determine the outstanding matters in dispute between the parties.

15.3 If the parties reach an agreement that the appeal should be allowed by consent, and that an order made by the Employment Tribunal should be reversed or varied or the matter remitted to the Employment Tribunal on the ground that the decision contains an error of law, it is usually necessary for the matter to be heard by the EAT to determine whether there is a good reason for making the proposed order. On notification by the parties, the EAT will decide whether the appeal can be dealt with on the papers or by a hearing at which one or more parties or their representatives should attend to argue the case for allowing the appeal and making the order that the parties wish the EAT to make.

15.4 If the application for permission to withdraw an appeal is made close to the hearing date the EAT may require the attendance of the Appellant and/or a representative to explain the reasons for delay in making a decision not to pursue the appeal.

16 Appellant's Failure to Present a Response

16.1 If the appellant in a case did not present a response (ET3) to the Employment Tribunal and did not apply to the Employment Tribunal for an extension of time for doing so, or applied for such an extension and was refused, the Notice of Appeal must include particulars directed to the following issues, namely whether:

16.1.1 there is a good excuse for failing to present a response (ET3) and (if that be the case) for failing to apply for such an extension of time; and
16.1.2 there is a reasonably arguable defence to the claim (ET1).

16.2 In order to satisfy the EAT on these issues, the appellant must lodge at the EAT, together with the Notice of Appeal, a witness statement explaining in detail the circumstances in which there has been a failure to serve a response (ET3) in time or apply for such an extension of time, the reason for that failure and the facts and matters relied upon for contesting the claim (ET1) on the merits. There should be exhibited to the witness statement all relevant documents and a completed draft response (ET3).

17 Hearings

17.1 Where consent is to be obtained from the parties pursuant to s 28(3) of the ETA 1996 to an appeal commencing or continuing to be heard by a judge together with only one lay member, the parties must, prior to the commencement or continuation of such hearing in front of a two-member court, themselves or by their representatives each sign a form containing the name of the one member remaining, and stating whether the member is a person falling within s 28(1)(a) or (b) of the ETA 1996.

17.2 **Video and Telephone Hearings:** facilities can be arranged for the purpose of holding short PHs or short Appointments for Directions by video or telephone link, upon the application (in writing) of an appellant or respondent who, or whose representative, has a relevant disability (supported by appropriate medical evidence). Such facilities will only be made available for a hearing at which the party or, if more than one party will take part, both or all parties is or are legally represented. An application that a hearing should be so held will be determined by a judge or the Registrar, and must be made well in advance of the date intended for the hearing, so that arrangements may be made. So far as concerns video conferencing facilities, they may not always be available, dependent on the location of the parties; as for telephone hearings or, especially, telephone conferencing facilities, consideration may need to be given as to payment by a party or parties of any additional expenditure resulting.

18 Handing Down of Judgments

(England and Wales)

18.1 When the EAT reserves judgment to a later date, the parties will be notified of the date when it is ready to be handed down. It is not necessary for a party or representative to attend.

18.2 Copies of the judgment will be available to the parties or their representatives on the morning on which it is handed down or, if so directed by a judge, earlier to the parties' representatives in draft subject to terms as to confidentiality.

18.3 The judgment will be pronounced without being read aloud, by the judge who presided or by another judge, on behalf of the EAT. The judge may deal with any application or may refer it to the judge and/or the Tribunal who heard the appeal, whether to deal with on the papers or at a further oral hearing on notice. Applications for permission to appeal should be made pursuant to para 21 below. Applications for costs should be made pursuant to para 19 below.

18.4 Transcripts of unreserved judgments at a PH, appeal against Registrar's Order, Appointment for Directions and Rule 3(10) hearing will not (save as below) be produced and provided to the parties:

- 18.4.1 Where an appeal, or any ground of appeal, is dismissed in the presence of the appellant, no transcript of the judgment is produced unless, within 14 days of the seal date of the order, either party applies to the EAT for a transcript, or the EAT of its own initiative directs that a judgment be transcribed (in circumstances such as those set out in para 18.5.2 below).
- 18.4.2 Where an appeal or any ground of appeal is dismissed in the absence of the appellant, a transcript will be supplied to the appellant.
- 18.4.3 Where an appeal is allowed to go forward to a PH or an FH, a judgment will not normally be delivered, but, if it is, the judge may order it to be transcribed, in which case a transcript is provided to the parties.

18.5 Transcripts of unreserved judgments at an FH: where judgment is delivered at the hearing, no transcript will be produced and provided to the parties unless:

18.5.1 either party applies for it to the EAT within 14 days of that hearing; or

18.5.2 the EAT of its own initiative directs that the judgment be transcribed, eg where it is considered that a point of general importance arises or that the matter is to be remitted to, or otherwise continued before, the Employment Tribunal.

18.6 Where judgment at either a PH or an FH is reserved, and later handed down in writing, a copy is provided to all parties, and to recognised law reporters.

(Scotland)

18.7 Judgments are normally reserved in Scotland and will be handed down as soon as practicable thereafter on a provisional basis to both parties who will thereafter have a period of 14 days to make any representations with regard to expenses, leave to appeal or any other relevant matter. At the expiry of that period or after such representations have been dealt with, whichever shall be the later, an order will be issued to conform to the original judgment.

EAT Website

18.8 All FH judgments which are transcribed or handed down will be posted on the EAT website. Any other judgment may be posted on the EAT website if so directed by the Registrar or a Judge.

19 Costs (referred to as Expenses in Scotland)

19.1 In this PD 'costs' includes legal costs, expenses, allowances paid by the Secretary of State and payment in respect of time spent in preparing a case. Such costs may relate to interim applications or hearings or to a PH or FH.

19.2 An application for costs must be made either during or at the end of a relevant hearing, or in writing to the Registrar within 14 days of the seal date of the relevant order of the EAT or, in the case of a reserved judgment, as provided for in paragraph 18.3 above, copied to all parties.

19.3 The party seeking the order must state the legal ground on which the application is based and the facts on which it is based and, by a schedule or otherwise, show how the costs have been incurred. If the application is made in respect of only part of the proceedings, particulars must be given showing how the costs have been incurred on that specific part. If the party against whom the order is sought wishes the EAT to have regard to means and/or an alleged inability to pay, a witness statement giving particulars and exhibiting any documents must be served on the other party(ies) and lodged with the EAT. Further directions may be required to be given by the EAT in such cases.

19.4 Such application may be resolved by the EAT on the papers, provided that the opportunity has been given for representations in writing by all relevant parties, or the EAT may refer the matter for an oral hearing, and may assess the costs either on the papers or at an oral hearing, or refer the matter for detailed assessment.

19.5 **Wasted Costs:** An application for a wasted costs order must be made in writing, setting out the nature of the case upon which the application is based and the best particulars of the costs sought to be recovered. Such application must be lodged with the EAT and served upon the party(ies) sought to be charged. Further directions may be required to be given by the EAT in such cases.

19.6 Where the EAT makes any costs order it shall provide written reasons for so doing if such order is made by decision on the papers. If such order is made at a hearing, then written reasons will be provided if a request is made at the hearing or within 21 days of the seal date of the costs order. The Registrar shall send a copy of the written reasons to all the parties to the proceedings.

20 Review

20.1 Where an application is made for a review of a judgment or order of the EAT, it can be considered on paper by a judge who may, if he or she heard the original appeal or made the original order alone, without lay members, make such order, granting, refusing, adjourning or otherwise dealing with such application, as he or she may think fit. If the original judgment or order was made by the judge together with lay members, then the judge may, pursuant to Rule 33, consider and refuse such application for review on the papers. If the judge does not refuse such application, he or she may make any relevant further order, but would not grant such application without notice to the opposing party and reference to the lay members, for consideration with them, either on paper or in open court. A request to review a judgment or order of the EAT must be made within 14 days of the seal date of the order, or must include an application, with reasons for an extension of time copied to all parties.

21 Appeals from the EAT

Appeals Heard in England and Wales

21.1 An application to the EAT for permission to appeal to the Court of Appeal must be made (unless the EAT otherwise orders) at the hearing or when a reserved judgment is handed down or in writing within seven days thereafter as provided in para 18.3 above. If not made then, or if refused, or unless the EAT otherwise orders, any such applications must be made to the Court of Appeal within 21 days of the sealed order. An application for an extension of time for permission to appeal may be entertained by the EAT where a case is made out to the satisfaction of a judge or Registrar that there is a need to delay until after a transcript is received (expedited if appropriate). Applications for an extension of time for permission to appeal should however normally be made to the Court of Appeal.

21.2 The party seeking permission must state the point of law to be advanced and the grounds.

Appeals Heard in Scotland

21.3 An application to the EAT for permission to appeal to the Court of Session must be made within 42 days of the date of the hearing where judgment is delivered at that hearing: if judgment is reserved, within 42 days of the date the transcript was sent to parties.

21.4 The party seeking permission must state the point of law to be advanced and the grounds.

22 Conciliation

22.1 Pursuant to Rule 36 and the overriding objective, the EAT encourages alternative dispute resolution. To this end it has agreed a pilot scheme with ACAS for ACAS to provide conciliation in certain cases. See 2007 Protocol.

22.2 In all cases the parties should, and when so directed must, consider conciliation of their appeals. The Registrar or a Judge may at any stage make such a direction and require the parties to report on steps taken, but not the substance, to effect a conciliated settlement with the assistance of an ACAS officer notified by ACAS to the EAT.

THE HONOURABLE MR JUSTICE ELIAS

PRESIDENT

Dated: 22 May 2008

FORM 1
Notice of Appeal From Decision of Employment Tribunal

1 The Appellant is (name and address of the Appellant):

2 Any communication relating to this appeal may be sent to the Appellant at (Appellant's address for service, including telephone number if any):

3 The Appellant appeals from (here give particulars of the judgment, decision or order of the Employment Tribunal from which the appeal is brought including the location of the Employment Tribunal and the date):

4 The parties to the proceedings before the Employment Tribunal, other than the Appellant, were (names and addresses of other parties to the proceedings resulting in judgment, decision or order appealed from):

5 Copies of:

the written record of the Employment Tribunal's judgment, decision or order and the Written Reasons of the Employment Tribunal
the Claim (ET1) and Response (ET3)

or

an explanation as to why any of these documents are not included are attached to this notice.

[If relevant.]

[If the Appellant has made an application to the Employment Tribunal for a review of its judgment or decision, a copy of such application, together with the judgment and Written Reasons of the Employment Tribunal in respect of that review application, or a statement by or on behalf of the Appellant, if such be the case, that a judgment is awaited, is attached to this Notice. If any of these documents exist but cannot be included, then a written explanation must be given.]

6 The grounds upon which this appeal is brought are that the Employment Tribunal erred in law in that

(here set out in paragraphs the various grounds of appeal):

Signed

Date:

N.B. The details entered on your Notice of Appeal must be legible and suitable for photocopying. The use of black ink or typescript is recommended.

PRACTICE STATEMENT

This is a Practice Statement handed down by the President of the Employment Appeal Tribunal on 3 February 2005.

1 The attention of litigants and practitioners in the Employment Appeal Tribunal is expressly drawn to the wording and effect of Rules 3(1)(b) and 3(3) of the Employment Appeal Tribunal Rules (1993) (as amended). As is quite clear from the terms of paragraph 2.1 of the Employment Appeal Tribunal Practice Direction 2004 handed down on 9 December 2004, a Notice of Appeal without the specified documentation will not be validly lodged. The documentation required to accompany the Notice of Appeal in order for it to be valid now includes a copy of the Claim (ET1) and the Response (ET3) in the Employment Tribunal proceedings appealed from, if such be available to the appellant, and in any event if such not be available for whatever reason then a written explanation as to why they are not provided. Paragraph 2.1 of the Practice Direction makes this entirely clear:

> 2.1 Copies of the judgment, decision or order appealed against and of the Employment Tribunal s written reasons, together with a copy of the Claim (ET1) and the Response (ET3) must be attached, or if not, a written explanation must be given. A Notice of Appeal without such documentation will not be validly lodged.

2 The reported decision of the Employment Appeal Tribunal in *Kanapathiar v London Borough of Harrow* [2003] IRLR 571 made quite clear that the effect of failure to lodge documents required by the Rules with the Notice of Appeal within the time limit specified for lodging of a Notice of Appeal would mean that the Notice of Appeal had not been validly lodged in time. The same now applies to the additional documents required by the amended Rule, namely the Claim and the Response.

3 It is apparent that both practitioners and litigants in person are not complying with the new Rules and Practice Direction, and not appreciating the consequences of their non-compliance. Between 2 and 26 January 2005, 20 Notices of Appeal were received by the Employment Appeal Tribunal and returned as invalid (compared with 4 during the similar period in 2004). Of those 20 Notices of Appeal, 7 would have been invalid in any event under the old Rules. 13 however were only invalid because they were neither accompanied by the Claim nor the Response nor by any explanation as to their absence or unavailability. If the Notices of Appeal are relodged well within the very generous 42-day time limit, there may still be time for the missing documents to be supplied and the time limit to be complied with. If however, as is very often the case, such Notices of Appeal are delivered either at, or only immediately before, the expiry of the time limit, the absence of the relevant documents is, even if speedily pointed out by the Employment Appeal Tribunal, likely to lead to the Notice of Appeal being out of time.

4 Of the 20 Notices of Appeal which were invalidly lodged during the period above referred to, only 10 were lodged by litigants in person and 10 by solicitors or other representatives: and it is plain that the latter ought certainly to have

known of the requirements, although, given the wide publication both of the Rules and the Practice Direction, together with the guidance given by the Employment Tribunals, both at the Tribunal and sent with their judgments, there can be no excuse for litigants in person either.

5 The reason for this Statement in open court is to re-emphasise these requirements and the consequence of failure to comply with them, namely that an appeal not lodged within the 42 days validly constituted, ie accompanied by the required documents, will be out of time, and extensions of time are only exceptionally granted (see paragraph 3.7 of the Practice Direction).

6 From the date of this Practice Statement, ignorance or misunderstanding of the requirements as to service of the documents required to make a Notice of Appeal within the 42 days valid will not be accepted by the Registrar as an excuse.

THE HON MR JUSTICE BURTON

PRESIDENT OF THE EMPLOYMENT APPEAL TRIBUNAL

3 February 2005

EMPLOYMENT APPEAL TRIBUNAL CONCILIATION PROTOCOL

1 Since its inception in 1976, the EAT has, by its Rules, had power to take any steps it thinks fit to enable the parties to avail themselves of conciliation, if it appears to the EAT that there is a reasonable prospect of agreement being reached between them: see Rule 36.

2. Conciliation by ACAS officers is an integral part of most claims presented to an Employment Tribunal: see s21 Employment Tribunals Act 1996. ACAS has unique experience and expertise involving its duties and powers to assist the parties to a Tribunal claim.

3 The modern approach to litigation requires parties at all stages to be alert to the possible settlement of cases without resort to a hearing, using, wherever possible, alternative methods of dispute resolution. It also involves firm case management so that cases can be heard efficiently and fairly, recognising that ET and EAT resources are limited and there are many claims to be heard. These are embodied in the overriding objective: see Rule 2A.

4 From its experience of appeals, the EAT considers that some may be amenable to conciliation, particularly those relating to monetary awards only, or where the overwhelmingly likely result of a successful appeal would be a remission to the ET, or the case concerns remedies, or the parties' employment relationship is continuing.

5 ACAS agrees in principle with this approach and has agreed to help the EAT to use its powers under Rule 36. It reflects in modified form the pilot scheme introduced in 2004/05, and it will take effect for one year from 1 June 2007 when this modified pilot scheme will be reviewed.

6 This Protocol has consequential effects upon the provisions of PD para 9 and will now be operated in the following way:

- 6.1 a case manager checks the Notice of Appeal to ensure compliance with rules on lodging of appropriate papers and time limits.
- 6.2 a judge sifts the Notice of Appeal and considers whether there are reasonable grounds for bringing an appeal. If the judge concludes that there are not, Rule 3(7) applies and the Appellant is notified that no further action is to be taken. Reasons are given.
- 6.3 if the judge considers more material is needed, either to form an opinion under Rule 3(7) or to send the case to a Preliminary Hearing or a Full Hearing, the judge may direct that more information is given of the ground; and in cases alleging bias or procedural irregularity may order a stay while the Appellant or a representative is ordered to provide an affidavit.
- 6.4 after deciding whether to sift the appeal to a hearing track, and whether or not to continue any stay, a direction may be given to:
    - 6.4.1 require the parties to consider conciliation by ACAS, and, if asked, to attend a meeting called by, or respond to other communications from, the nominated ACAS officer;

6.4.2 send the papers to the nominated ACAS officer, inviting the officer to conciliate a settlement of the appeal or of the ground;

6.4.3 require the Appellant to report back to the EAT on the outcome.

6.5 the judge will then consider the papers and decide what further steps should be directed in the appeal. If a settlement is achieved, the appeal, or any particular ground, will be dismissed by the Registrar on withdrawal by the Appellant. If the parties wish and so apply, the terms of the settlement may be annexed as a Schedule to the Registrar's Order. If the parties seek to have the appeal allowed by consent, they must give adequate reasons. Directions under PD para 15 will be considered by a judge.

7 To assist the parties and the ACAS officer, the judge may indicate brief reasons for considering why conciliation might be sought. In every appropriate case, the following paragraph will be included in an order made on the papers or at a hearing:

Pursuant to Rule 36 and the EAT/ACAS Protocol 2007, it is considered that there is potential for some or all of the matters at issue between parties being resolved by means of conciliation. The papers will be sent to an ACAS Officer. The parties are each directed to give consideration to any offer of conciliation and respond promptly to any invitation made by the ACAS Officer. The Appellant is directed within 28 days of the seal date of this Order to inform the EAT what has occurred, when any necessary further directions can be given.

8 After any hearing disposing of an appeal under Employment Tribunals Act 1996 s 35 when a further ET hearing is to take place, the EAT may exercise its power under EAT Rule 36 and give directions as to steps in relation to conciliation or other settlement.

9 This Protocol applies in Scotland, as it does in England and Wales.

THE HONOURABLE MR JUSTICE ELIAS

PRESIDENT

1 June 2007

Appendix 3

THE COURT OF APPEAL

CONTENTS

Employment Tribunals Act 1996
Supreme Court Act 1981
Access to Justice Act 1999
Civil Procedure Rules 1998 (SI 1998/3132), Pt 52

EMPLOYMENT TRIBUNALS ACT 1996

****

PART II
THE EMPLOYMENT APPEAL TRIBUNAL

37 Appeals from Appeal Tribunal

(1) Subject to subsection (3), an appeal on any question of law lies from any decision or order of the Appeal Tribunal to the relevant appeal court with the leave of the Appeal Tribunal or of the relevant appeal court.

(2) In subsection (1) the 'relevant appeal court' means –

(a) in the case of proceedings in England and Wales, the Court of Appeal, and
(b) in the case of proceedings in Scotland, the Court of Session.

(3) No appeal lies from a decision of the Appeal Tribunal refusing leave for the institution or continuance of, or for the making of an application in, proceedings by a person who is the subject of a restriction of proceedings order made under section 33.

(4) This section is without prejudice to section 13 of the Administration of Justice Act 1960 (appeal in case of contempt of court).

****

SUPREME COURT ACT 1981

PART I
CONSTITUTION OF SUPREME COURT

****

The Court of Appeal

2 The Court of Appeal

(1) The Court of Appeal shall consist of ex-officio judges and not more than thirty-seven ordinary judges.

(2) The following shall be ex-officio judges of the Court of Appeal –

- (a) (*repealed*)
- (b) any person who was Lord Chancellor before 12 June 2003;
- (c) any Lord of Appeal in Ordinary who at the date of his appointment was, or was qualified for appointment as, an ordinary judge of the Court of Appeal or held an office within paragraphs (d) to (g);
- (d) the Lord Chief Justice;
- (e) the Master of the Rolls;
- (f) the President of the Queen's Bench Division;
- (g) the President of the Family Division;
- (h) the Chancellor of the High Court;

but a person within paragraph (b) or (c) shall not be required to sit and act as a judge of the Court of Appeal unless at the request of the Lord Chief Justice he consents to do so.

(2A) The Lord Chief Justice may nominate a judicial office holder (as defined in section 109(4) of the Constitutional Reform Act 2005) to exercise his function under subsection (2) of making requests to persons within paragraphs (b) and (c) of that subsection.

(3) An ordinary judge of the Court of Appeal (including the vice-president, if any, of either division) shall be styled 'Lord Justice of Appeal' or 'Lady Justice of Appeal'.

(4) Her Majesty may by Order in Council from time to time amend subsection (1) so as to increase or further increase the maximum number of ordinary judges of the Court of Appeal.

(4A) It is for the Lord Chancellor to recommend to Her Majesty the making of an Order under subsection (4).

(5) No recommendation shall be made to Her Majesty in Council to make an Order under subsection (4) unless a draft of the Order has been laid before Parliament and approved by resolution of each House of Parliament.

(6) The Court of Appeal shall be taken to be duly constituted notwithstanding any vacancy in the office of Lord Chief Justice, Master of the Rolls, President of the Queen's Bench Division, President of the Family Division or Chancellor of the High Court.

Amendments—SI 1996/1142, SI 2002/2837, Courts Act 2003, s 63(1); Constitutional Reform Act 2005, ss 15(1), 146, Sch 4, Pt 1, paras 114, 115(1), (2)(a)-(d), (3), (4), (5)(a), (b), Sch 18, Pt 2.

****

ACCESS TO JUSTICE ACT 1999

****

PART IV
APPEALS, COURTS, JUDGES AND COURT PROCEEDINGS

Appeals

****

55 Second appeals

(1) Where an appeal is made to a county court or the High Court in relation to any matter, and on hearing the appeal the court makes a decision in relation to that matter, no appeal may be made to the Court of Appeal from that decision unless the Court of Appeal considers that –

- (a) the appeal would raise an important point of principle or practice, or
- (b) there is some other compelling reason for the Court of Appeal to hear it.

(2) This section does not apply in relation to an appeal in a criminal cause or matter.

****

CIVIL PROCEDURE RULES 1998

SI 1998/3132

PART 52
APPEALS

I General Rules about Appeals

52.1 Scope and interpretation

(1) The rules in this Part apply to appeals to –

- (a) the civil division of the Court of Appeal;
- (b) the High Court; and
- (c) a county court.

(2) This Part does not apply to an appeal in detailed assessment proceedings against a decision of an authorised court officer.

> (Rules 47.20 to 47.23 deal with appeals against a decision of an authorised court officer in detailed assessment proceedings)

(3) In this Part –

- (a) 'appeal' includes an appeal by way of case stated;
- (b) 'appeal court' means the court to which an appeal is made;
- (c) 'lower court' means the court, tribunal or other person or body from whose decision an appeal is brought;
- (d) 'appellant' means a person who brings or seeks to bring an appeal;
- (e) 'respondent' means –
  - (i) a person other than the appellant who was a party to the proceedings in the lower court and who is affected by the appeal; and
  - (ii) a person who is permitted by the appeal court to be a party to the appeal; and
- (f) 'appeal notice' means an appellant's or respondent's notice.

(4) This Part is subject to any rule, enactment or practice direction which sets out special provisions with regard to any particular category of appeal.

Amendments—Inserted by SI 2000/221; amended by SI 2000/2092; SI 2005/3515.

52.2 Parties to comply with the practice direction

All parties to an appeal must comply with the relevant practice direction.

Amendments—Inserted by SI 2000/221.

52.3 Permission

(1) An appellant or respondent requires permission to appeal –

(a) where the appeal is from a decision of a judge in a county court or the High Court, except where the appeal is against –
  (i) a committal order;
  (ii) a refusal to grant habeas corpus; or
  (iii) a secure accommodation order made under section 25 of the Children Act 1989; or
(b) as provided by the relevant practice direction.

(Other enactments may provide that permission is required for particular appeals)

(2) An application for permission to appeal may be made –

(a) to the lower court at the hearing at which the decision to be appealed was made; or
(b) to the appeal court in an appeal notice.

(Rule 52.4 sets out the time limits for filing an appellant's notice at the appeal court. Rule 52.5 sets out the time limits for filing a respondent's notice at the appeal court. Any application for permission to appeal to the appeal court must be made in the appeal notice (see rules 52.4(1) and 52.5(3)))

(Rule 52.13(1) provides that permission is required from the Court of Appeal for all appeals to that court from a decision of a county court or the High Court which was itself made on appeal)

(3) Where the lower court refuses an application for permission to appeal, a further application for permission to appeal may be made to the appeal court.

(4) Subject to paragraph (4A), where the appeal court, without a hearing, refuses permission to appeal, the person seeking permission may request the decision to be reconsidered at a hearing.

(4A) Where the Court of Appeal refuses permission to appeal without a hearing, it may, if it considers that the application is totally without merit, make an order that the person seeking permission may not request the decision to be reconsidered at a hearing. The court may not make such an order in family proceedings.

('Family proceedings' is defined by section 32 of the Matrimonial and Family Proceedings Act 1984)

(4B) Rule 3.3(5) will not apply to an order that the person seeking permission may not request the decision to be reconsidered at a hearing made under paragraph (4A).

(5) A request under paragraph (4) must be filed within 7 days after service of the notice that permission has been refused.

(6) Permission to appeal may be given only where –

(a) the court considers that the appeal would have a real prospect of success; or
(b) there is some other compelling reason why the appeal should be heard.

(7) An order giving permission may –

(a) limit the issues to be heard; and
(b) be made subject to conditions.

(Rule 3.1(3) also provides that the court may make an order subject to conditions)

(Rule 25.15 provides for the court to order security for costs of an appeal)

Amendments—Inserted by SI 2000/221; amended by SI 2005/3515; SI 2006/1689.

52.4 Appellant's notice

(1) Where the appellant seeks permission from the appeal court it must be requested in the appellant's notice.

(2) The appellant must file the appellant's notice at the appeal court within –

(a) such period as may be directed by the lower court (which may be longer or shorter than the period referred to in sub-paragraph (b)); or
(b) where the court makes no such direction, 21 days after the date of the decision of the lower court that the appellant wishes to appeal.

(3) Unless the appeal court orders otherwise, an appellant's notice must be served on each respondent –

(a) as soon as practicable; and
(b) in any event not later than 7 days,

after it is filed.

Amendments—Inserted by SI 2000/221; amended by SI 2005/3515.

52.5 Respondent's notice

(1) A respondent may file and serve a respondent's notice.

(2) A respondent who –

(a) is seeking permission to appeal from the appeal court; or
(b) wishes to ask the appeal court to uphold the order of the lower court for reasons different from or additional to those given by the lower court,

must file a respondent's notice.

(3) Where the respondent seeks permission from the appeal court it must be requested in the respondent's notice.

(4) A respondent's notice must be filed within –

(a) such period as may be directed by the lower court; or
(b) where the court makes no such direction, 14 days, after the date in paragraph (5).

(5) The date referred to in paragraph (4) is –

(a) the date the respondent is served with the appellant's notice where –
    (i) permission to appeal was given by the lower court; or
    (ii) permission to appeal is not required;

(b) the date the respondent is served with notification that the appeal court has given the appellant permission to appeal; or
(c) the date the respondent is served with notification that the application for permission to appeal and the appeal itself are to be heard together.

(6) Unless the appeal court orders otherwise a respondent's notice must be served on the appellant and any other respondent –

(a) as soon as practicable; and
(b) in any event not later than 7 days,

after it is filed.

Amendments—Inserted by SI 2000/221.

52.6 Variation of time

(1) An application to vary the time limit for filing an appeal notice must be made to the appeal court.

(2) The parties may not agree to extend any date or time limit set by –

(a) these Rules;
(b) the relevant practice direction; or
(c) an order of the appeal court or the lower court.

(Rule 3.1(2)(a) provides that the court may extend or shorten the time for compliance with any rule, practice direction or court order (even if an application for extension is made after the time for compliance has expired))

(Rule 3.1(2)(b) provides that the court may adjourn or bring forward a hearing)

Amendments—Inserted by SI 2000/221.

52.7 Stay

Unless –

(a) the appeal court or the lower court orders otherwise; or
(b) the appeal is from the Asylum and Immigration Tribunal,

an appeal shall not operate as a stay of any order or decision of the lower court.

Amendments—Inserted by SI 2000/221; amended by SI 2006/1689.

52.8 Amendment of appeal notice

An appeal notice may not be amended without the permission of the appeal court.

Amendments—Inserted by SI 2000/221.

52.9 Striking out appeal notices and setting aside or imposing conditions on permission to appeal

(1) The appeal court may –

(a) strike out the whole or part of an appeal notice;
(b) set aside permission to appeal in whole or in part;
(c) impose or vary conditions upon which an appeal may be brought.

(2) The court will only exercise its powers under paragraph (1) where there is a compelling reason for doing so.

(3) Where a party was present at the hearing at which permission was given he may not subsequently apply for an order that the court exercise its powers under sub-paragraphs (1)(b) or (1)(c).

Amendments—Inserted by SI 2000/221.

52.10 Appeal court's powers

(1) In relation to an appeal the appeal court has all the powers of the lower court.

> (Rule 52.1(4) provides that this Part is subject to any enactment that sets out special provisions with regard to any particular category of appeal – where such an enactment gives a statutory power to a tribunal, person or other body it may be the case that the appeal court may not exercise that power on an appeal)

(2) The appeal court has power to –

(a) affirm, set aside or vary any order or judgment made or given by the lower court;
(b) refer any claim or issue for determination by the lower court;
(c) order a new trial or hearing;
(d) make orders for the payment of interest;
(e) make a costs order.

(3) In an appeal from a claim tried with a jury the Court of Appeal may, instead of ordering a new trial –

(a) make an order for damages; or
(b) vary an award of damages made by the jury.

(4) The appeal court may exercise its powers in relation to the whole or part of an order of the lower court.

> (Part 3 contains general rules about the court's case management powers)

(5) If the appeal court –

(a) refuses an application for permission to appeal;
(b) strikes out an appellant's notice; or
(c) dismisses an appeal,

and it considers that the application, the appellant's notice or the appeal is totally without merit, the provisions of paragraph (6) must be complied with.

(6) Where paragraph (5) applies –

(a) the court's order must record the fact that it considers the application, the appellant's notice or the appeal to be totally without merit; and

(b) the court must at the same time consider whether it is appropriate to make a civil restraint order.

Amendments—Inserted by SI 2000/221; SI 2004/2072.

52.11 Hearing of appeals

(1) Every appeal will be limited to a review of the decision of the lower court unless –

(a) a practice direction makes different provision for a particular category of appeal; or
(b) the court considers that in the circumstances of an individual appeal it would be in the interests of justice to hold a re-hearing.

(2) Unless it orders otherwise, the appeal court will not receive –

(a) oral evidence; or
(b) evidence which was not before the lower court.

(3) The appeal court will allow an appeal where the decision of the lower court was –

(a) wrong; or
(b) unjust because of a serious procedural or other irregularity in the proceedings in the lower court.

(4) The appeal court may draw any inference of fact which it considers justified on the evidence.

(5) At the hearing of the appeal a party may not rely on a matter not contained in his appeal notice unless the appeal court gives permission.

Amendments—Inserted by SI 2000/221.

52.12 Non-disclosure of Part 36 offers and payments

(1) The fact that a Part 36 offer or payment into court has been made must not be disclosed to any judge of the appeal court who is to hear or determine –

(a) an application for permission to appeal; or
(b) an appeal,

until all questions (other than costs) have been determined.

(2) Paragraph (1) does not apply if the Part 36 offer or payment into court is relevant to the substance of the appeal.

(3) Paragraph (1) does not prevent disclosure in any application in the appeal proceedings if disclosure of the fact that a Part 36 offer or payment into court has been made is properly relevant to the matter to be decided.

> (Rule 36.3 has the effect that a Part 36 offer made in proceedings at first instance will not have consequences in any appeal proceedings. Therefore, a fresh Part 36 offer needs to be made in appeal proceedings. However, rule 52.12 applies to a Part 36 offer whether made in the original proceedings or in the appeal.)

Amendments—Inserted by SI 2000/221; amended by SI 2003/3361; SI 2006/3435.

52.12A Statutory appeals – court's power to hear any person

(1) In a statutory appeal, any person may apply for permission –

  (a) to file evidence; or
  (b) to make representations at the appeal hearing.

(2) An application under paragraph (1) must be made promptly.

Amendments—Inserted by SI 2007/2204.

II Special Provisions applying to the Court of Appeal

52.13 Second appeals to the court

(1) Permission is required from the Court of Appeal for any appeal to that court from a decision of a county court or the High Court which was itself made on appeal.

(2) The Court of Appeal will not give permission unless it considers that –

  (a) the appeal would raise an important point of principle or practice; or
  (b) there is some other compelling reason for the Court of Appeal to hear it.

Amendments—Inserted by SI 2000/221.

52.14 Assignment of appeals to the Court of Appeal

(1) Where the court from or to which an appeal is made or from which permission to appeal is sought ('the relevant court') considers that –

  (a) an appeal which is to be heard by a county court or the High Court would raise an important point of principle or practice; or
  (b) there is some other compelling reason for the Court of Appeal to hear it,

the relevant court may order the appeal to be transferred to the Court of Appeal.

> (The Master of the Rolls has the power to direct that an appeal which would be heard by a county court or the High Court should be heard instead by the Court of Appeal – see section 57 of the Access to Justice Act 1999.)

(2) The Master of the Rolls or the Court of Appeal may remit an appeal to the court in which the original appeal was or would have been brought.

Amendments—Inserted by SI 2000/221.

52.15 Judicial review appeals

(1) Where permission to apply for judicial review has been refused at a hearing in the High Court, the person seeking that permission may apply to the Court of Appeal for permission to appeal.

(2) An application in accordance with paragraph (1) must be made within 7 days of the decision of the High Court to refuse to give permission to apply for judicial review.

(3) On an application under paragraph (1), the Court of Appeal may, instead of giving permission to appeal, give permission to apply for judicial review.

(4) Where the Court of Appeal gives permission to apply for judicial review in accordance with paragraph (3), the case will proceed in the High Court unless the Court of Appeal orders otherwise.

Amendments—Inserted by SI 2000/221.

52.16 Who may exercise the powers of the Court of Appeal

(1) A court officer assigned to the Civil Appeals Office who is –

- (a) a barrister; or
- (b) a solicitor

may exercise the jurisdiction of the Court of Appeal with regard to the matters set out in paragraph (2) with the consent of the Master of the Rolls.

(2) The matters referred to in paragraph (1) are –

- (a) any matter incidental to any proceedings in the Court of Appeal;
- (b) any other matter where there is no substantial dispute between the parties; and
- (c) the dismissal of an appeal or application where a party has failed to comply with any order, rule or practice direction.

(3) A court officer may not decide an application for –

- (a) permission to appeal;
- (b) bail pending an appeal;
- (c) an injunction;
- (d) a stay of any proceedings, other than a temporary stay of any order or decision of the lower court over a period when the Court of Appeal is not sitting or cannot conveniently be convened.

(4) Decisions of a court officer may be made without a hearing.

(5) A party may request any decision of a court officer to be reviewed by the Court of Appeal.

(6) At the request of a party, a hearing will be held to reconsider a decision of –

- (a) a single judge; or
- (b) a court officer,

made without a hearing.

(6A) A request under paragraph (5) or (6) must be filed within 7 days after the party is served with the notice of the decision.

(7) A single judge may refer any matter for a decision by a court consisting of two or more judges.

> (Section 54(6) of the Supreme Court Act 1981 provides that there is no appeal from the decision of a single judge on an application for permission to appeal)
>
> (Section 58(2) of the Supreme Court Act 1981 provides that there is no appeal to the House of Lords from decisions of the Court of Appeal that –
>
> (a) are taken by a single judge or any officer or member of staff of that court in proceedings incidental to any cause or matter pending before the civil division of that court; and
>
> (b) do not involve the determination of an appeal or of an application for permission to appeal,
>
> and which may be called into question by rules of court. Rules 52.16(5) and (6) provide the procedure for the calling into question of such decisions)

Amendments—Inserted by SI 2000/221; amended by SI 2003/3361.

III Provisions about Reopening Appeals

52.17 Reopening of final appeals

(1) The Court of Appeal or the High Court will not reopen a final determination of any appeal unless –

(a) it is necessary to do so in order to avoid real injustice;
(b) the circumstances are exceptional and make it appropriate to reopen the appeal; and
(c) there is no alternative effective remedy.

(2) In paragraphs (1), (3), (4) and (6), 'appeal' includes an application for permission to appeal.

(3) This rule does not apply to appeals to a county court.

(4) Permission is needed to make an application under this rule to reopen a final determination of an appeal even in cases where under rule 52.3(1) permission was not needed for the original appeal.

(5) There is no right to an oral hearing of an application for permission unless, exceptionally, the judge so directs.

(6) The judge will not grant permission without directing the application to be served on the other party to the original appeal and giving him an opportunity to make representations.

(7) There is no right of appeal or review from the decision of the judge on the application for permission, which is final.

(8) The procedure for making an application for permission is set out in the practice direction.

Amendments—Inserted by SI 2003/2113.

****

PRACTICE DIRECTION
PART 52

Appeals

Contents of this Practice Direction

1.1 This practice direction is divided into four sections –

- Section I – General provisions about appeals
- Section II – General provisions about statutory appeals and appeals by way of case stated
- Section III – Provisions about specific appeals
- Section IV – Provisions about reopening appeals

Section I General Provisions about Appeals

2.1 This practice direction applies to all appeals to which Part 52 applies except where specific provision is made for appeals to the Court of Appeal.

2.2 For the purpose only of appeals to the Court of Appeal from cases in family proceedings this Practice Direction will apply with such modifications as may be required.

****

2A.3 A decision of a court is to be treated as a final decision for routes of appeal purposes where it:

(1) is made at the conclusion of part of a hearing or trial which has been split into parts; and

(2) would, if it had been made at the conclusion of that hearing or trial, have been a final decision.

Accordingly, a judgment on liability at the end of a split trial is a 'final decision' for this purpose and the judgment at the conclusion of the assessment of damages following a judgment on liability is also a "final decision" for this purpose.

2A.4 An order made:

(1) on a summary or detailed assessment of costs; or
(2) on an application to enforce a final decision,

is not a 'final decision' and any appeal from such an order will follow the routes of appeal set out in the tables above.

(Section 16(1) of the Supreme Court Act 1981 (as amended); section 77(1) of the County Courts Act 1984 (as amended); and the Access to Justice Act 1999 (Destination of Appeals) Order 2000 set out the provisions governing routes of appeal.)

2A.5

(1) Where an applicant attempts to file an appellant's notice and the appeal court does not have jurisdiction to issue the notice, a court

officer may notify the applicant in writing that the appeal court does not have jurisdiction in respect of the notice.

(2) Before notifying a person under paragraph (1) the court officer must confer –
 (a) with a judge of the appeal court; or
 (b) where the Court of Appeal, Civil Division is the appeal court, with a court officer who exercises the jurisdiction of that court under rule 52.16.

(3) Where a court officer in the Court of Appeal, Civil Division notifies a person under paragraph (1), rule 52.16(5) shall not apply.

Grounds for Appeal

3.1 Rule 52.11(3)(a) and (b) sets out the circumstances in which the appeal court will allow an appeal.

3.2 The grounds of appeal should –

(1) set out clearly the reasons why rule 52.11(3)(a) or (b) is said to apply; and
(2) specify, in respect of each ground, whether the ground raises an appeal on a point of law or is an appeal against a finding of fact.

Permission to Appeal

4.1 Rule 52.3 sets out the circumstances when permission to appeal is required.

4.2 The permission of –

(a) the Court of Appeal; or
(b) where the lower court's rules allow, the lower court,

is required for all appeals to the Court of Appeal except as provided for by statute or rule 52.3.

(The requirement of permission to appeal may be imposed by a practice direction – see rule 52.3(b).)

4.3 Where the lower court is not required to give permission to appeal, it may give an indication of its opinion as to whether permission should be given.

(Rule 52.1(3)(c) defines 'lower court'.)

4.3A

(1) This paragraph applies where a party applies for permission to appeal against a decision at the hearing at which the decision was made.
(2) Where this paragraph applies, the judge making the decision shall state –
 (a) whether or not the judgment or order is final;
 (b) whether an appeal lies from the judgment or order and, if so, to which appeal court;
 (c) whether the court gives permission to appeal; and

(d) if not, the appropriate appeal court to which any further application for permission may be made.

(Rule 40.2(4) contains requirements as to the contents of the judgment or order in these circumstances.)

4.3B Where no application for permission to appeal has been made in accordance with rule 52.3(2)(a) but a party requests further time to make such an application, the court may adjourn the hearing to give that party the opportunity to do so.

Appeals from case management decisions

4.4 Case management decisions include decisions made under rule 3.1(2) and decisions about –

(1) disclosure
(2) filing of witness statements or experts reports
(3) directions about the timetable of the claim
(4) adding a party to a claim
(5) security for costs.

4.5 Where the application is for permission to appeal from a case management decision, the court dealing with the application may take into account whether –

(1) the issue is of sufficient significance to justify the costs of an appeal;
(2) the procedural consequences of an appeal (eg loss of trial date) outweigh the significance of the case management decision;
(3) it would be more convenient to determine the issue at or after trial.

Court to which permission to appeal application should be made

4.6 An application for permission should be made orally at the hearing at which the decision to be appealed against is made.

4.7 Where:

(a) no application for permission to appeal is made at the hearing; or
(b) the lower court refuses permission to appeal,

an application for permission to appeal may be made to the appeal court in accordance with rules 52.3(2) and (3).

4.8 There is no appeal from the decision of the appeal court to allow or refuse permission to appeal to that court (although where the appeal court, without a hearing, refuses permission to appeal, the person seeking permission may request that decision to be reconsidered at a hearing). See section 54(4) of the Access to Justice Act and rule 52.3(2), (3), (4) and (5).

Second appeals

4.9 An application for permission to appeal from a decision of the High Court or a county court which was itself made on appeal must be made to the Court of Appeal.

4.10 If permission to appeal is granted the appeal will be heard by the Court of Appeal.

Consideration of Permission without a hearing

4.11 Applications for permission to appeal may be considered by the appeal court without a hearing.

4.12 If permission is granted without a hearing the parties will be notified of that decision and the procedure in paragraphs 6.1 to 6.6 will then apply.

4.13 If permission is refused without a hearing the parties will be notified of that decision with the reasons for it. The decision is subject to the appellant's right to have it reconsidered at an oral hearing. This may be before the same judge.

4.14 A request for the decision to be reconsidered at an oral hearing must be filed at the appeal court within 7 days after service of the notice that permission has been refused. A copy of the request must be served by the appellant on the respondent at the same time.

Permission hearing

4.14A

(1) This paragraph applies where an appellant, who is represented, makes a request for a decision to be reconsidered at an oral hearing.
(2) The appellant's advocate must, at least 4 days before the hearing, in a brief written statement –
 (a) inform the court and the respondent of the points which he proposes to raise at the hearing;
 (b) set out his reasons why permission should be granted notwithstanding the reasons given for the refusal of permission; and
 (c) confirm, where applicable, that the requirements of paragraph 4.17 have been complied with (appellant in receipt of services funded by the Legal Services Commission).

4.15 Notice of a permission hearing will be given to the respondent but he is not required to attend unless the court requests him to do so.

4.16 If the court requests the respondent's attendance at the permission hearing, the appellant must supply the respondent with a copy of the appeal bundle (see paragraph 5.6A) within 7 days of being notified of the request, or such other period as the court may direct. The costs of providing that bundle shall be borne by the appellant initially, but will form part of the costs of the permission application.

Appellants in receipt of services funded by the Legal Services Commission applying for permission to appeal

4.17 Where the appellant is in receipt of services funded by the Legal Services Commission (or legally aided) and permission to appeal has been refused by the appeal court without a hearing, the appellant must send a copy of the reasons the appeal court gave for refusing permission to the relevant office of the Legal Services Commission as soon as it has been received from the court. The court will require confirmation that this has been done if a hearing is requested to re-consider the question of permission.

Limited permission

4.18 Where a court under rule 52.3(7) gives permission to appeal on some issues only, it will –

(1) refuse permission on any remaining issues; or
(2) reserve the question of permission to appeal on any remaining issues to the court hearing the appeal.

4.19 If the court reserves the question of permission under paragraph 4.18(2), the appellant must, within 14 days after service of the court's order, inform the appeal court and the respondent in writing whether he intends to pursue the reserved issues. If the appellant does intend to pursue the reserved issues, the parties must include in any time estimate for the appeal hearing, their time estimate for the reserved issues.

4.20 If the appeal court refuses permission to appeal on the remaining issues without a hearing and the applicant wishes to have that decision reconsidered at an oral hearing, the time limit in rule 52.3(5) shall apply. Any application for an extension of this time limit should be made promptly. The court hearing the appeal on the issues for which permission has been granted will not normally grant, at the appeal hearing, an application to extend the time limit in rule 52.3(5) for the remaining issues.

4.21 If the appeal court refuses permission to appeal on remaining issues at or after an oral hearing, the application for permission to appeal on those issues cannot be renewed at the appeal hearing. See section 54(4) of the Access to Justice Act 1999.

Respondents' costs of permission applications

4.22 In most cases, applications for permission to appeal will be determined without the court requiring –

(1) submissions from, or
(2) if there is an oral hearing, attendance by

the respondent.

4.23 Where the court does not request submissions from or attendance by the respondent, costs will not normally be allowed to a respondent who volunteers submissions or attendance.

4.24 Where the court does request –

(1) submissions from or attendance by the respondent; or
(2) attendance by the respondent with the appeal to follow if permission is granted,

the court will normally allow the respondent his costs if permission is refused.

Appellant's Notice

5.1 An appellant's notice must be filed and served in all cases. Where an application for permission to appeal is made to the appeal court it must be applied for in the appellant's notice.

Human Rights

5.1A

(1) This paragraph applies where the appellant seeks –
  (a) to rely on any issue under the Human Rights Act 1998; or
  (b) a remedy available under that Act,
 for the first time in an appeal.
(2) The appellant must include in his appeal notice the information required by paragraph 15.1 of the practice direction supplementing Part 16.
(3) Paragraph 15.2 of the practice direction supplementing Part 16 applies as if references to a statement of case were to the appeal notice.

5.1B CPR rule 19.4A and the practice direction supplementing it shall apply as if references to the case management conference were to the application for permission to appeal.

(The practice direction to Part 19 provides for notice to be given and parties joined in certain circumstances to which this paragraph applies)

Extension of time for filing appellant's notice

5.2 Where the time for filing an appellant's notice has expired, the appellant must –

(a) file the appellant's notice; and
(b) include in that appellant's notice an application for an extension of time.

The appellant's notice should state the reason for the delay and the steps taken prior to the application being made.

5.3 Where the appellant's notice includes an application for an extension of time and permission to appeal has been given or is not required the respondent has the right to be heard on that application. He must be served with a copy of the appeal bundle (see paragraph 5.6A). However, a respondent who unreasonably opposes an extension of time runs the risk of being ordered to pay the appellant's costs of that application.

5.4 If an extension of time is given following such an application the procedure at paragraphs 6.1 to 6.6 applies.

Applications

5.5 Notice of an application to be made to the appeal court for a remedy incidental to the appeal (eg an interim remedy under rule 25.1 or an order for security for costs) may be included in the appeal notice or in a Part 23 application notice.

> (Rule 25.15 deals with security for costs of an appeal.)

> (Paragraph 11 of this practice direction contains other provisions relating to applications.)

Documents

5.6 (1) This paragraph applies to every case except where the appeal –
    (a)   relates to a claim allocated to the small claims track; and
    (b)   is being heard in a county court or the High Court.

(Paragraph 5.8 applies where this paragraph does not apply.)

(2) The appellant must file the following documents together with an appeal bundle (see paragraph 5.6A) with his appellant's notice –
    (a)   two additional copies of the appellant's notice for the appeal court; and
    (b)   one copy of the appellant's notice for each of the respondents;
    (c)   one copy of his skeleton argument for each copy of the appellant's notice that is filed (see paragraph 5.9);
    (d)   a sealed copy of the order being appealed;
    (e)   a copy of any order giving or refusing permission to appeal, together with a copy of the judge's reasons for allowing or refusing permission to appeal;
    (f)   any witness statements or affidavits in support of any application included in the appellant's notice;
    (g)   a copy of the order allocating a case to a track (if any).

5.6A

(1) An appellant must include in his appeal bundle the following documents:
    (a)   a sealed copy of the appellant's notice;
    (b)   a sealed copy of the order being appealed;
    (c)   a copy of any order giving or refusing permission to appeal, together with a copy of the judge's reasons for allowing or refusing permission to appeal;
    (d)   any affidavit or witness statement filed in support of any application included in the appellant's notice;
    (e)   a copy of his skeleton argument;
    (f)   a transcript or note of judgment (see paragraph 5.12), and in cases where permission to appeal was given by the lower court or

is not required those parts of any transcript of evidence which are directly relevant to any question at issue on the appeal;
 (g) the claim form and statements of case (where relevant to the subject of the appeal);
 (h) any application notice (or case management documentation) relevant to the subject of the appeal;
 (i) in cases where the decision appealed was itself made on appeal (eg from district judge to circuit judge), the first order, the reasons given and the appellant's notice used to appeal from that order;
 (j) in the case of judicial review or a statutory appeal, the original decision which was the subject of the application to the lower court;
 (k) in cases where the appeal is from a Tribunal, a copy of the Tribunal's reasons for the decision, a copy of the decision reviewed by the Tribunal and the reasons for the original decision and any document filed with the Tribunal setting out the grounds of appeal from that decision;
 (l) any other documents which the appellant reasonably considers necessary to enable the appeal court to reach its decision on the hearing of the application or appeal; and
 (m) such other documents as the court may direct.
(2) All documents that are extraneous to the issues to be considered on the application or the appeal must be excluded. The appeal bundle may include affidavits, witness statements, summaries, experts' reports and exhibits but only where these are directly relevant to the subject matter of the appeal.
(3) Where the appellant is represented, the appeal bundle must contain a certificate signed by his solicitor, counsel or other representative to the effect that he has read and understood paragraph (2) above and that the composition of the appeal bundle complies with it.

5.7 Where it is not possible to file all the above documents, the appellant must indicate which documents have not yet been filed and the reasons why they are not currently available. The appellant must then provide a reasonable estimate of when the missing document or documents can be filed and file them as soon as reasonably practicable.

Small claims

5.8 (1) This paragraph applies where –
 (a) the appeal relates to a claim allocated to the small claims track; and
 (b) the appeal is being heard in a county court or the High Court.
(1A) An appellant's notice must be filed and served in Form N164.
(2) The appellant must file the following documents with his appellant's notice –
 (a) a sealed copy of the order being appealed; and

(b) any order giving or refusing permission to appeal, together with a copy of the reasons for that decision.

(3) The appellant may, if relevant to the issues to be determined on the appeal, file any other document listed in paragraph 5.6 or 5.6A in addition to the documents referred to in sub-paragraph (2).

(4) The appellant need not file a record of the reasons for judgment of the lower court with his appellant's notice unless sub-paragraph (5) applies.

(5) The court may order a suitable record of the reasons for judgment of the lower court (see paragraph 5.12) to be filed –
    (a) to enable it to decide if permission should be granted; or
    (b) if permission is granted to enable it to decide the appeal.

Skeleton arguments

5.9 (1) The appellant's notice must, subject to (2) and (3) below, be accompanied by a skeleton argument. Alternatively the skeleton argument may be included in the appellant's notice. Where the skeleton argument is so included it will not form part of the notice for the purposes of rule 52.8.

(2) Where it is impracticable for the appellant's skeleton argument to accompany the appellant's notice it must be filed and served on all respondents within 14 days of filing the notice.

(3) An appellant who is not represented need not file a skeleton argument but is encouraged to do so since this will be helpful to the court.

Content of skeleton arguments

5.10 (1) A skeleton argument must contain a numbered list of the points which the party wishes to make. These should both define and confine the areas of controversy. Each point should be stated as concisely as the nature of the case allows.

(2) A numbered point must be followed by a reference to any document on which the party wishes to rely.

(3) A skeleton argument must state, in respect of each authority cited –
    (a) the proposition of law that the authority demonstrates; and
    (b) the parts of the authority (identified by page or paragraph references) that support the proposition.

(4) If more than one authority is cited in support of a given proposition, the skeleton argument must briefly state the reason for taking that course.

(5) The statement referred to in sub-paragraph (4) should not materially add to the length of the skeleton argument but should be sufficient to demonstrate, in the context of the argument –
    (a) the relevance of the authority or authorities to that argument; and
    (b) that the citation is necessary for a proper presentation of that argument.

(6) The cost of preparing a skeleton argument which –

(a) does not comply with the requirements set out in this paragraph; or
(b) was not filed within the time limits provided by this Practice Direction (or any further time granted by the court),
(7) A skeleton argument filed in the Court of Appeal, Civil Division on behalf of the appellant should contain in paragraph 1 the advocate's time estimate for the hearing of the appeal.
will not be allowed on assessment except to the extent that the court otherwise directs.

5.11 The appellant should consider what other information the appeal court will need. This may include a list of persons who feature in the case or glossaries of technical terms. A chronology of relevant events will be necessary in most appeals.

Suitable record of the judgment

5.12 Where the judgment to be appealed has been officially recorded by the court, an approved transcript of that record should accompany the appellant's notice. Photocopies will not be accepted for this purpose. However, where there is no officially recorded judgment, the following documents will be acceptable –

Written judgments

(1) Where the judgment was made in writing a copy of that judgment endorsed with the judge's signature.

Note of judgment

(2) When judgment was not officially recorded or made in writing a note of the judgment (agreed between the appellant's and respondent's advocates) should be submitted for approval to the judge whose decision is being appealed. If the parties cannot agree on a single note of the judgment, both versions should be provided to that judge with an explanatory letter. For the purpose of an application for permission to appeal the note need not be approved by the respondent or the lower court judge.

Advocates' notes of judgments where the appellant is unrepresented

(3) When the appellant was unrepresented in the lower court it is the duty of any advocate for the respondent to make his/her note of judgment promptly available, free of charge to the appellant where there is no officially recorded judgment or if the court so directs. Where the appellant was represented in the lower court it is the duty of his/her own former advocate to make his/her note available in these circumstances. The appellant should submit the note of judgment to the appeal court.

Reasons for Judgment in Tribunal cases

(4) A sealed copy of the tribunal's reasons for the decision.

5.13 An appellant may not be able to obtain an official transcript or other suitable record of the lower court's decision within the time within which the appellant's notice must be filed. In such cases the appellant's notice must still be completed to the best of the appellant's ability on the basis of the documentation available. However, it may be amended subsequently with the permission of the appeal court.

Advocates' notes of judgments

5.14 Advocates' brief (or, where appropriate, refresher) fee includes –

(1) remuneration for taking a note of the judgment of the court;
(2) having the note transcribed accurately;
(3) attempting to agree the note with the other side if represented;
(4) submitting the note to the judge for approval where appropriate;
(5) revising it if so requested by the judge;
(6) providing any copies required for the appeal court, instructing solicitors and lay client; and
(7) providing a copy of his note to an unrepresented appellant.

Transcripts or Notes of Evidence

5.15 When the evidence is relevant to the appeal an official transcript of the relevant evidence must be obtained. Transcripts or notes of evidence are generally not needed for the purpose of determining an application for permission to appeal.

Notes of evidence

5.16 If evidence relevant to the appeal was not officially recorded, a typed version of the judge's notes of evidence must be obtained.

Transcripts at public expense

5.17 Where the lower court or the appeal court is satisfied that:

(1) an unrepresented appellant; or
(2) an appellant whose legal representation is provided free of charge to the appellant and not funded by the Community Legal Service;

is in such poor financial circumstances that the cost of a transcript would be an excessive burden the court may certify that the cost of obtaining one official transcript should be borne at public expense.

5.18 In the case of a request for an official transcript of evidence or proceedings to be paid for at public expense, the court must also be satisfied that there are reasonable grounds for appeal. Whenever possible a request for a transcript at public expense should be made to the lower court when asking for permission to appeal.

Filing and service of appellant's notice

5.19 Rule 52.4 sets out the procedure and time limits for filing and serving an appellant's notice. The appellant must file the appellant's notice at the appeal court within such period as may be directed by the lower court which should not normally exceed 35 days or, where the lower court directs no such period, within 21 days of the date of the decision that the appellant wishes to appeal.

> (Rule 52.15 sets out the time limit for filing an application for permission to appeal against the refusal of the High Court to grant permission to apply for judicial review.)

5.20 Where the lower court judge announces his decision and reserves the reasons for his judgment or order until a later date, he should, in the exercise of powers under rule 52.4(2)(a), fix a period for filing the appellant's notice at the appeal court that takes this into account.

5.21 (1) Except where the appeal court orders otherwise a sealed copy of the appellant's notice, including any skeleton arguments must be served on all respondents in accordance with the timetable prescribed by rule 52.4(3) except where this requirement is modified by paragraph 5.9(2) in which case the skeleton argument should be served as soon as it is filed.

    (2) The appellant must, as soon as practicable, file a certificate of service of the documents referred to in paragraph (1).

5.22 Unless the court otherwise directs a respondent need not take any action when served with an appellant's notice until such time as notification is given to him that permission to appeal has been given.

5.23 The court may dispense with the requirement for service of the notice on a respondent. Any application notice seeking an order under rule 6.9 to dispense with service should set out the reasons relied on and be verified by a statement of truth.

5.24 (1) Where the appellant is applying for permission to appeal in his appellant's notice, he must serve on the respondents his appellant's notice and skeleton argument (but not the appeal bundle), unless the appeal court directs otherwise.

    (2) Where permission to appeal –
        (a) has been given by the lower court; or
        (b) is not required,
    the appellant must serve the appeal bundle on the respondents with the appellant's notice.

Amendment of Appeal Notice

5.25 An appeal notice may be amended with permission. Such an application to amend and any application in opposition will normally be dealt with at the hearing unless that course would cause unnecessary expense or delay in which case a request should be made for the application to amend to be heard in advance.

Procedure after Permission is Obtained

6.1 This paragraph sets out the procedure where –

(1) permission to appeal is given by the appeal court; or
(2) the appellant's notice is filed in the appeal court and –
    (a) permission was given by the lower court; or
    (b) permission is not required.

6.2 If the appeal court gives permission to appeal, the appeal bundle must be served on each of the respondents within 7 days of receiving the order giving permission to appeal.

(Part 6 (service of documents) provides rules on service.)

6.3 The appeal court will send the parties –

(1) notification of –
    (a) the date of the hearing or the period of time (the 'listing window') during which the appeal is likely to be heard; and
    (b) in the Court of Appeal, the date by which the appeal will be heard (the 'hear by date');
(2) where permission is granted by the appeal court a copy of the order giving permission to appeal; and
(3) any other directions given by the court.

6.3A

(1) Where the appeal court grants permission to appeal, the appellant must add the following documents to the appeal bundle –
    (a) the respondent's notice and skeleton argument (if any);
    (b) those parts of the transcripts of evidence which are directly relevant to any question at issue on the appeal;
    (c) the order granting permission to appeal and, where permission to appeal was granted at an oral hearing, the transcript (or note) of any judgment which was given; and
    (d) any document which the appellant and respondent have agreed to add to the appeal bundle in accordance with paragraph 7.11.
(2) Where permission to appeal has been refused on a particular issue, the appellant must remove from the appeal bundle all documents that are relevant only to that issue.

Appeal Questionnaire in the Court of Appeal

6.4 The Court of Appeal will send an Appeal Questionnaire to the appellant when it notifies him of the matters referred to in paragraph 6.3.

6.5 The appellant must complete and file the Appeal Questionnaire within 14 days of the date of the letter of notification of the matters in paragraph 6.3. The Appeal Questionnaire must contain:

(1) if the appellant is legally represented, the advocate's time estimate for the hearing of the appeal;

(2) where a transcript of evidence is relevant to the appeal, confirmation as to what parts of a transcript of evidence have been ordered where this is not already in the bundle of documents;
(3) confirmation that copies of the appeal bundle are being prepared and will be held ready for the use of the Court of Appeal and an undertaking that they will be supplied to the court on request. For the purpose of these bundles photocopies of the transcripts will be accepted;
(4) confirmation that copies of the Appeal Questionnaire and the appeal bundle have been served on the respondents and the date of that service.

Time estimates

6.6 The time estimate included in an Appeal Questionnaire must be that of the advocate who will argue the appeal. It should exclude the time required by the court to give judgment. If the respondent disagrees with the time estimate, the respondent must inform the court within 7 days of receipt of the Appeal Questionnaire. In the absence of such notification the respondent will be deemed to have accepted the estimate proposed on behalf of the appellant.

Respondent

7.1 A respondent who wishes to ask the appeal court to vary the order of the lower court in any way must appeal and permission will be required on the same basis as for an appellant.

(Paragraph 3.2 applies to grounds of appeal by a respondent.)

7.2 A respondent who wishes only to request that the appeal court upholds the judgment or order of the lower court whether for the reasons given in the lower court or otherwise does not make an appeal and does not therefore require permission to appeal in accordance with rule 52.3(1).

(Paragraph 7.6 requires a respondent to file a skeleton argument where he wishes to address the appeal court.)

7.3 (1) A respondent who wishes to appeal or who wishes to ask the appeal court to uphold the order of the lower court for reasons different from or additional to those given by the lower court must file a respondent's notice.

(2) If the respondent does not file a respondent's notice, he will not be entitled, except with the permission of the court, to rely on any reason not relied on in the lower court.

7.3A Paragraphs 5.1A, 5.1B and 5.2 of this practice direction (Human Rights and extension for time for filing appellant's notice) also apply to a respondent and a respondent's notice.

Time limits

7.4 The time limits for filing a respondent's notice are set out in rule 52.5 (4) and (5).

7.5 Where an extension of time is required the extension must be requested in the respondent's notice and the reasons why the respondent failed to act within the specified time must be included.

7.6 Except where paragraph 7.7A applies, the respondent must file a skeleton argument for the court in all cases where he proposes to address arguments to the court. The respondent's skeleton argument may be included within a respondent's notice. Where a skeleton argument is included within a respondent's notice it will not form part of the notice for the purposes of rule 52.8.

7.7 (1) A respondent who –
        (a)   files a respondent's notice; but
        (b)   does not include his skeleton argument within that notice,
   must file and serve his skeleton argument within 14 days of filing the notice.
(2)   A respondent who does not file a respondent's notice but who files a skeleton argument must file and serve that skeleton argument at least 7 days before the appeal hearing.

(Rule 52.5(4) sets out the period for filing and serving a respondent's notice.)

7.7A

(1)   Where the appeal relates to a claim allocated to the small claims track and is being heard in a county court or the High Court, the respondent may file a skeleton argument but is not required to do so.
(2)   A respondent who is not represented need not file a skeleton argument but is encouraged to do so in order to assist the court.

7.7B The respondent must –

(1)   serve his skeleton argument on –
        (a)   the appellant; and
        (b)   any other respondent,
   at the same time as he files it at the court; and
(2)   file a certificate of service.

Content of skeleton arguments

7.8 A respondent's skeleton argument must conform to the directions at paragraphs 5.10 and 5.11 with any necessary modifications. It should, where appropriate, answer the arguments set out in the appellant's skeleton argument.

Applications within respondent's notices

7.9 A respondent may include an application within a respondent's notice in accordance with paragraph 5.5 above.

Filing respondent's notices and skeleton arguments

7.10 (1) The respondent must file the following documents with his respondent's notice in every case:

(a) two additional copies of the respondent's notice for the appeal court; and
(b) one copy each for the appellant and any other respondents.
(2) The respondent may file a skeleton argument with his respondent's notice and –
(a) where he does so he must file two copies; and
(b) where he does not do so he must comply with paragraph 7.7.

7.11 If the respondent wishes to rely on any documents which he reasonably considers necessary to enable the appeal court to reach its decision on the appeal in addition to those filed by the appellant, he must make every effort to agree amendments to the appeal bundle with the appellant.

7.12

(1) If the representatives for the parties are unable to reach agreement, the respondent may prepare a supplemental bundle.
(2) If the respondent prepares a supplemental bundle he must file it, together with the requisite number of copies for the appeal court, at the appeal court –
(a) with the respondent's notice; or
(b) if a respondent's notice is not filed, within 21 days after he is served with the appeal bundle.

7.13 The respondent must serve –

(1) the respondent's notice;
(2) his skeleton argument (if any); and
(3) the supplemental bundle (if any),
on –
(a) the appellant; and
(b) any other respondent,
at the same time as he files them at the court.

****

Disposing of Applications or Appeals by Consent

12.1 These paragraphs do not apply where –

(1) any party to the proceedings is a child or protected party; or
(2) the appeal or application is to the Court of Appeal from a decision of the Court of Protection.

12.2 Where an appellant does not wish to pursue an application or an appeal, he may request the appeal court for an order that his application or appeal be dismissed. Such a request must contain a statement that the appellant is not a child or protected party and that the appeal or application is not from a decision of the Court of Protection. If such a request is granted it will usually be on the basis that the appellant pays the costs of the application or appeal.

12.3 If the appellant wishes to have the application or appeal dismissed without costs, his request must be accompanied by a consent signed by the respondent or his legal representative stating –

(1) that the respondent is not a child or protected party and that the appeal or application is not from a decision of the Court of Protection; and
(2) that he consents to the dismissal of the application or appeal without costs.

12.4 Where a settlement has been reached disposing of the application or appeal, the parties may make a joint request to the court stating that –

(1) none of them is a child or protected party; and
(2) the appeal or application is not from a decision of the Court of Protection,

and asking that the application or appeal be dismissed by consent. If the request is granted the application or appeal will be dismissed.

('Child' and 'protected party' have the same meaning as in rule 21.1(2).)

Allowing unopposed appeals or applications on paper

13.1 The appeal court will not normally make an order allowing an appeal unless satisfied that the decision of the lower court was wrong, but the appeal court may set aside or vary the order of the lower court with consent and without determining the merits of the appeal, if it is satisfied that there are good and sufficient reasons for doing so. Where the appeal court is requested by all parties to allow an application or an appeal the court may consider the request on the papers. The request should state that none of the parties is a child or protected party and that the application or appeal is not from a decision of the Court of Protection and set out the relevant history of the proceedings and the matters relied on as justifying the proposed order and be accompanied by a copy of the proposed order.

Procedure for consent orders and agreements to pay periodical payments involving a child or protected party or in applications or appeals to the Court of Appeal from a decision of the Court of Protection

13.2 Where one of the parties is a child or protected party or the application or appeal is to the Court of Appeal from a decision of the Court of Protection –

(1) a settlement relating to an appeal or application;...
(2) in a personal injury claim for damages for future pecuniary loss, an agreement reached at the appeal stage to pay periodical payments; or
(3) a request by an appellant for an order that his application or appeal be dismissed with or without the consent of the respondent,

requires the court's approval.

Child

13.3 In cases involving a child a copy of the proposed order signed by the parties' solicitors should be sent to the appeal court, together with an opinion from the advocate acting on behalf of the child.

Protected party

13.4 Where a party is a protected party the same procedure will be adopted, but the documents filed should also include any relevant reports prepared for the Court of Protection.

('Child' and 'protected party' have the same meaning as in rule 21.1(2).)

Periodical payments

13.5 Where periodical payments for future pecuniary loss have been negotiated in a personal injury case which is under appeal, the documents filed should include those which would be required in the case of a personal injury claim for damages for future pecuniary loss dealt with at first instance. Details can be found in the Practice Direction which supplements Part 21.

Summary Assessment of Costs

14.1 Costs are likely to be assessed by way of summary assessment at the following hearings:

(1) contested directions hearings;
(2) applications for permission to appeal at which the respondent is present;
(3) dismissal list hearings in the Court of Appeal at which the respondent is present;
(4) appeals from case management decisions; and
(5) appeals listed for one day or less.

14.2 Parties attending any of the hearings referred to in paragraph 14.1 should be prepared to deal with the summary assessment.

Other Special Provisions Regarding the Court of Appeal

Filing of Documents

15.1 (1) The documents relevant to proceedings in the Court of Appeal, Civil Division must be filed in the Civil Appeals Office Registry, Room E307, Royal Courts of Justice, Strand, London, WC2A 2LL.

(2) The Civil Appeals Office will not serve documents and where service is required by the CPR or this practice direction it must be effected by the parties.

15.1A

(1) A party may file by e-mail –
    (a) an appellant's notice;

(b) a respondent's notice;
  (c) an application notice,
  In the Court of Appeal, Civil Division, using the e-mail account specified in the 'Guidelines for filing by E-mail' which appear on the Court of Appeal, Civil Division website at www.civilappeals.gov.uk.
  (2) A party may only file a notice in accordance with paragraph (1) where he is permitted to do so by the 'Guidelines for filing by E-mail'.

15.1B

  (1) A party to an appeal in the Court of Appeal, Civil Division may file –
    (a) an appellant's notice;
    (b) a respondent's notice; or
    (c) an application notice,
    electronically using the online forms service on the Court of Appeal, Civil Division website at *www.civil appeals.gov.uk*.
  (2) A party may only file a notice in accordance with paragraph (1) where he is permitted to so do by the 'Guidelines for filing electronically'. The Guidelines for filing electronically may be found on the Court of Appeal, Civil Division website.
  (3) The online forms service will assist the user in completing a document accurately but the user is responsible for ensuring that the rules and practice directions relating to the document have been complied with. Transmission by the service does not guarantee that the document will be accepted by the Court of Appeal, Civil Division.
  (4) A party using the online forms service in accordance with this paragraph is responsible for ensuring that the transmission or any document attached to it is filed within any relevant time limits.
  (5) Parties are advised not to transmit electronically any correspondence or documents of a confidential or sensitive nature, as security cannot be guaranteed.
  (6) Where a party wishes to file a document containing a statement of truth electronically, that party should retain the document containing the original signature and file with the court a version of the document on which the name of the person who has signed the statement of truth is typed underneath the statement.

Core Bundles

15.2 In cases where the appeal bundle comprises more than 500 pages, exclusive of transcripts, the appellant's solicitors must, after consultation with the respondent's solicitors, also prepare and file with the court, in addition to copies of the appeal bundle (as amended in accordance with paragraph 7.11) the requisite number of copies of a core bundle.

15.3 (1) The core bundle must be filed within 28 days of receipt of the order giving permission to appeal or, where permission to appeal was granted by the lower court or is not required, within 28 days of the date of service of the appellant's notice on the respondent.

  (2) The core bundle –

(a) must contain the documents which are central to the appeal; and
(b) must not exceed 150 pages.

Preparation of bundles

15.4 The provisions of this paragraph apply to the preparation of appeal bundles, supplemental respondents' bundles where the parties are unable to agree amendments to the appeal bundle, and core bundles.

(1) **Rejection of bundles**. Where documents are copied unnecessarily or bundled incompletely, costs may be disallowed. Where the provisions of this Practice Direction as to the preparation or delivery of bundles are not followed the bundle may be rejected by the court or be made the subject of a special costs order.

(2) **Avoidance of duplication**. No more than one copy of any document should be included unless there is a good reason for doing otherwise (such as the use of a separate core bundle – see paragraph 15.2).

(3) **Pagination**
   (a) Bundles must be paginated, each page being numbered individually and consecutively. The pagination used at trial must also be indicated. Letters and other documents should normally be included in chronological order. (An exception to consecutive page numbering arises in the case of core bundles where it may be preferable to retain the original numbering).
   (b) Page numbers should be inserted in bold figures at the bottom of the page and in a form that can be clearly distinguished from any other pagination on the document.

(4) **Format and presentation**
   (a) Where possible the documents should be in A4 format. Where a document has to be read across rather than down the page, it should be so placed in the bundle as to ensure that the text starts nearest the spine.
   (b) Where any marking or writing in colour on a document is important, the document must be copied in colour or marked up correctly in colour.
   (c) Documents which are not easily legible should be transcribed and the transcription marked and placed adjacent to the document transcribed.
   (d) Documents in a foreign language should be translated and the translation marked and placed adjacent to the document translated. The translation should be agreed or, if it cannot be agreed, each party's proposed translation should be included.
   (e) The size of any bundle should be tailored to its contents. A large lever arch file should not be used for just a few pages nor should files of whatever size be overloaded.
   (f) Where it will assist the Court of Appeal, different sections of the file may be separated by cardboard or other tabbed dividers so long as these are clearly indexed. Where, for example, a document is awaited when the appeal bundle is filed, a single

sheet of paper can be inserted after a divider, indicating the nature of the document awaited. For example, 'Transcript of evidence of Mr J Smith (to follow)'.

(5) **Binding**
  (a) All documents, with the exception of transcripts, must be bound together. This may be in a lever arch file, ring binder or plastic folder. Plastic sleeves containing loose documents must not be used. Binders and files must be strong enough to withstand heavy use.
  (b) Large documents such as plans should be placed in an easily accessible file. Large documents which will need to be opened up frequently should be inserted in a file larger than A4 size.

(6) **Indices and labels**
  (a) An index must be included at the front of the bundle listing all the documents and providing the page references for each. In the case of documents such as letters, invoices or bank statements, they may be given a general description.
  (b) Where the bundles consist of more than one file, an index to all the files should be included in the first file and an index included for each file. Indices should, if possible, be on a single sheet. The full name of the case should not be inserted on the index if this would waste space. Documents should be identified briefly but properly.

(7) **Identification**
  (a) Every bundle must be clearly identified, on the spine and on the front cover, with the name of the case and the Court of Appeal's reference. Where the bundle consists of more than one file, each file must be numbered on the spine, the front cover and the inside of the front cover.
  (b) Outer labels should use large lettering eg ' Appeal Bundle A' or 'Core Bundle'. The full title of the appeal and solicitors' names and addresses should be omitted. A label should be used on the front as well as on the spine.

(8) **Staples etc**. All staples, heavy metal clips etc, must be removed.

(9) **Statements of case**
  (a) Statements of case should be assembled in 'chapter' form – ie claim followed by particulars of claim, followed by further information, irrespective of date.
  (b) Redundant documents, eg particulars of claim overtaken by amendments, requests for further information recited in the answers given, should generally be excluded.

(10) **New Documents**
  (a) Before a new document is introduced into bundles which have already been delivered to the court, steps should be taken to ensure that it carries an appropriate bundle/page number so that it can be added to the court documents. It should not be stapled and it should be prepared with punch holes for immediate inclusion in the binders in use.

(b) If it is expected that a large number of miscellaneous new documents will from time to time be introduced, there should be a special tabbed empty loose-leaf file for that purpose. An index should be produced for this file, updated as necessary.

(11) **Inter-solicitor correspondence**. Since inter-solicitor correspondence is unlikely to be required for the purposes of an appeal, only those letters which will need to be referred to should be copied.

(12) **Sanctions for non-compliance**. If the appellant fails to comply with the requirements as to the provision of bundles of documents, the application or appeal will be referred for consideration to be given as to why it should not be dismissed for failure to so comply.

Master in the Court of Appeal, Civil Division

15.5 When the Head of the Civil Appeals Office acts in a judicial capacity pursuant to rule 52.16, he shall be known as Master. Other eligible officers may also be designated by the Master of the Rolls to exercise judicial authority under rule 52.16 and shall then be known as Deputy Masters.

Respondent to notify Civil Appeals Office whether he intends to file respondent's notice

15.6 A respondent must, no later than 21 days after the date he is served with notification that –

(1) permission to appeal has been granted; or
(2) the application for permission to appeal and the appeal are to be heard together,

inform the Civil Appeals Office and the appellant in writing whether –

(a) he proposes to file a respondent's notice appealing the order or seeking to uphold the order for reasons different from, or additional to, those given by the lower court; or
(b) he proposes to rely on the reasons given by the lower court for its decision.

(Paragraph 15.11B requires all documents needed for an appeal hearing, including a respondent's skeleton argument, to be filed at least 7 days before the hearing.)

Listing and hear-by dates

15.7 The management of the list will be dealt with by the listing officer under the direction of the Master.

15.8 The Civil Appeals List of the Court of Appeal is divided as follows:

- *The applications list* – applications for permission to appeal and other applications.
- *The appeals list* – appeals where permission to appeal has been given or where an appeal lies without permission being required where a hearing date is fixed in advance. (Appeals in this list which require special listing arrangements will be assigned to the special fixtures list)

- *The expedited list* – appeals or applications where the Court of Appeal has directed an expedited hearing. The current practice of the Court of Appeal is summarised in *Unilever plc v Chefaro Proprietaries Ltd* (Practice Note) 1995 1 WLR 243.
- *The stand-out list* – Appeals or applications which, for good reason, are not at present ready to proceed and have been stood out by judicial direction.
- *The second fixtures list* – see paragraph 15.9A(1) below.
- *The second fixtures list* – if an appeal is designated as a 'second fixture' it means that a hearing date is arranged in advance on the express basis that the list is fully booked for the period in question and therefore the case will be heard only if a suitable gap occurs in the list.
- *The short-warned list* – appeals which the court considers may be prepared for the hearing by an advocate other than the one originally instructed with a half day's notice, or such other period as the court may direct.

Special provisions relating to the short-warned list

15.9 (1) Where an appeal is assigned to the short-warned list, the Civil Appeals Office will notify the parties' solicitors in writing. The court may abridge the time for filing any outstanding bundles in an appeal assigned to this list.

(2) The solicitors for the parties must notify their advocate and their client as soon as the Civil Appeals Office notifies them that the appeal has been assigned to the short-warned list.

(3) The appellant may apply in writing for the appeal to be removed from the short-warned list within 14 days of notification of its assignment. The application will be decided by a Lord Justice, or the Master, and will only be granted for the most compelling reasons.

(4) The Civil Appeals Listing Officer may place an appeal from the short-warned list 'on call' from a given date and will inform the parties' advocates accordingly.

(5) An appeal which is 'on call' may be listed for hearing on half a day's notice or such longer period as the court may direct.

(6) Once an appeal is listed for hearing from the short warned list it becomes the immediate professional duty of the advocate instructed in the appeal, if he is unable to appear at the hearing, to take all practicable measures to ensure that his lay client is represented at the hearing by an advocate who is fully instructed and able to argue the appeal.

Special provisions relating to the special fixtures list

15.9A

(1) The special fixtures list is a sub-division of the appeals list and is used to deal with appeals that may require special listing arrangements, such as the need to list a number of cases before the same constitution, in a particular order, during a particular period or at a given location.

(2) The Civil Appeals Office will notify the parties' representatives, or the parties if acting in person, of the particular arrangements that will apply. The notice –
  (a) will give details of the specific period during which a case is scheduled to be heard; and
  (b) may give directions in relation to the filing of any outstanding documents.
(3) The listing officer will notify the parties' representatives of the precise hearing date as soon as practicable. While every effort will be made to accommodate the availability of counsel, the requirements of the court will prevail.

Requests for directions

15.10 To ensure that all requests for directions are centrally monitored and correctly allocated, all requests for directions or rulings (whether relating to listing or any other matters) should be made to the Civil Appeals Office. Those seeking directions or rulings must not approach the supervising Lord Justice either directly, or via his or her clerk.

Bundles of authorities

15.11

(1) Once the parties have been notified of the date fixed for the hearing, the appellant's advocate must, after consultation with his opponent, file a bundle containing photocopies of the authorities upon which each side will rely at the hearing.
(2) The bundle of authorities should, in general –
  (a) have the relevant passages of the authorities marked;
  (b) not include authorities for propositions not in dispute; and
  (c) not contain more than 10 authorities unless the scale of the appeal warrants more extensive citation.
(3) The bundle of authorities must be filed –
  (a) at least 7 days before the hearing; or
  (b) where the period of notice of the hearing is less than 7 days, immediately.
(4) If, through some oversight, a party intends, during the hearing, to refer to other authorities the parties may agree a second agreed bundle. The appellant's advocate must file this bundle at least 48 hours before the hearing commences.
(5) A bundle of authorities must bear a certification by the advocates responsible for arguing the case that the requirements of sub-paragraphs (3) to (5) of paragraph 5.10 have been complied with in respect of each authority included.

Supplementary skeleton arguments

15.11A

(1) A supplementary skeleton argument on which the appellant wishes to rely must be filed at least 14 days before the hearing.
(2) A supplementary skeleton argument on which the respondent wishes to rely must be filed at least 7 days before the hearing.
(3) All supplementary skeleton arguments must comply with the requirements set out in paragraph 5.10.
(4) At the hearing the court may refuse to hear argument from a party not contained in a skeleton argument filed within the relevant time limit set out in this paragraph.

Papers for the appeal hearing

15.11B

(1) All the documents which are needed for the appeal hearing must be filed at least 7 days before the hearing. Where a document has not been filed 10 days before the hearing a reminder will be sent by the Civil Appeals Office.
(2) Any party who fails to comply with the provisions of paragraph (1) may be required to attend before the Presiding Lord Justice to seek permission to proceed with, or to oppose, the appeal.

Disposal of bundles of documents

15.11C

(1) Where the court has determined a case, the official transcriber will retain one set of papers. The Civil Appeals Office will destroy any remaining sets of papers not collected within 21 days of –
    (a) where one or more parties attend the hearing, the date of the court's decision;
    (b) where there is no attendance, the date of the notification of court's decision.
(2) The parties should ensure that bundles of papers supplied to the court do not contain original documents (other than transcripts). The parties must ensure that they –
    (a) bring any necessary original documents to the hearing; and
    (b) retrieve any original documents handed up to the court before leaving the court.
(3) The court will retain application bundles where permission to appeal has been granted. Where permission is refused the arrangements in sub-paragraph (1) will apply.
(4) Where a single Lord Justice has refused permission to appeal on paper, application bundles will not be destroyed until after the time limit for seeking a hearing has expired.

Availability of Reserved judgments before hand down

15.12 This section applies where the presiding Lord Justice is satisfied that the result of the appeal will attract no special degree of confidentiality or sensitivity.

15.13 A copy of the written judgment will be made available to the parties' legal advisers by 4 p.m. on the second working day before judgment is due to be pronounced or such other period as the court may direct. This can be shown, in confidence, to the parties but only for the purpose of obtaining instructions and on the strict understanding that the judgment, or its effect, is not to be disclosed to any other person. A working day is any day on which the Civil Appeals Office is open for business.

15.14 The appeal will be listed for judgment in the cause list and the judgment handed down at the appropriate time.

Attendance of advocates on the handing down of a reserved judgment

15.15 Where any consequential orders are agreed, the parties' advocates need not attend on the handing down of a reserved judgment. Where an advocate does attend the court may, if it considers such attendance unnecessary, disallow the costs of the attendance. If the parties do not indicate that they intend to attend, the judgment may be handed down by a single member of the court.

Agreed orders following judgment

15.16 The parties must, in respect of any draft agreed orders –

  (a) fax a copy to the clerk to the presiding Lord Justice; and
  (b) file four copies in the Civil Appeals Office,

no later than 12 noon on the working day before the judgment is handed down.

15.17 A copy of a draft order must bear the Court of Appeal case reference, the date the judgment is to be handed down and the name of the presiding Lord Justice.

Corrections to the draft judgment

15.18 Any proposed correction to the draft judgment should be sent to the clerk to the judge who prepared the draft with a copy to any other party.

Application for leave to appeal

15.19 Where a party wishes to apply for leave to appeal to the House of Lords under section 1 of the Administration of Justice (Appeals) Act 1934 the court may deal with the application on the basis of written submissions.

15.20 A party must, in relation to his submission –

  (a) fax a copy to the clerk to the presiding Lord Justice; and
  (b) file four copies in the Civil Appeals Office,

no later than 12 noon on the working day before the judgment is handed down.

15.21 A copy of a submission must bear the Court of Appeal case reference, the date the judgment is to be handed down and the name of the presiding Lord Justice.

****

Section IV Provisions about Reopening Appeals
Reopening of Final Appeals

25.1 This paragraph applies to applications under rule 52.17 for permission to reopen a final determination of an appeal.

25.2 In this paragraph, 'appeal' includes an application for permission to appeal.

25.3 Permission must be sought from the court whose decision the applicant wishes to reopen.

25.4 The application for permission must be made by application notice and supported by written evidence, verified by a statement of truth.

25.5 A copy of the application for permission must not be served on any other party to the original appeal unless the court so directs.

25.6 Where the court directs that the application for permission is to be served on another party, that party may within 14 days of the service on him of the copy of the application file and serve a written statement either supporting or opposing the application.

25.7 The application for permission, and any written statements supporting or opposing it, will be considered on paper by a single judge, and will be allowed to proceed only if the judge so directs.

Appendix 4

THE HOUSE OF LORDS AND SUPREME COURT

CONTENTS

Appellate Jurisdiction Act 1876
Administration of Justice Act 1934
Constitutional Reform Act 2005
House of Lords Practice Directions Applicable to Civil Appeals

APPELLATE JURISDICTION ACT 1876

****

3 Cases in which appeal lies to House of Lords

Subject as in this Act mentioned an appeal shall lie to the House of Lords from any order or judgment of any of the courts following; that is to say,

(1) Of Her Majesty's Court of Appeal in England; and

(2) Of any Court in Scotland from which error or an appeal at or immediately before the commencement of this Act lay to the House of Lords by common law or by statute; and

(3) (*repealed*).

****

ADMINISTRATION OF JUSTICE ACT 1934

1 Restrictions on appeals from Court of Appeal to House of Lords

(1) No appeal shall lie to the House of Lords from any order or judgment made or given by the Court of Appeal after the first day of October nineteen hundred and thirty-four, except with the leave of that Court or of the House of Lords.

(2) The House of Lords may by order provide for the hearing and determination by a Committee of that House of petitions for leave to appeal from the Court of Appeal:

Provided that section five of the Appellate Jurisdiction Act 1876, shall apply to the hearing and determination of any such petition by a Committee of the House as it applies to the hearing and determination of an appeal by the House.

(3) Nothing in this section shall affect any restriction existing, apart from this section, on the bringing of appeals from the Court of Appeal to the House of Lords.

CONSTITUTIONAL REFORM ACT 2005

****

Jurisdiction, relation to other courts etc

40 Jurisdiction

(1) The Supreme Court is a superior court of record.

(2) An appeal lies to the Court from any order or judgment of the Court of Appeal in England and Wales in civil proceedings.

(3) An appeal lies to the Court from any order or judgment of a court in Scotland if an appeal lay from that court to the House of Lords at or immediately before the commencement of this section.

(4) Schedule 9 –

- (a) transfers other jurisdiction from the House of Lords to the Court,
- (b) transfers devolution jurisdiction from the Judicial Committee of the Privy Council to the Court, and
- (c) makes other amendments relating to jurisdiction.

(5) The Court has power to determine any question necessary to be determined for the purposes of doing justice in an appeal to it under any enactment.

(6) An appeal under subsection (2) lies only with the permission of the Court of Appeal or the Supreme Court; but this is subject to provision under any other enactment restricting such an appeal

****

HOUSE OF LORDS PRACTICE DIRECTIONS APPLICABLE TO CIVIL APPEALS

PART I

Directions on Petitions for Leave to Appeal

****

2 Time Limits

2.1 Time limits apply as follows:

(a) Except for applications under direction 2.4, a petition for leave to appeal to the House of Lords should be lodged at the Judicial Office within one month from the date of the order appealed from. The one month period runs from the date of the substantive order appealed from, not from the date on which the order is sealed or the date of any subsequent procedural order (e g an order refusing permission to appeal).

(b) If a petitioner has applied for public funding, the above period is extended to one month after the decision whether funding should be granted, including any appeals. The Judicial Office must be informed in writing within the original one month period that public funding has been applied for (direction 41).

(c) Petitions for leave to appeal out of time are admissible.

Petitions out of time

2.2 A petition for leave to appeal lodged outside the one month period is accepted by the Judicial Office for presentation to the House provided that:

(a) it has been drafted in the style required for such petitions and seeks leave to appeal out of time; and

(b) it sets out in the first paragraph the reason(s) why it was not lodged within the time limit; and

(c) it is in order in all other respects.

The reason(s) should not normally exceed one paragraph in length.

2.3 In considering a petition for leave to appeal out of time, the Appeal Committee may reject it solely on the ground that it is out of time; but the Appeal Committee may grant an extension of time and decide the application for leave on the merits.

Contempt of court

2.4 A petition for leave to appeal in a case involving civil contempt of court must be lodged in the Judicial Office within 14 days (not one month), beginning with the date of the refusal of leave by the court below (not the following day).

3 Lodgment of Petition

Form of petition

3.1 A petition for leave to appeal should be produced on A4 paper, securely bound on the left, using both sides of the paper. The petition should set out briefly the facts and points of law; and conclude with a summary of the reasons why leave should be granted. Petitions which are not legible or which are not produced in the required form are not accepted. A petition should not contain annexes or appendices. Parties may consult the Judicial Office at any stage of preparation of the petition, and may submit petitions in draft for approval.

3.2 Supporting documents other than those set out in direction 4.2 are not normally accepted.

3.3 Amendments to petitions and the lodging of supplementary petitions are allowed only in exceptional circumstances. The Head of the Judicial Office may allow amendments to petitions and the lodging of supplementary petitions if he is satisfied that this will assist the Appeal Committee and will not unfairly prejudice the respondents or cause undue delay. Any such amendments and supplementary petitions must be served on the respondents (see direction 3.12).

3.4 If a petition for leave to appeal

(a) asks the House to depart from one of its own decisions;
(b) raises issues relating to the Human Rights Act 1998; or
(c) seeks a reference to the Court of Justice of the European Communities, the point should be stated clearly in the petition.

3.5 A petition for leave to appeal must be signed by the petitioners or their agents.

3.6 On the back of the petition for leave, below the certificate of service, there should be inserted the neutral citation of the judgment petitioned against, the references of any law report in the courts below, and subject matter catchwords for indexing (whether or not the case has been reported).

Case title

3.7 Petitions for leave to appeal to the House of Lords carry the same title as in the court below, except that the parties are described as petitioner(s) and respondent(s). For reference purposes, the names of parties to the original action who are not parties to the appeal should nevertheless be included in the title: their names should be enclosed in square brackets. The names of all parties should be given in the same sequence as in the title used in the court below.

3.8 Petitions in which trustees, executors etc. are parties are titled in the short form, for example Trustees of John Black's Charity (Respondents) v White (Petitioner).

3.9 In any petition concerning minors or where in the court below the title used has been such as to conceal the identity of one or more parties to the action, this fact should be clearly drawn to the attention of the Judicial Office at the time the petition is lodged, so that the title adopted in the House of Lords can take account of the need for anonymity. Petitions involving minors are normally given a title in the form In re B (see also direction 9.9).

3.10 In case titles involving the Crown, the abbreviation "R" meaning "Regina" is used. "R" is always given first. So case titles using this abbreviation take the form R v Jones (Petitioner) or R v Jones (Respondent) (as the case may be) or R (on the application of Jones) (Petitioner) v Secretary of State for the Home Department (Respondent).

3.11 Apart from the above, Latin is not used in case titles.

Service

3.12 A copy of the petition must be served on the respondents or their agents, either by delivery in person or by first class post, before it is lodged at the Judicial Office. A certificate of such service (noting the full name and address of the respondents or their agents) must be endorsed on the back of the original petition and signed.

Lodgment

3.13 Two original copies of the petition must be lodged at the Judicial Office, together with a copy of the order appealed against and, if separate, a copy of the order of the court below refusing leave to appeal. If the substantive order appealed against is not immediately available, the petition should nevertheless be lodged within the required time limits, and the order lodged as soon as possible thereafter.

3.14 An agent who attends the Judicial Office to lodge a petition for leave to appeal or accompanying papers must be familiar with the subject matter of the petition.

3.15 A petition for leave to appeal is presented to the House and recorded in the House of Lords Business on the day it is lodged or on the next sitting day of the House.

Waiver of fees

3.16 Standing Order XIII provides that a fee is payable when a petition for leave to appeal is lodged. For the present level of fees, see Appendix C.

3.17 In circumstances where a petitioner would suffer financial hardship by the payment of fees to the House, the requirement to pay fees may be waived. Application should be made to the Judicial Office. In order to provide an objective test, and to keep in step with the courts below, the Judicial Office applies the provisions of the Civil Proceedings Fees Order 20042 to determine financial hardship for the purposes of Standing Order XIII. Waivers of fees are also granted to petitioners who have been granted a remission of fees in the court below.

The fee paid by a petitioner on a petition for leave to appeal is not refunded, even if the Appeal Committee dismiss the petition as inadmissible.

Appearance for respondents

3.18 Respondents or their agents should enter appearance to a petition for leave as soon as they have received service. The respondents or their agents enter appearance by informing the Judicial Office by post of their name and address or that of their firm and paying the prescribed fee. The fee is refunded if the petition is dismissed as inadmissible.

3.19 Respondents who do not intend to take part in the proceedings do not need to enter appearance, but the Judicial Office sends communications concerning a petition for leave to appeal only to those who have entered appearance.

3.20 An order for costs will not be made in favour of a respondent who has not entered appearance.

Interventions in petitions for leave to appeal

3.21 Save in exceptional circumstances, no application may be made to intervene in support of a petition for leave to appeal.

Communications by fax/e-mail

3.22 See direction 26.2.

4 Appeal Committee

4.1 Petitions for leave to appeal to the House of Lords are considered by an Appeal Committee consisting of three Lords of Appeal. Petitions are generally decided on the papers alone, without a hearing.

Additional papers

4.2 The following additional papers for use by the Appeal Committee must be lodged within seven days

of lodgment of the petition:
- (a) four copies of the petition;
- (b) four copies of the order appealed against;
- (c) if separate from the order at (b) above, four copies of the order of the court below refusing leave to appeal to the House of Lords;
- (d) four copies of the official transcript of the judgment of the court below;
- (e) four copies of the final order(s) of all other courts below;

(f) four copies of the official transcript of the final judgment(s) of all other courts below;

(g) four copies of any unreported judgment(s) cited in the petition or judgment of a court below.

No other papers are required, and documents other than those listed above are not accepted unless requested by the Appeal Committee.

4.3 Papers lodged in accordance with direction 4.2 should be lodged as individual documents, double sided, single-stapled and not inserted into ring binders. Documents which are not clearly legible or which are not in the required style or form (see direction 3.1) are not accepted.

4.4 Where the required papers are not lodged within three months of presentation of the petition and no good reason is given for the delay, the petition may at the direction of the Head of the Judicial Office be referred to an Appeal Committee without the required accompanying papers.

Consideration on the papers

4.5 The Appeal Committee decides first whether a petition for leave to appeal is admissible. The rules on admissibility are set out in direction 1.14. If the Appeal Committee determines that a petition is inadmissible, it may refuse leave on that ground alone and not consider the content of the petition. The Appeal Committee gives a reason for deciding that the petition is inadmissible.

4.6 If the Appeal Committee decides that a petition is admissible, the Committee may then:

(a) refuse leave (see direction 4.8);
(b) give leave outright (see direction 4.9);
(c) invite the respondents to lodge objections to the petition (see directions 4.10–4.14);
(d) give leave on terms (see direction 4.15);
(e) refer the petition for an oral hearing (see directions 4.16–4.21).

4.7 Leave to appeal is granted to petitions that, in the opinion of the Appeal Committee, raise an arguable point of law of general public importance which ought to be considered by the House at this time, bearing in mind that the matter will already have been the subject of judicial decision and may have already been reviewed on appeal. A petition which in the opinion of the Appeal Committee does not raise such a point of law is refused on that ground. The Appeal Committee gives brief reasons for refusing leave to appeal but does not otherwise explain its decisions.

Leave refused

4.8 If the Appeal Committee is unanimous that a petition should be refused, the parties are notified that the petition is dismissed.

Leave given outright

4.9 If the Appeal Committee is unanimous that a petition should be allowed without further proceedings, the House grants leave outright (without inviting respondents' objections).

Respondents' objections

4.10 Respondents may submit written objections giving their reasons why leave to appeal should be refused. They may do this:

(a) within 14 days of the date of service on them of the petition for leave to appeal; or
(b) within 14 days of any invitation by the Appeal Committee to do so; or
(c) within 14 days of a petition for leave to appeal being referred for an oral hearing.

4.11 Respondents' objections set out briefly the reasons why the petition should be refused or make submissions as to the terms upon which leave should be granted (for example, on costs). One master plus four copies of the respondents' written objections must be lodged at the Judicial Office. The objections must be produced on A4 paper, securely fastened, using both sides of the paper.

4.12 A copy of the respondents' objections should be sent to the agents for the other parties. In certain circumstances the Appeal Committee may invite further submissions from the petitioners in the light of the respondents' objections, but petitioners do not have a right to comment on respondents' objections. Where the Appeal Committee does not require further submissions, and provided the Committee is unanimous in its decision to grant or refuse leave, it reports its decision to the House and the parties are informed. Where the Appeal Committee proposes terms for granting leave, direction 4.15 applies.

4.13 Respondents' objections are subject to any order for costs made by the Appeal Committee or, if leave to appeal is granted, become costs in the appeal (see direction 5).

4.14 Respondents unable to meet the deadlines set out in direction 4.10 must write to the Head of the Judicial Office requesting an extension of time for lodging their written objections.

Leave given on terms

4.15 If the Appeal Committee decides that leave to appeal should be given on terms:

(a) the Committee proposes the terms and the parties have the right to make submissions on the proposed terms within 14 days of the date of the Committee's decision to give leave to appeal;
(b) prospective appellants who are granted leave to appeal subject to terms that they are unwilling to accept may decline to pursue the appeal;
(c) in an application for leave to appeal under the "leapfrog" procedure (see direction 6), prospective appellants who decline to proceed on the

basis of the terms proposed by the Appeal Committee may instead pursue an appeal to the Court of Appeal in the usual way.

Petition referred for oral hearing

4.16 In all cases where the members of the Appeal Committee are not unanimous, or where further argument is required, a petition for leave to appeal is referred for an oral hearing.

4.17 If the respondents have not already lodged written objections, they may do so within 14 days of being informed that the petition has been referred for a hearing (direction 4.10(c)).

4.18 When a petition is referred for an oral hearing, the petitioners and all respondents who have entered appearance are notified of the date of the hearing before the Appeal Committee.

4.19 Parties may be heard before the Appeal Committee by counsel, by agent, or in person, but one only may be heard on each side.

4.20 If counsel is briefed, agents should ensure that the Judicial Office is notified of their name. Only a junior counsel's fee is allowed on taxation (direction 1.23).

4.21 Authorities are not normally cited before the Appeal Committee or provided for the Committee's use at the hearing.

Lodgment of petition of appeal

4.22 If leave to appeal is given, the petition of appeal (direction 9) must be lodged with the prescribed fee within 14 days of the date of the Appeal Committee's decision. Failure to meet this deadline results in the petition of appeal being lodged out of time and referred to an Appeal Committee pursuant to direction 7.3.

Order of the House

4.23 Copies of the House of Lords Business recording the report of the Appeal Committee and the order of the House are sent to all parties who have entered appearance.

4.24 A formal order of the Appeal Committee is not normally issued but will be issued on written request and on payment of a fee. A formal order is not required for taxation of costs arising from the application for leave to appeal.

Expedition

4.25 Once the required papers are lodged at the Judicial Office (direction 4.2), the procedure described above is normally completed within eight sitting weeks (excluding any oral hearing). In cases involving liberty of the subject, urgent medical intervention or the well-being of children (see direction 4.26), application for expedition may be made in writing to the Judicial Office.

Expeditious hearing of proceedings under the Hague Convention etc

4.26 The Convention on the Civil Aspects of International Child Abduction (the Hague Convention) deals with the wrongful removal and retention of children from their habitual country of residence. The Revised Brussels II Regulation also deals with these matters. In the House of Lords an expedited timetable applies. The parties must therefore inform the Judicial Office that the proceedings fall under the Convention or Regulation. The House normally gives judgment within six weeks of the commencement of proceedings in the House. This can only be achieved with the fullest co-operation of the parties.

4.27 The following timetable may be taken as a general guideline:

(a) an application for leave to appeal is decided by an Appeal Committee within 7 days of being lodged;
(b) an appeal is heard within 21 days of a decision to give leave to appeal;
(c) the result of the appeal is given immediately after the end of the hearing with reasons given later or, if judgment is reserved, the result of the appeal and the reasons are given within 2 weeks of the end of the hearing.

4.28 In order to achieve the timetable in direction 4.27 the House makes dispensing orders to set aside or vary the practice directions that normally apply to applications and appeals to the House.

4.29 Abridged procedures and special rules for the production of documents are applied to meet the circumstances of each application and appeal. The following timetable for the production of documents is therefore indicative only:

(a) the Statement of facts and issues is lodged within seven days of the decision to give leave to appeal;
(b) the appellant's case is lodged within 10 days of the decision to give leave to appeal (or, if the relevant day falls on a Saturday or Sunday, the following Monday);
(c) the respondent's case is lodged within 14 days of the decision to give leave to appeal;
(d) the Bound Volumes (if required) and the authorities' volumes are lodged within 17 days of the decision to give leave to appeal (or, if the relevant day falls on a Saturday or Sunday, the following Monday).

5 Costs

5.1 Where a petition for leave to appeal is determined without an oral hearing, costs may be awarded as follows:

(a) to a publicly funded or legally aided petitioner, reasonable costs incurred in preparing papers for the Appeal Committee;
(b) to a publicly funded or legally aided respondent, only those costs necessarily incurred in attending the client, attending the petitioner's agents, perusing the petition, entering appearance and, where applicable, preparing respondent's objections to the petition 2;

(c) to an unassisted respondent where the petitioner is publicly funded or legally aided, payment out of the Community Legal Service Fund (pursuant to s 11 of the Access to Justice Act 1993) of costs as specified at (b) above;

(d) to a respondent where neither party is publicly funded or legally aided, costs as specified at (b) above.

Where costs are sought under (c) or (d) above, the application may be made by letter addressed to the Judicial Office or may be included in a bill of costs lodged in the Judicial Office conditional upon the application being granted.

5.2 Where a petition for leave to appeal is referred for an oral hearing and is dismissed, application for costs must be made by the respondent at the end of the hearing. No order for costs is made unless requested at that time.

5.3 Where a petition for leave to appeal is allowed, costs of the petition become costs in the appeal.

5.4 Bills of costs for taxation must be lodged within three months from the date of the decision of the Appeal Committee or the date on which a petition for leave is withdrawn in accordance with direction 45.1. If an extension of the three month period is desired, application must be made in writing to the Taxing Officer and copies of all such correspondence sent to all interested parties. In deciding whether to grant an application for an extension of time made after the expiry of the three month period, the Taxing Officer takes into account the circumstances set out in the practice directions applicable to judicial taxations.

5.5 The practice directions relating to judicial taxations and forms of bills of costs are available from the Judicial Office and on the internet at www.parliament.uk. Fees are payable on taxation of a bill of costs.

Withdrawal of petitions for leave to appeal

5.6 See direction 45.1.

PART II
DIRECTIONS APPLYING IN ALL CIVIL APPEALS

7 Time Limits

7.1 A petition of appeal must be lodged at the Judicial Office within three months of the date on which the order appealed against was made.

7.2 However, this time limit may be varied by an order of the House when granting leave or by an order of the court below. The order appealed against is the substantive order complained of.

Out of time appeals

7.3 Where a petition of appeal is not lodged within the time allowed, a petition for leave to present the appeal out of time may be lodged. This petition is referred to an Appeal Committee.

Fees

7.4 A fee is payable on a petition of appeal and on a petition for leave to present a petition of appeal out of time (see Appendix C).

8 London Agents

8.1 Solicitors outside London may appoint London agents. Those who decide not to do so should note that any additional costs incurred as a result of that decision may be disallowed on taxation (assessment of costs).

9 Lodgment of Appeal

Form of petition of appeal

9.1 Petitions of appeal must be produced on A4 paper, securely bound on the left, using both sides of the paper.

9.2 Where leave to appeal has been obtained, it is enough for the petition of appeal to be signed by the appellants or their agents. In appeals where leave to appeal is not required (for example, in most Scottish appeals) the petition of appeal must be certified as reasonable by two counsel from the relevant jurisdiction and signed by them. In Scottish appeals a certificate of difference of opinion must also be included where appropriate.

9.3 On the back page of the petition, below the certificate of service, there should be inserted the neutral citation of the judgment appealed against, the references of any law report of the case in the courts below and subject matter catchwords for indexing (whether or not the case has been reported).

Case title

9.4 Petitions of appeal to the House of Lords carry the same title as in the court below, except that the parties are described as appellant(s) and respondent(s). For reference purposes, the names of parties to the original action who are not parties to the appeal should nevertheless be included in the title: their names should be enclosed in square brackets. The names of all parties should be given in the same sequence as in the title used in the court below.

9.5 Petitions in which trustees, executors, etc. are parties are titled in the short form, for example Trustees of John Black's Charity (Respondents) v White (Appellant).

9.6 In any petition concerning minors or where in the court below the title used has been such as to conceal the identity of one or more parties to the action, this fact should be clearly drawn to the attention of the Judicial Office at the time the petition is lodged, so that the title adopted in the House of Lords can take account of the need for anonymity. Petitions involving minors are normally given a title in the form In re B (see also direction 9.9).

9.7 In case titles involving the Crown, the abbreviation "R" meaning "Regina" is used. "R" is always given first. Case titles using this abbreviation take the form R v Jones (Appellant) or R v Jones (Respondent) (as the case may be) or R (on the application of Jones) (Appellant) v Secretary of State for the Home Department (Respondent).

9.8 Apart from the above, Latin is not used in case titles.

Anonymity and reporting restrictions

9.9 In any appeal concerning children, the parties, in addition to considering the case title to be used,

should also consider whether it would be appropriate for the House to make an order under s 39 of the Children and Young Persons Act 1933. The parties should always inform the Judicial Office if such an order has been made by a court below. A request for such an order to be made by the House should be made in writing, preferably on behalf of all parties to the appeal, as soon as possible after the appeal has been presented and not later than 14 days before the start of the hearing.

9.10 Direction 9.9 also applies to a request for an order under s 4 of the Contempt of Court Act 1981.

Human Rights Act 1998

9.11 Appellants must notify the Judicial Office in writing when:

(a) the House is to be asked to consider whether to make, uphold or reverse a declaration that a provision of primary or subordinate legislation is incompatible with a European Human Rights Convention right, or is to be asked to consider any issue which may lead the House to make such a declaration, or where such an issue is or may be raised in respect of a judicial act;

(b) a party seeks to challenge an act of a public authority under the Human Rights Act 1998; or

(c) a party relies in whole or in part on the provisions of the Human Rights Act 1998.

Appellants should indicate whether notification is made under (a), (b) or (c) above (see direction 33.1). They should set out briefly the arguments involved; and state whether the point was taken in the courts below. In appeals in which (a) above is an issue, the Crown has a right to be joined as a party to the appeal (see direction 33.2).

Service

9.12 A copy of the petition of appeal must be served on the respondents or their agents, either by delivery in person or by first class post, before lodgment at the Judicial Office. A certificate of such service noting the full name and address of the respondents or their agents must be endorsed on the back of the original petition and signed by the appellants or their agents.

Lodgment

9.13 The original petition of appeal together with seven copies must be lodged at the Judicial Office with the prescribed fee. If leave to appeal was granted by the court below, a copy of the order appealed against must also be lodged and, if separate, a copy of the order granting leave to appeal to the House of Lords. If the order is not immediately available, the petition should be lodged in time and the order lodged as soon as possible thereafter.

9.14 Once the petition of appeal has been lodged, it is presented to the House and recorded in the House of Lords Business. A copy of the House of Lords Business is sent to all parties who have entered appearance (direction 9.15).

Appearance for respondents

9.15 Respondents or their agents should enter appearance to an appeal as soon as they have received service of the petition of appeal, by informing the Judicial Office by post of their name and address or that of their firm and paying the prescribed fee.

9.16 Respondents who do not intend to take part in the proceedings do not need to enter appearance, but the Judicial Office sends communications concerning the appeal only to those who have entered appearance. An order for costs will not be made in favour of a respondent who has not entered appearance.

10 Security for Costs

10.1 Within seven days of the presentation of an appeal, appellants must give security for costs by paying into the House of Lords Security Fund Account the sum fixed by the House. Failure to do so results in the appeal being dismissed by default (unless public funding or legal aid has been applied for: see direction 41.3).

10.2 Payment is made by banker's draft or cheque made payable to 'House of Lords Security Fund Account'. If an appellant wishes to pay in cash, the Judicial Office may only accept cash up to £10,000, in order to comply with money laundering regulations. No interest is payable on security money.

Waiver of security

10.3 Provided that all the respondents agree that security for costs should be waived, the appellants may lodge a consent form asking the House to release the appellants from the obligation to pay security for costs. The consent must be signed by all the respondents and lodged with the prescribed fee within seven days of the presentation of the appeal. An order is then made absolving the appellants from giving security. A copy of the form of consent is available from the Judicial Office.

10.4 The following are not required to give security for costs and no waiver is necessary:

(a) an appellant who has been granted a certificate of public funding/legal aid;
(b) an appellant in an appeal under the Child Abduction and Custody Act 1985;
(c) a Minister or Government department.

10.5 No security for costs or waiver is required in cross-appeals.

10.6 The House has the power to vary or dispense with the requirement to give security for costs when the respondents do not agree to a waiver, but uses this power rarely, and only after an Appeal Committee has recommended that the requirement for security should be waived. The Appeal Committee normally takes this decision on the papers alone, without an oral hearing.

11 Statement of facts and Issues

11.1 It is the appellants' responsibility to lodge a Statement of the facts and issues (with an Appendix (see direction 12)). The Statement should be a succinct account of the main facts of the case, including an account of judicial proceedings up to that point and an account of the issues raised by the appeal. The appellants are responsible for drawing up the Statement in draft and they must submit it to the respondents for discussion and agreement. The Statement must be a single document agreed between the parties. In the event of disagreement, disputed material should be removed from the draft Statement and included instead in each party's case (see direction 15). The Statement must be signed on behalf of each party by at least one counsel who appeared in the court below or who will appear at the hearing before the House.

Form of Statement of facts and issues

11.2 The Statement of facts and issues should be produced on A4 paper, securely bound on the left, and incorporate:

(a) pages printed on both sides of the paper;
(b) capital letters down the inside margins;
(c) references on the outside margins to relevant pages of the Appendix;
(d) on the front cover, the reference of every law report of the case in the courts below, together with the catchword summary of one of the reports;
(e) on the front cover, a headnote summary, whether or not the case has been reported;
(f) on the front cover, a statement of the time occupied in the courts below;
(g) on the front cover, addresses of parties at foot of page; and
(h) at the end, the signatures of counsel for both parties above their printed names.

12 Appendix

12.1 It is the appellants' responsibility, in consultation with the respondents, to prepare and lodge an Appendix of documents considered necessary for the appeal. These documents include all the documents used in evidence or recording proceedings in the courts below.

12.2 The appellants bear the cost of preparing the Appendix, although these costs are ultimately subject to the decision of the House as to the costs of the appeal.

Contents of Appendix

12.3 The Appendix contains only documents or extracts from documents that are necessary to support and understand the argument when the appeal is heard by the Appellate Committee. No document which was not used in evidence or does not record proceedings relevant to the action in the courts below may be included. Transcripts of arguments in the courts below may not be included unless remarks by a judge are relied on by any party or the arguments refer to facts which are admitted by all parties and as to which no evidence was called.

12.4 The Appendix consists of one or more parts. Part 1 must contain:

(a) formal originating documents;
(b) case stated (if any);
(c) judgments and orders relating to the decisions at first instance and on appeal;
(d) relevant legislative provisions including delegated legislation; and
(e) any relevant document on which the action is founded (such as a will, contract, map, plan etc.) or an extract from such document.

12.5 For judgments that have been published, unbound parts of the relevant Law Reports or the Weekly Law Reports should be used if available; otherwise the All England Reports, Tax Cases, Simons' Tax Cases, Reports of Patent Cases and Lloyd's List Reports may be used. In Scottish appeals, Session Cases should be used where available; otherwise, Scots Law Times and Scottish Civil Case Reports may be used. Where, at the time of preparation of the Appendix, a judgment of a court below has not been published, a transcript must be included, which may later be replaced by the published version. In such circumstances, 15 copies of the published version should be submitted to the Judicial Office. Judgments in draft are not accepted. If the printed Act or set of Regulations is conveniently small, it should be used; if the provisions are bulky or numerous, the relevant provisions should be copied. Halsbury's Statutes may be used.

12.6 Other documents should be included in Part 2 of the Appendix and, if the bulk of the documents makes it necessary, in Parts 3, 4 etc. The Appendix volume should only be numbered Part 1 if there is more than one Part.

Form of Appendix

12.7 The Appendix takes the following form:

(a) it must be A4 size bound with a plastic comb binding and blue card covers (blue indicating a civil appeal);

(b) documents must be printed on both sides of the paper;
(c) documents must be numbered;
(d) original documents smaller than A4 may be enlarged to A4 size with a broad outside margin;
(e) the Appendix must contain an index; and if there is more than one Part, Part 1 of the Appendix must also contain an index to all the other Parts;
(f) in addition to the requirement at (e) above, if the Appendix has more than one Part, each Part must contain a list of its own contents;
(g) documents of an unsuitable size or form for binding (for example, booklets or charts) should be included in a pocket attached to the inside back cover of the appropriate Appendix volume;
(h) no tabs should be included in the Appendix.

Examination of Appendix

12.8 The Appendix is for the use of all parties and the contents of the Appendix must be agreed by appellants and respondents. Disputed documents (see direction 12.9) should not be included in the Appendix. As soon as proofs of the Appendix are available they should be examined against the originals by all parties, if possible at one joint examination. As soon as practicable after the examination, a final proof of the Appendix should be provided to each party.

Documents in readiness at hearing

12.9 Disputed documents and any document not included in the Appendix which may be required at the hearing should be held in readiness and, subject to leave being given by the Appellate Committee, may be introduced at an appropriate moment. Fifteen copies are required. All such documents are subject to previous examination by the other parties. Where the appellants refuse to include in the Appendix any documents that the respondents consider necessary, the respondents must prepare and reproduce the documents at their own expense, subject to the final order on costs.

Scottish Record

12.10 In all Scottish appeals, appellants are required to include in Part 1 of the Appendix:

(a) a copy of the Record as authenticated by the Deputy Principal Clerk of Session or a Clerk of Session delegated by him;
(b) a supplement containing an account, without argument or statement of other facts, of the further steps which have been taken in the appeal since the Record was completed; and
(c) copies of the interlocutors (or parts of interlocutors) complained of.

13 Lodgment of Statment and Appendix

Time limits

13.1 The Statement and Appendix must be lodged by the appellants within six weeks of the presentation of the appeal, or within such longer period as may be allowed on petition (see direction 13.3).

13.2 If this time limit expires during a parliamentary recess, it is automatically extended to the third next sitting day of the House of Lords; and if any party has applied for public funding/legal aid, the time limit is automatically extended to one month after the notification of the result of the funding decision, provided that the Judicial Office has been informed of the application.

Petitions for extension of time—first extension

13.3 Appellants who are unable to complete preparation of the Statement and Appendix within the initial six weeks' period may apply by petition for an extension of that time. The petition takes the form common to all formal documents of the House. It should explain briefly the reason(s) why an extension is needed. Application may be made for an extension of up to six weeks from the original expiry date, and the petition must specify the date to which the extension is requested. If that date seems likely to fall in a parliamentary recess, the petition may request extension until '[specify date] or the third sitting day of the next ensuing meeting of the House'.

13.4 A petition for extension of time must be signed by the appellants. It must be submitted to those respondents who have entered appearance for the endorsement of their consent, and it must bear their signature. One master of the petition plus one copy and the prescribed fee must be lodged before the expiry of the six weeks initially allowed for lodging the Statement and Appendix.

Petitions for extension of time—second and subsequent extensions

13.5 Up to three extensions of time are granted, provided that they do not prejudice the preparation for the hearing or its proposed date. A petition for a fourth extension of time, and any subsequent petitions, may, at the discretion of the Head of the Judicial Office, be referred to an Appeal Committee.

Respondents' consent

13.6 Respondents are expected not to withhold unreasonably their consent to a petition for extension of time. If consent is refused, the petition must be endorsed with a certificate that it has been served on the respondents. The petition is then referred to an Appeal Committee. In that event, eight copies of the petition must be lodged, together with the prescribed fee.

Lodgment

13.7 When the Statement and Appendix are ready, one master plus seven copies of the Statement, eight copies of Part 1 of the Appendix and 15 copies of

Parts 2 etc. (if any) must be lodged at the Judicial Office with the prescribed fee. The appellants must at the same time apply to set down the appeal for hearing.

14 Setting Down for Hearing

14.1 An appeal is set down for hearing at the same time as the appellants lodge the Statement and Appendix.

14.2 Once an appeal has been set down for hearing, it may be called on at any time. Certain directions, for example directions 15.13–15.14, may be dispensed with to enable an appeal to be called on at short notice.

Estimates of length of time needed for hearing of appeal

14.3 Within seven days of the setting down of an appeal, each party must notify the Judicial Office of the number of hours that their counsel estimate to be necessary for each of them to address the Appellate Committee. Subject to any directions by the Appellate Committee before or at the hearing, counsel are expected to confine their submissions to the time indicated in their estimates. The Judicial Office should be informed at once of any alteration to the original estimate.

14.4 The average length of appeals before the Appellate Committee is two days, and appeals are listed for hearing on this basis. Estimates of more than two days must be explained in writing to the Head of the Judicial Office and may be referred to the Law Lords.

15 Appellant's and Respondent's Cases

15.1 The case is the statement of a party's argument in the appeal.

15.2 The case should be confined to the heads of argument that counsel propose to submit at the hearing and omit material contained in the Statement of facts and issues. The members of the Appeal Committee who gave leave to appeal may not be sitting on the Appellate Committee; and so it cannot be assumed that the members of the Appellate Committee will be familiar with the arguments set out in the petition for leave to appeal.

15.3 Page 1 of the case should set out the title of the party on whose behalf it is lodged.

15.4 If either party is abandoning any point taken in the courts below, this should be made plain in their case. If they intend to apply in the course of the hearing for leave to introduce a new point not taken below, this should also be indicated in their case and the Judicial Office informed. If such a point involves the introduction of fresh evidence, application for leave must be made either in the case or by lodging a petition for leave to adduce the fresh evidence.

15.5 If a party intends to invite the House to depart from one of its own decisions, this intention must be clearly stated in a separate paragraph of their case, to which special attention must be drawn. A respondent who wishes to contend that a decision of the court below should be affirmed on grounds other than those relied on by that court must set out the grounds for that contention in their case.

15.6 Transcripts of unreported judgments should only be cited when they contain an authoritative statement of a relevant principle of law not to be found in a reported case or when they are necessary for the understanding of some other authority.

15.7 All cases must conclude with a numbered summary of the reasons upon which the argument is founded, and must bear the signature of at least one counsel for each case to the appeal who has appeared in the court below or who will be briefed for the hearing before the House.

15.8 The lodgment of a case carries the right to be heard by two counsel, one of whom may be leading counsel. The fees of two counsel only for any party are allowed on taxation unless the Appellate Committee orders otherwise on application at the hearing.

Separate cases

15.9 All the appellants must join in one case. All the respondents must also join in one case, unless it can be shown that the interests of one or more of the respondents are distinct from those of the rest. If the respondents' interests are distinct, the agents who first lodge their case must certify in a letter to the Judicial Office as follows:

(a) 'We, as agents for the respondent(s) [name particular parties], certify that opportunity has been offered by us for joining in one case to the respondent(s) [name particular parties] whose interests are, in our opinion, similar to those set out in the case lodged by us'; or

(b) 'We, as agents for the respondent(s) [name particular parties], certify that the interests represented in the case lodged by us are, in our opinion, distinct from those of the remaining respondent(s).'

15.10 When one of the foregoing certificates has been given, all remaining respondents wishing to lodge a case must respectively petition to do so in respect of each of their separate cases. Such petitions (which must be lodged with the prescribed fee) must be consented to by the appellants, and must set out the reasons for separate lodgment.

15.11 Parties whose interests in the appeal are passive (for example, stakeholders, trustees, executors, etc.) are not required to lodge a separate case but should ensure that their position is explained in one of the cases lodged.

Joint case

15.12 The lodgment of a joint case on behalf of both appellants and respondents may be permitted in certain circumstances.

Lodgment and exchange of cases

15.13 No later than five weeks before the proposed date of the hearing, the appellants must lodge at the Judicial Office one master plus seven copies of their case and serve it on the respondents.

15.14 No later than three weeks before the proposed date of the hearing, the respondents must serve on the appellants a copy of their case in response and lodge at the Judicial Office one master plus seven copies of their case, as must any other party lodging a case (for example, an intervener or advocate to the court).

15.15 The number of copies of cases exchanged should be enough to meet the requirements of counsel and agents and should not usually exceed eight. To enable the appellants to lodge the bound volumes, the respondents and any other party who has lodged a case must also provide the appellants with 15 further copies of their case.

15.16 Following the exchange of cases, further arguments by either side may not without leave be submitted in advance of the hearing.

Form of cases

15.17 Cases must be produced on A4 paper, securely bound on the left, with:
- (a) numbered paragraphs;
- (b) capital letters down the inside margins;
- (c) references to Appendix and authorities on the outside margins; and
- (d) signatures of counsel at the end, above their printed names.

Scottish cases

15.18 Each party must include in their case to the House a copy of the case presented by them to the Court of Session, with a short summary of any additional reasons on which they propose to insist. If no case was presented to the Court of Session, each party must set forth in their case as shortly and succinctly as possible the reasons upon which they found their argument.

16 Bound Volumes

16.1 As soon as all cases have been exchanged, and no later than 14 days before the proposed date of the hearing, the appellants must lodge (in addition to the documents already lodged on setting down) 15 bound volumes, each containing:
- (a) petition(s) of appeal;
- (b) petition(s) of cross-appeal (if any);
- (c) Statement of facts and issues;
- (d) appellants' and respondents' cases, with cross-references on the outside margins to the Appendix and authorities volume(s);
- (e) case of the advocate to the court or intervener, if any;
- (f) Part 1 of the Appendix; and
- (g) index to the authorities volume(s).

Form of bound volumes

16.2 The bound volumes:

- (a) should be bound in the same manner as the Appendix, with plastic comb binding and blue card covers;
- (b) must include cut-out tabs for each of the documents set out in direction 16.1, with the name of the document on the tab;
- (c) must show on the front cover a list of the contents and the names and addresses of the agents for all parties;
- (d) must indicate on a sticker attached to the plastic spine the volume number and the short title of the appeal; and
- (e) should include a few blank pages at either end.

Provision of documents

16.3 To enable the appellants to produce the bound volumes, the respondents must provide the appellants' agents with a further 15 copies of the respondents' case in addition to the cases already exchanged.

16.4 Respondents should arrange with the appellants' agents for the delivery to them of such bound volumes as the respondents' counsel and agents require.

17 Authorities

17.1 Ten copies of all authorities that may be needed during the hearing must be lodged at the same time as the bound volumes. The authorities should be collected together into one or more volumes. The appellants are responsible for producing the authorities volumes and lodging them at the Judicial Office. To enable the appellants to lodge the volumes, the respondents must provide the appellants with ten copies of any authorities which the respondents require but which the appellants do not, or arrange with the appellants for their photocopying. Respondents should arrange with the appellants for the delivery to them of such authorities volumes as the respondents' counsel and agents require.

Form and content of authorities volumes

17.2 The authorities volumes should:

- (a) be A4 size, comb bound with green card covers;
- (b) have flexible covers;
- (c) separate each authority in the volume by numbered dividers;
- (d) contain an index to that volume; the first volume must also contain an index to all the volumes;
- (e) be numbered consecutively on the cover and spine with numerals at least point 72 in size for swift identification of different volumes during the hearing;
- (f) have printed clearly on the front cover the title of the appeal and the names of the agents for all parties;
- (g) have affixed to the plastic spine a sticker indicating clearly the volume number and short title of the appeal;

(h) include a few blank pages at either end;
(i) not be more than 2½cm (1 inch) thick.

17.3 The first volume(s) should contain citations from the C and L series of the Official Journal of the European Union; the Law Reports; the All England Reports; the Weekly Law Reports; Session Cases; the Scots Law Times; and the current edition of Halsbury's Laws. Subsequent volumes should contain all other material. In an appeal where there is a large number of authorities volumes, it is helpful to produce an index of indexes, separate from the index contained in the first authorities volume.

17.4 The authorities volumes should be lodged in the Judicial Office in separate containers from the bound volumes.

17.5 Where a case is not reported in the Law Reports or Session Cases, references to other recognized reports may be given (see direction 15.6). In Revenue appeals, Tax Cases may be cited but, wherever possible, references to the case in the Law Reports or Session Cases should also be given.

17.6 In order to produce the authorities volumes, parties may download text from electronic sources; but the authorities volumes may only be lodged in paper form.

17.7 In certain circumstances (for example, when during the hearing before the Appellate Committee it becomes apparent that a particular authority is needed but is not in the authorities volume), the House of Lords Library can arrange for copies of authorities to be made available at the hearing. Parties must themselves provide ten copies of any other authority or of unreported cases. They must similarly provide copies of any authority of which notice has not been given.

17.8 The cost of preparing the authorities volumes falls to the appellants, but is ultimately subject to the decision of the House as to the costs of the appeal.

18 Notice of Hearing

18.1 Once an appeal has been set down, it may be called on at any time, possibly at short notice.

18.2 The Judicial Office lists appeals to meet the convenience of all the parties. Provisional dates are agreed with the parties well in advance of the hearing and every effort is made to keep to these dates. Counsel, agents and parties are however advised to hold themselves in readiness during the week before and the week following the provisional date given. Agents receive formal notification shortly before the hearing.

18.3 Parties should inform the Judicial Office as early as possible of the names of counsel they have briefed.

18.4 Appellate Committees usually hear appeals on Mondays from 11am–1pm and from 2–4pm, and on Tuesdays to Thursdays from 10.30am–1pm and 2–4pm. Hearings take place in Committee Room 1.

19 Costs

19.1 If counsel seek an order other than that costs should be awarded to the successful party, they may make written submissions within 14 days of the conclusion of the hearing. One master plus seven copies of the written submissions must be lodged at the Judicial Office. Copies should also be sent to the other parties to the appeal.

Conditional fee agreements

19.2 Conditional fee agreements may properly be made by parties to appeals before the House of Lords It is open to the Taxing Officer to reduce the percentage uplift recoverable under a conditional fee agreement if he considers it to be excessive. The Taxing Officer decides questions of percentage uplift in accordance with the principles set out in Designers Guild Limited v Russell Williams (Textiles) Limited (trading as Washington DC) [2003] 2 Costs LR 204. If a party appearing before the House seeks a ruling that the percentage uplift provided for in a conditional fee agreement should be wholly disallowed on legal grounds, such a ruling should (unless otherwise ordered) be expressly sought from the House before the end of the hearing.

Submissions at judgment

19.3 If submissions on costs have not been made pursuant to direction 19.1, it may be appropriate for submissions on costs to be made in the light of the result of the appeal. In such cases the House postpones making an order for costs in order to allow the parties to make written submissions, usually within 14 days of the date on which judgment is given. One master plus seven copies of the submissions must be lodged at the Judicial Office, and copies sent to the other parties to the appeal.

19.4 The costs submissions are considered on the papers alone.

20 Judgment

Place and time of judgment

20.1 Judgments are given in the Chamber of the House of Lords, usually on Wednesdays at 9.45 am. Agents are notified of the date. One week's notice is normally given.

Attendance of counsel

20.2 One junior of counsel for each party or group of parties who have lodged a case is required to attend at the Bar of the House when judgment is delivered. Queen's Counsel may attend instead, but only a junior's fee is allowed on taxation. It is the convention that Queen's Counsel wear full-bottomed wigs when appearing at the Bar of the House. Counsel instructed to attend judgment must be familiar with the subject matter of the appeal and with the options for its disposal.

Conditions under which judgments are released in advance

20.3 The opinions of the Law Lords who sat on the Appellate Committee and the questions to be put to the House to dispose of the appeal are available to certain persons before judgment is given. When judgment is given on a Wednesday morning, these documents are made available to counsel from 10.30 am on the previous Friday morning. They may be collected from the Judicial Office. In releasing these documents, the House gives permission for their contents to be disclosed to counsel, agents (including solicitors outside London who have appointed London agents) and in-house legal advisers in a client Government department. The contents of the documents and the result of the appeal must not be disclosed to the client parties themselves until judgment is given in the House.

20.4 It is the duty of counsel to check that the questions to be put to the House dispose of the appeal in accordance with the opinions of the members of the Appellate Committee. In the case of apparent error or ambiguity in the opinions, counsel are requested to inform the Judicial Office as soon as possible. This can be done at any time by e-mail to lawlords@parliament.uk, and no later than 4 pm on the Monday before judgment.

20.5 Accredited members of the media may also be given in advance of judgment the Appellate Committee's opinions and the questions to be put to the House to dispose of the appeal. The contents of these documents are subject to a strict embargo, and are not for publication, broadcast or use on club tapes before judgment has been delivered. The documents are issued in advance on the strict understanding that no approach is made to any person or organisation about their contents before judgment is given.

21 Order of the House

Draft order

21.1 After the House has given judgment, drafts of the order of the House are sent to all parties who lodged a case. The drafts must be returned to the Judicial Office within seven days of the date of receipt (unless otherwise directed), either approved or with suggested amendments. If amendments are proposed, they must be submitted to the agents for the other parties, who should indicate their approval or disagreement both to the agents submitting the proposals and to the Judicial Office. Where the amendments proposed are contrary to the questions put to and agreed by the House, a petition must be lodged.

Final order

21.2 The final order is sent free of charge to the agents for the successful parties.

21.3 Prints of the final order are sent free of charge to the agents for all parties who have entered appearance.

22 Bills of Costs

22.1 Bills of costs for taxation (assessment of costs) should be lodged within three months from the date of judgment or the date on which a petition of appeal is withdrawn (see direction 45).

22.2 The practice directions relating to judicial taxations and forms of bills of costs are available from the Judicial Office and at www.parliament.uk. Fees are payable on taxation of a bill of costs.

23 Disposal; of Security Money

23.1 When the appellants are ordered to pay the costs of the appeal, the respondents' costs are met in whole or in part by direct payment to the respondents of the money deposited in the Security Fund (see direction 10), unless the parties have come to some other arrangement.

23.2 If the total amount of the respondents' costs can be met from the money paid into the Security Fund, any balance is repaid to the party who paid it in.

23.3 If the respondents' costs are only partly met by such payment, any certificate of taxation which is forwarded to the respondents takes account of the amount so paid.

23.4 In appeals where more than one bill of respondents' costs is to be paid by the appellants, and the money deposited as security is not enough to meet all the bills, the money is divided between the bills in proportion to their amounts as allowed on taxation or in proportion to the amounts agreed by the respondents.

23. If the appellants are not ordered to pay the costs of the appeal, money paid into the Security Fund is returned to them when the final judgment order has been issued.

23.6 If an appeal is withdrawn before setting down or is dismissed for want of prosecution, or if the respondent fails to lodge a bill of costs or an application for extension of time within three months of the date of judgment (see direction 22), the appellants may apply in writing to the Judicial Office for the return to them of the money deposited in the Security Fund. The application must be accompanied by the written consent of all the respondents who have entered appearance. If any respondent refuses consent, the appellants may send them a written demand to lodge a bill of costs within four weeks from the date of notice. If the Clerk of the Parliaments is satisfied that such a demand was duly sent and if the respondent fails to lodge a bill of costs within the time specified, the money in the Security Fund is returned to the appellants.

****

29 Consolidation and Conjoinder

29.1 Where the issues in two or more appeals are similar, it may be appropriate for them to be consolidated or conjoined.

29.2 Consolidation results in the appeals being conducted as a single cause with one set of counsel and one case only on each side and with a single Appendix of documents.

29.3 Conjoinder is a looser linking of two or more appeals, and a number of variations is possible. Common forms of conjoinder are where: the appellants lodge separate cases with a separate junior for each appellant but a single leader; or the appellants lodge a single case with a single set of counsel but the respondents lodge separate cases and are separately represented.

29.4 The Judicial Office should be consulted on whether consolidation or some form of conjoinder is likely to be appropriate. A principal consideration should be to avoid wherever possible separate representation by counsel, or any duplication in the submissions made or in documents produced for the hearing.

29.5 Applications to consolidate or to conjoin appeals are made by petition. The petition must be signed by the agents for all petitioners and must be submitted to the agents for all the other parties who have entered appearance for the endorsement of their consent. If consent is refused, the petition must be endorsed with a certificate that it has been served on the agents in question.

29.6 If all parties consent to or join in the petition, one master plus one copy of the petition should be lodged, together with the prescribed fee.

29.7 If any party refuses their consent, one master plus five copies of the petition should be lodged, together with the prescribed fee. The petition is then referred to an Appeal Committee and may be determined after a hearing.

30 Cross-Appeals

30.1 The presentation of an appeal does not entitle a respondent to an appeal to present a cross-appeal. Leave to appeal is required. If leave to appeal has been given to the appellants by an Appeal Committee of the House, application for leave to cross-appeal may be made by the respondents directly to the Appeal Committee. If leave to appeal has been given by the Court of Appeal, then the respondents must first apply to the Court of Appeal for leave to cross-appeal and, if leave is refused, then to apply to the House.

30.2 A petition for leave to cross-appeal may only be lodged after leave to appeal has been granted to the original petitioner for leave to appeal. One master plus five copies of the petition for leave to cross-appeal must be lodged.

If leave to cross-appeal is granted, the petition of cross-appeal must be lodged with the prescribed fee within six weeks of the presentation of the original appeal. One master plus seven copies of the petition of cross-appeal must be lodged. In a petition of cross-appeal, the original appellant in the House of Lords is designated as original-appellant/cross-respondent and the original respondent is designated as original respondent/ cross-appellant.

A cross-appeal may be presented out of time in accordance with direction 7.3.

30.3 No security for costs is required in cross-appeals (direction 10.5).

30.4 Argument in respect of a cross-appeal must be included by each party in their case in the original appeal. Such an inclusive case must clearly state that it is lodged in respect of both the original and cross-appeals.

30.5 In a cross-appeal, the cases on the original appeal must be lodged in accordance with direction 15.13, ie five weeks before the hearing. The cross-appellants' case for the cross-appeal must be lodged in accordance with direction 15.14, ie three weeks before the hearing as part of their reply to the original appellants' case. The original appellants/cross-respondents may reply to the case for the cross-appeal in their case lodged in the bound volumes.

30.6 There is only one Appendix for the original appeal and cross-appeal, and documents in respect of the appeal and cross-appeal must be included in the same Appendix. The original-appellants/crossrespondents are responsible for lodging the Statement and Appendix and setting the appeal and cross-appeal down for hearing (including payment of the fee).

31 Death of a Party

31.1 If a party to an appeal dies before the hearing, the appeal abates from the date of death (Standing Order X). Immediate notice of the death must be given in writing to the Judicial Office and to the other parties. The addition of a new party to represent the deceased person's interest cannot proceed until a petition for reviving the appeal has been agreed to by the House.

31.2 The petition for revivor must be lodged with the prescribed fee within three months of the date of notice of death. It must be accompanied by an affidavit explaining the circumstances in which it is being lodged. It must be endorsed with a certificate of service on the respondents.

31.3 If abatement takes place after the case for the deceased person has been lodged but before the appeal has been heard, the appellants must lodge a supplemental case setting out the orders of the House on reviving the appeal and information about the newly-added parties.

32 Dispute between parties settled

32 1It is the duty of counsel and solicitors in any pending appeal, if an event occurs which arguably disposes of the dispute between the parties, either to ensure that the appeal is withdrawn by consent or, if there is no agreement on that course, to bring the facts promptly to the attention of the House and to seek directions.

33 European Convention on Human Rights

Appeals notified under direction 9.11(a), (b) or (c).

33.1 Where an appeal involves a point notified under direction 9.11, the petition of appeal must include the words 'in accordance with the Human Rights Act 1998' at the appropriate place in the prayer of the petition. Details of the Convention right which it is alleged has been infringed and of the infringement must be set out in the Statement of facts and issues and dealt with in a separate paragraph of the cases of all parties to the appeal.

Appeals notified under direction 9.11(a)

33.2 The Crown has the right to be joined as a party in any appeal where the House is considering whether to declare that a provision of primary or subordinate legislation is incompatible with a Convention right. In any appeal where the House is considering, or is being asked to consider, whether to make, uphold or reverse such a declaration, whether or not the Crown is already a party to the appeal, the Head of the Judicial Office notifies the appropriate Law Officer(s)3.

33.3 Where such an issue is raised in respect of a judicial act, the Head of the Judicial Office notifies the Crown through the Treasury Solicitor as agent for the Lord Chancellor.

33.4 The person notified under direction 33.2 or 33.3 must within 21 days of receiving such notice, or such extended period as the Head of the Judicial Office may allow, serve on the parties and lodge at the Judicial Office a notice stating whether or not the Crown intends to intervene in the appeal; and the identity of the Minister or other person who is to be joined as a party to the appeal.

33.5 If a Minister or other person has already been joined to proceedings in the court below in accordance with the provisions of s 5 of the Human Rights Act 1998, the leave of the House is not required for the continued intervention of the Crown.

33.6 Once joined to the appeal, the case for the Minister or other person must be lodged in accordance with direction 15.

33.7 The House may order the postponement or adjournment of the hearing of the appeal for the purpose of giving effect to the provisions of this direction or the requirements of the Act. Appeals notified under direction 9.11(b) or (c).

33.8 Except as prescribed in direction 33.1, no special steps are required for appeals notified under direction 9.11(b) or 9.11(c).

34 European Court of Justice

34.1 Article 234 of the Treaty establishing the European Community provides:

1 The Court of Justice shall have jurisdiction to give preliminary rulings concerning:
    (a)   the interpretation of this Treaty;
    (b)   the validity and interpretation of acts of the institutions of the Community and of the European Central Bank;
    (c)   the interpretation of the statutes of bodies established by an act of the Council, where those statutes so provide.

2 Where such a question is raised before any court or tribunal of a Member State, that court or tribunal may, if it considers that a decision on the question is necessary to enable it to give judgment, request the Court of Justice to give a ruling thereon.

3 Where any such question is raised in a case pending before a court or tribunal of a Member State against whose decisions there is no judicial remedy under national law, that court or tribunal shall bring the matter before the Court of Justice.

34.2 When the House refuses leave to appeal to a petition which includes a contention that a question of Community law is involved, the House gives additional reasons for its decision not to grant leave to appeal (see direction 4.7). These reasons reflect the decision of the Court of Justice in CILFIT v Ministry of Health (Case C-283/81) which laid down the categories of case where the Court of Justice considered that no reference should be made to it, namely:

(a) where the question raised is irrelevant;
(b) where the Community provision in question has already been interpreted by the Court of Justice;
(c) where the question raised is materially identical with a question which has already been the subject of a preliminary ruling in a similar case; and
(d) where the correct application of Community law is so obvious as to leave no scope for any reasonable doubt.

34.3 The House may order a reference to the Court of Justice before determining whether to grant leave to appeal. In such circumstances proceedings on the petition for leave to appeal are stayed until the answer is received. The directions below apply as appropriate.

34.4 When the House intends to make a reference, the hearing is adjourned and the parties are invited to submit an agreed draft of the question(s) to be referred. A further Statement of facts and issues, for the use of the Court of Justice, may also be appropriate. The House then makes the reference, with or without opinions. At this stage the appeal may also be disposed of in part.

34.5 Within one month of the judgment of the Court of Justice, the parties must make written submissions to the Judicial Office on whether a further hearing before the Appellate Committee is necessary or on how the appeal is to be disposed of.

Further proceedings in the House of Lords

34.6 If a further hearing is required before the Appellate Committee, the parties may lodge supplemental cases.

34.7 If supplemental cases are lodged, then:

(a) no later than five weeks before the expected date of the further hearing, the appellants must lodge in the Judicial Office one master and seven copies of their supplemental case and also serve it on the respondents;
(b) no later than three weeks before the expected date of the further hearing, the respondents must lodge in the Judicial Office one master and seven copies of their supplemental case and also serve it on the appellants;
(c) no later than three weeks before the expected date of the further hearing, any other party lodging a case (eg an intervener or advocate to the court) must lodge in the Judicial Office one master and seven copies of their supplemental case, and also provide copies to the appellants and respondents.

34.8 As soon as all the supplemental cases have been exchanged, and no later than two weeks before the date of the expected hearing, the appellants must lodge 15 additional sets of bound volumes containing:

(a) appellants' and respondents' cases;
(b) cases of interveners etc, if any;
(c) judgment of the European Court of Justice;
(d) any additional authorities relied on that are not included in the original authorities volumes.

34.9 The Judicial Office supplies the Appellate Committee with the original bound volumes, appendices and authorities volumes.

Costs

34.10 The Court of Justice does not make orders for costs. The costs of the reference are included in the order of the House disposing of the appeal; and, if necessary, are taxed by the House's Taxing Officer.

Appendix 5

REFERENCES TO THE EUROPEAN COURT OF JUSTICE

CONTENTS

Article 234 EC Treaty pre-Treaty of Lisbon
Article 234 EC Treaty post-Treaty of Lisbon
Civil Procedure Rules 1998 (SI 1998/3132), Pt 68

ARTICLE 234 EC TREATY PRE-TREATY OF LISBON

The Court of Justice shall have jurisdiction to give preliminary rulings concerning:

(a) the interpretation of this Treaty;
(b) the validity and interpretation of acts of the institutions of the Community and of the ECB;
(c) the interpretation of the statutes of bodies established by an act of the Council, where those statutes so provide.

Where such a question is raised before any court or tribunal of a Member State, that court or tribunal may, if it considers that a decision on the question is necessary to enable it to give judgment, request the Court of Justice to give a ruling thereon.

Where any such question is raised in a case pending before a court or tribunal of a Member State against whose decisions there is no judicial remedy under national law, that court or tribunal shall bring the matter before the Court of Justice.

****

ARTICLE 234 EC TREATY POST-TREATY OF LISBON

The Court of Justice of the European Union shall have jurisdiction to give preliminary rulings concerning:

(a) the interpretation of the Treaties
(b) the validity and interpretation of acts of the institutions, bodies, offices or agencies of the Union and of the European Central Bank;
(c) the interpretation of the statutes of bodies established by an act of the Council, where those statutes so provide.

Where such a question is raised before any court or tribunal of a Member State, that court or tribunal may, if it considers that a decision on the question is necessary to enable it to give judgment, request the Court to give a ruling thereon.

Where any such question is raised in a case pending before a court or tribunal of a Member State against whose decisions there is no judicial remedy under national law, that court or tribunal shall bring the matter before the Court.

****

CIVIL PROCEDURE RULES 1998

SI 1998/3132

PART 68
REFERENCES TO THE EUROPEAN COURT

68.1 Interpretation

In this Part –

(a) 'the court' means the court making the order;
(b) 'the European Court' means the Court of Justice of the European Communities;
(c) 'order' means an order referring a question to the European Court for a preliminary ruling under –
 (i) article 234 of the Treaty establishing the European Community;
 (ii) article 150 of the Euratom Treaty;
 (iii) article 41 of the ECSC Treaty;
 (iv) the Protocol of 3 June 1971 on the interpretation by the European Court of the Convention of 27 September 1968 on Jurisdiction and the Enforcement of Judgments in Civil and Commercial Matters; or
 (v) the Protocol of 19 December 1988 on the interpretation by the European Court of the Convention of 19 June 1980 on the Law applicable to Contractual Obligations.

Amendments—Inserted by SI 2002/2058.

68.2 Making of order of reference

(1) An order may be made at any stage of the proceedings –

(a) by the court of its own initiative; or
(b) on an application by a party in accordance with Part 23.

(2) An order may not be made –

(a) in the High Court, by a Master or district judge;
(b) in a county court, by a district judge.

(3) The request to the European Court for a preliminary ruling must be set out in a schedule to the order, and the court may give directions on the preparation of the schedule.

Amendments—Inserted by SI 2002/2058.

68.3 Transmission to the European Court

(1) The Senior Master will send a copy of the order to the Registrar of the European Court.

(2) Where an order is made by a county court, the proper officer will send a copy of it to the Senior Master for onward transmission to the European Court.

(3) Unless the court orders otherwise, the Senior Master will not send a copy of the order to the European Court until –

(a) the time for appealing against the order has expired; or
(b) any application for permission to appeal has been refused, or any appeal has been determined.

Amendments—Inserted by SI 2002/2058.

68.4 Stay of proceedings

Where an order is made, unless the court orders otherwise the proceedings will be stayed until the European Court has given a preliminary ruling on the question referred to it.

Amendments—Inserted by SI 2002/2058.

PRACTICE DIRECTION
PD68 REFERENCES TO THE EUROPEAN COURT

This Practice Direction supplements CPR Part 68 (PD68)

References to the European Court

Wording of References

1.1 Where the court intends to refer a question to the European Court it will welcome suggestions from the parties for the wording of the reference. However the responsibility for settling the terms of the reference lies with the English court and not with the parties.

1.2 The reference should identify as clearly and succinctly as possible the question on which the court seeks the ruling of the European Court. In choosing the wording of the reference, it should be remembered that it will need to be translated into many other languages.

1.3 The court will incorporate the reference in its order. Scheduled to the order should be a document –

(1) giving the full name of the referring court;
(2) identifying the parties;
(3) summarising the nature and history of the proceedings, including the salient facts, indicating whether these are proved or admitted or assumed;
(4) setting out the relevant rules of national law;
(5) summarising the relevant contentions of the parties;
(6) explaining why a ruling of the European Court is sought; and
(7) identifying the provisions of Community law which it is being requested to interpret.

1.4 Where, as will often be convenient, some of these matters are in the form of a judgment, passages of the judgment not relevant to the reference should be omitted.

Transmission to the European Court

2.1 The order containing the reference, and the document scheduled to it, should be sent to The Senior Master, Room E115, Queen's Bench Division, Royal Courts of Justice, Strand, London WC2A 2LL, for onward transmission to the European Court.

2.2 The relevant court file should also be sent to the Senior Master at the above address.

European Court Information Note

3 There is annexed to this Practice Direction an Information Note issued by the European Court. The reference in the opening passage to Article 177 of the EC Treaty should now be read as a reference to Article 234.

Court of Justice of the European Communities

Information Note on References by National Courts
For Preliminary Rulings

The development of the Community legal order is largely the result of cooperation established between the Court of Justice of the European Communities and the national courts and tribunals through the preliminary ruling procedure provided for in Article 177 of the EC Treaty and the corresponding provisions of the ECSC and Euratom Treaties.[1]

1   A preliminary ruling procedure is also provided for by the protocols to several conventions concluded by the Member States, in particular the Brussels Convention on Jurisdiction and the Enforcement of Judgments in Civil and Commercial Matters.

In order to make this cooperation more effective, and thus to enable the Court of Justice to meet the expectations of national courts more suitably by providing answers to preliminary questions which are of assistance to them, this Note provides information for all interested parties, in particular the national courts.

The Note is for information only and does not have any regulatory or interpretative effect in relation to the provisions which govern the preliminary ruling procedure. It merely contains practical information which, in the light of experience accumulated in the application of the preliminary ruling procedure, may help to prevent the kind of difficulties which the Court has sometimes encountered.

1 Any court or tribunal of a Member State may ask the Court of Justice to interpret a rule of Community law, whether contained in the Treaties or in acts of secondary law, if it considers that that is necessary for it to give judgment in a case pending before it.

Courts against whose decisions there is no judicial remedy under national law must refer questions of interpretation arising before them to the Court of Justice, unless the Court has already ruled on the point or unless the correct application of the rule of Community law is obvious.[1]

1   Judgment in Case 283/81 *CILFIT v Ministry of Health* 1982 ECR 3415.

2 The Court of Justice has jurisdiction to rule on the validity of acts of the Community institutions. National courts may reject a pleas challenging the validity of an act. All national courts – even those whose decisions are still open to appeal – raising the question of the validity of a Community act must refer that question to the Court of Justice.[1]

1   Judgment in Case 314/85 *Foto-Frost v Hauptzollamt Lübeck-Ost* 1987 ECR 4199.

However, if a national court has serious doubts about the validity of a Community act on which a national measure is based, it may exceptionally suspend application of that measure temporarily or grant other interim relief with respect to it. It must then refer the question of validity to the Court of Justice, stating the reasons for which it considers that the Community act is not valid.[1]

1   Judgments in Joined Cases C-143/88 and C-92/89 *Zuckerfabrik Süderdithmarschen and Zuckerfabrik Soest* 1991 ECR I-415 and in Case C-465/93 *Atlanta Fruchthandelsgesellschaft* 1995 ECR I-3761.

3 Questions referred for a preliminary ruling must concern the interpretation or validity of a provision of Community law only, since the Court of Justice does not have jurisdiction to interpret national law or assess its validity. It is for the referring court to apply the relevant provision of Community law in the specific case pending before it.

4 The decision by which a national court or tribunal refers a question to the Court of Justice for a preliminary ruling may be in any form allowed by national law as regards procedural steps. The reference of a question or questions to the Court of Justice generally causes the national proceedings to be stayed until the Court gives its ruling, but the decision to stay proceedings is one which the national court alone must take in accordance with its own national law.

5 The decision making the reference and containing the question or questions referred to the Court will have to be translated by the Court's translators into the other official languages of the Community. Questions concerning the interpretation or validity of Community law are frequently of general interest and the Member States and Community institutions are entitled to submit observations. It is therefore desirable that the decision making the reference should be drafted as clearly and precisely as possible.

6 It must contain a statement of reasons which is succinct but sufficiently complete to give the Court, and those to whom the decision must be notified (the Member States, the Commission, and in certain cases the Council and the European Parliament), a clear understanding of the factual and legal context of the main proceedings.[1]

[1] Judgment in Joined Cases C-320/90, C-321/90 and C-322/90 *Telemarsicabruzzo* 1993 ECR I-393.

In particular, it must include an account of the facts which are essential for understanding the full legal significance of the main proceedings, an account of the points of law which may apply, a statement of the reasons which prompted the national court to refer the question or questions to the Court of Justice and, if need be, a summary of the arguments of the parties. The purpose of all this is to put the Court of Justice in a position to give the national court an answer which will be of assistance to it.

The decision making the reference must also be accompanied by copies of the documents needed for a proper understanding of the case, especially the text of the applicable national provisions. However, as the case-file or documents annexed to the decision making the reference are not always translated in full into the other official languages of the Community, the national court must make sure that its decision includes all the relevant information.

7 A national court or tribunal may refer a question to the Court of Justice for a preliminary ruling as soon as it finds that a ruling on the point or points of interpretation or validity is necessary to enable it to give judgment. It must be stressed, however, that it is not for the Court of Justice to decide issues of fact or differences of opinion as to the interpretation or application of rules of national law. It is therefore desirable that a decision to make a reference should not be taken until the national proceedings have reached a stage where the national court is able to define, if only hypothetically, the factual and legal context of the question. In any event, the administration of justice may well be best served by waiting to refer a question for a preliminary ruling until both sides have been heard.[1]

[1] Judgment in Case 70/77 *Simmenthal v Amministrazione delle Finanze dello Stato* 1978 ECR 1453.

8 The decision making the reference and the relevant documents are to be sent by the national court directly to the Court of Justice, by registered post (addressed to the Registry of the Court of Justice of the European Communities, L-2925 Luxembourg, telephone 352-43031). The Court Registry will stay in contact with the national court until judgment is given, and will send it copies of the various documents (written observations, Report for the Hearing, Opinion of the Advocate General). The Court will also send its judgment to the national court. It would be grateful to receive word that its judgment has been applied in the national proceedings and a copy of the national court's final decision.

9 Proceedings for a preliminary ruling before the Court of Justice are free of charge. The Court does not rule on costs.

Appendix 6

THE EUROPEAN COURT OF HUMAN RIGHTS

CONTENTS
European Convention on Human Rights

EUROPEAN CONVENTION ON HUMAN RIGHTS

****

Article 34 – Individual applications

The Court may receive applications from any person, non-governmental organisation or group of individuals claiming to be the victim of a violation by one of the High Contracting Parties of the rights set forth in the Convention or the protocols thereto. The High Contracting Parties undertake not to hinder in any way the effective exercise of this right.

Article 35 – Admissibility criteria

1 The Court may only deal with the matter after all domestic remedies have been exhausted, according to the generally recognised rules of international law, and within a period of six months from the date on which the final decision was taken.

2 The Court shall not deal with any application submitted under Article 34 that

(a) is anonymous; or
(b) is substantially the same as a matter that has already been examined by the Court or has already been submitted to another procedure of international investigation or settlement and contains no relevant new information.

3 The Court shall declare inadmissible any individual application submitted under Article 34 which it considers incompatible with the provisions of the Convention or the protocols thereto, manifestly ill-founded, or an abuse of the right of application.

4 The Court shall reject any application which it considers inadmissible under this Article. It may do so at any stage of the proceedings.

****

Article 41 – Just satisfaction

If the Court finds that there has been a violation of the Convention or the protocols thereto, and if the internal law of the High Contracting Party concerned allows only partial reparation to be made, the Court shall, if necessary, afford just satisfaction to the injured party.

****

Article 46 – Binding force and execution of judgments

1 The High Contracting Parties undertake to abide by the final judgment of the Court in any case to which they are parties.

2 The final judgment of the Court shall be transmitted to the Committee of Ministers, which shall supervise its execution

****

EUROPEAN COURT OF HUMAN RIGHTS RULES OF COURT

Rule 47 – Contents of an individual application

1 Any application under Article 34 of the Convention shall be made on the application form provided by the Registry, unless the President of the Section concerned decides otherwise. It shall set out

(a) the name, date of birth, nationality, sex, occupation and address of the applicant;
(b) the name, occupation and address of the representative, if any;
(c) the name of the Contracting Party or Parties against which the application is
made;
(d) a succinct statement of the facts;
(e) a succinct statement of the alleged violation(s) of the Convention and the relevant arguments;
(f) a succinct statement on the applicant's compliance with the admissibility criteria (exhaustion of domestic remedies and the six-month rule) laid down in Article 35 § 1 of the Convention; and
(g) the object of the application; and be accompanied by
(h) copies of any relevant documents and in particular the decisions, whether judicial or not, relating to the object of the application.

2 Applicants shall furthermore

(a) provide information, notably the documents and decisions referred to in paragraph 1 (h) of this Rule, enabling it to be shown that the admissibility criteria (exhaustion of domestic remedies and the six-month rule) laid down in Article 35 § 1 of the Convention have been satisfied; and

(b) indicate whether they have submitted their complaints to any other procedure of international investigation or settlement.

3 Applicants who do not wish their identity to be disclosed to the public shall so indicate and shall submit a statement of the reasons justifying such a departure from the normal rule of public access to information in proceedings before the Court. The President of the Chamber may authorise anonymity in exceptional and duly justified cases.

4 Failure to comply with the requirements set out in paragraphs 1 and 2 of this Rule may result in the application not being examined by the Court.

5 The date of introduction of the application shall as a general rule be considered to be the date of the first communication from the applicant setting out, even summarily, the object of the application. The Court may for good cause nevertheless decide that a different date shall be considered to be the date of introduction.

6 Applicants shall keep the Court informed of any change of address and of all circumstances relevant to the application.

****

Rule 49 – Individual applications

1 Where the material submitted by the applicant is on its own sufficient to disclose that the application is inadmissible or should be struck out of the list, the application shall be considered by a Committee unless there is some special reason to the contrary.

2 Where an application is made under Article 34 of the Convention and its examination by a Chamber seems justified, the President of the Section to which the case has been assigned shall designate a judge as Judge Rapporteur, who shall examine the application.

3 In their examination of applications Judge Rapporteurs

(a) may request the parties to submit, within a specified time, any factual information, documents or other material which they consider to be relevant;
(b) shall, subject to the President of the Section directing that the case be considered by a Chamber, decide whether the application is to be considered by a Committee or by a Chamber;
(c) shall submit such reports, drafts and other documents as may assist the Chamber or its President in carrying out their functions.

****

Rule 54 – Procedure before a Chamber

1 The Chamber may at once declare the application inadmissible or strike it out of the Court's list of cases.

2 Alternatively, the Chamber or its President may decide to

(a) request the parties to submit any factual information, documents or other material considered by the Chamber or its President to be relevant;

(b) give notice of the application to the respondent Contracting Party and invite that Party to submit written observations on the application and, upon receipt thereof, invite the applicant to submit observations in reply;

(c) invite the parties to submit further observations in writing.

3 Before taking its decision on the admissibility, the Chamber may decide, either at the request of a party or of its own motion, to hold a hearing if it considers that the discharge of its functions under the Convention so requires. In that event, unless the Chamber shall exceptionally decide otherwise, the parties shall also be invited to address the issues arising in relation to the merits of the application.

****

Rule 59 – Individual applications

1 Once an application made under Article 34 of the Convention has been declared admissible, the Chamber or its President may invite the parties to submit further evidence and written observations.

2 Unless decided otherwise, the parties shall be allowed the same time for submission of their observations.

3 The Chamber may decide, either at the request of a party or of its own motion, to hold a hearing on the merits if it considers that the discharge of its functions under the Convention so requires.

4 The President of the Chamber shall, where appropriate, fix the written and oral procedure.

****

Appendix 7

PRECEDENTS

CONTENTS

Notice of Appeal from Decision of Employment Tribunal
Rule 3(10) Letter
EAT Form 3
EAT Respondent's Answer
CA Form N161
Court of Appeal Grounds
CA Form N162
Order Remitting Appeal to EAT
Reference to ECJ order
Petition for Leave to Appeal
Petition to Appeal
Application to ECtHR

NOTICE OF APPEAL FROM DECISION OF EMPLOYMENT TRIBUNAL

EAT Form 1

Note: The Grounds set out in Section 7 can be provided in a separate document if they are lengthy, stating 'see attached grounds' in Section 7.

1. The appellant is (name and address of appellant).

FANNY SMITH, 6 FIREBRAND LANE, LITTLE PAIN, WILTS, WW2 3FF

2. Any communication relating to this appeal may be sent to the appellant at (*appellant's address for service, including telephone number if any*).

ADDRESS ABOVE

3. The appellant appeals from (here give particulars of the judgment, decision or order of the employment tribunal from which the appeal is brought including the location of the employment tribunal and the date).

JUDGMENT OF THE EMPLOYMENT TRIBUNALS, SITTING AT GREAT WORTHING, SENT TO THE PARTIES ON 16 JANUARY 2007

4. The parties to the proceedings before the employment tribunal, other than the appellant, were (names and addresses of other parties to the proceedings resulting in judgment, decision or order appealed from).

RESPONDENT: FRESCO PLC, FRESCO TOWERS, NOWHERE TECHNO PARK, BIG CITY

5. Copies of:

(a) the written record of the employment tribunal's judgment, decision or order and the written reasons of the employment tribunal;
(b) the claim (ET1);
(c) the response (ET3); and/or (*where relevant*);
(d) an explanation as to why any of these documents are not included; are attached to this notice.

PLEASE FIND ATTACHED A COPY OF THE JUDGMENT OF THE EMPLOYMENT TRIBUNAL, THE ET1 AND ET3

6. If the appellant has made an application to the employment tribunal for a review of its judgment or decision, copies of:

(a) the review application;
(b) the judgment;
(c) the written reasons of the employment tribunal in respect of that review application; and/or
(d) a statement by or on behalf of the appellant, if such be the case, that a judgment is awaited;

are attached to this Notice. If any of these documents exist but cannot be included, then a written explanation must be given.

NO APPLICATION HAS BEEN MADE FOR A REVIEW

7. The grounds upon which this appeal is brought are that the employment tribunal erred in law in that (*here set out in paragraphs the various grounds of appeal*).

(1) **Continuity of employment:** The Tribunal failed to apply the provisions of the Employment Rights Act 1996 relating to continuity of employment properly or at all and wrongly found the Claimant not to have the necessary continuity of employment to bring a claim for unfair dismissal:-

(a) The Tribunal found that the Claimant had been dismissed without notice on the 364th day of continuous employment with the Respondent.

(b) Based on this finding of fact the Tribunal went on to wrongly find that the Claimant did not have the requisite 1 year of continuous employment to bring a claim for unfair dismissal (section 108 ERA 1996).

(c) The Tribunal erred in failing to apply section 97(2) ERA 1996 which extended the Claimant's period of continuous employment beyond the date she was dismissed to the end of the minimum notice period she was otherwise entitled to under section 84 ERA 1996, being one week after the 364th day. The effective date of termination was therefore 1 year and 6 days after she commenced employment and the Tribunal was therefore wrong in law to find that she did not have the necessary continuity of employment to bring a claim for unfair dismissal under section 108 ERA 1996.

(2) **Reason for dismissal:** The Tribunal erred in finding the Claimant's conduct to have been the relevant potentially fair reason for the Claimant's dismissal. The decision was perverse:-

(a) The Claimant's conduct was not the reason out in the dismissal letter relied on by the Respondent, which stated the reason to be redundancy.

(b) No witness contended that conduct was the reason for the dismissal, nor was this suggested in any documentary evidence before the Tribunal.

(c) There was no evidence at all before the Tribunal of two of the three aspects of misconduct by the Claimant, relied upon by the Tribunal as the conduct in question (paragraph 54(ii) and (iii) of the written reasons). Those two matters appeared to be at the forefront of the Tribunal's reasoning, but the Tribunal failed to make a finding as to which was the principal reason for the dismissal. The absence of any evidence of two of the three aspects of misconduct is therefore a material error in the Tribunal's reasoning.

(d) In the premises, the Tribunal's conclusion that conduct was the reason for the dismissal was perverse, in that:

(i) it not the reason contended for by either party

(ii) it was unsupported by any evidence at all

(iii) it was unsupported by any findings of fact that the respondent had any such belief at the time of dismissal.

(3) **Fairness:** The Tribunal's finding that the dismissal was fair was perverse:-

(a) The only issue of possible misconduct of which there was any evidence before the Tribunal was the Claimant's failure to say good morning to Mr Smug, her line manager.

(b) It was common ground before the Tribunal that the Claimant had an impeccable disciplinary record and that Mr Smug was often rude and offensive to employees and had been rude and offensive to the Claimant the previous day.

(c) No Tribunal could reasonably regard a dismissal for not saying good morning as fair. To so find would fly in the face of recognised employment practice.

(d) In the premises, if this was the conduct which the Tribunal had in mind, the Tribunal's decision that the dismissal was fair is perverse.

(e) Alternatively, in so far as the Tribunal had in mind the two other aspects of misconduct mentioned in its reasons, as stated above, its findings on those aspects were perverse and the Tribunal's conclusion on fairness is therefore in error.

(4) **Reasons:** The Tribunal failed to give intelligible reasons for its findings as to misconduct by the Claimant or as to conduct having been the reason (or if more than one) the principal reason for the Claimant's dismissal.

    (a) The Tribunal gave no, or no adequate, reasons for those findings of misconduct:

        (i) the Tribunal made no findings of fact that the respondent held any belief that the Claimant had misconducted herself as set out at paragraph 54 of the Tribunal's written reasons;

        (ii) against that background, the Tribunal gave no reasons at all for concluding that the respondent held such a belief;

        (iii) the Tribunal made no findings and gave no reasons as to how such conduct set out in paragraph 54 could reasonably be characterise as misconduct, let alone gross misconduct.

    (b) As a result the Claimant is unable to ascertain why the Tribunal found as it did and why she lost.

    (c) The Tribunal have failed to give the reasons required by Rule 30 of the Employment Tribunal Rules of Procedure and the decision fails to comply with the requirements in *Meek v Birmingham City Council* [1987] IRLR 251.

Signed:

Date:

NB: The details entered on your Notice of Appeal must be legible and suitable for photocopying or electronic scanning. The use of black ink or typescript is recommended.

RULE 3(10) LETTER

Fanny Smith
6 Firebrand Lane
Little Pain
Wilts
WW2 3FF

The Registrar
Employment Appeal Tribunal
Audit House
58 Victoria Embankment
London
EC4Y 0DS

1 March 2008

Dear Madam,

RE: Fanny Smith v Fresco Plc

Thank you for your letter dated 27 February 2008, informing me that HHJ Harsh QC has directed that no further action be taken on my appeal pursuant to Rule 3(7) of the Employment Appeal Tribunal Rules and giving the judge's reasons for his opinion that my appeal discloses no reasonable grounds and/or is an abuse of process.

I write to express my dissatisfaction with the reasons given by HHJ Harsh QC and to request that the matter be heard before a judge under Rule 3(10) of the Employment Appeal Tribunal Rules.

Yours faithfully,

Ms F Smith

EAT FORM 3

EAT Form 3

Ref:

Appeal from decision of employment tribunal / certification officer

Respondent's Answer

Case name: .... v ....

1   The respondent is (*name and address of respondent*).

2   Any communication relating to this appeal may be sent to the respondent at (*respondent's address for service, including telephone number if any*).

3   The respondent intends to resist the appeal of (*here give the name of appellant*).

The grounds on which the respondent will relay are [the grounds relied upon by the employment tribunal/Certification Officer for making the judgment, decision or order appealed from] [and] [the following grounds]: (*here set out any grounds which differ from those relied upon by the employment tribunal or Certification Officer, as the case may be*).

4   The respondent cross-appeals from (*here give particulars of the decision appealed from*).

5   The respondent's grounds of appeal are: (*here state the grounds of appeal*).

Signed:

Date:

EAT RESPONDENT'S ANSWER

Note: The Respondent's Answer must be substantially in accordance with Form 3 (Rule 6(2)).

Appeal No: UKEAT/1110/06/ZT

IN THE EMPLOYMENT APPEAL TRIBUNAL

BETWEEN:

FANNY SMITH

Appellant

and

FRESCO PLC

Respondent

RESPONDENT'S ANSWER

The Respondent is FRESCO PLC, Fresco Towers, Nowhere Techno Park, Big City BB1 1GG.

Any communication relating to this appeal may be sent to the Respondent's solicitors whose address is as follows:

Smash, Grabbit and Run LLP
Flash House
Big City
DX 666 Big City
Tel: 020 9565 4526
Fax: 020 9565 8686

1. The Respondent intends to resist, in part, the appeal of Fanny Smith. The Employment Tribunal was right to find that Mrs Smith was fairly dismissed. The Employment Tribunal was not right to find that Mrs Smith did not have the requisite period of service for bringing a claim of unfair dismissal.

2. In resisting the appeal, the grounds on which the Respondent will rely are the grounds relied upon by the Employment Tribunal in its Judgment and the following grounds:

ANSWER TO APPEAL

3. The Tribunal made findings of fact which were (at the very least) permissible; crucially, that the Respondent's reason for dismissal was conduct. That finding of fact was properly supported by the evidence including the implied allegations as to the Appellant's conduct to be

found in the dismissal letter. It is not understood what the Appellant means by the decision not according with industrial relations practices.

4. In the premises, the Tribunal's decision was not perverse and discloses no error of law.

5. It is not right to dress up an appeal on the facts as an appeal on the law, merely because the appellant is dissatisfied with the result: *Hollister v National Farmers' Union* [1979] ICR 542 per Lord Denning MR at 552, 553.

ROBUSTER PLEADER

Date:

Signed:

Appeal No: UKEAT/1110/06/ZT

IN THE EMPLOYMENT APPEAL TRIBUNAL

BETWEEN:

COMPUTERSHARE INVESTOR SERVICES PLC

Appellant

and

MRS A JACKSON

Respondent

RESPONDENT'S ANSWER

Patrick Green
Henderson Chambers
2 Harcourt Buildings
Temple
London EC4Y 9DB
Tel: 020 7583 9020

Bevans
Grove House
Grove Road
Redland
Bristol BS6 6UL
DX 99880 Bristol Redland
Tel: 0117 923 7249
Fax: 0117 923 7253

CA FORM N161

Appellant's Notice

In the COURT OF APPEAL

Notes for guidance are available which will help you complete this form. Please read them carefully before you complete each section.

For Court use only	
Appeal Court Reference No.	
Date filed	

Seal

Section 1 — Details of the claim or case

Name of court: EMPLOYMENT APPEAL TRIBUNAL

Case or claim number: UKEAT/0007/08

Names of claimants/applicants/petitioner: FANNY SMITH

Names of defendants/respondents: FRESCO PLC

In the case or claim, were you the *(tick appropriate box)*

- [x] claimant
- [ ] applicant
- [ ] petitioner
- [ ] defendant
- [ ] respondent
- [ ] other *(please specify)* _____

Section 2 — Your (appellant's) name and address

Your (appellant's) name: Ms Fanny Smith

Your solicitor's name: n/a   *(if you are legally represented)*

Your (your solicitor's) address:

6 Firebrand Lane,
Little Pain,
Wilts,
WW2 3FF

reference or contact name:

contact telephone number: 01777 321 321

DX number:

N161 Appellant's Notice (10.00)

Printed on behalf of The Court Service

CA Form N161

Section 3	Respondent's name and address

Respondent's name: Fresco Plc

Solicitor's name: Smash, Grabbit and Run LLP   *(if the respondent is legally represented)*

Respondent's (solicitor's) contact address:

Flash House
Big City
BB1 2GG

reference or contact name:

contact telephone number: 0209 565 4526

DX number: 666 Big City

Details of other respondents are attached ☐ Yes ☑ No

Section 4	Time estimate for appeal hearing

Do not complete if appealing to the Court of Appeal

How long do you estimate it will take to put your appeal to the appeal court at the hearing?   Days / Hours / Minutes

Who will represent you at the appeal hearing?   ☐ Yourself   ☐ Solicitor   ☐ Counsel

Section 5	Details of the order(s) or part(s) of order(s) you want to appeal

Was the order you are appealing made as the result of a previous appeal?   Yes ☑   No ☐

Name of Judge: HHJ Harsh QC

Date of order(s): 28 May 2008

If only part of an order is appealed, write out that part (or those parts)

Was the case allocated to a track?   Yes ☐   No ☑

If Yes, which track was the case allocated to?   ☐ small claims track   ☐ fast track   ☐ multi-track

Is the order you are appealing a case management order?   Yes ☐   No ☑

Section 6 — Permission to Appeal

Has permission to appeal been granted?

        Yes ☐   complete box **A**   No ☑   complete box **B**

if you are asking for permission or it is not required

A
Date of order granting permission _____
Name of judge _____
Name of court _____

B
☐ I do not need permission
☑ I Fanny Smith _____
appellant seek permission to appeal the order(s) at **section 5** above.

Are you making any other applications?   Yes ☐   No ☑
If Yes, complete section 10

Is the appellant in receipt of legal aid certificate or a community legal service fund (CLSF) certificate?   Yes ☐   No ☑

Does your appeal include any issues arising from the Human Rights Act 1998?   Yes ☐   No ☐

Section 7 — Grounds for appeal

I (the appellant) appeal(s) the order(s) at **section 5** because:

see attached

CA Form N161   433

| Section 8 | Arguments in support of grounds |

My skeleton argument is:-

☐ set out below   ☐ attached   ☑ will follow within 14 days of filing this notice

I (the appellant) will rely on the following arguments at the hearing of the appeal:-

| Section 9 | What decision are you asking the appeal court to make? |

I (the appellant) am (is) asking that:-

(tick appropriate box)

- [✓] the order(s) at **section 5** be set aside

- [ ] the order(s) at **section 5** be varied and the following order(s) substituted :-

- [ ] a new trial be ordered

- [✓] the appeal court makes the following additional orders :-

> That I have permission to appeal in the Court of Appeal on my appeal;
>
> Alternatively, that my appeal be remitted to the Employment Appeal Tribunal to be heard there.

CA Form N161

| Section 10 | **Other applications** |

I wish to make an application for additional orders ☐ in this section

☐ in the Part 23 application form (N244) attached

Part A
I apply (the appellant applies) for an order (a draft of which is attached) that :-

because :-

Part B
I (we) wish to rely on :

☐ evidence in Part C
☐ witness statement (affidavit)

COURT OF APPEAL GROUNDS

Note: These grounds can either be set out in Section 7 of Form N161 (or in the case of a cross-appeal, Section 6 of Form N162) or, if separate, should be referred to in the relevant section 'see attached grounds' and filed and served together.

Case No: UKEAT/0007/08

IN THE COURT OF APPEAL
ON APPEAL FROM
THE EMPLOYMENT APPEAL TRIBUNAL

BETWEEN:

FRESCO PLC

Appellant

and

FANNY SMITH

Respondent

GROUNDS OF APPEAL

The Appellant appeals from the Order of the Employment Appeal Tribunal dated 28 May 2008, allowing Mrs Smith's appeal against the Judgment of the Employment Tribunal sitting at Great Worthing, sent to the parties on 30 May 2008, on the following grounds:

1. The Employment Appeal Tribunal was wrong to hold that the findings as to misconduct by the Employment Tribunal were perverse. There was some evidence of the misconduct found by the Tribunal, and the Tribunal was entitled to make the succinct findings of fact at paragraph 54.
2. The Employment Appeal Tribunal found that the Employment Tribunal's conclusions were contrary to the weight of the evidence. This is the wrong test and not a permissible basis upon which to hold that the Employment Tribunal has erred in law: *Chiu v British Aerospace plc* [1982] ICR 156, [1982] IRLR 83.
3. There was no 'overwhelming case' such as to justify the Employment Appeal Tribunal's conclusion that the Employment Tribunal's decision was perverse: *Yeboah v Crofton* [2002] EWCA Civ 794, [2002] IRLR 634.
4. Equally, the Employment Tribunal's finding that conduct was the principal reason for the Claimant's dismissal was a permissible one on the evidence and there was, again, both some evidence to support it and no overwhelming case to justify the Employment Appeal Tribunal holding the Employment Tribunal's finding to have been perverse.

5. Alternatively, if the Employment Appeal Tribunal was correct to allow the appeal, it was wrong to substitute a finding of unfair dismissal, when it had not itself heard the evidence. The proper course, if the appeal was to be allowed was to remit the case to be determined by either the original or a newly constituted Employment Tribunal.

ARABELLA SNIPE

Dated: 5 June 2008

CA FORM N162

Respondent's Notice

In the
Appeal Court Reference No.

Notes for guidance are available which will help you complete this form. Please read them carefully before you complete each section.

	For Court use only
Date filed	

Seal

Section 1 — Details of the claim or case

Name of court _____   Case or claim number _____

Name or title of case or claim _____

In the case or claim, were you the
(tick appropriate box)

- [ ] claimant
- [ ] applicant
- [ ] petitioner
- [ ] defendant
- [ ] respondent
- [ ] other *(please specify)* _____

Section 2 — Your (respondent's) name and address

Your (respondent's) name _____

Your solicitor's name _____ *(if you are legally represented)*

Your (your solicitor's) address

Your reference or contact name _____

Your contact telephone number _____

DX number _____

Details of other respondents are attached [ ] Yes   [ ] No

Section 3 — Time estimate for appeal hearing

Do not complete if appealing to the Court of Appeal

	Days	Hours	Minutes
How long do you estimate it will take to put your case to the appeal court at the hearing?			

Who will represent you at the appeal hearing?   [ ] Yourself   [ ] Solicitor   [ ] Counsel

N162 Respondent's Notice (04.07)   © Crown copyright 2007

CA Form N162

Section 4 — Details of the order(s) or part(s) of order(s) you want to appeal

Name of Judge

Date of order(s)

If only part of an order is appealed, write out that part (or those parts)

Section 5 — Permission to file a respondent's notice

Has permission to appeal been granted?

☐ Yes   complete box **A**   ☐ No   complete box **B**
if you are asking for permission or it is not required

A

Date of order granting permission _____

Name of judge _____

Name of court _____

B

☐ I do not need permission

☐ I _____ respondent('s solicitor) seek permission to appeal the order(s) at **section 4** above.

Are you making any other applications? If Yes, complete section 9	☐ Yes	☐ No
Is the respondent in receipt of legal aid certificate or a community legal service fund (CLSF) certificate?	☐ Yes	☐ No
Does your appeal include any issues arising from the Human Rights Act 1998?	☐ Yes	☐ No

| Section 6 | Grounds for appeal or for upholding the order |

I (the respondent)

☐ appeal(s) the order   ☐ wish(es) the appeal court to uphold the order on different or additional grounds

because:-

CA Form N162

Section 7	Arguments in support of grounds

My skeleton argument is:-

☐ set out below ☐ attached ☐ will follow within 14 days of receiving the appellant's skeleton arguments

I (the respondent) will rely on the following arguments at the hearing of the appeal:-

Section 8 — What decision are you asking the appeal court to make?

I (the respondent) am (is) asking that:-

(*tick appropriate box*)

☐ the order(s) at **section 4** be set aside

☐ the order(s) at **section 4** be varied and the following order(s) substituted :-

☐ a new trial be ordered

☐ the appeal court makes the following additional orders :-

☐ the appeal court upholds the order but for the following different or additional reasons

CA Form N162

Section 9	Other applications

I wish to make an application for additional orders ☐ in this section

☐ in the Part 23 application form (N244) attached

Part A
I apply (the respondent applies) for an order (a draft of which is attached) that :-

because :-

Part B
I (the respondent) wish(es) to rely on :

☐ evidence in Part C

☐ witness statement (affidavit)

Part C
I (the respondent) wish(es) to rely on the following evidence in support of this application:-

Statement of Truth	
I believe (the respondent believes) that the facts stated in Section 9 are true.	
Full name _____	
Name of respondent's solicitor's firm _____	
Signed _____	position or office held _____
Respondent ('s solicitor)	(if signing on behalf of firm or company)

CA Form N162

| Section 10 | Supporting documents |

Please tick the papers you are filing in your bundle:-

- ☐ your respondent's notice and any skeleton arguments (if separate);
- ☐ any witness statements or affidavits in support of any application included in section 5 or 9 of your notice or in a separate Part 23 application notice;
- ☐ any other affidavit or witness statement filed in support of your arguments;
- ☐ a copy of the legal aid or CLSF certificate (if legally represented); and
- ☐ any other documents directed by the court to be filed in your appeal *(give details)*.

Reasons why you have not supplied a document and date when you expect it to be available:-

Signed_____   Respondent/'s Solicitor

Click here to print form

ORDER REMITTING APPEAL TO EAT

*Note: This is a draft order to be used when the Court of Appeal gives permission to an appeal which seeks to overturn an appeal against an interim order of the EAT which would be best disposed by a consent order remitting that matter back to the EAT. For more details see para **4.90**.*

Appeal No: A2/2008/20025

IN HER MAJESTY'S COURT OF APPEAL (CIVIL DIVISION)
ON APPEAL FROM THE EMPLOYMENT APPEAL TRIBUNAL

BETWEEN:

LOOPY LOU

Appellant

and

LOPPY LIE

Respondent

MINUTE OF ORDER

UPON His Honour Judge Harsh QC having ordered that the Appellant's appeal should not proceed to a final hearing before the Employment Appeal Tribunal pursuant to rule 3(7) of the Employment Appeal Tribunal Rules of Procedure.

AND UPON the Appellant appealing that order.

AND UPON Lord Justice Fair granting the Appellant permission to appeal to the Court of Appeal, by an Order dated 16 April 2008.

AND UPON Lord Justice Fair giving as his reasons:

'The Employment Appeal Tribunal was wrong not to permit the Appellant's appeal to proceed to a full hearing, as the appeal discloses reasonably arguable grounds that the Employment Tribunal erred in law in finding the dismissal to be fair. The appeal should be heard before the Employment Appeal Tribunal.'

BY CONSENT:

IT IS ORDERED THAT:

1. The appeal against the Order of His Honour Judge Harsh QC be allowed.
2. The Order of His Honour Judge Harsh QC be varied to direct that the Appellant's appeal before the Employment Appeal Tribunal do proceed to a full hearing.
3. For the avoidance of doubt, the Appellant's appeal therefore be remitted to the Employment Appeal Tribunal for such hearing.

4. No Order for costs.

DATED this 25th day of April 2008

REFERENCE TO ECJ ORDER

IN THE COURT OF APPEAL
(ENGLAND AND WALES)

Claim No:

Before

Claimant

Respondent

An application was made by [application notice/letter] dated (*date*) *or* by [Counsel][solicitor] for (*party*) and was attended by (*insert text*).

The Judge [or Tribunal]

IT IS ORDERED that:

1. the question[s] set out in the Schedule to this Order concerning the interpretation [or validity] of (*specify Treaty provision or Community instrument or act concerned*) be referred to the Court of Justice of the European Communities for a preliminary ruling in accordance with Article 234 (formerly Article 177) of the Treaty establishing the European Economic Community.
2. all further proceedings in this claim be stayed until the Court of Justice has given its ruling on the said question[s] or until further order.

Schedule

Request for Preliminary Ruling of the Court of Justice of the European Communities

(Here set out a clear and succinct statement of the case giving rise to the request for the ruling of the European Court of Justice in order to enable the European Court of Justice to consider and understand the issues of Community Law raised and to enable Governments of member States and other interested parties to submit observations.

The statement of the case should:

(a) *identify the parties and summarise the nature and history of the proceedings;*
(b) *summarise the salient facts, indicating whether these are proved or admitted or assumed;*
(c) *make reference to the rules of national law (substantive and procedural) relevant to the dispute;*
(d) *summarise the contentions of the parties;*
(e) *explain why a ruling of the Court of Justice is sought, identifying the European Community provisions whose effect is in issue;*

(f) formulate, without avoidable complexity, the question(s) to which an answer is requested.)

The preliminary ruling of the Court of Justice of the European Communities is accordingly requested on the following question(s):

(here set out the questions, without avoidable complexity, on which the ruling is sought, identifying the Treaty provisions or other Acts, Instruments or Rules of Community Law concerned).

Dated:

PETITION FOR LEAVE TO APPEAL

IN THE HOUSE OF LORDS
ON APPEAL FROM HER MAJESTY'S COURT OF APPEAL (CIVIL DIVISION)
(ENGLAND)

Court of Appeal Ref: B3/2008/0066

Neutral citation of judgment appealed against: [2008] EWCA Civ 1575

BETWEEN:

FRESCO PLC

Respondents

and

FANNY SMITH

Petitioners

PETITION FOR LEAVE TO APPEAL

TO THE RIGHT HONOURABLE THE HOUSE OF LORDS

THE HUMBLE PETITION OF FANNY SMITH OF 6 FIREBRAND LANE, LITTLE PAIN, WILTS

PRAYING FOR LEAVE TO APPEAL SHOWS–

1. The Petitioner was a in the employ of the Respondent. The Respondent dismissed her without notice on 1st December 2007. She was given a dismissal letter on the same day which stated nothing more than *'You're sacked, get off the premises now!'*
2. The Petitioner brought a claim for unfair dismissal pursuant to Part X Employment Rights Act 1996 (ERA).
3. The Employment Tribunal found (a) that the Petitioner did not have the requisite 1 year's service to bring a claim for unfair dismissal (section 108 ERA) and (b) even if the Petitioner could bring such a claim, her dismissal, was in any event, fair.
4. The Petitioner appealed those findings to the EAT on the following grounds:

    (1) **Continuity of employment:** The Tribunal failed to apply the provisions of the Employment Rights Act 1996 relating to continuity of employment properly or at all and wrongly found the Claimant not to have the necessary continuity of employment to bring a claim for unfair dismissal:

(a) The Tribunal found that the Claimant had been dismissed without notice on the 364th day of continuous employment with the Respondent.

(b) Based on this finding of fact the Tribunal went on to wrongly find that the Claimant did not have the requisite 1 year of continuous employment to bring a claim for unfair dismissal (section 108 ERA 1996).

(c) The Tribunal erred in failing to apply section 97(2) ERA 1996 which extended the Claimant's period of continuous employment beyond the date she was dismissed to the end of the minimum notice period she was otherwise entitled to under section 84 ERA 1996, being one week after the 364th day. The effective date of termination was therefore 1 year and 6 days after she commenced employment and the Tribunal was therefore wrong in law to find that she did not have the necessary continuity of employment to bring a claim for unfair dismissal under section 108 ERA 1996.

(2) **Reason for dismissal:** The Tribunal erred in finding the Claimant's conduct to have been the relevant potentially fair reason for the Claimant's dismissal. The decision was perverse:

(a) The Claimant's conduct was not the reason out in the dismissal letter relied on by the Respondent, which stated the reason to be redundancy.

(b) No witness contended that conduct was the reason for the dismissal, nor was this suggested in any documentary evidence before the Tribunal.

(c) There was no evidence at all before the Tribunal of two of the three aspects of misconduct by the Claimant, relied upon by the Tribunal as the conduct in question (paragraph 54(ii) and (iii) of the written reasons). Those two matters appeared to be at the forefront of the Tribunal's reasoning, but the Tribunal failed to make a finding as to which was the principal reason for the dismissal. The absence of any evidence of two of the three aspects of misconduct is therefore a material error in the Tribunal's reasoning.

(d) In the premises, the Tribunal's conclusion that conduct was the reason for the dismissal was perverse, in that:

(i) it not the reason contended for by either party

(ii) it was unsupported by any evidence at all

(iii) it was unsupported by any findings of fact that the respondent had any such belief at the time of dismissal.

(3) **Fairness**: The Tribunal's finding that the dismissal was fair was perverse:

(a) The only issue of possible misconduct of which there was any evidence before the Tribunal was the Claimant's failure to say good morning to Mr Smug, her line manager.

(b) It was common ground before the Tribunal that the Claimant had an impeccable disciplinary record and that Mr Smug was often rude and offensive to employees and had been rude and offensive to the Claimant the previous day.

(c) No Tribunal could reasonably regard a dismissal for not saying good morning as fair. To so find would fly in the face of recognised employment practice.

(d) In the premises, if this was the conduct which the Tribunal had in mind, the Tribunal's decision that the dismissal was fair is perverse.

(e) Alternatively, in so far as the Tribunal had in mind the two other aspects of misconduct mentioned in its reasons, as stated above, its findings on those aspects were perverse and the Tribunal's conclusion on fairness is therefore in error.

(4) **Reasons:** The Tribunal failed to give intelligible reasons for its findings as to misconduct by the Claimant or as to conduct having been the reason (or if more than one) the principal reason for the Claimant's dismissal.

(a) The Tribunal gave no, or no adequate, reasons for those findings of misconduct:

(i) the Tribunal made no findings of fact that the respondent held any belief that the Claimant had misconducted herself as set out at paragraph 54 of the Tribunal's written reasons;

(ii) against that background, the Tribunal gave no reasons at all for concluding that the respondent held such a belief;

(iii) the Tribunal made no findings and gave no reasons as to how such conduct set out in paragraph 54 could reasonably be characterise as misconduct, let alone gross misconduct.

	(b)	As a result the Claimant is unable to ascertain why the Tribunal found as it did and why she lost.
	(c)	The Tribunal have failed to give the reasons required by Rule 30 of the Employment Tribunal Rules of Procedure and the decision fails to comply with the requirements in *Meek v Birmingham City Council* [1987] IRLR 251.
5.		The Respondent did not seek to uphold the Tribunal's findings set out in ground (1) above but did resist grounds (2) to (4).
6.		The EAT's judgment dated 28th May 2008 (UKEAT/0007/08) was to the effect that the Tribunal had erred in law as set out in grounds 1 to 4 above and held that the Tribunal's conclusion was perverse and unsupported by primary findings of fact. The Employment Appeal Tribunal also found that the Employment Tribunal had given inadequate reasons for its decision.
7.		The EAT substituted the judgment of the Employment Tribunal with one finding that the Petitioner had been unfairly dismissed and remitted that matter back to the Tribunal for a remedies hearing.
8.		The Respondent appealed that judgment to the Court of Appeal. That appeal was resisted by the Petitioner.
9.		The Respondent's grounds of appeal were:
	(1)	The Employment Appeal Tribunal was wrong to hold that the findings as to misconduct by the Employment Tribunal were perverse. There was some evidence of the misconduct found by the Tribunal, and the Tribunal was entitled to make the succinct findings of fact at paragraph 54.
	(2)	The Employment Appeal Tribunal found that the Employment Tribunal's conclusions were contrary to the weight of the evidence. This is the wrong test and not a permissible basis upon which to hold that the Employment Tribunal has erred in law: *Chiu v British Aerospace plc* [1982] ICR 156, [1982] IRLR 83.
	(3)	There was no 'overwhelming case' such as to justify the Employment Appeal Tribunal's conclusion that the Employment Tribunal's decision was perverse: *Yeboah v Crofton* [2002] EWCA Civ 794, [2002] IRLR 634.
	(4)	Equally, the Employment Tribunal's finding that conduct was the principal reason for the Claimant's dismissal was a permissible one on the evidence and there was, again, both some evidence to support it and no overwhelming case to justify the Employment Appeal Tribunal holding the Employment Tribunal's finding to have been perverse.
	(5)	Alternatively, if the Employment Appeal Tribunal was correct to allow the appeal, it was wrong to substitute a finding of unfair dismissal, when it had not itself heard the evidence. The proper

course, if the appeal was to be allowed was to remit the case to be determined by either the original or a newly constituted Employment Tribunal.
10. The Court of Appeal acceded to the Respondent's argument that if a reason for dismissal can be inferred from the terms of a dismissal letter, an Employment Tribunal is entitled to treat that implied reason as the reason for the dismissal and held that the decision was therefore not perverse and was adequately reasoned.
11. The Court of Appeal therefore set aside the EAT's judgment and restored the original judgment of the Employment Tribunal.
12. It is respectfully submitted that the Court of Appeal's judgment as set out above was wrong.
13. It is respectfully submitted that an employer cannot rely on a reason for dismissal which is not expressly stated in such a letter and, at best, can only be inferred from the terms of a dismissal letter, in particular where the reason found by the Tribunal is not contended for by either party and is unsupported by any evidence (at least on two aspects of the supposed misconduct set out in paragraph 54 of the Employment Tribunal's reasons).
14. The first point of law is in two parts and will affect the unfair dismissal rights of all employees. It goes to the fundamental nature of protection from unfair dismissal; namely, that:

(1) a dismissed employee is entitled to a clear and explicit statement of the reasons for dismissal; and

(2) in the absence of such a statement, an employment tribunal must not speculate by inference not contended for by either party.

15. The second point of law raised is the proper approach to the question of perversity of decisions of Employment Tribunals, upon which there are several differing decisions of the Court of Appeal, upon which authoritative guidance is desirable.
16. Accordingly it is respectfully submitted that this appeal raises important points of law of general public importance which ought to be considered by Your Lordships' House at this time.

YOUR PETITIONER HUMBLY SUBMITS that leave to appeal to Your Lordships' House

Should be granted for the following among other REASONS

(1) That the Court of Appeal's judgment was wrong
(2) That the appeal raises an important point of law of general public importance which ought to be considered by the House at this time.

AND YOUR PETITIONER WILL EVER PRAY

Signed: FANNY SMITH

Signature of petitioner

PETITION TO APPEAL

IN THE HOUSE OF LORDS

ON APPEAL FROM HER MAJESTY'S COURT OF APPEAL (CIVIL DIVISION)

(ENGLAND)

Court of Appeal Ref: B3/2008/0038

Neutral citation of judgment appealed against: [2008] EWCA Civ 1575

BETWEEN:

FRESCO PLC

Respondents

and

FANNY SMITH

Petitioners

PETITION OF APPEAL

TO THE RIGHT HONOURABLE THE HOUSE OF LORDS

THE HUMBLE PETITION AND APPEAL OF FANNY SMITH OF 6 FIREBRAND LANE, LITTLE PAIN, WILTS

YOUR PETITIONER

humbly prays that the matter of the Order set forth in the Schedule hereto may be reviewed before Her Majesty the Queen, in Her Court of Parliament, and that the said Order may be reversed, varied or altered or that the petitioner may have such other relief in the premises as to Her Majesty the Queen, in Her Court of Parliament, may seem meet.

Signed: FANNY SMITH

[signature of appellant(s) or their agents or counsel, as appropriate]

THE SCHEDULE REFERRED TO ABOVE

FROM HER MAJESTY'S COURT OF APPEAL (CIVIL DIVISION) (ENGLAND)

In a certain cause wherein FANNY SMITH OF 6 FIREBRAND LANE, LITTLE PAIN, WILTS was Claimant and FRESCO PLC was Respondent

The Order of Her Majesty's Court of Appeal (Civil Division) (England) appealed from is in the words following:

1. Appeal allowed

2. The order of the Employment Tribunal dated 16 January 2007 is restored and the order of the Employment Appeal Tribunal dated 28th May 2008 is set aside.

And your Lordships gave leave to appeal to your Lordships' House on 14 October 2008.

APPLICATION TO ECTHR

Voir Note explicative
See Explanatory Note

Numéro de dossier
File-number

COUR EUROPÉENNE DES DROITS DE L'HOMME
EUROPEAN COURT OF HUMAN RIGHTS

Conseil de l'Europe – *Council of Europe*
Strasbourg, France

REQUÊTE
APPLICATION

présentée en application de l'article 34 de la Convention européenne des Droits de l'Homme,
ainsi que des articles 45 et 47 du règlement de la Cour

*under Article 34 of the European Convention on Human Rights
and Rules 45 and 47 of the Rules of Court*

IMPORTANT: La présente requête est un document juridique et peut affecter vos droits et obligations.
This application is a formal legal document and may affect your rights and obligations.

I. LES PARTIES
THE PARTIES

A. LE REQUÉRANT/LA REQUÉRANTE
THE APPLICANT

(Renseignements à fournir concernant le/la requérant(e) et son/sa représentant(e) éventuel(le))
(Fill in the following details of the applicant and the representative, if any)

1. Nom de famille ....
   Surname

2. Prénom(s)
   First name(s)

   Sexe : masculin / féminin   *Sex: male / female*

3. Nationalité ....
   Nationality

4. Profession
   Occupation

5. Date et lieu de naissance
   Date and place of birth

6. Domicile
   Permanent address

7. Tel. N°

8. Adresse actuelle (si différente de 6.)
   Present address (if different from 6.)

9. Nom et prénom du/de la représentant(e)[1]
   *Name of representative**

10. Profession du/de la représentant(e)
    Occupation of representative

11. Adresse du/de la représentant(e)
    Address of representative

12. Tel. N° ....   Fax N°

B. LA HAUTE PARTIE CONTRACTANTE
THE HIGH CONTRACTING PARTY

(Indiquer ci-après le nom de l'Etat/des Etats contre le(s)quel(s) la requête est dirigée)
(Fill in the name of the State(s) against which the application is directed)

13.

---

[1] Si le/la requérant(e) est représenté(e), joindre une procuration signée par le/la requérant(e) et son/sa représentant(e).
If the applicant appoints a representative, attach a form of authority signed by the applicant and his or her representative.

II. EXPOSÉ DES FAITS
STATEMENT OF THE FACTS

(Voir chapitre II de la note explicative)
(See Part II of the Explanatory Note)

14.

Si nécessaire, continuer sur une feuille séparée
Continue on a separate sheet if necessary

- 4 -

III. EXPOSÉ DE LA OU DES VIOLATION(S) DE LA CONVENTION ET/OU DES PROTOCOLES ALLÉGUÉE(S), AINSI QUE DES ARGUMENTS À L'APPUI
STATEMENT OF ALLEGED VIOLATION(S) OF THE CONVENTION AND/OR PROTOCOLS AND OF RELEVANT ARGUMENTS

(Voir chapitre III de la note explicative)
(See Part III of the Explanatory Note)

15.

IV. EXPOSÉ RELATIF AUX PRESCRIPTIONS DE L'ARTICLE 35 § 1 DE LA CONVENTION
STATEMENT RELATIVE TO ARTICLE 35 § 1 OF THE CONVENTION

(Voir chapitre IV de la note explicative. Donner pour chaque grief, et au besoin sur une feuille séparée, les renseignements demandés sous les points 16 à 18 ci-après)
(See Part IV of the Explanatory Note. If necessary, give the details mentioned below under points 16 to 18 on a separate sheet for each separate complaint)

16. Décision interne définitive (date et nature de la décision, organe – judiciaire ou autre – l'ayant rendue)
    Final decision (date, court or authority and nature of decision)

17. Autres décisions (énumérées dans l'ordre chronologique en indiquant, pour chaque décision, sa date, sa nature et l'organe – judiciaire ou autre – l'ayant rendue)
    Other decisions (list in chronological order, giving date, court or authority and nature of decision for each of them)

18. Dispos(i)ez-vous d'un recours que vous n'avez pas exercé? Si oui, lequel et pour quel motif n'a-t-il pas été exercé?
    Is there or was there any other appeal or other remedy available to you which you have not used? If so, explain why you have not used it.

Si nécessaire, continuer sur une feuille séparée
Continue on a separate sheet if necessary

V. EXPOSÉ DE L'OBJET DE LA REQUÊTE
STATEMENT OF THE OBJECT OF THE APPLICATION

(Voir chapitre V de la note explicative)
(See Part V of the Explanatory Note)

19.

VI. AUTRES INSTANCES INTERNATIONALES TRAITANT OU AYANT TRAITÉ L'AFFAIRE
STATEMENT CONCERNING OTHER INTERNATIONAL PROCEEDINGS

(Voir chapitre VI de la note explicative)
(See Part VI of the Explanatory Note)

20. Avez-vous soumis à une autre instance internationale d'enquête ou de règlement les griefs énoncés dans la présente requête? Si oui, fournir des indications détaillées à ce sujet.
Have you submitted the above complaints to any other procedure of international investigation or settlement? If so, give full details.

VII. PIÈCES ANNEXÉES (PAS D'ORIGINAUX, UNIQUEMENT DES COPIES ; PRIÈRE DE N'UTILISER NI AGRAFE, NI ADHÉSIF, NI LIEN D'AUCUNE SORTE)

LIST OF DOCUMENTS (NO ORIGINAL DOCUMENTS, ONLY PHOTOCOPIES, DO NOT STAPLE, TAPE OR BIND DOCUMENTS)

(Voir chapitre VII de la note explicative. Joindre copie de toutes les décisions mentionnées sous ch. IV et VI ci-dessus. Se procurer, au besoin, les copies nécessaires, et, en cas d'impossibilité, expliquer pourquoi celles-ci ne peuvent pas être obtenues. Ces documents ne vous seront pas retournés.)
(See Part VII of the Explanatory Note. Include copies of all decisions referred to in Parts IV and VI above. If you do not have copies, you should obtain them. If you cannot obtain them, explain why not. No documents will be returned to you.)

21. a)

b)

c)

VIII. DÉCLARATION ET SIGNATURE
DECLARATION AND SIGNATURE

(Voir chapitre VIII de la note explicative)
(See Part VIII of the Explanatory Note)

Je déclare en toute conscience et loyauté que les renseignements qui figurent sur la présente formule de requête sont exacts.
I hereby declare that, to the best of my knowledge and belief, the information I have given in the present application form is correct.

Lieu/*Place*

Date/*Date*

(Signature du/de la requérant(e) ou du/de la représentant(e))
(Signature of the applicant or of the representative)

INDEX

References are to paragraph numbers.

Agreed bundle 3.333
  documents required 3.334, 3.335
  lodging of 3.336, 3.337
  number of copies required 3.336
  parties unable to agree 3.338
Amendments
  grounds of appeal to 3.243–3.247
Appeals
  agreed bundle 3.333–3.338
  bias 1.8, *see also* Bias
  case tracks 3.158, 3.159, 3.161
  chairmen 3.262
  consent to withdraw or
    abandon 3.387–3.390
  costs 3.392–3.401
  Court of Appeal to *see* Court of
    Appeal
  cross-appeals 1.16, 3.185, 3.186, 3.188,
    3.216–3.218, 3.220–3.222
  debarring orders 3.304, 3.305
  decisions 3.7
    reasons 3.12–3.14
  Employment Appeal Tribunal *see*
    Employment Appeal
    Tribunal
  employment judge 3.262
  employment tribunals, from 1.25
  enforcement of awards 3.417
  extension of time limits 3.84–3.110
  full hearings 1.16, 3.200, 3.327,
    3.328, 3.329, 3.330, 3.331,
    3.332, *see also* Full hearings
  funding
    Equality and Human Rights
      Commission 3.424, 3.425
    insurance 3.419, 3.420
    legal aid 3.421–3.423
    legal expenses 3.418
  grounds of appeal 1.30, 1.31, 1.32,
    1.33, 1.45, 1.46, 1.47, 1.48,
    3.120, 3.121, 3.122, 3.123,
    3.124, 3.125, 3.126, 8.1, *see
    also* Grounds of appeal
  House of Lords to *see* House of
    Lords
  illustrative example 1.14, 1.15
  initiating proceedings 1.16

Appeals—*continued*
  interim applications 3.34–3.36, 3.296, 3.297
  introduction 1.1–1.7, 1.10–1.13, 1.16, 3.1–3.6
  joinder of parties 3.323
  judgments 3.8–3.11, 3.374–3.380
  judicial precedent 1.54–1.57
  key practice points 1.8
  last minute appeals 3.127–3.129
  litigants in person 3.290–3.292
  lodging of appeal 3.49
    documents required 3.50
  national security 3.324–3.326
  nature of 1.30, 1.31
  new evidence 3.254–3.261
  new points of law 3.248–3.253
  not contested 3.204
  not validly lodged 3.130, 3.131, 3.133
  notice of appeal 3.116–3.118
    documents accompanying 3.130, 3.131, 3.133, 3.135–3.137
      copies acceptable 3.134
    lodged early 3.111–3.115
    lodges out of time 1.18
    particulars 3.119
    receipt by EAT 3.76–3.80
    service 3.81–3.83
  oral evidence 1.17
  orders 3.8, 3.10, 3.11
  overlapping, both parties by 1.18
  parallel appeals 3.223–3.226, 3.228–3.242
  preliminary hearings 1.16, 3.183, 3.184
  preparation of documents 1.16
  question of law 1.8, 1.30, 3.2, 3.15, 8.4–8.15
    material errors 3.16–3.18
  remission of cases 3.381–3.386
  response to claims 1.16, 3.202, 3.203
  restricted reporting orders 3.307–3.316
  review of judgments and
    decisions 2.7–2.10
  rules of procedure 3.22–3.28
    early applications 3.31, 3.32
    non-compliance 3.29–3.32
  service of documents 3.154–3.157
  sifting and filtering 1.16, 3.162–3.172
  'slip' rule 3.403
  source of materials 1.9
  stay of proceedings 3.160, 3.298

Appeals—*continued*
   time limits 1.8, 1.16, 1.19–1.24, 3.51–3.55,
                                              3.57
      lodging of notice of appeal   1.8, 1.16,
                            1.18, 1.20, 1.42, 3.56
        orders and judgments   3.58–3.66
          illustrative examples   3.67–3.75
   'unless orders'   3.10
   vexations proceedings   3.317–3.322
   waiver of rules   3.301–3.303
   withdrawal of   3.205
   witness orders   3.299, 3.300
   written reasons of employment
      tribunal   3.138, 3.139, 3.151–3.153
        not available   3.140–3.142
          powers of EAT   3.142
        not sought   3.144–3.146
        reasons refused   3.150
        waiting for   3.147–3.149

Bias *see also* Grounds of appeal
   appeals   1.8
   grounds of appeal   1.48, 3.123–3.126,
                         8.123, 8.125–8.128
      evidence   8.129–8.131
      excessive intervention   8.139
      financial interest and   8.133, 8.134
      personal relationships and   8.132
      pre-judging   8.136, 8.137
      prejudices   8.138
      previous conduct   8.135
***Burns/Barke* procedure**   3.189–3.191,
        8.174–8.186, 8.202, 8.203, 10.4,
                                      10.5

Case tracks   3.158, 3.159, 3.161
Chairmen *see also* Employment judge
   new title of employment judge   3.262
   notes of   3.262
      directions from EAT   3.288
      parties disputing   3.293–3.295
      practical application of   3.268–3.274,
                                       3.286
        provision to parties   3.289
        requirement for   3.263–3.267
Civil Procedure Rules
   costs of assisted person   3.401
   guidance for EAT, as   3.48
   overriding objective   3.46
   references to ECJ   6.9–6.11
Commencing proceedings
   lodging an appeal   3.49
   documents required   3.50
Convention for the Protection of
   Human Rights and Fundamental
   Freedoms 1950
   employment proceedings and   7.1
Costs
   assessment   3.396, 4.145
   assisted person   3.401, 4.148
      Civil Procedure Rules   3.401
   EAT order   3.392–3.394
   generally   3.392–3.394, 4.143

Costs—*continued*
   House of Lords   5.63, 5.64
   litigants in person   3.400
   misconceived proceedings   3.392
   orders   4.144
   procedure   3.395
   unreasonable delay   3.392
   vexatious conduct   3.392
   wasted costs order   3.397–3.399
Court of Appeal
   appeals against decision of   1.29
      permission to appeal   1.29
   appeals by consent   4.139–4.141
   appeals to
      EAT interim hearing from   4.90, 4.91
      EAT preliminary hearing from   4.90,
                                         4.91
      extension of time limits   4.83–4.88
      introduction   4.1–4.9
      new argument   4.127
      new evidence   4.126
      no 'leapfrog' to House of Lords 3.415,
                                        3.416
      not classified as 'second appeal' 3.410,
                               3.411, 4.11, 4.12
      statistics   4.150
      time limits   3.409
   appeals without merit   4.142
   case management
      amendments to notices   4.115
      Deputy Master, role of   4.117, 4.118
      Master, role of   4.117, 4.118
      powers of   4.114
      security for costs   4.116
   composition   4.152
   costs
      assessment   4.145
      assisted person   4.148
      generally   4.143
      litigants in person   4.147
      orders   4.144
      re-opening of appeal   4.149
   cross-appeals   4.75–4.81
   final hearing   4.132–4.135
   full hearing of appeal   4.119, 4.120
      appeal questionnaire   4.96–4.98
      appellant's supplementary
         skeleton argument   4.101
      bundles of authorities   4.105–4.108,
                                       4.113
      filing of documents   4.109–4.112
      listing   4.99, 4.100
      respondent's skeleton
         argument   4.102–4.104
      service of appeal bundle   4.91, 4.93
      service of core bundle   4.95
      service of supplemental bundle 4.94
   nature of appeal   4.121–4.124
   no re-hearing   4.125
   oral evidence, no use of   4.125
   permission to appeal   1.22, 1.23,
                3.412–3.414, 4.1–4.9, 4.13,
                                 4.23–4.25
      appeal bundle   4.31, 4.34

Index

Court of Appeal—*continued*
  permission to appeal—*continued*
    appellant's notice 4.27, 4.28
    appellant's skeleton
      argument 4.35–4.38
    conditional permission 4.70–4.72, 4.74
    decision to grant 4.47–4.50, 4.58
    documents required 4.29, 4.30, 4.32, 4.33
    EAT from 4.61, 4.62
    grounds 4.40–4.46
    hearing simultaneous with
      appeal 4.89
    limited permission 4.63
      Court of Appeal by 4.67–4.69
      EAT by 4.64–4.66
    obtaining permssion from
      EAT 4.14–4.21
    oral hearing 4.53–4.57
    refusal to grant 4.51, 4.52, 4.59
    service on respondent 4.39
    setting aside 4.60
    time limits 4.26
  powers following appeal 4.128
    remission to EAT 4.130, 4.131
    remission to employment
      tribunal 4.129
  reference to ECJ
    procedure 6.12
  references to ECJ 6.5
  reserved judgment 4.136–4.138
  respondent's notice 4.82
  right of appeal 4.10
  time limits for appeal 1.23
  wasted costs orders 4.146
Cross-appeals 1.16, 3.185
  appellant's response 3.220
  directions 3.221, 3.222
  form of 3.216
  grounds 3.217
  procedure 3.188
  sift of 3.218
  written submissions 3.186

Debarring orders 3.304, 3.305
Default judgements
  review 2.2
Delay
  grounds of appeal 8.153

Employment Appeal Tribunal
  administrative justice tribunal
    service 9.48
  appeals against decision of 1.26
    permission to appeal by Court
      of Appeal 1.28
    refusal of permission to appeal
      by Court of Appeal 1.27
  appeals to 1.2
  background 9.42
  composition 9.43
  conduct of proceedings 3.21

Employment Appeal Tribunal—*continued*
  constitution 9.44
  early applications 3.31, 3.32
  establishment 1.34, 9.42
  funding 1.49, 1.50
  grounds of appeal 1.45–1.48
  history of 1.41
  interim applications 3.34–3.36
  judge sitting alone 3.21
  judgments 3.374–3.380
  judicial member 9.44
  jurisdiction 1.35, 1.38, 1.39, 9.1–9.7
    appellate 9.39
    original 9.39–9.41
  lay members 3.21, 9.44
  limited powers 1.37, 1.39
    effect of appeal cases 1.40
  national security 9.52
  number of appeals to 1.43, 1.44
  overriding objective 3.46, 3.47
  permission to appeal from 4.14–4.21
  powers 9.50
  president 3.20, 9.45
  procedure 1.42
  references to ECJ 6.5
    procedure 6.12
  registrar 3.20, 9.46
    appeals from decision of 3.43
    register of cases 3.44, 3.45
  representation at 1.51, 1.52
  review of its decisions 3.402, 3.403, 9.53
    procedure 3.404–3.407
  rules of procedure 3.22–3.28
    non-compliance 3.29–3.32
    registrar 3.33
  sitting in private 3.306
  sittings 9.47
  status 3.19
  territorial jurisdiction 9.8–9.18, 9.20–9.28, 9.30–9.34
    human rights 9.37
  time limits for appeal 1.20, 1.21
  Tribunals, Courts and Enforcement
    Act 2007 and 9.48, 9.49
Employment judge
  formerly chairman 3.262
  notes of 3.262
    directions from EAT 3.288
    parties disputing 3.293–3.295
    practical application of 3.268–3.274, 3.286
    provision to parties 3.289
    requirement for 3.263–3.267
Employment tribunals
  appeals against decision of 1.25
  appeals to High Court 9.51
  chairman sitting alone 8.158–8.160, 8.162
  composition of 8.157
  employment judge sitting
    alone 8.158–8.160, 8.162
  judgments and decisions of 8.194–8.196
    correction of 8.197, 8.198
  jurisdiction 8.155, 8.156
    statutory provisions 8.194–8.198

468   The Manual of Employment Appeals

Employment tribunals—*continued*
oral evidence used   1.17
references to ECJ   6.5
procedure   6.12
review by 1.2, 1.11, 2.1, 2.2, *see also* Review of judgments and decisions
revocation of orders without a review   2.2
variation of orders without a review   2.2
Enforcement   3.417
Equality and Human Rights Commission
funding for EAT cases   3.424, 3.425
ET1 form
generally   3.135
ET3 form
generally   3.135
European Convention of Human Rights
employment proceedings and   7.5–7.9
admissibility of application   7.24–7.27
compensation   7.28
settlement   7.29
anonymity   7.15
criteria of admissibility   7.11–7.13
ECtHR's powers   7.32
hearing   7.30
inadmissible claims   7.18–7.20
judgment   7.31
action following   7.33–7.36
legal aid   7.10
procedure for application   7.21–7.23
time limits for complaint   7.14, 7.16, 7.17
European Court of Justice
jurisdiction of   6.1, 6.2
references to   1.11, 4.151, 5.75, 6.3–6.5, 6.7, 6.8
documents accompanying reference   6.11
judgment by   6.16, 6.19
further action following   6.17
procedure   6.9–6.12, 6.15
question of law   6.6
Treaty on the functioning of the European Union by the Treaty of Lisbon   6.18
Evidence
chairman's notes   3.262–3.274
directions from EAT   3.288
parties disputing   3.293–3.295
provision to parties   3.289
purpose of   3.286
costs risk   3.287
employment judge's notes   3.262–3.274
directions from EAT   3.288
parties disputing   3.293–3.295
provision to parties   3.289
purpose of   3.286

Evidence—*continued*
provisions of EAT Practice
Direction   3.275–3.285
litigants in person   3.290–3.292
purpose of chairman's notes   3.286
purpose of employment judge's notes   3.286
Extension of time limits
agreement between parties   3.107
appeals to Court of Appeal   4.83–4.88
applications for   3.88
representations following   3.89
right of appeal against registrar's decision   3.90
change in the law   3.108–3.110
criteria for   3.91–3.94
discretion of EAT   3.97–3.106
not before lodging notice of appeal   3.85–3.87
power of EAT   3.84
reason for failing to lodge notice on time   3.95
'good excuse'   3.96

Full hearings   3.200
agreed bundle   3.333–3.338
consultation of parties   3.342
EAT Practice Direction
citation of authorities   3.358
EAT Rules and Practice Direction   3.355–3.357
estimate of length   3.339, 3.340
introduction   1.16
judgments   3.374–3.380
listing of cases   3.327–3.330, 3.342
details of   3.332
listing officer   3.331, 3.342
notice of appeal for   3.201
parties to   3.352–3.354
preliminary hearing date   3.341
procedure   3.359, 3.360, 3.363–3.373
members of panel   3.359, 3.360
representation   3.361, 3.362
skeleton arguments   3.343–3.345, 3.348, 3.349
EAT Practice Direction
guidance   3.346, 3.347
lodging of   3.350, 3.351
Funding
Equality and Human Rights Commission   3.424, 3.425
insurance   3.419, 3.420
legal aid   3.421–3.423
legal expenses   3.418

Grounds of appeal
amendments to   3.243–3.247
bias   1.8, 1.48, 3.123–3.126, 8.123, 8.125–8.128
evidence   8.129–8.131
excessive intervention   8.139
financial interest and   8.133, 8.134

Grounds of appeal—*continued*
  bias—*continued*
    personal relationships and   8.132
    pre-judging   8.136, 8.137
    prejudices   8.138
    previous conduct   8.135
  Burns/Barke procedure   8.174–8.186,
    8.202, 8.203, 10.4, 10.5
  delay   8.153
  errors of jurisdiction   8.154–8.156,
    8.163–8.173
    case law   8.187, 8.188, 8.190–8.193
  generally   3.121, 3.122
  inadequate reasons for decisions   8.21,
    8.65–8.67, 8.99
    additional reasons   8.119, 8.120
    Anya v University of Oxford   10.3
    Barke v SEETEC   10.5
    Burns v Consignia (No 2)   10.4
    duty to give reasons   8.68–8.71,
    8.79–8.88, 8.90–8.97
      rule 30(1) duty   8.72–8.74
      rule 30(6) duty   8.75–8.77
    interim decisions   8.78
    Meek v City of Birmingham
      District Council   10.2
    no reasoning   8.98
  introduction   1.31, 1.45–1.48, 3.5, 3.6,
    8.1–8.3
  misdirection, misunderstanding or
    misapplication of law   8.21, 8.22
    illustrative cases   8.23
  perversity   1.31–1.33, 1.48, 3.123–3.126,
    8.21, 8.25–8.36
    agreement of evidence   8.44
    categories of perversity
      challenge   8.37
    exercise of discretion by
      tribunal   8.63, 8.64
    inferences admissible   8.49–8.54
    no evidence   8.39–8.42
    overlap with 'inadequate
      reasons' appeals   8.38
    particulars of allegation   8.43
    relevant documents required   8.45,
    8.46
    some evidence   8.39–8.42
    tribunal's overall conclusion   8.55–8.62
    Yeboah v Crofton   10.1
  procedural irregularity   8.21, 8.121, 8.122
  question of law   1.8, 1.30, 3.15–3.18,
    3.120, 8.4–8.20
  unfairness of hearing   8.140, 8.145, 8.146,
    8.148–8.150
    evidence   8.142–8.144
    failure to hold public hearing   8.152
    representation   8.141
    tribunal's inattention   8.151

House of Lords
  appeal hearing
    procedure
      appellant's submission of
        case   5.47–5.50
      documents, lodging of   5.57, 5.58
      intervention by parties   5.34
      lodging of petition   5.28–5.30
      notice of hearing   5.59
      notification to Judicial
        Office   5.32, 5.33
      petition to cross-appeal,
        lodging of   5.36
      petition, lodging of   5.31
      respondent's submission of
        case   5.52–5.56
      security, lodging of   5.35
      statement of fact and
        appendix, lodging
        of   5.37–5.42
      submission of time
        estimates   5.46
    procedure at hearing   5.60–5.62
    setting down   5.43–5.45
  appeals to   1.29, 4.151, 5.1
  costs   5.63, 5.64
  judgment   5.66–5.68
  leave to appeal   5.5
    consolidation and conjoinder   5.25,
    5.26
    cross-appeals   5.27
    disposal by consent   5.71–5.73
    granting of   5.19, 5.20
    on Court of Appeal's refusal   5.7
    out of time   5.23, 5.24
    petition
      appeal committee, decisions   5.13,
      5.15–5.17
      lodging   5.21
      procedure   5.9–5.11
      time limit   5.8
      respondent's response   5.12, 5.14
    refusal of   5.18
    with Court of Appeal's leave   5.22
  new submissions to   5.65
  no power to stay Court of Appeal's
    order   5.6
  order of the House   5.70
  permission to appeal
    EAT unable to give permission   4.22
  references to ECJ   6.13
    procedure   6.14
  right of appeal   5.2
    procedure   5.3, 5.4
  time limits for appeal to   1.24
  transfer of judicial jurisdiction   5.76, 5.77
Human rights
  employment proceedings and   7.1
  jurisdiction   9.37
Human Rights Act 1998
  employment proceedings and   7.2–7.4

Inadequate reasons for decisions *see also* Grounds of appeal
Burns/Barke procedure 8.174–8.186, 8.202, 8.203, 10.4, 10.5
grounds of appeal 8.21, 8.65–8.67
Anya v University of Oxford 10.3
Barke v SEETEC 10.5
Burns v Consignia (No 2) 10.4
Meek v City of Birmingham District Council 10.2
'Interests of justice'
review of judgments and decisions 2.6, 2.8
Interim applications 3.36, 3.37
appeals 3.34, 3.35
consideration by registrar 3.40
form of 3.296
in writing 3.39
no specific form 3.38
registrar
from 3.297
notice of appeal 3.297
procedure 3.297
time limits 3.297
to 3.296
restricted reporting orders 3.41

Joinder of parties 3.323
Judgments 3.374
enforcement 3.417
House of Lords 5.66–5.68
reserved judgments 3.375, 3.377–3.380
handing down procedure 3.376
Jurisdiction
employment tribunals 8.155, 8.156
errors of 8.154–8.156, 8.163–8.165
of House of Lords
transferred to Supreme Court of the United Kingdom 5.76
remission on 8.166–8.173, 8.199, 8.200
errors of
case law 8.187, 8.188, 8.190–8.193
Jurisdiction of tribunals 9.1–9.7
territorial jurisdiction 9.8–9.18, 9.20–9.28, 9.30–9.34
human rights 9.37

Lay members
Employment Appeal Tribunal 3.21, 3.359, 9.44
Legal aid 3.421–3.423
Litigants in person 3.290–3.292
costs 3.400, 4.147

Misdirection, misunderstanding or misapplication of law 8.21, 8.22,
see also Grounds of appeal
illustrative cases 8.23

National security
appeals 3.324, 3.325

National security—*continued*
Employment Appeal Tribunal 9.52
hearing procedure 3.326
Natural justice
general rule 8.147
presentation of evidence 8.147
New evidence
admissibility 3.254–3.256
applications to use 3.257
Court of Appeal 4.126
discretion of EAT 3.260, 3.261
objection to application 3.259
overriding objective and 3.260, 3.261
review of judgments and decisions 2.5
statement, form of 3.258
New points of law
appeals, generally 3.248
procedure of EAT 3.250–3.253
respondent's objection to 3.249
Notice of appeal
documents accompanying 3.130, 3.131, 3.133, 3.136
applications made to
employment tribunal 3.135
copies acceptable 3.134
employment tribunal's written reasons 3.135
ET1 form 3.135
ET3 form 3.135
judgment, decision or order appealed against 3.135
judgments made by
employment tribunal 3.135
relevant orders made 3.135
request for particular directions 3.137
extension of time after lodged 3.85–3.87
form of 3.116–3.119
full hearing for 3.201
grounds of appeal 3.120–3.122
last minute appeals 3.127–3.129
lodged early 3.111–3.115
lodged out of time 1.18
not validly lodged 3.130, 3.131, 3.133
receipt by EAT, time limits 3.76–3.80
service 3.81–3.83
time limits 1.8, 1.16, 3.56

Overriding objective
and use of new evidence 3.260, 3.261
appeals 3.46, 3.47
EAT 3.46, 3.47
interim applications 3.40
restricted reporting orders and 3.316

Parallel appeals 3.223
guidance in Plummer Parsons v Wight 3.228–3.235
separate parallel appeals 3.224–3.226, 3.236–3.242
unitary parallel appeals 3.224–3.226
Perversity *see also* Grounds of appeal
agreement of evidence 8.44

Perversity—continued
  categories of perversity challenge 8.37
  exercise of discretion by tribunal 8.63, 8.64
  grounds of appeal 1.31–1.33, 1.48, 3.123–3.126, 8.21, 8.25–8.36
    Yeboah v Crofton 10.1
  inferences admissible 8.49–8.54
  no evidence 8.39–8.42
  overlap with 'inadequate reasons' appeals 8.38
  particulars of allegation 8.43
  relevant documents required 8.45, 8.46
  some evidence 8.39–8.42
  tribunal's overall conclusion 8.55–8.62

Preliminary hearings 1.16, 3.183
  Burns/Barke procedure 3.189–3.191
  directions from EAT 3.185
  no further action on appeal 3.192
  purpose 3.184
  rule 3(10) hearing, following 3.183
  sift, following 3.183

President of the Employment Appeal Tribunal 3.20, 9.45

Procedural irregularity
  grounds of appeal 8.21, 8.121, 8.122

Question of law
  grounds of appeal 1.8, 1.30, 3.2, 3.15–3.18, 3.120, 8.4–8.20
  references to ECJ 6.6

Remission for rehearing
  jurisdiction of tribunals 3.349, 3.381–3.388, 8.166–8.173, 8.199, 8.200
  Lambe v 186K Ltd 3.198, 10.7
  Sinclair Roche and Temperley 3.349, 3.382, 3.383, 3.386, 10.6

Representation
  appeals 1.51–1.53
  non-lawyers 3.361
  pro bono representation 3.362

Respondent's answer 1.16
  content 3.210, 3.212, 3.213, 3.215
  cross-appeals and 3.214
  documents received from registrar 3.207
  form of 3.209
  lodging of 3.208
  service of 3.211
  when required 3.202–3.204, 3.206

Restricted reporting orders
  full restricted reporting order 3.312
  interim applications 3.41
  notice of 3.314
  overriding objective and 3.316
  particulars 3.311
  representations from parties 3.315
  revocation by EAT 3.313
  temporary restricted reporting order 3.312
  when used 3.307–3.310

Review of judgments and decisions 3.402
  appeals 2.7–2.10
  applications by party 2.12–2.14
  default judgments 2.2
  EAT by 3.403
    procedure 3.404–3.407
  general rule 2.2
  grounds 2.3, 2.4
  'interests of justice' 2.6, 2.8
  introduction 2.1
  new evidence become available 2.5
  powers of tribunal 2.15
  procedure 2.11
  review by tribunal's own motion 2.16
  simultaneous appeal to EAT 2.17–2.20
  'slip' rule 2.21

Revocation of orders 2.15

Rule 3(7) cases
  procedure 3.173–3.176

Rule 3(10) cases
  appeals on decision 3.193–3.199
  no further action on appeal 3.192
  oral hearing 3.177, 3.178, 3.181, 3.182
    participation by the respondent 3.180
    submissions by respondent 3.179

Service
  notice of appeal 3.81–3.83
  time limits 3.154–3.157

Sifting and filtering 3.162
  introduction 1.16
  procedure 3.163–3.168, 3.170–3.172
    oral hearing 3.169
  rule 3(7) cases 3.173–3.176
  rule 3(10) cases 3.177–3.182

'Slip' rule 2.21, 3.403

Stay of proceedings 3.160
  judge by 3.298
  registrar by 3.298

Supreme Court of the United Kingdom
  draft rules for 5.77

Territorial jurisdiction 9.8–9.18, 9.20–9.28, 9.30–9.34
  errors of 8.163–8.165
  human rights 9.37

Time limits 1.8, 1.16, 1.19–1.24
  appeals 3.51–3.55, 3.57
    lodging notice of appeal 3.56
    orders and judgments 3.58–3.66
      illustrative examples 3.67–3.75
    extension of 3.84–3.110
    receipt of notice by EAT 3.76–3.80
  service of documents 3.154–3.157
  service of notice of appeal 3.81–3.83

Time limits for starting proceedings 1.16, 1.20–1.24
  general rule 3.51–3.55
  introduction 1.8
  lodging notice of appeal 3.56
  orders and judgments 3.58–3.66
    illustrative examples 3.67–3.75
  receipt of notice by EAT 3.76–3.80

Time limits for starting proceedings—*continued*
  regimes   3.57

Treaty on the functioning of the European Union by the Treaty of Lisbon   6.18

Unfairness of hearing *see also* **Grounds of appeal**
  grounds of appeal   8.140, 8.145, 8.148–8.150
    evidence   8.142–8.144, 8.146
    failure to hold public hearing   8.152
    representation   8.141
    tribunal's inattention   8.151

Vexation proceedings   3.317–3.322
Vexatious conduct   3.317–3.322

Waiver of rules
  appeals   3.301–3.303
Wasted costs order   3.397–3.399
  Court of Appeal from   4.146
Witness statements
  new evidence   3.258
Witnesses
  production of documents   3.299, 3.300
Written reasons
  employment tribunal from   3.138, 3.139, 3.151–3.153
    not sought   3.144–3.146
    reasons refused   3.150
    waiting for   3.147–3.149
    when not available   3.140–3.142
      powers of EAT   3.142
Written reasons for judgments or decisions   8.75–8.77, 8.100–8.105, 8.107–8.118, 8.194–8.196
  correction of   8.197, 8.198